Time Out

Florence
& the best of Tuscany

timeout.com/florence

Penguin Books

PENGUIN BOOKS

Published by the Penguin Group
Penguin Books Ltd, 80 Strand, London WC2R ORL, England
Penguin Books USA Inc., 375 Hudson Street, New York, New York 10014, USA
Penguin Books Australia Ltd, Ringwood, Victoria, Australia
Penguin Books Canada Ltd, 10 Alcorn Avenue, Toronto, Ontario, Canada M4V 3B2
Penguin Books (NZ) Ltd, 182-190 Wairau Road, Auckland 10, New Zealand

Penguin Books Ltd, Registered Offices: Harmondsworth, Middlesex, England

First published 1997
Second edition 1999
10 9 8 7 6 5 4 3 2 1

Colour reprographics by Icon, Crown House, 56-58 Southwark Street, London SE1
and Precise Litho, 34-35 Great Sutton Street, London EC1
Printed and bound by Cayfosa-Quebecor, Ctra. de Caldes, Km 3 08 130 Sta, Perpètua de Mogoda, Barcelona, Spain

Edited and designed by
Time Out Guides Limited
Universal House
251 Tottenham Court Road
London W1T 7AB
Tel + 44 (0) 20 7813 3000
Fax + 44 (0) 20 7813 6001
Email guides@timeout.com
www.timeout.com

Editorial

Editor Ruth Jarvis
Deputy Editor Rhonda Carrier
Copy Editing Christi Daugherty, Nadia Durani, Kevin Ebbutt
Consultant Editor Nicky Swallow
Listings Editor Helen Holubov
Proofreader Marion Moisy
Indexer Selena Cox

Editorial Director Peter Fiennes
Series Editor Ruth Jarvis
Deputy Series Editor Jonathan Cox
Guides Co-ordinator Jenny Noden

Design

Art Director John Oakey
Art Editor Mandy Martin
Senior Designer Scott Moore
Designers Benjamin de Lotz, Lucy Grant, Kate Vincent-Smith
Picture Editor Kerri Miles
Deputy Picture Editor Olivia Duncan-Jones
Scanning & Imaging Dan Conway
Ad make-up Glen Impey

Advertising

Group Commercial Director Lesley Gill
Sales Director/Sponsorship Mark Phillips
International Sales Co-ordinator Ross Canadé
Advertisement Sales Manager (Florence)
Margherita Tedone
Advertisement Sales Executive (Florence) Sara de Martini
Advertising Assistant Sabrina Ancilleri

Administration

Publisher Tony Elliott
Managing Director Mike Hardwick
Group Financial Director Kevin Ellis
Marketing Director Christine Cort
Marketing Manager Mandy Martinez
Group General Manager Nichola Coulthard
Production Manager Mark Lamond
Production Controller Samantha Furniss
Accountant Sarah Bostock

Features in this guide were written and researched by:
Introduction Ruth Jarvis. **History** Anne Hanley *Who they? Matilda of Canossa* Michèle Kahn Spike. **Florence Today** Caroline Burdet *The future starts here* Nicky Swallow. **Architecture** Richard Fremantle. **Food in Tuscany** Kate Singleton, Kate Carlisle *Who they? The butcher of Panzano, Larding it* Nicky Swallow. **Tuscan Wine** Kate Singleton. **Accommodation** Nicky Swallow. **Sightseeing** Julia Burdet. Outside the City Gates and *Beyond the beaten track* Nicky Swallow. **Restaurants** Nicky Swallow *Who they? David Gardner* Lee Marshall. *Wine Bars* Nicky Swallow. **Cafés & Bars** Julia Burdet. **Shopping & Services** Julia Burdet. **Tuscany by Season** Nicky Swallow. **Children** Elena Brizio. **Film** Julia Burdet. **Galleries** Julia Burdet. **Gay & Lesbian** Bruno Casini. **Music: Classical & Opera** Nicky Swallow. **Music: Rock, Roots & Jazz** Dahlia Roemer. **Nightlife** Julia Burdet. **Theatre & Dance** Keith Ferrone, Nicky Swallow. **Sport & Fitness** Dahlia Roemer. **Tuscany** Daniel Scott, Marco Bianchini, Kate Carlisle, Monica Larner. **Directory** Julia Burdet.

The Editor would like to thank Sophie Blacksell, Cath Phillips, Nicholas Royle, Julia Walker, Will Fulford-Jones and all contributors from previous editions, whose work formed the basis for parts of this book.

Maps by JS Graphics, 17 Beadles Lane, Old Oxted, Surrey RH8 9JG.

All photography by Adam Eastland except for: page 7 Hulton Getty; page 9, 10, 11, 12, 13, 15, 19, 79, 91, 93, 94, 199, 261 AKG; page 32 Associated Press; page 104 The Italian State Tourist Board (ENIT); page 36, 155, 156 Luca Moggi; page 189 Allsport; pages 40, 191, 196, 197, 198, 200, 201, 205, 208, 211, 214, 215, 219, 221, 223, 227, 228, 229, 231, 232, 234, 236, 238, 239, 240, 243, 244, 245, 246, 249, 250, 252, 253, 254, 256, 258, 260, 263, 264, 265, 266, 267, 268, 269, 271, 272, 275, 276, 279 Daniel Scott.

The following photographs were supplied by featured establishments/artists; page 39, 164, 165, 166, 167, 169, 171, 185, 255

Contents

Introduction

Florence made the Renaisance and in return the Renaissance made Florence. It gave the city the self-esteem to survive conquest and relegation to a cultural backwater; the international cachet to attract lucrative foreign visitors (and residents); and, of course, more than anything else, an unmatched artistic and architectural heritage. Florence induced a libertarian sensuality that still remains clearly evident among its residents, particularly in the pleasures of food, drink and art and a primacy of the aesthetic that makes light fall on a bridge more beautifully here than anywhere else in the world, even if it were the same light, the same bridge.

All of which contributes to the city's unfailing magnetism: still people abandon other lives to come and live here, and still they visit in such droves that at high season their massed ranks contrast unfavourably with the ethereal art around which they swarm. It's an easy town to visit, its attractions unending and closely clustered but also easy to escape for the cool olive groves of the countryside when they start, as they inevitably will, to overwhelm. But it can also be a difficult town to 'get': those hoping to be seduced for the first time by Renaissance art may find it instead impenetrable; those who enjoy spontaneity may find it too precious; and those who like to get to know people as well as place may find that after 500 years of hosting the world and its easel, locals are not always communicative. It overheats in summer and overcharges for hotel rooms (though compensates with cheap admission to its churches and museums). There's a conservatism to the place that is both its charm and its downfall. Florence remains defined by and steeped in an event that happened over half a millennium ago – some would argue that maybe it's time to move on.

And some reply that Florence has, a little. That its contemporary arts are beginning to thrive; that its satellite new town to the west, Firenze Nova, is now being built, not merely promised; that its bars, clubs and restaurants are opening up to international influence. And that in these days of global homogeneity, that's enough, *mille grazie*.

ABOUT THE TIME OUT CITY GUIDES

The *Time Out Florence Guide* is one of an expanding series of *Time Out* City Guides produced by the people behind London and New York's successful listings magazines. Our guides are all written and updated by resident experts who have striven to provide you with all the most up-to-date information.

THE LOWDOWN ON THE LISTINGS

Above all, we've tried to make this book as useful as possible. Addresses, telephone numbers, websites, transport, opening times, admission prices and credit card details were all checked and correct at the time we went to press. However, owners can change their arrangements at any time. Before you go out of your way, we'd advise you to telephone and check opening times and other particulars. While every effort has been made to ensure the accuracy of the information contained in this guide, the publishers cannot accept responsibility for any errors it may contain.

PRICES AND PAYMENT

We have noted whether venues such as shops, hotels and restaurants accept credit cards but have only listed the major cards – American Express (**AmEx**), Diners Club (**DC**), Japanese credit cards (**JCB**), MasterCard (**MC**) – also known as EuroCard – and Visa (**V**). Many hotels and the more salubrious shops and restaurants will also accept travellers' cheques in all denominations; some also take pounds and US dollars.

THE LIE OF THE LAND

Florence has few easily identifiable areas. For convenient orientation, we have divided the city into six areas, most based around their principal church. These areas are clearly marked on the map on page 314 and echoed in the titles of our sightseeing chapters. Bear in mind, however, that central Florence is very compact and so it's often easy to walk between destinations. For this reason, we have given public transport only for addresses beyond the old city walls: in the central area, a combination of short walks and using the four electric bus circuits marked on the page 314 map should get you everywhere quickly.

> There is an online version of this guide, as well as weekly events listings for 35 international cities, at **www.timeout.com**.

The Euro

From 1 March 2002 the lira will be withdrawn and replaced by the Euro, which comes into circulation on 1 January 2002. The rate of exchange has been set at L1,936.27 to one Euro. Prices will be conversted exactly to the nearerst cent to avoid inflation by upward adjustment, but over the life of this guide they are expected to settle slightly to sensible figures. We have given both currencies, adjusting the Euro figure up or down to the nearest 50c at most and to the nearest 10c for sums under €10. Though the aim is a stable transition, the introduction of the Euro may affect the prices given.

39, leaving the initial zero. In the shorter listings, the accommodation rates are for a double room unless otherwise stated and the average price for a meal is for the full four courses, even though you're unlikely to order them all.

Note that the city's famously complex street numbering system can be confusing. Residential addresses are 'black' numbers (*nero*) and take an 'n' suffix when calling from outside the country. Most commercial addresses are 'red' (*rosso*), with an 'r' suffix. This means that in any one street there can be multiple addresses of the same number, but in different colours, sometimes far apart.

TELEPHONE NUMBERS
The area code for Florence is 055; do not drop the zero when calling from outside the country. The international code for Italy is 39. Numbers preceded by 800 can be called free of charge from Florence. For more details of phone codes and charges, *see page 293*.

ESSENTIAL INFORMATION
For all the practical information you might need for visiting the city – including visa and customs information, disabled access, emergency telephone numbers, a list of useful websites and the lowdown on the local transport network – turn to the **Directory** chapter at the back of this guide. It starts on page 280.

TUSCANY
A third of this guide is devoted to the highlights of Tuscany. Again, phone numbers are given in their entirety as dialled locally and throughout Italy – for international calls preface them with

MAPS
We've included a series of fully indexed colour maps to the city at the back of this guide – they start on page 312. Where possible, we've printed a grid reference against all venues that appear on the maps. There's a map of Tuscany on page 308 and individual city maps in the relevant chapters.

LET US KNOW WHAT YOU THINK
We hope you enjoy the *Time Out Florence Guide*, and we'd like to know what you think of it. In addition, we also welcome tips for places that you consider we should include in future editions, and take notice of your criticism of our choices. There's a reader's reply card at the back of this book – or you can email us on florenceguide@timeout.com.

Sponsors & advertisers

We would like to stress that no establishment has been included in this guide because it has advertised in any of our publications and no payment of any kind has influenced any review. The opinions given in this book are those of *Time Out* writers and entirely independent.

Targasys.

A world of services.

Targasys is always with you, ready to assure you all the tranquillity and serenity that you desire for your journeys, 24 hours a day 365 days a year.

Roadside assistance always and everywhere, infomobility so not to have surprises, insurance... and lots more.

To get to know us better contact us at the toll-free number **00-800-55555555**.

...and to discover Targa Connect's exclusive and innovative integrated infotelematic services onboard system visit us at:

www.targaconnect.com

In Context

Luxury
in the heart
of Florence

HOTEL SAVOY
FIRENZE

L'INCONTRO BAR AND RESTAURANT

Italian soldiers help clear debris after the flood of 1966.

History

Guelphs, Ghibellines and miscellaneous Medici: unravelling Florence's history is not for the faint-hearted.

From around the eighth century BC, much of central Italy was controlled by the Etruscans, who may have been natives or may have drifted in from Asia Minor. Whatever their origins, they settled in Veio and Cerveteri close to Rome and further north – in what is now Tuscany – in Volterra, Populonia, Arezzo, Chiusi and Cortona. They entirely overlooked the site we now know as Florence, making hilltop Fiesole their northernmost stronghold.

Tantalisingly little evidence remains of Etruscan history and culture before they were clobbered out of existence by the Romans. One of the main reasons we can be sure of so little about them is that they constructed almost everything from wood. Everything, that is, except their tombs. Because of this, their tombs and the objects recovered from them constitute most of the evidence on their civilisation. With so little to go on, mythologisers have had a field day. Enchanting frescoes of feasts, festivals, dancing and hunting that adorn many of the tombs led DH Lawrence to conclude that

'…death to the Etruscan was a pleasant continuance of life.' Others say the opposite: that the Etruscans were terrified of death and the seemingly carefree paintings were a desperate plea for the gods to go easy with them on the other side.

The historical bones of what we know about the Etruscans are as follows. They were certainly a spiritual people, but they were also partial to a good war, against either other tribes or rival Etruscan cities. Their civilisation reached its peak in the seventh and sixth centuries BC, when their loose federation of cities dominated much of what is now southern Tuscany and northern Lazio. Women played an unusually prominent role, apparently having as much fun as the lads; writing in the fourth century BC, Theopompos said: 'Etruscan women take particular care of their bodies and exercise often, sometimes along with the men, and sometimes by themselves. It is not a disgrace for them to be seen naked. They do not share their couches with their husbands but

with other men who happen to be present…
They are expert drinkers and very attractive.'

Etruscan cities grew wealthy on the proceeds of mining and trading copper and iron. Their art and superbly worked gold jewellery display distinctive Oriental influences, adding credence to the theory that the Etruscans migrated to Italy from the East, though such influences could have been due to their extensive trading in the eastern Mediterranean.

At the end of the seventh century BC, the Etruscans captured the small town of Rome and ruled it for a century before being expelled. The next few centuries witnessed city against city, tribe against tribe, all over central Italy until the emerging Roman republic overwhelmed all-comers by the third century BC. As the virulently pro-Etruscan, anti-Roman Lawrence put it: 'The Etruscans were the people who occupied the middle of Italy in early Roman days and whom the Romans, in their usual neighbourly fashion, wiped out entirely in order to make room for Rome with a very big R.'

The Romans absorbed many aspects of Etruscan society, such as Etruscan gods and divination by entrails, but when the Etruscans were awarded Roman citizenship in 90BC, all distinct signs of their civilisation had vanished.

ETRUSCAN TO TUSCAN

In 59 BC Julius Caesar established a colony for army veterans along the narrowest stretch of the Arno, and Florentia was born. Strategically located at the heart of Italian territory, it grew into a flourishing commercial centre, becoming the capital of a Roman province in the third century AD. In the fifth century, the Roman Empire in the west finally crumbled before the pagan hordes (some of whom were no less cultured than the dissolute Romans they displaced). Italian unity collapsed as Ostrogoths, Visigoths, Huns then Lombards rampaged through the peninsula.

The Goths who swept into central Italy in the fifth century were dislodged by the Byzantine forces of the Eastern emperor in conflicts that left the area badly battle-scarred. The Goth King Totila seized Florence again in 552, only to be ejected two decades later when the Lombards stormed across the Alps and established a regional HQ at Lucca.

In the eighth century Charlemagne and his Frankish forces crushed the last of the Lombard kings of Italy. To thank him for his intervention and ensure his future support (a move that backfired badly, leading to centuries of conflict between pontiff and emperors), Pope Leo III crowned Charlemagne Holy Roman Emperor. Much of the country then came under (at least nominal) control of the emperor. In practice,

local warlords carved out feudal fiefs for themselves and threw their weight around much as they pleased.

The imperial margravate of Tuscany began to emerge as a region of some promise during the 10th and 11th centuries, when it came under the control of the Canossa family (*see p9* **Who they? Matilda of Canossa**). Initially, the richest city was Lucca, but it was Pisa's increasingly profitable maritime trade that brought the biggest impetus of ideas and wealth into the region.

'The murder of Florentine nobleman Buondelmonte was the spark that ignited the flames across Tuscany.'

As a prosperous merchant class developed in cities all over Tuscany, the region sought to throw off the constraints and demands of its feudal overlords. By 1200 the majority had succeeded (Florence, Siena and Lucca had been established as independent city states or *comuni* by the redoubtable Matilda di Canossa on her death in 1115) and Tuscany had become a patchwork of tiny but increasingly self-confident and ambitious, self-ruling entities. The potential for conflict was huge, and by the 13th century it crystallised into an intractable struggle between Guelph and Ghibelline.

GUELPH VS GHIBELLINE

The names Guelph and Ghibelline came from the Italian forms of Welf (the family name of the German emperor Otto IV) and Waiblingen (a castle belonging to the Welfs' rivals for the role of Holy Roman Emperor, the Hohenstaufen) respectively, but by the time the appellations crossed the Alps into Italy (probably in the 12th century) their significance had changed.

'Guelph' became attached primarily to the increasingly influential merchant classes. In their continuing desire to be free from imperial control, they looked around for a powerful backer. The only viable candidate was the emperor's enemy, the pope, who by this time had recognised the error of creating a rival ruler and was peddling the theory that the fourth-century Roman emperor Constantine (who sat by in his new Eastern capital at Constantinople as the Western Empire fell from the hands of the last Roman emperors into the ruthless ones of barbarian invaders) had assigned not just spiritual but also temporal power in Italy to the papacy. The Guelphs could thus add a patriotic and religious sheen to their own self-interest.

Anyone keen to uphold imperial power and opposed to papal designs and rising commercial

Who she? Matilda of Canossa

Though her name is rarely mentioned by present-day historians, Matilda was one of the great women of the Middle Ages – her rebellion against the German kings liberated the towns of Italy from the yoke of German feudalism and she defended Gregory VII's reforms of the Roman Church to establish the revolutionary principle that all men are equal in the eyes of God. She began the tradition of building a legacy in stone that culminated with the Medici princes of Florence: the historic Duomo of Modena as well as numerous small *pieves* throughout the Tuscan countryside are the fruits of her generosity. Five hundred years after her death, Pope Urban VIII gave her the Roman Church's highest honour – she's one of only three women whose bones are buried in the nave of Saint Peter's in Rome.

Matilda was in her late 20s when Hildebrand became Pope Gregory VII. Widely regarded as the greatest of the medieval popes, Gregory is credited with the transformation of the Roman Church from a weak, corrupt and spiritually impoverished institution to a world political power. He did so in alliance with monks from the monastery of Cluny and with Matilda, who found in him a willing ally in her battle against the violence and lawlessness of the German feudal state.

In the decades after Gregory VII's death, Matilda financed the monks dedicated to reform of the Roman Church. She continued to oppose the German king Henry IV for control of the Italian peninsula even after the battles had exhausted her wealth and her bishops advised her to surrender. After her victory she took the title Countess of Saint Peter to emphasise her dedication to a new state centred in Rome.

It is from her death in 1115 that the history of the Italian *comune* dates. During her conflicts with the Germans, Matilda empowered the citizens of the walled cities in northern Italy to govern themselves.

In 1088, she founded the University of Bologna and sponsored the scholarship of Inerius, who revived the study and practice of Roman law. He trained the townsmen who acted as her chancellors and judges in a system of written laws that replaced the ad hoc pronouncements of German feudal nobility. In her name, the townsmen subdued the aggressive nobles who lived in castle hilltops in the surrounding countryside, thus encouraging the revival of trade and commerce.

When Matilda died, these citizens founded the city councils that established and governed the *comune*. The Germans did not willingly relinquish Italy and her death initiated the famous strife between the Guelphs (papal) and the Ghibellines (imperial).

interests – mainly the old nobility – became known as Ghibellines. That, at least, was the theory. It soon became clear, however, that self-interest and local rivalries were of far greater importance than theoretical allegiances to emperor or pope.

Although bad feeling had been simmering for decades, the murder of Florentine nobleman Buondelmonte dei Buondelmonti is traditionally seen as the spark that ignited flames across Tuscany. On his wedding day in 1215, Buondelmonte was stabbed to death by a member of the Amidei family for having previously jilted an Amidei maiden. The subsequent trial dissolved into a test of wills – and soon of arms – between the pro-Empire Amidei and the pro-*comune* faction mourning the demise of the groom. The Ghibelline Amidei

finally prevailed with help from Emperor Frederick II in 1248, but were ousted with Guelph aid two years later, when semi-democratic government by the merchant class known as the *piccolo popolo* was established.

Ten years on, Ghibellines from Siena had dislodged the *piccolo popolo* and came close to razing the town; a decade on, the Guelphs were back in the driving seat, with the major craft guilds running the show through an administration called the *secondo popolo*. In 1293 the body passed a regulation effectively banning the nobility from government in Florence, giving power to a *signoria* made up of representatives of the guilds.

The situation was no less complex in other Tuscan towns: Lucca was generally Guelph-dominated, while Siena and Pisa tended to

Who they? The Medici

The name Medici (pronounced with the stress on the first e) is all but synonymous with Florence and Tuscany. It suggests that family's origins probably lie in the medical profession, though their later wealth was built on banking.

Giovanni di Bicci (1360-1429)

The fortune Giovanni di Bicci quietly built up through his banking business – boosted immensely by the fact that it handled the papal account – provided the basis for the Medici's later clout. While filling the family coffers, Giovanni acted with the utmost discretion, wary of the Florentines' habit of picking on those who got above themselves.

Cosimo 'il Vecchio' (1389-1464)

Cosimo (pictured right) ran Florence informally from 1434, presiding over one of its most prosperous and prestigious eras. An even more astute banker than his father, he pacified opponents and his conscience by spending lavishly on charities and public building projects, introducing a progressive income tax system and balancing the interests of the volatile Florentine classes relatively successfully. Cosimo was also an intellectual; he encouraged the new Humanist

learning and developments in art that were sweeping Florence. He built up a wonderful public library (the first in Europe), financed scholars and artists, gave architectural commissions and founded a school along the lines of Plato's Academy – he was the epitome of the Renaissance *uomo universale*. The name *il Vecchio* (the Elder) was a mark of respect. When he died, the Florentines inscribed on his tomb the words *Pater Patriae* ('father of the nation').

Piero 'il Gottoso' (1416-69)

All the Medici suffered from gout, but poor Piero the Gouty's joints gave him such gyp that he had to be carried around for half his life. During his short spell at the helm he proved a surprisingly able ruler: he crushed an anti-Medici conspiracy, maintained the success of the Medici bank and patronised the city's best artists and architects.

Lorenzo 'il Magnifico' (1449-92)

Cosimo's grandson Lorenzo was the big Medici, famous in his own time and legendary in later centuries. His rule marked the peak of the Florentine Renaissance, with artists such as Botticelli and the young Michelangelo producing superlative works. Lorenzo was

favour the Ghibellines, but this had as much to do with mutual antagonisms as deeply held beliefs. Siena started off Guelph, but couldn't bear the thought of having to be nice to its traditional enemy, Florence, and so swapped to the Ghibelline cause. Similarly, the Guelph/Ghibelline splits within cities were more often class- and grudge-based than ideological.

Throughout the 14th century, power ebbed and flowed between the two (loosely knit) parties across Tuscany and from city to city. When one party was in the ascendant its supporters would tear down its opponents' fortified towers (the Guelphs' with their square crenellations, the Ghibellines' with swallow-tail ones), only to have its own towers levelled in turn as soon as the pendulum swung back.

Once firmly in command of Florence at the end of the 13th century, the Guelphs started squabbling internally. In around 1300 open conflict broke out between the virulently anti-Imperial 'Blacks' and the more conciliatory 'Whites'. After various to-ings and fro-ings, the Blacks booted the Whites out for good. Among those sent into exile was Dante Alighieri (*see p70* **Who he?**).

Eventually the Guelph/Ghibelline conflict ran out of steam. It says much for the energy, innovation, graft and skill of the Tuscans (or for the relative harmlessness of much medieval warfare in Italy) that throughout this stormy period, the region was booming economically.

By the beginning of the 14th century Florence was one of the five biggest cities in Europe, with a population of almost 100,000.

a gifted poet, and gathered round him a supremely talented group of scholars and artists. The climate of intellectual freedom he fostered was a major factor in some of the greatest achievements of the Renaissance.

Lorenzo's reign was a time of relative peace, thanks in part to his diplomatic skills. As a businessman, however, he wasn't a patch on his predecessors and the Medici bank suffered a severe decline. Lorenzo maintained a façade of being no more than *primus inter pares* (first among equals), but he made sure he always got his way, and he could be ruthless with his enemies.

Piero di Lorenzo
(1471-1503)
Piero couldn't live up to his father: ruthless, charmless and tactless, he had a violent temper, no sense of loyalty and a haughty wife. His father described him as foolish, and he certainly did nothing to help his cause when he surrendered the city to the French in 1494 (*see p14*). He spent the rest of his days skulking around Italy, trying to persuade unenthusiastic states to help him regain power in a Florence that had no wish to see his mug again.

Giuliano, Duke of Nemours
(1478-1516)
The third son of Lorenzo *il Magnifico* and an improvement on his brother Piero only in the sense that he was more nonentity than swine,

Giuliano was ruler of Florence in name only, being little more than a puppet of his brother Cardinal Giovanni, later Pope Leo X.

Lorenzo, Duke of Urbino
(1492-1519)
Son of Piero di Lorenzo, Lorenzo was puny, arrogant, high-handed and corrupt. No one was anything but relieved when he succumbed to tuberculosis, aggravated by syphilis. His only significant legacy was his daughter, Catherine, who as wife then widow of Henri II wielded considerable power in France.

Giovanni; Pope Leo X
(1475-1521)
Lorenzo *il Magnifico*'s second son (pictured left) wasn't such a loser as his brothers, perhaps because the night before his birth his mother dreamed she would have not a baby but a huge lion. Lorenzo decided early on that Giovanni was destined for a glittering ecclesiastical career, and serious papal ear-bending ensured that he became a monk at eight and a cardinal aged 16. He elbowed his way into the papacy in 1513. Pope Leo (spot the lion reference) was a remarkably likeable, open character, and though lazy and fond of the good life ('God has given us the Papacy so let us enjoy it', he's reported to have said), he was a generous host and politically conciliatory. But his shameless exploitation ▶

It went through a rocky patch in the middle of the century, when England's King Edward III defaulted on his debts (1342), bankrupting several Florentine lenders, and a plague epidemic (1348) carried off an estimated half of the city's population. But it soon bounced back: its currency – the florin, first minted in 1252 – remained one of Europe's strongest; and with fewer illness-prone poor to employ and feed, Florence may even have benefited economically from the Black Death.

The city's good fortune was due in no small part to its woollen cloth industry. Taxes to finance the costly conflict known as the War of the Eight Saints against Pope Gregory XI in 1375-78 hit the *ciompi* – wool carders – hardest, and they revolted, gaining representation in city government. By the mid 1380s, however, the three guilds formed in the wake of the uprising began to lose ground to the *popolo grasso*, a small group of the wealthiest merchant families, who had united with the Guelphs to form an oligarchy in 1382. The *popolo grasso* held sway in the *signoria* (government) for 40 years, during which time intellectuals and artists were becoming increasingly involved in political life.

Not all of Florence's business community backed the *popolo grasso*. Banker Cosimo de' Medici's stance against the extremes of the *signoria* gained him the support both of other dissenting merchants and the *popolo minuto* from the less influential guilds. Cosimo's mounting popularity alarmed the *signoria*, and the dominant Albizzi family clan had him exiled on trumped-up charges in 1433. A year later he returned to Florence by popular consent and

▶ Who they? The Medici (continued)

of the sale of indulgences to ease his permanent debts added fuel to the fires of critics of papal corruption, while a chronic anal fistula meant he wasn't the most fragrant company.

Giulio; Pope Clement VII

(1478-1534)

Lorenzo *Il Magnifico*'s illegitimate nephew, Giulio had honours heaped on him by his cousin Pope Leo. Though this didn't endear him to other cardinals (his disagreeable personality didn't help much either), he swung the papacy in 1524. Pope Clement was notorious for his indecision, irresolution and disloyalty. He abandoned his alliance with Charles V only to regret it when the emperor's troops sacked Rome in 1527 (*see p14*).

Alessandro (1511-37)

Thought to be Clement's illegitimate son, Alessandro proved to be a bastard by nature too, abandoning all pretence of respecting the Florentines' treasured institutions and freedoms. Increasingly authoritarian, he tortured and executed his opponents and outraged the good Florentine burghers by his appalling rudeness and sexual antics. He had a

penchant for dressing in women's clothes and riding about town with his bosom buddy and distant cousin, the equally alarming Lorenzaccio. A deputation of senior figures complained to Charles V, to no avail. It was left to Lorenzaccio to put everyone out of their misery by luring Alessandro to bed and stabbing him to death.

Cosimo I (1519-74)

With no heir in the direct Medici line, the Florentines chose this obscure 18-year-old

(grandson of Lorenzo *il Magnifico*'s daughter Lucrezia), thinking they could manipulate him. How wrong they were – cold, secretive and cunning, Cosimo set about ruling with merciless efficiency. His unpleasantness didn't stop him restoring stability in Florence and boost the city's international image. He also built up a navy and threw off the dependence on imperial troops to maintain order. After relentless lobbying he was granted the title Grand Duke of Tuscany by Pope Paul V in 1569.

Francesco I (1541-87)

Short, skinny, graceless and sulky, Francesco (pictured above) had little in common with his father Cosimo. He retreated into his own little world at any opportunity, to play with his pet reindeer, dabble in alchemy and invent a new process for porcelain production.

with handy military backing from his allies in Milan, and he was immediately made first citizen, becoming 'king in all but name'. For most of the next 300 years, the Medici dynasty remained more or less firmly in Florence's driving seat (*see p10* **Who they?**).

KINGS IN ALL BUT NAME

Cosimo's habit of giving large sums to charity and endowing religious institutions with artworks helped make Florence a centre of artistic production, while by persuading representatives of the Eastern and Western churches to try to mend their schism at a conference in Florence in 1439, he hosted Greek scholars who could sate his intellectual hunger for classical literature. This artistic and intellectual fervour gathered steam

through the long 'reign' of his grandson Lorenzo *il Magnifico*.

Under his *de facto* leadership, Florence enjoyed a long period of relative peace, aided to some extent by Lorenzo's diplomatic skills in minimising squabbles between Italian states. Which isn't to say that all went smoothly: Lorenzo's relations with Pope Sixtus IV were famously bitter, resulting in excommunication and war; the pope also backed the Pazzi Conspiracy, an assault financed by rival banking clan the Pazzi in which Lorenzo was injured and his brother Giuliano killed during Easter Sunday mass in 1478. Moreover, Lorenzo was more scholar-prince than all-round leader: his lack of economic prowess was to bankrupt the family business and come close to doing the same to his city-state. Though his personal

Ferdinando I (1549-1609)

Ferdinando was a huge improvement on his brother Francesco. He reduced corruption, improved trade and farming, encouraged learning, and developed the navy and the port of Livorno. By staging lavish popular entertainments and giving dowries to poor girls, he became the most-loved Medici since Lorenzo *il Magnifico*.

Cosimo II (1590-1621)

The son of Ferdinando I, Cosimo (pictured right) protected Galileo from a hostile Catholic church. This was about the only worthwhile thing he did.

Ferdinando II
(1610-70)

Porky, laid-back, moustachioed Ferdinando did little to pull Florence from the backwater into which it had sunk. He loved to hunt, eye up boys and collect bric-a-brac.

Cosimo III (1642-1723)

Though trade was drying up and plague and famine stalked the land, Cosimo – a joyless, gluttonous, anti-Semitic loner who hung out with monks (his sulky wife Marguerite-Louise must take some blame for this) – did nothing to improve Tuscany's lot during his 53 years at the helm. Instead, intellectual freedom took a nosedive, taxes soared and public executions were a daily occurrence.

Gian Gastone (1671-1737)

Cosimo's disaster of a son was forcibly married to a spectacularly offensive woman, Anna Maria Francesca of Saxe-Lauenberg, who dragged him off to her gloomy castle near Prague, where he drowned his sorrows in taverns, whoring about with stable boys before escaping back to Florence in 1708. He was shocked to find himself Grand Duke in 1723. In the surprisingly coherent early years of his rule, he tried to relieve the tax burden and reinstate citizens' rights but quickly lapsed into chronic apathy and dissolution. When his relations tried to get him back on the straight and narrow he disgraced himself by, for instance, vomiting into his napkin at a respectable dinner, then taking off his wig and wiping his mouth with it. Eventually he wouldn't even get out of bed, and had troops of rowdy boys entertain him by cavorting about and shouting obscenities.

Anna Maria
(died 1743)

Every visitor to Florence since the mid 18th century has reason to be grateful to the straight-laced, pious Anna Maria, who was Gian Gastone's sister and the very last surviving Medici – in her will she bequeathed all Medici property and treasures to the Grand Duchy in perpetuity, on the sole condition that they never leave Florence.

popularity endured until his death in 1492, it didn't spill over on to his son Piero di Lorenzo, who in 1494 handed Florence to the French King Charles VIII as he passed through on the way to conquer Naples, then fled.

In a violent backlash against the splendour of Lorenzo's times, Florence turned for inspiration and guidance to a fire-and-brimstone-preaching monk who railed against paintings that made the Virgin Mary 'look like a harlot' and against Humanist thought, which he said would prompt the wrath of the one true and very vengeful God. Girolamo Savonarola (1452-98) perfectly caught the end-of-century spirit, winning the fanatical devotion not only of the poor and uneducated but of the leading minds of Lorenzo's magificent court. Artists and art patrons willingly threw their works and finery on to the monk's Bonfire of the Vanities in piazza della Signoria in 1497.

For Savonarola, Charles VIII represented the 'sword of the Lord': the city's capitulation was a just punishment. Savonarola set up a semi-democratic government, firmly allied to him, then allowed his extremist tendencies to get the better of him, alienating the Borgia pope Alexander VI and getting himself excommunicated. Had Florence been in a better economic state, the pope's gesture may have had little resonance; as it was, the region was devastated by pestilence and starvation. Resentment turned on Savonarola, who was summarily tried and burned at the stake in piazza della Signoria in May 1498.

The republic created after his death was surprisingly democratic but increasingly ineffective, making a stronger leadership look enticing to disaffected Florentines. In 1502 Piero Soderini, from an old noble family, was elected *gonfaloniere*-for-life, along the model of the Venetian doge. His pro-French policies brought him into conflict with the pro-Spanish pope Julius II, who had Cardinal Giovanni de' Medici whispering policy suggestions in his ear. In 1512 Soderini went into exile. Giuliano de' Medici, duke of Nemours, was installed as Florence's most prominent citizen, succeeded by his nephew Lorenzo, Duke of Urbino. Their clout was reinforced in 1513 when Giovanni became Pope Leo X.

The Medici clan got a second crack at the papacy in 1524, when Giulio, Lorenzo's illegitimate nephew, became Clement VII. Renowned for his vacillating nature, Clement withdrew his support from Europe's most powerful ruler, the Habsburg emperor Charles V, then dithered for months without reinforcing Rome's fortifications; in 1527 Charles dispatched some troops to show the Medici pope who was who, Rome was sacked and

Clement was forced to slink back to Charles' side, crowning him Holy Roman Emperor in 1529. Meanwhile, back in Florence the local populace had exploited the Medici ignominy in Rome to reinstall the republic. It was short-lived: Clement had agreed to crown Charles in exchange for a promise of help to get Florence back into Medici hands. The city fell in 1530.

When Clement installed the frizzy-haired Alessandro in power in Florence in 1530 and Charles V made him hereditary duke of Florence, the city entered one of its darkest and most desperate periods. Buoyed by support from Charles, whose daughter he had married, the authoritarian Alessandro trampled on Florentines' traditional rights and privileges while indulging in some shocking sexual antics.

His successor Cosimo had different, though no less unpleasant, defects; nor was he much cop at reversing Tuscany's gentle slide into the economic doldrums. Still, this dark horse – whom the pope made the first Grand Duke of Tuscany in 1569 – at least gave the city a patina of action, extending the writ of the *granducato* to all of Tuscany save Lucca, and adorning the city with vast new *palazzi*, including the Uffizi and the Palazzo Pitti.

BACKWATER

Cosimo's descendants continued to rule for 150 years: they were fittingly poor rulers for what was a very minor statelet in the chessboard of Europe. The *granducato*'s farming methods were backwards; the European fulcrum of its core industry, wool-making, like that of its main service industry, banking, had shifted definitively to northern Europe, leaving it to descend inexorably into depression. Its glory – and a very dusty glory it was – hung on its walls and adorned its palaces, with only the occasional spark of intellectual fervour (such as Cosimo II's spirited defence of Galileo Galilei when the astronomer was accused of heresy) to recall what the city had once represented. One 17th-century visitor described Florence as 'much sunk from what it was [...] one cannot but wonder to find a country that has been a scene of so much action now so forsaken and so poor.'

The male Medici line came to a squalid end in the shape of Gian Gastone, who died in 1737. His frantically pious sister Anna Maria couldn't wait to offload the *granducato*, handing it over to the house of Lorraine, cousins of the Austrian Habsburgs. Grand Duke Francis I and his successors spruced up the city, knocked its administration into shape, introduced new farming methods and generally shook the place out of its torpor.

Napoleon's triumphant romp down the peninsula at the end of the 18th century

The Renaissance and Humanism

The guiding doctrine of the Renaissance (*Rinascimento*, rebirth) was Humanism – the revival of the language and art of the ancient Greeks and Romans, and the reconciliation of this pagan heritage with Christianity. And although the most visible manifestation of the Renaissance in Florence was the astonishing outpouring of art in the 15th century, it was classical studies that lit the spark of the new age.

The groundwork had been done by a handful of exceptional men: Dante (1265-1321), Petrarch (1304-74) and Boccaccio (1313-75) had all collected Latin manuscripts, which shaped their approach to writing. But it was mounting Florentine wealth that paid for dedicated manuscript detectives such as Poggio Bracciolini (1380-1459) to dig through neglected monastery libraries across Europe.

A few classical works had never been lost, but those that were known were usually corrupted versions only available to clerics who forbade their dissemination or discussion. The volume of unknown works discovered was astonishing – and their effect was intellectual dynamite, causing the Florentines to reassess the way they thought about almost every field of human endeavour. In the first few decades of the 15th century, there came to light Quintilian's *The Training of an Orator*, which detailed the Roman education system, Columella's *De Re Rustica* on agriculture, key texts on Roman architecture by Vitruvius and Frontinus, and Cicero's *Brutus* (a justification of Republicanism). Very few Greek works were known in western Europe; suddenly, almost simultaneously, most of Plato, Homer, the plays of Sophocles, Aeschylus, Euripedes, Aristophanes, histories by Herodotus, Xenophon and Thucydides, the speeches of Demosthenes and many other classics were discovered.

The Renaissance focus on a pre-Christian age did not mean that God was under threat: just as Renaissance artists had no compunction about enhancing the beauty of their forms and compositions with classical features and allusions, Renaissance Humanists sought explanations beyond the Scriptures that were complementary to accepted religion rather than a challenge to it. Much effort was made to present the wisdom of the ancients as a precursor to the ultimate wisdom of God. The main players of the Renaissance did not perceive it as 'recanting' when they went on to embrace the millennial rantings of Savonarola (*see p14*) with enthusiasm.

Nor did the Renaissance fascination with things semi-scientific – Leonardo's anatomical drawings (pictured left) or the widespread obsession with the mathematics of Pythagorus – mean that this was a scientific age. The 15th century was an era when ideas were still paramount: science, as a process of deduction based on observation and experimentation, didn't really get going until the 17th century. In medicine, the theory of the four humours still held sway; astronomy and astrology were all but synonymous; mathematics was an almost mystical art; alchemy, the attempt to transform base metals into gold, flourished.

Magnificent while it lasted, Florence's pre-eminence in art and ideas was abruptly snuffed out on the death of Lorenzo *il Magnifico* in 1492: the invasion by Charles VIII of France in the 1490s and Savonarola's Bonfires of the Vanities (*see p14*) saw to that. In the early 16th century, the cutting edge switched to Rome, where Michelangelo, Bramante and Raphael were creating their finest works; thence, after Emperor Charles V sacked Rome in 1527, to Venice, where masters such as Palladio and Titian practised.

The Renaissance and art

By the time Giorgio Vasari coined the expression *rinascita* (rebirth) for the extraordinary flowering of art that took place in Tuscany in the 14th and 15th centuries, artistic primacy had passed to Rome. His seminal work *Lives of the Most Eminent Painters, Sculptors and Architects* (1550), the basis for much later assessment of the Renaissance, was as much a piece of propaganda for a declining city as a true reflection of the development of art in Italy.

The Renaissance was not a spontaneous Florentine outburst but a development in an unbroken tradition, the fulcrum of which shifted to Florence when the *caput mundi*, Rome, became so strife-ridden that the papacy fled into exile in Avignon (1305-1378). The innovations of Giotto (pictured left) – the so-called father of the Renaissance – owe as much to his contact with the great but neglected Romans Pietro Cavallini and his contemporary Jacopo di Torriti as they do to the stiff, Byzantine art of Cimabue, whom Vasari describes as Giotto's teacher.

There's no doubt, however, that events conspired to ensure that, with Rome out of the artistic picture, Florence was ready to fill the gap. With trade booming and enlightened leaders splashing their great wealth on beautifying their city, the arts bloomed. Spurred by Humanist studies into classical texts in which artists were lauded to the skies, the 'artisans' who had long been designing or daubing superlative works became highly regarded personages; rather than ordering decorations by the yard, patrons would seek the top names to create or decorate *palazzi* and churches worthy of their status. The 'artist' was reborn.

In architecture the leap from Arnolfo di Cambio's Duomo in Florence to Filippo Brunelleschi's magnificent dome for the same building is a good example of the transition from the late Gothic to the resoundingly classically inspired Renaissance. For sculpture, follow the progress in the doors of the Baptistery from Nicolo Pisano's glorious Gothic quatrefoils to Lorenzo Ghiberti's two sets of perfectly Renaissance ones, with their arresting use of perpective. Ghiberti's student Donatello (pictured middle) took his innovations to new heights in his *David* and *St George*, both now in the Bargello.

In painting Masaccio (1401-28) was the first of the Tuscan artists to make a complete break with the past, introducing the revolutionary vocabulary of naturalism and profoundly human emotion that would come to be synonymous with Renaissance art. Along with Fra Angelico, he laid the groundwork for a new generation, including Domenico Ghirlandaio, Filippo Lippi, Andrea del Verrocchio and the lyrical Sandro Botticelli. Outside Florence, Piero della Francesca and Luca Signorelli drew on that same vocabulary to extraordinary effect.

From Verrocchio's workshop came Leonardo da Vinci (pictured right), from Ghirlandaio's came Michelangelo Buonarotti. The heavyweights of the Renaissance, they waded in at the end of Florence's Golden Age and left their mark as much elsewhere as in this city: the former in Milan, the latter in his unforgettable works in a Rome that by then was picking up the pieces of its shattered glory, eclipsing Florence and becoming the world centre of art once more.

brought him into possession of Tuscany in 1799, to the joy of liberals and the horror of local peasantry, who drove the French out in the Viva Maria uprising, during which they also wreaked their revenge on unlucky Jews and anyone suspected of Jacobin leanings.

But it wasn't long before the French returned, installing Louis de Bourbon of Parma as head of the Kingdom of Etruria in 1801. Napoleon's sister Elisa Baciocchi was made Princess of Piombino and Lucca in 1805, and Grand Duchess of Tuscany from 1809 to 1814 – a time that saw much constitutional reform and much pilfering from Florence's art collections. Many of the works spirited off to Paris were returned to Tuscany after the restoration of the Lorraine dynasty in the shape of Ferdinand III in 1816.

FLORENCE IN THE *RISORGIMENTO*

By the 1820s and 1830s Tuscany was an agreeable, benign place. Under the laid-back if not overly bright Grand Duke Leopold II, the region enjoyed a climate of tolerance that attracted intellectuals, dissidents, artists and writers from all over Italy and Europe. They would meet in the Gabinetto Scientifico-Letterario in the Palazzo Buondelmonti in piazza Santa Trinità, frequently welcoming prominent foreigners such as Heine and Byron.

For a time Leopold and his ministers kept the reactionary influence of the Grand Duke's uncle, Emperor Francis II of Austria, at arm's length while playing down the growing populist cry for Italian unification. But by the 1840s it was clear that the nationalist movement posed a serious threat to the status quo. Even relaxed Florence was swept up in nationalist enthusiasm, causing Leopold to clamp down on reformers and impose some censorship.

In 1848, a tumultuous year of revolutions, insurrections in Livorno and Pisa forced Leopold to grant concessions to the reformers, including a Tuscan constitution.

When news reached Florence that the Milanese had driven the Austrians out of their city, and that Carlo Alberto, King of Sardinia-Piedmont, was determined to push them out of Italy altogether, thousands of Tuscans joined the cause. In 1849, the pendulum seemed to be swinging back in favour of the better-trained Austrians. But radicals in Florence dug in and bullied the Grand Duke into appointing the activist reformer Giuseppe Montanelli, a professor of law at Pisa University, to head a new government. Montanelli went to Rome to attend a constituent assembly, but the alarmed Pope Pius IX threatened to excommunicate anyone attending such an assembly.

Leopold panicked, and fled in disguise to Naples. A provisional government was set up but, in the absence of armed support, collapsed. The Florentines invited Leopold back; he returned in July 1849 but brought Austrian troops to keep order. Grim times followed for a city just recovering from one of its worst ever floods. On his return, Leopold seemed content to be an Austrian puppet and clamped down on the press and dissent; his popularity vanished.

In April 1859, Piedmont's Count Camillo Cavour persuaded Napoleon III's France to join him in expelling the Austrians. The French and Piedmontese swept the Austrian armies before them, while in Florence nationalist demos forced the government to resign. On 27 April Leopold left Florence and his family for the last time, his former subjects watching in silence. The following year the Tuscan people voted for unification with the Kingdom of Piedmont.

'A formation of American bombers tried to destroy Campo di Marte station: the operation was bungled.'

CAPITAL OF ITALY

Five years later, with Rome holding out against the forces of unification, Florence was declared capital of Italy, much to the annoyance of the Piedmontese capital of Turin – 200 people died in riots there when the shift was announced. The Florentines greeted their new king with enthusiasm when he arrived in February 1865 to take up residence in the Palazzo Pitti, but the influx of northerners was met with mixed feelings: business boomed, but the Florentines didn't take to Piedmontese flashiness.

Huge changes were wrought in the city. Ring roads encircled the old centre, avenues, squares (such as piazza della Repubblica) and residential suburbs were built and parks were laid out. Intellectuals and socialites crowded the salons and cafés.

When war with Prussia forced the French (who had swapped sides) to withdraw their troops from Italy in 1870, Rome finally fell to Vittorio Emanuele's troops and Italy was united for the first time since the fall of the Roman Empire. Florence's brief reign as capital ended.

THE 20TH CENTURY

Florence began the 20th century much as it ended it – as a thriving tourist centre. In the early 1900s it drew an exclusive coterie of writers, artists, aesthetes and the upper-middle classes. Queen Victoria, Oscar Wilde, Henry James, EM Forster and DH Lawrence were among its famous visitors. An English-speaking

A load of bankers

As international trade flourished in the 13th century, merchants were faced with two problems: finding capital for investments, and devising methods of moving money without having to haul bags of bullion with them. A major commercial centre, Florence was among the first European city to come up with handy solutions, thus establishing itself a role as one of the continent's biggest banking centres.

The first problem was partially solved by money-lenders, many of whom were successful merchants themselves with cash to spare. But a papal ban on usury – charging interest on loans – meant that simply handing out money made little sense except to Jews, who were not affected by Church law. Florence's original bankers, therefore, hailed from the city's thriving Jewish community, with the Da Pisa, Da Rieti and Abrabanel families leading the pack.

It wasn't long before gentiles sought a way to get into this high-yielding field: by the mid 13th century, the pope had come up with a handy cavil allowing Christians to charge a levy on loans where risk was involved – meaning practically any. Soon Florence's excellent bankers were handling the huge papal accounts and collecting taxes for the pope.

In the 1290s the Florentine Bardi and Peruzzi banking families set up offices around Europe, and in London in particular, overcoming that second problem – moving cash – by instituting the system of bankers' drafts that formed the basis of modern banking. By the 1320s, these two, along with the Acciaiuoli – another Tuscan family – had become Europe's biggest bankers.

Twenty years later – when Florence boasted more than 80 banks functioning internationally – the Bardi, Peruzzi and Acciaiuoli paid the price of over-concentrating their assets, in this case in England. Major financers of the Hundred Years' War, they were all bankrupted when Edward III defaulted on the debts accumulated over long periods of conflict fought by expensive mercenary soldiers.

The older banks' downfall provided a solid lesson for another up-and-coming banking dynasty, the Medici, who learned not to place all their florins in one basket. Firmly in charge of the papal account, and diversifying operations around the continent, they dominated the city's banking scene for well over a century.

Florence's downfall as a banking heavyweight came in the second half of the 15th century. He may have been *Magnifico* in many ways, but Lorenzo, the grandest of the Medici (*see p10* **Who they? The Medici**), didn't have the Midas touch, and his family fortunes had been eroded well before his son Piero di Lorenzo sealed the fate of Florentine banking for good. The luckless Piero capitulated before the French king Charles VIII in 1494, the Medici bank effectively shut up shop, and the focus of the political, commercial and banking world shifted definitively to northern Europe.

industry sprang up to cater for the needs of these wealthy foreigners.

The city was neither occupied nor attacked in World War I, though it inevitably suffered the social repercussions. Post-war hardship inspired a fierce middle-class rage for order that found expression in the black shirt of Fascism. Groups of *squadristi* were already forming in 1919, organising parades and demonstrations in the streets of Florence.

When Mussolini was elected in 1923, there began in Florence a campaign to expunge the city of foreign elements and influences. Hotels and shops with English names were put under pressure to sever their Anglo-Saxon affiliations. The Florence that had been described as a '*ville toute Anglaise*' by the French social-historian Goncourt brothers was under threat.

When Italy entered the war at Germany's side on 10 June 1940, Florentines were confident that the Allies would never attack their city from the air: Florence was a museum, a testament to artistic evolution; its monuments were its best protection. Nevertheless, the Fascist regime, perhaps for propaganda reasons, began protecting the city's art. Photos of the period show statuary disappearing inside comically inefficient wooden sheds, while the Baptistery doors were bricked up and many of the main treasures from the Uffizi and Palazzo Pitti, including Botticelli's *Primavera*, were taken to Castello di Montegufoni – owned by the British Sitwell family – in the Tuscan countryside for safekeeping.

The Germans occupied Florence on 11 September 1943, just weeks after Mussolini's arrest and the armistice was signed. Only when it became necessary to hinder the Nazis' communications line to Rome were aesthetic scruples set aside. In September 1943 a

By 1944 Allied commanding officers had extracted permission from leaders to attack Florence using only the most experienced squadrons, in ideal weather conditions. On 11 March the Americans began unleashing their bombers on the city, causing casualties but leaving the *centro storico* and its art intact. On 1 August 1944 fighting broke out in various parts of the city but poorly armed Florentine patriots couldn't prevent the Germans from destroying all the Arno bridges except Ponte Vecchio. Along with the bridges, the old quarter around Ponte Vecchio was razed to the ground.

The Val D'Orcia and Monte Amiata areas in southern Tuscany were key theatres for partisans, who held out with considerable loss of life until British and US infantry reinforced their lines on the Arno on 1 September 1944. The German army abandoned Fiesole on 7 September. When the Allies reached Florence they found a functioning government formed by the partisan *Comitati di liberazione nazionale* (CLN). Within hours of the Germans' departure, work started to put the bridges back into place – Ponte Santa Trinità was rebuilt, stone by stone, in exactly the same location.

DAMAGED GOODS

Two decades later the Florentine skill at restoration was required again, this time for a calamity of an altogether different nature: in the early hours of the morning of 4 November 1966 citizens awoke to find their homes flooded by the Arno, which had broken its banks, and soon all the main *piazze* were under water. An estimated 15,000 cars were destroyed, 6,000 shops put out of business, and almost 14,000 families left homeless. Many artworks, books and archives were damaged, treasures in the refectory of Santa Croce were blackened by mud, and in the church's nave Donatello's *Cavalcanti Annunciation* was soaked with oil up to the Virgin's knees. As word of the disaster spread around the world, public and private funds were pumped into repairing and restoring some of the damage.

The city's cultural heritage took another direct hit in 1993 when a bomb planted by the Mafia exploded in the city centre, killing five people. It caused structural damage to the Uffizi, destroying the Gregoriophilus library and damaging the Vasari Corridor.

Not that you'd know it now: in a restoration job carried out in record time, one of the world's most-visited art repositories was returned to its pristine state and tourists began queuing outside again, confirming the modern city's vocation for living off its past.

Hitler and Mussolini, Florence 1940.

formation of American bombers swooped in to destroy Florence's Campo di Marte station: the operation was bungled, leaving 218 civilians dead while the station remained in perfect working order. Further air raids were banned by orders from the highest levels.

At the beginning of the war Florence had a Jewish population of more than 2,000. The chief rabbi saved the lives of many Jews in the city by advising them to hide in convents or little villages under false names.

Three raids were carried out by Nazis and Fascists on the night of 27 November 1943. The largest was on the Franciscan Sisters of Mary in piazza del Carmine, where dozens of Jews were concealed. The second train to leave Italy bound for the gas chambers set out from Florence, carrying at least 400 Jews from Florence, Siena and Bologna; not one of them is known to have returned.

Key events

7th-6th centuries BC Height of Etruscan civilisation.

3rd century All Etruria under Roman control.

59 BC Foundation of Florentia by Julius Caesar.

56 BC Caesar, Crassus and Pompey form first triumvirate at Lucca.

AD 540s Tuscany contested in Goth vs Byzantine campaigns.

552 Florence falls to the Goths under Totila.

c800 New walls erected around Florence.

10th-12th centuries Pisa becomes wealthy port; Lucca, seat of margraves of Tuscany, is region's most important city.

1076 Matilda becomes countess of Tuscany.

1115 Matilda bequeaths all her lands to the Pope except Florence, Lucca and Siena, which become independent *comuni*.

1125 Florence captures Fiesole.

1173-5 More new walls for Florence.

1215 Murder of Buondelmonte ignites Guelph/Ghibelline conflict.

1252 First gold florin minted.

1289 Florence defeats Arezzo at Campaldino.

1293 Nobility excluded from government, *signoria* created.

1296 Foundations laid for new Duomo.

1329 Florence takes over Pistoia.

1342 Florence's biggest banks collapse when English king Edward III defaults on debts.

1348 Black Death ravages Tuscany.

1351 Florence buys Prato from Naples.

1375-8 War of the Eight Saints frees Florence from papal influence. Guelphs join with *popolo grasso* to exclude guilds from power.

1406 Florence captures Pisa.

1411 Florence gains Cortona.

1421 Florence buys Livorno from Genova.

1428 War between Florence and Lucca.

1432 Florence beats Siena at San Romano, immortalised by artist Paolo Uccello.

1433 Cosimo de Medici exiled by Albizzi clan during unpopular Lucchese war.

1434 Return of Cosimo from exile; overthrow and exile of the Albizzi.

1436 Brunelleschi finishes the Duomo dome.

1437 Florence defeats Milan at Barga.

1452 Naples and Venice declare war on Milan and Florence.

1454 Threat of the Turks brings Pope, Venice, Florence and Milan together in Holy League.

1466 Piero quashes conspiracy to oust Medici.

1478 Piero's son Lorenzo escapes murder in Pazzi conspiracy. Papacy and Naples declare war on Florence.

1479 Lorenzo goes alone to Naples to negotiate peace treaty with King Ferrante.

1494 Wars of Italy begin – France's Charles VIII invades Italy. Inept Piero, son of Lorenzo, surrenders Florence then flees.

1512 Papal and Spanish armies sack Prato and force return of Medici to Florence.

1524 Giulio de' Medici becomes Pope Clement VII; continues to run Florence from Rome.

1527 Horrific sacking of Rome by Habsburg emperor Charles V's army. Medici expelled; new republic declared.

1529 Charles V, now allied with Clement VII, besieges and takes Florence.

1530 Alessandro de' Medici installed as head of government then Duke by Charles V.

1537 Alessandro murdered. Obscure Cosimo defeats Florentine rebels at Montemurlo.

1555 With imperial help, Cosimo crushes Siena after a devastating war.

1569 Cosimo buys the title Grand Duke of Tuscany from Pope Paul V.

16th-17th centuries Steady decline of Tuscan agriculture and industry overseen by succession of Medici Grand Dukes.

1723 Gian Gastone, last of the Medici rulers, takes the reins.

1735 Grand duchy of Tuscany given to Francis, duke of Lorraine. Enlightened regime begins.

1737 Death of Gian Gastone's sister, Anna Maria, who leaves all Medici art and treasures to Florence in perpetuity.

1799 French troops enter Florence. Revival of interest in Tuscany, which becomes major stop on the 'Grand Tour'.

1801-7 Grand Duchy absorbed into Kingdom of Etruria.

1809 Napoleon installs his sister Elisa Bacciochi as Grand Duchess of Tuscany.

1816 Grand Duke Ferdinando III returns to Tuscany on defeat of Napoleon.

1824 Genial Leopold II succeeds father.

1859 Leopold allows himself to be overthrown in the *Risorgimento*.

1865-70 Florence becomes first capital of united Italy.

1943 Germans enter Florence, establish Gothic Line on the Arno.

1944 Germans blow up all Pisa's bridges and all but the Ponte Vecchio in Florence. Allies liberate Florence.

1966 The Arno floods, causing huge damage.

1993 Bomb destroys Gregoriophilus library and damages Vasari Corridor.

New law courts are part of Florence's urban renewal. *See p23.*

Florence Today

The laissez-faire attitude of the Tuscan capital.

Florence is famous in Italy for its tolerance. Life is sweet; anywhere you look, the eye alights on beauty and harmony. Culture is vibrant, but love of tradition has kept the city looking much the same as it has done for 500 years, while modern development is chased out of town. Football, politics and personal compliments are favourite topics of conversation, while uglier issues of city life are swept under the carpet.

In a country that has the seat of the Roman Catholic empire embedded in its capital, Florence has a remarkably easy-come easy-go relationship with the Church. The Vatican is another country. Religion is something depicted in Renaissance art, rather than an arbiter of contemporary morality. While the Pope's proclamation that the Pill is chemical abortion caused a moral dilemma in many areas of Italy, in Florence it was a distant furore.

The Mafia too has a low profile in Florence, and tales of bribery and corruption stand out against a backdrop of polite decency. Deputy mayor Cioni has been known to wire his office with listening devices to entrap contract-hunters offering bribes – oiling palms just

doesn't wash here. You're more likely to see genuine handshakes than funny ones: the suave mayor, or Sindaco, Leonardo Domenici, pops up in the papers on matters of civic pride, inviting celebrities like Michael Douglas and Catherine Zeta Jones to stop off at the Palazzo Vecchio before a shopping trip at Gucci. When Sindaco Domenici suggested a modest tourist tax of L2,000 on hotel and restaurant bills to allow the 11 million tourists annually to help pay for the upkeep of the entire city as an open-air art museum, art critic Vittorio Sgarbi led the shockwave against such blatant commercialism of the city's heritage. 'Certain values have no price,' Sgarbi proclaimed proudly.

CONSERVE AND SURVIVE

Politics is constantly debated – particularly during the Berlusconi election campaign, as Florence, along with much of Tuscany and Emilia Romagna, is communist and vehemently opposed to the right-wing media tycoon's march to power. However, for a 'communist' city, Florence is deeply conservative – with a small 'c'. Conservation and preservation of museums and monuments is a priority, in no small part because of the money they bring in from the tourist trade. But leftist politics protects workers' family life – rather than seeking to maximise profits. Post may take three weeks – as part of a job creation programme, mail is diverted to southern Italy for sorting – but workers' rights are considered more important than efficiency. A fast food outlet staged a strike when staff insisted they should get an afternoon siesta like everyone else – which went down like a lead balloon in McBurger land.

Manual work proceeds at a leisurely pace – a long stretch of roadworks to repair gas leaks closed via dei Fossi for a year recently – and the city is stoical about bus strikes, although the biggest grumble is traffic and getting around in a city where private cars are restricted. Nevertheless, there is public – if not commercial – support for keeping cars out of the centre.

There have been pilot schemes to make electric cars available at hotels and introduce buses that run on gas. There are bigger ideas too, though they often have credibility problems, partly because of failures in the past. Plans for a tramway were temporarily derailed when it was pointed out that the vehicles would not fit in the narrow streets. Similarly, the university unveiled a proposal for a subway system in May 2001, a one-way figure of eight: miss your stop and you would have to change twice and complete the circuit. However, a clutch of new projects may finally have gained enough momentum to make a significant impact (*see p23* **The future starts here**).

PERSONAL COMFORTS

Florentines grow up surrounded by beauty, and perhaps vanity is the side effect. In Florence, it's believed that promotion goes to the best-groomed man. Not that promotion is taken too seriously. There is little overt ambition; a job that necessitates foreign travel is viewed as an infringement not a fringe benefit. Nor have Florentines adopted the New Yorker's time-saving approach to double-dinner deals (swapping tables after the starter to do business with another associate). Though there are signs that this is changing. Whereas lunch used to be a sacrosanct three-hour affair, bar and café menus reveal a quick plate of pasta is becoming popular, and fewer shops now close for lunch.

Another area where things have started to change is in the home. Property tends to stay in the family as the younger generation inherit a home from their grandparents (and move directly there from their parents' homes); until recently you'd never hear Notting Hill dinner party talk of house prices or property renovations. But changes in the finance markets means that mortgage rates have fallen to

around UK levels, with a smaller deposit required: more young people are buying properties, and Bologna's IKEA is packed with homebodies on Sunday afternoons

IMMORAL MINORITY

The pleasure industry has changed in the past few years. The wide leafy *viali* leading out of the city have long been a place where transvestite and transsexual 'ladies' of the night proudly displayed their designer plastic surgery. The city turned a blind eye, a generously liberal, broadly tolerant attitude in the spirit of the Venusian arts that define the city's mentality. But it's no longer a carnival of individual vanity and fluttering false eyelashes but a sleazy business allegedly organised by a criminal underworld.

The girls available for sale really are girls – many as young as 13 or 14 – procured to order for the city's wealthy indigenous and visiting businessmen. The polite response is still a faltering 'if that's how they want to live… let them get on with it'. But it would seem that the girls didn't choose to live that way, and now turning a blind eye seems more of an immoral weakness than a moral strength. And the official attitude has swung that way too recently, with a big clamp-down on prostitution resulting in a wave of arrests.

The papers say illegal immigration rackets, drug dealing and prostitution are being run by a new – Albanian – mafia. Inner city problems are anathema to Florentines. Illegal immigration is a pressing human rights issue, but a public brought up in the bosom of its family is out of its depth when faced with harsh facts. The Church takes an active role in secular social issues while the local authorities look the other way. A priest, Don Benzi, has been raising awareness of the plight of girls whose asylum-seeking parents have been duped into selling them into sex slavery and attempting to rescue them from the streets – not so much to save their souls as their bodies and their lives.

The change in tone has made Florentines uneasy, but rather than facing the awkward questions it raises about their own family men – apparently willing customers in this trade – they are directing their indignation into xenophobia. Immigrants aren't warmly welcomed in Florence. Italy is not a naturally multicultural society; it has a history not of colonies but of warring principalities and regional insularity is deeply entrenched.

Racism towards the African street pedlars – often students or graduates here because the money is good – is covert. The pedlars live in cramped conditions – often ten to a room, in tenements in the industrial hinterland outside the city. They are tolerated (grudgingly by businesses), but this doesn't mean they are welcomed with open arms by Florentines – who besides their tolerance are also renowned for their snobbery and superciliousness. But hostility is reserved for Albanians – who are widely feared. Street crime has seen a spate of muggings and handbag snatches by thieves on scooters. Car crime is accelerating and residents of Settignano, on the leafy slopes above the city, say their villas have been raided. They also worry their student children are being sold drugs. While cocaine has acceptance in clubbing and fashion circles, the drug that parents fear is heroin. Police have attempted to clean up the action in bohemian left-bank Piazza Santo Spirito and Piazza Santa Maria Novella, near the station, where dealing was rife under the shadowy cloisters. But tour guides complain that drug deals are now conducted openly in front of the Duomo – dealers operating in the safety of numbers as thousands of tourists pass by.

SWEET NOTHINGS

But little really disturbs people going about their daily lives in this prosperous city. Even a bomb scare in May 2001, on the eve of the eighth anniversary of the bombing of the Georgofili library which killed five people and damaged the Uffizi in 1993 – hardly caused a stir. The suitcase of bullets and electrical wiring planted outside a bank was disposed of as passers-by stopped to stare. 'A thousand precautions taken' yelled the headlines. In reality a newsstand outside the bank was evacuated, as people squeezed past and convened in a bar nearby to gossip.

Ciao, Bella. *La dolce vita* goes on as Florentines insist on a state of grace.

The future starts here

Forget conservative consolidation. Assuming everything goes according to plan, the urban development projected for Florence over the next ten years or so could change the face of the city forever. Of course, we are talking Italy here, so plans come and plans go, money materialises and then seems to disappear, but the present state of play would seem to suggest that things are indeed moving.

Some of the projects are national, such as the new high speed railway designed to improve rail links between Milan and Rome that will pass under Florence with an underground station near Santa Maria Novella, but others focus on Florence itself. Several 'lost' areas on the periphery of the city are being reclaimed and developed as residential areas, the most ambitious of which is Firenze Nova. The 'satellite city', which is being built to the north-west of the city in Novoli on land which was once occupied by a huge Fiat factory, has been on the drawing-board for years with its fair share of scandal attached, but funding is now in place and building work has started.

An area covering some 320,000 square metres (3.44 million square feet) will eventually incorporate three faculties of the University of Florence, new law courts and relevant departmental offices all under the same roof for the first time (they are at present spread all over the centre of town), a hotel, a big park, extensive housing and all the infrastructure required to support a large residential area. So far, the university buildings are materialising fast (it is hoped to get students in there by the end of 2001), and the foundations of the court building (which will provide work space for about 4,000 people) have been dug. The state is financing the latter while private money is accounting for the rest.

The ever-present problem of traffic continues to be a major headache for the urban planners. A three-line tram network (or *tranvia*) should reduce the number of fume-belching buses that plague the city, and cut down on the number of private cars used. Aimed towards commuters, the project has received funding and preliminary work has started. It will serve the new satellite city and other peripheral residential areas as well as Peretola airport; one line will be linked with the *centro storico*. The first phase should be completed by 2004, while the third line (still only partially financed at this point) should be functional by the end of 2006. There are also plans for a subway system, though these seem less likely to come to fruition.

Florence is notoriously lacking in green space, but the traffic-clogged *viale* (the ring road) around Porta al Prato is being moved below ground via an underpass, thereby freeing up an extensive space which is to be turned into a public park; work is already disrupting the area. Just north of here, the present customs house will be turned into the city's first purpose-built auditorium, to be used mainly for classical concerts. Will it all happen? Time will tell.

Scuola del Cuoio

FIRENZE
The Leather School
manufacturers of fine leather goods
Inside the monastery of Santa Croce

Opening Hours:
from 15 March to 15 November 9.00am-6.30pm Sunday: 10.30-12.30am-3-6.00pm
from 16 November to 14 March 9.30-12.30am-3-6.30pm Sunday closed
Entrance:
Through the Church-Piazza Santa Croce, 16
Through the Garden-Via San Giuseppe, 5r (on Sunday mornings)
Phones: 055 244533 - 055 244534 - Fax: 055 2480337
http://www.leatherschool.it/ email: leatherschool@leatherschool.it

The magnificent interior of Brunelleschi's landmark Duomo cupola. *See p27.*

Architecture

The harmonious, simple and simply magnificent buildings of Firenze.

The roots of Florentine builders are primarily Etruscan. It was the Etruscans, in the third or fourth century before Christ, who first used the arch. And it was their sense of proportion and colour that reappeared during the Middle Ages as Florentine architecture found its form. The Romans were important too, but since some of the early kings of Rome were Etruscans, the distinction is somewhat blurred. Besides, Rome was located on the southern border of Etruria near many of the main Etruscan centres and may have originally been an Etruscan city. So when, during the Renaissance, Imperial Rome and Christian Rome infused Florentine architecture, it was to a great extent a rebirth.

Fiesole, the hill town just to the north of Florence, was the first major settlement in the area. It was one of the league of major Etruscan cities and, as such, would have been settled to protect the pass coming south out of the Apennines, and the crossing point over the Arno, more or less where the Ponte Vecchio

now stands. Extensive sections of walls survive there – some with the massive blocks of stone for which the Etruscans were famous – and there are considerable remains from both Etruscan and later Roman times. The Roman theatre is still used for shows in the summer.

Only when the Romans began to absorb Etruscan civilisation was Roman Florence, probably on the site of a razed Etruscan village. Laid out in the grid pattern still visible on any map, the town was apparently founded by Julius Caesar in 59 BC. Not much of Roman Florence remains above ground, but it is known that the theatre was just behind Palazzo Vecchio, while the amphitheatre's shape can still be seen in the shape of the streets and buildings just west of piazza Santa Croce.

It was along one of the main axes of Roman Florence, now via dei Calzaiuoli, that medieval Florence grew up. At one end of the axis was the religious centre with the Baptistery and Santa Reparata (the church that once stood where the Duomo now stands); at the other, the civil centre of piazza della Signoria, where

Palazzo Vecchio stands. Between the two, just as today, was the commercial centre, now piazza della Repubblica.

There are a number of medieval towers still standing, the oldest of which is the round **Torre della Pagliazza** in via Santa Elisabetta, just off via del Corso. There are others in via Dante Alighieri, opposite Dante's house, in piazza di San Pier Maggiore, and in borgo San Jacopo, near the Ponte Vecchio.

'Brunelleschi not only gave the Duomo its cupola, he also designed two of the city's finest churches.'

As Florence expanded, new walls had to be built, principally between 1259 and 1333. The newly enclosed area came to include the *borghi*, service areas for industry and storage that grew up along the roads leading out of early medieval towns. The *borghi* suddenly became fairly straight, wide streets, and the owners of industrial property found themselves sitting on prime development land. Many of them moved their commercial premises outside the new walls, knocked down the old ones, now inside the city, and built large townhouses in their place – eventually to be called *palazzi* – with ample gardens behind.

IT STARTS HERE

Florentine architecture – as opposed to architecture in Florence – began in the 11th century with the completion of the Baptistery of San Giovanni, the green and white structure just in front of the Duomo. It is is characterised by a search for harmony. The buildings are balanced and simple. They are sharp-edged, with wide, overhanging roofs. The almost black shadows they cast onto the hard stone streets have no gradation at all between light and dark. Any baroque that you may see in Florentine architecture is certainly an import from Rome.

Its distinct style partly arises from the fact that the prominent architects who worked in Florence were all local: Arnolfo di Cambio (c1245-1302); Giotto (1266/7-1337); Filippo Brunelleschi (1377-1446); Michelozzo di Bartolommeo Michelozzi (1396-1472); Leon Battista Alberti (1404-72); Giuliano da Sangallo (c1445-1535); Il Cronaca (1454-1508); Michelangelo Buonarroti (1475-1564); Giorgio Vasari (1511-74); Bartolommeo Ammanati (1511-92); Bernardo Buontalenti (1531-1608) and, in the 19th century, Giuseppe Poggi (1811-1901). Even the best modern building in Florence, the railway station at Santa Maria Novella, was built in the 1930s by a local fellow: Giovanni Michelucci (1891-1991) from Pistoia.

ROMANESQUE AND GOTHIC

Along with San Miniato al Monte – the wonderful green and white faced church that looks down on the city from above piazzale Michelangelo – and Santissimi Apostoli, the **Baptistery** (*see p69*) is the main Romanesque church in Florence. It was built some time between the sixth and the 11th centuries; both the stupendous mosaics inside and the marble decoration outside seem to have been finished in the late 12th or early 13th century, indicating that the building was completed by that time. **San Miniato** (*see p105*) is an 11th-century building, also finished at the beginning of the 13th century and, together with the Baptistery, among the finest Romanesque churches in Europe. **Santissimi Apostoli** (c1080; *see p81*) is hidden away on the north bank of the Arno, between Ponte Vecchio and Ponte Santa Trinita. It's also an early building, less spectacular perhaps, but purely Romanesque in its plan and the way it conveys the beauty of medieval culture.

Gothic construction followed, using a pointed arch instead of the earlier half-moon Roman one that enabled builders to make higher and wider structures. There are five major Gothic churches in Florence, four of which were influenced by the one built slightly earlier: **San Remigio**, a French pilgrims' church of the 12th century, located just behind Palazzo Vecchio. It retains, as does much Florentine building, an external simplicity that belies its interior. In 1278 the building of **Santa Maria Novella** (*see p84*) was started. This vast and beautiful Domenican church near the railway station is perhaps the loveliest structure ever put up by that order of monks.

The cathedral of **Santa Maria del Fiore**, better known as the Duomo (*see p65*), was begun in 1297, perhaps designed by Arnolfo di Cambio. It carried medieval construction to a yet higher and larger scale, while retaining the essential Gothic principles of construction. (The great size of the building's cupola was not actually envisaged in the original plan.)

The famous bronze doors of the **Baptistery**.

The fourth major Gothic church in Florence is **Santa Croce** (1298; *see p96*), also attributed to Arnolfo. Although this Franciscan building has wide, pointed arches along both sides of the nave, springing diagonally across it, the flat, timber ceiling inside Santa Croce, supported on the two rows of parallel nave arches means that, upon entering the church, the eye is drawn along the nave to the main altar and to the wall of stained glass behind it, rather than upwards.

At the end of the 14th century, the grain market and store that was San Michele in Orto (now known as **Orsanmichele**; *see p77*) had its ground-floor loggia closed on all sides to create a small, rather gloomy church for the guilds of Florence. At the beginning of the 15th century each guild commissioned a statue to place in each of the 14 niches around the building's exterior. These statues, modelled as they were on humans rather than on traditional medieval Christian figures, were an important impetus to the development of the early Renaissance. Many of the originals are housed in the Museo di Orsanmichele and the Bargello and have been replaced here by replicas.

Another Gothic structure is the bell-tower of the Duomo, the **Campanile** (*see p69*). Designed and begun by Giotto in about 1330, it was completed only after his death. The **Bargello** (originally the Palazzo del Popolo, begun 1250; *see p93*) and the **Palazzo Vecchio** (begun 1299; *see p78*) are two more civil structures that were built in the Gothic period, this latter another structure apparently designed by Arnolfo di Cambio, Florence's early sculptor and architect.

EARLY RENAISSANCE

Brunelleschi, Michelozzo and Alberti are the three most important names of early Renaissance architecture in Florence. Brunelleschi not only gave the Duomo its cupola – the largest such construction since Ancient Roman times – he also designed two of the city's finest churches: **San Lorenzo** (constructed 1422-69; *see p88*), including its especially fine, almost independent Old Sacristy (1422-9) and **Santo Spirito** (1444-81; *see p100*). He also built the **Pazzi Chapel** (begun 1442; *see p96*), a small private family building in the garden of Santa Croce. Breaking with the past, these buildings embrace human thought even more than Christian faith. They turn back to ideas and forms of the pagan world before Christianity. Their very roots spring from a new, lay Christianity, centred on the individual. The cupola of the Duomo is really already the ideal Renaissance central-plan church, built on top of an earlier 14th-century structure. Many later churches, dating from the High Renaissance

Where to see...

Palazzi
Florence contains more than 200 private *palazzi*, which are among the most beautiful buildings anywhere. Among the best streets to spot these are **via Maggio**, **via di Santo Spirito**, **via dei Tornabuoni**, **via dei Gori**, **via San Gallo** and **borgo degli Albizi**.

Loggias
There are many beautiful loggias and porches hidden away in private courtyards or monasteries, but many can also be seen from the street. Those in **piazza della Signoria** and **piazzale degli Uffizi**, in **piazza della Santissima Annunziata**, in **piazza San Marco**, behind the Uffizi at the corner of **via dei Neri**, and at the **Mercato Nuovo** are all easily accessible.

Libraries
Besides Michelangelo's Laurentian Library (*see p28*), there are two libraries of merit: the beautiful one by Michelozzo in the **San Marco** monastery (after 1437), and the less beautiful **Biblioteca Nazionale** (begun 1911) – the largest in Italy – at Piazza Cavalleggeri.

Cast iron
The cast-iron markets near piazzas **San Lorenzo** and **Sant'Ambrogio** are two fine 19th-century structures.

Non-Catholic churches
The large **Jewish Synagogue** (begun 1874) in via Farini, and the smaller, exquisite **Russian Church** (1902) in viale Leone X.

and even baroque periods, descend directly from this amazing structure. St Peter's cupola in Rome, begun about 100 years later by Michelangelo, has roughly the same interior diameter: 42 metres (546 feet). But both structures are marginally narrower than the dome of the Pantheon in Rome, built over 1,200 years earlier, a structure that itself descends from the still much earlier design of large Etruscan domed tombs.

Michelozzo worked often for Cosimo de' Medici (Cosimo il Vecchio), the founder of the Medici family's fortunes. He built Cosimo's town residence, now called **Palazzo Medici Riccardi** (1444; *see p88*), where he developed the traditional Florentine *palazzo* so that it had two façades, as well as strongly rusticated orders. He also built for Cosimo a number of castellated villas in 13th-century style, including **Careggi** (*see p104* **Medici villas**).

Although Florentine, Alberti grew up elsewhere and worked mostly outside Florence. His usual taste tended almost to ape the architectural forms of Ancient Rome, but in Florence he completed the façade of Santa Maria Novella (1470) in such a harmonious manner that it has remained a symbol of the city to this day. He also built for the Rucellai family the *palazzo* in the via della Vigna Nuova (c1446-51; *see p83*), where they still live, and the lovely loggia opposite (1463). To the palazzo's façade Alberti introduced pilasters and capitals of the three classical orders that appear to support the three storeys, strongly separated with carved friezes. He completed the tribune started by Michelozzo at **Santissima Annunziata** (*see p92*) in an ornate style more compatible with Rome than Florence.

LATER RENAISSANCE

Other architects, especially Il Cronaca (Simone del Pollaiolo) and Giuliano da Sangallo, the preferred architect of Lorenzo il Magnifico, carried Brunelleschian and Albertian ideals to the end of the 15th and even into the 16th century. These were then developed in both Florence and Rome, principally by Michelangelo, whose work spanned the tense years in Florence before, during and after its subjugation by Habsburg emperor Charles V in 1530, which marked the beginning of the end for Florence's Renaissance spirit. Michelangelo left for Rome in 1534 never to return, to be followed in Florence by three main Medici court architects who all worked for Cosimo I, the first Duke of Tuscany after the siege and conquest of Florence: Vasari, Ammanati and Buontalenti.

Il Cronaca built the Santo Spirito vestibule and sacristy (1489-94), structures that carry the Renaissance imitation of the Ancient World almost to a culmination. He also built the **Museo** (formerly Palazzo) **Horne** (1495-1502; *see p95*), returning to an earlier, less rustic Florentine style. Sangallo could be a builder of great delicacy, as demonstrated by his cloister in **Santa Maria Maddalena dei Pazzi** (1492) in borgo Pinti. He also built two grand structures outside Florence: the beautiful **Medici villa** at Poggio a Caiano (begun 1480), and the tiny Renaissance church of **Santa Maria delle Carceri** in Prato (1484-95).

Michelangelo was certainly the greatest of these architects. He took the bold, classicising style that da Sangallo and Il Cronaca had inherited from Alberti and instilled it with a sense of uncertainty, but also of great energy and rhythm. Instead of the exterior reflecting

The nave of **Santa Croce**. *See p27*.

Ancient Rome, the very soul of his creations was pagan, oriented toward man's emotional state, rather than his Christianity. In this sense Michelangelo's architecture moved beyond the Renaissance. In neither of the projects he undertook in Florence, both in the church of San Lorenzo (*see p88*), the so-called **New Sacristy** (begun c1520) – a mausoleum for the Medici, as well as for Florence as a republic – and the **Laurentian Library** (begun 1524), is there even the slightest reference to Christianity. In the former, the use of levels that have nothing to do with floor structure, non load-bearing columns and arches and windows that don't give light instills a sense of the unreal. The overall effect is enhanced by large areas of cold, white wall. With its cupola so reminiscent of the Pantheon, the structure draws the curtain on that part of the Renaissance that posited that resurrecting the Antique would provide a new truth sufficient to supplant God. The Laurentian Library, with its inspiring vestibule calculated to raise the spirits of readers before they entered the reading-room, is similarly a structure so modern as to be mysterious.

Many fine things were built in Florence during the 16th and 17th centuries – churches, private *palazzi*, gardens, loggias, villas – but certainly nothing that continued the essence of Brunelleschi and Michelangelo. The tenure of the age is expressed on the one hand by the two fortresses built during the 16th century: the **Fortezza da Basso** (1534; *see p101*), which, symbolically, has its strongest side facing the city, and the **Forte di Belvedere** (1590; *see p98*), which dominates from just above the Ponte Vecchio. These, together with the vast **Palazzo Pitti** (1457; *see p99*), where the Medici moved in the mid-16th century, express the total dominance the Medici had attained over their fellow Florentines at this time. Also from this period date many marvellous formal gardens laid out by wealthy patrons employing Niccolo Pericoli, known as Il Tribolo (1500-58), and his pupils and followers.

Vasari built the **Uffizi** (1560; *see p79*) for Cosimo I and, with Buontalenti's help, filled it with offices and workshops for the city's administration. On the top floor was located the Gallery, which remains there still for the ever-expanding Medici collections. Vasari also built the raised corridor that runs from their office building across the Ponte Vecchio to their home at Palazzo Pitti, so that the family could travel without the dangers of the streets of Florence. Ammannati built the lovely **Ponte Santa Trinità** over the Arno to replace an earlier bridge that had collapsed in 1557. It was he who began the 300-year expansion of Palazzo Pitti. Buontalenti, besides extending Palazzo Vecchio to its present eastern limits and designing the Forte di Belvedere, built for the Medici the lovely villas at Petraia (1587) and (later demolished) Pratolino (1568).

THE LONG DECLINE

Not much happened in Florence, architecturally, between 1600 and 1860, at least not compared with the previous three centuries. The period from 1600 to the death of the last Medici ruler in 1737 was a long decline, and even after the Grand Duchy of Tuscany became property of the Habsburgs, with their capable reforms, the city remained a provincial appendage of the Austrian Empire. Napoleon, who destroyed so much, did little to damage Florence. Perhaps he

felt at home? His family had been minor Florentine nobles from the 14th century onwards, until their move to Corsica – when it was still part of Italy.

As time passed, gardens and *palazzi* were enlarged, grottos were fitted into hillsides, piazzas were decorated with fountains and statues, the vast and questionable **Cappella dei Principi** in San Lorenzo (c1604; *see p87*) was built. A few fine but unspectacular churches, necessarily in a Roman baroque style, were built: San Gaetano (1604), in via dei Tornabuoni, San Frediano in Cestello (1680-9), on the lungarno Soderini, San Giorgio alla Costa (1705-8), just up the hill from the Ponte Vecchio, and San Filippo Neri (1640-1715), in piazza San Firenze. Eventually, in the 19th century, the railway arrived in Florence and two stations were built: Leopolda (1847) and Maria Antonia near Santa Maria Novella (1848). Only the Leopolda still stands, just outside Porta al Prato, now a spectacular performance space.

DEVELOPMENT AND DESTRUCTION

Beginning with the period just before the unification of Italy in 1860, the city of Florence underwent a series of enormous architectural changes. First, much of the as yet undeveloped land inside the city walls was used for housing. Then, on the north side of the Arno, the walls themselves were pulled down (1865-9), leaving only some of the gates, standing isolated as they still do today. Where there had been walls, *viali* (avenues) were built for the carriages of the new householders, and two large open spaces were left as breaks in the *viali*: piazza C Beccaria, by Giuseppe Poggi, and piazza della

Florence's post-war architecture includes Spadolini's **Palazzo degli Affari**. *See p30*.

Liberta. Both were meant to be elegant openings in neo-classical and neo-Renaissance style, but today, like so much of Florence – and the *viali* – they are submerged in traffic.

The new avenues were continued on the south side of the river, from what is now piazza Ferrucci, up another tree-and-villa-lined *viale* to **piazzale Michelangelo** (1875), a large open space for carriages, where a magnificent panorama of Florence and its valley awaited the visitor. They continued along the side of the hills facing Florence and the Forte di Belvedere, and then came back down again to Porta Romana. This wonderful drive of approximately six kilometres (3.5 miles), one of the prettiest in Italy, is also due in great part to Poggi.

In these same years, parts of the old city were pulled down to make space for three covered, cast-iron market buildings. This was followed, from 1890 onwards, by the most thoughtless devastation of all: the area that had been the centre of the Roman and medieval city, piazza della Repubblica, and all the streets near it, was pulled down so that the city centre could be redeveloped. Then, soon after World War I, the central government at Rome, with much the same speculative mentality, pulled down yet more large sections of the city, particularly around the new station of Santa Maria Novella, and near Santa Croce.

Only 50 years after the centre of Florence had been gutted, yet another large area of destruction took place, once again removing scores of beautiful and irreplaceable ancient buildings. The Germans, partly out of fury with their former allies, and partly in a hopeless attempt to stem the Anglo-American advance, blew up all the bridges over the Arno except the Ponte Vecchio (1944), along with all the buildings to the immediate north and immediate south of the Ponte Vecchio. Ponte Santa Trinità was rebuilt in the 1950s to the original plans; the other three – Ponte alle Grazie, Ponte alla Carraia and Ponte alla Vittoria – were all replaced in modern style.

This means that, whereas just over 100 years ago most of the old centre of Florence was still intact, made up of buildings going back to the early Middle Ages, on foundations that went back at least to Ancient Rome, today you can walk all the way from the Duomo, down via Roma, across piazza della Repubblica, through via Calimala and via por Santa Maria, right down to the Ponte Vecchio without passing more than two or three buildings that are not late 19th- or 20th-century structures. What's more, the buildings that you pass, which were erected to replace those destroyed are, at best, banal.

THE SCHLOCK OF THE NEW

There are a few modern structures of note. The **railway station** near Santa Maria Novella, built in 1936 by Giovanni Michelucci, is exemplary. Another fine functional structure from between the wars is the **Stadio Artemio Franchi** (*see p187*), finished in 1932, and recently considerably restructured. The church of **San Giovanni Battista** at the crossing of the Autostrade del Sole and del Mare (1960), also by Michelucci, has vision and sensitivity. The inter-war Facist period produced a few other fine if typically grandiose structures: a reception building for the Italian royal family, attached to Santa Maria train station, called the **Palazzina Reale**; the **Istituto Aeronautica Militare** building in the Cascine park; and the **Cinema Puccini**, in piazza Puccini.

'The past 50 years have been an almost total architectural disaster.'

Other modern structures worthy of note are: the interior of the **Teatro Comunale** (*see p171*), rebuilt after World War II, the new bus terminal by Santa Maria Novella station, an overhead footway joining the station to a parking lot, the new buildings at **Amerigo Vespucci** airport, and Guido Spadolini's 1970s **Palazzo degli Affari** (part of the Palazzo dei Congressi complex).

Sadly, there's a total lack of quality in the modern building along the flatlands of the Arno valley. There are plans to develop new areas – whole towns, really, like the Firenze Nova area near Rifredi in Novloli (*see p23* **The future starts here**) – on open land beyond Peretola airport. Distinguished, internationally known architects have submitted proposals for these. But if the past is anything to go by, these plans are merely for show. The areas are likely to be developed piecemeal, even chaotically, to the financial advantage of a few interested parties.

One extremely bright note in this rather bleak picture is that the beautiful green landscape on three sides of Florence has been preserved. Although the past 50 years have been an almost total architectural disaster, somehow the speculation and ugliness have not spread to building on the hills. No other major town in Italy, or perhaps even Europe, can boast this proportion of green space.

▶ See p298 for a **glossary of art and architectural terms**.

Food in Tuscany

The word 'cuisine' is almost superfluous in Tuscany, where
fresh, seasonal foods are left to speak for themselves.

BASICS

The three staples of the Tuscan diet are bread,
olive oil and wine (*see chapter* **Tuscan Wines**).
While the wines are famously substantial and
the olive oil distinctively peppery, the bread
is deliberately bland: it is made without salt
to provide a neutral background for the food
it accompanies. A worthy intention – but
an acquired taste.

Tuscany claims to have Italy's best olive
oil – but don't tell that to growers in Puglia
or Umbria. And within Tuscany each region
claims superiority, though the consensus is that
the finest oil comes from groves located slightly
inland away from the varying temperatures
and high moisture levels of the coast. Judge
for yourself: touring the region, you will come
across many producers offering the public a
tour of their groves and a taste of their product.

L'ANTIPASTO

Meals generally start with the **antipasto**,
literally, 'before the meal'. In Tuscany, the
most common **antipasto** is **crostini**, chicken
liver pâté on bread or toast. Cured meats are a
regional speciality – usually pork and wild
boar, which are butchered or hunted during the
cold winter months. **Prosciutto crudo** comes
from a pig haunch that has been buried under
salt for three weeks, then swabbed with spicy

vinegar, covered with black pepper and hung
to dry for a further five months. **Capocollo** is
a neck cut cured the same way for three days,
then covered with pepper and fennel seed and
rolled round in yellow butcher's paper and tied
up with string so that it looks sausage-shaped.
It's ready for eating a few months later. The
most typical Tuscan salami is **finocchiona**,
made of pork and flavoured with fennel seed
and whole pepper corns. **Salamini di
cinghiale**, or small wild boar salamis, include
plenty of chilli pepper and a little fatty pork to
keep them from going too hard (wild boar is a
very lean meat). Look out as well for **milza**, a
delicious pungent pâté, made from spleen,
herbs, spices and wine.

IL PRIMO

The *primo*, or first course, is carbohydrate-
based. In most parts of Italy the carbohydrate
will be pasta or rice. Here in Tuscany it's as
likely to be a bread-based salad or soup. Old
bread is never thrown away, but is mixed with
what could be called the second tier of Tuscan
staples – tomatoes, garlic, cabbage and *fagioli*
(Tuscan white beans).

These form such dishes as **panzanella**
(stale bread that is soaked in water, squeezed
out, mixed with raw onion, fresh tomato, basil,
the odd salad leaf, and dressed with oil, salt and

Who they? The butcher of Panzano

He has been dubbed at various times the Michelangelo of Chiantishire, the Poet of the Bistecca and the Messiah of Meat. People come for miles to hear him speak and seek out his products across the land. Ladies and gentlemen, we give you... Dario Cecchini, the exuberant Macellaio di Panzano.

Dario's kingdom is a little butcher's shop on an unassuming street in the village of Panzano in the heart of Chianti. His family has sold meat for over 200 years, and although Dario originally started training as a vet, he abandoned his studies and took over the family business when his father died.

The goings-on inside this pristine, white-tiled shop are totally unexpected. Garlic, herbs, strings of sausages and *pepperoncini*, jars of spices and cookery books brighten the room; there are seats for weary acolytes; classical music or jazz blares from the CD player; wine and samples of in-house produce are offered on Sundays – while Cecchini, intense-eyed, disarmingly charismatic and standing tall behind the counter, holds forth to an adoring audience that packs the shop and spills over on to the street. While he expertly carves mountainous joints of meat

with one of his lethal-looking knives or cleavers, he recites Dante, discusses politics and local issues, ruminates on the state of food production today and, a favourite subject

pepper), **ribollita** (rich bean and cabbage soup with bread), **acqua cotta** (toasted bread rubbed with garlic and covered with crinkly dark green cabbage and the water it was cooked in – topped with premium olive oil, sometimes with an egg broken into it), **pappa al pomodoro** (an exquisite porridge-like mush of a soup made with onion, garlic, plenty of tomatoes, basil, a touch of chilli pepper and dressed with a swirl of olive oil). To say nothing

Delicious mush – **Pappa al pomodoro**.

of the ultimate winter ritual: **bruschetta** – toasted bread rubbed with garlic and soaked in freshly pressed olive oil with a sprinkle of salt on top.

Fresh pasta in Tuscany usually takes the form of **tagliatelle** (flat ribbons made with flour, water and egg), **ravioli** (envelopes of the same mixture containing ricotta and spinach); **tordelli** (from around Lucca, stuffed with chard, meat and ricotta); in the south you'll find **pici** (just flour and water extruded into fattish strings) and in the Mugello **tortelli** (a double carbohydrate whammy stuffed with potato and bacon). **Ravioli** are best eaten with a topping of **burro e salvia** (butter and sage) or with a sprinkling of Parmesan or Pecorino. Flat ribbony pastas (like *papardelle*) go well with gamey sauces such as **lepre** (hare) and **cinghiale** (wild boar), and also **anatra** (duck), as well as the ubiquitous **ragù** (made with tomato and minced beef or, occasionally, lamb) and **salsa di pomodoro** (tomato sauce, usually spiced up with chilli pepper).

IL SECONDO

Cacciagione (game), **salsicce** (sausages) and **bistecca** (beef steak) are the main meats eaten

in the wake of BSE, rails against the banning of one of Tuscany's signature foods, the Bistecca alla Fiorentina.

When the government decided to ban the sale of meat on the bone, Cecchini declared that 'taking away the Fiorentina from the Florentines is like taking the cupola from Brunelleschi's Duomo'. He marked the start of the ban (31 March 2001) by staging a high-profile funeral for the T-bone, complete with cortège, coffin and weeping widow, then auctioned off 200 vast steaks (each up to eight centimetres/three inches thick and some weighing in at over two and a half kilos/five and a half pounds), the first one going for L10,000,000 (€5,165) and another being sold over the phone to Elton John. Substantial proceeds went to a local hospital.

Cecchini was already well known for his superb organic meat in foodie circles internationally, but the bistecca issue has brought him to the attention of a wider audience. It is hard to resist his enthusiasm for life, his work and for the causes he believes in so passionately, among them the preservation of artisan values and the upholding of genuine Tuscan food traditions.

At the time of going to press, it is illegal to sell (in either shops or restaurants) steak on the bone from animals that are more than 12 months old, a ban that will probably be lifted by the end of 2001. But Italians are great rule-benders, so Bistecca alla Fiorentina remains on the menu of many restaurants, in some cases renamed along the lines of Bistecca all' Italiana.

Antico Macelleria Cecchini

Via XX Luglio, Panzano in Chianti (055 852 020). **Open** 9am-noon Mon, Tue, Thur; 9am-6pm Fri, Sat; 9am-1.30pm Sun. **No credit cards**.

FIORENTINA CECCHINI-STYLE

The steak must be cut to a thickness of no less than four fingers of his right hand (8-10cm/3-4in), should weigh between two and three kilos (4.4-6.6lb) and be brought to room temperature before cooking. The fire must be made of a rich wood such as oak and the grill must be placed near the embers; the meat should be cooked for five minutes per side, turned over by hand and then rested for 15 minutes before being placed on a slab of olive wood to bring to the table (no metal platters). It can be flavoured with salt and pepper and a drizzle of olive oil and should be cut into large chunks and eaten with the fingers.

---

in the region, though there is good lamb in some areas (look out for **agnellino nostrali**, which means young, locally raised lamb). Also common are **coniglio** (rabbit, usually roasted, sometimes with pine nuts, sometimes rolled around a filling such as egg and bacon) and **pollo** (chicken: look out for **ruspante**, free-range). During the winter you'll find plenty of slowly stewed and highly spiced **cinghiale**. This is a species that was cross-bred with the domestic pig about 20 years ago, producing a largely herbivorous creature so

---

The best Tuscan restaurants

for a Michelin-starred experience
Da Arnolfo (*see p231*), **Gambero Rosso** (*p271*) **La Tenda Rossa** (*p227*).

for modern Italian food
Osteria La Rendola (*see p264*), **La Mora** (*p247*), **Il Castagno di Pier Angelo** (*p197*).

for a rustic experience
Hostaria Costachiara (*see p264*), **Taverna del Guerrino** (*p228*), **Re di Puglia** (*p209*).

in unusual locations
Il Tufo Allegro (carved into tufa; *see p274*), **La Frateria di Padre Eligio** (in a monastery and run by ex-drug addicts; *see p234*), **Albergo Ristorante il Garibaldi** (in a petrol station; *see p238*).

for fish
La Darsena (*see p251*), **Da Antonio** (*p231*).

With a view from the terrace
La Cantinetta di Rignana (*see p228*).

For dishes with a past
La Trattoria dell' Orcio Interrato (*see p202*).

for a Tuscan blow-out
Locanda Castello di Sorci (*see p267*).

Understanding the menu

Techniques/descriptions

Al forno cooked in an oven; **affumicato** smoked; **arrosto** roast; **nostrali** locally grown/raised; **brasato** braised; **fatto in casa** home-made; **griglia** grill; **fritto** fried; **ripieno** stuffed; **ruspante** free-range; **vapore** steamed.

Basics

Aceto vinegar; **burro** butter; **bottiglia** bottle; **focaccia** flat bread made with olive oil; **ghiaccio** ice; **miele** honey; **olio** oil; **pane** bread; **panino** sandwich; **panna** cream; **pepe** pepper; **sale** salt; **salsa** sauce; **senape** mustard; **uovo** egg.

Antipasti

Antipasti misto mixed hors d'œuvres; **bruschetta** bread toasted and rubbed with garlic, sometimes drizzled with olive oil. Often comes with tomatoes or white tuscan beans; **crostini** small slices of toasted bread. *Crostini toscani* are smeared with chicken liver pâté; **crostone** big crostini; **fettunta** the Tuscan name for bruschetta; **prosciutto crudo** cured ham, either *dolce* (sweet, similar to Parma ham) or *salato* (salty).

Primi

Acquacotta cabbage soup usually served with a bruschetta, sometimes with an egg broken into it; **agnolotti** stuffed triangle-shaped pasta; **brodo** broth; **cacciucco** thick, chilli-spiked fish soup: Livorno's main contribution to Tuscan cuisine; **cecina** flat, crispy bread made of chick-pea flour; **fettuccine** long, narrow ribbons of egg pasta; **frittata** type of substantial omelette; **gnocchi** small potato and flour dumplings; **minestra** soup, usually vegetable; **pappa al pomodoro** bread and tomato soup; **pappardelle** broad ribbons of egg pasta, usually served with *lepre* (hare); **panzanella** Tuscan bread and tomato salad; **passato** puréed soup; **pasta e fagioli** pasta and bean soup; **ribollita** literally a twice-cooked soup of bean, bread, cabbage and vegetable; **taglierini** thin ribbons of pasta; **tordelli/tortelli** stuffed pasta; **zuppa** soup; **zuppa frantoiana** literally, olive press soup; another bean and cabbage soup, distinguished by being served with the very best young olive oil.

Fish & seafood

Acciughe/alici anchovies; **anguilla** eel; **aragosta** lobster; **aringa** herring; **baccalà** salt cod; **bianchetti** little fish, like whitebait; **bonito** small tuna; **branzino** sea bass; **calamari** squid; **capesante** scallops; **coda di rospo** monkfish tails; **cozze** mussels; **fritto misto** mixed fried fish; **gamberetti** shrimps; **gefalo** grey mullet; **gamberi** prawns; **granchio** crab; **insalata di mare** seafood salad; **merluzzo** cod; **nasello** hake; **ostriche** oyster; **pesce** fish; **pesce spada** swordfish; **polpo** octopus; **ricci** sea urchins; **rombo** turbot; **san Pietro** John Dory; **sarde** sardines; **scampi** langoustines; **scoglio** shell- and rockfish; **sgombro** mackerel; **seppia** cuttlefish or squid; **sogliola** sole; **spigola** sea bass; **stoccafisso** stockfish; **tonno** tuna; **triglia** red mullet; **trota** trout; **trota salmonata** salmon trout; **vongole** clams.

Meat, poultry & game

Agnellino young lamb; **agnello** lamb; **anatra** duck; **animelle** sweetbreads; **arrosto misto**

prolific that it has become a threat to crops and has to be culled. Other common game includes **lepre** and **fagiano** (pheasant). The famous **bistecca fiorentina** is a vast T-bone steak that tends to be served very rare and is quite enough for two or even three people. Though a *fiorentina*, grilled over a herby wood fire, might now seem synonymous with Tuscany, the habit of eating huge beef steaks was in fact, introduced in the 19th century by English aristocrats homesick for roast beef. Have no qualms: the Chianina breed of cattle found locally are a salubrious lot.

IL CONTORNO

To accompany your meat course you're normally offered a side plate of vegetables or a salad. **Bietole** (Swiss chard) is available almost throughout the year. It is scalded in salted water and tossed in the pan with olive oil, garlic and chilli pepper. **Fagiolini** (green beans) are more likely to be boiled and dressed with oil and lemon or vinegar. The ubiquitous and sublime white Tuscan **fagioli** are served lukewarm with a swirl of good olive oil and a sprinkle of black pepper on top. **Patatine** mixed roast meats; **beccacce** woodcock; **bistecca** beef steak; **bresaola** cured, dried beef, served in thin slices; **caccia** general term for game; **carpaccio** raw beef, served in thin slices; **capretto** kid; **cervo** venison; **cinghiale** wild boar; **coniglio** rabbit; **cotoletta/costoletta** chop; **fagiano** pheasant; **fegato** liver; **lepre** hare; **maiale** pork; **manzo** beef; **ocio/oca** goose; **ossobucco** veal shank stew; **pancetta** like bacon; **piccione** pigeon; **pollo** chicken; **porchetta** roast pork; **rognone** kidney; **salsicce** sausages; **tacchino** turkey; **trippa** tripe; **vitello** veal.

Herbs, pulses & vegetables

Aglio garlic; **asparagi** asparagus; **basilico** basil; **bietola** Swiss chard; **capperi** capers; **carciofi** artichokes; **carote** carrots; **castagne** chestnuts; **cavolfiore** cauliflower; **cavolo nero** red cabbage; **ceci** chick-peas; **cetriolo** cucumber; **cipolla** onion; **dragoncello** tarragon; **erbe** herbs; **fagioli** Tuscan white beans; **fagiolini** green, string or French beans; **farro** spelt (a hard wheat), a popular soup ingredient around Lucca and the Garfagnana; **fave or baccelli** broad beans (NB 'Fava' in Tuscany means the male 'organ'; so use 'baccelli'); **finocchio** fennel; **fiori di zucca** courgette flowers; **funghi** mushrooms; **funghi porcini** ceps; **funghi selvatici** wild mushrooms; **lattuga** lettuce; **lenticchie** lentils; **mandorle** almonds; **melanzane** aubergine; **menta** mint; **patate** potatoes; **peperoncino** chilli pepper; **peperoni** peppers; **pinoli** pine nuts; **pinzimonio** selection of raw vegetables to be dipped in olive oil; **piselli** peas; **pomodoro** tomato; **porri** leeks; **prezzemolo** parsley; **radice/ravanelli** radish; **ramerino/rosmarino** rosemary; **rapa** turnip; **rucola/rughetta** rocket (UK), rugola (US); **salvia** sage; **sedano** celery; **spinaci** spinach; **tartufo** truffles; **tartufato** cut thin like a truffle; **zucchini** courgette.

Fruit

Albicocche apricots; **ananas** pineapple; **arance** oranges; **banane** bananas; **ciliege** cherries; **cocomero** watermelon; **datteri** dates; **fichi** figs; **fragole** strawberries; **lamponi** raspberries; **limone** lemon; **macedonia di frutta** fruit salad; **mele** apples; **melone** melon; **more** blackberries; **pera** pear; **pesca** peach; **pompelmo** grapefruit; **uva** grapes.

Desserts & cheese

Cantuccini almond biscuits; **castagnaccio** chestnut flour cake, made around Lucca; **cavallucci** spiced biscuits from Siena; **gelato** ice-cream; **granita** flavoured ice; **mandorlata** almond brittle; **panforte** cake of dried fruit; **Pecorino** sheep's milk cheese; **ricciarelli** almond biscuits from Siena; **torrone** nougat; **torta** tart, cake; **zabaglione** egg custard mixed with Marsala; **zuppa Inglese** trifle.

Drinks

Acqua water; *gassata* (fizzy) or *senza gas* (still); **birra** beer; **caffè** coffee; **cioccolata** hot chocolate; **latte** milk; **succo di frutta** fruit juice; **tè** tea; **vino rosso/bianco/rosato** red/white/rosé wine; **Vin Santo** dessert wine.

General

May I see the menu? **Posso vedere il menù?** May I have the bill, please? **Mi fa il conto, per favore?**

---

fritte (French fries) are available almost everywhere, though boiled potatoes dressed with oil, pepper and capers are often much tastier. **Pomodori** (tomatoes) and **cipolle** (onions) that are sliced, spiced and baked *al forno* (in the oven) are recommended. To those accustomed to watery lettuce, radicchio salads may at first seem bitter: an acquired taste that will lead you to an appreciation of the many wild salad varieties. In early summer artichokes are often eaten raw, stripped of their tough outer leaves and dipped into olive oil and salt.

IL FORMAGGIO

The one true Tuscan cheese is Pecorino, made with ewe's milk. In fact the sheep you see grazing on the hillsides are more often than not there for their milk rather than mutton, lamb or wool.

Thirty years ago each small farm would have raised enough sheep to provide the household with sufficient rounds of Pecorino, which can be eaten *fresco* (up to a month old), *semi-stagionato* after about a month of ripening, or up to six months later when the

Larding it

The word lard doesn't conjure up a particularly appetising culinary image, but make that 'Lardo di Colonnata' and, to the initiated, it becomes a whole different ballgame. Slightly glistening, opaque white, flavour-imbued slabs of pig fat, sometimes shot with the thinnest streak of pink lean, are sliced into wafer-thin slivers and eaten on lightly toasted bread (the warmth slightly melting the fat and bringing out the spiciness) or used as a flavour-enhancer in recipes. Jack Spratt would not have been a happy lad.

Colonnata is an unassuming village (population 300) located just inland from the north-west Tuscan coast, perched some 530 metres (1,700 feet) above sea level in the foothills of the Apuanian Alps. The whole area is, of course, world famous for its quarries, but to foodies, Colonnata's lard is just as important as nearby Carrara's marble.

The history of lard production goes back a long way, but methods have changed little. Slabs of fat are taken from the backs of suitably chubby pigs and layered in rectangular marble vats with salt, pepper, rosemary, garlic and other herbs and spices. The vats are then stored in basement rooms at a natural temperature of between 9°C and 14°C for six months or more. Marble, being a porous stone, is essential to the proper curing process.

In the old days, whole pigs were jointed and pickled in the vats; the lean meat would be eaten first and the lard, which lasted longer, kept until the end. Today, only lard is used, but a piece of lean pig is added as this was found to accelerate the curing process.

In Colonnata itself, some 8,000 kilograms (17,600 pounds) of lard are produced each year by 14 villagers. A large proportion of this is vacuum-packed and sent far afield – but that doesn't mean that the lard you buy originated in this far-flung corner of Tuscany. Throughout Italy, fake versions are being produced. In some cases the end result is perfectly acceptable, but the Colonnatese are fighting for what would amount to a patent to protect their rather singular cottage industry. If and when they succeed, any lard you buy without the magic words 'di Colonnata' on the label will not be the Real Thing.

---

cheese is fully *stagionato*, and thus drier, sharper and tastier. Nowadays sheep farming, milk collecting and cheese-making are mostly the province of Sardinians, who came over to work the land abandoned by the Tuscans drawn to towns and factory employment.

Fresh **ricotta**, which is made from whey and is thus not strictly speaking a cheese, is soft, mild and wet and should be eaten with black pepper and a few drops of olive oil on top.

LA FRUTTA

Cherries, then apricots and peaches, are readily available in the summer, grapes in the late summer, and apples and pears in the early autumn. Although citrus fruits imported from the south now take pride of place in the winter months, the indigenous fruits are quinces (**mele cotogne**, excellent baked, stewed or turned into a sort of jelly) and persimmons (**cachi**) – each sloppy sweet spoonful of which helps keep out the winter cold. However, for visitors to Tuscany fruit is perhaps at its most interesting in sweet/savoury combinations: **il cacio con le pere** (cheese with pears), **i fichi con il salame** (figs with salami), **melone** (or **popone**) **con prosciutto** (melon and cured ham).

IL DOLCE

Although the Tuscans are not great purveyors of desserts, they do like to conclude festive meals with a glass of a dry raisin wine called **Vin Santo** into which they dunk **cantucci**, little dry biscuits packed with almonds. Vin Santo is made with a special white grape variety which is dried out in bunches for a month, then crushed to obtain a sweet juice which is aged for at least five years. All this is highly uneconomical (you could get five bottles of wine out of the grapes you need for one bottle of Vin Santo), so that to offer a glass of Vin Santo is to honour a guest with the essence of hospitality.

In Context

Tuscan Wine

Forget Chianti-in-a-basket. Tuscany's wines have developed a reputation for quality and diversity.

If mere quantity is your measure, then Tuscany is not Italy's foremost wine producing region. For a long time now it has ceased to produce bulk wines. For plonk you can turn to the highly mechanised viticulture of the Veneto and Emilia Romagna regions to the north-east, or Puglia in the south. But if quality is your goal, then Tuscany has a uniquely wide range of options to offer. And what the vine-clad hillsides of Chianti, the Maremma, Montalcino and Montepulciano also produce is value. No other Italian region can compete with Tuscany for the overall value of the wines it exports. They are quality products that often command very high prices.

The quest for quality means getting the best from a particular grape variety in a certain type of soil within a given microclimate. Such territorial specificity ensures what is known as 'tipicità': a distinct character pertaining to a given place. In other words, individuality versus bland sameness. *Tipicità* is to some extent defined by the various DOCs (Denominazione di Origine Controllata, which regulate wines from a specific,

controlled area), the ultra-select category of DOCGs (Denominazione di Origine Controllata e Garantita) and IGTs (Indicazione Geografica Tipica, table wines from a well-defined area). These certified names are the equivalent of the French Appellation, each with its own production rules and regulations to which producers must adhere. Tuscany has 39 such appellations, more than any other region in the country.

During the past 15 years wine production in the region has evolved to such a degree that the change is as evident in the landscape as in the glass. Take note wherever you see an orchard of fruit trees interspersed with a few rows of tall, exuberant vines, their tendrils embracing sturdy trees for support: this is viticultural archaeology, destined to disappear entirely before long. With the demise of this sort of vine dressing went much of the quaffing wine in large bottles. For growers, choosing the right vine-stock and clone for a particular soil and exposure has become an art, indeed a science, often pursued in collaboration with the Departments of Agronomy from the

Universities of Florence and Pisa. Moreover, even a cursory visit to the wine havens of Tuscany will reveal that the emphasis is now on densely planted vineyards. Vibrant green geometries have replaced the softer contours and mixed hues of the sparsely planted orchards tended by yesteryear's sharecrop farmers. Vines need to be 'stressed' by competition. That way they will concentrate on survival, which means focusing energy on seed production, in other words on sturdy, healthy fruit. The bunches of grapes grown on vines that are radically pruned in winter and again in the spring will often be thinned out to improve their sugar content and ensure that the ripening process proceeds evenly. The goal is to grow smaller quantities of quality grapes that can all be harvested in prime condition.

The best Wines

Chianti Classico (moderate)
Castello di Fonterutoli 1995, 1997; Castello di Brolio 1997; Grosso Sanese 1995, 1997: all between L35,000 (€18) and L55,000 (€28.50).

Chianti Classico (expensive)
La Casuccia 1997: L220,000 (€113.50).

Chianti Rufina DOCG
Selvapiana Riserva 1997: L33,000 (€17).

Carmignano DOCG
Piaggia Riserva 1996: L44,000 (€22).

Brunello DOCG
Siro Pacenti 1997; Fuligni 1997; Casanova di Neri 1997; Piancornello 1997: all L80,000-L100,000 (€41.50-€51.50). To spend between L25,000 (€13) and L33,000 (€17), try the excellent Rosso di Montalcino by the same winemakers.

SuperTuscans
Le Pergole Torte 1997; Sammarco 1997; Percarlo 1997; Flaccianello 1997: all well over the L100,000/€51.50 mark.

If someone else is buying
Solaia 1997 SuperTuscan: about L500,000 (€258).

Vintages
For all categories mentioned above: 1985, 1988, 1990, 1995, 1997, 1998, 1999.

All prices are approximate.

PRODUCTION VALUES
To match the changes in vineyards, much more attention is now also paid to the cellar. Though there are still plenty of individuals who make wine for family consumption more or less in their own back yard, the demand for quality wines with some degree of guarantee for performance after bottling has meant that the sale of *vino sfuso*, or wine on tap, has diminished. The peasant winemaker of a few years ago now either sells his grapes to larger wineries or has embarked on a programme of investment in new vineyards and appropriate winemaking facilities: spotless new cellars, temperature-controlled steel fermentation tanks, expensive pumps that shift the deep red liquid from one container to another without bruising it, small French oak barrels (called *barriques*) for oxygenating and ageing the wine, immaculate bottling equipment and as often as not a tasting room as well. To say nothing of the role of the modern-day wine wizard: the omnipresent oenologist, the wine technician whose expertise is essential when it comes to balance, structure, bouquet, consistency…

'With SuperTuscans the idea was to open up the way for wines that could satisfy changing tastes.'

A number of small growers instead sell their grapes to the remaining co-operative wineries. Since these producers are placing their wines in an increasingly competitive market, in the past few years they have had to improve their act considerably or go under. Mere quaffing wines are no longer good enough. With the help of agronomists who advise the co-operative growers and the oenologists who work miracles in the cellar, the better co-operative winemakers are producing perfectly acceptable wines whose good price to quality ratio helps overlook what might otherwise be perceived as a lack of individuality. Cases in point include **Agricoltori del Chianti Geografico**, which produces an excellent **Chianti Classico** (especially the 1998); the **Cantina di Montalcino**, whose Brunello '95 meets with considerable acclaim (the Montalcino co-operative growers are paid for their grapes in relation to quality, and prices may vary by as much as 20 per cent, a policy that is certainly paying off in the end product); the **Cantina Cooperativa del Morellino**, which has a good **Morellino di Scansano**, one of the relatively new Tuscan red DOCs; **Redi**, the flagship for the Vecchia Cantina co-operative winery at Montepulciano; and

Women in wine

Winemaking in Italy has traditionally been a male universe. So to help open up the sphere to women, in 1988 an organisation called **Le donne del vino** (The Women of Wine) was launched by female winemakers, wine writers, sommeliers etc. Their objective was to increase awareness, self-esteem and their professional profile. In 15 years things have changed a lot, and now there are several prominent female winemakers forging a name for themselves. **Lorenza Sebasti** at the **Castello di Ama** winery at **Gaiole in Chianti** has been their forerunner since 1976, and **Donatella Cinelli Colombini**, now producing wine at the **Fattoria del Colle** at **Trequanda**, has long been active in promoting women's involvement in this field. The younger generation includes **Caterina Dei**, who abandoned a musical career to devote her creative energies to the family winery at **Montepulciano** (her first offspring is the **Sancta Catherina** red, a blend of Syrah, Sangiovese, Cabernet Sauvignon and Petit Verdot). Another impressive protagonist is **Emanuela Stucchi Prinetti** who runs the winery at the **Badia a Coltibuono** and is also president of the Consortium of Chianti Classico producers. The female roll of honour should also include **Laura Bianchi**, who produces a **Chianti Classico Riserva** at **Castello di Monsanto** near **Barberino Val d'Elsa**. Although the country's foremost oenologists are all still men, **Giovanna**

Morganti, a highly competent oenologist who also produces **Chianti Classico le Trame** at **Le Boncie** at **Castelnuovo Berardenga**, is bearing a promising standard for women. Indeed, surveying the burgeoning talent, Donatella Cinelli Colombini has warned her oenologist (male) that his days with her are probably numbered.

Le Chiantigiane, producing the white Vernaccia di San Gimignano. Such products are widely distributed, both at supermarket level in Italy and in wine stores and chains abroad.

Right at the other end of the spectrum are the great aristocratic wine dynasties: names such as **Antinori**, **Ricasoli**, **Frescobaldi**, **Mazzei** and **Folonari** (the owners of Ruffino). With their many generations of experience, they have gradually expanded from the area south of Florence, where they principally produce Chianti Classico, to other parts of Tuscany, and indeed Umbria. They have the clout, financially and socially, to espouse quality and shape palates in far-sighted anticipation of market and consumer trends. A case in point was the development of Galestro back in the late 1970s. In a region that was largely identified with reds, these producers saw that the time was ripe for a white wine in which the emphasis was more on freshness and

lightness than aroma and body. Made up largely of the Trebbiano Toscano grape variety, with small amounts of Malvasia del Chianti, Vernaccia di San Gimignano, Chardonnay, Pinot Blanc and Rhine-Riesling, it involved pioneering vinification techniques. In 20 years it has grown in structure to become – well, perhaps not a connoisseur's choice, but a thoroughly acceptable aperitif or accompaniment to lighter summer cuisine.

THE SUPER MARKET

Still more impressive and influential has been the development from the mid-1980s of what go by the name of SuperTuscans, which were also pioneered by the great wine estates. The idea was to open up the way for wines that could satisfy changing tastes, particularly on the international market. The quality of Tuscan table wines was perceived as being poor, whereas the production of DOC wines was stultified by excessive strictures and regulations. Surely there was room for wines that did not conform to the models established by Chianti Classico, Brunello di Montalcino or Vino Nobile di Montepulciano, all of which owe their being entirely or largely to the Sangiovese grape that is widespread in Tuscany. Wouldn't it be worth experimenting with the grape varieties that have contributed to the renown of French viticulture? The Cabernets, the Merlot, the Chardonnay and the Sauvignon? Alongside the enterprising producers there was a new

generation of highly trained wine technicians who could hardly wait to get involved in the creation of innovative wines.

The fruits of their labours were beautifully made, commanded relatively high prices, and for consumers abroad were initially somewhat perplexing. Why should an 'ordinary' wine cost more than certain DOCs? Was there anything beyond the thick glass of the bottle and the refined label? The British and American wine press decreed that reds such as the **Tignanello** (Sangiovese and Cabernet

Intensive viticulture at **Montalcino**.

New DOCs

The great Tuscan appellations such as Chianti Classico, Brunello di Montalcino and Vino Nobile di Montepulciano have long overshadowed some interesting, quality wines that lacked an official identity. One absurd case in point was the famous Sassicaia wine that has brought international renown to the winemaking potential of Bolgheri, just inland from the northern Maremma coast. Until 1994 this most elect and select of niche products was categorised as a table wine. Happily that is now all history, and Sassicaia currently enjoys the absolute privilege of being a DOC that comprises just one wine and producer: Bolgheri Sassicaia DOC. The other SuperTuscans made in the same area have now come home to roost in the newly created Bolgheri DOC.

In more recent years the creation of a number of new DOCs has contributed to a better understanding of what the varied soils, climates and grape varieties now grown in Tuscany are able to produce. While the Denomination itself is more a guarantee of *tipicità* than of excellence, there is no doubt that some of the new DOCs are very promising, and still reasonably priced, at least in relation to the established SuperTuscans.

For the **Bolgheri Rosso** DOC, keep an eye out for Michele Satta's Piastraia. A little further south is the **Montescudaio** DOC, and below this the **Morellino di Scansano** DOC, which boasts some good reds, especially from the Le Pupille and Moris Farm wineries. A little further inland is the recently defined **Montecucco** DOC, also producing promising, well-structured reds. Two other new southern Tuscan DOCs are **Capalbio** on the coast and **Sovana**, between the southern slopes of Mount Amiata and the coast. Due east and slightly north of here is the fairly extensive and variegated area devoted to the production of **Orcia** DOC, whose flagship in the early years is likely to be Donatella Cinelli Colombini at the **Fattoria del Colle** near Trequanda. Another producer who should prove promising in coming years is Simonelli-Santi at the **Malintoppo** winery at San Quirico d'Orcia.

The well-established Tuscan whites are the Vernaccia di San Gimignano DOC and the Bianco di Pitigliano DOC. However, a number of the new DOCs also embrace white wines and it will be interesting to see whether these will be able to stand up to comparisons with the very few Tuscan whites of excellence, the Batàr Pinot Bianco made by Agricola Querciabella at Greve in Chianti and the Cabreo La Pietra Chardonnay made by Ruffino at Pontassieve.

Sauvignon) and **Solaia** (Cabernet plus a small percentage of Sangiovese) made by the Marchesi Antinori in Chianti deserved the epithet SuperTuscans, and the name stuck. Similar enthusiasm greeted Nicolò Incisa della Rocchetta's **Sassicaia** (90 per cent Cabernet Sauvignon, 10 per cent Cabernet Franc) and Lodovico Antinori's **Ornellaia** (90 per cent Cabernet Sauvignon, 10 per cent Merlot), both made at Bolgheri, near the northern Maremma coast, an area hitherto devoted entirely to Sangiovese and Trebbiano.

The new wines soon spread in range, reaching areas as distant from the original Chianti region as the western foothills of Mount Amiata and Montalcino. A number of the SuperTuscans have joined the Indicazione Geografica Tipica (IGT) category, some have continued to call themselves 'vini da tavola', and others still have achieved a more specific geographical identity of their own by associating with the newly created DOCs (*see above* **New DOCs**). Moreover, even the traditional native Sangiovese grape variety has proved to have plenty to say for itself, both on its own and in discerning combination with varieties from further afield.

THE YOUNG PRETENDERS

The true newcomers to the scene are the new DOCS and a generation of younger winemakers who are opening up new vistas by fine-tuning a particular feature within a given DOC. Many of these latter are the sons of the sharecrop farmers whose own winemaking methods were pretty much those of their medieval forebears. Better educated and travelled than their fathers, these youngsters have been keen to experiment with new clones, grape varieties, vinification methods and ageing techniques. At Bolgheri Eugenio Campolmi's winery, **Le Macchiole**, has made quite a name for itself with Paleo, Messorio and Scrio, all excellent reds; not far distant at Suvereto is Rita Tua's winery (called **Tua Rita**) that produces Redigaffi and Giusto di Notri, which practically have cult followings. Around Montalcino the number of 'contadini' (peasant farmers, but the term has no negative connotations in Italian) who have become prestigious producers of Brunello is even greater: Giancarlo Pacenti at the winery that still bears his father's name (**Pelagrilli di Pacenti Siro**); Paolo Bartolommei at the **Caprili** winery; Vincenzo Abbruzzese at **Val di Cava**; Giacomo Neri at **Casanova di Neri**. All of these winemakers have enormously transcended their parents' horizons, but with touching respect for what their fathers have taught them.

TASTE AND SEE

The wine map of Tuscany is thus far more varied than a visit to a wine shop in the UK or US would ever lead you to believe. So rich, in fact, that Tuscany is at the forefront of 'il turismo enogastronomico' (devoting part of your holiday to visiting wineries and sampling local foods) – over 90 per cent of Italy's wine and food tourism focuses on Tuscany. Such tourism is seen as eminently sustainable, as good for the visitor as it is for the local economy and a delightful way of getting to know the countryside as well as its products. To win discerning palates to the lesser-known reaches of Tuscan viticulture the Movimento del turismo del vino (www.wineday.org) has helped set up and co-ordinate a number of specialised offices in most of the wine-producing areas. They are called Strade del Vino and organise guided tasting tours, visits to cellars, meals revolving around local produce and so on. Often they have staff who can also cope in English.

> **'Enoteche are usually run by appassionati who will provide you with a number of glasses for a "vertical" or "horizontal" tasting.'**

The alternative is to go it alone, which can be both interesting and frustrating. While most wineries welcome visitors if they are given due warning by phone, not all of them have a proper tasting facility, or staff who speak English and have the time to devote to this sort of PR. For our picks of wineries open to the public, *see p232*. Well-run local *enoteche* will be in a position to advise, both by providing a tasting experience in their own premises and by phoning their contacts in particular wineries. These wine shops are usually run by *appassionati* who will happily provide you with a number of glasses for a 'vertical' tasting of different vintages of the same wine, or a 'horizontal' tasting (no reference to your final

Straw dogs: nice packaging, but an inferior interior.

posture) of wines of the same variety and/or year made by different producers. The *enoteche* also sell wine, by the case or as individual bottles. Prices may be higher than at the wineries, but then you may well find that the smaller wineries have no product left to sell, or are so far away that it's not worth the time and petrol slogging over there.

DRINKING OUT

The Strade del Vino di Toscana organisation is gradually working on restaurateurs to improve the level of wine expertise of their staff. In an expensive gourmet restaurant you're bound to find a waiter who really knows their wine, but in simpler eateries this is not generally the case. Where suggestions are not readily to hand, you have three choices. You could arm yourself pre-emptively with the annually updated English edition of *Italian Wines Guide* published by Slow Food and Gambero Rosso (by far the most reliable publication on the subject) and pick something from the wine list. You could choose a bottle made by one of the old established wine estates. Or you might discover what the local DOC is and opt for a medium-priced bottle, an approach that could lead to some gratifying discoveries. Clearly if you are staying in a place for a number of days, it would be worth doing some agreeable groundwork in the local *enoteca*.

Accommodation

Accommodation

Hotel prices are on the up, but so are standards, and there's bags of choice for the discerning visitor.

Florence is one of the most expensive Italian cities in which to lay your head. On the positive side, there are no international chains and lots of privately owned or family-run establishments with character. There are many options: you can stay in anything from a humble *pensione* in a crumbling *palazzo* with bits of faded fresco on the wall to the grandest of hotels. In between, there are far too many bog-standard places with no character and hostile staff, charging outrageous prices.

Hotels are given a rating of between one and five stars, but these are an indication of the facilities offered and are nothing to do with atmosphere or standards. There's also an enormous disparity between hotels in the same star rating, so it pays to shop around. The hotels listed in this guide have all been chosen for their value for money within their category or simply because they are great places to stay.

We've noticed an improvement in standards since the last edition of this guide, probably due to government-funded facelifts for millennium year. This turned out to be a damp squib, but the benefits in terms of hotel standards are lasting. Even the modest one-star places listed here have had a lick of paint since we last visited.

FACILITIES

Rooms in most hotels vary considerably. It is your right to refuse a room if you don't like it and ask to see another one; don't be put off by grumpy owners. If you feel you've been taken for a ride, there's an office for complaints (*see* **Directory: Tourist information**).

If you're staying in the centre of the city in summer, look for a room with a private terrace or some kind of communal outside space; it can make a huge difference after a long day's sightseeing to be able to relax al fresco with a Campari. If you want more than a scrap of terrace, there are great places to stay in the nearby hills (*see p57* **Outside the City Gates**) which, while only spitting distance from the sights, give you a sense of being away from the rat pack – and, unlike in the centre, they often have pools.

Very few central hotels have their own parking, and about as many have even heard of no-smoking areas or rooms. Facilities for the disabled are improving a little, partly due to a law requiring hotels to have a certain number

of adapted rooms. This law does not extend to all facilities, however, resulting in the absurd situation where many rooms for the disabled are only accessible by a lift that's too narrow to fit a wheelchair. Staff may be willing to help but most places have so many steep stairs there's little they can do. We've indicated the few places that do have special facilities. All the luxury and expensive hotels have telephones in the bedrooms, but for moderate and budget options we list whether or not the rooms have them.

OTHER OPTIONS

If you prefer to self-cater, you could try a *residences* – these offer apartments of various sizes, usually in the same building, with some kind of concierge service. They are rentable by the night or the week and are advertised in the accommodation booklet produced by the tourist office. Or rent an apartment independently; the minimum stay is usually a week. See the list of agencies below.

Affittacamere (rooms for rent) denotes accommodation that doesn't qualify as an official hotel (it has too few rooms, for example); it can be either a private house that rents out a couple of rooms or something that is to all intents and purposes a hotel. Some are very cheap, others less so. Some of the establishments listed below are *affittacamere*.

ADVANCE BOOKINGS

Florence is busy most of the year, but there's particular pressure on rooms from mid March to mid June (with Easter probably the busiest weekend of the year) and in September. Christmas and New Year are also crowd-pullers. Book well in advance. If you arrive without a place to stay, go to the APT office (*see* **Directory: Tourist information**) or the Ufficio Informazione Turistiche in Piazza Stazione or at Peretola airport; they provide lists but no booking service. The ITA office in the station will find and book you a hotel for a fee.

RATE RELATED

Many hotels slash their prices by as much as 50 per cent off-season, but even outside these times, a hotel may give you a better price if it has plenty of room; it's worth haggling.

Unless stated, prices (which are subject to change) are for a room with en suite bathroom,

Helvetia & Bristol – arguably central Florence's finest small hotel.

and include breakfast. Breakfast in cheaper hotels is rarely worth eating: you'd be better off with a brioche and cappuccino from a stand-up *pasticceria* on a street corner. Most hotels and *pensioni* will put at least one extra bed in a double room, for a fee.

The APT booklet *Guida all' ospitalità* available at tourist offices is a good source of cheap accommodation. It gives a list of *affittacamere* and religious institutions (often single sex with a curfew) that provide beds.

Duomo & around

Luxury

Brunelleschi

Via dei Calzaiuoli, Piazza Santa Elisabetta, off Via del Corso (055 27370/fax 055 219 653/ www.hotelbrunelleschi.it). **Rates** single L420,000 (€217); double L570,000 (€294.50); suite L900,000 (€465). **Credit** AmEx, DC, JCB, MC, V. **Map** p314 B4.
It's hard to believe that the Byzantine tower forming part of this hotel was once a prison (it's thought to be the city's oldest standing structure). Many objects of archaeological interest unearthed during its reconstruction in the 1980s are displayed in a museum in the basement. The 95 bedrooms are comfortably if uniformly furnished; most were refurbished in 2000. Part of the restaurant is in the tower, and two penthouse suites enjoy 360° city views.
Hotel services *Babysitting. Bar. Car park (nearby garage, extra charge). Conference facilities (up to 140).*

Fax. Laundry. Lifts. No-smoking rooms. Restaurant. **Room services**. *Air-conditioning. Dataport. Hairdryer. Jacuzzi (penthouse suites). Minibar. Radio. Room service (24hr). Safe. TV (satellite).*

Gallery, Hotel Art

Vicolo del'Oro 2 (055 27263/fax 055 268557/ www.lungarnohotels.com). **Rates** double L450,000-L590,000 (€232.50-€304.50); suites L490,000-L650,000 (€253-€335.50). **Credit** AmEx, MC, V. **Map** p314 C3.
Located in a tiny piazza right near Ponte Vecchio, Gallery made waves when it opened in 1999 – it's Florence's first 'hip hotel' and as such very different from anything else in the city. The look is East-meets-West, with a cosy library with squashy sofas and lots of arty books to browse, and a stylish bar that serves 'fusion sushi' and that extends into the piazza in the summer. Bedrooms are business-like but comfy; bathrooms are a dream. The penthouse suite has two terraces with stunning views. *See also p48* **Who they? Ferragamo**.
Hotel services *Babysitting. Car park (nearby garage, extra charge). Bar. Fax. Laundry. Lift. No-smoking rooms.* **Room services** *Air-conditioning. Hairdryer. Room service. Safe. TV (satellite).*

Helvetia & Bristol

Via dei Pescioni 2 (055 287 814/fax 055 288 353/ www.thecharminghotels.it). **Rates** single L420,000 (€217); double L670,000-L790,000 (€346-€408); suite L760,000-L1,900,000 (€392.50-€981); breakfast L40,000 (€20.50). **Credit** AmEx, DC, MC, V. **Map** p314 B3.
With Stravinsky, Gabriele d'Annunzio, Pirandello and Bertrand Russell among past guests, the

Helvetia & Bristol has a distinguished history. With some 70 rooms and suites, it's arguably central Florence's finest small hotel, exclusive without being stuffy. The salon has a fireplace and velvet sofas and armchairs; breakfast and lunch are served in the delightful Winter Garden, which was once a meeting place for '20s intelligentsia. Bedrooms are sumptuous (sometimes to excess), with swathes of ornate fabrics everywhere (interiors are by Gaetani and Ruspoli, responsible for some of Italy's finest hotels). The elegant restaurant serves above-average food at above-average prices.
Hotel services *Bar. Car park (nearby garage, extra charge). Fax. Laundry. Lift. No-smoking rooms. Restaurant.* **Room services** *Air-conditioning. Hairdryer. Jacuzzi (some rooms). Minibar. Radio. Room service (24hr). Safe. TV (satellite).Video.*

The Savoy

Piazza Repubblica 7 (055 283 313/fax 055 284 840/ www.rfhotels.com). **Rates** double L750,000-L880,000 (€387.50-€454.50); suite L1,500,000-L2,500,000 (€774.50-€1291). **Credit** AmEx, DC, JCB, MC, V. **Map** p314 B3.
The Savoy was a bit of a crumbling eyesore when it was bought by the Rocco Forte group, but re-opened in May 2000 after a multi-million pound refurbishment and is popular with both a business clientele and well-heeled tourists. The decor is modern but a little soulless. The bar/bistro with tables out in the piazza is great for people-watching.
Hotel services *Babysitting. Bar. Car park (nearby garage, extra charge). Conference facilities. Fax. Laundry. Lifts. Restaurant.* **Room services** *Air-conditioning. Dataport. Hairdryer. Minibar. Radio. Room service (24hr). Safe. TV (satellite).*

Expensive

Beacci Tornabuoni

Via Tornabuoni 3 (055 212 645/fax 055 283 594)/ www.bthotel.it). **Rates** single L240,000-L260,000 (€124-€134.50); double L300,000-L400,000 (€155); suites L680,000 (€351). **Credit** AmEx, DC, JCB, MC, V. **Map** p314 B2.
A hotel with an Edwardian feel in the middle of shopping heaven, the Beacci Tornabuoni is on the top two floors of the 15th-century Palazzo Minerbetti Strozzi. Its wonderful flower-filled roof garden is used for meals in summer, while inside the old parquet floors creak and groan amid the kind of furniture you would normally expect to find at your grandma's. It's beautifully maintained and very comfortable with loads of character.
Hotel services *Babysitting. Bar. Car park (nearby garage, extra charge). Conference facilities. Dataport. Fax. Laundry. Lifts. Restaurant. Roof garden.* **Room services** *Air-conditioning. Hairdryer. Minibar. Room service (24hr). Safe. TV (satellite).*

Hermitage

Vicolo Marzio 1, Piazza del Pesce (055 287 216/ fax 055 212 208/www.hermitagehotel.com). **Rates** double L390,000-L410,000 (€201.50-€212);

triple L470,000 (€242.50); quad L530,000 (€273.50). **Credit** MC, V. **Map** p314 C3.
This delightful little hotel with its superb location (practically on the Ponte Vecchio), warm welcome and superior facilities is always popular. In summer, breakfast on the plant-filled roof garden is a must. The reception and public rooms are on the top floors, with the comfortable bedrooms (some rather small) on the lower four floors. Some rooms have a river view but can be noisy. Prices are a little above average for this category, but it's worth it.
Hotel services *Babysitting. Bar. Car park (nearby garage, extra charge). Fax. Laundry. Lift. No-smoking rooms. Roof garden.* **Room services** *Air-conditioning. Hairdryer. Jacuzzi (8 rooms). Room service. Safe. TV (satellite).*

Guelfo Bianco

Via C Cavour 29 (055 288 330/fax 055 295 203/ www.ilguelfobianco.it). **Rates** single L235,000 (€121.50); double L320,000-L385,000 (€165.50-€199); triple L445,000 (€230); family L500,000 (€258); apartment L750,000 (€387.50). **Credit** AmEx, MC, V. **Map** p314 A4.
The renovation of two adjacent 15th-century houses has preserved many original features in this attractive hotel with its helpful staff. The 43 bedrooms are comfortable; the more spacious ones allow for a lounge area or two extra beds. Those on Via Cavour are soundproofed, the ones at the back are quieter. One double room has a terrace. There's also a two-bedroomed self-catering apartment. Two courtyards offer respite from city noise.
Hotel services *Babysitting. Bar. Bicycle hire. Car park (nearby garage, extra charge). Fax. Laundry. Lift. No-smoking rooms.* **Room services** *Air-conditioning. Dataport (some rooms). Hairdryer. Minibar. Radio. Room service. Safe. TV (satellite).*

Torre Guelfa

Borgo SS Apostoli 8 (055 239 6338/fax 055 239 8577/www.torreguelfa.3000.it). **Rates** single L200,000 (€103.50); double L300,000 (€155). **Credit** AmEx, JCB, MC, V. **Map** p314 C3.
Enjoy an aperitif while marvelling at the 360° view from the top of the tallest privately owned tower in Florence. In spite of the building's great age, decor is contemporary: rooms have wrought-iron beds (there are several four-posters), white cotton curtains and hand-painted furniture. One room has its own roof garden. The hotel has recently extended into the floor below; there are now 18 rooms. It's popular with the fashion-show crowd.
Hotel services *Bar. Car park (nearby garage, extra charge). Fax. Laundry. Lift. No-smoking rooms. Terrace.* **Room services** *Air-conditioning. Hairdryer. Minibar. Room service. TV (satellite).*

Moderate

Alessandra

Borgo SS Apostoli 17 (055 283 438/282 156/ fax 055 210 619/www.hotelalessandra.com). **Rates** single L120,000-L190,000 (€62-€98); double

Who they? Ferragamo

Book ahead – the library of Ferragamo's hip hotel **Gallery, Hotel Art**.

As the style hotel continues its well-documented and profitable rise, it was inevitable that a fashion company should move in on the business. In conservative Florence, there were no international contenders, leaving the market wide open for local luminary Ferragamo.

The name Ferragamo is synonymous throughout the world with feet, or shoes to be more precise, and the story of Salvatore Ferragamo's rise from rags to riches is a familiar one. Born into poverty near Naples in 1898, the 11th of 14 children, he travelled to America in 1914 and was soon making shoes for movie stars in Hollywood. On his return to Italy in 1927, he settled in Florence where he opened his first workshop in Palazzo Spini Ferone; his reputation as master shoemaker of the highest order was assured.

From these modest beginnings, today's fashion empire was born with glitzy shops selling superbly made (if rather stuffy) shoes, accessories and clothes; home-from-home to Japanese tourists the world over. Testimony to Salvatore's life and work is the **Museo Ferragamo** in Palazzo Spini-Ferone (*see p81*); although he was not born in the city, Florentines have adopted him as one of theirs.

Salvatore died in 1960, leaving the company in the capable hands of his six children, five of whom survive today. Business has boomed, but in the mid-'90s the Ferragamos decided to diversify and bought up a group of small hotels in Florence; the Lungarno Hotels group was born. The sites of these three hotels couldn't have been better; the **Lungarno** (*see p55*) was right on the river bank in the Oltrarno, the **Continental** on the opposite bank practically on top of the Ponte Vecchio, and the **Augustus** a few metres from the Continental.

The Lungarno was immediately given a smart facelift, the Augustus was gutted and transformed into the hip **Gallery, Hotel Art** (*see p45*), a boutique hotel of a kind never before seen in Florence and the Continental is due for an overhaul in winter 2002.

The family deliberately chose establishments that were small enough and with sufficient character to be run individually rather than as a big chain. Leonardo Ferragamo is in charge of the hotel business and oversees all the planning, restructuring and decorating, but his siblings are involved too; it is still very much a family firm. Plans are afoot to expand beyond Florence with hotels being sought in Rome, Venice, Milan and London according to strict criteria; none must have more than 100 rooms, and all must have the potential for an individual personality.

L190,000-L250,000 (€98-€129). **Credit** AmEx, MC, V. **Map** p314 C3.

This modest hotel on the second and third floors of an old *palazzo* is well located on a quiet backstreet between Santa Trinità and the Ponte Vecchio. The best rooms are quite spacious, with antiques and polished parquet floors. All but eight have bathrooms.
Hotel services *Babysitting. Currency exchange. Fax. Laundry. Lift.* **Room services** *Air-conditioning (some rooms). Dataport. Hairdryer. Room service. Safe (some rooms). Telephone. TV (satellite).*

Casci

Via C Cavour 13 (055 211 686/fax 055 239 6461/www.hotelcasci.com). **Rates** single L180,000 (€93); double L240,000 (€124); triple L320,000 (€165.50); quad L400,000 (€206.50). Closed three weeks Jan. **Credit** AmEx, DC, JCB, MC, V. **Map** p314 A4.

This 15th-century *palazzo*, which once belonged to Giacomo Rossini, is now run by the Lombardi family as a cheerful *pensione*. There are 25 bedrooms, many with new bathrooms; those at the back are quieter and look onto a beautiful garden. The breakfast room and bar have elaborately frescoed ceilings and shelves stocked with guidebooks and maps.
Hotel services *Babysitting. Bar. Car park (nearby garage, extra charge). Currency exchange. Fax. Laundry. Lift.* **Room services** *Air-conditioning. Dataport. Hairdryer. Radio. Room service. Safe. Telephone. TV (satellite).*

Dei Mori

Via D Alighieri 12 (tel/fax 055 211 438/ www.bnb.it/deimori). **Rates** single L110,000-L150,000 (€57-€77.50); double L130,000-L170,000 (€67-€88); reduced rates for longer stays. **Credit** AmEx, MC, V. **Map** p314 B4.

Daniele and Franco welcome guests into this 15th-century townhouse as they might friends into their home. Rooms are small but attractive; six new rooms added in late 2000 are more spacious and modern. Nice touches (unusual at this price) include feather duvets and dressing gowns on request. A kitchen links the two 'wings' of the hotel; breakfast is served here and guests can also use it to make drinks and snacks. The comfy sitting room has a TV, stereo and lots of books and mags. There's a terrace from which you can just see the top of the Duomo – it's the only place to smoke in this non-smoking hotel.
Hotel services *Fax. Kitchen. Laundry.* **Room services** *Air-conditioning. Hairdryer (on request). Safe (some rooms). Room service. Telephone.*

Hotel Maxim

Via dei Medici 4 (055 217 474/fax 055 283 729/ www.firenzealbergo.it/home/hotelmaxim). **Rates** single L160,000 (€82.50); double L180,000 (€93); triple L240,000 (€124); quad L290,000 (€150). **Credit** AmEx, MC, V. **Map** p314 B4.

Another budget hotel that's undergone a remarkable transformation since our last edition. The modern two- and three-bedded rooms are now well furnished with cherrywood and have private baths – one even

has a jacuzzi (amazing for a one-star place). There's also a welcoming reception/sitting area.
Hotel services *Car park (nearby garage, extra charge). Fax. Lift.* **Room services** *Air-conditioning. Hairdryer (some rooms). Telephone.*

Budget

Scoti

Via dei Tornabuoni 7 (tel/fax 055 292 128/hotelscoti @hotmail.com). **Rates** single L75,000 (€38.50); double L110,000 (€57); triple L140,000 (€72.50); quad L170,000 (€88). **No credit cards. Map** p314 B2.

This simple *pensione* on the second floor of a 15th-century *palazzo* is one of the best bargains in town if you're more concerned with atmosphere than luxury. Bedrooms are airy if basic (none have private baths). The sitting room, with its floor-to-ceiling frescoes, is out of this world. Australian Maureen and her Italian husband bend over backwards to be helpful. Book well ahead.
Hotel services *Lift. Safe.*

Santa Maria Novella

Luxury

Excelsior

Piazza Ognissanti 3 (055 264 201/fax 055 210 278/ www.westin.com/excelsiorflorence). **Rates** single L590,000-L718,000 (€304.50-€371); double L905,000-L1,074,000 (€467.50-€554.50); suite L1,900,000-L4,300,000 (€981-€2,221); supplement for Arno view L145,000 (€75); breakfast L48,000 (€25). **Credit** AmEx, DC, JCB, MC, V. **Map** p314 B1.

More olde worlde in style than the Grand (*see below*), the Excelsior offers luxury without pomp. The restored public rooms have polished marble floors, neo-classical columns, painted wooden ceilings and stained glass. The 168 rooms and suites are sumptuously appointed; some boast terraces with views over the river to the rooftops of Oltrarno. Popular with upmarket tour groups.
Hotel services *Babysitting. Bar. Car park (nearby garage, extra charge). Conference facilities (up to 180). Dataport. Fax. Laundry. Lifts. No-smoking rooms. Restaurant.* **Room services** *Air-conditioning. Hairdryer. Minibar. Radio. Room service (24hr). Safe. TV (satellite).*

Grand Hotel

Piazza Ognissanti 1 (055 288 781/fax 055 217 400/www.luxurycollection.com/grandflorence). **Rates** single L590,000-L718,000 (€304.50-€371); double L905,000-L1,074,000 (€467.50-€554.50); suite L1,900,000-L4,300,000 (€981-€2221); supplement for Arno view L145,000 (€75); breakfast L48,000 (€25). **Credit** AmEx, DC, JCB, MC, V. **Map** p314 B1.

Smaller than its sister hotel, the Excelsior (*see p49*) across Piazza Ognissanti, the Grand is equal in grandeur but different in character. Renovated in the mid '90s, it is unashamedly luxurious. The vast hall, with its stained-glass ceiling, marble floor, *pietra*

serena columns, brocades, statues and palms, contains a restaurant, bar, salon and piano bar. Many of the 107 bedrooms look over the Arno and are decorated in early Florentine style with frescoes.
Hotel services *Babysitting. Bar. Car park (nearby garage, extra charge). Conference facilities (up to 250). Fax. Laundry. Lifts. No-smoking rooms. Restaurant.* **Room services** *Air-conditioning. Dataport. Hairdryer. Minibar. Radio. Room service (24hr). Safe. TV (satellite).*

Expensive

Kraft
Via Solferino 2 (055 284 273/fax 055 239 8267/ www.krafthotel.it). **Rates** single L245,000-L380,000 (€126.50-€196.50); double L310,000-L560,000 (€160-€289); triple L620,000-L1,140,000 (€320-€589). **Credit** AmEx, DC, JCB, MC, V.
This 80-room hotel west of the city centre, near the Arno and convenient for Santa Maria Novella station, is an excellent choice if you are in town for the opera – the Teatro Comunale is just across the road, and conductors and singers frequently stay here. The bedrooms are fairly traditionally furnished in bright, warm colours, and the five junior suites enjoy panoramic views. An added bonus is the rooftop garden with swimming pool (open from Easter until the end of September).
Hotel services *Babysitting. Bar. Car park (nearby garage, extra charge). Conference facilities (up to 50 people). Fax. Laundry. Lift. No-smoking rooms. Pool. Restaurant. Roof garden. Safe.* **Room services** *Air-conditioning. Hairdryer. Minibar. Room service. Radio. Safe. TV (satellite).*

Aprile
Via della Scala 6 (055 216 237/055 289 147/fax 055 280 947/www.aprile@italyhotel.com). **Rates** single L160,000-L200,000 (€82.50-€103.50); double L240,000-L300,000 (€124-€155); suite L290,000-L300,000 (€150-€191). **Credit** AmEx, JCB, MC, V. **Map** p314 B2.
The bust of Cosimo I above the entrance of the Aprile is a reminder that this building was once a Medici palace. Conveniently placed for the station, this place has an old-fashioned feel. Some bedrooms feature frescoes or scraps of 15th-century graffiti, and, though others are a bit on the gloomy side, the recently acquired *palazzo* next door has rooms with a more modern touch. There's an attractive bar and breakfast room, and plans are afoot to create a winter garden in the shady courtyard.
Hotel services *Babysitting. Bar. Car park (nearby garage, extra charge). Fax. Laundry. Lift.* **Room services** *Air-conditioning (some rooms). Hairdryer (some rooms). Minibar. Room service.TV (satellite).*

Moderate

Palazzo Vecchio
Via B Cennini 4 (055 212 182/055 216 445/fax 055 216 445/www.hotelpalazzovecchio.it). **Rates** single L150,000 (€77.50); double L230,000 (€119); triple

The **Kraft**'s cool pool has fine city views.

L220,000 (€113.50); quad L260,000 (€134.50). **Credit** AmEx, DC, MC, V.
A surprisingly pleasant hotel given its two-star status and proximity to the station, Vecchio's recent facelift has resulted in modern spacious bedrooms with spruce bathrooms.
Hotel services *Babysitting. Bar. Car park. Lift. Laundry.* **Room services** *Hairdryer. Room service. Telephone. TV (satellite).*

Budget

Anna
Via Faenza 56 (055 239 8322/hotelazzi@hotmail. com). **Rates** single L70,000 (€36); double L110,000 (€57); triple L150,000 (€77.50). **Credit** AmEx, MC, V. **Map** p314 A2.
On the floor above the Azzi (*see below*), Anna has only eight rooms, none with a private bathroom. As with so many old Florentine buildings, the basic level of the accommodation is offset by the occasional frescoed ceiling. Some rooms are quite spacious, others pokey, but everything is clean.
Hotel services *Car park (nearby garage, extra charge).*

Azzi
Via Faenza 56 (tel/fax 055 213 806/hotelazzi@ hotmail.com). **Rates** single L70,000 (€36); double L140,000 (€72.50), L110,000 (€57) no bath; triple L180,000 (€93), L150,000 (€77.50) no bath. **Credit** AmEx, MC, V. **Map** p314 A2.
This friendly *pensione* near the train station is set in a crumbling building that has been smartened up a

Palazzo Castiglione – a new hotel in a 16th-century *palazzo*. Half the rooms have frescoes.

bit since our last visit. Rooms are geared towards students, but one or two stand out, and all now have pretty bedcovers. Breakfast is served in the homely sitting room and there's a big terrace.
Hotel services *Bar. Car park (nearby garage, extra charge). Telephone. Terrace.*

San Lorenzo

Expensive

Palazzo Castiglione
Via del Giglio 8 (055 214 886/fax 055 2740521/ www.venere.it/firenze/palazzocastiglione). **Rates** double L300,000 (€155); suites L380,000 (€196.50). **No credit cards. Map** p314 A3.
This new guesthouse located near San Lorenzo market and on the second floor of a 16th-century *palazzo* is under the same management as the Torre Guelfa (*see above*). In fact, Palazzo Castiglione feels more like an elegant private apartment than a hotel, with its reception area doubling as a breakfast and sitting room, and six individually decorated and comfortable bedrooms, half of which have elaborate frescoes (one is entirely painted as a *trompe-l'oeil* of a fortified castle courtyard).
Hotel services *Babysitter. Bar. Car park (nearby garage, extra charge). Laundry. Lift.* **Room services** *Air-conditioning. Hairdryer. Minibar. TV.*

Moderate

Belletini
Via dei Conti 7 (055 213 561/055 282 980/fax 055 283 551/www.firenze.net/hotelbellettini). **Rates** single L170,000 (€88); double L210,000 (€108.50). **Credit** AmEx, DC, MC, V. **Map** p314 A3.
This bustling hotel near the Medici Chapels and San Lorenzo is great value for money. Dating from the 15th century, it holds one of the oldest hotel licences

in the city. Signora Gina is a warm hostess who goes out of her way to please, offering games and videos for bored children, a theatre-booking service and travel arrangements. The 27 rooms have been smartened up recently, and the two at the top have close-up views of the Duomo. A room in the new annexe round the corner is one of the best buys in Florence; elegant fabrics combine with marble, stunning colours and soft lighting.
Hotel services *Babysitting. Bar. Car park (nearby garage, extra charge). Currency exchange. Fax. Laundry. Lift (to first floor). No-smoking rooms.*
Room services *Air-conditioning. Minibar. Room service. Telephone. TV (satellite).*

San Marco

Expensive

Loggiato dei Serviti
Piazza SS Annunziata 3 (055 289 592/fax 055 289 595/www.venere.it/firenze/loggiato_serviti). **Rates** single L250,000 (€129); double L370,000 (€191); suite L420,000-L570,000 (€217-€294.50). **Credit** AmEx, DC, JCB, MC, V. **Map** p314 A5.
This delightful 29-room hotel is in one of Florence's most beautiful piazzas (now, thankfully, traffic-free, but sadly blighted by junkies). Occupying a building that was a convent in the 16th century, its interior tastefully combines original architectural features and antique furniture with the comforts of an upmarket hotel. Bedrooms vary in size and style; the four suites are ideal for families. Breakfast is served in a bright, elegant room with vaulted ceilings, and there's an additional cosy bar area.
Hotel services *Babysitting. Bar. Car park (nearby garage, extra charge). Fax. Laundry. Lift.* **Room services** *Air-conditioning. Dataport. Hairdryer. Minibar. Radio. Room service (24hr). Safe. TV (satellite).*

Moderate

Morandi alla Crocetta

*Via Laura 50 (055 234 4747/fax 055 248 0954/
www.hotelmorandi.it).* **Rates** single L180,000 (€93);
double L290,000 (€150); triple L350,000 (€181);
breakfast L20,000 (€10.50). **Credit** AmEx, DC,
MC, V. **Map** p314 A5.

Book well in advance for a bed in this quiet ten-room
hotel, housed in a former 16th-century convent in
the university area and offering comfortable accommodation at reasonable prices. Kathleen Doyle
Antuono has handed the running of the hotel to her
son Paolo, but the caring and friendly approach has
not changed. Plans are being made to expand on to
the floor below, which will eventually alleviate the
scramble for rooms. As things stand, you'll have to
fight for one of the two rooms with a private terrace.
Hotel services *Babysitting. Bar. Car park
(nearby garage, extra charge). Fax. Laundry.*

B&B: Florence's women-only hotel.

Room services *Air-conditioning. Dataport.
Hairdryer. Minibar. Radio. Room service. Safe.
TV (satellite).*

B&B

*Borgo Pinti 31, San Marco/Santa Croce (055 248
0056/fax 055 238 1260/www.bnb.it/beb).* **Rates**
single L90,000 (€46.50); double L150,000 (€77.50).
Credit MC, V. **Map** p314 B5.

Florence's tiny women-only, non-smoking hotel is a
simple but stylish retreat from the city heat and dust.
The four rooms on the top floor of a *palazzo* are airy
and quiet, with views over an internal garden and
surrounding rooftops. The two communal bathrooms are spotless. Breakfast is help-yourself.

Residenza Johlea Uno

Via San Gallo 80 (055 463 3292/fax 055 463 4552).
Rates single L130,000 (€67); doubles L160,000-
L180,000 (€82.50-€93). **No credit cards**.
Map p314 A4.

Sister hotel to *residenzas* Johanna and Johanna
Cinque Giornate (*see p60* **Chic and cheap**) and,
like them, too small to be officially classified as a
hotel, the Johlea opened in March 2001. The owners
strive to offer value for money, which they achieve
here even more spectacularly than in the other two
(and only ten minutes' walk from the Duomo).
Standards of comfort and service are those of a
three-star hotel but the atmosphere is discreet.
Rooms are decorated in soft pastel colours, furnished
partly with antiques and have excellent bathrooms.
Breakfast is laid on elegant lacquer trays. Upstairs
there's a cosy little sitting room with an 'honesty
fridge' and a roof terrace with a 360° city view.
Hotel services *Lift. Roof terrace.* **Room services**
Air-conditioning. Hairdryer. Kettle. Safe. TV.

Santa Croce

Luxury

J and J

*Via di Mezzo 20 (055 234 5005/fax 055 240 282/
www.jandjhotel.com).* **Rates** double L490,000-
L650,000 (€253-€335.50); suite L550,000-L800,000
(€284-€454.50). **Credit** AmEx, DC, MC, V.
Map p314 B6.

The simple façade of this former convent gives little clue to the chic rooms within, where old and new
are combined. Many original architectural features
are visible in the public rooms and the cool arched
cloister, where breakfast is served in summer. No
two bedrooms are alike – some are huge, with split
levels and seating areas – but all feature antiques,
rich fabrics and immaculate bathrooms. J and J is
supremely comfortable and discreet; its only defect
is that it has numerous steep stairs and no lift.
Hotel services *Babysitting. Bar. Car park
(nearby garage, extra charge). Fax. Laundry.
No-smoking rooms.* **Room services** *Air-
conditioning. Dataport. Hairdryer. Minibar. Room
service. Safe. TV (satellite).*

Expensive

Monna Lisa
Borgo Pinti 27 (055 247 9751/fax 055 247 9755/www.monnalisa.it). **Rates** single L220,000-L350,000 (€113.50-€181); double L330,000-L530,000 (€170.50-€273.50). **Credit** AmEx, DC, JCB, MC, V. **Map** p314 B5.
Florence is full of grand *palazzi* hiding behind plain façades, and the upmarket Monna Lisa is a prime example of this. The maze of public rooms, many with original waxed terracotta floors and wooden ceilings, is crammed with the owners' priceless collection of paintings, sculptures and furniture. It's not the friendliest hotel in Florence, but has a delightful courtyard garden. The 30 bedrooms range from huge and ornate to cramped and ordinary; the best look on to the garden, and some have balconies.
Hotel services *Babysitting. Bar. Car park (extra charge). Laundry. Lift (in annexe). No-smoking rooms.* **Room services** *Air-conditioning. Hairdryer. Jacuzzi (6 rooms). Minibar. Room service. Safe. TV (satellite).*

Moderate

Liana
Via Alfieri 18 (055 245 303/fax 055 234 4596/www.venere.it/firenze/liana). **Rates** single L160,000-L220,000 (€82.50-€113.50); double L230,000-L290,000 (€119-€150); triple L300,000-L385,000 (€115-€199); quad L380,000-L480,000 (€196.50-€248); quin L440,000-L550,000 (€227-€284). **Credit** AmEx, DC, MC, V.
Once the British Embassy, this 19th-century house is worth considering if you're travelling by car and would like to be within reach of the sights but not in the centre. Marie-Thérèse Blot has done a great job of redecorating and generally raising standards to transform the Liana from a crumbling two- to a very pleasant three-star hotel, restoring faded frescoes and filling the place with antiques, fresh flowers and stylish fabrics. Rooms are now more comfortable, especially in the case of the elegant Count's Room. Classical music is played in the first-floor breakfast room.
Hotel services *Babysitting. Bar. Car park (extra charge). Fax. Hairdryer. Garden. Laundry. Safe.* **Room services** *Minibar. Room service. TV (satellite).*

Budget

Locanda Orchidea
Borgo degli Albizi 11 (tel/fax 055 248 0346/hotelorchidea@yahoo.it). **Rates** single L75,000 (€38.50); double L110,000 (€57); triple L160,000 (€82.50). Closed 3wks Aug. **No credit cards. Map** p314 B5.
Dante's wife was born in the 12th-century *palazzo* that houses the simple, cosy Orchidea with its seven bright rooms, the best overlooking a wonderful overgrown garden. Only one room has a shower; the rest share two communal bathrooms that have just been renovated. Friendly Anglo-Italian owners.
Hotel services *Lift. Telephone.*

Oltrarno

Luxury

Lungarno
Borgo San Jacopo 14 (055 27261/fax 055 268 437/www.lungarnohotels.com). **Rates** single L410,000 (€212); double L650,000-L880,000 (€335.50-€454.50); suite L980,000-L1,500,000 (€506-€774.50). **Credit** AmEx, DC, JCB, MC, V. **Map** p314 C3.
The most coveted rooms in this recently refurbished hotel, owned by the Ferragamos and in the smart part of the Oltrarno, have terraces overlooking the Arno. The 1960s building incorporates a medieval tower. The sitting-room/bar has huge windows, taking advantage of the waterside setting, as does the elegant ground-floor restaurant. There's a little outside seating area right on the river, too. Bedrooms are stylish and comfy but not that big. Those in the medieval tower have original stone walls.
Hotel services *Bar. Babysitting. Car park (nearby garage, extra charge). Fax. Laundry. Lifts. No-smoking rooms. Restaurant.* **Room services** *Air-conditioning. Dataport (some rooms). Hairdryer. Minibar. Radio. Room service. Safe. TV (satellite).*

Moderate

Annalena
Via Romana 34 (055 222 439/fax 055 222 403/www.hotelannalena.it). **Rates** single L160,000-L200,000 (€82.50-€103.50); double L250,000-L290,000 (€129-€150). **Credit** AmEx, DC, MC, V. **Map** p314 D1.
If buildings could speak, the 15th-century *palazzo* housing this hotel would never stop. Annalena, a young Florentine noblewoman, inherited the house from the Medici, but tragic circumstances (outlined in the hotel brochure) obliged her to donate it to nuns to use as a refuge for young widows. During the Mussolini years, refugees from the Fascist police were lodged here. Today it's a comfortable, old-fashioned *pensione*. Bedrooms vary in size; the best have balconies and views over a garden centre.
Hotel services *Bar. Car Park (nearby garage, extra charge). Hairdryer (on request). Fax. Laundry. Safe.* **Room services** *Room service. TV (satellite).*

Hotel Boboli
Via Romana 63 (055 229 8654/fax 055 233 7169/giottiroberto@tiscalinet.it). **Rates** single L180,000 (€93); double L240,000 (€124). **Credit** MC, V. **Map** p314 D1.
This perfectly adequate little hotel near the Boboli Gardens is being spruced up a bit. There's no lift, so the sunniest of the pleasant rooms (on the fourth floor with skyline views) require quite a climb.

About half the rooms look over an inner courtyard and are very quiet. The bathrooms are all relatively new, though some are only big enough to swing a small mouse in. In warm weather breakfast is served in the pretty little courtyard garden.
Hotel services *Bar. Car park (nearby garage, extra charge). Fax.* **Room services** *Dataport. Hairdryer (on request). Telephone.*

Silla
Via dei Renai 5 (055 234 2888/fax 055 234 1437/www.hotelsilla.it). **Rates** single L210,000 (€108.50); double L290,000 (€150); triple L360,000 (€186). **Credit** AmEx, DC, MC, V. **Map** p314 D5.
This old-fashioned *pensione*, which is housed in a 16th-century *palazzo* south of the river has a roof terrace overlooking the Arno. The decor hints at the owner's Venetian origins, but recent renovation work has compromised the character. The bedrooms are clean but rather uniform, and those facing the Lungarno can be noisy.
Hotel services *Babysitting. Bar. Car park (extra charge). Fax. Lift (two flights of stairs to get to it). Terrace.* **Room services** *Air-conditioning (most rooms). Dataport. Hairdryer. Minibar. Room service. TV (satellite).*

La Scaletta
Via dei Guicciardini 13 (055 283 028/055 214 255/fax 055 289 562/www.lascaletta.com). **Rates** single L170,000 (€88), L90,000 (€46.50) no bath; double L240,000 (€124), L180,000 (€93) no bath; triple L280,000 (€144.50), L160,000

The best Rooms with a view

From their roof garden
Beacci Tornabuoni (*p47*), **Kraft** (*p51*), **La Scaletta** (*p56*), **Silla** (*p56*).

Of the city
Bencistà (*p58*), **Villa Belvedere** (*p58*), **Villa Poggio San Felice** (*p59*), **Torre di Bellosguardo** (*p57*), **Torre Guelfa** (*p47*).

Of the river
Excelsior (*p49*), **Grand Hotel** (*p49*), **Hermitage** (*p47*), **Lungarno** (*p55*).

Of frescoed ceilings
Aprile, rooms 8, 13 & 16 (*p51*), **Belletini** annexe, rooms 52 & 53 (*p52*), **Grand Hotel**, 34 rooms (*p49*), **Liana**, most second-floor rooms (*p55*), **Morandi alla Crocetta**, room 29 (*p53*), **Palazzo Castiglione**, rooms 1, 2 & 4 (*p52*). Ask for *camera con gli affreschi*.

(€82.50) no bath; quad L300,000 (€155); dinner L25,000 (€13). **Credit** MC, V, JCB. **Map** p314 D2.
The 15th-century building that houses this 11-room, two-star hotel is near Boboli Gardens (over which the back rooms have wonderful views) and has a delightful roof garden. It's a simple, friendly place with a lived-in feel. Recent improvements have resulted in brighter colours and air-conditioning in most rooms. It's one of the few small hotels in Florence to provide an evening meal (not obligatory but excellent value). Rooms on the noisy Via de' Guicciardini have double-glazing.
Hotel services *Babysitting. Bar. Car park (garage nearby, extra charge). Currency exchange. Fax. Lift. Restaurant. Roof garden. Safe.* **Room services** *Air-conditioning. Hairdryer. Room service. Telephone.*

Sorelle Bandini
Piazza Santo Spirito 9 (055 215 308/fax 055 282 761). **Rates** double L186,000 (€96), L162,000 (€83.50) no bath; triple L257,000 (€132.50), L182,000 (€94) no bath; breakfast L20,000 (€10.50). **No credit cards. Map** p314 D1.
The charm of the Sorelle Bandini comes from its superb setting on Piazza Santo Spirito and a sense that little has changed since the Bandini sisters opened it in the '20s. The loggia that runs along two sides of the building (Room 4 has direct access) makes up for the dilapidated interior with its faded mirrors, dusty chandeliers and lumbering old furniture. Owners Antonio and Mimmo stick doggedly to the one-star formula but make the odd improvement such as new bathrooms and fresh paintwork.
Hotel services *Currency exchange. Fax. Lift. Safe. Terrace.* **Room services** *Hairdryer. Room service (breakfast). Telephone.*

Budget

Istituto Gould
Via dei Serragli 49 (055 212 576/fax 055 280 274/gould.reception@dada.it). **Open** office 9am-1pm, 3pm-7pm Mon-Fri; 9am-1pm Sat. **Rates** single L65,000 (€33.50), L55,000 (€28.50) no bath; double L90,000 (€46.50), L78,000 (€40.50) no bath; triple L114,000 (€59), L99,000 (€51) no bath; quad L148,000 (€76.60). **No credit cards. Map** p314 D1.
This budget accommodation run by the Valdese Church is popular: book ahead. The 17th-century *palazzo* with its courtyard, stone staircases and terracotta floors has plenty of atmosphere. If you want to avoid noisy Via dei Serragli, ask for a room at the back; some have access to a terrace. All rooms are non-smoking. You have to check in during office hours, but once that's done you get your own key. Sadly, guests don't have access to the lovely garden.
Hotel services *All rooms no-smoking. Safe (at reception).* **Room services** *Telephone.*

Pensionato Pio X
Via dei Serragli 106 (055 225 044). **Open** 24hrs daily. **Rates** single L30,000 (€15.50); doubles,

The superb loggia of the **Sorelle Bandini** gives it a unique charm. *See p56.*

triples, quads & quins L27,000 (€14) per person. **No credit cards. Map** p314 D1.

This church-owned *pensione* in a 13th-century former convent is a quiet, pleasant alternative to a youth hostel. The two singles offer amazing value, but most of the rooms are three- and four-bedded. There's a cheerful sitting room and a dining room where guests can picnic. Only two rooms have private bathrooms (and they cost a little extra), but the communal showers have recently been re-done and are spotless. There's a midnight curfew, but unlike most hostels the place is open all day. The minimum stay is two nights, the maximum five. All rooms are no-smoking.
Hotel services *Hairdryers. Safe. Vending machines.*

Outside the City Gates

Luxury

Grand Hotel Villa Cora
Viale N Machiavelli 18 (055 229 8451/fax 055 229 086/www.villacora.com). Bus 13. **Rates** single L520,000 (€268.50); double L830,000-L950,000 (€428.50-€490.50); suite L1,300,000-L2,400,000 (€671.50-€1239.50). **Credit** AmEx, DC, JCB, MC, V.

A relatively small size (49 rooms) and friendly staff give the Villa Cora the feel of a grand country house. The 19th-century villa is set in gardens ten minutes' walk south-west of Porta Romana; a courtesy limo service provides transport into town. Public rooms are lavish with ornate plasterwork,

gold, frescoes, chandeliers, huge mirrors, intricate woodwork and rich fabrics. The bedrooms vary in style from clean and classical to formal and grand. Anthony Hopkins stayed here during the filming of *Hannibal* in 2000.
Hotel services *Bar. Car park. Conference facilities (up to 120). Fax. Garden. Laundry. Lifts. No-smoking rooms. Pool. Restaurant.* **Room services** *Air-conditioning. Dataport. Hairdryer. Minibar. Radio. Room service (24hr). Safe. TV (satellite). Video (on request).*

Expensive

Torre di Bellosguardo
Via Roti Michelozzi 2 (055 229 8145/fax 055 229 008/www.members.aol.com/puterbugzz/tbellos.html). Bus 36 or 37 then 15-min walk. **Rates** single L290,000 (€150); double L490,000 (€253); suite L590,000 (€304.50); breakfast L35,000 (€18).
Credit AmEx, DC, MC, V.

Up in the hills west of the traffic hell of Porta Romana, Bellosguardo is a collection of villas among olive groves and cypresses that makes for a retreat from the summer heat. Amerigo Franchetti has lovingly restored his family's Renaissance villa, preserving its atmosphere while offering supreme comfort. The suite in the top of the tower enjoys a 360° view of the Florentine hills, while the Italianate garden with its 'pool with a view' is a delight. There are no TVs on the premises. Staff can be very rude.
Hotel services *Babysitting. Bar. Car park. Fax. Garden. Laundry. Lift. Pool. Safe.* **Room**

Villa Poggio San Felice has been restored to its 15th-century glory. *See p59.*

services *Air-conditioning (three suites). Dataport. Hairdryer. Room service.*

Villa Belvedere

Via Benedetto Castelli 3 (055 222 501/502/fax 055 223 163/www.villa-belvedere.com). Bus 11, then 10min walk. **Rates** single L250,000 (€129); double L330,000-L390,000 (€170.50-€201.50); suite L490,000 (€253). Closed mid Nov-mid Mar. **Credit** AmEx, DC, MC, V.

Though located in a very uninspiring '30s building, the Belvedere is set in an attractive garden with a swimming pool on a quiet residential street above Porta Romana, with wonderful views of Florence. A family-run hotel, it has 26 comfy, spacious rooms with parquet floors and wood furnishings. All have brand-new bathrooms and some have terraces and city views. Prices are very reasonable for a four-star place.

Hotel services *Babysitting. Bar. Car park. Fax. Garden. Laundry. Lift. No-smoking rooms. Pool. Restaurant (light meals). Tennis court.* **Room services** *Air-conditioning. Dataport. Hairdryer. Room service. Safe. TV (satellite).*

Moderate

Bencistà

Via Benedetto di Maiano 4, Fiesole (tel/fax 055 59163/pensionebencista@uol.it). Bus 7. **Rates** (per person, obligatory half-board) single L180,000 (€93), without bath L140,000 (€72.50); double L160,000 (€82.50), without bath L140,000 (€72.50). Full board L15,000 (€7.80) extra. **No credit cards.**

This former convent, run as a *pensione* by the Simoni family since 1925, has an unparalleled setting on a hillside just below Fiesole. Of the three salons furnished with antiques, one has a fireplace and shelves stuffed with some early editions of English books. The 47 bedrooms are arranged off

a rabbit warren of passages and stone stairways; those at the front of the building enjoy fabulous city views. Room prices include either lunch or dinner in the restaurant overlooking Florence but the food is pretty average.

Hotel services *Bar service. Car park. Fax. Garden. Laundry. Restaurant. Safe. TV.* **Room services** *Room service (breakfast only).*

Cimabue

Via B Lupi 7 (055 471 989/fax 055 475 601/ www.hotelcimabue.it). Bus 11, 36, 37 to Piazza San Marco. **Rates** single L150,000-L170,000 (€77.50-€88); double L200,000-L240,000 (€103.50-€124); triple L260,000-L300,000 (€134.50-€155); quad L300,000-L350,000 (€155-€181). **Credit** AmEx, DC, MC, V.

This two-star hotel ten minutes' walk north of the Duomo is at the upper end of its category thanks to the welcoming Rossis. The 16 rooms have their own well-equipped bathrooms. The generous breakfast buffet is served in a bright little ground-floor room.

Hotel services *Babysitting. Bar. Car park (nearby garage, extra charge). Currency exchange. Fax.* **Room services** *Hairdryer. Room service. Safe. TV.*

Classic Hotel

Viale N Machiavelli 25 (055 229 351/fax 055 229 353/www.classichotel.it). Bus 11, 36, 37 to Porta Romana. **Rates** single L160,000 (€82.50); double L250,000 (€129); suite L330,000 (€170.50). **Credit** AmEx, MC, V.

In a lush garden five minutes' walk south-west of the old city walls at Porta Romana, this attractive villa has been tastefully refurbished with pristine results. Breakfast is either served in a basement room or, more pleasantly, a conservatory leading to a garden full of mature trees and shrubs. For romantics, an annexe suite with its own terrace is tucked away in a corner of the garden. Prices are still very reasonable, standards high and the staff are friendly and helpful.

Hotel services *Babysitting. Bar. Car park. Fax. Garden. Laundry. Lift.* Room services *Air-conditioning (some rooms). Room service. Safe.*

Villa Betania
Viale del Poggio Imperiale 23 (tel/fax 055 222 243/www.villabetania.it). Bus 11, 36, 37 to Porta Romana, then 10min walk south. Rates single L140,000-220,000 (€72.50-113.50); double L190,000-L280,000 (€98-€144.50). Credit AmEx, DC, MC, V.
Hidden away in a secret garden, this 15th-century building had become dilapidated but redecoration in 1998 brought it up to scratch. The most pleasant of the 15 rooms are in the tower. The generous breakfast buffet can be taken on one of two shady terraces. Hotel services *Bar. Car park. Fax. Garden. Laundry. TV (satellite).* Room services *Air-conditioning. Dataport. Hairdryer (on request). Room service. Safe.*

Villa Poggio San Felice
Via San Matteo in Arcetri 24 (055 220 016/fax 055 233 5388/www.wel.it/Sanfelice). Free shuttle to city centre. Rates double L300,000 (€155); suite L400,000 (€206.50). Credit AmEx, DC, MC, V.
This mellow 15th-century villa in beautiful gardens in the hills behind Porta Romana was once the summer home of a Swiss hotel magnate; his descendants recently rescued it from decay and turned it into a relaxed B&B. The public rooms and bedrooms, decorated with taste and imagination, are full of family antiques and pictures. One bedroom has a big terrace. The cool, peaceful garden has city views. Hotel services *Babysitting. Bar. Car park. Garden. Fax. Laundry.* Room services *Dataport. Hairdryer (on request). Room service.*

Budget

Residence Johanna
Via B Lupi 14 (055 481 896/fax 055 482 721/ www.johanna.it). Bus 1, 17 to Via Mischeli, then 10min walk. Rates single (no bath) L80,000 (€41.50); double L130,000 (€67). No credit cards.
The owners of this discreet home from home in a residential area north of the city centre have kept prices admirably low since the last edition of this guide, offering comfortable, stylish rooms at rock-bottom prices. The makings of breakfast is provided on a tray in each room and there's a good supply of books and mags. Neither single has a bathroom. Hotel services *Car park (nearby garage, extra charge). Fax. Lift. Mobile phones for hire. Safe.* Room services *Kettle.*

Residence Johanna Cinque Giornate
Via delle Cinque Giornate 12 (055 473 377/www.johanna.it). Bus 4, 28 to Via dello Statuto. Rates double L140,000 (€72.50). No credit cards.
Under the same management as Residence Johanna (*see p60* Chic & cheap) and offering the same set-up, this small villa (in a residential area north-west of the city centre) has its own garden. Considering

the low prices, the six bedrooms are elegantly furnished – and each has its own bathroom. Hotel services *Car park. Fridge. Laundry (external).* Room services *Air-conditioning (some rooms). Hairdryer (on request). Kettle. TV.*

Hostels

Hostel Archi Rossi
Via Faenza 94r, Santa Maria Novella (055 290 804/ fax 055 230 2601/ostelloarchirossi@hotmail.com). Open 6.30-11am, 2.30pm-12.30am daily. Rates *per person* L27,000-L30,000 (€14-€15.50) dorm; L40,000 (€20.50) quad with bath (L30,000/€15.50 no bath); breakfast L3,000-L4,500 (€1.60-€2.30); dinner from L12,000 (€6.20). No credit cards. Map p314 A2.
Ten minutes from the station, with a reception area covered with garish modern versions of famous frescoes. Rooms are spacious and light; some have bathrooms. Facilities for the disabled are unusually good for Italy. All rooms are no-smoking. Services *Bar. Hairdryer (on request). Internet point. Laundry. Lift. Restaurant. Terrace. Vending machines.*

Ostello per la Gioventù (YHA)
Viale A Righi 2/4, Outside the City Gates (055 601 451/fax 055 610 300). Bus 17A or 17B. Rates per person L25,000 (€13) in dorm; family rooms (double) from L70,000 (€36); extra meals L15,000 (€7.80). No credit cards.
Not as central as other hostels but more pleasant in the heat, this lies just below Fiesole in an impressive setting with a loggia and ranks of lemon trees in its extensive grounds. Most beds are in dorms, but there are smaller rooms for families. There are also camping facilities. It's worth the 20-minute bus ride (it's a trek up the hill from the stop) from the city centre if you want some peace. There's a midnight curfew. Services *Bar. Disabled: toilet. Restaurant. TV.*

Santa Monaca
Via Santa Monaca 6, Oltrarno (055 268 338/fax 055 280 185/www.ostello.it). Rates per person L30,000 (€15.50). Credit AmEx, DC, MC, V. Map p314 C1.
This 15th-century convent building is convenient for those wanting to stay south of the river but is a little gloomy. Beds have been moved around a bit recently to make the rooms less crowded and dispensers provide drinks, snacks and hot meals. All rooms are no-smoking. There's a 1am curfew. Services *Internet points (2). Kitchen. Laundry. TV.*

Youth Residence Firenze 2000
Viale Raffaello Sanzio 16, Outside the City Gates (055 233 5558/fax 055 230 6392/scatizzi@dada.it). Bus 12; get off just after Piazza Pier Vettori. Rates per person L45,000 (€23) in rooms with shower only; L60,000 (€34) with full bath; triples L45,000 (€23) with full bath. No credit cards.
A new-ish hostel some way from the centre, with better facilities than standard hostels – there's an indoor pool (for which you have to pay), and bathrooms with all rooms (2-5 beds) – but a total lack of character. It's not that cheap but often has room

when more central hostels are full. Rooms must be pre-booked and groups of ten or more get free breakfast. There is a blanket no-smoking policy.
Services *Car park (limited, extra charge). Currency exchange. Disabled: toilet. Fax. Lift. Pool. Vending machine.*

Campsites

Camping Panoramico
Via Peramondo 1, Fiesole (055 599 069/fax 055 59186/www.florencecamping.com). Bus 7, then walk. **Open** *office* 8am-10pm daily. **Rates** *per person* L15,000 (€7.80); per tent L25,000 (€13); per camper van L25,000 (€13). **No credit cards.**
With some 120 pitches, this is probably the most picturesque site within easy reach of Florence (it's about 8km/5 miles north of the city centre). Facilities include a bar, restaurant, supermarket and pool. There are also 21 self-catering bungalows that sleep four, and some caravans to rent. It gets packed in summer.

Camping Michelangiolo
Viale Michelangiolo 80, Outside the City Gates (055 681 1977/www.ecvacanze.it). Bus 12, 13. **Open** *office* 7am-midnight daily. **Rates** *per person* L14,000 (€7.20); children 5-12yrs L8,000 (€4.10); under-4s free; per tent L9,000 (€4.70); per camper van L19,000 (€9.80); incl electricity. **No credit cards.**
Though noisy in summer (there's a disco till 1am), this campsite has room for 240 tents/caravans and 960 people. It has fabulous city views, a bar, restaurant and supermarket. It's situated just below Piazzale Michelangiolo, within easy walking distance of the city centre.

Villa Camerata
Viale A Righi 2-4, Outside the City Gates (055 601 451/fax 055 610 300). **Open** *office* 7am-midnight daily. **Rates** *per person* L10,000 (€5.20); per tent L9,000/L20,000 (€4.70/€10.50) depending on size; per camper van L20,000 (€10.50); incl electricity. **No credit cards.**
In the grounds of the YHA's Ostello per la Gioventù *(see p59).*

Long-term accommodation

Florence & Abroad
Via San Zanobi 58, San Lorenzo (055 487 004/fax 055 490 143/www.florenceandabroad.com). **Open** 10am-12.30pm, 3-6.30pm Mon-Fri. **No credit cards.** For a one-bedroomed flat, expect to pay L2,000,000-L5,000,000 (€1,033-€2,582) per month on a holiday let, L1,500,000 (€774.50) plus for longer rentals in the city centre. English-speaking staff

Milligan & Milligan Rentals
Via degli Alfani 68, San Marco (055 268 256/fax 055 268 260/www.italy-rentals.com). **Open** 9am-noon, 1-4pm Mon-Fri. **No credit cards. Map** p314 A4. Staffed by English speakers; specialises in student-type accommodation.

Chic and cheap

The idea of a comfortable, classy and cheap hotel in notoriously pricey Florence would seem to be a pipedream. But thanks to Lea Gulmanelli and her business partner Vitta Johanna, there are now four such places.

Lea and Vitta were driven by the desire to offer visitors a positive impression of the city and to send them home without feeling they'd been fleeced by their hotel. They bought their first 'residenza', the **Johanna** (*see p59*), in 1995, establishing a template that was copied in the **Johanna Cinque Giornate** (*p59*): a small property in a quiet residential area some way from the centre of town but with good public transport, decorated in the style of a comfortable private apartment, with few hotel 'trappings', no more than six rooms, no porter, no 24-hour room service, no phones in the rooms and no breakfast room (breakfast is a generous DIY job left in the rooms on a prettily laid tray).

Two *residenzes* on, the guidelines remain the same; a high degree of comfort and extraordinarily reasonable prices. The last acquisition, the **Johlea Uno** (*see p53*), is slightly more expensive than the others but offers more facilities and creature comforts. The **Johlea Due** is set to open in summer 2001 in the *palazzo* next door to its sister; this time the rooms will be furnished with elegant antiques. Word is spreading fast, particularly among business clients, so book well in advance.

Johlea – a step away from the ordinary.

Sightseeing

Introduction

Art heaven, tourist hell. Here's how to cope.

Home to the Duomo, piazza della Signoria, the Uffizi and a number of renowned parish churches, the historic centre of Florence contains statistically more art treasures per square metre than any other city in the world. EM Forster wrote that 'the traveller who has gone to Italy to study the tactile values of Giotto… may return remembering nothing but the blue sky and the men and women who live under it', but this is Florence, and Florence defies its visitors to leave without an abiding memory of a favourite artwork, sight or building. And this is in spite of the haze of *piazze* full of backpackers, streets lined with fake designer goods sellers and stalls selling posters, postcards and T-shirts printed with famous images from Botticelli, Leonardo, Michelangelo et al.

Sightseeing in Florence has more to offer than the feats of genius you'll see in the form of monuments and inside world-famous museums. Getting the true feel of a city that is so steeped in history, where the walls speak of ancient feuds and alliances, where heavy stone family crests allude to the strength of historic noble families and each street name holds a fable of its own, means unravelling the secrets of an intricate and powerful past. Stolen glimpses through iron-studded doors of orange-scented courtyard gardens in forbidding *palazzi*, tiny tabernacles on street corners with candles and fresh flowers left to icons of the Madonna, images of shell-shaped windows reflected in a river lit by art nouveau street lamps, and the rooftop worlds of hanging gardens, medieval bell-towers and fresco-ceilinged rooms built into suspended arches – all of these beg onlooking eyes to read between the lines and reach the essence of the city. How can you refuse?

ORIENTATION

The city centre is compact and manageable, and it's practically impossible to get lost, with the ever-visible dome of the Duomo and the River Arno and its four central bridges acting as reference points. The majority of the main sights and museums are clustered north of the two central bridges in the area around the Duomo, and most other important sites circling this rectangle in the Santa Maria Novella, San Lorenzo, San Marco, Santa Croce and Oltrarno zones. We've organised our sightseeing chapters (along with the divisions of many

of our other chapters) into these areas, though be aware that in Florence nothing is very far from anything else. The main central area sits in the river valley, so is practically flat, while the surrounding hills rise steeply on both sides, creating challenging walks and rewarding views, easily accessible by foot or bus.

MUSEUMS AND GALLERIES

During the summer and around Easter, Florence spills over with visitors, so the sights are crowded and huge queues can form at the main museums. The best times to sightsee in relative ease are the inbetween seasons, from January to March (avoiding Easter), and from mid September to mid December. If you're intending to visit all of the main museums, it could be worth aiming for the week when state museums give free entrance (*see below*).

Many of Florence's unrivalled museum collections have private collections at their core, whether that of a mega-family such as the Medici (**Uffizi** and **Palazzo Pitti**) or of a lone connoisseur (**Bardini**, **Horne** and **Stibbert** museums), while other major museums were founded to preserve treasures too precious to expose to the elements (**Accademia**, **Bargello** and **Museo dell'Opera del Duomo**). Administratively, they fall into three categories: private, state or municipal. A collective ticket is available for municipal museums that entitles you to a 50 per cent discount on entry on paying an initial L10,000 (€5.20); the ticket is valid for one year and allows one visit to each museum (call 055 262 8325 for more information). The main participants are the Brancacci Chapel, Cenacolo di Santo Spirito, Museo Firenze com'era, Palazzo Vecchio, Collezione della Ragione and Museo Bardini.

The state museums don't give concessions, except for one week of the year ('Settimana dei Beni Culturali'), which varies but is generally in February or March, when they are all free. For general information on the state museums and for booking, call Firenze Musei on 055 294 883.

Firenze Musei recommends booking for the **Uffizi** and the **Accademia**, which could save you a two-hour wait, though the wait on the phone can sometimes be almost as long as the queue. Booking costs L3,000 (€2) and tickets are collected from a window beside the normal ticket office, or, in the case of the Palazzo Pitti, from an office in the corner of the courtyard.

Full to bursting: Florence's historic heart contains more art treasures than any other city.

Don't expect to be able to book tickets there directly; you will be told to phone the central number. Last issuing times for tickets vary (and we have given the closing time in our listings, not last admission) – try to get to the ticket office an hour before the museum closes. The closing time for at least half of the city's museums is 1.50pm.

Art-lovers should note that works of art are often lent to other museums or to exhibitions, and restoration can be carried out with little or no notice, so call first if you want to view a specific piece, or pick up the leaflet at the museum ticket office with the list of exhibits not currently on show.

Temporary exhibitions are regularly held at a few locations in Florence, among them Palazzo Vecchio, Palazzo Medici Riccardi and Palazzo Strozzi; see the magazine *Firenze Spettacolo* or the local newspapers for details.

MONDAY BLUES

For occupants of more accommodating metropolises it can be a shock – and a spanner in the planning works – to find that some of

Florence's major museums close on Monday. These include the Uffizi, the Accademia and the Galleria Palatina in the Palazzo Pitti. If you're lucky and it's the first, third or fifth Monday of the month, you could go to the Galleria dell'Arte Moderna, the Bargello or the Museo di San Marco, or if it's the second or fourth, the Capelle Medicee and the minor museums of Palazzo Pitti. Or plan in a visit to a smaller, less intense museum or church: not a bad idea, anyway, given how easy it is to overload.

GUIDED TOURS

There's not a great deal to choose between Florence's various tour companies, all of which offer pretty standard itineraries with English-

► For info on climate and public holidays, *see* **Directory: When to go**, and for tourist offices, *see* **Directory: Tourist information**.
► The **Icons of art** box on page 106 gives background on Florentine's major artists, and there's an art and architecture glossary on page 298.

Electric dreams

Walk over any of the bridges in Florence that are open to traffic, close your eyes, and you could be forgiven for thinking that you're experiencing the start of a Grand Prix, choked as you are with exhaust fumes and deafened by the constant roar of speeding motors.

The central tourist honeypot is a traffic-exclusion zone, but otherwise the city is one of the most air-polluted in Europe, and noise pollution is endemic, thanks largely to the Florentines' love affair with the moped, especially if it's been *truccato* – souped up with holes in the exhaust to make even more noise and go even faster. To add insult to injury, huge diesel buses thunder down central streets barely wide enough to contain them, scattering tourists caught in their paths.

The effects are tangible; the marble sculptures in the Loggia dei Lanzi are crumbling like Athens's Parthenon, the incidence of respiratory problems has more than doubled in the past ten years, and it's no longer odd to see pedestrians going about their business wearing white hospital masks.

The council has hummed and hawed over the problem for years, making sporadic efforts to improve matters by offering practically free bicycle hire (snubbed by the Florentines), bringing in regularly flouted regulations to keep daytime traffic out of the centre, and sometimes holding token traffic-free days when the pollution levels are announced to be at risk of exceeding the European limits. Cynics point out that the machines installed to measure the levels mysteriously disappeared from those strategic points in the city where it's rumoured that pollution does sometimes fall below the limits.

So what's to do? Well, an unusual knight in shining armour could be on its way in the shape of a move towards the use of blissfully quiet and fume-free forms of electric transport.

A network of small electric buses covering most of the city centre is already up and running (*see p282* **Directory: Getting Around**); the perfect foil to sightseeing on foot, it's one of the best ways to see the city, as you trundle along cocooned from the elements and the hard cobbles. There are four interlinking routes, which between them provide pretty much the grand central tour.

The council has also started to wheel out incentive schemes for anyone buying electric mopeds or cars, including free charge-ups, and has unveiled plans to install many more recharging columns at sites all over the city. Whether the initiatives, along with rising fuel costs, will be enough to coax environmentally unenlightened Florentines away from using their beloved combustion engines in the centre of town remains to be seen. Judging by the true story of one traffic offender who drove his Ferrari round the seriously out-of-bounds piazza del Duomo and when fined by the traffic police offered to pay double if they'd let him do another lap, it doesn't look promising.

In the meantime, an alternative for visitors has emerged: car hire company Biancaneve (*see p283* **Directory: Getting Around**) now offers the ultimate in sightseeing comfort and convenience and the most fun you've had since bumper cars – electric golf carts for four with roll-up roof and sides for sun-basking, and permission to drive through any of the streets and squares of central Florence.

language options covering the main monuments and museums by foot or by bus. The highly reputable **Association of Tourist Guides** (055 210 641/www.florencetouristguides.com), the **Association of Florentine Tourist Guides** (055 422 0901) and the **Cultural Association of Guides** (055 787 7744/www.firenze-guide.com) all offer a vast selection of standard tours. Two firms that provide a little more variety are **Walking Tours of Florence** (055 264 5033/www.artviva.com), which offers a morning jaunt into Tuscany and a views tour, and **CAF** (055 283 2000/www.caftours.com), which runs a

Florence by night tour. Prices obviously vary depending on the type of tour that you choose, but you should expect to pay approximately L40,000 (€20.50) for a three-hour walk and L60,000 (€34) for a tour of a major museum, including admission.

If you prefer to do it yourself when it comes to sightseeing, some excellent ways in which to see the city are to hire a bike or moped (*see p283* **Directory: Getting Around**) or – if you want to be environmentally friendly – to take a ride on the electric buses that cover the central areas of the city or to hire an electric golf cart (*see above* **Electric dreams**).

Duomo & Around

The inner city's inner sanctum.

Florence's historic heart stretches from the north side of the Duomo down to the river bank, bordered by the exclusive designer shops of via dei Tornabuoni and the heavy, fortified *palazzi* and Gothic pride of via del Proconsolo.

Around piazza del Duomo

Central Florence is dominated by the splendid piazza del Duomo. The **Duomo**, the city's cathedral, its exterior inlaid with intricately patterned pink, white and green marble, soars above the surrounding buildings; it's so huge that there's no point nearby from which you can see the whole church, though a walk through nearby streets will be peppered with tantalising glimpses of its magnificent red-tiled dome. The square itself is constantly thronged with visitors circling the cathedral, in awe of its magnitude. The areas outside the entrance and around the south of the Duomo are pedestrianised, but mopeds and buses roar around the north and east sides.

Directly west of the Duomo, piazza San Giovanni, named after John the Baptist, skirts his **Baptistery**; it also houses the tiny **Museo di Bigallo** (*for both, see p69*). Following the curve of the piazza on the north side of the Duomo, the **Museo dell'Opera del Duomo** (*see p70*), which houses the treasures of the Duomo, is on the north-east of the piazza. Leading south from the façade of the Duomo is via dei Calzaiuoli, a heaving pedestrian shopping street flanked by self-service restaurants, shops and *gelaterie*. Running down from the south-west corner of the **Baptistery** is the more upmarket via Roma, which opens into the pompous **piazza della Repubblica**.

This rather ungainly piazza was built in 1882, when the ancient heart of Florence, the so-called Mercato Vecchio (Old Market), was demolished and replaced in a massive urban clean-up following a cholera outbreak. Now the only remnant from before that time is the Colonna dell'Abbondanza, which used to mark the spot where two principal Roman roads crossed; it was reinstated to its original position after World War II. Vasari's Loggia, which had formed the central meeting-place of the square, was moved to piazza dei Ciompi. In the medieval period the area covered by the piazza was given over to a huge market where you could change money, buy a hawk or falcon, pay over the odds for a quack remedy, or pick up a prostitute (distinguished by the bells on their hats and their gloves). Further back, the ancient Roman Forum once occupied a quarter of the piazza, and the Campidoglio and Temple of Jupiter covered the rest. The piazza is now surrounded by pavement cafés and dominated at night by street artists and strollers.

Duomo

Ufficio del Duomo (055 230 2885). **Open** *Church* 10am-5pm Mon-Fri; 10am-4.45pm Sat; 1.30-4.45pm Sun; 10am-3.30pm 1st Sat of month. *Crypt of Santa Reparata* 10am-5pm Mon-Sat. **Admission** free; crypt of Santa Reparata L5,000 (€2.60). **No credit cards. Map** p314 B4.

In the 13th century a hugely successful and expanding wool industry gave the Florentine population such a boost that several new churches had to be built, among them Santa Croce and Santa Maria Novella, but most important of all Santa Maria del Fiore, or the Duomo, which replaced the small church of Santa Reparata. The construction was commissioned by the Florentine Republic, who saw the project as an opportunity to show Florence as indisputably the most important Tuscan city. A competition held to find an architect was won by Arnolfo di Cambio, a sculptor from Pisa who had trained with Nicola Pisano. The first stones were laid on 8 September 1296 around the exterior of Santa Reparata so that the Florentines could continue to use the church. The remains of the medieval structure can still be seen under the crypt. Building continued for the next 170 years, with the guidance and revision of three further architects, though the church was consecrated 30 years before its completion in 1436. The visionary Francesco Talenti had sufficient confidence in future architectural achievements to enlarge the cathedral and prepare the building for Brunelleschi's inspired dome. The last significant change came in the 19th century when Emilio de Fabris designed a neo-Gothic façade to replace the bland temporary façade. When Luigi del Moro took over the project after the death of de Fabris, the problem arose of how to crown the façade. Some wanted the cuspidal spires of the Siena Duomo, others a flat balustraded balcony. One of each solution was built, and a referendum was held to decide the outcome. Happily, the balconies outvoted the spires.

Cupola/Dome

Open 8.30am-7pm Mon-Fri; 8.30am-5.40pm Sat; 8.30am-4pm 1st Sat of month. **Admission** L10,000 (€5.20). **No credit cards. Map** p314 B4.

The vast **Duomo** dominates the historic centre. *See p65.*

Walk 1 The beaten track

Set off in style by Alberti's shapely scrolls on the façade of the church of Santa Maria Novella, then turn right up via de' Banchi and walk along the busy shopping street of via Cerretani past the ubiquitous Stefanels and Benettons to piazza San Giovanni, faced by the Baptistery, and piazza del Duomo, with the Campanile and Duomo. Queues permitting, step into the fourth largest church in the world to experience the cupola inside-out, then stop to admire it from the outside before heading down via Calzaiuoli as far as the well-disguised but ornate church of Orsanmichele on the right. Circle the building to admire its tabernacles and overpass, then take via Calimala down to the loggia of the Mercato Nuovo, where fans of Florence should rub the (by now shiny) bronze boar's nose and throw him a coin if they want a return visit, and fledgling fans of the Fiorentina football club can buy a cheap Viola scarf to please the locals.

Walk on down via Por Santa Maria, then take a left into via Vacchereccia for a double-take view of the clock-tower of the Palazzo Vecchio. In the piazza della Signoria, take time to give *Perseus* and *The Rape of the Sabines* in the Loggia dei Lanzi the once-over, then saunter down the daunting piazzale degli Uffizi, hiding any double-chins and Roman noses from the caricature artists lining up to give you a lifelong complex. At the river, admire the view of San Miniato on the hill to the left, then turn right towards the Ponte Vecchio. Follow the arches of the Vasari Corridor to the bridge, and keep going along Lungarno Accaiuoli till you reach Ponte Santa Trinità. Here turn right and walk up via dei Tornabuoni past the church of Santa Trinità on the left and carry on up via the designer boutiques to the rusticated Palazzo Strozzi. Follow its corner right into via Strozzi and trudge through the arch into piazza della Repubblica to enjoy a rest at one of its cafés.

The Duomo's most celebrated feature needs distance if one is to appreciate how it towers above the city – it is, as Alberti put it, 'large enough to cover every Tuscan with its shadow'. But the dome is not just visually stunning, it's also an incredible feat of engineering, thanks to Brunelleschi, who had dreamed of completing the dome since childhood and studied architecture in Rome with it in mind. Brunelleschi won the commission for the cupola with the more experienced Ghiberti but soon found that while he was doing the important work Ghiberti was taking the glory. He pulled a sickie, bringing work to a halt, and got the recognition he deserved.

At first Brunelleschi considered designing the classic semi-spherical dome used in existing churches around Italy, but the sheer size of the structure precluded the traditional method of laying tree-trunks across the diameter to build around. The idea was toyed with of filling the space with earth and building up around it, then sprinkling the earth with gold florins to encourage locals to take it away, an idea that was used with great public approval for the outside ramps. In the end, a revolutionary design for an elongated dome was followed. Brunelleschi made the dome support itself by building two domes, one on top of the other, and more importantly by laying the bricks in herringbone-pattern rings to integrate successive layers that could consequently support themselves. The design was so efficient that it risked becoming a victim of its success; the ribs around the dome were in danger of 'springing' open at the top, so a much heavier lantern than normal was designed, to hold

the ribs in place. As innovative as the design were the tools used and the organisation of the work: Brunelleschi designed pulley systems to winch materials up to the dome. Between the two shells of the dome he installed a canteen so workers wouldn't waste time going to ground level to eat, bringing construction time down to a mere 16 years (1420-36).

After the splendour of the exterior, the interior looks dark and dreary, though decorating the world's fourth largest cathedral was never going to be easy. It's actually full of fascinating oddities, notably the clock on the inner side of the Paolo Uccello façade, which marks 24 hours, operates anti-clockwise and starts its days at sunset (expect it to be between four and six hours fast). Also by Uccello is a monument to English mercenary Sir John Hawkwood, painted in 1436 and rather a muddle (it has a perspective problem). More coherent is Andrea del Castagno's *Niccolo da Tolentino*, painted in 1456 and illustrating the heroic characteristics of a Renaissance man. Beyond these two is Domenico di Michelino's well-known *Dante Explaining the Divine Comedy*, featuring the poet dressed in pink and the recently completed Duomo vying for prominence with the Mountain of Purgatory.

A couple of strides forward and across puts you directly underneath the dome, which is possibly even more breathtaking inside than out. The lantern in the centre is 90m (295ft) above you and the diameter of the inner dome is 43m (140ft) across, housing within it one of the largest frescoed surfaces in the world. Brunelleschi had intended that the cupola be mosaic, so it would mirror the Baptistery ceiling, but

Why is the construction of Brunelleschi's cathedral dome still not completely understood by experts?

What happened in 1348 to radically change the style of Italian art?

Why are the Three Graces dancing in Botticelli's 'Primavera'?

Who ordered the fig leaves that originally covered Michelangelo's David?

Why not enrol on the History of Art courses at the British Institute of Florence to find out?

The courses comprise lectures and tours which can be taken individually or in full (from one afternoon to eight weeks). The Institute, which has been active in the heart of Florence for over 80 years, also offers Italian language courses, Dante, wine tasting, film appreciation, cooking, drawing and opera, as well as English as a foreign language.

During August, the Institute runs a summer school offering Italian language and cultural courses with open-air opera on the Tuscan coast.

Computer and study facilities are at the Language Centre and in the Institute's Harold Acton Library which holds over 50,000 books, the largest collection of English books in Italy.

The Institute organises social events and can also help to arrange accommodation for those taking courses.

For more information
please contact:
The British Institute of Florence
Piazza Strozzi 2
I-50123 Firenze
Tel.: +39 055 267 782 00
Fax: +39 055 267 782 22

www.britishinstitute.it
info@britishinstitute.it

Bridging Cultures since 1917

THE BRITISH INSTITUTE OF FLORENCE

Michelangelo's emotional **Pietà**. *See p70.*

interior work began some 125 years after his death in 1572. The frescoes were started under the supervision of Giorgio Vasari, who died two years after starting and was succeeded by Federigo Zuccaro, who worked for a further five years until completion. The subject of the frescoes is the Last Judgement; the huge space of the dome suggests visitors are looking up into Heaven.

There's a separate side entrance to get to the top of the dome (463 steps, about 20 minutes up and down) with its fantastic city views.

Campanile
Open 8.30am-7.30pm daily. **Admission** L10,000 (€5.20). **No credit cards. Map** p314 B4.
The Campanile – the cathedral's bell tower – was designed by Giotto in 1334, though his plans weren't followed faithfully (the original drawing, held in the Museo dell'Opera Metropolitana in Siena, can be seen on request). Andrea Pisano, who continued the work three years after Giotto's death, took the precaution of doubling the thickness of the walls, while Francesco Talenti, who saw the building to completion in 1359, inserted the large windows high up the tower. Inlaid, like the Duomo, with pretty pink, white and green marble, the campanile is decorated with 16 sculptures of prophets, patriarchs and pagans (the originals are in the Museo dell'Opera del Duomo; *see p70*), bas-reliefs designed by Giotto and executed by Pisano recounting the *Creation* and *Fall of Man* and his *Redemption Through Industry*; look carefully and you'll make out Eve emerging from Adam's side and a drunken Noah. There are great views of the Duomo and the city from the top, which is occasionally used by suicides, who

somehow avoid the netting hung as a precaution against this (some years ago a man landed splat in a throng of tourists below).

Baptistery
Open noon-7pm Mon-Sat; 8.30am-2pm Sun.
Admission L5,000 (€2.60). **No credit cards.**
Map p314 B3.
For centuries, Florentines (including such well-educated characters as Brunelleschi and Alberti) believed the Baptistery was converted from an ancient Roman temple dedicated to Mars. In fact, although there are the relics of an ancient pavement below it, these probably belonged to a bakery. The Baptistery of St John the Baptist was actually built to an octagonal design between 1059 and 1128 as a remodelling of a sixth- or seventh-century version. The octagon reappears most obviously in the shape of the cathedral dome, but also on the buttresses of the Campanile, which constitute its corners. Today, the striped octagon is best known for its bronze doors, though you might want see the vibrant *Last Judgement* mosaic lining the vault. In the 1330s Andrea Pisano completed the south doors, with 28 Gothic quatrefoil-framed panels depicting stories from the life of St John the Baptist and the eight theological and cardinal virtues. In the winter of 1400, the Calimala guild held a competition to find an artist to create a pair of bronze doors for the north entrance and, having seen pieces by Brunelleschi, Ghiberti and five others, gave the commission to Ghiberti, then just 20 years old. Relief panels displaying a masterful use of perspective retell the story of Christ from the Annunciation to the Crucifixion. The eight lower panels show the four evangelists and four doctors. Even more remarkable are the east doors, known as the Gates of Paradise. No sooner had the north doors been installed than the Calimala commissioned Ghiberti to make another pair. The doors you see here are copies (the originals are in the Museo dell'Opera del Duomo) but the casts are fine enough to appreciate Ghiberti's work.

Museo di Bigallo
Piazza San Giovanni 1 (055 230 2885). **Open** 8am-noon Mon; 4-6pm Thur. **Admission** L5,000 (€2.60). **No credit cards. Map** p314 B3.
The city's tiniest museum is in a beautiful Gothic loggia built in 1358 for the Misericordia, which was a charitable organisation that cared for unwanted children and plague victims. The loggia was later renovated for another fraternity, the Bigallo, and the Misericordia moved to piazza del Duomo 19, from where it still works as a voluntary ambulance and medical service. The main room has frescoes depicting the work of the two fraternities, though the two scenes on the left wall as you enter were badly damaged while being transferred from the façade in the 18th century. The *Madonna della Misericordia*, an anonymous work of 1342, has the Virgin suspended above the earliest known depiction of Florence, showing the Baptistery, the original façade to the domeless Duomo and an incomplete campanile.

Sightseeing

Who they? Dante

Dante Alighieri was born in 1265 into a noble family that had fallen on hard times. In common with most minor nobles and merchants, the Alighieris were affiliated to the Guelphs, and their fortunes in the 13th century were thus dictated by the ups and downs of their party. Most of Dante's early life coincided with a period of Guelph domination of Florence. The young Dante did his bit to preserve peace, fighting for the city in the victory against Ghibelline Arezzo at Campaldino in 1289, and later taking part in the siege of the Pisan fortress of Caprona.

His expulsion from Florence with the other White Guelphs in 1302 was a bitter blow and despite repeated attempts to return he never saw the city again, dying in Ravenna in 1321.

It was while he was in exile that Dante wrote his greatest work, *La Commedia*, known to posterity as the *Divine Comedy*. This multi-levelled poetic epic is the story of Dante the Pilgrim's journey through Hell, Purgatory and Paradise to God. On the way, Dante the Poet incorporates countless references to the tumultuous events of the preceding century, lamenting the injustices inflicted by the Ghibellines and the plight of Florence.

Dante was a firm believer that temporal and spiritual power should be kept separate. He viewed the Pope's increasing domination of Italian politics as an ominous sign. In Canto XVI of *Purgatorio* he warns: 'The sword is now one with the crook – and fused together thus, must bring about misrule.' Yet he was deeply religious, and outraged by clerical corruption (outspoken criticism of which was one of the causes of the split between 'Black' and 'White' Guelphs). In Canto XIX of *Inferno* he condemns the simonists (who obtained or dispensed religious offices for money) to be shoved down tubes and have flames flicker across the soles of their feet. Popes Nicholas III and Benedict VIII (who was instrumental in bringing about Dante's exile) are found here, lambasted by Dante the Pilgrim: 'Those things of God that rightly should be wed to holiness, you, rapacious creatures, for the price of silver and gold prostitute.'

Museo dell'Opera del Duomo

Piazza Duomo 9 (055 230 2885). **Open** 9am-7.30pm Mon-Sat; 9am-1.40pm Sun. **Admission** L10,000 (€5.20). **No credit cards. Map** p314 B4.

This recently enlarged and improved museum contains instruments that were used to build the Duomo, the original wood models of the cupola, and sculptures deemed too precious and vulnerable to be left to the mercy of the elements.

On the ground floor are some of the recently restored original east Baptistery bronze door panels, the so-called Porta del Paradiso (Gates of Paradise) sculpted by Lorenzo Ghiberti over the 27 years between 1425 and 1452 and considered by some to be the work of art that initiated the Renaissance. There are also bits and pieces from Santa Reparata, the earlier church on the site of the Duomo, including a classical-style *Madonna* with spooky glass eyes by Arnolfo di Cambio.

Halfway up the stairs is the *Pietà Bandini*, a heart-rending late work by Michelangelo showing Christ slithering from the grasp of Nicodemus. The sculpture was intended as Michelangelo's tombstone, and he sculpted his own features on the face of Nicodemus, showing that his lifelong obsession with the story of the pieta had become too much for him to bear. In true tortured-artist style, frustrated and dissatisfied with the piece, he smashed Christ's left arm, and it was supposedly left to his servant to pick up the fragments and save the masterpiece.

Upstairs are brick stamps and forms, the pulleys and ropes by which building materials (and workers) were winched up to the dome. The wood sculpture of Mary Magdalene by Donatello, dishevelled and ugly, with coarse, dirty hair so realistic you can almost smell it, is extraordinary. His *Habbakuk*, bald, emancipated and caught in vision, is another uncomfortable work: Donatello himself is said to have gripped it and screamed 'Speak, speak, speak!'

It's a relief to turn to the *cantorie* (choir lofts). One is by Donatello, with cavorting *putti*; the other, by Luca della Robbia, is full of angel musicians. Beyond are some reliefs that Giotto carved for the Campanile.

Around piazza della Signoria

Florence's civic showpiece piazza is dominated by the crenellated and corbelled **Palazzo Vecchio** (formerly Palazzo della Signoria; *see p77*), built at the end of the 13th century (probably to a design by Arnolfo di Cambio) as the seat of the Signoria, the top tier of the city's government. The piazza itself was the focus of civic activity. Life in medieval Florence was beset with political and personal vendettas, and it didn't take much to ignite a crowd; on one occasion in the 14th century, a scrap in the piazza led to a man being eaten by the mob.

It was in this piazza that the religious and political reformer Girolamo Savonarola (*see p14*) lit his Bonfire of the Vanities in 1497, throwing onto it all the trappings of culture and wealth he and his followers could muster, many donated by such luminaries as Botticelli and Fra Bartolomeo. Savonarola ended up burned at the stake on 23 May 1498, on the exact spot of his prophetic bonfire a year earlier (marked by a plaque in front of the *Neptune* fountain).

The piazza was also the seat of civic defence, however; whenever Florence was threatened by an external enemy, the bell of the Palazzo della Signoria (known as the 'Vacca', or cow, after its moo-ing tone) was tolled to summon the citizens' militia. Part of the militia's training included playing *calcio* on the piazza – an almost homicidal version of rugby that's still 'played' in original costumes in piazza Santa Croce every June.

In the mid 1980s it was decided that the piazza's ancient paving stones should be taken up and restored. The state-run Sovrintendenza dei Beni Archeologici, which oversees the city's archaeological works, took the opportunity to carry out excavations on the area. In the course of the work, the ruins of 12th-century Florence were discovered beneath the piazza, built over the thermal baths of Roman Florentia and bits and pieces of the Etruscans' outpost, and the remains were signposted for bemused tourists

Orsanmichele and **Palazzo dell'Arte** (*p74*).

expecting to find the Renaissance piazza della Signoria. The Sovrintendenza ordered further excavation of the ruins and there was talk of the site becoming an underground museum; local government, fearing its showpiece piazza becoming a building site and losing it valuable tourist income, objected. The result was a shambles. The company taken on to restore the ancient slabs (and later alleged to have won the contract through bribery), catalogued the position of the stones using chalk, which was washed away on the first rainy day. They also managed to 'lose' some of the slabs, which now apparently grace the courtyards of various Tuscan villas. Given that most of Florence lies over the ruins of the Roman city, the decision to replace the paving with artificially aged stones and re-seal the Roman site was predictable.

Dominating the piazza are a copy of Michelangelo's *David* and an equestrian bronze of Cosimo I by Giambologna, who also created some sexy nymphs and satyrs for Ammanati's *Neptune* fountain, a Mannerist monstrosity of which Michelangelo is reputed to have said 'Ammanato, Ammanato, che bel marmo ha rovinato' ('Ammanati, what beautiful marble you have ruined'). Even Ammanati eventually admitted the piece was a failure, in part because the block of marble used for Neptune lacked width, forcing him to give the god narrow shoulders and keep his right arm close to his body. Beyond is a copy of Donatello's *Marzocco* (the original of the city's heraldic lion is in the Bargello), and his *Judith and Holofernes* (the original is in the Palazzo Vecchio). Judith, like David, was a symbol of the power of the people over tyrannical rulers, a Jewish widow who inveigled her way into the camp of Holofernes, Israel's enemy, got the man drunk, then sliced off his head.

Beyond *David* is *Hercules and Cacus* by Bandinelli, much ridiculed by the exacting Florentines and described by rival sculptor Benvenuto Cellini as a 'sack of melons'. The marble block it's carved from fell into the river in transit to Bandinelli's workshop, leading to the running joke that it had tried to commit suicide rather than end up in his hands. Cellini himself is represented by another monster-killer, a fabulous *Perseus* holding the snaky head of Medusa, standing victorious in the adjacent **Loggia dei Lanzi**. On the edge of the Palazzo Vecchio nearest the Loggia, on one of the cornerstones, is the etched graffiti of a hawk-nosed man, said to be a tongue-in-cheek self-portrait by Leonardo, keen to leave his mark.

The Loggia, whose name derives from the *lanzichenecchi*, a private army of Cosimo I, was built in the late 14th century to shelter civic bigwigs during ceremonies. By the mid-15th

Sightseeing

century it had become a favourite spot for old men to gossip and shelter from the sun, which, the architect Alberti noted with approval, had a restraining influence on the young men engaging in the 'mischievousness and folly natural to their Age'. Also in the Loggia is Giambologna's spiralling *Rape of the Sabine Women* (1582), a virtuoso attempt to outdo Cellini and the first sculpture to have what John Pope Hennessy described as no dominant viewpoint. The marble is now crumbling in the polluted air of the city, and the decision has been made to move the piece to the Accademia and place a copy in the Loggia.

Leading down to the river from piazza della Signoria, the piazzale degli Uffizi is home to the greatest museum of Renaissance art in the world (*see p78*). Also here is the separate entrance to the **Corridoio Vasariano** (*see p75*), the Vasari Corridor. Halfway down the piazzale on the right in via Lambertesca is the entrance to the **Collezione Contini-Bonacossi** (*see p74*) and the Georgofili library, where a Mafia bomb exploded in 1993.

Turning left from the river bank leads to the **Museo della Storia e della Scienza** (*see p75*). Via Castellani heads north from this fascinating museum to reach piazza San Firenze with the imposing law courts and the entrance to the **Badia Fiorentina** (*see p74*), which lies along via Proconsolo. This is home on its east side to the National Museum, the scupture-laden **Bargello** (*see p93*). We are now in Danteland: just behind the Badia is the uninspiring **Museo Casa di Dante** (*see p75*).

Back at the river end of the Uffizi and on the right is the whimsical **Ponte Vecchio**. There has been a bridge spanning this point of the Arno – its narrowest within the city – since Roman times, though the first bridge was slightly upstream, where canoe club members now bask on their riverside sanctuary. The current structure was completed in 1345 to replace a bridge swept away by a flood in 1333. By the 13th century there were wooden shops on the bridge; these frequently caught fire, so when the bridge was reconstructed, the shops were built of stone. The bridge was originally favoured by butchers and tanners, whose trade involved soaking the hides in the Arno for eight months, then curing them in horse urine, but in 1593 Grand Duke Ferdinando I, fed up with retching every time he walked along the Vasari Corridor on his way to or from the Pitti Palace, banned all 'vile trades' and permitted only jewellers and goldsmiths on the bridge. In the centre of the bridge is a newly restored bust (by Raffaello Romanelli) of Benvenuto Cellini, who is considered by many to have been the most talented goldsmith of all time.

Don't miss Artworks

Allegoria della Primavera
Read Botticelli's painting *The Allegory of Spring* (displayed in the Uffizi; *see p78*) like a book in Arabic, from right to left, trying to coax out its secrets, or play spot the flower – there are 190 different species to find.

The Duomo cupola
The mystery remains of exactly how Brunelleschi managed to pull off this daring stunt remains (*see p66*).

Noli me Tangere
Pure spiritualism is encapsulated in the brushstrokes of the 'good monk', Fra Angelico, in this other-worldly fresco in the Museo di San Marco (*see p92*).

The Baptistery's bronze panels
Ghiberti's panels for the east doors of the Baptistery (*see p69*) are so stunning as to have been dubbed 'the gates of Paradise' by Michelangelo. The originals are in the Museo dell'Opera del Duomo (*see p70*).

Brancacci Chapel
In Santa Maria del Carmine (*see p92*, this was the first fusion of humanism and perspective and was later used as a study aid by Leonardo, Botticelli and Ghirlandaio.

Michelangelo's Pietà
It's impossible not to be moved by the piece that proved to be the master's obsession and that he intended for his own tomb, now in the Museo dell'Opera del Duomo (*see p70*).

San Miniato al Monte
The simplest and most exquisite of Florence's churches and legendary resting place of the first Florentine Christian martyr, who carried his own severed head up the hill to lie down and die among the graves of other early Christians (*see p105*).

Directly north of Ponte Vecchio is the predominantly modern architecture of via Por Santa Maria, much of which had to be rebuilt after the war. At the top of this busy shopping street is the **Mercato Nuovo** ('new market', but often called the 'straw market'), a fine stone loggia erected between 1547 and 1551 on a site where there had been a market since the 11th century (the Mercato Vecchio or 'old market'

Who they? Galileo

Galileo Galilei, the founder of modern science, was born in Pisa in 1564. Son of a court musician and descendant of a noble Florentine family, he entered the University of Pisa as a medical student, having received his early education at the monastery of Vallombrosa near Florence. He abandoned medicine for mathematics and physics but was unable to finish his degree because his father could no longer afford the fees.

In 1589 he was given a post at the University of Pisa, where he taught mathematics. In 1590 he completed a book, De Motu ('On Motion'), in which he took exception to the Aristotelian doctrines of motion based on weight. In 1592, by then well known for various revolutionary scientific treatises, he was given a chair at Padua.

In 1609 news came to him of a Dutch invention: the telescope. He quickly built one of his own, and before the year was out had produced a telescope that enabled him to see

mountains on the moon and identify four stars circling Jupiter. In 1610 he published these discoveries in a book entitled The Sidereal Messenger, which laid the foundations for his scientific reputation.

Also in 1609, Galileo was called to do the astrological chart for the Grand Duke Ferdinando I. In the best high-street tradition, he predicted a long, happy life for him. Ferdinando died a few months later, putting paid to Galileo's fortune-telling career.

Some years later he demonstrated his telescope at Rome. By then, however, the ecclesiastical authorities had become alarmed by his defence of the Copernican theory of the solar system in contradiction of the scriptures. It was at this stage of his career that he was invited by Ferdinando's son Cosimo to come to Florence as First Philosopher and Mathematician to the Grand Duke of Tuscany. Grateful for the chance to continue his studies and experiments under

occupied the area now covered by piazza della Repubblica). It now houses stalls selling leather and straw goods and cheap souvenirs, but in the 16th century it was full of silk and gold merchants and money-changers. The market is popularly known as the Porcellino, or piglet, after a bronze statue of a boar by Pietro Tacca, a copy of an ancient marble now in the Uffizi (in fact, the copy there now is a copy of Tacca's statue; Tacca's was replaced a couple of years ago). It's considered good luck to rub the boar's nose and put a coin in its mouth – proceeds go to a children's charity, and the legend goes that the donor is assured a return trip to the city.

A block up via Calimala on the right, named after the Greek words for 'beautiful fleece', is the portico-and-ramparts grandeur of the **Palazzo dell'Arte della Lana**, the Renaissance home to the filthy-rich guild of clothmakers. This fairytale castle is connected by an arched overpass to **Orsanmichele** church (see p77), the main entrance of which is on via Calzaiuoli, the pedestrian thoroughfare between piazza della Signoria and the Duomo.

Badia Fiorentina

Via del Proconsolo (055 283 451/0347 910 1784). **Open** 3-6pm Mon. **Admission** donation to Eucharist. **Map** p314 4C.
Recently reopened after restoration, the Badia, a Benedictine abbey founded in the tenth century by Willa, mother of Ugo, Margrave of Tuscany, was the

richest religious institution of medieval Florence. Willa had been deeply influenced by Romuald, a monk who travelled round Tuscany denouncing the wickedness of the clergy, flagellating himself, and urging the rich to build monasteries. Eventually Romuald persuaded Willa to found an abbey within Florence, in 978. Ugo also lavished money and land on the abbey, and was eventually buried there in a Roman sarcophagus, later replaced by a tomb by Renaissance sculptor Mino da Fiesole. It was in the Badia, just across the street from Dante's probable birthplace, that the poet first set eyes on Beatrice Portinari attending a May feast in 1274. He was nine, she eight, and he fell instantly in love with 'the glorious Lady of my mind'. His life was forever blighted when her family arranged her marriage at the age of 17 to one Simone de Bardi. Beatrice died seven years later at the age of 24 and Dante attempted to forget his pain by throwing himself into war, fighting in battles against Arezzo and Pisa. As for the Badia, it has been rebuilt many times since Dante's day but retains a graceful Romanesque campanile. The Chiostro degli Aranci, where the Benedictine monks grew oranges (*aranci*), dates from 1430 and is frescoed with scenes from the life of St Bernard. Inside the church Bernard is celebrated again, in a painting by Filippino Lippi.

Collezione Contini-Bonacossi

Uffizi, entrance via Lambertesca (055 294 883/ 055 238 8618). **Open** by appointment 8.45am-12.30pm Tue-Sun. **Ticket** included in Uffizi ticket. **Map** p314 C3.

Ducal protection, Galileo moved, as the Medici's guest, to a house in Bellosguardo and repaid his patron's kindness by naming the satellites of Jupiter Sidera Medicea.

His book *The Assayer* incensed the Jesuits, who were then enjoying a certain power in the Papal Court. The Thirty Years' War was in full swing and accusations of heresy abounded as the Counter-Reformation struggled to spread its influence. But it was the next book, Dialogue on Two World Systems, that really got him into trouble. In it he posited – erroneously, as it happened – that the ebb and flow of the tides is due to the three-fold Copernican motions of the Earth. For this he was summoned to Rome to stand trial for heresy, the Jesuits having insisted that his theories would have more catastrophic consequences for the Church than 'Luther and Calvin put together'. In June 1633, he was pronounced 'vehemently suspected of heresy', condemned to formal imprisonment

and forced to sign a recantation of his theories: 'I abandon completely the false opinion that the sun is at the centre of the world and does not move and that the Earth is not the centre of the world and moves…' His sentence was commuted by the Pope, however, and later that year he returned to Tuscany under house arrest. He spent the last eight years of his life on a small estate at Arcetri. His last book, Discorsi, discusses the problems of matter and local motion.

He died on 8 January 1642. The Church forbade a Christian burial, but in 1737 the Medici arranged for his remains to be transferred to the Novice's Chapel at Santa Croce, where a memorial can be seen. There is also a room devoted to him in the Museo di Storia della Scienza (*see p75*), where, along with various of his instruments, the bones of his right middle finger are displayed.

A Vatican commission cleared Galileo of heresy over 500 years after his death, in 1992.

Save some energy during a tour of the Uffizi for this impressive collection, which was donated to the state by the Contini-Bonacossi family in 1974. There are *Madonna and Child*s by Duccio, Cimabué and Andrea del Castagno and a room of artistic VIPs, containing works by Bernini, Veronese and Tintoretto. Among the foreigners prestigious enough to find their way into the collection are El Greco, Velázquez and Goya.

Collezione della Ragione

Piazza della Signoria 5 (055 283 078). **Open** 9am-1.30pm Mon, Wed-Sun. **Admission** L4,000 (€2.10). **No credit cards. Map** p314 C4.

The collection of Alberto della Ragione, an engineer from Sorrento, follows the Italian artistic movements that fought the restrictions of Fascism to rival modern art in France and Germany between 1920 and 1960. There are Futurist and Surrealist works, including a De Chirico in Room 9 (not one of his trademark dreamscapes). More interesting are Ottone Rosai's works, indicative of a post-Fascist artistic freedom. This sense of freedom can also be seen in the work of Emilio Vedova, labelled the Venetian brother of Kline and Pollock; his Tintoretto-inspired pieces have a disarming array of colour and form.

Museo Casa di Dante

Via Santa Margherita 1 (055 219 416). **Open** *Summer* 10am-6pm Mon, Wed-Sat; 10am-2pm Sun. *Winter* 10am-4pm Mon, Wed-Sat; 10am-2pm Sun. **Admission** L5,000 (€2.60). **No credit cards. Map** p314 B4.

This museum, located where Dante is thought to have lived, is full of facsimiles of archive material (including a photocopy of a document in which the poet's great great grandfather promised to cut down a fig tree). Barely worth the entrance fee.

Corridoio Vasariano

Loggiato degli Uffizi 6 (055 265 4321). **Open** by appointment 3-5pm Wed, Fri. **Admission** free with ticket to Uffizi. **No credit cards. Map** p314 C3.

This kilometre-long corridor running the length of the Uffizi, over the Ponte Vecchio and down to the Palazzo Pitti and the Boboli gardens was built by Vasari in only five months to enable Grand Duke Cosimo I to walk from his home, the Palazzo Pitti, to work in the Palazzo Vecchio, without having to mix with the plebs. It's lined with the self-portraits of illustrious artists such as Delacroix, Titian, Bernini, Andrea del Sarto, Raphael and Rembrandt. The views over the river are breathtaking. Book early as visits are now limited to groups of 30.

Museo della Storia e della Scienza

Piazza dei Giudici 1 (055 239 8876). **Open** *Summer* 9.30am-5pm Mon, Wed-Fri; 9.30am-1pm Tue, Sat. *Winter* 9.30am-5pm Mon, Wed-Sat; 9.30am-1pm Tue. **Admission** L12,000 (€6.20). **No credit cards. Map** p314 C4.

This is one of the best museums in Florence, offering a view of the Renaissance and beyond that, for once, is not limited to stone and pigment. Two of the most fascinating rooms are those devoted to Galileo; they include a morbid reliquary of his right-hand

HOTEL RESERVATIONS CENTER

Leonardo's unofficial signature on the **Palazzo Vecchio**. *See p71.*

middle finger (the rest of his body is in Santa Croce) and one of his telescopes, bound in leather.

In the following rooms are a collection of prisms and optical games. Art continues to mingle with science in Room 7, which is devoted to armillary spheres and dominated by a gold-leaf decorated model commissioned by Federico II in 1593. Most of them have the earth emphatically placed at the centre of the universe, surrounded by seven spheres of the planets. Also look out for the stunning collection of spiralling 18th-century thermometers.

The second floor has an eclectic mix of machines, mechanisms and models, including a 19th-century clock (*pianola*) that writes a sentence with a mechanical hand, and a selection of electromagnetic and electrostatic instruments (Room 14). More pleasing are the pneumatic pumps decorated with inlaid wood by Nollet (famous for his globe machine) and the carefully constructed illustration of the mechanical paradox of two spheres ascending a plane. The display of amputation implements and models of foetuses adorning the walls are gruelling.

In addition to the hours given above, the museum is open on the morning of the second Sunday of every month, from 10am to 1pm.

Orsanmichele & the Museo di Orsanmichele

Via dell'Arte della Lana (055 284 944/055 284 715). **Church open** 9am-noon, 4-6pm daily. **Museum tours** 9am, 10am, 11am daily. Closed 1st & last Mon of month. **Admission** free. **Map** p314 C3.

The relationship between art, religion and commerce is seldom closer than in the church of Orsanmichele. In 1290 a loggia intended as a grain store was built to a design by Arnolfo di Cambio, the original architect of the Duomo, in the garden (*orto*) of the Monastery of San Michele, hence the name Orsanmichele. The loggia burned down in 1304 along with a painting, the *Madonna of the Trumpet*,

said to have been invoked to put out a previous fire. The Madonna's tabernacle is on the corner of via dell'Arte della Lana.

The place was rebuilt in the mid 1300s by Talenti and Fioravante and used as grain market. Two upper floors were later added to store grain at the same time as the monks were walling up the loggia's arches so they could use it for religious services. From the outset, the council intended Orsanmichele to be a magnificent advertisement for the wealth of the city's guilds and, in 1339, each guild was instructed to fill one of the loggia's niches with a statue of its patron saint. Only the wool guild obliged (with a stone statue of St Stephen) so in 1406 the council presented the guilds with a ten-year deadline. In 1412 the Calimala, the wealthiest guild (of cloth importers), commissioned Ghiberti to create a life-sized bronze of John the Baptist, the largest statue ever to have been cast in Florence. The other major guilds now fell over themselves to produce the finest statue. The guild of armourers was represented by a tense *St George* by Donatello (now in the Bargello), one of the first psychologically realistic sculptures of the Renaissance; the Parte Guelfa had Donatello gild their bronze, a St Louis of Toulouse, later removed by the Medici to Santa Croce in their drive to expunge all memory of the Guelphs from the public face of the city. Most of the statues are now replicas – the originals are on display either in the museum or in the Bargello.

Inside the church a restored elaborate glass and marble Orcagna tabernacle frames a *Madonna* by Bernardo Daddi, painted in 1347 to replace the supposedly fireproof Madonna.

Palazzo Vecchio

Piazza Signoria (055 276 8465). **Open** *Summer* 9am-11pm Mon, Fri; 9am-7pm Tue, Wed, Sat; 9am-2pm Thur, Sun. *Winter* 9am-7pm Mon, Wed, Fri, Sat; 9am-2pm Thur, Sun. **Admission** L11,000 (€5.70). **No credit cards. Map** p314 C4.

The imposing exterior of the **Uffizi** doesn't deter its public.

Still Florence's town hall, the 13th-century Palazzo Vecchio was the seat first of the Signoria, the city's ruling body, then, for nine years, of the Medici (1540-9). The Medici's stay may have been brief, but they nonetheless instigated a massive Mannerist makeover of the palace's interior, under Giorgio Vasari, court architect from 1555 to 1574.

The Salone dei Cinquecento ('Hall of the Five Hundred'), where members of the Great Council met, should have been decorated with battle scenes by Michelangelo and Leonardo, not the zestless scenes of victory over Siena and Pisa by Vasari that cover the walls. Leonardo, frustrated by attempts to develop new mural techniques, abandoned the project. Michelangelo had only finished the cartoon for the *Battle of Cascine* when he was summoned to Rome by Pope Julius II. One of Michelangelo's commissions did end up here: *Victory*, a statue carved for the Pope's never-finished tomb.

Off the Salone is the Studiolo di Francesco I, the office where Francesco hid away to conduct alchemical experiments. Also decorated by Vasari, it includes a scene from the alchemist's laboratory and illustrations of the four elements. From the vaulted ceiling, Bronzino's portraits of Francesco's parents, Cosimo I and Elenora di Toledo, look down.

Upstairs, the Quartiere degli Elementi contains Vasari's allegories of the elements. The Quartiere di Eleonora (the wife of Cosimo I) has two entirely frescoed chapels; the first was partly decorated by Bronzino, who uses intense pastel hues to depict a surreal *Crossing the Red Sea*, while the Cappella dei Priori is decorated with fake mosaics and an idealised *Annunciation*.

Beyond is the garish Sala D'Udienza with a carved ceiling dripping in gold; more subtle is the Sala dei Gigli, so named because of the gilded lilies (the symbol of the city) that cover the walls. Decorated in the 15th century, it has a ceiling by Guiliano and Benedetto da Maiano, and frescoes of Roman statesmen by Ghirlandaio opposite the door. Equally appealing is Donatello's *Judith & Holofernes*, rich in political significance, Judith representing Savonarola's new republic triumphing over the Medici.

The Uffizi

Piazzale degli Uffizi 6 (055 23885). **Open** *Summer* 8.15am-6.05pm Tue-Fri, Sun; 8.15am-9pm Sat. *Autumn-spring* 8.15am-6.05pm Tue-Sun. **Admission** L15,000 (€7.80). **No credit cards**. **Map** p314 C3/p314 C4.

The Uffizi building was designed by Vasari in the mid-16th century as a public administration centre for Cosimo I (hence the name 'Uffizi', meaning 'offices'). To make way for the pietra serena and white plaster building, inspired by Michelangelo's Laurentian Library in San Lorenzo, most of the 11th-century church of San Piero Scheraggio was demolished (the remains can still be seen beyond the main entrance hall), and the Old Mint, the Palazzo della Zecca, was incorporated into the design. The Uffizi's existence as an office building was short-lived – as early as 1581, Francesco I had begun turning the top floor into a new home for his art collection, and the habit caught on; a succession of Medici added to the collection, culminating in the bequest of most of the family's artworks by the last of the family, Anna Maria, on her death in 1743.

When the specialist art museums of the city were opened in the 18th and 19th centuries, the silver, sculptures and scientific exhibits were transferred from the Uffizi, leaving the gallery we see today.

If you're at all fond of Renaissance art prepare to step into heaven, albeit a crowded one. Off the corridors lined with magnificent ancient Greek and Roman wrestlers, flawless Apollos and eminent-looking busts, the collection begins, gloriously, with three *Maestàs* by Giotto, Cimabué and Duccio in **Room 2,** painted in the 13th and early 14th centuries, all three still part of the Byzantine tradition. Stepping into **Room 3** is to enter the world of 14th-century Siena, most exquisitely evoked by Simone Martini's *Annunciazione* with a breathtaking angel and coy yet fearful Virgin. Such delight in detail reached its zenith in the international Gothic movement (**Rooms 5 & 6**), most particularly the work of Gentile da Fabriano (1370-1427), whose *Adorazione dei Magi* (otherwise known as the Strozzi altarpiece) seems a wonderful excuse to paint sumptuous brocades and intricate gold jewellery.

It is something of a surprise, then, to turn to a strikingly contemporary *Madonna e Bambino con Sant'Anna* by Masolino and Masaccio (1401-28) in **Room 7**. Though Masolino was not averse to a little international Gothic frivolity (note some of the costumes he dreamed up for the Brancacci Chapel), here he's entirely restrained. Masaccio painted the Virgin, whose severe expression and statuesque pose make her an indubitable descendant of Giotto's *Maestà*. In the same room is the *Altare di Santa Lucia dei Magnoli* by Domenico Veneziano (1400-61), a Venetian artist who died a pauper in Florence

and who had a remarkable skill for rendering the way light affects colour. His influence on his pupil Piero della Francesca's work is clear in the younger artist's portraits of the Duke and Duchess of Urbino. Still in Room 7, Paolo Uccello (1396-1475) is represented by the *Battaglia di San Romano*, a triptych whose other thirds are in London's National Gallery and Paris's Louvre. A work of tremendous energy and power, it reinforces the chaos of battle with its intense, distorted perspective.

Rooms 8 and **9** are dominated by Filippo Lippi and the Pollaiuolo brothers. The Madonna in Lippi's *Madonna con Bambino e Angeli* is a portrait of the astonishingly beautiful Lucrezia Buti, a nun whom he abducted and married once he had given up the Carmelite vows, painted with their son Filippino, who was also to become a famous painter. The more talented of the brothers, Antonio, was one of the first artists to dissect bodies in order to study anatomy. His small panels of the Labours of Hercules (*Le Fatiche di Ercole*) evidence his familiarity with the skeletal form and musculature.

The two most famous paintings in the Uffizi and in Italy are in **Room 10**. Botticelli's *Nascita di Venere*, the epitome of Renaissance romance, depicts the birth of the goddess from a sea impregnated by the castration of Uranus – an allegory of the birth of beauty from the mingling of the physical world (the sea) and the spiritual (Uranus). Scholars have been squabbling about the true meaning of the other, Botticelli's *Allegoria della Primavera*, since it was painted in 1478. Many now agree that it was intended to represent the onset of spring (reading from right to left) and to signify the triumph of Venus

Botticelli's enigmatic **Allegoria della Primavera**: read from right to left.

Truly Original

(centre) as true love, with the Three Graces representing her beauty and Zephyr, on the right, as lust, pursuing the nymph Chloris, who is transformed into Flora, Venus's fecundity. The painting is believed to have been a wedding present from Lorenzo il Magnifico to his cousin Lorenzo di Pierfrancesco dei Medici, and many of the 190 different flowers under Flora's feet symbolise marriage.

In **Room 15** are several paintings by Leonardo da Vinci, including a collaboration with his teacher Verrocchio, *Il Battesimo di Cristo* (Verrocchio never painted again, reputedly because his work couldn't match up to Leonardo's). The octagonal **Room 18**, with its mother-of-pearl ceiling, is dominated by portraits by Bronzino, most strikingly that of Eleonora di Toledo, assured, beautiful and very Spanish in an opulent gold and black brocade gown.

In **Room 25** the gallery makes its transition to Mannerism, championed by Michelangelo's *Tondo Doni*, which shows the sculptural bodies, virtuoso composition and luscious palette that characterised the new wave. The **Pontormo and Rosso Fiorentino** room again shows Michelangelo's legacy, most clearly in *Mose' Difende le Figlie di Jetro* by Rosso Fiorentino. Also here is his ubiquitous cherub with a lyre, the *Angelo Musicante*. **Room 28** has works by Titian including his masterpiece *Venere d'Urbino*, whose questionably chaste gaze has disarmed viewers for centuries. For more Venetian works skip to **Rooms 31-35**, but don't miss the visually challenging *Madonna dal Collo Lungo* by Parmigianino en route. For an Old Masters cherry on the Renaissance cake, visit **Room 41**, with its classic row of portraits and self-portraits by Rubens, Van Dyck and Velázquez.

In summer and during holiday times, the Uffizi is almost always hellishly crowded; if you've booked your ticket (*see p62*) one of the best times to go is lunchtime, when the tour groups are unlikely to be around; otherwise, aim for opening time, when the queues at the ticket office are shorter and you can jump to the rooms you're most interested in. To see the whole collection would take either several hours or a return visit – allow at least three hours for the unmissables. Several organisations provide guided tours (*see p64*); there are also audio tours in seven languages for L3,000 (€11.60) from the ticket office.

Around via dei Tornabuoni

The elegant shopping mecca of via dei Tornabuoni sweeps down from piazza Antinori to piazza Santa Trinità and the Santa Trinità bridge, tracing the line of the ancient Roman city wall. It's crowned by Palazzo Antinori, an austere mid 15th-century palace of neat stone blocks, bought by the Antinoris in 1506 and still inhabited by the winemaking family. The church opposite is the baroque San Gaetano.

Halfway down the road, on the corner with via degli Strozzi, stands stately **Palazzo**

Strozzi (*see p82*), its mammoth fortification stones embellished with the three crescent-moon motif of the family crest. Passing Gucci, Prada and other designer names, you'll come to piazza Santa Trinità. Just before it is via Porta Rossa, home to Renaissance house museum **Palazzo Davanzati**, while off it is Borgo Santissimi Apostoli. In the middle of that is piazza del Limbo, so-called because it occupies the site of a graveyard for unbaptised babies. The tiny church to the left is **Santissimi Apostoli**.

Piazza Santa Trinità itself is little more than a bulge in via Tornabuoni, dominated by the extraordinary curved ramparts of Palazzo Spini Ferroni, home to Ferragamo and the **Museo Ferragamo** (*see p82*), and by an ancient column taken from the Baths of Caracalla in Rome, a gift to Cosimo I from Pope Pius I in 1560. The statue of Justice on top was designed by Ammanati. Opposite Palazzo Spini-Ferroni on the west side of via dei Tornabuoni is the church of **Santa Trinità**, built in the 13th century over 11th-century churches and home to the Ghirlandaio frescoes in the Sassetti chapel.

The Ponte Santa Trinità, an elegant bridge with an elliptical arch, links piazza Santa Trinità with the Oltrarno. It was first built in 1252 on the initiative of the Frescobaldi family but was swept away by floodwaters in 1333.

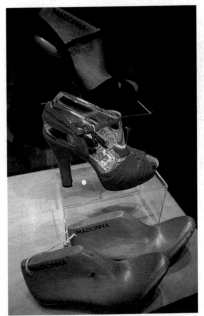

Museo Ferragamo: one for foot fetishists.

Sightseeing

Rebuilt in 1346, it was carried away by the river again in 1557 and was made in its present form by Ammanati in 1567, possibly to a design by Michelangelo, and is considered by many to be the most beautiful bridge in the world. The statues at either end, which represent the four seasons, were placed there in 1608 to celebrate Cosimo II's marriage to Maria of Austria. Bombed on the night of 3 August 1944 by retreating Germans, the statues were fished up from the riverbed; in 1955 the bridge was rebuilt in the same position and to the same design. The head of the most famous, *Spring*, by Pietro Francavilla, which graces the north-east side of the bridge, remained lost until 1961, when a council employee dredged it up during a routine clean-up and claimed the reward offered for its return years before by a US newspaper.

Museo Ferragamo

Via Tornabuoni 2 (055 336 0456). **Open** by appointment 9am-1pm, 2-6pm Mon-Fri. Closed Aug & 2 wks Christmas. **Admission** free. **Map** p314 C2.
The small museum above Ferragamo's shop in the Palazzo Spini Ferroni displays just a fraction of the company's 10,000 archive shoes, but still affords an opportunity to drool over some of the world's most beautiful footwear. Ferragamo, born in a small village outside Naples in 1898, opened his first shop at the age of 14, emigrated to the US at 16, and was soon designing shoes for the movies. Commissions for Cecil B DeMille's *Cleopatra* gave him the opportunity to experiment. In 1927 he moved to Florence to start a factory producing hand-made shoes *en masse*; since then the family business has flourished (*see p48* **Who they? Ferragamo**).

Palazzo Davanzati & the Museo dell'Antica Casa Fiorentina

Palazzo Davanzati, Via Porta Rossa 13 (055 238 8705). **Open** call for post-restoration times. **Admission** free. **Map** p314 C3.
This fascinating museum decked out as a mid-Renaissance family home is closed until 2002/3.

Palazzo Strozzi

Piazza Strozzi (055 288 342). **Open** varies according to exhibitions; library 9am-1pm, 3-6pm Mon-Fri; 9am-1pm Sat. **Admission** free to ground-floor courtyard; exhibitions vary. **Map** p314 B3.
Mercantile Florence was at its zenith in the 1400s, and during that century more than 100 palaces were built. The most magnificent was Palazzo Strozzi; its three tiers of golden rusticated stone still dominate via Tornabuoni. Work began on the palace in 1489 on the orders of Filippo Strozzi. The family had been exiled from Florence in 1434 for opposing the Medici but made good use of the time, moving south and becoming bankers to the King of Naples. By the time they returned to Florence in 1466 they had amassed a fortune. In 1474 Filippo began buying up property in the centre of Florence, until he had acquired

enough to build the biggest palace in the city. Fifteen buildings were demolished to make room for it, playing havoc with local traffic and covering the city in dust. An astrologer asked to choose an auspicious day to lay the foundation stone came up with 6 August 1489. Conveniently, a few months earlier Lorenzo de' Medici had passed a law exempting anyone who built a house on an empty site from taxes.
Three architects were involved in the design of the Palazzo: Giuliano da Sangallo, Benedetto da Maiano and Simone del Pollaiolo. When Filippo died in 1491, he left his heirs the responsibility of completing the project; it eventually bankrupted them. The palace now houses several institutions and stages prestigious exhibitions.

Santissimi Apostoli

Piazza del Limbo (055 290 642). **Open** 10am-noon, 3.30-7pm Mon-Sat; 10am-1pm, 4-6pm Sun. **Admission** free. **Map** p314 C3.
Santissimi Apostoli, the design of which, like that of the early Christian churches of Rome, is based on that of a Roman basilica (rectangular, with columns and a flat ceiling), retains much of its 11th-century façade. The third chapel on the right holds an *Immaculate Conception* by Vasari, and in the left aisle is an odd glazed terracotta tabernacle by Giovanni della Robbia. The church used to hold pieces of flint reputed to have come from Jerusalem's Holy Sepulchre, which were awarded to Pazzino de'Pazzi for his bravery during the Crusades (though his name, 'Little Mad Man of the Mad Men', suggests his actions may have been more foolhardy than brave). These flints were used on Easter Day to light the 'dove' that sets off the fireworks display at the Scoppio del Carro. Note that the church has a tendency to close in the afternoon without prior notice.

Santa Trinità

Piazza Santa Trinità (055 216 912). **Open** 8am-noon, 4-6pm Mon-Sat; 4-6pm Sun. **Admission** free. **Map** p314 C2.
A plain church built in the 13th century over the ruins of two earlier churches belonging to the Vallombrosans. The order was founded by San Giovanni Gualberto Visdomini in 1038, following a miraculous incident 20 years earlier in the church of San Miniato al Monte: while kneeling in front of a crucifix, he saw the head of Christ nod in approval of his prayer, starting his conversion from nobleman to monk. He then spent a great deal of time attempting to persuade pious aristocrats to surrender their wealth and live a life of austerity. The said crucifix was supposedly that held in San Miniato's Ficozzi Chapel and moved to Santa Trinita in 1671. The order became extremely wealthy and powerful, reaching a peak in the 16th and 17th centuries when its huge fortress abbey at Vallombrosa, in the Casentino countryside north of Arezzo, was built. The church is worth a visit for the Sassetti Chapel, luminously frescoed by Ghirlandaio with scenes from the life of St Francis, including one set in the piazza della Signoria featuring Lorenzo il Magnifico and his children.

Santa Maria Novella

Sleaze and more subtle pleasures.

This richly varied area stretches from the striking modernist main railway station (designed by Michelucci in 1935) through the antiques emporia of via dei Fossi and the designer clothes shops of via della Vigna Nuova to elegant lungarno Corsini and the statue-topped Palazzo Corsini in the east, and the fine white mansion blocks around the Teatro Comunale and the dark maze of ancient streets where ageing prostitutes wait for trade on plastic garden chairs to the west. At its centre is lively piazza Santa Maria Novella and the church of Ognissanti.

Round the train station and adjacent bus terminus, as in so many European cities, sleaze is prevalent: amid the chestnut sellers, business travellers and backpackers picking their way through the choked traffic system is a chaos of tramps, beggars and men on the pull. The hellish underpass, supposedly a safe alternative to the road, is a case of out of the frying pan into the fire. Hold on to bags and wallets.

Across from the station, Alberti's façade for the church of **Santa Maria Novella** (see p84) looks out on a piazza where tourists strain to hear the guide through the cacophony of school-trip children sitting on the 'Keep off the grass' signs and singing Italian pop songs, pub-goers basking in the sun and groups of immigrant workers catching up on the latest gossip.

The triangle formed by via dei Fossi, via della Spada and via della Vigna Nuova brings you the more civilised pleasures of the fine **Palazzo Rucellai**, the **Capella Rucellai** and the adjacent modern art museum, the **Museo Marino Marini** (for all three, see below).

Alberti had already designed the **Palazzo Rucellai** in via della Vigna Nuova, then the most refined in the city, for the Rucellai family when he created the façade of Santa Maria Novella. Its subtle façade was inspired by Rome's Colosseum: the pilasters that section the bottom storey have Doric capitals, those on the middle storey Ionic capitals, and those on the top storey are based on the Corinthian style. There's no rustication; Alberti considered it pompous and fit only for tyrants. The Rucellai were wool merchants who had grown rich by importing from Majorca a red dye derived from lichen, known as *oricello*, from which their surname derives and which they then grew in the Orti Oricellari garden at the far end of via della Scala.

Up past piazza Goldoni, lungarno Vespucci and shopping street borgo Ognissanti open out into piazza Ognissanti, flanked by prestigious hotels and topped by the church of **Ognissanti** (see below). Further up, elegant residential roads arrive at the main avenues, Porta al Prato and the mammoth park, the **Cascine** (see p101).

Cappella Rucellai

Via della Spada (055 216 912). **Open** tours 10am-12.30pm Mon-Fri. **Admission** free. **Map** p314 B2.
This tiny chapel was part of the church of San Pancrazio, now the Museo Marino Marini, and contains the tombs of many of the family of 15th-century wool magnate Giovanni Rucellai, including that of his wife Iacopa Strozzi. It's worth a visit to see the copy by Alberti of the *Holy Sepulchre of Jerusalem*, commissioned in 1467 by Giovanni in an attempt to ensure his own salvation.

Museo Marino Marini

Piazza San Pancrazio (055 219 432). **Open** *Summer* 10am-5pm Mon, Wed, Fri, Sat; 10am-11pm Thur. *Winter* 10am-5pm Mon, Wed-Sat; 10am-1pm Sun. **Admission** L8,000 (€4.10). **No credit cards**. **Map** p314 B2.
This Albertian church was redesigned to accommodate the work of sculptor Marino Marini (1901-80), and the equine rigidity and monumentality of the pieces are reflected in its design and spaciousness. Many of the first-floor sculptures are a variation on the theme of horse and rider, championed by the central exhibit, the 6m (20ft) *Composizione Equestre*. The second floor has a series of other sculptural subjects, including the hypnotic *Nuotatore* (Swimmers) plus fabulous paintings of dancers and jugglers.

Ognissanti

Via Borgognissanti 42 (no phone). **Open** 8am-12.30pm, 5-7.30pm daily; *Last Supper* 9am-noon Mon, Tue, Sat. **Admission** free. **Map** p314 B1.
The recently restored church of Ognissanti (All Saints) was founded in the 13th century by the Umiliati, a group of monks from Lombardy. They introduced the wool trade to Florence, and as the city's subsequent wealth was built on wool, it could be argued that without them there would have been no Florentine Renaissance. By the 14th century, the Umiliati were so rich they commissioned Giotto to paint the *Maestà* (now in the **Uffizi**; see p78) for their high altar. Fifty years later they commissioned Giovanni da Milano to create a flashier altarpiece with more gold (now also in the Uffizi). Ognissanti was also the parish church of the

Vespucci, a family of merchants from Peretola (near the airport) who dealt in silk, wine, wool, banking and goods from the Far East. They included 15th-century navigator Amerigo, who sailed to the Venezuelan coast in 1499 and had two continents named after him. The church has been rebuilt numerous times, and is now visited mainly for paintings by Ghirlandaio. Amerigo himself appears as a young boy dressed in pink in the *Madonna della Misericordia*. Other frescoes worth seeing are a *St Augustine* by Botticelli and a *St Jerome* by Ghirlandaio. Off the cloister on a refectory wall is Ghirlandaio's most famous *Last Supper* (1480). As in his work in San Marco, he uses religious iconography to load it with deeper meaning; here, however, his Apostles' expressions are more realistic. Also here is a museum of Franciscan bits and pieces, and in the church is the tomb of Botticelli, marked with his family name, Filipepi.

Santa Maria Novella

Piazza Santa Maria Novella (055 215 918/cloisters & museum 055 282 187). **Open** *Church* 9.30am-5pm Mon-Thur, Sat; 1-5pm Fri, Sun. *Cloisters & museum* 9am-2pm Mon-Thur, Sat, Sun. **Admission** L5,000 (€2.60) church; L5,000 (€2.60) cloisters & museum. **No credit cards. Map** p314 B2.

This was the Florentine seat of the Dominicans, a fanatically inquisitorial order fond of leading street brawls against suspected heretics and encouraging the faithful to strip and whip themselves before the altar. The piazza outside, one of Florence's biggest, was enlarged in 1244-5 to accommodate the crowds who came to hear St Peter the Martyr, one of the viler members of the saintly canon, who made his name persecuting so-called heretics in northern Italy (and ended up with one of their axes in his head).

The church interior, designed by the order's monks, is suitably cheerless, but the façade is light with elegant green and white marble. This is thanks to Alberti, who in 1465, at the request of the Rucellai family, incorporated the Romanesque lower storey into a refined Renaissance scheme. To the right of the church is a cemetery surrounded by the grave niches of Florence's wealthy families. Until Vasari had them whitewashed in the mid 16th century, the church walls were covered with frescoes; fortunately Vasari left Masaccio's *Trinità* of 1427 (recently restored), in which we can see the first application of Brunelleschi's mathematical rules of perspective to a painting – the result is a triumph of *trompe-l'œil*, with God, Christ and two saints appearing to stand in a niche, watched by the patrons, Lorenzo Lenzi and his wife. The inscription above the skeleton on the sarcophagus reads 'I was what you are and what I am you shall be'.

Over the next few decades the Dominicans appear to have loosened up. In 1485 they let Ghirlandaio cover the walls of the Cappella Tornabuoni with scenes from the life of John the Baptist, featuring lavish contemporary Florentine interiors and a supporting cast from the Tornabuoni family. Ghirlandaio also found the time to train a young man by the name of Michelangelo while working on the chapel. At about the same time, Filippino Lippi was at work next door in the Cappella di Filippo Strozzi, painting scenes from the life of St Philip.

The church is also home to the *Crocifisso* by Giotto, a simple, otherworldly wooden crucifix that sparked off a massive political row – after a 12-year restoration, in the run-up to the general election of 2001 bureaucratic jobsworths decided it could be perceived as political manoeuvring to reinstall it before voting had taken place, and asked for the *Trinità* to be unveiled before the election and the

Crocifisso afterwards. After national ridicule, the mayor gallantly stepped in to halt the 'comedy of errors' and replace the masterpiece in the church.

To compare Masaccio's easeful use of perspective with the contorted struggles of Paolo Uccello, pop outside to the Chiostro Verde ('green cloister') left of the church, so-called because of the green base pigment Uccello used, which gave the flood-damaged frescoes a chill, deathly hue. The best-preserved example of how not to do perspective is *The Flood*, which looks as if it was painted from down a plughole. Beyond the Chiostro is the Cappella degli Spagnoli, whose name derives from Cosimo I's wife Eleonora di Toledo using it for her Spanish cronies and decorating it with vibrant scenes celebrating the triumph of Dominicans and the Catholic Church. There's also a small Museo di Santa Maria Novella just off the Chiostro Verde.

Walk 2 Off the beaten track

Florence's almost continous slew of tourists tend to follow one another along the well-worn paths between major monuments like sheep. All you have to do to avoid the river of people is dive down the nearest alleyway and follow your instincts.

There's plenty to see for the curious on such wanderings: cool churches, quiet *piazze*, hidden courtyards, windowboxes dripping with colourful blooms, gardens revealed through open doors, glimpses of frescoes and elaborate ceilings in apartments, eccentric doorknobs, stone gargoyles, modest artisan workshops and lots more. Just keep your eyes peeled.

Start in lovely piazza Santo Spirito, preferably in the morning when the square is dominated by bustling local life. Wander round any of the sidestreets here and you'll see a variety of artisans at work in their *botteghe*. If the church is open, pop inside to see Filippino Lippi's *Madonna & Saints* with its background of nearby Porta San Frediano (in the right transept), then walk straight across via Maggio by way of via Michelozzo and into sdrucciolo dei Pitti. Take a left down via Toscanella, a quiet street lined with ancient buildings that brings you out in delightful piazza della Passera. A zigzag (right down via dello Sprone, left down via de' Ramagliante and right again into via Barbadori) takes you out by the Ponte Vecchio. For a quick detour, double back along via Guicciardini and pop into the church of Santa Felicità to see Pontormo's amazing *Deposition*.

Going back to the river, head upstream for 50 metres until the road forks then bear right into via de' Bardi, lined with rather austere palaces. Palazzo Capponi at No.36 achieved notoriety as the fictitious home of Dr Lecter in *Hannibal* – a number of scenes in the film were shot there in May 2000. The Capponi family crest – a distinctive black and white diagonal design – is above the door. A little further on, at No.28, a wall plaque testifies to the fact that art historian John Pope Henessey lived in the street until his death in 1994, while on the opposite side of the street another commemorates a visit by St Francis of Assisi in 1211.

Where via de' Bardi becomes via San Niccolò, turn left and cross the Arno on Ponte alle Grazie, which affords a great view upstream, past what may well be the most spectacularly located rowing club in the world (on the right), as far as the Ponte Vecchio. It's an ideal vantage point for sunset shots of the bridge.

Once you're over the river, turn left into traffic-free via de' Neri, the hub of a busy working neighbourhood with a real sense of Florentine life in spite of its proximity to piazza Santa Croce; it's full of bakeries, grocers, rustic wine bars and plenty of local characters. The first narrow lane on the right (via delle Brache) leads into piazza de' Peruzzi, from where, starting at the far left corner, you can follow the outline of the inner arcade of the old Roman amphitheatre along via Bentaccordi (look out for the plaque marking Michelangelo's boyhood home) and via Torta; you'll emerge opposite Santa Croce.

Go back down to via de' Neri, following it to the end this time, cross via de' Castellani (perhaps swerving briefly to the right to have a look at what could be the smallest luthier's workshop in the world) and piazza Signoria, then turn left into via Por Santa Maria and take the second right into borgo SS Apostoli, lined by impressive *palazzi*. Towards the end, on the left, you'll come to the 11th-century Romanesque church of Santi Apostoli and the sunken piazza del Limbo, a quiet, sad little place so named because it is built on a burial ground for unbaptised babies.

The street emerges in piazza Santa Trinità, between Palazzi Spini-Feroni and Buondelmonti. Finish your walk by nipping into the church opposite with a L100 coin at the ready to light up Ghirlandaio's superb *Adoration of the Shepherds* over the altar in the Sassetti chapel.

Sightseeing

San Lorenzo

The old Medici 'hood is now dominated by the city market.

This vibrant area extends north from the huge market round the church of **San Lorenzo** (*see p88*), with its streets full of stalls selling cheap clothes, mediocre leather goods and tacky souvenirs, and huge covered market in the piazza del Mercato Centrale, chock-a-block with fresh fruit and vegetables, fish, cheese and meat stalls. The overpowering smells inside and out are joined by those of the bakeries, delis, cafés and fresh doughnut stands in neighbouring streets and the piles of refuse.

Roads lead off the *piazze* around San Lorenzo in a star-shape – north-east up via dei Ginori alongside the gardens at the back of the **Palazzo Medici Riccardi** (entrance on via Cavour; *see p88*), past craft and gift shops to the corner of via San Gallo and the Benedictine refectory **Cenacolo di Sant'Apollonia** (*see p87*) as far as the old city gate Porta a San Gallo; south, by the busy shoe and clothes shops in borgo San Lorenzo (*see p88* **Bargain chic**) to the Duomo; south-west, via the tiny food stores towards the station; north-west past the **Cappelle Medicee** (*see p87*) up via dell'Ariento and via Faenza with their simple *pensioni* towards the dingy via Nazionale; and north to the main market square.

Further up via Nazionale, the roads widen into piazza dell'Indipendenza, and the smell of boiled cabbage disappears. The double square, with a main road running through the middle, a few stone seats scattered round the edges, bald

Who they? Mark-makers

Crests mark the territory of Florence's historic power-players.

Antinori

Family crest: Simple harlequin pattern designating mercantile status.
Historic heyday: Long history of winemaking dating back to 1180 over 26 generations, Renaissance trade in silks, and banking. Giovanni di Piero was accepted into the Vintners' Guild in 1385.
Now live: Palazzo Antinori – having sold it, the family triumphantly bought it back after the war.
Last seen: Treading grapes in Chianti and serving *pappa al pomodoro* with some of the finest wines in Italy at upper-crust restaurant Cantinetta Antinori in the Palazzo, and buying up and converting Tuscan villages for *agriturismo*.

Corsini

Family crest: Three red bands and a blue stripe that have kept heraldry experts guessing for centuries, although the red stands for courage, passion and cruelty and the blue for absolute purity and happiness.
Historic heyday: 1644, when the Medici rewarded their support with a title; 1700s, when Lorenzo became pope and Neri president.
Now live: Palazzo Corsini al Prato is home to the head of the family, Prince Don Filippo; Palazzo Corsini is owned by the female line, so is theoretically no longer 'Corsini'; Prince Giovanni owns Mezzomonte, a stunning villa in Impruneta that he hires out to a fortunate few for parties, weddings and congresses. There's even a website – www.villacorsini.com.
Last seen: Incognito as architects, lawyers and doctors, and organising posh parties.

and a couple of trees, is a bad excuse for
~~k~~, but it does take you a step closer to the
pond and flowerbeds of the gardens of the
~~w~~ise unspectacular **Fortezza da Basso**
~~●~~*101*) on the other side of the viale.

~~●~~elle Medicee
~~ı~~ *Madonna degli Aldbrandini (055 238 8602).*
~~●~~ 8.15am-5pm Tue-Sat, 1st, 3rd, 5th Sun & 2nd,
~~●~~on of month. **Admission** L11,000 (€5.70).
~~●~~redit cards. **Map** p314 A3.
~~●~~most important Medici were laid to rest in these
~~●~~te chapels. Designed by Michelangelo (from
~~●~~ as the Medici mausoleum, the floor plan of the
~~●~~ella dei Principi was based on that of Florence's
~~●~~istery, and possibly of the Holy Sepulchre in
~~●~~alem. Inlaid with brilliantly hued *pietra dura*,
~~●~~h kept the workers of the Opificio delle Pietre
~~●~~ busy for several centuries, it's made of huge
~~●~~s of porphyry and ancient Roman marbles
~~●~~d into the city and sawn into pieces by Turkish
~~●~~es. At one time it was hoped that the tombs
~~●~~d be joined by that of Christ, but unfortunate-
~~●~~ the Medici the authorities in Jerusalem refused

to sell it. This chapel houses the six sarcophagi of
the Medici Grand Dukes buried in the crypt. These
include Giovanni dalle Bande Nere, Cosimo I and the
last of the Medicis, Anna Maria.

The adjoining Sagrestia Nuova is dominated by
the tombs of Lorenzo il Magnifico's far from magnificent cousins, Giuliano, Duke of Nemours, and
Lorenzo, Duke of Urbino, designed by Michelangelo
with the allegorical figures of Night and Day, plus
Dawn and Dusk reclining atop, the females Night
and Dawn leaving no doubt that the sculptor was
more used to chiselling nude men. Also here is
the incomplete tomb of Lorenzo il Magnifico and
his brother Giuliano, who are buried beneath it.
The coffered dome of the chapel, an architectural
masterpiece that was built directly on to a square
base, was designed to contribute to Michelangelo's
allegory within the tomb of the inevitability of
death, symbolising the 'sun' of salvation.

Cenacolo di Sant'Apollonia
Via XXVII Aprile 1 (055 23885). **Open** 8.15am-
1.50pm Tue-Sat, 2nd & 4th Sun of month, 1st, 3rd &
5th Mon of month. **Admission** free.

Della Gherardesca
Family crest: The eagle, a symbol of
spirituality, strength and astuteness.
Historic heyday: Ugolino was Podestà of Pisa
in the late 1200s, until he was betrayed by a
nephew and starved to death with his children
and grandchildren in a prison tower (some
legends say he ate them and survived).
Now live: The most conspicuous member
of the family, Count Gaddo, lives in Milan.
Last seen: Count G has often been spotted by
the press escorting Duchess Sarah Ferguson
to polo matches and showing worthy
visitors round his
country estate,
Castagneto
Carducci in the
Maremma;
sister Sibilla
writes books
on etiquette.

Frescobaldi
Family crest: Three fleur-de-lis motifs,
probably symbolising the lily of Florence.
Historic heyday: Thirty-generation wine reign,
including shipments to Henry VIII in the
1500s; served the Medici (1616-22).
Now live: Many of the *marchesi* (marquesses)
live in Palazzo Frescobaldi; Ludovico owns the
vineyards of Tenuta dell'Ornellaia.
Last seen: In a lucrative joint venture with
Californian grape magnate Mondavi making
the high-class hybrid 'Luce', and in another
with Gianfranco Ferre (who designed the
packaging). Prince Charles's friend Bona, wife
of Vittorio, writes upmarket guides and acts
as PR supremo for the family. ▶

The works in this Benedictine refectory, such as the frescoes of the passion of Christ, were covered over during the baroque period and only came to light during restoration work. The most important is Andrea del Castagno's *Last Supper* (1445-50), in which the painter reverts to a 14th-century seating plan, with Judas alienated on our side of the table. The vibrant colours and enclosed space intensify the scene. There are also other works by del Castagno, including a *Pietà*.

Palazzo Medici-Riccardi

Via Cavour 1 (055 276 0340). **Open** 9am-7pm Mon, Tue, Thur-Sun. **Admission** L8,000 (€4.10). **No credit cards. Map** p315 B4.

A demonstration of both Medici muscle and Medici subtlety, Palazzo Medici Riccardi was home to the Medici until they moved into the Palazzo Vecchio in 1540. Not wishing to appear too ostentatious, Cosimo il Vecchio rejected a design by Brunelleschi as too extravagant. He plumped instead for one by Michelozzo, who had just proved his worth as a heavyweight architect in the rebuilding of the San Marco convent complex. Michelozzo designed a façade with a heavily rusticated lower storey in the style of many military buildings, but a smoother, more refined, first storey and a yet more restrained second storey, crowned by an overhanging cornice. The *palazzo* doubled as fortress and home, and was widely copied throughout Italy. It was massively expanded and revamped in the 17th century by its new owners, the Riccardi, but retains Michelozzo's charming chapel, accessed via steps off the main courtyard. Almost entirely covered with frescoes by Benozzo Gozzoli, a student of Fra' Angelico, the chapel features a vivid *Journey of the Magi*, which is actually a portrait of 15th century Medici. The palace now hosts art and cultural exhibitions.

San Lorenzo

Piazza San Lorenzo (055 216 634). **Open** 10am-5pm Mon-Sat. **Admission** free. **Map** p314 A3.

San Lorenzo was the parish church of the Medici family, who largely financed its construction, and for centuries the ruling family continued to lavish money on the place. It was built between 1419 and 1469 to a design by Brunelleschi, sprawling heavy and imposing between piazza di San Lorenzo and

▶ # Who they? Mark-makers (continued)

Medici

Family crest: The balls on the shield, used to rally supporters with cries of 'Palle! Palle!', probably represented pills or cupping glasses as the Medici name, which means 'doctors' and suggests their origins, would suggest.
Historic heyday: Where to start? Popes, dukes, grand dukes and master bankers, all descended from the first Medici from the Mugello, who between them ran the place for centuries. The zenith arrived with Lorenzo il Magnifico, the revered patron of Renaissance art.
Last seen: Lorenza de' Medici runs prestigious cookery courses much favoured by awestruck Americans and writes books for foodies from her husband Stucchi Prinetti's abbey, restaurant and similarly prestigious wine estate, Badia a Coltibuono, in Chiantishire.

Ricasoli

Family crest: A lion rampant, symbol of power and ferocity.
Historic heyday: Winemakers since 1141; achieved the political pinnacle of success in the days of Baron Bettino, who succeeded Cavour as prime minister in 1861.
Now live: Palazzo Ricasoli and the family estate of Brolio near Siena, with its famous castle.
Last seen: three guesses... OK then, making wine on the estate.
Did you know?: They're still moving in rarefied circles: the late wife of Bettino Ricasoli was the sister of the queen of Belgium.

piazza di Madonna degli Aldobrandini, with a dome almost as prominent as that of the Duomo.

Despite the fortune spent on the place, the façade was never finished, hence the digestive biscuit bricks. In 1518, the Medici pope Leo X commissioned Michelangelo to design a façade (the models for it can be seen in the Casa Buonarroti; *see p94*); he ordained that the marble should be mined at Pietrasanta, which was part of Florence's domain, but Michelangelo disagreed, preferring high-quality Carrara marble. In the end it didn't matter – in 1520 the scheme was cancelled.

San Lorenzo was the first church to which Brunelleschi applied his theory of rational proportion. Like Santo Spirito, it's a church to stroll round and savour, though there are a couple of artworks you might want to look at more closely. The first of these is Donatello's bronze pulpits, from which Savonarola snarled his tales of sin and doom. The reliefs are powerful too: you can almost hear the crowds scream in the *Deposition*. On the north wall is a *Martyrdom of St Lawrence* by Mannerist painter par excellence Bronzino, a decadent affair in which the burning of the saint is attended by

musclebound men and hefty women with red-gold hair, dressed in pink, lime green, yellow and lilac. In the second chapel on the right is another Mannerist work, a *Marriage of the Virgin* by Rosso Fiorentino, and in the north transept there is an *Annunciation* by Filippo Lippi, which displays a clarity of line and a depth of perspective that make it perfect for this interior.

Opening off the north transept is the Sagrestia Vecchia ('old sacristy'), another Brunelleschi design with a dome segmented like a tangerine and proportions based on cubes and spheres, and fabulous painted tondi by Donatello. The doors, which are also by Donatello, feature martyrs, apostles and church fathers, while to the left of the entrance there is an elaborate tomb made out of serpentine, porphyry, marble and bronze containing the remains of Lorenzo il Magnifico's father and uncle, by Verrocchio.

The Biblioteca Laurenziana was built to house the Medici's large library and is reached via the door to the left of the façade and up one of Europe's most elegant stairwells, a slick three-sweep Michelangelo mannerist design in *pietra serena*.

Strozzi-Guicciardini

Family crest: Three crescent moons on the Strozzi crest, symbolising knowledge; the Guicciardini crest (right) has three hunting horns, symbolising power.

Historic heyday: Guicciardinis – the early 1500s, when the highly cultured Francesco had Machiavelli as friend and secretary; Strozzis – their triumphant return to Florence from Naples in 1466 after a 32-year exile imposed by the Medicis, and as papal bankers in the 1500s.

Now live: Next-door neighbours to the Palazzo Pitti, in the charming Palazzo Guicciardini in the Oltrarno.

Last seen: Playing impeccable hosts to Tony, Cherie and family in an annual (and mutual) photo op in their Tuscan villa near Poggibonsi.
In case you were wondering: Prince Girolamo is a Guicciardini but was adopted by his aunt Princess Strozzi, who made him take her name before his, hence the double-whammy of nominative nobility. So that's two crests for the price of one from now on – lucky masons.

San Marco

Must-see museums are San Marco's big draw.

This student quarter buzzes with backpack- and drawing-tube-laden clones hanging round the piazzas or making their way to or from the nearby architecture and law faculties. At its heart is **Santissimi Annunziata**, one of the most aesthetically pleasing piazzas in the city – it's surrounded on three sides by delicate arcades, while the centre contains a powerful equestrian statue of Grand Duke Ferdinando I by Giambologna. On its eastern side, the **Spedale degli Innocenti** (*see p92*), opened in 1445 and the first foundling hospital in Europe, was commissioned by the Guild of Silk Weavers and designed by Brunelleschi (a guild member). The building is one of the most significant examples of early-Renaissance design in the city in that it marks the advent of Renaissance 'town-planning', with the hospital designed to fit into Brunelleschi's greater plan for the whole square. The powder-blue medallions in the spandrels, each showing a swaddled baby, are by Andrea della Robbia – unwanted babies, often those of domestic servants, were left in a small revolving door set in the wall on the left to be collected by the nuns. Brunelleschi had envisioned a perfectly symmetrical piazza (to be modern Europe's first) but died before he could realise the dream. In the 17th century, the

porticos were continued around (only) two other sides of the square, giving the piazza a human scale and unity absent elsewhere in the city.

Passing under the northernmost arch of the Spedale is via della Colonna, which contains the **Museo Archeologico** (*see p91*), while on the west side of the piazza is upmarket hotel **Loggiato dei Serviti** (*see p52*) and, on the north, the church of **Santissima Annunziata** (*see p92*). The street between the two, via Battisti, leads directly into piazza San Marco, best known as a bus hub and as the site of the church of **San Marco** (on the north), with the unmissable **Museo di San Marco** (*see p92*), once home to Fra Angelico and Savonarola, next door. On the via Ricasoli corner of the piazza Annunziata a never-ending, snaking queue denotes the **Accademia** (*see below*), the second most visited museum in the city after the Uffizi.

North of the piazza is via la Pira, containing the **Museo di Geologia e Paleontologia** (*see p91*) and **Museo di Mineralogia e Lithologia** (*see p91*), the delightfully eclectic geology and mineralogy museums, and just round the corner is the perfect resting place after a hard morning's culture – the **Giardino dei Semplici** (*see p91*).

North and east of the gardens is a genteel residential area, and south-west are the streets leading back down to the piazza del Duomo.

Galleria dell'Accademia

Via Ricasoli 58-60 (055 238 8609). **Open** 8.15am-6.50pm Tue-Sun. **Admission** L12,000 (€6.20). **No credit cards. Map** p314 A4.

Home to Michelangelo's monumental *David* (1504), the Accademia attracts millions of visitors a year. The famous sculpture started life as a serious political icon portraying strength and resolve and designed to encourage Florentines to support their fledgling constitution, but Michelangelo also undoubtedly considered it a monument to his genius – he managed to carve a figure from a 5m (16ft) high, exceptionally narrow slab of marble. You'll notice that the sculpture is top heavy; this is because Michelangelo intended it to be placed on a high column and shaped it so that it would look its best from the viewpoint of the beholder. When it was moved from piazza della Signoria in 1873, it was decided to keep the plinth low so visitors could see his curves close-up.

But the museum is not all about *David*; lining the walls of the salon where it is kept are Michelangelo's so-called slaves – masterly but unfinished sculptures struggling to escape from their marble prisons. They were intended for Pope Julius II's tomb, a project that

San Marco is packed with students.

Fra Angelico's glorious *Deposition from the Cross* in **San Marco** church. *See page 92.*

Michelangelo was forced to abandon, much to his irritation, in order to paint the Sistine Chapel ceiling in Rome. On the right of *David* is the *Pietà Palestrina*, also attributed to Michelangelo (the stilted lines of the figures surrounding Jesus have led many to believe that it was taken over halfway through by a student of the master).

The Salone dell'Ottocento is full of sculptural reproductions intended to provide budding artists with examples to copy. The Accademia will also soon be home to the original *Rape of the Sabines* by Giambologna, to be moved from piazza della Signoria, as David was. The gallery also houses a mixed bag of late-Gothic and Renaissance paintings, including two of Botticelli's Madonnas, bible scenes by Perugino, Fra Bartolomeo and Filippino Lippi, and a moving *Pietà* (1365) by Giovanni da Milano.

A very important collection of musical instruments has just opened in the Accademia, too.

Giardino dei Semplici

Via Micheli 3 (055 275 7402). **Open** 9am-1pm Mon-Fri. **Admission** L6,000 (€3.10). **No credit cards.**
Set up for the cultivation of exotic plants and research into their uses, the 'garden of samples' was planted in 1545 on the orders of Cosimo I, on lands seized from an order of Dominican nuns. Essential oils were extracted, perfumes distilled and cures and antidotes sought for various ailments and poisons.

Museo Archeologico

Via della Colonna 38 (055 23575). **Open** 2-7pm Mon; 8.30am-7pm Tue, Thur; 8.30am-2pm Wed, Fri, Sun. **Admission** L8,000 (€4.10). **No credit cards.** Map p314 A5.
The place to come for a break from the Renaissance. The Etruscan art includes jewellery, funerary sculpture and bronzes, including the important *Chimera*, *Orator* and *Minerva*, all dating from about the fifth century BC. The Egyptian rooms exude a pyramidal mysticism with sedate cube-statues from the Middle Kingdom and precisely decorated tombs, complete with mummified bodies. On the second floor is an extensive collection of Greek ceramics.

Museo di Geologia e Paleontologia

Via la Pira 4 (055 275 7536). **Open** 9am-1pm Tue-Sat; 9am-1pm 2nd Sun of month (except June-Sept 2001). **Admission** L3,000 (€1.60). **No credit cards.**
Old-fashioned museum with one of the best fossil collections in Italy, resembling an unusually orderly hoard belonging to an eccentric uncle. In Room 4 the remains of an elephant-like creature found in the Valdarno towers above visitors.

Museo di Mineralogia e Lithologia

Via la Pira 4 (055 275 7537). **Open** 9am-1pm Mon-Fri; 9am-1pm 2nd Sun of the month (except June-Sept 2001). **Admission** free Mon-Sat; L6,000 (€3.10) Sun. **No credit cards.**

Simple arrangement and clear explanations make this collection accessible to the least scientifically minded. It's packed full of strange and lovely gems, including 12 huge Brazilian quartzes opposite the entrance. Fantastic agates, chalcedony, tormaline, opals and iridescent limonite line the cabinets. There are also glass models of famous stones such as the Koh-i-noor and items from Cosimo III's collection.

Museo di San Marco

Piazza San Marco 1 (055 238 8608). **Open** 8.15am-6.50pm Tue-Fri; 8.15am-1.50pm Sat; 8.15am-1.50pm 1st, 3rd & 5th Mon of month; 8.15am-7pm 2nd & 4th Sun of month. **Admission** L8,000 (€4.10). **No credit cards**.

This museum, housed in the monastery where Fra Angelico (known to Florentines as Beato Angelico) and Fra Girolamo Savonarola lived with their fellow monks, is largely dedicated to the ethereal paintings of Angelico, arguably the most spiritual artist of the 15th century. You're greeted on the first floor by one of the most famous images in Christendom – an *Annunciation* that is, for once, entirely of another world. The same is true of the other images Fra Angelico and his assistants frescoed on the walls of the monks' white vaulted cells. Most of the cells on the outer wall of the left corridor are by Fra Angelico himself; particularly outstanding are a lyrical *Noli Me Tangere*, showing Christ appearing to Mary Magdalene in a field of flowers, and the surreal *Mocking of Christ*, in which Christ's torturers are represented simply by relevant fragments of their anatomy (a hand holding a whip, another holding a sponge, a face spitting). The cell that was occupied by Savonarola is adorned with portraits of the rabid reformer by Fra Bartolomeo.

Museo dello Spedale degli Innocenti

Piazza SS Annunziata (055 249 1708). **Open** 8.30am-2pm Mon, Tue, Thur-Sun. **Admission** L5,000 (€2.60). **No credit cards. Map** p314 A5.

This collection, housed in the former recreation room of Brunelleschi's foundlings hospital, received a substantial blow in 1853, when several important works were auctioned off (for a relative pittance) to raise money for the hospital. What remains constitutes a harmonious collection, with an unsurprising concentration of *Madonna & Child* pieces, including a Botticelli and a vivid Luca della Robbia. The highlight is Ghirlandaio's *Adoration of the Magi*, commissioned for the high altar of the hospital's church.

Opificio delle Pietre Dure

Via degli Alfani 78 (055 265 111/055 287 123). **Open** 8.15am-7pm Mon, Wed-Sat; 8.15am-2pm Tue. **Admission** L4,000 (€2.10). **No credit cards. Map** p314 A4.

The 'workshop of hard stones' was founded in 1588 by Grand Duke Ferdinando I. *Pietra dura* is the craft of inlaying gems or semi-precious stones in intricate mosaics. Nowadays most work is restoration, but some beautifully intricate pieces are exhibited here.

San Marco

Piazza San Marco (055 287628). **Open** 8.30am-noon, 4-6pm Mon-Sat; 4-6pm Sun. **Admission** free. **Map** p314 A4.

The Medici lavished even more money on the church and convent of San Marco than on San Lorenzo. In 1434 Cosimo il Vecchio returned from exile and organised the handing over of the monastery of San Marco to the Dominicans. He then funded the renovation of the decaying church and convent by Michelozzo; whether he did so to ease his conscience (banking was still officially forbidden by the church) or to cash in on the increasing popularity of the Dominicans is uncertain. He also founded a public library full of Greek and Latin works, which had a great influence on Florentine humanists. Ironically, later in the 15th century San Marco became the base of religious fundamentalist Savonarola.

On the ground floor are more works by Fra Angelico in the Ospizio dei Pellegrini (pilgrims' hospice), many collected from churches around the city. His first commission, the *Madonna dei Linaiuoli*, painted in 1433 for the Guild of Linen Makers, is here, along with a superb *Deposition* and a *Last Judgement* in which the blessed dance among the flowers and trees of paradise while the damned are boiled in cauldrons and pursued by monsters.

By way of contrast, pop into the refectory, which is dominated by a Ghirlandaio *Last Supper*, where the disciples, by turn bored, praying, crying or haughty, pick at a frugal repast of bread, wine and cherries against a background of orange trees, a peacock, a Burmese cat and flying ducks (the oranges are the fruits of paradise, the peacock symbolises the resurrection, the cat is a symbol of evil – that's why it's near Judas – and the ducks represent the heavens).

Santissima Annunziata

Piazza SS Annunziata (055 239 8034). **Open** 7.30am-12.30pm, 4-6.30pm Mon-Sun. **Admission** free. **Map** p314 A5.

Santissima Annunziata, the church of the Servite Order, is a place of popular worship rather than perfect proportion. There's a frescoed baroque ceiling and an opulent shrine built around a miraculous *Madonna*, said to have been painted by a monk called Bartolomeo in 1252 and finished by angels (it's from this legend that the church derives its name). Surrounding the icon are flowers, silver lamps and pewter body parts – ex-votives left in the hope that the *Madonna* will cure the dicky heart or gammy leg of loved ones. Despite its baroque appearance, the church was actually built by Michelozzo in the 15th century, as can be seen in the light, arcaded atrium. It was frescoed early the following century by Pontormo, Rosso Fiorentino and, most strikingly, Andrea del Sarto, whose *Birth of the Virgin* is set within the walls of a Renaissance *palazzo*, with cherubs perched on a mantelpiece and the festooned canopy of the bed. There's another del Sarto fresco in the Chiostro dei Morti ('cloister of the dead'), but you need permission from the sacristan to see it.

Santa Croce

The diverse parish of Florence's richest medieval church.

The huge area around Santa Croce naturally divides into specific districts, each with its own distinct flavour. On the western edge, opposite and above the bulk of the Palazzo Vecchio, piazza San Firenze houses the **Bargello** (*see below*), heavy with the atmosphere of its history, on the north-east corner, and via Proconsolo heads north with its **Museo di Antropologia e Etnologia** (*see p95*). Up north, close to the Duomo, is the **Museo di Firenze com'era** (*see p95*), stuffed with the city archives.

Between this western border and piazza Santa Croce, with the matchless Gothic church of **Santa Croce** (*see p96*) and its mediocre mock-Gothic façade, lie myriad winding streets, some built over the ruins of the Roman amphitheatre of Florentia and still following its curve. These narrow pedestrian lanes are mostly given over to leather factories and tiny souvenir shops, but borgo degli Albizi is a main shopping street with local designer clothes, shoe and gift shops housed on the ground floors of the dour *palazzi*.

Back at the head of piazza Santa Croce, via dei Benci runs down towards the Arno, dotted with crafts shops and bohemian restaurants, past the eclectic **Museo Horne** (*see p96*) to Ponte alle Grazie. Until they were demolished in the 19th century, there were several oratories and chapels and a few workshops on its piers. One of them, devoted to Santa Maria delle Grazie, was much visited by distraught lovers seeking solace, and gave the bridge its name. Also on the bridge was a tiny convent where several nuns cloistered themselves for life.

The architect Alverti died in another of its chapels. The original stone bridge, which was built in 1227, was the only one in Florence to survive a flood in 1333. It was destroyed during World War II and replaced by the present structure in 1957.

Follow lungarno delle Grazie or corso dei Tintori, named after the dyers who lived here in medieval times, to the point where the roads open out into a main parking square, dominated by the **Biblioteca Nazionale**. The national library, built to house the three million books and two million documents that were held in the Uffizi until 1935, has two towers with statues of Dante and Galileo, nicknamed by Florentines 'the asses' ears' in mock disrespect.

Behind Santa Croce up past the **Casa Buonarroti** in via Ghibellina, it's a different scene, with a young, alternative element manifesting itself in ads for tattooists, graffiti and flyers for gigs and benefits at the student centres. At the heart of this district are the fruit and veg market of **Sant' Ambrogio** (*see p150*), piazza dei Ciompi, and the shops, bars, *pizzerie* and restaurants of borgo La Croce and piazza Ghiberti, including the renowned **Cibreo** (*see p115*). Borgo La Croce extends as far as piazza Beccaria and the east city gate, the Porta alla Croce.

Named after the dyers' and wool-workers' revolt of 1378, piazza dei Ciompi is given over to a junk/antiques market during the week and a huge day-long flea-market on the last Sunday of the month. It's dominated by the **Loggia del Pesce**, built by Vasari in 1568 for the Mercato Vecchio, which occupied the site of piazza della Repubblica. Taken apart in the 19th century and re-erected here, it now shelters a bookstand.

On the north-east of the Santa Croce area is the synagogue in via Farina, and above it the children's playground in piazza d'Azeglio, a light, spacious garden surrounded by prestigious apartment blocks and hotels.

Bacchus. *See p94.*

Bargello

Via del Proconsolo 4 (055 238 8606). **Open** 8.15am-1.50pm Tue-Sat, 2nd & 4th Sun, 1st, 3rd & 5th Mon of month. **Admission** L8,000 (€4.10). **No credit cards**. **Map** p315 C4.

This dour, fortified building started life as the Palazzo del Popolo in 1250 and soon became the seat of the Podestà, the chief magistrate. In the 14th century the

Giambologna's aviary includes his **Adler**.

eclectic and prestigious, ranging from prime sculptures by the likes of Michelangelo, Donatello, Cellini and Giambologna to Scandinavian chess sets and Egyptian ivories. The most famous pieces are Michelangelo's androgynous *Bacchus* and Giambologna's fleet-of-foot *Mercury*, and the *David*s of Donatello. The first-floor loggia in the courtyard has Giambologna's virtuoso aviary of bronze birds, including a madly exaggerated turkey. This leads to the Salone Donatello with his two triumphant *David*s and tense *Saint George*, the original sculpture that once adorned one of the tabernacles on the outside of Orsanmichele. Also fascinating are the two bronze panels of the *Sacrifice of Isaac*, sculpted by Brunelleschi and Lorenzo Ghiberti for a competition to design the north doors of the Duomo Baptistery.

bodies of executed criminals were displayed in the courtyard and in the 15th century law courts, prisons and torture chambers were set up inside. It didn't get its present name until the 16th century, when the Medici made it the seat of the chief of police, the Bargello. In 1865 it opened as a museum.

The museum has done its utmost to purge itself of its past; the collection is one of the city's most

Casa Buonarroti

Via Ghibellina 70 (055 241 752/fax 055 241 698). **Open** 9.30am-2pm Mon, Wed-Sun. **Admission** L12,000 (€6.20). **No credit cards. Map** p315 C5.
Michelangelo owned but never actually lived in this house, and this collection of memorabilia, which was put together by the artist's great-nephew Filippo, is

Walk 3 Beyond the beaten track

The fact that Florence is surrounded by hills on three sides means it has a humid climate, but it also means it's easy to get out of the city and into the 'country' relatively quickly. Most visitors at some point trek up toward piazzale Michelangelo, San Miniato or Fiesole, but there are plenty of other walks along the maze of narrow lanes that lace the nearby hills to carry you far away from the heat and the crowds.

The walk suggested below starts right in the centre of town, but it's just one of dozens of routes that take in some surprisingly rural scenery and plenty of to-die-for villas and gardens. South of the river, where there's little suburban sprawl, such walks begin almost immediately.

Ponte Vecchio to Porta Romana
About 45min

Set off down via Guicciardini from the south side of the Ponte Vecchio, keeping to the left-hand side of the road. After a few metres, turn left into piazza Santa Felicità and from the far right-hand side of the square, pick up cobbled costa San Giorgio, which climbs steeply above the river. At the top, the road passes under the old city gate of Porta San Giorgio and Forte di Belvedere on the right.

Continue straight on and the road becomes via di San Leonardo, essentially a country

lane that's heavy with the scents of wisteria and hawthorn in spring. If you're tall enough, peek over the high walls on either side for a glimpse of olive groves, fields and open vistas, not to mention the superb villas that line the road. After about a kilometre, just before you reach viale Michelangelo, there's a little road to the right (via Schiaparelli) that comes out on busy viale Machiavelli. Turn right, and after about 50 metres (55 yards) hang another right into via del Bobolino. Follow this lane downhill and you'll arrive in a magical little collection of houses grouped around a quiet *piazzetta*, that seem quite cut off from the rest of the city.

Bear left down via Madonna della Pace and at the end of the road you'll come to an iron fence. Look for a little gate along the fence that is open daily all year from 7am to 8pm. This will take you into the overgrown garden of the Istituto d'Arte, which is full of students during school hours and a favourite haunt of dog-walkers and mothers with babies at weekends. Trees provide shade, and it's a good place for a picnic.

From here you'll find that the southern boundary of the Boboli gardens is now on your right; follow the fence to come out at Porta Romana. A short walk (or buses 11, 36 or 37) brings you back to the centre of town.

a bit contrived, though there are some interesting reproductions of scenes from the painter's life painted on the walls of La Galleria, and two original works, a bas-relief *Madonna della Scala* breastfeeding at the foot of a flight of stairs and an unfinished *Battaglia dei Centauri*.

Museo di Antropologia e Etnologia

Via del Proconsolo 12 (055 239 6449). **Open** 9am-1pm Mon, Wed-Sun. **Admission** L6,000 (€3.10). **No credit cards.** Map p315 B4.

A mixed bag of goodies from all over the world – a collection of Peruvian mummies, an Ostyak harp in the shape of a swan from Lapland, an engraved trumpet made from an elephant tusk from the former Belgian Congo, Ecuadorian shrunken heads complete with a specially designed skull-beating club (called a *tupinamba*), and a Marini-meets-Picasso equestrian monument.

Museo Fiorentino di Preistoria

Via Sant'Egidio 21 (055 295 159). **Open** 9.30am-12.30pm Mon-Sat; guided tours by appointment. **Admission** L6,000 (€3.10). **No credit cards.** Map p315 B4.

This museum traces humanity's development from the Paleolithic to the Bronze Age. The first floor follows hominid physical changes, and also examines Italy's prehistoric artistic legacy. Unfortunately, the evidence is for the most part in caves, so the museum has to make do with photos and illustrations. The second floor covers the rest of the world and includes a collection of stone implements found by Frenchman Boucher de Perthes, who ascertained that rocks previously believed to have been shaped by weathering and glacial movment were actually the work of prehistoric humans.

Museo di Firenze com'era

Via dell'Oriuolo 24 (055 261 6545). **Open** 9am-2pm Mon-Wed, Fri, Sat; 8am-1pm Sun. **Admission** L5,000 (€2.60). **No credit cards.** Map p315 B5.

This charmingly named museum of 'Florence as it was' traces the city's development through collections of maps, paintings and archaeological discoveries. There's a room devoted to Giuseppe Poggi's plans from the 1860s to modernise Florence by creating Parisian-style boulevards; the famous lunettes of the Medici villas painted in 1599 by Flemish artist

Sightseeing

The view from San Miniato.

Giusto Utens; and a room charting the history of the region from 200 million years ago to Roman times. New exhibits include a model of 'Florentia', showing how the city must have been in Roman times, with the Forum right underneath present-day piazza della Repubblica and a Roman theatre buried under the Palazzo Vecchio.

Museo Horne

Via dei Benci 6 (055 244 661). **Open** 9am-1pm Mon-Sat. **Admission** L10,000 (€5.20). **No credit cards**. **Map** p315 C4.

The 15th-century Palazzo Corsi-Alberti was bought by English architect and art historian Herbert Percy Horne in the late 19th century. When he died he left it and his vast, magpie-like collection to the state, and in 1922 it opened as a museum. Objects on the ground floor range from ceramics and Florentine coins to a coffee grinder and pair of spectacles. Upstairs is a damaged wooden panel from a triptych attributed to Masaccio, relating the story of San Giuliano, a medieval Oedipus who came home early one day to find his mother in bed with a man and killed them both before realising the man was his father. In repentance he cut off his right arm and became a devout Christian. Also here is an *Exorcism* by the Maestro di San Severino and, the pride of the Horne collection, a gold-back *Santo Stefano* by Giotto. Other famous works include a limbless statue of an athlete by Giambologna and a painted wedding chest by Filippino Lippi.

Museo dell'Opera di Santa Croce

Piazza Santa Croce 16 (055 244 619). **Open** 10am-7pm Mon, Tue, Thur-Sun. **Admission** L8,000 (€4.10). **No credit cards**. **Map** p315 C5.

A ticket into the cloisters of Santa Croce is worth it, even if the museum is not the highlight. The backbone of the collection is in the former refectory with Taddeo Gaddi's *Last Supper*, the impact of which is reduced due to its bad condition and the imposing yet poetic *Albero della Vita* ('Tree of Life') above. In equally poor condition is Cimabué's *Crucifixion*, which hung in the basilica until the flood of 1966. On the opposite wall is a pious *St Louis of Toulouse* cast in bronze by Donatello. There's also a small permanent exhibition of the woodcuts and engravings of Pietro Parigi, whose reawakening of the Tuscan realism in religious illustrations earned him fame.

Santa Croce

Piazza Santa Croce (055 244 619). **Open** *Summer* 9.30am-5.30pm Mon-Sat; 3-5.30pm Sun. *Winter* 9.30am-12.30pm, 3-5.30pm Mon-Sat; 3-5.30pm Sun. **Admission** free. **Map** p315 C5.

Santa Croce is filled with the tombs of the city's illustrious; oddly so, given that the church belonged to the Franciscans, the most unworldly of the religious orders. They founded it in 1228, ten years after arriving in the city. A recently established order, they were supposed to make their living by manual work,

preaching and begging. At the time, Santa Croce was a slum, full of the city's grossly underpaid dyers and wool-workers. Franciscan preaching, with its message that all men were equal, had a huge impact on the poor people of the quarter, and it was in part due to the confidence given them by the Franciscans that, in 1378, the dyers and wool-makers revolted against the guilds and were allowed to organise their own. As for the Franciscans, their vow of poverty slowly eroded. By the late 13th century, the old church was felt to be inadequate and a new church was planned – intended to be one of the largest in Christendom, and probably designed by Arnolfo di Cambio, architect of the Duomo and the Palazzo Vecchio. It was financed partly by property confiscated from Ghibellines who had been convicted of heresy.

Santa Croce remains the richest medieval church in the city, with frescoes by Giotto, a chapel by Brunelleschi and one of the finest of all early Renaissance tombs. At first sight the interior is too big, too gloomy, with too many overbearing marble tombs clogging the walls. Not all the tombs contain bodies: Dante's (right aisle) is simply a memorial to the writer, who is buried in Ravenna. In the niche alongside is the tomb of Michelangelo – he actually died in Rome, but his body was brought back to Florence. Further down is the tomb of Leonardo Bruni by Bernardo Rossellini. Back at the top of the left aisle is Galileo's tomb, a polychrome marble confection that was created more than a century after the astronomer's death, when the Church finally permitted him a Christian burial, having previously branded him a heretic (*see p74* **Who he?**).

Cappelle Bardi and Cappelle Peruzzi, which were completely frescoed by Giotto, are more interesting, although they're not in brilliant condition – a result of Giotto painting on dry instead of wet plaster (a technique that's known as *secco*) and them being daubed with whitewash in the 18th century. The most striking of the two chapels is the Bardi, with scenes from the life of St Francis in haunting, virtual monotone, the figures just stylised enough to make them otherworldly yet individual enough to make them human. On the far side of the high altar is the Cappella Bardi di Vernio, frescoed by one of Giotto's most interesting followers, Maso di Banco, and recently restored in fresh, vibrant colours.

To get to the Cappella dei Pazzi, Brunelleschi's geometric *tour de force*, you have to leave the church and go through the cloister. Planned in the 1430s and completed 40 years later, it's based on a central square topped by a cupola, flanked by two barrel-vaulted bays with decorative arches on the white walls echoing the structural arches. Across the courtyard is **Museo dell'Opera di Santa Croce**, a small museum of church treasures, including a 13th-century crucifix by Cimabué that was badly damaged in the 1966 flood and Donatello's *St Louis of Toulouse* from Orsanmichele.

Oltrarno

The grand Palazzo Pitti aside, the easy-to-reach Oltrarno is locals' Florence.

The Oltrarno, which literally means 'beyond the Arno', spans the width of the city centre south of the river, tapering down to Porta Romana, the city gate leading out to Rome.

Borgo San Jacopo, on the river between Ponte Vecchio and Ponte Santa Trinità, is an odd mix of medieval towers and *palazzi*, shops and '60s council-block-style monstrosities built to replace the *palazzi* bombed in the war. The street leads, via a warren of tiny alleys bordered by the splendid *palazzi* of the antique-shop-lined via Maggio, to via dei Guicciardini with its expensive paper, crafts and jewellery shops and the grandeur of the Medici's gargantuan **Palazzo Pitti** (*see p99*).

The Palazzo's chunkily rusticated façade bears down on its sloping forecourt, dwarfing the tourists who've come to visit its museums or wander around the **Boboli Gardens** behind it. It was built in 1457 for Luca Pitti, a rival of the Medici, probably to a design by

Brunelleschi that had been rejected by Cosimo il Vecchio as too grandiose. It was also too grandiose for the Pitti, and less than a century later they were forced to sell to the doubtless gleeful Medici. The palace was more luxurious than draughty old Palazzo Vecchio and in 1549 Cosimo I and his wife Eleonora di Toledo moved in. Huge as it was, it wasn't big enough for the Medici, and Ammanati (he of the dubious *Neptune* fountain, *see p71*) was charged with remodelling the façade and creating the courtyard, with columns threaded through huge stone doughnuts. The façade was extended in the 17th century and two further wings added in the 18th century. The *palazzo* now holds the vast, opulent Medici collection.

South-east of Ponte Vecchio, snaking steeply uphill towards **Forte di Belvedere** (*see p98*), the Medici's summer retreat, are the *costas* – picturesque lanes with a country feel reaching as far as Porta San Giorgio. Past piazza dei Mozzi, with the **Museo Bardini** (*see p98*), and behind lungarno Serristori and its **Museo di Casa Siviero** (*see p99*), is San Niccolò, a sleepy village district until the evenings, when the wine bars and Tuscan *osterie* fill and the bars on via dei Renai overflow on to the pavements of the pretty riverside square. The edge of San Niccolò is signalled by Porta di San Niccolò in piazza Poggi, but turn right before then into via San Miniato and cross Porta San Miniato to via del Monte alle Croci to get to a delightful short cut on the left – a long trail of lichen-covered steps that come straight out into the famed tourist pilgrimage destination, **piazzale Michelangiolo** (*see p105*).

West of Ponte Vecchio, the bohemian areas Santo Spirito and San Frediano are named after their churches. **Piazza Santo Spirito** is a lively but low-key and laid-back space that – by day at least – still very much belongs to the locals. Furniture restorers have workshops just off the square, nearby *trattorie* serve good, cheap food, there's a daily market, and organic food markets and fleamarkets often spill across the piazza on Sundays. The bars and al fresco restaurants serve as meeting places for a pre-clubbing, arty crowd, and in summer a huge bar is set up in the middle of the square and crowds sit on the steps of the remarkable church of **Santo Spirito** (*see p100*), drinking beer and playing guitars. A constant police presence

Sightseeing

Life in the slow lane in **Piazza Poggi**.

Corridoio Vasariano and behind it the **Duomo** seen from via de' Guicciardini.

keeps an eye out for the dealers who frequent the piazza in the evenings, as well as the winos and homeless people looking for a place to sleep.

That said, both Santo Spirito and San Frediano have become gentrified over the past ten years. Santo Spirito in particular is now one of the most desirable residential areas in the city, and property prices have skyrocketed.

South of the piazza, via Romana is a narrow main road lined with unusual craft and antiques shops and **La Specola** (*see p100*), the zoology museum. On the far side of via dei Serragli, in San Frediano, things are even more villagey but not much quieter; by day local artisans bustle around with picture frames or weird pieces of furniture under their arms; by night piazza del Carmine, home to **Santa Maria del Carmine** church and the **Brancacci Chapel** (*for both, see p100*) fills up in direct correlation with the temperature, with the smart set congregating outside the **Dolce Vita** bar (*see p132*). For a genuine taste of Florence, walk west into borgo San Frediano, which extends to Porta San Frediano, home to the gate itself (built in 1332 by Andrea Pisano), the 18th-century baroque church and a couple of small *trattorie*, mainly frequented by locals.

Cenacolo di Santo Spirito

Piazza Santo Spirito 29 (055 287 043). **Open** 9am-2pm daily. **Admission** L4,000 (€2.10). **No credit cards. Map** p314 D1.

The *Last Supper* by Andrea Orcagna is not the foremost reason for visiting this former Augustinian refectory – the fresco was butchered

by an 18th-century architect commissioned to build some doors into it so it could be used as a carriage depot. Today only the fringes remain, although there's a more complete but heavily restored *Crucifixion* above. Otherwise, the museum houses an eclectic collection of sculptures given to the state in 1946 on the death of sailor Salvatore Romano, who considered his body in its sarcophagus a worthy partner to sculptures by Tino di Camaino and reliefs by Donatello.

Forte di Belvedere

Via San Leonardo (055 27681). **Map** p314 D3.
This star-shaped fortress was built by Bernardo Buontalenti in 1590. Originally intended to protect the city from foreign enemies or insurgent natives, it soon became a refuge for the Medici grand dukes. Ongoing restorations mean that the fort is unlikely to reopen to visitors during the life of this guide.

Museo Bardini

Piazza dei Mozzi 1 (055 234 2427). **Open** 9am-2pm Mon, Tue, Thur-Sat; 8am-1pm Sun. Closed for restoration until 2002. **Admission** L6,000 (€3.10). **No credit cards. Map** p314 D4.

Art dealer Stefano Bardini, who built this *palazzo* in 1881 on the foundations of a ruined 13th-century church, using ceilings, doors and fireplaces salvaged from other palaces, bequeathed his huge collection to the city on his death in 1922. It's partly uncatalogued – Bardini, no fan of writing, saw no need to record details. The eccentric pieces on display include muskets, daggers, musical instruments and Persian and Anatolian carpets. There are also some pleasing Etruscan sculptures and two unusual Donatello *Madonna*s (Room 14).

Museo di Casa Siviero

Lungarno Serristori 1/3 (055 234 5219/guided tours 055 293 007). **Open** 9.30am-12.30pm Mon; 3.30-6.30pm Sat. **Admission** free. **Map** p314 D4.
This museum was previously the house of Rodolfo Siviero, dubbed 'the James Bond of art' for his relentless efforts to prevent the Nazis plundering Italian masters during the war; those that were taken he subsequently retrieved. The paintings and antiques on display reflect his appreciation of various artistic styles. Visits are supervised by friendly guides.

Palazzo Pitti

Piazza Pitti, Via Romana. **Map** p314 D1.

Boboli Gardens

055 290 832/3. **Open** *June-Aug* 8.15am-7.30pm daily. *Nov-Feb* 8.15am-5pm daily. *Mar* 8.15am-5.30pm daily. *Apr, May, Sept, Oct* 8.15am-7pm daily. Closed 1st & last Mon of month. **Admission** including entrance to Museo di Porcellana L4,000 (€2.10). **No credit cards**. **Map** p314 D1-3.
The Giardini di Boboli, the only park in central Florence and much loved as a place to chill out on summer days, was laid out by a number of artists for Eleonora di Toledo and Cosimo I. Bandinelli created a grotto for Eleonora, complete with casts of Michelangelo's *Prigionieri* and Ammanati- and Giambologna-designed fountains. The gardens, which run up to the Forte di Belvedere (no access) and down to the Porta Romana, are beautifully kept, and the hilly site is taken full advantage of. Be sure to wander along the Viottolone, a long avenue lined with cypresses, and stop at the rococo Kaffeehaus (1776) to gaze out over the city. Other highlights include L'Isolotto, a miniature island in a circular lake with a copy of Giambologna's *Oceanus* charging through the waters; the Amphitheatre, created in the gap left after stone had been quarried for the Palazzo and the venue where Jacopo Peri's and Giulio Caccini's *Euridice* (widely acknowledged to be the first ever opera) was staged for the Medici in 1600; and the repulsive Bacchus fountain, a copy of a 16th-century statue showing Cosimo I's dwarf as a nude Bacchus. On summer evenings the gardens host prestigious ballets, plays and fashion shows.

Galleria d'Arte Moderna

055 238 8616. **Open** 8.15am-1.50pm Tue-Sat (last entry 1.15pm), 2nd & 4th Mon of month, 1st, 3rd & 5th Sun of month. **Admission** L8,000 (€4.10). **No credit cards**.
The newly ordered and arranged 30 rooms on the top floor of the Pitti that now constitute Florence's modern art museum were royal apartments until 1920. The varied collection, which comprises works bought by the state, those belonging to the Florentine grand dukes and paintings donated by private collectors, has everything from neo-classical to early 20th-century art (modern being a relative term in Florence). Among the highlights are Giovanni Dupré's forceful bronze sculptures of Cain and Abel in Room 5 and Ottone Rosai's simple *Piazza del Carmine* in Room 30. There are also some

disaster areas – Rooms 11, 12, 18 and 19 all house work by the Macchiaioli school, which built up paintings using dots (*macchie*).

Museo del Costume

055 238 8713. **Open** 8.15am-1.50pm Tue-Sat (last entry 1.15pm), 2nd & 4th Mon of month, 1st, 3rd & 5th Sun of month. **Admission** L8,000 (€4.10). **No credit cards**.
The costume museum is next to Palazzina della Meridiana, which periodically served as residence to members of the Lorraine family and the House of Savoy and is marked out for a permanent exhibition of the works no longer on show in the Modern Art Museum, painted by the Romantic artists whose work also decorates the rooms. The archives include early 15th-century costumes, early 18th-century *robes a la française* and *fin de siècle* attire by Rosa Genoni, inspired by Botticelli and Pisanello. Due to go on display by 2002 is a collection of women's clothes from the early 1900s to the 1950s.

Galleria del Palatina & Appartamenti Reali

055 238 8614. **Open** 8.15am-6.50pm Tue-Sun. **Admission** L12,000 (€6.20). **No credit cards**.
The Galleria has paintings hung four or five high on its damask walls, in rooms busy with *pietra dura* and malachite tables. Included in the collection are a beautiful Filippo Lippi, *Madonna and Child*, which shows his sophisticated understanding of line, colour and form, and several works by Raphael – the coyly sweet *Madonna della Seggiola*, the serene *Madonna del Granduca* and the innovative *Holy Family*, his last painting and one that shows his susceptibility to the influences of Michelangelo. In addition, there are some inspired works by Titian.
There are 28 rooms in all; linger longest over the 'Planet Rooms' – five rooms named after Venus, Mercury (Apollo), Mars, Jupiter and Saturn, supposedly in honour of Galileo Galilei. The Venus Room, the Sala di Venere, is dominated by a statue of the goddess by Canova and crowned by a gilded stucco ceiling, and contains Titian's regal *La Bella*; the Sala di Apollo, over-decorated like the other planet rooms by Pietro da Cortona, houses the nine Muses in the pendentives and is crowded with works by Rosso Fiorentino and Andrea del Sarto, and with yet more Titian masterpieces. Mars, the Sala di Marte, houses Rubens' *Consequences of War* and his *Four Philosophers*, which contains a suitably detached self-portrait (the standing figure on the left). The best place to look in the Jupiter Room, the Sala di Giove, is up, in order to admire the depiction of Jupiter with his eagle and his lightning, surrounded by the Virtues, Hercules and Chance. Also look out for Raphael's lover, the 'baker girl' Margherita Luti, in his *La Velata*. The Sala di Saturno, the last of the Planet Rooms, contains some of Raphael's best-known works, including the *Madonna del Granduca*, showing a distinct Leonardo influence. The other rooms of the Palatine also follow a noticeably classical style, with names such as Allegory, Prometheus, Hercules, Ulysses and Iliad.

Museo degli Argenti

055 238 8710. **Open** 8.30am-6.30pm Tue-Sat, 2nd & 4th Mon of month. **Admission** L4,000 (€2.10). **No credit cards**.

A two-storey museum full of treasures amassed by the Medici, from beautiful vases and ornate crystal cups to a breathtakingly banal collection of miniature animals. There's also a fabulous display of Chinese and Japanese ceramics.

Museo delle Porcellane

055 238 8710. **Open** same as Boboli Gardens. **Admission** *included in ticket for Boboli Gardens* L4,000 (€2.10). **No credit cards**.

At the top of the Boboli Gardens, this former reception room for artists, built by Leopoldo de' Medici, offers inspiring views over the Tuscan hills. The museum displays china used by the various occupants of Palazzo Pitti and includes the largest selection of Viennese china outside Vienna. Look out for the rare oyster stand from Sèvres and the teapot in the shape of a hen from the Meissen factory.

Museo delle Carrozze

055 238 8614. **Closed for restoration**.

A collection of carriages once belonging to the Medici, Lorraine and Savoy houses.

Santa Felicità

Piazza Santa Felicità (055 213 018). **Open** 9am-noon, 3-6pm Mon-Sat; 9am-1pm Sun except 9am & noon services. **Admission** free. **Map** p314 D2.

This little church occupies the site of the first church in Florence, founded in the second century by Syrian Greek tradesmen who settled in the area, but there are no traces of its ancient beginnings – the interior is largely 18th century. The portico was built by Vasari in 1564 to support the Corridoio Vasariano, the overhead walkway that connected Palazzo Pitti with Palazzo Vecchio and the Uffizi. The main reason to visit is Pontormo's *Deposition* altarpiece.

Santa Maria del Carmine & the Brancacci Chapel

Piazza del Carmine (055 238 2195). **Open** chapel 9am-5pm Mon, Wed-Sat; 1-5pm Sun. **Admission** L6,000 (€3.10). **No credit cards**. **Map** p314 C1.

Santa Maria del Carmine is a blowsy baroque church dominated by a huge single nave, adorned with pilasters and pious sculptures overlooked by a ceiling fresco of *The Ascension*. It was built in 1782 to replace a medieval church belonging to the Carmelite order, most of which burned down in 1771. Miraculously, the Brancacci Chapel, matchlessly frescoed in the 15th century by Masaccio and Masolino, escaped damage.

The artists were an odd pair with little in common other than the fact that they were both born in the Val d'Arno; Masolino was a court painter, his graceful style still in tune with the decorative international Gothic traditions of artists such as Gentile da Fabriano, while Masaccio was a more modern, innovative painter who worked mostly for monks and local priests – his work is more realistic,

driven and emotive. When he died aged just 27 he'd changed the direction of art forever (*see p107*). Compare Masolino's elegant Adam and Eve in The Temptation with Masaccio's masterpiece, the grief-stricken couple in the Expulsion from Paradise, or Masolino's dandified Florentines in their silks and brocades with Masaccio's simple saints. There are two themes to the paintings: the redemption of sinners, and scenes from the life of St Peter. Work on the frescoes stopped for 60 years after Masaccio's death, and was then taken up again by Filippino Lippi, whose most striking contribution was *The Release of St Peter*. The frescoes were restored in the 1980s (the work was financed by Olivetti), and there are strict rules about how many people can visit (visits are limited to 15 minutes).

Santo Spirito

Piazza Santo Spirito (055 210 030). **Open** 8am-noon, 4-6pm, Mon, Tue, Thur-Sun; 8am-noon Wed. **Admission** free. **Map** p314 D2-3.

One of Brunelleschi's most remarkable buildings, though you wouldn't know it from the consummately plain cream 18th-century façade. Step inside, however, and you enter a world of perfect proportions, a Latin-cross church surrounded by a continuous colonnade of dove grey *pietra serena* columns. There had been an Augustinian church on the site since 1250, but in 1397 the monks decided to replace it, cutting out one meal a day to finance the project. Eventually they commissioned Brunelleschi to design it. Work started in 1444, two years before Brunelleschi died, and the façade and exterior walls were never finished; Vasari reckoned that had the church been completed as planned it would have been 'the most perfect temple of Christianity'. It's hard to disagree. To the left of the church is the Cenacolo di Santo Spirito museum (*see p98*).

La Specola

Via Romana 17 (055 228 8251). **Open** 9am-1pm Mon, Tue, Thur-Sun. **Admission** L6,000 (€3.10). **No credit cards**. **Map** p314 D1.

Known as La Specola ('observatory') because of the telescope on the roof, this is actually Florence's zoology museum. The first 23 rooms are crammed with stuffed and pickled animals, including a hippopotamus given to Grand Duke Pietro Leopoldo that used to be kept in the Boboli Gardens. Room 9 has a repulsive collection of hunting trophies donated by the Count of Turin, including an elephant-skin sofa. From Room 24 onwards, the exhibits become still more grotesque – in a Frankensteinesque laboratory, wax corpses lie on satin beds, each a little more dissected than the last, and walls are covered with dismembered and perfectly realistic body parts: (limbs, organs and sections) crafted as teaching aids between 1771 and the late 1800s by artist Clemente Susini and physiologist Felice Fontana. Also look out for the gory tableaux devoted to Florence during the plague, made by Sicilian wax sculptor Giulio Gaetano Zumbo. Not for sensitive souls.

Outside the City Gates

Break out of the centre for a balanced view of Florence.

Though there's not much left of Florence's medieval walls, eight of the 16 original gates into the city are still standing and are now more or less linked to each other by the ring road or *viale*, allowing for a natural division. Most visitors stick to the relatively small area inside the gates without realising that there's a lot to see beyond them.

To the north, south and east, Florence is hemmed in by hills – this fact is largely responsible for the damp climate but also means there's a natural barrier against urban sprawl and allows you to get up into what feels like the country – narrow lanes winding through olive groves and dotted with fabulous villas – quickly. This is particularly true south of the river, where hills practically rise from the banks of the Arno. To the north genteel suburbia extends further before being thwarted by the hills that lead up to Fiesole and Settignano, while to the east development follows the Arno for some kilometres.

This isn't to say that Florence is devoid of suburban ugliness – to the west and north-west of the centre unimaginative housing and industrial development have claimed swathes of land, creating such *quartieri* as Brozzi, Campi Bisenzio, Scandicci and Sesto Fiorentino. Firenze Nova, a 'new' satellite city and administrative centre, is being built on reclaimed land to the west (*see p23* **The future starts here**). But even these areas have odd rays of light in the form of elegant villas built in the countryside but now incongruously flanked by uninspiring blocks of flats.

North of the river

Any round-up of attractions beyond the city walls has to begin with the **Parco delle Cascine** in the west. A green oasis just beyond Porta al Prato and outside the carbon-monoxide hell of the *viale*, this 3.5 kilometre (two mile) long public park stretches along the north bank of the Arno. Its name comes from *cascina*, meaning dairy farm, which is what the Medici originally used the area as. Later it became a hunting park and, simultaneously, a space for theatre and public spectacles. Shelley wrote his 'Ode to the West Wind' here in 1819, and in 1870 the body of the Maharaja of Kohlapur (who died in Florence) was burned on a funeral

pyre at the far end of the park marked by an equestrian statue. Today the park is full of children on bikes, rollerbladers, joggers and Florentines out for a stroll. It hosts a huge market on Tuesday mornings (*see p150*) and contains a riding school, racetrack and tennis courts. At night transvestites strut their stuff along the parallel *viale*.

North-east of the Cascine along viale Rosselli is the restored but monstrous **Fortezza da Basso**, Florence's main exhibition centre. Commissioned from Antonio da Sangallo by Alessandro de' Medici (who met his death within its ugly walls) in 1534, it's a prototype of 16th-century military architecture.

Five minutes' walk beyond the Fortezza, among elegant residential *palazzi*, are the five rather incongruous polychrome onion domes of Florence's exquisite **Russian Orthodox church** (via Leone X). Designed by Russian architects and completed in 1904, it's a reminder that the city was once popular with such wealthy Russians as Dostoevsky, Tchaikovsky, Maxim Gorky et al as a retreat from harsh winters back home. The only access to the interior is during the monthly (third Sunday) Russian-language service.

Directly north of here is **Museo Stibbert** (via Stibbert 26, 055 475 520, admission L8,000/€4.10, closed Mon-Wed afternoon, Thur), whose bizarre collection of everything from paintings to snuff boxes once belonged to Fredrick Stibbert (1838-1906), a brother-in-arms with Garibaldi in the name of Italian unification. Stibbert was born of an English father and Italian mother, who left him her 14th-century house; he bought the neighbouring mansion and had the two joined together to house his collection. The linking room between the *palazzi*, Sala della Cavalcata, houses a troop of horses with fully clad knights and footmen – Freddie had a penchant for war memorabilia and weaponry. Among the 50,000 items crammed into 64 rooms are a handpainted harpsichord, chalices and crucifixes and even an attributed Botticelli. The garden, which is really a small park, is a delightfully cool escape in the summer months.

Piazza della Libertà, the focal point of northern access to the city, is home to the massive and rather graceless triumphal arch built to mark the arrival in Florence of the

Secret gardens

Florence can seem less than lush, but in fact it's full of secret oases of green hidden away behind thick walls and iron gates but perfectly accessible to visitors in the know.

Good starting points are the universities, many of which will allow free visits by appointment. The formal garden of **Villa Le Balze** (via Vecchia Fiesolana 26, Fiesole, fax 055 599 584 for appointment, bus 7), Florence base of Georgetown University, was designed by English landscape gardener Cecil Pinsent and gives one of the best views in the whole city. Another Pinsent-designed delight, with its boxwood hedges, sweeping stone steps and mosaic pebble paths, can be found at **Villa I Tatti** (via di Vincigliata 26, Fiesole, call 055 603 251 ten days in advance for a Tuesday or Wednesday appointment, bus 7).

Florence University's **Orto Botanico** and **Giardino dei Semplici** (see p91), open to any museum-weary feet, house myriad rare plants, herbs and trees. For hilltop adventurers the University's **Villa La Quiete** (via di Boldrone 2, 055 450 634, due to re-open Nov 2001, bus 28), named after a 1633 fresco by Giovanni da San Giovanni called *Stillness Dominating the Winds*, lives up to its title in its calming Italian garden and lemon groves. **Villa La Pietra** (via Bolognese 120, 055 50071, due to open in 2002, bus 25), with its cypress boulevard and moss-covered statues, was once owned by the Capponi family, then used as the Prussian Embassy, and later became the property of Lord Acton, who bequeathed it to New York University. Visitors need to get written permission from the director.

Capponi is a recurring name in gardens – the family-owned **Villa Capponi** (via Pian dei Giullari 3, 055 223 465 for group visits, bus 12, 13) was home to Lady Scott, grandmother of the Queen Mother, and its garden is a wonderland of secret and griffin-guarded rose gardens, topiaries and a pool

(see p102)

eighth grand duke of Tuscany in 1744. From here, the 7 bus (the stop is on the north-eastern side of the piazza or you can catch it from the station) goes up to **Fiesole** (*see p102*), passing some of the superb villas and gardens that dot the hillside on the way up.

Back down in town and east of piazza della Libertà is Pier Luigi Nervi's huge football stadium, the **Stadio Comunale** near Campo di Marte. Built in 1932 and used for football matches (most notably those involving home team Fiorentina; *see p189*) plus the odd rock concert, it has a capacity of 66,000 and is one of the few modern buildings in Florence with any architectural merit.

Not far south-east is the **Museo del Cenacolo di Andrea del Sarto** (via San Salvi 16, 055 238 8603, admission free, opening times vary). Another refectory cum museum, this was part of the monastery of San Salvi, used by the Vallombrosan order. The highlight is the *Last Supper* (1526-7) by Andrea del Sarto, a godfather of mannerism, whose careful study of form, movement and colour give the work a tangible tension. There are also works by his pupil Pontormo, whose mannerist tendencies are even stronger. The adjacent monastery buildings now house a psychiatric hospital.

Back on the *viale* is the **Cimitero degli Inglesi** or English cemetery (piazzale Donatello 38, 055 582 608, admission by donation, closed Tue-Fri morning, Sat, Sun, Mon afternoon).

Opened in 1827, it tries in vain to be a tree-filled oasis. All sorts of Anglo-Florentines were buried here, among them Elizabeth Barrett Browning, Walter Savage Landor and Frances Trollope (Anthony's mum).

Fiesole & around

This lovely little town, now essentially part of Florence, can get as packed as the city, though fortunately the masses that invade Faesulae (as it was known to the Etruscans) come mainly in high summer, and most of them leave at night.

Without Fiesole there would have been no Florence – the stubborn Etruscan hill-town proved so difficult for the Romans to subdue that they set up camp in the river valley below. When they eventually took Fiesole, it became one of the most important towns in Etruria, remaining independent until the 12th century, when Florence finally vanquished it in battle.

Fiesole soon found a new role as a refined suburb where aristocrats could escape the heat and hoi polloi of Florence. In the 14th century it was to its villas that Boccaccio sent his courtly raconteurs to escape the plague and tell the stories of *The Decameron*; half a millennium later, it was here that EM Forster had his corsetted Edwardians picnic and Lucy have her first kiss in *Room with a View*.

Some 14,000 people live in Fiesole today. The main square, **piazza Mino**, named after the

Villa Camponi.

surrounded by cypress trees and Hellenic statues. The Capponis had a hand in making another privately owned garden, that of the **Villa Gamberaia** (via del Rossellino 72, Settignano, 055 697 205, bus 10, admission L15,000/€7.80) with its ilex groves and Italian garden water parterres flanked by impassive stone guard dogs.

For true enthusiasts, Florence and Fiesole councils (055 234 0444 and 055 59611 respectively) organise special visits during the spring to private gardens not normally open to the public, including **Giardino Torrigiani** (via dei Serragli 144) with its spectacular heptagonal observatory tower and tens of thousands of botanical specimens; **Orti Oricellari** (via della Scala 85), where the Rucellai made their fortune in red lichen and where you can admire a giant statue of Polyphemus; and the **Giardino Della Gherardesca**, which was the first Florentine garden to grow mandarins.

artist Mino da Fiesole, is lined with cafés and restaurants and dominated by the immense honey-stone campanile of the 11th-century **Duomo**. Inside the Duomo, columns are topped with capitals dating from Fiesole's period under Roman occupation. **Museo Bandini** (via Duprè 1, 055 59477, admission L12,000/€6.20 including Teatro Romano and Museo Archeologico, closed Tue in winter) contains a collection of 13th- to 15th-century Florentine paintings, while down the hill are more relics of Roman Fiesole – a 3,000-seater theatre, the **Teatro Romano** (via Portigiani 1, 055 59477, admission included in Museo Bandini ticket, closed Tue in winter). This was built in 1 BC and is still used for concerts and plays in summer and a complex with the remains of two temples, partially restored Roman baths and a stretch of Etruscan walls. The **Museo Archeologico** (same details as Teatro Romano; admission included in Museo Bandini ticket) houses a haul of finds from Bronze Age, Etruscan and Roman Fiesole and the Constantini collection of Greek vases.

Head up via San Francesco to see the church of **Sant'Alessandro**, founded in the fifth or sixth century on the site of Roman and Etruscan temples. There are great views from its terrace and vibrant onion marble columns within. **San Franceso**, further up, has Chinese souvenirs brought back by missionaries.

There are some lovely walks around Fiesole;

the best is down steep, twisting via Vecchia Fiesolana to the hamlet of **San Domenico**. On the way, you pass the **Villa Medici** (to the left), built by Michelozzo for Cosimo il Vecchio and the childhood home of Anglo-American writer Iris Origo. At the bottom of the hill is the 15th-century church and convent where painter Fra Angelico was a monk, which retains a delicate *Madonna and Angels* (1420) by him. In the chapter house of the adjacent monastery is a fresco by him (ring the bell at No.4 for entry).

Opposite the church is a lane leading down to **Badia Fiesolana** (via Roccettini 9, 055 59155, admission free, closed Sat afternoon & Sun), Fiesole's cathedral until 1028, when it was enlarged. The façade incorporates the original front of the older church, elegant with its green and white marble inlay. Enter via the cloister when the church doors are closed.

The village of **Settignano** lies on the hill to the east of Fiesole. There's no public transport from Fiesole (the 10 bus goes from Florence station to Settignano) but the (long-ish) walk or drive between the two through woods and cypresses is very pleasant. There's nothing special to see, but Settignano makes for a almost tourist-free trip out of town and has a history littered with eminent names – sculptors Desiderio da Settignano and the Rossellini brothers were born here, and Michelangelo spent part of his childhood at Villa Buonarotti. It's just a pity no one left any art.

Medici villas

The area north and north-west of Florence is dotted with villas built or bought by Florence's first family. Most were used as retreats from the heat, but some were originally hunting lodges or farmhouses. The ones listed are accessible by bus (some require a bit of a walk too) from central Florence.

Villa della Petraia

Via della Petraia 40 (055 451 208). Bus 28 from station to 1st stop in via Sestese, then 10-min walk (villa is signposted). **Open** 9am-4.30pm daily (extended summer hours). Closed 2nd & 3rd Mon of month. **Admission** L4,000 (€2.10). **No credit cards**.
About 5km (3 miles) from the city centre, on a hill in the industrial suburban sprawl that characterises north-west Florence, this villa provides splendid relief from its surrounds – the terraced gardens with a bit of moat and a formal *giardino all'Italiana* are lovely. A large rectangle with a solid tower sticking out of the top, the villa was acquired by the Medici family in 1530, and frescoes depicting its history adorn the ornate glassed-in internal courtyard. There's nothing much to see within the vast rooms, though the Sala dei Giochi has a collection of 600 games, and look out for the statue with what must be the longest name in Tuscany – Giambologna's *Venus-Florence Wringing the Waters of the Arno and the Mugnone from her Hair*.

Villa di Castello

Via del Castello 40 (055 454 791). Bus 28 to 2nd stop in via Sestese. **Open** 9am-4.30pm daily (extended summer hours). Closed 2nd & 3rd Mon of month. **Admission** incl in fee for Villa della Petraia (*see above*).
Just down the hill from La Petraia, this villa is famous for its gardens laid out by Tribolo, who also designed the central fountain with its statue by Ammannati. Another of the sculptor's monumental figures, *L'Appennino* or *Gennaio* ('January'), emerges dripping and frozen from a shady pool on the terrace. But the main attraction here has go to be the bizarre Grotta degli Animali, an artificial cave with walls lined with seashells, pebbles and stalactites, filled with statues by Ammanati and Giambologna of an amazing variety of lifelike birds and animals.
The house (not open to the public), bought by the Medici in 1477, was badly damaged in the seige of 1530 and restored by Cosimo I,

Villa della Petraia: nice gaff.

who commissioned the great garden. Today it's the headquarters of the strangely named Accademia della Crusca ('Academy of Bran'), dedicated to the study of Italian.

Villa Demidoff

Via Fiorentina 6, Pratolino (055 409 427). Bus 25A. **Open** *Mar-Oct* 10am-8.30pm Thur-Sun. *Nov-Feb* 10am-6pm Sun. **Admission** L5,000 (€2.60). **No credit cards**.
Villa Demidoff, 12km (7.5 miles) north of Florence on the winding old road to Bologna, was bought by Duke Francesco in 1568 as a gift for his mistress. Buontalenti designed the gardens on a grand scale, filling the vast spaces with the water tricks and other marvels he was famous for. None survive, but you can wonder at Giambologna's massive icicle-hung statue *L'Appennino*, which looms out of a still, murky pond and seems to be part of the rock out of which it's hewn. There's no access to the villa, but the park is a green and leafy escape.

Villa Careggi

Viale Pieraccini 17 (055 427 9501). Bus 14C to penultimate stop. **Admission** free.
Probably the best-known of the Medici lodgings in the countryside (or erstwhile countryside) near Florence, Careggi began life as a fortified farmhouse. Located to the north, it now lies within the messy sprawl of the city's biggest hospital; in fact it's used by the health board as offices. Extensions were made by Michelozzo in 1434, and in the 1460s it became the headquarters of the Accademia Platonica Fiorentina, a group of scholars whose philosophical discussions are generally agreed to have resulted in humanism. Three prominent Medicis died here – Cosimo il Vecchio, Piero and Lorenzo il Magnifico. After the latter's demise, the villa was burned by republicans in 1529, and though rebuilt never regained its former glory.

South of the river

The hilly area south of the Arno, a short walk
from the city centre, is characterised by olive
groves, cypresses, the odd farmhouse and a
maze of steep lanes lined with high walls and
impenetrable gates protecting beautiful villas.

The most famous viewpoint in Florence is
probably **piazzale Michelangiolo** directly
above piazza Poggi. 'Il Piazzale' is Florence's
balcony, a large, open square with vistas over
the entire city. Its stone balustrade is usually
crowded with tourists having their photo taken
against the spectacular backdrop. Laid out in
1869 by Giuseppe Poggi, it's dominated by a
bronze replica of Michelangelo's *David* and
crammed all day with coaches. Buses 12 and 13
come here, but the best way up is to walk along
via San Niccolo to Porta San Miniato, then
climb via del Monte alle Croci, winding between
gardens and villas. Alternatively, walk up the
rococo staircase that Poggi designed to link
piazzale Michelangiolo with his piazza below.

From the Piazzale it's a short walk to the
church of **San Miniato al Monte** (via delle
Porte Sante 34, 055 234 2731, admission free),
whose façade, delicately inlaid with white
Carrara and green Verde di Prato marble, looks
down on the city. There's been a chapel on the
site since at least the fourth century, on the spot
where, legend has it, San Miniato took up his
lopped-off head and walked from the banks of
the Arno up the hill, where he finally expired.
The chapel was replaced with a Benedictine
monastery in the early 11th century, built on
the orders of reforming Bishop Hildebrand.

The church's interior is one of Tuscany's
loveliest, its walls patchworked with faded
frescoes, its choir raised above a serene 11th-
century crypt. Occasionally a door from the
crypt is open, leading to an even earlier chapel.
One of the church's most remarkable features is
the marble pavement of the nave, inlaid with
signs of the zodiac and stylised lions and lambs.
It's worth timing your trip to coincide with the

Gregorian chant sung by the monks (4.30pm
in winter daily, 5.30pm in summer).

From San Miniato, take viale Galileo Galilei
then turn left up via San Leonardo to see the
astrophysical observatory at Arcetri, its
receiver dishes incongruous among the olive
and cypress trees. Nearby **Villa di Poggio
Imperiale** was acquired by Cosimo I in 1565
and remained in Medici hands for many years.
It's now principally occupied by a girls' school.

For contemporary art fans, the **Dutch
Institute** (viale Torricelli 5, 055 221 612, closed
Sat, Sun & 3wks Aug, admission free) has a
garden of 20th-century sculpture that seems in
perfect harmony with its surroundings, most
notably Leo Vroegindewey's interpretation of
land art in *Untitled* and Yvonne Kracht's post-
Mondrian sculpture *Acute Angles*.

On a nearby hill just above Porta Romana
lies the hamlet of **Bellosguardo** ('beautiful
view'), set among olive groves and cypresses.
It's a 20-minute slog by foot, but you can catch
your breath at a viewpoint just before the
piazza that affords a glimpse of every important
church façade in central Florence. At the top
there's a collection of old houses and grand
villas grouped round a quiet, shady square.
The only sign of modern life (apart from the
inevitable cars) is a postbox on a wall.

The most impressive of the villas is the **Villa
Bellosguardo**, down a little turning to the left.
It was built in 1780 for the Marchese Orazio
Pucci (ancestor of fashion designer Emilio
Pucci) and bought, more than a century later,
by the great tenor Enrico Caruso, who lived
there for just three years before his death in
1921. Just past it is another of the hamlet's
gorgeous villas – the 16th-century **Torre di
Bellosguardo**, now the home of the Franchetti
family and a luxurious hotel (*see p57*).

About five kilometres (3.5 miles) south-
west of Porta Romana and accessible by bus
36 or 37, the **Certosa del Galuzzo** (via Buca
di Certosa 2, Galluzzo, 055 204 9226, admission
by donation, closed Mon) looms like a fortress
above the busy Siena road. The imposing
complex was founded in 1342 as a *certosa*
(Carthusian monastery) by Renaissance big-wig
Niccolò Acciaiuoli and is the third of six built
in Tuscany in the 14th century. Inhabited since
1958 by a small group of Cistercian monks, it's
full of artistic interest; the main entrance leads
into a large courtyard and the Church of San
Lorenzo, which is said to be by Brunelleschi
(also thought to be responsible for the double-
arched lay brothers' cloister). In the crypt are
some imposing tombs. Around the Chiostro
Grande (main cloister) are the 12 monks' cells,
which are almost mini-houses, each with a well,
vegetable garden and study room.

San Miniato's fading frescoes.

Icons of art

Giotto di Bondone

Born c1267 Vespignano, died 1337 Florence

According to legend, Cimabué saw the child Giotto sketching sheep on stones and immediately apprenticed him in his studio. In his lifetime, the pupil's reputation far outweighed his master's, and he is still considered an inspiration for his treatment of human experience in his portrayal of expression and gesture.

The first artist to break from Byzantine art by introducing an inkling of humanism and space, Giotto earned himself commissions from princes and popes, has some of the most sublime works of art in history, frescoes in the Upper Church of San Francesco at Assisi, attributed to him, and though not primarily an architect, was even asked to design the Duomo's Campanile. Vasari tells how Pope Boniface VIII asked Giotto for a demonstration of his skills, and when he drew a perfect freehand circle, known as the 'Giotto O', 'instantly perceived that Giotto surpassed all other painters of his time'.

In Florence: Bardi/Peruzzi Chapels, Santa Croce; *Maestà*, Uffizi; *Crocifisso*, Santa Maria Novella.

Lorenzo Ghiberti

Born 1378, died 1455, Florence

With his innovations of style and subject matter, Ghiberti was to provide a basis for many of the ideals and practices of the High Renaissance. He studied as a goldsmith, but his big break came when he beat Filippo Brunelleschi to the commission for the second (north) Baptistery doors. (Brunelleschi later got his revenge by proving his architectural superiority in the building of the Cupola.) During his 20 years' work on these bronze panels, Ghiberti began to move away from the Gothic style, introducing deep pictorial space and an emphasis on figures, which many consider the first signs of Renaissance art, perfected in his masterpiece, the east doors, known as the Gates of Paradise. He later wrote the earliest known autobiography by an artist, *Commentarii*.

In Florence: *Sacrificio di Isacco* (trial for north door commission), Bargello; Baptistery north doors; Baptistery east doors (originals in Museo dell'Opera del Duomo); Saints John the Baptist, Matthew, Stephen (Orsanmichele).

Donatello

Born 1386, died 1466, Florence

The greatest sculptor of the Early Renaissance, Donatello (born Donato di Niccolò) had a life that was full of firsts since classical antiquity: the first free-standing nude statue (the bronze *David*), the first bronze equestrian statue (*Gattamelata*, Padua), and the first shallow relief, a technique he invented in order to give depth to relatively flat sculptured friezes. He was also the first artist to free sculpture from Gothic limitations, introducing naturalism and displaying each subject's individual character. He studied with a number of artists who were working on the Duomo in around 1400 in the workshop of Lorenzo Ghiberti, whose influence is evident in Donatello's marble sculture of David, but his greatest influence was Roman art, studied on trips to Rome with one-time friend, then fierce rival Brunelleschi.

In Florence: Saint Mark and Saint George (original in Bargello) statues for niches of Orsanmichele; prophets for Campanile niches, Magdalene, Habbakuk, Cantoria relief (Museo dell'Opera del Duomo); marble *David*, bronze *David*, Bargello.

Fra' Angelico

Born c1400 Vicchio, died 1455 Rome

'Not an artist... but an inspired saint' (Ruskin), 'A simple and most holy man' (Vasari) – the patronising voices of critics have sometimes encouraged people to overlook the contribution to Renaissance art of the monk so loved he was known as 'Beato' centuries before his official 1984 beatification. Though his life was spent as a monk, mostly in Fiesole, then in San Marco and finally in Rome to paint the Vatican's Chapel of Pope Nicholas, his devoted monastic life was also an art apprenticeship, and having learned his trade painting manuscript illuminations, his most spiritual work was carried out during his inspired redecorations at San Marco. Masaccio and Alberti influences are evident in Fra' Angelico's treatment of linear perspective, and his pioneering use of light and colour to depict movement and expression ensure him his place in the Renaissance Hall of Fame.

In Florence: cell frescoes, *Noli me Tangere*, *Annunciazione*, *Deposizione*, *Tabernacolo dei Linaioli*, all Museo di San Marco.

Masaccio

Born 1401 San Giovanni Valdarno, died 1428 Rome

Masaccio was born Tommaso di ser Giovanni di Mone Cassai. In his short life, he would become a prodigious forerunner to the Renaissance, picking up the painting baton where Giotto had left off. He studied in the studio of Masolino, later his sidekick on most of his few projects, but was more master than apprentice, the older painter acknowledging his superior abilities. His *Trinità* was the first painting with true perspective (a skill developed from studying Brunelleschi's mathematical rules of proportion), and his fresco cycle in the Brancacci Chapel reached new heights of a naturalism of colour and expression, showing Donatello's influence, and a completely innovative use of light.

Having kick-started the Renaissance, Masaccio died at 27 in mysterious circumstances, leaving work that would be studied and admired by, among others, Leonardo and Michelangelo.

In Florence: *Trinità*, Santa Maria Novella; *Sant'Anna Metterza*, Uffizi; fresco cycle, Brancacci Chapel, Santa Maria del Carmine.

Sandro Botticelli

Born 1445, died 1510, Florence

Nicknamed 'Botticelli'(Little Barrels) after his rotund elder brother, the artist who, for most, epitomises the spirit of the Renaissance, was born Alessandro Filipepi. After a life of prestigious commissions from the Medici and ecclesiastical dignitaries, his work remained relatively unknown until its rediscovery by the Pre-Raphaelites in the 19th century.

Botticelli's linear style owed much to the Pollaiolo brothers, and his detached sense of beauty to his teacher Filippo Lippi, but he took both to new heights with a technical understanding of perspective and anatomy. His religious paintings and Sistine Chapel wall frescoes are red herrings – he was actually part of an intellectual Medici court aiming to reconcile Christianity with paganism in neo-Platonism, as reflected in his best-known masterpieces, *Birth of Venus* and *Allegory of Spring*.

In Florence: *Nascita di Venere*, *Allegoria della Primavera*, *Adorazioni dei Magi*, *Madonna del Melagrano*, *Madonna del Magnificat*, *Annunciazione del Cestello*, all Uffizi.

Leonardo da Vinci

Born 1452 Vinci, died 1519 Cloux, France
See p199.

Michelangelo Buonarroti

Born 1474 Caprese, died 1564 Rome

'The greatest danger is not to set too high a target and miss it, but to set too low a target and reach it' sums up in his own words the attitude to life and work of the most influential artist of all time. Michelangelo apprenticed under Ghirlandaio, then studied in Lorenzo il Magnifico's court. After a spell in Rome sculpting his first *Pietà* for St Peter's, the now famous artist returned to Florence to work on the *David*. Despite his protestations – 'I cannot live under pressure from patrons, let alone paint – he was press-ganged by Pope Julius II to return to Rome to design his tomb and start work on the Sistine Chapel, a project interrupted by a period in Florence, his last, to work on San Lorenzo. In Rome again, he completed the *Last Judgement* and worked on his obsession, the *Pietà*, intended for his own tomb in Santa Croce where he had insisted on a view towards the Duomo's Cupola for eternity.

In Florence: *David*, *Dying Slaves*, *Pietà*, Accademia; *Tondo Doni*, Uffizi; *Pietà*, Museo dell'Opera del Duomo; *Bacchus*, Bargello; Medici tombs, San Lorenzo.

Giorgio Vasari

Born 1511 Arezzo, died 1574 Florence

Vasari's prowess as a painter and sculptor pales into insignificance compared to his infinitely greater achievements as architect of the Uffizi and Corridoio Vasariano, and fame as the most important chronicler of artists' lives. He studied mannerist methods in Florence, hopeful of surpassing the heights reached by his idol Michelangelo but failing miserably. His social climbing in Rome brought him his first major painting commission (the Vatican Chancellery) from Cardinal Farnese, whose chance remark at a dinner party asking him to produce 'a catalogue of the artists and their works, in chronological order' led to the publication in 1550 of *The Lives of the Most Eminent Italian Architects, Painters & Sculptors*. Returning to Florence, he worked for Cosimo I on his major architectural projects, and oversaw the redecoration of the Palazzo Vecchio's Salone dei Cinquecento.

Sightseeing

Eat, Drink, Shop

Restaurants

A gentle wave of updating is refreshing Florence's superb but sometimes staid eating scene.

Food in Florence has, on the whole, improved over the past few years. While this doesn't mean that there aren't still plenty of worse-than-mediocre joints preying on the unwary (avoid anywhere full of tourists, anywhere with *menu turistico* written outside the door in five languages including Japanese, and anywhere on the main tourist drags), a random dip into a trattoria is more likely to result in a reasonable meal than it was ten years ago.

But if you want more than just a 'reasonable' meal, there's plenty on offer. The emergence of mid-priced, 'new generation' restaurants, where the food is based proudly on Tuscan traditions but given a contemporary interpretation ('cucina Toscana rivisitata'), has done much to improve general culinary standards. There's also been a revival of traditional *trattorie* and *osterie*, which, though no longer run by archetypal mammas but by their sons and daughters, stick faithfully to traditional recipes offered in a rustic (and sometimes antiseptic) ambience at fair prices.

Rule number one in your search for the perfect eaterie is to use this guide, but if you're faced with a place not listed here, gauge the standard by looking for a sticker by a respected Italian restaurant guide, especially Gambero Rosso's *Ristoranti d'Italia*; Veronelli; L'Espresso; or Slow Food's *Osterie d'Italia*. And don't forget to check that there are plenty of locals eating there.

Where 15 years ago the only non-Italian options in Florence were a handful of Chinese restaurants, now there are more than 20 Chinese eateries (most of them mediocre, granted), several Indian, Japanese, Middle Eastern and Mexican joints, an African and a Vietnamese. The situation has also improved for vegetarians, and though many waiters still look aghast when they hear the words 'Sono vegetariano' ('I'm vegetarian'), most restaurants offer plenty of vegetable-based pasta and rice dishes, a greater number of non-meat choices among the *secondi*, and plenty of salads and side-vegetables (*contorni*).

If you're looking for a quick bite between museums and galleries rather than a full meal, there are plenty of alternatives to the endless 'tavola calda' (hot buffet) joints that infest the centre of town. Wine bars (*see chapter* **Wine bars**) are a good option, offering anything from a sandwich to a more substantial meal, and are less formal than restaurants. A lot of bars serve a limited selection of hot and cold dishes of the day, providing a quick and cheap lunch option (*see chapter* **Cafés & Bars**).

Italian restaurants are, on the whole, refreshingly informal, and you can be casual in all but the most upmarket establishments. Children are almost always welcome, and staff do their best to find something for them to eat: a simple *pasta al pomodoro* is never a problem, nor are half-portions ('una mezza porzione'). Booking is advisable in most of the restaurants listed, especially in summer, and certainly if you want a table outside.

We've given the average price per person for a meal. It covers *antipasto* or *primo*, *secondo*, *contorno* and *dolce* but not wine or water, but don't feel pressured into eating all the courses unless you see a sign saying 'solo pasti completi' ('only complete meals served'). In a pizzeria, average price covers beer, pizza and a dessert.

Bills usually include a cover charge ('pane e coperto') per person of anything from L2,000 (€1) to an outrageous L6,000 (€3.10) – this is to cover bread consumption and should also reflect the standard of service and table settings. There'll also be a service charge (by law included in the bill, but sometimes listed separately). Some places now include both of the above in the price of the meal. One consolation is that you're not expected to leave a hefty tip – leave ten per cent if you're truly happy with your service, or, in a modest place, round the bill up a few thousand lire. By law you must be given a *ricevuta fiscale* (receipt) and keep it when you leave.

The price of your meal will be heavily influenced by the wine you choose. Budget and moderate restaurants all offer *vino della casa* or house wine in quarter, half or litre flasks; this can be anything from some ghastly gut-rot to a quaffable country wine. If you find a wine undrinkable, ask for a better, bottled alternative or look at the wine list, which will usually be weighted towards Tuscan labels.

The restaurants here have been chosen either for their value for money within each category or simply because the food is good. Bear in mind that even the most expensive restaurants listed will cost little more than what you would pay for a pizza and a bottle of wine in London or New York, so be sure to take advantage.

For translations of menu items and a description of Tuscan cooking, *see chapter* **Food in Tuscany**.

The best Restaurants

...for alfresco dining
Bibe (*p121*), Da Stefano (*p122*), Enoteca Pinchiorri (*p115*), Il Guscio (*p118*), Osteria Santo Spirito (*p119*).

...for wine lists
Beccofino (*p117*), Caffè Concerto (*p121*), Enoteca Pinchiorri (*p115*), Il Guscio (*p118*), Oliviero (*p111*), Osteria del Caffè Italiano (*p115*), Pane e Vino (*p119*).

...for a Florentine atmosphere
Da Ruggero (*p121*), Da Sergio (*p113*), Latini, in spite of all the tourists... (*p111*), Nerbone (*p113*), Sabatino (*p121*), Trattoria del Carmine (*p121*).

...for a romantic evening
Alle Murate (*p114*), Caffè Concerto (*p121*).

...for when you can't face pasta
Cibrèo (*p115*), Momoyama (*p119*), Nin Hao (*p113*), Ruth's (*p117*), Salaam Bombay (*p122*).

...for fish
Da Sergio, on Tuesdays and Fridays (*p113*), Da Stefano (*p122*), Fuor d'Acqua (*p122*), Zibibbo (*p123*).

...for a truly beautiful setting
Cibrèo (*p115*), Enoteca Pinchiorri (*p115*), Osteria del Caffè Italiano (*p115*).

...for really cheap eats
Tavola Caldo da Rocco (*p117*), Nerbone (*p113*), Ruth's (*p117*), I Tarocchi (*p121*).

...for modern Italian cooking
Alle Murate (*p114*), Beccofino (*p117*), Caffè Concerto (*p121*).

...for pizza
Il Pizzaiuolo (*p117*), Santa Lucia (*p122*).

...for avoiding tourists
Mastrobuletto (*p122*), Santa Lucia (*p122*), Zibibbo (*p123*).

Duomo & Around

Antico Fattore
Via Lambertesca 1/3r (055 288 975). **Open** 12.15-2.30pm, 7.15-10.15pm Mon-Sat. Closed last 2wks Aug. **Average** L50,000 (€26). **Credit** AmEx, DC, MC, V. **Map** p314 C3.

Closed for three years after damage by the Uffizi bomb in 1993, Antico Fattore was founded in 1908 and has always been a favourite haunt of literary Florentines. Some of its olde-worlde appeal was lost through re-building, but it's still comfortably traditional, and a great place to try Florentine classics: soups, papardelle served with juniper-spiked *cinghiale* (wild boar) or venison sauce, delicate *crespelle* (pancakes), excellent *involtini* (meat wraps) with artichoke hearts. 'Il Fritto' (deep-fried chicken, rabbit, calves' brains and vegetables) is a speciality, as are grilled meats. The all-Tuscan wine list is fairly modest, with a nicely rounded Ruffino Riserva Ducale for L30,000 (€15.50) and a very presentable house red, Ruffino Torgaio, at L14,000 (€7.20). Prices are surprisingly contained given the location.

Oliviero
Via delle Terme 51r (055 212 42/ristoliv@tin.it). **Open** 7.30pm-1am Mon-Sat. Closed Aug. **Average** L85,000 (€44). **Credit** AmEx, DC, MC, V. **Map** p314 C3.

Oliviero has a curious *Dolce Vita* atmosphere (red velvet banquette seats, pink candles), but the food is great: generous portions of inventive Tuscan and southern Italian dishes executed with real skill and served formally. A glass of complimentary prosecco helps while you peruse the menu, which always offers something interesting to kick things off: duck terrine subtly flavoured with black truffle, or artichoke hearts stuffed with sea bass. To follow, there's an unusual leek soup with frogs' legs, chick pea soup with giant prawn-tails, pigeon with chestnuts, and steak with sage, rosemary and lardo di Colonnata (the ingredient *du jour*) and cooked in Chianti. The obnoxious *pane e coperto* is included in the price.

Santa Maria Novella

Latini
Via dei Palchetti 6r (055 210 916/www.illatini.com). **Open** 12.30-2.30pm, 7.30-10.30pm Tue-Sun. Closed last wk July & 1st wk Aug. **Average** L55,000 (€28.50). **Credit** AmEx, DC, MC, V. **Map** p314 B2.

Though the Tuscan fare is nothing exceptional, Latini is a legend in Florence and there's always a huge crowd of both tourists and Italians clamouring to get in (no bookings after 8pm). Narciso Latini (the octagenarian head of the family) will slosh you a glass of house wine if you're in for a wait, but once you're seated things speed up, often without the benefit of a menu. Among the gargantuan portions dished up, soups (*ribollita, pappa al pomodoro, zuppa di farro*) are good, pastas less so. The meat-oriented *secondi* are excellent on the whole; avid carnivores should try the 'gran pezzo', a gargantuan rib roast. The Latini family are prolific producers of a fine, sludgy green olive oil, and some good wines – the house red is very drinkable. Chances are that you'll be sharing one of the long communal tables – not ideal for that romantic *cena à due*.

Eat, Drink, Shop

Sample *La Dolce Vita* at **Oliviero**. *See p111.*

Marione

Via della Spada 27r (055 214 756). **Open** 7-10pm
Mon-Sat. Closed mid July-mid Aug. **Average** L35,000
(€18). **Credit** AmEx, DC, MC, V. **Map** p314 B2.
Surprisingly for a trattoria just off fashionable Via
Tornabuoni, Marione is frequented mainly by a
refreshingly un-fashionable clientele, who come for
honest home cooking and reasonable prices. At
lunchtime lots of the white-clothed tables are occupied by lone lunchers embedded in their newspapers; in the evenings there are more tourists. Tuscan
classics are the order of the day, including an excellent *ribollita*, *bollito misto* served with salsa verde
and pickled vegetables, and fish on Fridays.

Nin Hao

Borgo Ognissanti 159r (055 210 770). **Open** 6.30-
11pm Mon; 11.30am-3pm, 6.30-11pm Tue-Sun.
Average L30,000 (€15.50). **Credit** AmEx, DC, MC,
V. **Map** p314 B1.
One of the best, most upmarket Chinese restaurants
in the city, Nin Hao is often full. If you don't waste
energy on comparisons with similar eateries in
London or New York, you can have a cheap, satis-
fying meal. The yards-long menu includes tasty dim
sum, *gamberoni* (giant prawns) cooked in various
ways, duck, and fish, chicken or meat prepared *alla
piastra* (brought sizzling to the table on a hot plate).

Osteria dei Cento Poveri

Via Palazzuolo 31r (055 218 846). **Open** 7.30pm-
midnight Mon, Thur-Sun; 12.30-2.30pm, 7.30pm-
midnight Wed. Closed 2nd & 3rd wks Aug.
Average L75,000 (€38.50). **Credit** AmEx, DC,
MC, V. **Map** p314 A1-B1.
Try not to be put off by the number of tourists
squeezed into this tiny restaurant, or go late, when
they've all finished. The food – mainly Tuscan with
a creative twist – is excellent. Both permanent and
seasonal menus feature lots of fish. Antipasti are delicately flavoured and beautifully presented, while
primi include fabulous *gnocchi all'astice* (with lobster) and subtle *taglierini* with mussels and courgette
flowers. Fresh *maccheroni* come with a ragu of rabbit with fresh broad beans and parmesan. For fish-
lovers the catch of the day is roasted on a bed of
potatoes, tomatoes and olives. The wine list includes
some Super Tuscans and other extravagances.

San Lorenzo

Da Sergio

Via della Ruosina 2r (055 218 550). **Open** 11am-
2.30pm Mon-Sat. **Average** L35,000 (€18). **No credit
cards. Map** p314 A3.
This busy but untouristy trattoria, where the Colzi
family have been serving lunch for more than 40
years, is hidden away behind the market stalls in
San Lorenzo. If it's a simple, cheap and tasty meal
with a 'real' Florentine feel that you're after, this is
the place. The no-frills menu varies little; expect
pappa al pomodoro, *ribollita* and *minestra di farro*
followed by roast beef, roast veal or *bistecca alla
Fiorentina*. There's tripe on Mondays and
Thursdays and fresh fish on Tuesdays and Fridays.
The *seppie in inzimino* (a rich stew of sweet, tender
squid and Swiss chard) is superb. The sole dessert
is *cantucci e Vin Santo*, and – lo and behold, in one
of the few innovations of the last four decades –
there's now a coffee machine.

Nerbone

Mercato Centrale (055 219949). **Open** 7am-2pm
Mon-Sat. **Average** L10,000 (€5.20). **No credit
cards. Map** p314 A3.
If you're looking for local colour, this combination of
food stall and trattoria dating from 1872 and located
within the covered part of the central market is the
place to come to. From breakfast onwards it's packed
with market workers, who even at the godforsaken
hour of 7am can be found munching on *lampredotto*
(tripe) sarnies and knocking back a glass of wine –
an offal sandwich washed down with a glass of rough
red plonk is about L10,000 (€5.20). The more faint-
hearted can opt for a plate of simple pasta or a soup.

San Marco

Taverna del Bronzino

Via delle Ruote 25r (055 495 220).
Open 12.30-2.30pm, 7.30-10.30pm Mon-Sat.
Closed 3wks Aug. **Average** L100,000 (€51.50).
Credit AmEx, DC, MC, V.
The 16th-century *palazzo* housing the Bronzino, located in an unremarkable street ten minutes' walk north
of San Lorenzo, has a classic Tuscan interior of vaulted ceilings and terracotta floors. Now much-frequent-
ed by well-heeled tourists, it was a favourite haunt of
the late Sandro Pertini, a one-time Italian president.
Primi include rigatoni with courgette flowers, and gor-
gonzola and *cappelacci* (a kind of ravioli) in a delicate
lemon sauce. For more carnivorous types there's hefty
fillet of beef cooked with Brunello, entrecôtes with artichoke hearts, and rack of lamb, plus fish dishes. The
menu changes regularly. The more than ample wine
list has a leaning towards Brunello.

Il Vegetariano

Via delle Ruote 30r (055 475 030). **Open** 12.30-
2.30pm, 7.30-10.30pm Tue-Fri; 7.30-10.30pm Sat, Sun.
Closed 3wks Aug. **Average** L25,000 (€13). **No
credit cards.**

Eat, Drink, Shop

Nerbone – the market place for tripe and wine at 7am. *See p113.*

Reminiscent of British veggie restaurants in the '70s, this is a rare breed in Florence, and though more interesting vegetarian dishes are often on offer at 'normal' restaurants, it's a pleasant and cheap, if complicated, option – you have to take your pick from the long list on the blackboard, pay at the desk and get a written receipt, then show your order at the counter and carry it to your table. Food is pretty standard vegetarian fare with the odd Asian or Middle Eastern dish thrown in; the salad bar is fabulous.

Santa Croce

Alle Murate

Via Ghibellina 52r (055 240 618/www.florence-gourmet.it). **Open** 7.45pm-midnight Tue-Sun. Closed 15-28 Dec. **Average** L120,000 (€62). **Credit** AmEx, DC, MC, V. **Map** p314 C6.

Definitely on Florence's most desirable restaurant list, Alle Murate is intimate and discreet. The background music is normally jazz, the staff are efficient and food is very good, if rather overpriced. You can eat à la carte or choose one of two set menus (only served if everyone at the table participates) – the Menu Toscano (L100,000/€51.50) and the Menu Creativo (L120,000/€62). Staff maintain a rather exaggerated secrecy about the latter until the dishes appear, but if you're expecting something really different, you may be disappointed: on our last visit it included a velvety bean soup with plump and juicy shrimp tails, a deliciously sweet *inzimino* (squid stew with Swiss chard), a delicate courgette *sformato* and a rather bland piece of beef braised in

Brunello. Desserts are impressive: the *crostata di limone* is a tangy lemon cream on a light pastry base with strawberry coulis, and there's a deeply sinful chocolate mousse cake with whipped cream. January and February menus are devoted to fish. The wine list has more than 300 labels, predominantly Tuscan; prices start at L40,000 (€20.50) but expect to pay L60,000 (€34) and way up for most vintages. Wine buffs can book to eat in the brick vaulted cellar surrounded by racks of stupendous wines.

Baldovino

Via San Giuseppe 22r (055 241 773). **Open** 11.30am-2.30pm, 7-11.30pm Tue-Sun. **Average** L50,000 (€26). **Credit** MC, V. **Map** p314 C5.

Baldovino is the type of restaurant that's now quite common in Florence – a place you can eat just about anything, from a salad to a full meal, without hassle. Its unique atmosphere is down to David Gardner (*see box* **Who they?** *p123*), one of the few foreigners to make a success in the Florentine restaurant business. The refreshing decor takes in modern colours and interesting art, mostly by a Sicilian artist friend of David's. Part of the menu changes monthly; depending on the season, you may find asparagus soup topped with ricotta Romana, gnocchi with shrimps and artichokes, ravioli stuffed with rabbit and chick-peas, roast rabbit flavoured with thyme, leeks and lemon, or tuna steak with peppers and peas. Good pizzas (Napoli-style, with thick, puffy crusts), excellent *bistecca* (from Chianina beef) and main-course salads are permanent features. Early evenings in season are often packed with tour groups, but they usually leave by 8pm.

Cibrèo

Via de' Macci 118r (055 234 1100/cibreo.fi@tin.it).
Open 12.50-2.30pm, 7.30-11.15pm Tue-Sat. Closed
Aug. **Average** restaurant L100,000 (€51.50);
trattoria L40,000 (€20.50). **Credit** AmEx, DC, JCB,
MC, V. **Map** p314 C6.

A legend among the world's foodies (there's even a
branch in Tokyo), and justifiably so – food here is a
refreshingly unpretentious combination of traditional Tuscan and creative cuisines, based on the use of
prime ingredients. Owner Fabio Picchi understands
that people who love food want to relax and enjoy it,
not pose. Cibrèo has two dining rooms: a non-book-
ing trattoria (known locally as Cibreino) with rustic
tables and benches, and an elegant, panelled restaurant that costs twice as much. On the negative side,
prices have gone up significantly recently, and the
place is often full of (well-behaved) tourists. There are
no antipasti at Cibrèo, but a generous selection of
amuse-gueules is included in the price: these could
include a soft tomato jelly gently spiced with basil
and chilli, a ricotta and parmesan soufflé, or a gelati-
nous spicy tripe salad. Unusually there's no pasta, but
there is a fantastic selection of soups (including a velvety yellow pepper number) and polentas. *Secondi* to
look out for include stuffed pigeon, stuffed chicken
neck and *inzimino* (a superbly rich and spicy stew of
squid, spinach and chard). Dessert is a must: cheesecake with tangerine marmalade, a famous flourless
chocolate cake and a raspberry tart that you'll probably remember on your deathbed.

Enoteca Pinchiorri

Via Ghibellina 87 (055 242 777). **Open** 7.30-10pm
Mon, Wed; 12.30-2pm, 7.30-10pm, Tue, Thur-Sat
Closed Aug. **Average** L250,000 (€129). **Credit**
AmEx, MC, V. **Map** p314 C5.

Famous throughout Italy and one of only a handful
of restaurants in the country with two Michelin
stars, Enoteca Pinchiorri is in a class of its own. The
setting, a *palazzo* near Santa Croce with an inner
courtyard scented with jasmine and roses and several elegant rooms laid with the finest linens, porcelain and crystal, is captivating. Though it's hovering
waiter and silver domes territory, the result is
charming rather than intimidating. Food is exquisite, though the running local joke is that you need to
book a table at a pizzeria after a meal here – portions, in true nouvelle style, are tiny. There are several set menus, all involving at least eight or nine
superbly executed and beautifully presented courses. The Enoteca is as famous for its wine cellar as
its food, and Giorgio Pinchiorri has amassed a collection second to none (with prices to match).

Osteria dei Benci

Via de'Benci 13r (055 234 4923). **Open** 1-2.45pm, 8-
10.45pm Mon-Sat. **Average** L45,000 (€23). **Credit**
AmEx, DC, JCB, MC, V. **Map** p314 C4.

A lively young management serves up delicious,
imaginative food on cheerful ceramic plates in brick
vaulted rooms. There are daily specials, and the
menu changes monthly: in summer the emphasis is

on light, fresh ingredients (carpaccio of swordfish
on a bed of rocket; mozzarella di bufala with cherry
tomatoes; tagliolini with home-made pesto) while in
autumn and winter hearty soups and stews are a feature. *Carne sulla brace* (meat grilled over an open
fire) is a year-round treat. Desserts include exquisite tarts made by the superlative Dolce Dolcezze.

Osteria del Caffè Italiano

*Via Isola delle Stinche 11/13r (055 289 368/
www.florence-gourmet.it).* **Open** noon-1am Tue-Sat.
Average L70 000 (€36). **Credit** AmEx, DC, MC, V.
Map p314 C5.

On the ground floor of Palazzo da Cintoia, this is one
of the loveliest restaurants in Florence, with three
rooms that are the epitome of rustic elegance – high
vaulted ceilings, wrought-iron light fittings, the odd
well-placed oil painting and sparkling crystal –
though notoriously slow and sloppy service lets it
down. It's from Umberto Montano, the owner of Alle
Murate (*see p114*), who sets out to provide simple
Tuscan dishes of the highest quality in beautiful surroundings. All the classics are there on the short
menu: four soups, pasta with wild boar or a smooth
duck sauce, roasted veal shank, *rosticciana* and *bollito misto* (with pungent salsa verde). The wine list
is exceptional. Prices begin at L30,000 (€15.50) for
a Chianti Colli Fiorentini, with Chianto Classici starting at L40,000 (€20.50) and Super Tuscans and
other great vintages representing good value for
money – splash out on a '97 Solaia at L200,000
(€103.50). There are snacks all day, and after
10.30pm pizzas (from Umberto's next door).

Go Neapolitan at **Il Pizzaiuolo**. *See p117.*

CREATIVE COOKING AND A SPLENDID LOCATION
FOR THIS RESTAURANT IN FIESOLE RUN BY
DANIELE RADDI, HEIR TO A FLORENTINE
RESTAURANT FAMILY ("LA POSTA", "IL
CAMPIDOGLIO"), WITH CHEF GIANLUCA DANESE.

RISTORANTE
45
piazza Mino

FRESH FISH AND TUSCAN "DOC" CERTIFIED
SPECIALTIES, HIGH QUALITY WINES ALSO BY
THE GLASS, AND WONDERFUL DESSERTS.
OUTDOOR TERRACE OFFERING AN
EXTRAORDINARY VIEW OF FLORENCE.

PIAZZA MINO DA FIESOLE, 45
FIESOLE - FIRENZE - TEL. 055 599854
e-mail: rist45piazzamino@hotmail.com

Restaurants

La Pentola dell'Oro
Via di Mezzo 24r (055 241 821/ www.terraditoscana.com/cucina/alessi). **Open** 7.30-midnight Mon-Sat. Closed Aug. **Average** L70 000 (€36). **Credit** MC, V. **Map** p314 B6.
Fed up with cooking for the nobs at his posh Fiesole restaurant, Giuseppe Alessi moved to a more lowly neighbourhood near Santa Croce, but his menus still reflect his knowledge of food (about which he is happy to talk all night) and his love of intriguing dishes. In his (somewhat uncomfortable) basement, you'll experience new flavour combinations such as warm crostini topped with herring and bitter greens, tagliolini with fresh green beans and pine nuts, and linguine *mare incanto* ('charmed sea'), with crab, squid and prawns. Main courses include *peposo* (a braised beef stew flavoured with black pepper and pears dating back to the Renaissance), duck with orange, and rabbit with olives and pine nuts. There are also a number of vegetarian options.

Il Pizzaiuolo
Via de'Macci 113r (055 241 171). **Open** 12.30-3.30pm, 7.30pm-1am Mon-Sat. Closed Aug. **Average** L25,000 (€13). **No credit cards**. **Map** p314 C6.
One of the few places in Florence where you can get genuine Neapolitan pizzas (Florentine bases are usually thin and crisp, whereas the Naples version comes steaming from the wood oven with light, puffy edges and a thin, slightly soggy middle). There are about 20 pizza varieties costing from L9,000 (€4.70) to L17,000 (€8.80); make sure you specify mozzarella di bufala, which is much tastier. Pizzas aside, there are plenty of other choices at this fun, noisy place with communal tables. Book ahead because it's always full.

Ruth's
Via Farini 2a (055 248 0888). **Open** 12.30-2.30pm, 8-10.30pm Mon-Thur; 12.30-2.30pm Fri. **Average** L35,000 (€18). **No credit cards**. **Map** p314 B6.
Next to Florence's synagogue, this kosher and vegetarian ('vegetarian' in this instance embraces fish) restaurant is a pleasant, brightly lit room with the kitchen in full view. The cooking has a strong Middle Eastern influence; the generous Piatto Ruth's (L16,000/€8.30) consisting of falafel, houmous, brik, rice and spicy Tunisian salad and various sauces is enough for lunch on its own. There's also fish or vegetable couscous, spicy aubergine and chick-pea stew, crisp-fried kefté and bagels with smoked salmon. There are always vegetarian pasta choices and lots of salads. Excellent value.

Tavola Calda da Rocco
Mercato di Sant'Ambrogio (no phone). **Open** noon-2.30pm Mon-Sat. **Average** L20,000 (€10.50). **No credit cards**. **Map** p314 C6.
Lunching at one of the formica-topped tables set out in a double row next to Rocco's tiny kitchen is a bit like eating in a glassed-in train carriage right in the middle of Sant'Ambrogio market, but this is a great place for a cheap, no-frills meal. You'll be seated wherever there is space, which usually means sharing a table with market workers or savvy shoppers. Rocco and his kids dole out the grub, the menu's written on a board on the wall, and prices are rock-bottom. Pastas or soup start at about L7,000 (€3.60). The robust *pasta con i ceci* (chick-peas) is delicious, while for *secondi* try the *polpette* (meatballs fried or in tomato sauce *alla pizzaiola*), or *spezzatino con le patate*, a rich meat stew with potatoes. House wine, in plastic cups, is rough but ready. A full meal with wine will set you back about L20,000 (€20.50).

Oltrarno

All'Antico Ristoro Di Cambi
Via Sant'Onofrio 1r (055 217 134). **Open** noon-2.30pm, 7.30-10.30pm Mon-Sat. Closed 3wks Aug. **Average** L40,000 (€20.50). **Credit** MC, V.
The Cambi family, who've been running a restaurant on this site near the river since the '40s, serve traditional Florentine dishes in a noisy, rustic setting. Popular with the local intelligensia, its only drawback is the uncomfy wooden seating. *Bistecca* continues to be a speciality, but there's lots more on each day's menu, including, in season, a simple but delicious salad of raw artichoke hearts and parmesan shavings dressed with olive oil and lemon juice. Traditional Tuscan soups are good, as is tagliatelle with *cinghiale* sauce. *Bocconcini* (mouthfuls) of chicken cooked in lemon is another house special. Finish off with home-made apple cake. The house wine (L12,000/€6.20 a litre) slips down nicely.

Alla Vecchia Bettola
Viale Ariosto 32/34r (055 224 158). **Open** noon-2.30pm, 7.30-10pm Tue-Sat. **Average** L45,000 (€23). Closed 3wks Aug. **Average** L45,000 (€23). **No credit cards**.
Just over the viale from Piazza Tasso in the Oltrarno, this is a popular place with locals, who sit on stools and benches at marble tables and pay for what they drink from a flask of house wine placed before them. The traditional menu includes daily specials, but regulars include *taglierini con funghi porcini* in summer, the house speciality *penne all Bettola* (with tomato, chilli pepper, vodka and a dash of cream) in winter, *topini al pomodoro* (gnocchi – literally 'little mice' – with tomatoes) and a superb beef carpaccio topped with rocket or artichoke hearts. On Fridays there's *baccalà* (salt cod), either *alla Livornese* (in tomato sauce) or with chick peas. For dessert, try the ice-cream, which comes from Vivoli.

Beccofino
Piazza degli Scarlatti (055 290 076/ baldovino.beccofino@inwind.it). **Open** *wine bar* 12.30-3.30pm, 7pm-midnight daily; *restaurant* 12.30-3pm, 7-11.30pm daily. **Average** L75,000 (€38.50). **Credit** MC, V. **Map** p314 C2.
When Beccofino opened in 1999, crowds flocked to try out the latest project by David Gardner (*see p123* **Who they?**), who combined a stylish contemporary decor that would be at home in any cosmopolitan

Eat, Drink, Shop

Beccofino: a new kid on the block for innovative Tuscan fare. *See p117.*

city, innovative cooking by one of Tuscany's most talented chefs and a hefty wine list. They're still coming for Francesco Berardinelli's food, which employs the season's freshest ingredients for Tuscan-based dishes with a twist, usually to superb effect (there's the odd off night). Chick-pea soup with shrimp tails, terrine of foie gras with dried fig chutney, gnocchi with melted pecorino cheese and thyme, pigeon stuffed with dried fruit and flavoured with juniper and rosemary, and roast guinea fowl with black olives have all been memorable. A lighter wine bar menu features snacks, salads, pasta dishes and risottos. The 500-strong wine list has an emphasis on Tuscany and Piemonte; mark-ups are quite steep. Staff are friendly, but the service can be sloppy and there have been complaints of long waits.

La Casalinga

Via del Michelozzo 9r (055 218 624). **Open** noon-2.30pm, 7-9.45pm Mon-Sat. Closed 3wks Aug. **Average** L35,000 (€18). **Credit** AmEx, DC, MC, V. **Map** p314 D2.

One of Florence's best local restaurants, run for decades by a family that's become an essential part of the Oltrarno, the vibrant Casalinga is always full of budget travellers (it's in all the guidebooks), but there are still plenty of regulars (usually eating an early lunch around noon) to save the atmosphere. *Bollito misto* comes with a deliciously fresh and pungent salsa verde that's good enough to eat spread on bread. Not every dish is a success, but the *ribollita* and *minestra del giorno* are excellent, home-made lasagne and cannelloni and roast meats good (try guinea fowl or beef) and tiramisù divine.

Diladdarno

Via dei Serragli 108r (055 225 001). **Open** 7.30-11pm Wed-Sun. Closed July. **Average** L35,000 (€18). **No credit cards. Map** p314 D1.

Known locally as Carlino after the cook and owner, this reliable neighbourhood trattoria serves Florentine classics in a bright, modern-rustic setting peppered with curious artworks. Some of the pasta dishes are a bit bland, but *ribollita* is good, and *arista* (a juicy hunk of roast pork served with garlicky spinach) is excellent. For an unusual salad, try the Roman *puntarelle*, a crunchy and bitter chicory-like leaf that is dressed with a sublime mixture of anchovies, capers and olive oil. There is a pretty little garden at the back, but in really hot weather it's cooler indoors. Useful on Sunday evenings, when a lot of places are closed.

Il Guscio

Via dell'Orto 49 (055 224 421). **Open** 8-11pm Tue-Sat. Closed Aug. **Average** L60,000 (€31). **Credit** DC, MC, V.

Another excellent choice in the Oltrarno, Il Guscio used to serve classic Tuscan food in a typical Tuscan ambience but these days offers something a little more interesting. The wine list, for instance, is long and varied, with labels from all over Italy and beyond, and an admirably wide choice of bottles for under L35,000 (€18). Food is consistently good, with creative twists given to familiar dishes: mixed antipasti include a daily-changing *sformato* (which may be flavoured with parmesan and topped with a lick of truffle cream), exquisite *crespelle* perfumed with truffle oil, tagliatelle tossed with

Sabatino serves up high-quality, honest home cooking – at great prices. *See p121.*

salsicce and broccoli. The meat in the classic *peposo* (beef stew) cuts like butter and is coated with a richly reduced gravy, while fish features in a tasty Mediterranean stew served in a pan directly from stove to tabletop. Puddings are divine; if you're lucky they'll include a sinful chocolate tart with a warm pear cream.

Momoyama
Borgo San Frediano 10r (055 291 840/
www.fionline.it/worldbusiness/yama.htm).
Open 8-11.30pm Tue-Sat; noon-3.30pm, 8-11.30pm Sun; brunch noon-3.15pm Sun. Closed 2wks Aug. **Average** 70,000 (€36). **Credit** AmEx, MC, V. **Map** p314 C1.
One of the new generation of Florentine restaurants, Momoyama is sleek and chic. Downstairs there are two massive glass chandeliers, a long beech table and a Japanese sushi chef slicing away behind glass, while other tables are arranged in a series of intimate rooms. The clientele is made up of a mix of Japanese diners (a good sign) and well-heeled trendies. The menu offers 'Sushi Bar + Inventive Food': the sushi and sashimi are beautifully presented (there's tempura on Tuesdays), but the 'Inventive' offerings are perplexing and overpriced. We sampled a bland shrimp and onion soup, and rabbit with tomato and rosemary, which, while good, was incongruously accompanied by peppered goat's cheese.

Osteria Santo Spirito
Piazza Santo Spirito 16r (055 238 2383). **Open** 12.30-2.30pm, 7.30-11.30pm daily. **Average** L50,000 (€26). **Credit** AmEx, MC, V. **Map** p314 D1.

This popular osteria with its flame-red walls and contemporary lighting was one of the first Florentine eateries to abandon the white walls and tablecloths of the traditional trattoria. Nibble at a plate of cheese and salami or a generous salad (chicken breast and pine nuts is very good), or go for a full meal, but bear in mind that portions are huge. Part of the menu (such as the simple yet delicious *spaghetti alla chitarra* with fresh tomatoes and basil) is fixed, with a daily menu reflecting the season. Fish dishes are an option at weekends. The choice of wines is not huge and there's no house wine, but you can order by both the glass and the bottle. When the weather allows, tables are set in the wonderful piazza.

Pane e Vino
Via di San Niccolò 70r (055 247 6956/
panevino@yahoo.it). **Open** 7.30pm-midnight Mon-Sat. Closed 2wks Aug. **Average** L65,000 (€33.50). **Credit** AmEx, DC, JCB, MC, V. **Map** p314 D5.
A calm, informal restaurant that started out as a wine bar and *enoteca*, with amenable staff, good wines and an enticing menu. The day's multi-course set *degustazione* menu is excellent value at L50,000 (€26), and you can choose wines by the glass to match each course. The à la carte menu is short; highlights have included porcini mousse, deep-fried courgette flowers stuffed with mozzarella, and tender young lamb with rosemary-spiked broad bean purée. For dessert there's an excellent pear and almond tart. The constantly updated wine list is particularly fine – one advantage for solitary diners and wine browsers is that you will only be charged for what you consume of a bottle.

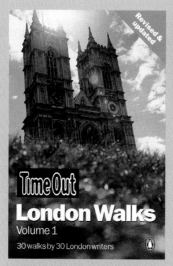
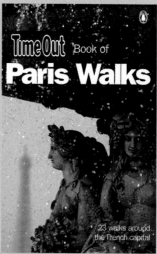
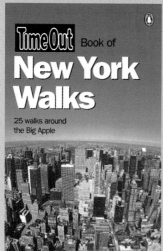

Restaurants

Sabatino

Via Pisana 2r (055 225 955). **Open** noon-2.30pm,
7.30-10pm Mon-Fri. Closed Aug. **Average** L30,000
(€15.50). **No credit cards.**
Located for decades on Borgo San Frediano,
Sabatino's moved down the road – it's now tucked
beneath Porta San Frediano. The Buccioni family
have maintained the unique atmosphere of the trattoria – the pre-war fridge, flood-damaged chairs,
'50s tiles and, most importantly, the customers all
moved with the premises. The honest home cooking (Italian and Florentine specialities) is of the
same high quality and still remarkably good value.

I Tarocchi

Via dei Renai 12/14 (055 234 3912). **Open** noon-
2.30pm, 7pm-1am Tue-Sun. **Average** L25,000 (€13).
Credit MC, V. **Map** p314 D4.
This lively, perennially popular pizzeria is a great
place for a good, cheap, late-night pizza (eat-in or
take-away) or plate of pasta and a beer. Pizzas are
Florentine-style (crisp, thin, slightly charred crusts)
and cost from L9,000 (€4.70) for a simple margherita (tomato and mozzarella) to L15,000 (€7.80) for a
hefty *tronchetto* (doubled over and stuffed with ham,
cheese, mushrooms, artichoke hearts and rocket).
Beer on tap (*alla spina*) costs L3,500 (€1.80) for a
small glass, L7,000 (€3.60) for a medium. The daily
menu has a few pasta dishes, salads and the odd
seafood or meat *secondo*.

Trattoria del Carmine

Piazza del Carmine 18r (055 218 601). **Open** noon-
2.30pm, 7-10.30pm Mon-Sat. Closed 3wks Aug.
Average L40,000 (€20.50). **Credit** AmEx, DC, MC,
V. **Map** p314 C1.
Another traditional neighbourhood trattoria that,
though popular with tourists, continues to attract
locals and has thus maintained its informal vibe and
fair prices. Though a car park now occupies Piazza
del Carmine, the few tables squeezed on to the terrace are still a pleasant place for a meal. The long
menu has plenty of choice, including dishes of the
day; try *coniglio alla Maremmana* (rabbit stewed in
a rich tomato sauce), or, in season, the decadent fillet steak topped with grilled porcini mushrooms.
The home-made desserts are delicious.

Trattoria 4 Leoni

Via dei Vellutini 1r (055 218 562/www.4leoni.com).
Open noon-2.30pm, 7-11pm daily. **Average** L50,000
(€26). **Credit** AmEx, DC, MC, V. **Map** p314 C2.
Once a simple, spit-on-the-floor local trattoria, the 4
Leoni – set in the delightful little Piazza della Passera
just south of the river – is now a trendy version of its
old self (red and white checked tablecloths, flasks,
rustic tables and chairs, and music that's just a bit
too loud for some). It buzzes with a mixed crowd who
turn up for the friendly atmosphere and acceptable
Tuscan food. *Primi* were rather bland on our visit,
but *secondi* had more character – try the *peposo* beef
stew, the deep-fried lamb with artichoke hearts, or
something from the grill. Booking is advised.

Outside the City Gates

Bibe

Via delle Bagnese 1r (055 204 9085). Bus 36, 37,
then taxi. **Open** 12.30-1.45pm, 7.30-9.45pm Mon, Tue,
Fri-Sun; 7.30-9.45pm Thur. Closed last wk Jan & 1st
wk Feb; 1st 2wks Nov. **Average** L50,000 (€26).
Credit AmEx, V.
Worth the 3km (2 mile) trip south from Porta
Romana, this old *casa colonica* (farmhouse) in a lovely flower-filled garden (with outside tables in summer) serves interesting traditional food such as *torta
di caprino e olive nere* (black olive paste sandwiched
in goats' cheese) and oven-baked garlicky tomatoes.
One of the best *primi* is the *zuppa di porcini e ceci*
(cep soup with chick-peas), but the delicate *crespelle*
with porcini mushrooms are excellent, as is the pappardelle with hare sauce. *Secondi* are classic Tuscan:
excellent steak or veal done over an olive wood grill,
roast guinea fowl, and deep-fried chicken, rabbit and
brains (a speciality). Puddings such as home-made
ice-cream in a honeycomb case are a dream. The
wine list is unusually good for such a rustic place,
but the fruity house red is fine.

Caffè Concerto

*Lungarno C Colombo 7 (055 677
377/caffeconcerto@tiscalinet.it).* Bus 31, 32.
Open noon-2.30pm, 8-11pm Mon-Sat. Closed 1st
3wks Aug. **Average** L90,000 (€46.50). **Credit**
AmEx, DC, MC, V.
Gabriele Tarchiani lived in the US for some years,
and the decor of his eaterie on the north bank of the
Arno about 2km east of the Ponte Vecchio reflects
this: warm wood, picture windows, low lighting,
background jazz and informal service. French chef
Ludovic Langlois has been heading the kitchen for
some years now, creating menus that are inventive
without being fussy, based on seasonal variation
and the freshest ingredients. If you want fish, the
hearty Livornese soup *cacciucco* is lightened with
spring veg and herbs, or try papardelle with braised
endive and lobster. For carnivores, boned pigeon is
stuffed with honeyed apples. Interestingly, antipasti,
primi and *secondi* all cost about the same. The extraordinarily rich chocolate mille-feuille with tart raspberry sauce is worth leaving room for. The drinks
list has some 800 wines, 127 whiskies (Scotch is a
passion of Gabriele's) and countless grappas,
cognacs and other after-dinner drinks.

Da Ruggero

Via Senese 89r (055 220 542). Buses 11, 36, 37 to
Porta Romana, then 5min walk south. **Open** noon-
2.30pm, 7.30-10.30pm Mon, Thur-Sun. Closed mid
July-mid Aug. **Average** L40,000 (€20.50). **No
credit cards.**
Don't risk the trek to Porta Romana without booking at the tiny and popular Da Ruggero – the kind
of place that's full of Florentine families for weekend lunch, it's one of the few genuine trattorias left
in Florence, and is always packed. Food is local and
home-cooked, and prices are low. Traditional soups

Eat, Drink, Shop

The inventive **Caffè Concerto**. See p121.

are always on the menu; the *ribollita* is particularly good, as is the *paperdelle alla lepre*. Roast meats always include tasty and tender pigeon flavoured with rosemary, plus beef, pork and lamb. Puddings are home-made, and there's a short wine list.

Da Stefano

Via Senese 271 (055 204 9105). Bus 36, 37 to Galuzzo. **Open** 7.30-11pm Mon-Sat. Closed Aug. **Average** L90,000 (€46.50). **Credit** AmEx, DC, JCB, MC, V.

It's worth making the trip to Galluzzo about 2km south of Porta Romana to eat in this casual, noisy and slightly chaotic restaurant. The charismatic Stefano, whose motto is 'Solo pesce, solo la sera, solo fresco' ('Only fish, only in the evening, only fresh'), or one of his young staff will help you through the excellent menu, highlights of which include spaghetti allo Stefano (with buttery, chilli-spiked lobster, langoustines and prawns) and the *gran tegame*, a vast pan full of molluscs cooked with tomatoes and garlic. Equally impressive are the platters of mixed seafood and the sushi and sashimi. After 10pm a bistro menu allows you to choose just one dish accompanied by a glass of wine, with cover charges waived. There's a jasmine-scented terrace.

Fuor d'Acqua

Via Pisana 37r (055 222 299/pesce@fuordacqua.it). **Open** 8-11.30pm Mon-Sat. Closed 3wks Aug. **Average** L110 000 (€57). **Credit** AmEx, DC, MC, V.

Just outside the old city gate of San Frediano and discreetly hidden behind smoked glass doors, Fuor d'Acqua is the best of several new fish restaurants in the city, and though the elegant modern decor isn't to everybody's taste, the place is relaxed and busy. There's no menu: the chef cooks what is considered to be the best of the day's catch when the trawler arrives in Viareggio at about 6pm, so if there's a delay on the *autostrada* coming into Florence, you may have to wait for your meal. But once it arrives, fish will be jumping fresh and prepared simply, using only olive oil, lemon juice and seasonings to enhance the flavours. Mixed antipasto is a mini meal in itself: warm, baby calemari with rocket and cherry tomatoes; carpaccio of sea bass; fat, juicy scampi with borlotti beans and tomatoes; tender fillets of John Dory topped with a purée of artichoke hearts and lemon juice… The *secondi* includes the catch of the day *all'isolana* (roasted in the oven on a bed of thinly sliced potatoes and tomatoes). Incredibly simple and incredibly good.

Mastrobuletto

Via Cento Stelle 27r (055 571 275). Bus 11, 17. **Open** 12.30-2.30pm, 7.30-10.30pm Mon-Sat. Closed Aug. **Average** L45,000 (€23). **No credit cards**.

You won't find many tourists in this trattoria just behind the north-eastern end of the football stadium: your fellow diners are more likely to be members of the Fiorentina football team and journalists who come for the Florentine cooking and lively atmosphere overseen by the outgoing Marco and his chef wife Roberta. The menu features just about everything you would want from a Tuscan meal, including excellent meat from the Valdichiana (try beef braised in Chianti, entrecôte with green pepper, or rabbit rolled in bacon and roasted). Wind up with a plate of *biscotti da Prato* dunked in Vin Santo.

Salaam Bombay

Viale Rosselli 45r (055 357 900). **Open** 7.30-11pm Tue-Sun. Closed 3wks Aug. **Average** T/C (range 30,000-45,000). **Credit** AmEx, DC, MC, V.

One of several Indian restaurants in Florence, Salaam Bombay, which lies ten minutes' walk north-west of the train station, serves decent if unthrilling fare. It's often full of Italians for whom ethnic cooking is still something of an adventure. The standard north-Indian food includes tandoori dishes and a number of veggie options; staff are very friendly.

Santa Lucia

Via Ponte alle Mosse 102r (055 353 255). Bus 30, 35. **Open** 7.30pm-1am Mon, Tue, Thur-Sun. Closed Aug. **Average** L25,000 (€13). **No credit cards**.

Some say the pizza at Santa Lucia, ten minutes' walk north-west of Porta al Prato, is the best in town, and one can rarely get a table on spec. Service is notoriously slow, but if you dare complain you risk being relegated to the bottom of the list – all Florentines know this. Like the atmosphere, the pizza is authentically Neapolitan, topped with the sweetest

Who they? David Gardner

The idea of a Scotsman building a small restaurant empire in Florence has something decidedly coals-to-Newcastle about it. But that is exactly what David Gardner has done. Gardner, a former tour operator, arrived in Florence in 1994 with his lawyer wife Catherine ostensibly to take time out from work and study Italian. Soon enough, though, the two were scouting around for a little trattoria in the Chianti countryside to renovate and relaunch – they found the trat of their dreams – and were promptly gazumped.

But the Gardners soon shifted their aim to Florence itself, having discovered the kind of gap in the market that business school graduates dream of. Until relatively recently, eating in Florence was binary. Either you went to a cheap-and-cheerful osteria, where you could recite most of the menu (*ribollita, bistecca fiorentina, panna cotta*...) even before you'd seen it; or else you went to a posh restaurant serving more refined versions of the same traditional dishes, accompanied by comforting pan-Italian classics. There were few creative trattorias, only a handful of decent pizzerias, and barely even a salad bar.

So when the couple bought up an ailing osteria on a corner of piazza Santa Croce and opened it in the spring of 1996 as **Baldovino** (*see p114*), their anything-you-want menu, which offered creative pasta dishes alongside thick Neapolitan pizzas, big salads and one or two more exotic dishes, made the place an instant hit. Other local restaurateurs soon jumped on the bandwagon; but the Gardners kept up the momentum by opening a wine bar (**Enoteca Baldovino**, *see p125*) on an adjacent corner in January 1998.

Their riskiest gamble to date came with **Beccofino** (*p117*), a modern, vaguely Conran-esque restaurant and wine-bar in a chic neighbourhood on the south bank of the

Arno. Backed by a small cartel of local wine families and with prestige signing Francesco Berardinelli from top Chianti restaurant Osteria di Rendola near Montevarchi wearing the chef's hat, Beccofino opened with a big media splash in May 1999. Florentines and splurging tourists took to it enthusiastically, and Italian restaurant guides were forced to admit that a Scot could make it in Florence (though with the help – to the locals' relief – of an Italian cook). Ever the diplomat, David Gardner is keen to point out that some of his best friends are Florentine restaurateurs – though he admits that his onward march has given rise to 'a little bit of jealousy' in the trade. If a Florentine takes over a Scottish malt whisky distillery anytime soon, you'll know why.

tomatoes and milkiest mozzarella, but if you don't fancy that, there's excellent seafood. There are no outside tables, but air-con makes summer eating bearable in spite of the heat from the pizza oven.

Zibibbo

Via di Terzollina 3r (055 433 383). Bus 14. **Open** 1-3pm, 8-11pm Mon-Sat. Closed Aug. **Average** L70,000 (€37). **Credit** AmEx, DC, MC, V.
Benedetta Vitali moved on from Cibrèo (*see p115*), where she was co-founder and chef, to open this delightful restaurant about 3km (2 miles) north of

the city centre. The decor (stylish but simple pink-varnished floorboards, blue chairs, picture windows overlooking the city) is refreshingly different but the food is classic, with superbly cooked fuss-free Florentine and Italian stalwarts. Houmous, home-made breads and a glass of wine (all on the house) help you through the menu, which features *baccalà mantecato* (a creamy salt cod pâté), spaghetti with swordfish or mussels and clams, stuffed calamari in tomato sauce, rabbit stewed with peppers, stuffed duck in orange sauce and roast pigeon. The menu is divided between fish and meat. Worth the trek.

Wine Bars

Drink, eat and watch the locals at play.

Wine and the drinking of it has played an important part in Florentine life for centuries, ever since the time when 'holes in the wall' (arch-shaped openings carved into the side of a building at waist level and still in evidence in parts of the city, though now unfortunately dry) began to serve glasses of rough plonk in exchange for a few coins.

Local wine bars have long provided a focus for neighbourhood life, but these days wine bars are even more popular than ever, particularly among young people, and are often full at *aperitivo* time.

There are various types of wine bar in Florence, from the tiny street booths (*fiaschetteria*, *vineria* or *mescita*) with no seating, serving basic Tuscan wines and rustic food, to the new, upmarket *enoteche* that offer a huge range of labels from all over Italy and beyond. Between the two extremes are a host of traditional places where you can eat and drink in reasonable comfort.

All the wine bars listed in this chapter will have a selection of wines by the glass (*alla mescita*) and eats of some description, ranging from basic panini and crostini to sophisticated snacks and complete meals.

Old-fashioned places tend to open throughout the day until dinner time; new ones stay open until late. The difference in price between a bottle consumed on the premises and one taken away will be about 20-30 per cent in most wine bars.

Duomo & Around

Cantinetta dei Verrazzano
Via dei Tavolini 18-20r (055 268 590/ www.verrazzano.com). **Open** 8am-9pm Mon-Sat. **Credit** AmEx, DC, MC, V. **Map** p315 B4.
Located between the Duomo and Palazzo Vecchio, this wine bar belongs to the Castello da Verrazzano estate, one of Chianti's major vineyards. The wood-panelled rooms are always crowded; on one side is the bakery (complete with wood oven) and coffeeshop, while on the other is the wine bar serving exclusively estate-produced wines. These are excellent value, both by the glass and by the bottle; the latter start at L25,000 (€13) for a Rosso Toscano and L55,000 (€28.50) for a Riserva '97 and go up to L150,000 (€77.50) for a Riserva '90. Snack on unusual crostini and sandwiches prepared behind the bar or a filled focaccia straight from the oven.

Vini
Via dei Cimatori 38r (no phone). **Open** 8am-8pm Mon-Sat. **No credit cards. Map** p315 C4.
Founded in 1875 and, literally, a hole in the wall, this *vinaio* squeezed between a brass engraver and a jeweller is one of the last of its kind in the city. Join the other customers standing on the road or squatting on the pavement for a glass of whatever's open and a liver-topped crostino, bruschetta with sweet red tomatoes and basil or a great slab of *porchetta* (rosemary-flavoured roast pork) on a hunk of bread.

San Lorenzo

Casa del Vino
Via dell' Ariento 16r, San Lorenzo (055 215 609/ www.casadelvino.it). **Open** 8am-2.30pm, 5-8pm Mon-Fri; 9am-2.30pm Sat. Closed Aug. **Credit** MC, V. **Map** p314 A3.
Tucked behind the market stalls in the busy Mercato Centrale, this is a lively place for a glass of wine, a snack or something from the excellent selection of bottles on the laden shelves. Stand or sit at one of the bar stools and munch on a variety of crostini and panini with *finocchiona* (salami flavoured with fennel), prosciutto and various cheeses.

Zanobini
Via Sant'Antonino 47r (055 239 6850). **Open** 8am-2pm, 3.30-8pm Mon-Sat. **Credit** over L50,000/€26 AmEx, MC, V. **Map** p314 A3.
In the narrow street that leads from the station to the Mercato Centrale, right opposite the *friggitoria* (fried food stall), this wood-panelled bar is always crowded with early-starting locals. It's good for a quick slurp and a snack before you repair to the back room with its shelves full of interesting bottles to buy.

Santa Croce

L'Antico Noè
Volta di San Piero 6r (055 234 0838). **Open** 10.30am-9.30pm Mon-Sat. Closed 2wks Aug. **No credit cards. Map** p315 B5.
Situated in a pedestrianised area near Santa Croce, in a small seedy passageway often frequented by the winos, junkies and scruffy dogs, this tight squeeze of a wine bar serves a predictable range of Tuscan reds at reasonable prices at the stand-up bar, along with snacks. Drinkers usually spill out into the passageway, and there's a cheap trattoria that's popular with students next door.

Eat, Drink, Shop

Vini – a fine wine and snack spot. *See p124.*

All'Antico Vinaio

Via dei Neri 65r (no phone). **Open** 8am-8pm Tue-Sat; 8am-1pm Sun. Closed Aug. **Credit** AmEx, MC, V. **Map** p315 C4.

Situated in a street that's relatively untouched by tourists and has a real neighbourhood feel, All'Antico Vinaio has been selling wine for a century or so. It was recently bought by Daniele, owner of a *rosticceria* across the road, who has modernised the interior without forsaking the basic, old-fashioned character of the place. It's still predominantly frequented by locals, who perch on the high stools to while away the time drinking and exchanging the day's news. Wines, which are all Tuscan (bar the odd Sicilian white), range from house plonk at L2,500 (€1.30) and some excellent Chianti Classicos at a very reasonable L5,000 (€2.60) up to Brunellos for L10,000 (€5.20) plus. There are crostini with various toppings in the evenings and more substantial fare (brought in from over the road) at lunchtime.

Boccadama

Piazza Santa Croce 25-26r (055 243 640). **Open** *Summer* 8.30am-1pm Mon; 8.30am-midnight Tue-Sun. *Winter* 8.30am-midnight Tue-Sun. **Credit** AmEx, DC, MC, V. **Map** p314 C5.

Right on the piazza with outside tables in summer, Boccadama is chock-a-block with tourists at lunchtimes in season, but don't let that put you off: it's a delightful place where serious wine lovers are given a run (and value) for their money, and the food is good too. The wine list comprises more than 1,000

labels, of which 90% are Italian; 40% of those are Tuscan, though the southern Italian section is growing. There's also a wide selection of aromatic dessert wines. The first room serves bar fare and snacks; next door is the restaurant for quick, light lunches or more substantial evening meals. The latter includes the six-course set *degustazione* menu (L55,000/€28.50); accompanying wines are another L35,000 (€18). This is remarkably reasonable.

Enoteca Baldovino

Via San Giuseppe 18r (055 234 7220). **Open** *Summer* noon-midnight daily. *Winter* noon-4pm, 6pm-midnight Tue-Sun. **Credit** MC, V. **Map** p315 C5/6.

Annexe to the popular Baldovino trattoria (*see p114*), Enoteca Baldovino has recently started serving a wider range of food and wine. In its bright serving area a marble-topped counter is backed by shelves laden with jars, and salamis and hams hang from butchers' hooks. There are some 35 varieties of hot crostini, sandwiches, *carpacci* (including a carpaccio of wild boar with juniper berries, Parmesan, pink peppercorns and gin vinegar), plates of cheeses, cured meats and interesting salads. Hot dishes of the day are flagged on a board. Ceramic-topped tables, wooden floors, mellow lighting and honey-coloured walls show off bright paintings, while in summer you can sit outside. Wines by the glass range from the cheap and cheerful to some heavy-duty Super Tuscans or Brunellos at around L14,000 (€7.20). The full list now features about 500 labels, including a huge section of Piedmont reds.

Enoteca de' Giraldi

Via dei Giraldi 4r (055 216 518/www.vinaio.com). **Open** noon-4pm, 7pm-1am Mon-Sat. Closed 2wks Aug. **Credit** MC, V. **Map** p315 C4.

Hidden in a narrow street off via Ghibellina in the erstwhile stables of Palazzo Borghese, Giraldi is owned by Tuscan Andrea Moradei and his Swiss wife, who are passionate about seeking out lesser-known wines, especially from Tuscany and central Italy (Umbria, Le Marche, Lazio, Campania); the result is a refreshing collection of bottles. Recommended purchases include a fabulous crisp Vermentino di Luni produced in small quantities by Nanni Barbero for L22,000/€11.50 and a 1996 Carmignano Riserva Elzana with all the classic characteristics of a Tuscan red at a reasonable L38,000 (€19.50). Some 25 wines are sold by the glass, and hot and cold snacks and light meals are served all day. The atmosphere is pleasing, with mellow background jazz and art on the walls. Wine courses and country gastro-trips are organised.

Fiaschetteria Balducci

Via dei Neri 2r (055 216 887). **Open** 9.30am-9.30pm Mon-Sat. **No credit cards. Map** p315 C4.

Dusty bottles stacked on dark wood shelves, a counter laden with goodies and a fair spattering of local types and their dogs – Balducci's has a traditional feel. It's a popular spot for a quick lunch

The famed (and often full) **Fuori Porta**.

among a range of Florentines, from builders to bank directors. The choice of wines by the glass (cheap plonk out of a plastic-bound flask all the way up to Brunello) is fairly run of the mill. Ask for a *gottino di rosso* and you'll get a stubby little glass of honest red for only L1,500 (c77). The munchies – crostini with various toppings, *frittate*, salads, a couple of daily pasta dishes and truffle panini – are excellent.

Oltrarno

Enoteca Le Barrique

Via del Leone 40r (055 224 192). **Open** 4.30pm-1am Tue-Fri, Sun; 4.30pm-2am Sat. Closed 2wks Aug. **Credit** AmEx, DC, MC, V.

Situated on an unassuming sidestreet, this little wine bar has a 'new rustic' atmosphere. Hot and cold dishes of the day (such as pasta with rocket and speck, and duck-breast salad) are listed on a blackboard and cost around L50,000 (€26) for two courses; there's also a great selection of cheeses, Italian and French, and other snacks. Have a quick glass of wine from a selection of open bottles at the wooden counter or enjoy a bottle from the list at one of the tables in the back; the choice ranges from Tuscan to Californian, familiar to little-known.

Pitti Gola e Cantina

Piazza Pitti 16 (055 212 704). **Open** *Summer* 10am-9pm daily. *Winter* 10am-9pm Mon-Sat. Closed 2wks Aug. **Credit** AmEx, MC, V. **Map** p314 D2.

This little wine bar opposite the Pitti Palace is inevitably full of tourists, and prices are thus on the high side, but the atmosphere is very pleasant, with background jazz, and there's a good choice of wines (heavily weighted towards Tuscany) and excellent nibbles: marinated vegetables (olives, artichokes, aubergines, stuffed chillies), pâtés made by Dario Cecchini, the famous Butcher of Panzano (*see p32*), and salamis and hams from Gaiole. There are also soups, *frittate*, cheeses and desserts.

Le Volpi e L'Uva

Piazza dei Rossi 1r (055 239 8132). **Open** 11am-8pm Mon-Sat. **Credit** AmEx, JCB, MC, V. **Map** p314 C3.

Tucked away in a little piazza just behind the Ponte Vecchio, this new generation *enoteca* always looks inviting from the outside, with its mellow clientele perched on high stools around the marble-topped bar. If you're looking for unusual labels, this is a good place to start, for experts Emilio and Riccardo search out small, little-known producers that give the best value for money. They also take great pleasure in recommending wines, of which about 35 are available by the glass. Try a generous *calice* of the Prosecco di Valdobbiadene for just L3,500 (€1.80) or an aromatic Shickenburg from Alto Adige (L4,500/€2.30). Bottle-wise, there are interesting wines from all over Italy, along with some French labels and the occasional New World bottle. Limited but delicious nibbles include a great selection of French and Italian cheeses, marinated fish, *panini tartufati* (stuffed with truffle cream), smoked duck breast and some rich pâtés, all of them designed to *stuzzicare* (whet) the appetite.

Outside the City Gates

Enotria

Via delle Porte Nuove 50 (055 354 350/ www.enotriawine.it). Short walk from Porta al Prato. **Open** 8am-3.30pm Mon, Sun; 8am-3.30pm, 7pm-midnight Tue-Sat. Closed 2wks Aug. **Credit** AmEx, MC, V.

You're unlikely to stumble upon this new-ish *enoteca* in the course of a day's sightseeing, located as it is on a busy arterial road leading west from Porta al Prato. It's not that far from the city centre, however, and it's well worth a visit for its convivial atmosphere, serious selection of wines and excellent food. The wine list features both familiar and lesser-known labels, with plenty of choice for less than L30,000 (€15.50), including a robust and unusual Rosso delle Miniere 1997 from the mining region of Tuscany near Massa Marittima – great value at L26,000 (€13.50). There are snacks all day, including interesting French and Italian cheeses, a short daily lunch menu and more substantial dinners.

Fuori Porta

Via Monte alle Croci 10r (055 234 2483/ www.fuoriporta.it). Bus D. **Open** 12.30-3.30pm, 7pm-12.30am Mon-Sat. Closed 2wks Aug. **Credit** AmEx, MC, V.

Just outside one of the old city gates in San Niccolò, south of the river, this is the most famous wine bar in Florence and as such nearly always full. The list offers more than 600 labels from Italy and France, plus a formidable choice of grappas and Scotch. Every six days, the 40-strong selection of wines available by the glass (L3,500-L15,000/€1.80-€7.80) changes, with *novità* added continually. The daily menu has a choice of pastas, vegetable *sformati*, *carpacci* and a range of nibbles and snacks to complement the wine; one of the huge choice of crostini – vast slabs of Tuscan bread topped with, for example, Asiago cheese and sun-dried tomatoes – is just the thing to pad out that second bottle. In warm weather the few tables outside are in great demand.

Cafés & Bars

Where to get your fix.

Astor Caffè: a gleaming newcomer to the caffeine-consuming scene.

There are three things Italians take very seriously: clothes, cars and coffee. In Italy, being a coffee barman is a well-respected profession, and Illy even runs a university course in Sao Paolo, Brazil, dedicated to the art of making a good espresso.

When a café displays the type of coffee served, this is not so much advertising a brand as displaying their good taste, and many coffee shops have house blends that are a particular source of pride.

The Italian habit is to have a small shot of espresso at a bar two or three times a day, plus a concentrated hit of sweet black coffee after an evening meal. If you want more to drink than a knock-it-back coffee, ask for a *lungo* (diluted with a little hot water) or *caffè americano* (weaker than an Italian would normally allow), and if you want a drop of milk in your espresso (acceptable locally), ask for a *caffè macchiato caldo* or *freddo* (with hot or cold milk).

If you have trouble getting used to the short, sharp shock of espresso note that in more upmarket places it often comes with a complimentary sweetener, a small cube of chocolate or a biscuit perched on the saucer.

Bars come in many guises, depending on their licence: in *caffe' bars* you can usually sit down for a full lunch; in *bar tabacchi* you can also buy cigarettes, bus tickets and stamps, in *latterie* milk and dairy products, and in *drogherie* groceries; and in many other shops, especially patisseries, there's also a bar. In bigger bars and cafés you pay for coffee at the till before you order it from the barman, unless you want to sit down. Location is everything when it comes to the bill; it costs far less if you stand at the bar rather than sit at a table, and you pay more to sit outside.

Duomo & around

Astor Caffè
Piazza Duomo (055 239 9000). **Open** 7am-1am Mon-Sat. Closed 2wks Aug. **Credit** MC, V. **Map** p314 B4.
A vast, contemporary chrome and glass bar with light flooding in from a central skylight. Perch on a padded barstool for an aperitif or a freshly made veg or fruit juice, or linger for a lunch of smoked trout salad or steaming olive and cherry tomato pasta. Some evenings there's jazz in the downstairs bar, while upstairs you can sip cocktails or eat a full Tuscan dinner. *See also p180.*

Chiaroscuro draws plenty of customers with its light lunches and dark delights. *See p129.*

Bar Perseo

Piazza della Signoria 16r (055 239 8316). **Open** 7am-midnight Mon-Sat. Closed 3wks Nov. **Credit** MC, V. **Map** p314 C4.

Though the centrepiece of this bar is its sculptural art deco light fitting, most eyes are drawn to the mountains of home-made ice-cream topped with cherries, berries and chocolate curls. Stand at the bar for an aperitif, or refuel on the likes of an artichoke and ham filled croissant (L2,500-L5,000/€1.30-€2.60) after a morning in the museums. Cappucinos are L2,200 (€1.10) at the bar, L8,500 (€4.40) outside.

Bar San Firenze

Piazza di San Firenze 1r (055 211 426). **Open** *Summer* 7am-8pm daily. *Winter* 7am-8pm Mon-Sat. **Credit** DC, MC, V. **Map** p314 C4.

This bar in a restored 15th-century Renaissance palace has ample seating and an impressive range of culinary delights that includes chocolates, ice-creams, pizzas and three-course meals. You can also buy some *cantucci* (almond biscuits) to dip in vin santo and marzipan fruits, a Sicilian speciality. A cappuccino costs L1,800 (93c) at the bar; L5,000 (€2.60) at a table.

Caffè Concerto Paszkowski

Piazza della Repubblica 31-35r (055 210 236). **Open** 7am-1.30am Tue-Sun. **Credit** AmEx, DC, JCB, MC, V. **Map** p314 B3.

Founded in 1846 as a beer hall and a meeting point for artists in the second half of the 19th century, the Concerto was declared a national monument in 1991. A cappuccino costs L1,800 (93c) at the bar, L6,000 (€3.10) seated. There's outside seating in summer.

Caffè Fiorenza

Via dei Calzaiuoli 9r (055 216 651). **Open** 7am-1am daily. **No credit cards. Map** p314 B3.

A compact mirrored premises offering 24 home-made ice-cream flavours (L8,000/€4.10 if you sit at one of the few tables). Alternatively, enjoy an aperitif at the bar or sit down for a coffee and watch the whole world go by. It's L1,800 (93c) for a cappuccino at the bar, L5,000 (€2.60) seated.

Caffè Italiano

Via della Condotta 56r (055 291 082). **Open** 8am-8pm Mon-Sat (lunch 1-3pm). Closed Aug. **No credit cards. Map** p314 C4.

A hidden treasure that's central but tranquil, and popular with locals at lunchtime. The lower level is for stand-up service, the upper for those wishing to sit for a salad or pasta lunch. Dark-wood tables, red velvet seats and mellow sounds make for a classy atmosphere. Regular exhibitions line the walls and there are papers and books to browse. Coffee and desserts are superb, but service can be poor. The 'caffè-choc' – espresso laced with pure bitter chocolate powder – is a must. Cappuccinos cost L1,800 (93c) at the bar, L5,000 (€2.60) at tables (with a free plate of home-made *biscotti*).

Caffè Rivoire

Piazza della Signoria 5r (055 214 412). **Open** 8am-midnight Tue-Sun. Closed 2nd 2wks Jan. **Credit** AmEx, DC, JCB, MC, V. **Map** p314 C4.

The *grande dame* of Florentine cafés, this was founded in 1872 as a steamed chocolate factory and is still famous for its chocs – the best in town. Its displays of chocolate sculptures are as breathtaking as the view of the Palazzo Vecchio from the outside tables. No trip to Florence is complete without a coffee from Rivoire's silver filigree cups. Cappuccinos are L2,000 (€1) at the bar, L8,000 (€4.10) seated.

Chiaroscuro
Via del Corso 36r (055 214 247). **Open** 7.30am-11.30pm Mon-Wed, Fri-Sun; 7.30am-8.30pm Thur. **No credit cards. Map** p314 B4.
The window display of espresso machines, coffee cups and coffee-bean resin trays (all for sale) shows that this place is serious about its coffee. At the back tables beyond the narrow bar you can have a light lunch or indulge in a slice of gateau. A cappuccino costs L1,800 (93c) at the bar, L3,500 (€1.80) seated.

Coquinarius
Via delle Oche 15r (055 230 2153). **Open** 9am-11pm Mon-Thur, Sun; 9am-11.30pm Fri, Sat (food from noon). Closed 2wks Aug. **Credit** MC, V. **Map** p314 B3.
A vaulted bar with cushioned bench seating. Simple, tasty dishes include fettucine with salmon and orange zest (L10,000/€5.20), big salads, crostini with pâté and spicy spreads (L5,000/€2.60) and smoked fish platters (L18,000/€9.30). Let the chocolate fondue with fresh fruit finish you off (L18,000/€9.30 for two). The bar has an exotic range of teas and speciality hot chocolate with fudge or meringues.

Gilli
Piazza della Repubblica 36-39r (055 213 896). **Open** 8am-midnight Mon, Wed-Sun. **Credit** AmEx, DC, JCB, MC, V.
Gilli's belle époque interior is original and its staff delightful. Not to be missed are its rich hot chocolates – cacao, *gianduia* (hazelnut), almond, mint, orange and coffee, and an irresistible spread of *spuntini* (nibbles) on the bar at aperitif time. A cappuccino's L2,000 (€1) at the bar, L6,000 (€3.10) seated. There's outside seating in warmer weather.

Giubbe Rosse
Piazza della Repubblica 13-14r (055 212 280). **Open** 7.30am-2am daily. **Credit** AmEx, DC, JCB, MC, V. **Map** p314 B3.
This café dates from the end of the 19th century and became an intellectuals' haunt in 1909, when the Futurist Manifesto was launched from here. Though always popular with the international literati, it went into decline after World War II until new management took over in 1991. Its tables on the elegant piazza are now one of Florentines' favourite places for a bowl of pasta at lunch. It costs L2,000 (€1) for a cappuccino at the bar, L7,000 (€3.60) at a table.

Amerini
Via della Vigna Nuova 63r (055 284 941). **Open** 8.30am-8.30pm Mon-Sat. **No credit cards. Map** p314 B2.
Smart but cosy with a gravity-defying display of the finest Tuscan wines, this is a lunchtime favourite

for local designer-emporium shop assistants. Choose from sandwiches such as marinated artichoke or grilled vegetables with brie (L6,000/€3.10), or order a bowl of fresh pasta (L7,000/€3.60), but be prepared to find other customers placed at your tiny table. At tea-time you can sample luscious lemon tart (L6,000/€3.10) relatively undisturbed or enjoy an aperitif at the bar loaded with snacks. A cappuccino costs L1,800 (93c) at the bar, L5,000 (€2.60) seated.

Bar Curtatone
Borgo Ognissanti 167r (055 210 772). **Open** 7am-1am Mon, Wed-Fri, Sun; 7am-2am Sat. Closed 2wks Aug. **No credit cards. Map** p314 B1.
A vast but stylish café serving a decadent selection of pastries, cakes and savouries. Have a three-course meal (12.30-2.30pm) or sip on a selection of liqueurs and aperitifs. Though it's always busy, service is efficient. Cappuccinos are L2,000 (€1) at the bar, L5,000 (€2.60) seated.

Top five Brunch bets

Brunch is a burgeoning phenomenon in Italy. Though the degree of authenticity varies, you'll often find hash browns, scrambled eggs, freshly squeezed orange juice and chocolate fudge brownies.

Capocaccia
Choose between classic American-style bagels and pancakes or a full English breakfast for L20,000 (€10.50) on Saturday; on Sunday there's a buffet, too. See *p131.*

Hemingway
Buffet brunch with an international flavour for L32,000 (€16.50). See *p132.*

Momoyama
Mainly organic dishes, including crostini with potato and seitan, tofu and vegetables, plus sushi and sashimi, for L35,000 (€18). See *p119.*

Rose's
A Saturday brunch of hamburgers, roast turkey, carrot and courgette bread and veggie options, followed by grandma's apple pie and cookies. L15,000-L20,000 (€7.80-€10.50). See *p131.*

The Westin Excelsior
A glass of champagne, plus smoked salmon, palm hearts, lemon shrimps, pastries, desserts and coffee (L68,000/€35), all to the strains of a live jazz band. See *p49* .

timeout.com

The World's Living Guide

Caffè Megara

Via della Spada 15-17r (055 211 837). **Open** 8am-2am Mon-Sat (lunch 11.30am-3pm). **No credit cards**. **Map** p314 B2.
Crowds flock here for lunch dishes such as *farfalle con pomodori, melanzane e noci* for L8,000 (€4.10). There are also substantial breakfasts and sumptuous cheesecakes. At happy hour (5-8pm) cocktails are L5,000 (€2.60), and there are student discounts after 9pm. It's L1,800 (93c) for a cappuccino at the bar, L5,000 (€2.60) seated. There are mounds of international newspapers and magazines and satellite TV on a huge screen.

Capocaccia

Lungarno Corsini 12/14r (055 210 751). **Open** noon-4pm Mon; noon-2am Tue-Sun. **Credit** MC, V. **Map** p314 C2.
With doors opening from a tiled central bar room on to the *lungarno*, this is one of Florence's most desirable café-bars. In the frescoed non-smoking salon, the US-biased menu is a big draw. Brunch is legendary, so be sure to book; another highlight is the radicchio risotto (L15,000/€7.80). There are also simple *panini* (L12,000/€6.20), smoked fish plates (L20,000/€10.50), champagne (L10,000/€10.50) and an extensive whisky collection. Cappuccino (L3,000/€1.65) and espresso come with handmade chocolate ice-cream. *See also p181*.

Latteria Moggi

Via del Parione 44r (0349 755 2330). **Open** 7.30am-8pm Mon-Sat. **No credit cards**. **Map** p314 C2 .
This relaxed no-smoking café with bleached wood tables and benches is a handy spot for salad or sandwiches, and is very popular with students from the university across the road. Try a yoghurt, milk pudding or one of the rich home-made ice-creams from the chiller cabinet.

San Lorenzo

Nannini Coffee Shop

Via Borgo S Lorenzo 7r (055 212 680). **Open** 7.30am-8pm daily. **Credit** MC, V. **Map** p314 B3.
Perennially bustling, this is a perfect stop for coffee and *panforte*, a sticky Sienese cake. It's owned by ex-racing driver Alessandro Nannini, who has a confectionery factory in Siena, and you can buy *cantuccini* (almond biscuits), *ricciarelli* (choc-covered marzipan petits fours) and hexagonal panfortes.

Porfirio Rubirosa

Viale Strozzi 38r (055 490 965). **Open** 8am-2am Tue-Sun. Closed 2wks Aug. **Credit** MC, V.
Across from the Fortezza da Basso and overlooking the park with its duck pond and fountains, this chic bar was named after a Brazilian playboy and is a monument to hedonism. Lunch on truffle mozzarella or smoked tuna salad, sit on the balcony mezzanine with a slice of passionfruit cheesecake at tea-time, or come back in the evening to make a night of it (*see also p183*).

Rose's

Via del Parione 26r (055 287 090). **Open** 8am-1.30am Mon-Sat, 5pm-1.30am Sun (brunch 12.30-3.30pm Sat). Closed 2wks Aug. **Credit** MC, V. **Map** p314 C2.
This spacious, informal salon with its sleek modern decor and smoke-free, air-conditioned atmosphere, is invariably packed with a young crowd. Lunch is decent pastas and salads (L10,000-L13,000/€5.20-€6.70); in the evening it's one of the trendiest sushi bars in town; *see p183*. Cappuccinos are L1,800 (93c) at the bar, L3,000 (€1.60) seated.

San Marco

Caffèllatte

Via degli Alfani 39r (055 247 8878). *Bus 6*. **Open** 8am-midnight Mon-Sat. **No credit cards**. **Map** p314 A4.
Licensed in 1920 to sell 'coffee and milk beverages', Caffèllatte continues to supply the neighbourhood's milk. In 1984, an organic bakery was added and the current café – one tiny room kitted out with rustic wood tables and chairs – was born. There are exhibits and magazines to peruse. The *caffèlatte*, served piping hot in giant bowls, are the city's best (L2,000/€1 at the bar; L3,500/€1.80 seated).

Santa Croce

Bar La Ribotta

Borgo degli Albizi 80/82 (055 234 5668). **Open** 9am-1am Mon-Sat. Closed 2wks Aug. **No credit cards**. **Map** p314 B4.
A friendly, busy café with plenty of tables and delicious sandwiches, plus more substantial hot food and salad offerings at lunch. The seating is in alcoves so you can have a fairly peaceful meal. Staff are lively and efficient, and there's plenty of info about local clubs, music and events. A cappuccino is L1,700 (88c) at the bar; L4,000 (€2.10) seated.

Caffè Cibreo

Via Andrea del Verrocchio 5r (055 234 5853). **Open** 8am-1am Tue-Sat; lunch served 1-2.30pm. Closed Aug. **No credit cards**. **Map** p314 C6.
A peaceful, elegant café offering phenomenal desserts, notably a dense chocolate torte and a cheesecake served with *arancia amara* (bitter orange) sauce. Call a day in advance for a cake (from L25,000/€13) to take home. A cappuccino is L1,800 (93c) at the bar, L4,000 (€2.10) seated. There are tables outside in summer.

Caffeteria Piansa

Borgo Pinti 18r, nr Piazza G Salvemini (055 234 2362). **Open** 7am-8pm Mon-Sat; lunch served noon-3pm. Closed Aug. **No credit cards**. **Map** p314 B5.
Set on a quiet street, this is a favourite with students and businessfolk, but seating is rarely a problem outside the lunch period. It's self-service, so prices are low (cappuccino L1,800/93c, sarnies L3,000-L5,000/€1.60-€2.60, set lunch L14,000/€7.20).

Oltrarno

Caffè degli Artigiani
Via dello Sprone 16r (055 287 141). **Open** 10am-midnight Tue-Sun. Closed 2wks Sept. **Credit** AmEx, DC, JCB, MC, V. **Map** p314 C2.
On the corner of one of Florence's least-known piazzas, this charming and laid-back rustic-chic café is well worth seeking out for its back salon with its fraying, beautifully carved antique chairs. Hip multilingual staff serve a predominantly art-school clientele. Cappuccino is L1,600 (83c) at the bar, L3,000 (€1.60) seated.

Caffè Notte
Via delle Caldaie 28r (055 223 067). **Open** 8am-2am Tue-Thur, Sun; 8am-3am Fri, Sat. Closed Aug. **No credit cards. Map** p314 D1.
With its earthy, nicotine-drenched ambience, this is a great place for a wake-up call, a pasta lunch, or (best of all) a glass of port and a chat in the early hours. Play a board game at one of the large wooden tables or pull down one of the old theatre seats for a prime view of the television. Cappuccinos cost L1,800 (93c) until 8.30pm.

Caffè Ricchi
Piazza Santo Spirito 9r (055 215 864). **Open** *Summer* 7am-1am Mon-Sat. *Winter* 7am-8pm Mon-Sat. Closed 1st 2wks Jan. **Credit** MC, V. **Map** p314 D2.
One of the most pleasant settings for al fresco drinking in Florence (it's on a traffic-free piazza), this has been a popular local hangout for years and is central to life in the area. The lunch menu, which

---

Top five
Bar snacks

Amerini
Filo pastry bites, anchovy-stuffed olives and mini pizzas, all home-made. *See p129.*

Caffè Ricchi
Salted nuts, fresh capers, canapés, cheeses, hot and cold spreads for *crostini sformatini*, bits-on-sticks and so on. *See p132.*

Capocaccia
Crostini, pâtés, pastas, biscuits with raspberry coulis, mini-muffins and the like. *See p131.*

Gilli
Crisps, tortilla chips, almonds, olives and bite-sized sandwiches on cocktail sticks. *See p129.*

The Fusion Bar, Gallery Hotel
Crunchy-coated macadamia nuts, sesame crackers and other oriental nibbles. *See p45.*

---

changes daily, runs from sandwiches to hearty pasta dishes and speciality *sformati* (hot vegetable terrines) in the restaurant room next to the bar. From 6pm a counter groans with nibbles to help the Campari go down.

Dolce Vita
Piazza del Carmine (055 284 595). **Open** 10am-2am Mon-Sat; 6pm-2am Sun. **Credit** AmEx, JCB, MC, V. **Map** p314 C1.
Though Dolce Vita is known mainly as the supreme pre-club hangout (*see p182*), a lunchtime or evening aperitif sipped outside in the square, shaded from the sun at the canopied tables, is a hallowed Florentine institution best savoured by following the lead of the locals and donning designer shades to sit alone and talk business into the hands-free of your last-model Nokia. Pretentious? You bet. Compulsive viewing? Definitely. A cappuccino is L2,000 (€1) at the bar, L4,000 (€2.10) at a table.

Hemingway
Piazza Piattellina 9r (055 284 781). **Open** 4.30pm-1am Tue-Thur; 4.30pm-2am Fri, Sat; 11am-8pm Sun (brunch noon-2.15pm Sun). Closed Aug. **Credit** AmEx, DC, JCB, MC, V. **Map** p314 C1.
This beautiful non-smoking café has an extensive menu, with a huge selection of teas, at least 20 types of coffee and stunning tea cocktails. Proprietor Monica Meschini is the secretary of the Chocolate Appreciation Society, so cakes and chocolates are to die for – the *sette veli* chocolate cake (L8,500/€4.40) won the World Cake Championship in 1997. Cocktails are L10,000 (€5.20), tea is L8,000 (€4.10). Hemingway high tea (6-7.30pm, L23,000/€12) includes ten different nibbles. There's also a Sunday brunch, with booking advisable.

Il Rifrullo
Via San Niccolò 53/57 (055 234 2621). **Open** 8am-2am daily. Closed 2wks Aug. **Credit** MC, V. **Map** p314 D5.
Set in peaceful San Niccolò, this bar has a variety of newspapers to linger over as you sip your morning cappuccino. Things liven up later, when music comes on and the cocktail barman starts to perform some tricks. From 6pm till 9.30pm the counter is laden with dips and appetisers, included in the price of drinks. It's L1,800 (93c) for a cappuccino at the bar, L5,000 (€2.60) at a table.

Outside the City Gates

Chalet Fontana
Via S Leonardo 8r (055 221 187). Bus 12,13. **Open** 7am-2am Tue-Sun. **No credit cards**.
Enjoy the view of cypress trees on hills in the distance from this charming wooden chalet (on the bus route to Piazza Michelangelo from the station or 15 minutes on foot from the Forte Belvedere). Snack lunches include quiche, salads and sandwiches. The home-made succulent pear and chocolate cake is not to be missed. Stays open till late as a piano bar.

Ice surprises

Ice-cream parlours in Florence are open until 1am – it's habitual to go out at night for an ice-cream just as you might go out for a drink. In summer most bars wheel out an ice-cream counter to replace their stocks of melting chocolate bars as a sweet treat. You can pay anything from L2,500 (€1.30) to €20,000 (€10.50), depending on the size of the cone and on whether you sit down or stroll on. If you see *produzione proprio* or *artigianale* you know the ice-cream is home-made.

The most famous *gelateria* is **Vivoli**, in Santa Croce (via Isola delle Stinche 7r, 055 292 334; closed Monday), revered for its *semi-freddi*, creamier and softer than ice-cream, its ultra-rich chocolate varities and for its divine *riso* (rice-pudding flavour). Flavours are seasonal, though traditional ones such as caramelised pear go year round.

Perche' No! (Via Tavolini 19r, 055 239 8969) is a local institution. It's been open

since 1939, and is one of the best *gelaterie* in Florence (the pistachio and chocolate flavours are legendary among locals).

Gold (Piazza Pesce 3/5r, 055 239 6810) attracts crowds to its tiny serving hatch and offers them a prime position by the Ponte Vecchio to enjoy their treat.

Gelateria dei Neri (Via dei Neri 22r, 055 210 034) has soya ice-cream, allowing even vegans and people with a dairy intolerance to indulge.

A new arrival, *yogurterie* serve a healthy alternative to full-cream ices. Low-fat yoghurt is frozen with fresh fruit or chocolate plus toppings of nuts, chocolate-coated crispy rice and marshmallows. Some places mix the yoghurt to your own recipe. Good *yogurterie* include **Baby Yogurt** (Via Calzaiuoli 24r, 055 92071), **De' Ciompi** (Via dell'Agnolo 121r, 055 234 3994) and **Doctor Ciock** (Via Guelfa 10r, no phone).

Shopping & Services

Whether you have a nose for knick-knacks, a taste for truffles or a lust for leather, Florence aims to please.

There are very few small cities with the wealth of designer flagship stores, antique furniture, rugs and jewellery shops, and artisan and crafts shops that make shopping in Florence such a unique and varied experience.

Culture vultures adore the gilding, mosaics, inlaying and marquetry, picture framing, book-binding and paper-making by Oltrarno craftspeople, the furniture designs and contemporary sculptures, and the marvellous antiques shops clustered around Via Maggio and Via dei Fossi, while magpies are drawn to the tiny shops on the Ponte Vecchio dating back to the 13th century and once the domain of tanners and butchers, though home exclusively to jewellers since 1593.

Designer clothes and jewellery devotees prefer the area around Via Tornabuoni, Via della Vigna Nuova, Via dei Calzaiuoli and Via Roma, while bargain hunters head for Via Panzani, Via dei Neri, Via del Corso and Borgo San Lorenzo for their cheap and cheerful clothes and shoe shops (*see p151* **Bargain chic**). The markets and areas around Santa Croce brim with leather bags and jackets (*see p137* **Hell for leather**).

Foodies swoon at the *alimentari* (small food shops with deli counters) and markets, though in light of recent food scares, it's best to check with your airline if there are any restrictions on importing cured meats and fresh foods.

Some shops have a baffling 'entrata libera' ('free entrance') sign in the window; which means you're free to browse with no obligation to buy. Though this seems obvious, there are still a few places (mainly older, family-run shops) where you're expected to tell the assistant what you're looking for as soon as you enter, and provide a good excuse if you don't like what they offer. Ignore over-zealous or discourteous staff, and leave with a pleasant 'buongiorno' if they insist.

Non-EU visitors are entitled to a VAT rebate on purchases of goods over L300,000 (€155) and some shops keep the requisite forms: *see chapter* **Directory: Money**.

OPENING HOURS

While supermarkets and larger stores in the city centre now stay open through the day ('orario continuato'), most shops still operate standard hours, closing at lunchtime and (food shops excepted) on Monday mornings. Standard opening times are 3.30pm to 7.30pm on Monday, and 9am to 1pm and 3.30pm to 7.30pm Tuesday to Saturday, with clothes shops sometimes opening around 10am. Food shops open earlier in the morning and later in the afternoon and close on Wednesday afternoons. Many central stores now stay open for at least part of Sunday and several more open on the last Sunday of the month.

Hours alter slightly in mid-June until the end of August, with most shops staying open a bit later on weekday evenings and closing on Saturday afternoons. Small shops tend to shut completely at some point during July or August, for anything from a week to a month.

The times listed apply most of the year but they can vary, and some shops, especially small ones, may open or close more randomly.

Books

Many bookshops stock books in English, but prices are 15-40 per cent higher than in the UK. For children's books, *see chapter* **Children**.

Alinari

Largo Alinari 15, Santa Maria Novella (055 23951/ www.alinari.com). **Open** 9am-1pm, 2.30-6.30pm Mon-Fri; 9am-1pm, 3.30-7.30pm Sat. Closed 3wks Aug. **Credit** AmEx, DC, MC, V. **Map** p314 A2.
The world's first photographic firm, established in 1852. Stocks photography books and exhibition catalogues, and will order prints of virtually anything in the Alinari archives.

City Lights

Via San Niccolò 23, Oltrarno (055 234 7882). **Open** 5.30-10.30pm Mon-Fri but erratic (call beforehand). **No credit cards. Map** p314 D5.
Modelled on the San Francisco bookstore of the same name, City Lights stocks Beat literature, much of it in English, and organises literary events.

Edison

Piazza della Repubblica 27r, Duomo & Around (055 213 110). **Open** 9am-midnight daily. **Credit** AmEx, DC, MC, V. **Map** p314 B3.
This book superstore, with its video screens showing the latest news, Internet points, café and lecture area, also sells maps, mags, calendars and CDs. The travel section has lots of guides in English.

Seeber – get there before it closes.

Feltrinelli International

Via Cavour 12-20r, San Marco (055 219 524/ www.feltrinelli.it). **Open** 9am-7.30pm Mon-Sat. **Credit** AmEx, DC, MC, V. **Map** p314 A4.

Modern and well organised, with strong art, photography and comic book sections, plus a huge selection of titles in English, language-teaching books, original-language videos and a gift section.

Libreria delle Donne

Via Fiesolana 2b, Santa Croce (055 240 384/www. associaizoni.comune.firenze.it/cooperativadonne). **Open** 3.30-7.30pm Mon; 9.30am-1pm, 3.30-7.30pm Tue-Fri; 11am-1pm, 3.30-7.30pm Sat. Closed Aug. **Credit** MC, V. **Map** p314 B5.

This women's bookshop is a good reference point for women visiting the city. The feminist literature is mostly Italian, but there's a useful noticeboard.

Paperback Exchange

Via Fiesolana 31r, Santa Croce (055 247 8154/fax 055 247 8856/www.papex.it). **Open** 9am-7.30pm Mon-Fri; 10am-1pm, 3.30-7.30pm Sat. **Credit** AmEx, DC, MC, V. **Map** p314 B5.

Good choice of new English-language fiction and non-fiction, particularly art, art history and Italian culture. The noticeboard has info about literary events, courses, accommodation and language lessons. Second-hand books can be traded.

Seeber

Via Tornabuoni 70r, Duomo & Around (055 215 697). **Open** 9.30am-7.30pm Mon-Sat. **Credit** AmEx, DC, MC, V. **Map** p314 B2.

Florence's oldest bookshop, with mahogany stairs and frescoes, and well-informed staff. Good range of fiction in English; cookbooks and travel guides. Sadly, it's closing in late 2002 (*see p144* **Ousted**).

Communications

Centro AZ

Via degli Alfani 20r, San Marco (055 247 7855). **Open** 9am-1pm, 3-7pm Mon-Fri; 9am-12.30pm Sat. **No credit cards. Map** p314 A4.

Faxes carry a standard charge of L2,000 (€1) plus the cost of the call. Copies cost L80 (4c).

Department stores

COIN

Via dei Calzaiuoli 56r, Duomo & Around (055 280 531/www.coin.it). **Open** 9.30am-8pm Mon-Sat; 11am-8pm Sun. **Credit** AmEx, DC, MC, V. **Map** p314 B3.

Furnishings are the strong point of this mid-range store, with heavy tapestry throws and bright contemporary homeware. There are also crisp modern fashions, shoes, accessories and gifts.

Principe

Via del Sole 2, Santa Maria Novella (055 292 764/www.principedifirenze.com). **Open** 3.30-7.30pm Mon; 9.30am-7.30pm Tue-Sat. **Credit** AmEx, DC, MC, V. **Map** p314 B2.

Staff are having problems fitting their egos into their new doll's-house home since Principe moved from grand premises in Piazza Strozzi (*see p144* **Ousted**). The first port of call for the tweedy English country look, and twee linens, bath accessories and toiletries. Men's suits are made to measure.

La Rinascente

Piazza della Repubblica 1, Duomo & Around (055 219 113/www.rinascente.it). **Open** 9am-9pm Mon-Sat; 10.30am-8pm Sun. **Credit** AmEx, DC, MC, V. **Map** p314 B3.

Classic store with decent menswear, plus perfume counters, Versace bedding and vast lingerie section.

Fashion

For sports clothes and equipment, *see chapter* **Sport & Fitness**; for kids' clothes, *see chapter* **Children**; for budget clothing, *see p151* **Bargain chic**; for gloves and handbags *see p137* **Hell for leather**.

Designer

Most of Florence's designer shops are strung along Via Tornabuoni and Via Vigna Nuova in Santa Maria Novella (map p314 B2/C2).

Eat, Drink, Shop

Armani

Via della Vigna Nuova 51r (055 219 041/www. armani.com). **Open** 3.30-7.30pm Mon; 10am-7pm Tue-Sat. **Credit** AmEx, DC, JCB, MC, V.
Understated, elegant – just don't look at the pricetags.

Bulgari

Via Tornabuoni 61/63r (055 239 6786/ www.bulgari.com). **Open** 3-7.30pm Mon; 10am-7pm Tue-Sat. **Credit** AmEx, DC, JCB, MC, V.
The ultimate status-symbol designer jewellery.

Emporio Armani

Piazza Strozzi 16r (055 284 315/ www.emporioarmani.com). **Open** 3.30-7pm Mon; 10am-7pm Tue-Sat. **Credit** AmEx, DC, JCB, MC, V.
Still understated but younger and hipper than the Armani lines.

Dolce & Gabbana

Via della Vigna Nuova 27 (055 281 003). **Open** 3-7pm Mon; 10am-7pm Tue-Sat. **Credit** AmEx, DC, JCB, MC, V.
Eclectic collections by the Sicilian duo.

Ferragamo

Via Tornabuoni 14r (055 292 123/ www.salvatore ferragamo.it). **Open** 3.30-7.30pm Mon; 9.30am-7.30pm Tue-Sat. **Credit** AmEx, DC, JCB, MC, V.
The king of the shoemakers. The megastore on the ground floor of the Palazzo Spini Ferroni has mens- and womenswear and leather goods too.

Gai Mattiolo

Piazza S Trinita' 1r (055 265 4451). **Open** 3.30-7.30pm Mon; 10am-1.30pm, 3-7.30pm Tue-Sat. Closed 3wks Aug. **Credit** AmEx, DC, JCB, MC, V.
Whimsical frocks for it-girls.

Gianni Versace

Via Tornabuoni 13-15r (055 282 638/ www.gianniversace.com). **Open** 3-7pm Mon; 10am-7pm Tue-Sat. **Credit** AmEx, DC, JCB, MC, V.
Sparkle and flair by Gianni's sister Donatella.

Gucci

Via Tornabuoni 73r (055 264 011/www.gucci.it). **Open** 3-7pm Mon; 10am-7pm Tue-Sat. **Credit** AmEx, DC, JCB, MC, V.
Ever-expanding to accommodate the growing numbers of pilgrims. The avant-garde feel is reflected in the art-gallery-style window displays. Italians buy from the factory outlet (*see p151* **Bargain chic**).

Luisa

Via Roma 19-21r (055 217 826/ www.luisaviaroma.com). **Open** 10am-7.30pm Mon-Sat; 11am-7pm Sun. **Credit** AmEx, DC, MC, V.
Designer collections from Issey Miyake, Roberto Cavalli, Alessandro dell'Acqua and others.

Prada

Via Tornabuoni 51/55r, 67r (055 283 439/ www.prada.it). **Open** 3-7pm Mon; 10am-7pm Tue-Sat. **Credit** AmEx, DC, JCB, MC, V.
Chic minimalist clothing and the famous bags.

Pucci

Via Vigna Nuova 97r (055 294 028). Open 3.30-7.30pm Mon; 10am-1pm, 3.30-7.30pm, Tue-Sat. **Credit** AmEx, DC, MC, V.
Psychedelic printed shirts and leggings, little changed since the '50s designs by Emilio Pucci.

Raspini

Via Roma 25-9r (055 213 077), Via Martelli 3-7 (055 239 8336) & Via Por S Maria 72r (055 213 901/ www.raspini.com). **Open** 3.30-7.30pm Mon; 9.30am-7.30pm Tue-Sat. **Credit** AmEx, DC, JCB, MC, V.
One-stop shops for Romeo Gigli, Armani, Prada, Miu Miu, Anna Molinari, D&G and many others.

Womenswear

Andrea Sassi

Via Cerretani 2r, Duomo & Around (055 294 323). **Open** 3-7.30pm Mon; 9.30am-7.30pm Tue-Sat. **Credit** AmEx, DC, MC, V. **Map** p314 B3.
Sassi by name, sassy by nature. Beautifully made clothing in soft colours and textures such as velvets, organzas and tiny beads, plus sculpted knitwear, simple linens and matt-satin jeans.

BPStudio

Via della Vigna Nuova 15r, Santa Maria Novella (055 213 243). **Open** 3-7.30pm Mon; 10am-7.30pm Tue-Sat. **Credit** AmEx, DC, MC, V. **Map** p314 B2.
Mermaid dresses, rosebud-edged chiffon skirts and mohair stoles in an upmarket but youthful store.

Expensive!

Via Calzaiuoli 78r, Duomo & Around (055 265 4608). **Open** 10am-9pm Mon-Sat; 11am-8pm Sun. **Credit** AmEx, DC, MC, V. **Map** p314 B3.
Great colour-coded collections include simple dresses, jackets and accessories. Accessible prices.

Intimissimi

Via Calzaiuoli 99r, Duomo & Around (055 230 2609). **Open** 9.30am-8pm daily. **Credit** AmEx, MC, V. **Map** p314 B3.
Simple cotton lingerie plus jersey vests and trousers, silk satin pyjamas and boa-trimmed tops.
Branch: Via Cerretani 15/17, Duomo & Around (055 260 8806).

Miss Trench

Via Porta Rossa 16r, Duomo & Around (055 287 601). **Open** 3-7.30pm Mon; 10am-7.30pm Tue-Sat. **Credit** AmEx, DC, MC, V. **Map** p314 C3.
Rock chick chic. Stocks Miss Sixty accessories such as daisy bags and sequinned low-slung hip belts.

Zini

Via Calimala 16-18r, Duomo & Around (055 294 212). **Open** 2-7pm Mon; 10am-7.30pm Tue, Wed; 10am-8pm Sat; 1.30-7.30pm Sun. **Credit** AmEx, DC, MC, V. **Map** p314 B3.
Wearable styles from selected young designers. Well-cut bell-sleeved jackets, little black dresses, fine knits and printed chiffon and crêpe dresses.

Hell for leather

If you're skin-seeking in Florence – and it's a great place for it – you'll either feel spoiled for choice or daunted by the range of styles and the vast differences in quality and price. Here are some tips that should ensure that you don't get stitched up.

In the designer statement range, a bag from Gucci or Prada (*see p136*) will set you back upwards of L800,000/€4,132 (half that at factory shops; *see p151* **Bargain chic**) but along with the kudos and quality comes the knowledge that you can take it back to any of the worldwide branches for repairs.

For top-quality skins with slight natural imperfections that only serve to underline their superiority, plus classic styles and craftsmanship that's been passed down through generations, the renowned **Il Bisonte** (Via del Parione 31r, Santa Maria Novella, 055 215 722), **Cellerini** (Via del Sole 37r, Santa Maria Novella, 055 282 533) and **Bojola** (Via Rondinella 25r, Duomo & Around, 055 211 155) outclass most leather shops, though you'll need to pay around L400,000 (€206) for a bag alone.

More youthful, contemporary designs, decent workmanship and durable leather with a smooth finish are the trademarks of **Coccinelle** (Via Por S Maria 49r, Duomo & Around, 055 239 8782), **Furla** (Via Calzaiuoli 47r, Duomo & Around, 055 238 2883) and

Nannini (Via Porta Rossa 64r, Duomo & Around, 055 213 888); wallets cost around L130,000 (€67), bags start at L250,000 (€129). Fresh modern shapes in pastel patent leather by Byblos and Krizia cost around L300,000 (€155) in the **Pelleteria al Duomo** (Piazza Duomo 14/A-B, Duomo & Around, 055 239 8643). The area around Santa Croce also has rich pickings: try the **Scuola del Cuoio** (inside the cloisters of Santa Croce, Piazza S Croce 16, or Via S Giuseppe 5r on Sunday mornings, 055 244 533) and **Peruzzi** (Borgo dei Greci 8-22r, 055 289 039), which has shoes, bags (from around L200,000/€104) wallets and clothes by famous names.

Italpel (Via Charta77 34, Scandicci, 055 721 570) makes goods for Armani, Prada and Cerruti. At its small own-brand shop in the suburbs a calf bag is L180,000 (€93). The leather gloves shrine **Madova** (Piazza S Felicita'4, Oltrarno, 055 239 6526) makes every imaginable style and colour in the factory behind the shop. They cost L47,000-350,000 (€25-€181).

For rock-bottom prices and pleasant surprises, try a visit to the Mercato Centrale and Mercato Nuovo (*see p150* **Markets**). And remember, it's always worth shopping around, haggling and checking the seams before you buy.

Flower power: **Al Portico** is in the courtyard of a beautiful *palazzo*. *See p141.*

Menswear

Boston Tailor
Via Vecchietti 13, Duomo & Around (055 213 570).
Open 3.30-7.30pm Mon; 9.30am-1pm, 3.30-7.30pm
Tue-Sat. **Credit** AmEx, DC, MC, V. **Map** p314 B3.
Suits, shirts and ties in an 'English' style.

Eredi Chiarini
Via Roma 16r, Duomo & Around (055 284 478).
Open 3.30-7.30pm Mon; 9.30am-7.30pm Tue-Sat.
Credit AmEx, DC, MC, V. **Map** p314 B3.
A favourite with Florentines for its effortlessly styl-
ish polos, softly tailored jackets and cool wool suits.
Eredi Chiarini for women is at Via Porta Rossa 39r.

Massimo Rebecchi
*Via della Vigna Nuova 18/20r, Santa Maria Novella
(055 212 559).* **Open** 3.30-7.30pm Mon; 10am-
7.30pm Tue-Sat; 2.30-7.30pm last Sun of month.
Credit AmEx, DC, MC, V. **Map** p314 D2.
Quality cotton and wool jumpers and casual suits.

Matucci
*Via del Corso 71r, Duomo & Around (055 239
6420).* **Open** 3.30-7.30pm Mon; 10am-7.30pm Tue-
Sat. **Credit** AmEx, DC, MC, V. **Map** p314 B4.
Collections by Armani, Diesel, Hugo Boss and
Versace. Womenwear is in the shop opposite.

Dry-cleaners & launderettes

Dry-cleaners (*tintorie*) also do washing.

Lucy & Rita
Via della Chiesa 19r, Oltrarno (055 224 536). **Open**
7am-1pm, 2.30-7.30pm Mon-Fri. Closed 2wks Aug.
Credit AmEx, MC, V. **Map** p314 D1.
Expensive but good (L5,000/€2.60 per shirt,
L18,000/€9.30 per suit). Wet laundry done by hand.

Wash & Dry
Via Nazionale 129r, San Lorenzo (055 580 480). **Open**
8am-10pm daily. **No credit cards. Map** p314 A3.
A self-service wash and dry takes 50 minutes. Costs:
L6,000 (€3.10) for 8kg, L6,000 (€3.10) for a dry.
Branches: Via dei Servi 105r, San Marco; Via della
Scala 52/54r, Santa Maria Novella; Via dei Serragli
87r, Oltrarno; Via Ghibellina 143r, Santa Croce.

Jewellery

For shops selling items by Arezzo goldsmiths,
visit Via Por S Maria and the Ponte Vecchio.

Aprosio e Luthi
Via dello Sprone 1r, Oltrarno (055 290 534). **Open**
3-7pm Mon; 9am-1pm, 3-7pm Tue-Sat. **Credit**
AmEx, MC, V. **Map** p314 C2.

Eat, Drink, Shop

Intricate necklaces, bracelets, brooches, earrings, evening bags and belts made from tiny glass beads, plus trademark animal brooches and earrings.

Babette von Dohnanyi
Viale Petrarca 116 int, Oltrarno (055 223 697/0338 158 1209). Bus 12, 13. **Open** 10am-1pm, 3-7pm Mon-Fri. Closed 2wks Aug. **No credit cards.**
Delicately coloured handmade glass baubles, decorated with silver and gold and strung on silver or gold chains and earrings (silver L85,000/€44).

Demo
Via del Corso 12r, Duomo & Around (055 217 289). **Open** 3.30-7.30pm Mon; 10am-2pm, 2.30-7.30pm Tue-Sat. **Credit** AmEx, MC, V. **Map** p314 B4.
Silver jewellery with an urban tribe feel. From L120,000 (€62).

Parenti
Via Tornabuoni 93r, Duomo & Around (055 214 438). **Open** 3.30-7.30pm Mon; 9am-1pm, 3.30-7.30pm Tue-Sat. Closed Aug. **Credit** AmEx, DC, MC, V. **Map** p314 B2.
Christmas shopping kicks off with a visit to this treasure trove of Baccarat glass rings and star pendants, art nouveau, art deco and '50s Tiffany jewellery.

Pianegonda
Via dei Calzaiuoli 96r, Duomo & Around (055 214 941/www.pianegondaitalia.com). **Open** 3.30-7.30pm Mon; 10am-7.30pm Tue-Sat. **Credit** AmEx, DC, MC, V. **Map** p314 B3.
Desirable topaz gems, amethysts and citrines in silver rings, necklaces and earrings costing L50,000-L2,000,000 (€26-€1033), and unusual silver watches.

Repairs

Guido
Via Santa Monaca 9, Oltrarno (no phone). **Open** 7am-1pm, 3-6pm Mon-Fri. Closed 2wks Aug. **No credit cards.** **Map** p314 C1.
Guido, who lived in Oz for 25 years, loves to speak English to those bringing in museum-weary shoes.

Punto Maria
Via Santa Monaca 23, Oltrarno (0339 5489 669). **Open** 9am-12.30pm, 3.30-7pm Mon-Fri. **No credit cards.** **Map** p314 C1.
Alterations and repairs on garments in all materials, including leather.

Presto Service
Via Faenza 77, San Lorenzo (no phone). **Open** 3.30-7pm Mon; 9am-12.30pm, 3.30-7.30pm Tue-Sat. Closed 2wks Aug. **No credit cards.** **Map** p314 A3.
While-you-wait heel bar and key-cutting service.

Walter's Silver and Gold
Borgo dei Greci 11Cr, San Croce (055 239 6678). **Open** 9am-6pm daily. **Credit** AmEx, DC, MC, V. **Map** p314 C4.
English-speaking Walter does all jewellery repairs.

Shoes

Calvani
Via degli Speziali 7r, Duomo & Around (055 265 4043). **Open** 10am-7.30pm Mon-Sat; 3-7pm Sun. **Credit** AmEx, MC, V. **Map** p314 B3.

For all things olive head to **La Bottega dell'Olio**. See p141.

Watch this space

After an illustrious history reaching back nearly a century and a half, Panerai, the Florentine watchmaker par excellence, was recently snapped up by the international jeweller Cartier. After starting life as a watch shop and navigation instrument supplier to the Italian navy in 1860, operating from one of the tiny shops that lined the Ponte alle Grazie, Panerai climbed to fame when the navy asked it to produce a watch that could be used underwater and in the dark.

And so the Panerai watch, with its huge glow-in-the-dark digits and resistance to water and pressure, was born, originally using a Rolex mechanism and later moving on to develop its own.

There's always been a scrabble for Panerai's unique, chunky watches among the Florentine elite, with limited editions, which cost upwards of L9,000,000 (€4,649), quickly becoming collectors' items. Panerai's local popularity is now such that the shop is being redeveloped as a museum dedicated to the history of Florence's timekeeper.
Orologeria Svizzera di G Panerai e figli, Piazza S Giovanni 16r, Duomo & Around (055 215 795). **Open** 10am-7pm Mon-Sat. **Credit** AmEx, DC, MC, V. **Map** p314 B3.

Men's and women's shoes in hip styles and colours from young designers such as Roberto del Carlo, along with the sports casual line by Camper.

Divarese
Piazza Duomo 55r, Duomo & Around (055 212 890). **Open** 9am-7.30pm Mon-Sat. **Credit** AmEx, DC, MC, V. **Map** p314 B4.
Stocks a great range of well-made, well-priced shoes in a variety of up-to-the-minute styles for both men and women.

Fausto Santini
Via Calzaiuoli 95r, Duomo & Around (055 239 8536). **Open** 3.30-7.30pm Mon; 10am-7.30pm Tue-Sat. **Credit** AmEx, DC, MC, V. **Map** p314 B3.
Exquisitely made and unusual but simple shoes and bags in high-quality leathers.

JP Tod's
Via Tornabuoni 103r, Duomo & Around (055 219 423). **Open** 10am-7pm Mon-Sat. **Credit** AmEx, DC, JCB, MC, V. **Map** p314 B2.
Trademark bobbly soles that win first prize for comfort on Florence's cobbles.

Marco Candido
Piazza Duomo 5r, Duomo & Around (055 215 342). **Open** 10am-7.30pm Mon-Sat; 11am-2pm, 3-7.30pm Sun. **Credit** AmEx, DC, MC, V. **Map** p314 B4.
A purveyor of sexy but stylish modern women's shoes and boots and classic but modern shoes, some handmade, for men.

Stefano Bemer
Borgo San Frediano 143r, Oltrarno (055 211 356/ www.stefanobemer.com). **Open** 9am-1pm, 3.30-7.30pm Mon-Sat. Closed Aug. **Credit** AmEx, DC, JCB, MC, V.
The place to head for luxury handmade shoes by a young craftsman. This is where Daniel Day-Lewis took time out from being an actor to live the life of an artisan.

Florists

Al Portico
Piazza S Firenze 2, Duomo & Around (055 213 716/www.semialportico.it). **Open** 8.30am-7.30pm Mon-Sat; 10am-6pm Sun. **Credit** AmEx, DC, MC, V. **Map** p314 C5.
An extraordinary shop in the courtyard of a magnificent *palazzo*. The owner is delighted to show customers round, even if they don't want to buy.

Calvanelli
Via della Vigna Nuova 81r, Santa Maria Novella (055 213 742). **Open** 8am-1pm, 3.30-7.30pm Mon, Tue, Thur-Sat; 7am-1pm Wed. **No credit cards.** **Map** p314 B2.
A delightful shop tucked away off the main street, with flowers wrapped in a lovely crêpe paper sculpture posy. Delivery is free within the city centre.

Food & drink

For food markets, *see p150* **Markets**.

Arte Alimentare Meridionale
Piazza Ghiberti 33r, Santa Croce (no phone). **Open** 8.30am-8pm Mon-Sat. **No credit cards.** **Map** p314 C6.
Wonderful *mozzarella di bufala* and other excellent cheeses. Try the ricotta and parsley ravioli.

Bottega della Frutta
Via della Spada 58r, Santa Maria Novella (055 239 8590). **Open** 8am-7.30pm Mon, Tue, Thur-Sat; 8am-1.30pm Wed. Closed Aug. **Credit** MC, V. **Map** p314 B2.
Friendly fruit and veg shop with vintage balsamic vinegar, truffle scented oils and flavoured grappas.

La Bottega dell'Olio
Piazza del Limbo 2r, Duomo & Around (055 267 0468/www.labottegadellolio.it). **Open** 10am-2pm, 3-8pm Mon-Sat. Closed 2wks Jan. **Credit** DC, MC, V. **Map** p314 C3.

Eat, Drink, Shop

pressing all the right buttons

After 21 years, i-D is still the world's most indispensable fashion magazine. Keep on smiling with us by picking up a copy on your travels... To find i-D visit any good newsagent. To find a subscription visit subscriptions@i-dmagazine.co.uk. To find the limited edition i-D badges visit merchandise@i-dmagazine.co.uk. To find the i-D website visit www.i-dmagazine.com

La Bottega dell' Olio has everything from olive oil soaps, delicacies preserved in green gold, olive wood breadboards and pestle and mortars.

Dolceforte

Via della Scala 21, Santa Maria Novella (055 219 116). **Open** 10am-1pm, 3.30-8.30pm Mon-Sat. Closed 3wks Aug. **Credit** AmEx, DC, MC, V. **Map** p314 B2.
The best range of connoisseur chocolates in town includes chocolate Duomos and Ponte Vecchios. In hot months the melting stock is replaced with speciality jams, sugared almond flowers and jars of gianduja, a chocolate hazelnut spread from Turin.

Friggitoria

Via S Antonino 50r, San Lorenzo (055 211 630). **Open** 9am-7pm Mon-Fri; 8am-1pm Sat. Closed Aug. **No credit cards. Map** p314 A3.
Kiosk selling freshly made doughnuts, rice or apple fritters and *coccoli* (deep-fried dough balls).

Mariano Alimentari

Via del Parione 19r, Santa Maria Novella (055 214 067). **Open** 8am-3pm, 5-7.30pm Mon-Fri; 8am-3pm Sat. Closed 3wks Aug. **Credit** AmEx, MC, V. **Map** p314 C2.
Tiny, rustic food shop-cum-sandwich bar with sarnies filled with artichokes, marinated aubergines and oil-preserved pecorino cheeses, and an array of delicacies on display. You can drink a coffee at the bar or in the vaulted-ceilinged wine cellar next door.

Pane & Co

Piazza S Firenze 5r, corner via Condotta, Duomo & Around (055 213 063/www.paneeco.com). **Open** 8am-7.30pm Mon, Tue, Thur-Sat; 8am-1pm Wed. Closed 2wks Aug. **Credit** MC, V. **Map** p314 D4.
Enjoy a glass of wine or a pasta lunch after shopping in the deli. Regular wine and cheese tastings.

Pegna

Via dello Studio 8, Duomo & Around (055 282 701/ www.pegna.it). **Open** 9am-1pm, 3.30-7.30pm Mon, Tue, Thur-Sat; 9am-1pm Wed. **Credit** AmEx, MC, V. **Map** p314 B4.
Specialist pâté, coffee and cheeses as well as general provisions. One of the few places in town where you can find Cheddar and Stilton.

Procacci

Via Tornabuoni 64r, Duomo & Around (055 211 656). **Open** 10.30am-8pm Tue-Sat. Closed Aug. **Credit** AmEx, MC, V. **Map** p314 B2.
The place to buy truffles; in season (Oct-Dec) they come in daily at around 10am. The panelled bar is good for a glass of prosecco and a *panino tartufato*.

I Sapori del Chianti

Via dei Servi 10, San Marco (055 238 2071/www. isaporidelchianti.it). **Open** 9.30am-7.30pm daily. **Credit** AmEx, V. **Map** p314 A4.
Wines, grappas, olive oils, *cantuccini, cavallucci* and *ossi di morto* biscuits, salami, and jars of pesto, condiments and vegetables in extra virgin olive oil.

Dolceforte – sweet treat central.

Sugar Blues

Via dei Serragli 57r, Oltrarno (055 268 378). **Open** 9am-1.30pm, 4.30-8pm Mon, Tue, Thur-Sat; 9am-1.30pm Wed. **Credit** AmEx, DC, MC, V. **Map** p314 D1.
Organic veg, grains, pulses, bread plus eco-friendly detergents and cruelty-free beauty products.
Branch: Via XXVII Aprile 46/48r, San Lorenzo (055 483 666).

Bakeries

Il Forno di Stefano Galli

Via Faenza 39r, San Lorenzo (055 215 314). **Open** 7.30am-4am daily. **No credit cards. Map** p314 A3.
Open till dawn for pizza, bread and biscuits.

Forno Top

Via della Spada 23r, Santa Maria Novella (055 212 461). **Open** 7.30am-1.30pm, 5-7.30pm Mon, Tue, Thur-Sat; 7.30am-1.30pm Wed. **No credit cards. Map** p314 B2.
Tasty sandwiches, batches of hot *schiacciata* (Easter cake) every day, plus fabulous carrot cake.
Branch: Via Orsanmichele 8r, Duomo & Around (055 216 564).

Sartoni

Via dei Cerchi 34r, Duomo & Around (055 212 570). **Open** 8am-8pm Mon-Sat. **Credit** AmEx, JCB, MC, V. **Map** p314 B4.
Takeaway slices of hot pizza, plus filled focaccia.

Deliveries

See also p145 **Rosticcerie.**

Ciao
Via Masaccio 101A, Outside the City Gates (055 574 485). **Open** 10.30am-2.30pm, 5.30-10.30pm daily.
Credit V.
Good Chinese takeaway that also delivers (minimum order L30,000/€15.50). A set combination costs from L8,500 (€4.40), a full meal is about L18,000 (€9.30).

Runner Pizza
055 333 333. **Open** noon-2pm, 7-11pm Mon-Fri; 6.30-11pm Sat, Sun. **Credit** MC.
Pizzas cost L8,000-L12,000 (€4.10-€6.20), including a drink or ice-cream. Delivery is L2,000 (€1) if you order one pizza, free if you order more.

Ethnic

Asia Masala
Piazza SM Novella 22r, Santa Maria Novella (055 281 800/www.ramraj.org). **Open** 4-8pm Mon; 10am-1.30pm, 3.30-9pm Tue, Wed, Fri; 10am-9.30pm Thur, Sat, Sun. **Credit** MC, JCB, V. **Map** p314 B2.
A wonderful source of foods and spices from Asia.

Vivimarket
Via del Melarancio 17r, San Lorenzo (055 294 911). **Open** 9am-7.30pm Mon-Sat. **Credit** V. **Map** p314 A3.
Shelves groan with Indian, Chinese, Japanese, Thai, Mexican and North African specialities, including tofu and lemongrass. It stocks good quality kitchen equipment as well.

Pasta

Bianchi
Via del Albero 1r, Santa Maria Novella (055 282 246). **Open** 9am-1pm, 4.30-7.30pm Mon, Tue, Thur-Sat; 9am-1pm Wed. Closed mid July-end Aug. **No credit cards. Map** p314 A1.
Spinach and ricotta ravioli and potato gnocchi are among the delights on offer in this modest shop.

La Bolognese
Via dei Serragli 24, Oltrarno (055 282 318). **Open** 7am-1pm, 4.30-7.30pm Mon-Fri; 7am-1pm Sat. **No credit cards. Map** p314 C1.
Call in advance for smoked salmon tortelloni.

Patisseries

Most serve breakfast coffee and snacks, and takeaway cakes and savouries ('da portare via').

Dolci e Dolcezze
Piazza Beccaria 8r, Santa Croce (055 234 5458). **Open** 8.30am-8pm Tue-Sat; 9am-1pm, 4.30-7pm Sun. Closed Sun when football match in Florence (open next day); 2wks Aug. **No credit cards.**
The finest patisserie in town, with its story-book

Ousted

As far back as 1975, local newspapers were lamenting the demise of the artisan shops, stationers and apothecaries in Via Calzaiuoli and the surrounding streets, which were closing or leaving the centre in droves to move towards the Oltrarno and the new industrial areas around Florence. It was an exodus that had started after the devastating flood of 1966 destroyed many small shops and businesses. Some were able to pick themselves up, but after the massive clean-up operation, many found the going too tough and sold up.

Well, *plus ça change...* locals are up in arms again over the news that some of the best-loved shops and bars of Florence's historic centre are to close, making way for top international designer houses prepared to pay astronomical rents for prized sites. Giacosa, since the early 1920s the most genteel of Florentine bars, was one of the first casualties, giving way to the wild leopard-skin chiffons and jewel-studded jeans of Florentine designer Roberto Cavalli. The

elegant bookshop Seeber (*see p135* **Books**) will be sadly missed when Max Mara take over the frescoed *palazzo* in Via Tornabuoni in late 2002, while Principe (*see p135* **Department stores**) has already moved from palatial premises to a smaller shop in Via del Sole, apparently usurped by the Rifle jeans emperor, the Tuscan Fratini. There's even talk of Hogan and Tod's shoes swallowing up perfume emporium Profumeria Inglese, one of the oldest shops on Via Tornabuoni.

Smaller, less illustrious shops haven't been spared by 'progress' either; a huge block near Piazza Santa Maria Novella is to be developed as a luxury hotel, squeezing out a handmade lace shop, a well-loved *enoteca* and other family-run businesses. But the biggest changes are taking place in the Oltrarno, traditional home to most of the city's craftspeople. The latter, gradually driven to the outskirts by high rents and traffic restrictions, fear that isolation will impede the exchange of ideas and trade secrets, and that ultimately they will close.

Forget about calories and sample the perfect patisserie of **Dolci e Dolcezze**. *See p144.*

window displays, is famed for its delectable, flourless chocolate cake, but it's worth trying the orange water, strawberry meringue and saffron tarts too. Savouries, incuding Roquefort and mustard croissants, are as good.

I Dolci di Patrizio Cosi
Borgo degli Albizi 11r, Santa Croce (055 248 0367).
Open 7am-8pm Mon-Sat. Closed Aug. **No credit cards. Map** p314 B5.
Famed in Florence for its huge range of tempting sweet treats, including the hot doughnuts (*bomboloni caldi*) served at 5pm.

Marino
Piazza Nazario Sauro 19r, Oltrarno (055 212 657).
Open 6am-8pm Tue-Sun. Closed 2wks Aug. **No credit cards. Map** p314 C1.
Delicious buttery pastries are pulled steaming from the oven here at breakfast and teatime. Sicilian specialities include *cannoli siciliani* (ricotta and candied fruit pastry tubes), rum babas and cassata. The *meringata* (meringue and cream concoction) is a wonderful revelation.

Robiglio
Via dei Servi 112r, San Marco (055 214 501). **Open** 7.30am-7.30pm Mon-Sat. Closed 3wks Aug. **No credit cards. Map** p314 A4.
The place for superb old-fashioned patisserie. The thick *cioccolato caldo* is also worth a try. It has tables outside in summer.
Branch: Via Tosinghi 11r, Duomo & Around (055 215 013).

Rosticcerie

Rosticcerie offer everything you need for a full meal, ready-cooked: *crostini*, roast meat (including spit-roasted chickens, sold by the quarter, half or whole bird) and potatoes, veg and desserts, plus basic wines.

Ramraj
Via Ghibellina 61r, Santa Croce (055 240 999/ www.ramraj.org). **Open** 11.30am-3.30pm, 5-11pm Tue-Sun. Closed Aug. **Credit** MC,V. **Map** p314 C5.
Tandoori and moghul dishes from L5,000 (€2.60). Free delivery with orders over L20,000 €6.20.

Rosticceria Alisio
Via dei Serragli 75r, Oltrarno (055 225 192).
Open 8am-2pm, 5-9pm Tue-Sun. **No credit cards. Map** p314 D1.
Free delivery on orders over L20,000 (€6.20) in central Florence.

Rosticceria Giuliano
Via dei Neri 174r, Santa Croce (055 238 2723).
Open 8am-3pm, 5-9pm Tue-Sat; 8am-3pm Sun. Closed Aug. **Credit** AmEx, MC, V. **Map** p314 C4.
Huge choice of roast meats and savoury dishes.

Rosticceria La Spada
Via della Spada, Santa Maria Novella (055 218 757). **Open** 11.30am-2.30pm, 6.30-10pm daily.
No credit cards. Map p314 B2.
Pasta dishes are cooked while you wait here. There are roast spuds too.

Supermarkets

Co-Op
Viale Talenti 94/96, Outside the City Gates (055 702 073). Bus 1, 5. **Open** 8am-9pm Mon, Tue, Thur, Fri; 8am-1.30pm Wed; 8am-8pm Sat. **No credit cards**.
Very goof for fresh fruit and veg. There's also an ample deli and fresh fish.
Branches: Via Cimabue 49 (055 246 0199).

Esselunga
Via Pisana 130/132, Outside the City Gates (055 706 556). Bus 6, 12, 13. **Open** 2.30-9pm Mon; 8am-9pm Tue-Fri; 7.30am-8.30pm Sat. **Credit** AmEx, DC, MC, V.
A wide choice of general groceries, plus CDs, flowers and newspapers. Free parking.

Margherita Conad
Via L Alamanni 2/10r, Santa Maria Novella (055 211 544). **Open** 8am-7.30pm Mon, Tue, Thur-Sat; 8am-1pm Wed. **Credit** MC, V. **Map** p314 A1.
Small, family-run store beside the station, with fresh and frozen items, a deli serving sarnies and speciality oils and foods, all at supermarket prices.

Natura Si'
Viale Corsica 19/23, Outside the City Gates (055 366 024). Bus 23. **Open** 3.30-7.30pm Mon; 9am-1pm, 3.30-7.30pm Tue-Thur; 9am-7.30pm Fri, Sat. **Credit** MC, V.
Health supermarket with a good organic range.

Wine

See also p124 **Wine Bars**.

Alessi
Via delle Oche 27r, Duomo & Around (055 214 966). **Open** 9am-1pm, 4-6pm Mon-Sat. **Credit** AmEx, DC, MC, V. **Map** p314 B4.
An *enoteca* with a difference – half of it is piled with cakes, biscuits and chocolates, and coffee is ground on the spot. The wine selection is brilliant.

Enoteca Murgia
Via dei Banchi 55/57r, Santa Maria Novella (055 215 686). **Open** 3.30-7.30pm Mon; 9am-1pm, 3.30-7.30pm Tue-Sat. Closed Aug. **Credit** AmEx, DC, JCB, MC, V. **Map** p314 B2.
Long-established *enoteca* with a fine selection of olive oil, *limoncello* and grappa, as well as wines. Service is courteous and helpful. Also sells the highly collectable Illy coffee cups.

Millesimi
Borgo Tegolaio 33r, Oltrarno (055 265 4675). **Open** 3-8pm Mon-Fri; 10am-8pm Sat; 10am-8pm 2nd Sun in month. Closed 2wks Aug. **Credit** AmEx, DC, MC, V. **Map** p314 D2.
Home to one of the biggest selections in town. It specialises in Burgundy and Tuscan wines. Tastings are held by appointment. Door-to-door shipments can be arranged.

Health & beauty

Erborista Inglese
Via Tornabuorni 19, Duomo & Around (055 210 628). **Open** 3.30-8pm Mon; 10.30am-8pm Tue-Sat. Closed 2wks Aug. **Credit** AmEx, DC, JCB, MC, V. **Map** p314 B2.
The gifts, perfumes and skincare in this lovely shop with its frescoed ceilings include Diptych fragrances, Dr Hauschka skincare, Persian Rose organic toners and creams and Bach Flower Remedies.

Experimenta
Via dello Studio 25r, Duomo & Around (055 210 394/www.experimenta.it). **Open** 10am-1.30pm, 3-7pm Mon-Sat. Closed 2wks Aug. **Credit** MC, V. **Map** p314 B4.
Charming little shop with original gifts, including cappuccino- or Tuscan bread-scented bubble bath.

Farmacia del Cinghiale
Piazza del Mercato Nuovo 4r, Duomo & Around (055 282 128). **Open** 9am-1pm, 3.30-7.30pm Mon-Fri; Sat according to rota. **Credit** AmEx, MC, V. **Map** p314 A3.

Products for pampering at **Erborista Inglese**.

Founded in the 18th century by herbalist Guadagni, Cinghiale now has its own line of natural cosmetics.

Farmacia di Santa Maria Novella

Via della Scala 16, Santa Maria Novella (055 216 276/www.smnovella.it). **Open** 9.30am-7.30pm Mon-Sat; 10.30am-6.30pm Sun. Closed 2wks Aug. **Credit** AmEx, DC, MC, V. **Map** p314 B2.

Ancient pharmacy in a 13th-century frescoed chapel, Lotions and potions include Aqua di Santa Maria Novella, known for its calming properties.

Spezieria Erborista Palazzo Vecchio

Via Vaccherccia 9r, Duomo & Around (055 239 6055/www.space.tin.it/salute/gidimass). **Open** 9.30am-7.30pm Mon-Sat; open 1st & last Sun of month. **Credit** AmEx, DC, MC, V. **Map** p314 C3.

Old-fashioned frescoed apothecary specialising in home-made perfumes and floral eau de toilette such as Acqua di Caterina di Medici and Iris di Firenze.

Hairdressers/barbers

Hairdressers in Florence close on Mondays.

Carlo Bay Hair Diffusion

Via Marsuppini 18r, Oltrarno (055 681 1876). **Open** 9am-7pm Tue-Sat. **Credit** AmEx, DC, MC, V.

Unisex salon with English-speaking staff who specialise in colour. It costs L70,000 (€36) for a cut and blow dry. Also offers a range of beauty treatments.

Gabrio Staff

Via Tornabuoni 5, Duomo & Around (055 214 668). **Open** 9am-7pm Tue-Sat. **Credit** MC, V. **Map** p314 C2.

Unisex hair and beauty centre in an amazing atelier, with buffet snacks at lunchtime. A wash and cut is L100,000 (€51.50).

Jean Louis David

Lungarno Corsini 52r, Santa Maria Novella (055 216 760). **Open** 9am-7pm Tue-Sat. **Credit** MC, V. **Map** p314 C2.

A women's wash and cut here is L61,000 (€31.50); men are also welcome. There's a student discount of 20%, or ring for a free haircut in the school. The branch in via Ghibellina 202/204 (055 265 4461) offers an express service.

Pratesi

Borgo Pinti 47r, Santa Croce (055 247 9814). **Open** 9am-6.30pm Tue-Sat. **No credit cards.** Map p314.

Old-fashioned barber for good basic cuts.

Health/beauty treatments

Acquabel

Piazza Pier Vettori 12, Outside the City Gates (055 229 434). Bus 6, 12, 13. **Open** 10am-8.30pm Mon-Fri; 10am-7pm Sat. Closed 2wks Aug. **Credit** AmEx, DC, MC, V.

A beauty salon, gym, sauna, Turkish bath and Jacuzzi. Prices for a simple facial begin at L80,000

The best Shops

For bags & leather

Pelleteria al Duomo (*see p137*) for this season's Byblos and timeless briefcases.

For ceramics

Hand-painted rustic terracotta from **La Botteghina del Ceramista** (*see p149*).

For Florentine perfumes

Handmade fragrances from **Spezieria Erborista Palazzo Vecchio** (*see p147*).

For handmade marbled paper

Watch the bookbinding and paper marbling at **Il Torchio** (*see p152*).

For olive oil

Tuscany's liquid green gold from **La Bottega dell'Olio** (*see p141*).

For truffles

Sit down for a truffle brioche at **Procacci** (*see p143*), or take home a tiny jar.

For unusual souvenirs

Truly tasteful souvenir chocolates from **Dolceforte** (*see p143*).

For wine

Tuscan wines galore at **Millesimi** (*see p146*).

(€41.50). Membership for a day, which allows use of all the facilities (but doesn't include any of the treatments), costs L65,000 (€33.50). There are separate men's and women's areas.

Hito Estetica

Via de' Ginori 21, San Lorenzo (055 284 424). **Open** 9am-7.30pm Mon-Fri; 9am-7pm Sat. **Credit** AmEx, MC, V. **Map** p314 A4.

Natural treatments, including Ayurvedic techniques. Prices start at L60,000 (€31) for a facial.

Freni

Via Calimala, Duomo & Around (055 239 6647). **Open** 9am-7pm Mon-Fri; 9am-1pm Sat. **Credit** AmEx, MC, V. **Map** p314 A3.

If your feet give out after all tramping around all those museums, come to Freni for a foot treatment. Facials are L80,000 (€41.50), massages L50,000-L80,000 (€26/€41.50).

Opticians

Camera and optical lenses go hand in hand in Italy: photography shops sell glasses and opticians sell basic photo equipment. *See p150* **Photography**.

Eat, Drink, Shop

The flowery furniture of
Rosa Regale. *See p149.*

Pisacchi
Via Condotta 22/24r, Duomo & Around (055 214 542). **Open** 4-8pm Mon; 9am-1pm, 4-7.30pm Tue-Sat. **Credit** AmEx, DC, MC, V. Closed 2wks Aug. **Map** p314 C4.
This contact lens specialist carries out eye tests and sells a good range of prescription and sunglasses.

Sbisa
Piazza Signoria 10r, Duomo & Around (055 211 339). **Open** 3.30-7.30pm Mon; 9am-7.30pm Tue-Sat. **Credit** AmEx, DC, MC, V. **Map** p314 C4.
Designer frames include Armani, Gucci, Ralph Lauren, Valentino and Versace, plus a good range of optical and photo equipment.

Homeware

Ceramics & glass

La Bottega dei Cristalli
Via dei Benci, 51r, Santa Croce (055 234 4891/ www.labottegadeicristalli.com). **Open** 10am-7.30pm daily. Closed mid Jan-late Feb. **Credit** AmEx, DC, MC, V. **Map** p314 C5.
Murano and Tuscan-made plates, lamps and chandeliers, and tiny glass sweets and bottles.

La Botteghina del Ceramista
Via Guelfa 5r, San Lorenzo (055 287 367). **Open** 9.30am-1.30pm, 3.30-7.30pm Mon-Fri; 9.30am-1.30pm Sat. Closed 2wks Aug. **Credit** AmEx, DC, JCB, MC, V. **Map** p314 A4.
Superb hand-painted ceramics in intricate designs and vivid colours. Prices go up to L780,000 (€403) for a plate, but there are lots of cheaper alternatives.

Sbigoli Terrecotte
Via Sant' Egidio 4r, Santa Croce (055 247 9713). **Open** 3.30-7.30pm Mon; 9am-1pm, 3.30-7.30pm Tue-Sat. **Credit** AmEx, DC, MC, V. **Map** p314 B5.
Handmade Tuscan ceramics and terracotta in traditional designs. Terracotta casseroles (with heat-retaining qualities) start at L20,000 (€10.50).

Home accessories & gifts

Arredamenti Castorina
Via di Santo Spirito 13/15r, Oltrarno (055 212 885/www.castorina.net). **Open** 9am-1pm, 3.30-7.30pm Mon-Fri; 9am-1pm Sat. Closed Aug. **Credit** AmEx, DC, MC, V. **Map** p314 C1.
An extraordinary old shop with all things baroque: gilded mouldings, frames, cherubs, *trompe-l'œil* tables and fake malachite and tortoiseshell obelisks.

Atmosfere
Via della Vigna Nuova 69r, Santa Maria Novella (055 264 5274). **Open** 3.30-7.30pm Mon; 10am-2pm, 3.30-7.30pm Tue-Sat; 3.30-7.30pm last Sun of month. Closed 2wks Aug. **Credit** DC, MC, V. **Map** p314 B2.
Ethereal shop with huge glass vases and long-stemmed cups and goblets filled with rose petals or

orchids set in transparent gel candlewax, exquisite leaf-embossed candles and globes, plus other gifts.

Culti
Via Scipone Ammirato 4r, Outside the City Gates (055 674 400/www.culti.it). Bus 6. **Open** 3.30-7.30pm Mon; 9.30am-1pm, 3.30-7.30pm Tue-Sat. Closed Aug. **Credit** MC, V.
Minimalist home emporium with wood and metal lamps, candles and kitchen accessories, recycled-card office accessories, and bath oils and fragrances.

Fornasetti
Borgo degli Albizi 70r, Santa Croce (055 234 7398). **Open** 3.30-7.30pm Mon; 10am-1pm, 3.30-7.30pm Tue-Sat. Closed Aug. **Credit** AmEx, MC, V. **Map** p314 B4.
The moon, sun and doleful-looking girl designs of Fornasetti are collectors' items. Six espresso cups and saucers cost from L200,000 (€103.50).

Giraffa
Via Ginori 20r, San Lorenzo (055 283 652). **Open** 3.30-7.30pm Mon; 10am-1pm, 3.30-7.30pm Tue-Sat. Closed 3wks Aug. **Credit** AmEx, DC, MC, V. **Map** p314 A3.
Silk lamps, Italian and Moroccan ceramics, Japanese tableware, candles, candelabra and small fun gifts.

G Veneziano
Via dei Fossi 53r, Santa Maria Novella (055 287 925). **Open** 3-7pm Mon; 9am-12.30pm, 3-7pm Tue-Sat. Closed Aug. **Credit** AmEx, DC, MC, V. **Map** p314 B2.
Upmarket gift shop selling tiny flower-embroidered cushions and tablecloths, glass tableware and jewellery, and unusual gifts for the home.

N'Uovo
Via dei Fossi 21r, Santa Maria Novella (055 238 2290/www.nuovoitaly.com). **Open** 3.30-7pm Mon; 10am-7pm Tue-Sat. Closed 2wks Aug. **Credit** AmEx, DC, MC, V. **Map** p314 B2.
Ultra-modern objets d'art and furniture, including conical silver or gold lamps with mesh shades.

Passamaneria Toscana
Piazza S Lorenzo 12r, San Lorenzo (055 214 670). **Open** 9am-7.30pm Mon-Sat; 10am-7.30pm Sun. **Credit** AmEx, DC, MC, V. **Map** p314 A3.
Brocade cushions, tapestries and wall hangings, table runners, fringes and tassels.
Branch: Via Federighi 1r, Santa Maria Novella (055 239 8047).

Progetto Verde
Piazza Tasso 11, Oltrarno (055 229 8029). Bus 12, 13. **Open** 3.30-7.30pm Mon; 9am-1pm, 3.30-7.30pm Tue-Sat. Closed Aug. **Credit** AmEx, DC, MC, V.
A mecca for the eco-minded, selling everything from non-toxic paints to recycled paper and essential oils.

Rosa Regale
Volta Mazzucconi 3r, beside Via de' Tosinghi 1, Duomo & Around (055 267 0613). **Open** 3.30-7.30pm Mon; 10am-1pm, 2.30-7.30pm Tue-Sat.

Eat, Drink, Shop

Credit AmEx, DC, MC, V. Closed 10-20 Aug.
Map p314 B3.
Sculpted flower chairs (L1,800,000/€929.50) and 3D
rose-shaped cushions (L180,000/€93).

Signum
Borgo dei Greci 40r, Santa Croce (055 280 621/
www.signumfirenze.it). **Open** 10am-7.30pm daily.
Credit MC, V. **Map** p314 C4.
Mini models of shop windows and bookcases, tiny
tarot cards, Murano glass inkwells and more.
Branches: Lungarno Archibusieri 14r, Duomo &
Around (055 289 393), Via dei Benci 29r, Santa Croce
(055 244 590).

Via Toscana
Piazza N Sauro 16r, Oltrarno (055 219 948). **Open**
3.30-7.30pm Mon; 10am-1pm, 3.30-7.30pm Tue-Sat.
Closed Aug. **Credit** MC, V. **Map** p314 C1.
Ceramics, unbleached cotton clothes and bathrobes,
velvet slippers and other Tuscan handicrafts.

Picture framers

Leonardo Romanelli
Via Santo Spirito 16r, Oltrarno (055 284 794).
Open 9am-1pm, 3-7.30pm Mon-Fri; 9am-1pm Sat.
Closed Aug. **No credit cards. Map** p314 C2.
Excellent frames from about L30,000 (€15.50).

Markets

Cascine
*Parco dell Cascine, Viale Lincoln, Outside the City
Gates. Bus 1, 9, 12, 13.* **Open** 8am-1pm Tue.
More than 300 stalls sell everything from live chick-
ens to shoes. Lots of tack, the odd designer bargain.

Mercato Centrale
Piazza del Mercato Centrale & around, San Lorenzo.
Open clothes 8.30am-7pm Mon-Sat; food 7am-2pm
Mon-Fri; Sat pm in winter. **Map** p314 A3.
Food is sold in the 19th-century covered market;
clothes, souvenirs and accessories on stalls outside.

Mercato Nuovo (Mercato del Porcellino)
Loggia Mercato Nuovo, Duomo & Around. **Open**
9am-7pm daily. **Map** p314 A3.
Angled towards the tourists with plaster casts of
Michelangelo's David and other kitsch souvenirs;
leather goods; alabaster chess sets.

Mercato di Sant'Ambrogio
Piazza Ghiberti, Santa Croce. **Open** 7am-2pm Mon-
Sat. **Map** p314 C6.
Florence's foremost and cheapest produce market.
Outside are cheap clothes stalls.

Mercato delle Pulci
Piazza dei Ciompi, Santa Croce. **Open** 9am-7pm
Mon-Sat. **Map** p314 B6.
Good flea market with lots of genuine household and
wardrobe throw-outs and antiques/bric-a-brac stalls.

Plant Market
Piazza della Repubblica, Duomo & Around. **Open**
8am-1pm Thur. **Map** p314 B3.
This sweet-smelling, colourful, good-value plant
market is a pleasue to browse.

Santo Spirito
Piazza Santo Spirito, Oltrarno. **Open** 8am-6pm 2nd
& 3rd Sun of month. **Map** p314 D1 & D2.
On the second Sunday of the month there's a lively
flea market with the odd treasure among the bric-a-
brac and clothing. The third Sunday has stalls selling organic produce, handmade Tuscan clothing,
cosmetics and natural medicines.

Photography

Bongi
*Via Por Santa Maria 82/84r, Duomo & Around
(055 239 8811).* **Open** 3.30-7.30pm Mon; 9.30am-
7.30pm Tue-Sat. **Credit** AmEx, DC, MC, V.
Map p314 C3.
One of the best-equipped photographic shops in the
city centre, with a wide range of second-hand equipment in good condition.

Foto Ottica Fontani
Viale Strozzi 18/20A, San Lorenzo (055 470 981).
Open 2-7.30pm Mon; 8.30am-1pm, 2.30-7.30pm Tue-
Sat. **No credit cards.**
A mecca for photography enthusiasts. The prices
for processing and developing are the lowest in
town: L9,000 (€4.70) for 24 exposures (overnight ser-
vice). It also sells glasses by Armani, Byblos and
Ralph Lauren.

Records

Data Records
*Via dei Neri 15r, Santa Croce (055 287 592/
www.superecord.com).* **Open** 3.30-7.30pm Mon;
10am-1pm, 3.30-8pm Tue-Sat. Closed Aug. **Credit**
MC, V. **Map** p314 C4.
Home to more than 80,000 titles, new and second-
hand, with an emphasis on psychedelia, blues, R&B,
jazz and soundtracks. It also specialises in finding
the unfindable.

Disco Emporium
*Via dell Studio 11r, Duomo & Around (055 295
101).* **Open** 3.30-7.30pm Mon; 9am-1pm, 3.30-7.30pm
Tue-Sat. **Credit** MC, V. **Map** p314 B4.
A specialist shop for historic opera recordings and
classical music.

Ricordi
*Via Brunelleschi 8r, Duomo & Around (055 214
104).* **Open** 3.30-7.30pm Mon; 9.30am-7.30pm Tue-
Sat; 9.30am-7.30pm last Sun of month. **Credit**
AmEx, DC, MC, V. **Map** p314 B3.
Probably the best selection in town, with classical,
jazz, rock and dance sections and helpful English-
speaking staff. Also sells instruments, sheet music
and scores.

Cartoleria Ecologica La Tartaruga

Borgo Albizi 60r, Santa Croce (055 234 0845).
Open 1.30-7.30pm Mon; 9.30am-7.30pm Tue-Sat.
Credit DC, MC, V. **Map** p314 B5.
Unusual stationery and gifts made of recycled paper.

Le Dune

Piazza Ottaviani 9r, Santa Maria Novella (055 214 377). **Open** 9am-7pm Mon-Fri; 9am-1pm Sat. **Credit** AmEx, DC, JCB, MC, V. **Map** p314 B2.

Small, friendly gift and stationery shop with a good range of greetings cards, and photocopying, photo developing and faxing services.

Mandragora

Piazza Duomo 50r, Duomo & Around (055 292 559/www.mandragora.it). **Open** 10am-7.30pm Mon-Sat; 10.30am-6.30pm Sun. **Credit** DC, MC, V. **Map** 314 B4.

Stunning reproductions by local artists of famous Florentine works of art on furnishings, scarves, bags and ornaments, plus great books, cards and prints.

Bargain chic

The abundance of designer flagship stores in central Florence makes for fabulous window shopping, but one look at the price tags may well have you reaching for your Farmacia di Santa Maria Novella smelling salts. If so, be consoled by the factory outlets just outside Florence, where last season's Gucci or Prada collections, plus samples, seconds and some current lines, are sold at 30%-60% discounts.

A private minibus service (for a minimum of four people) is available for **Gucci** (via Arentina 63, Leccio, Reggello, 055 865 7775), **Prada/Miu Miu** (Localita' SS Levanella, Montevarchi, 055 919 6528) and many others, at a return fare of L50,000 (€26) per person per outlet. Call 0347 837 4131 for info, or book by fax on 055 612 0249.

Cashmere company **Malo** has a factory shop for affordable knitwear at via Limite 164, localita Campi Bisenzio (055 894 5308) – up the road from the upmarket casuals **Conte of Florence** outlet (via Limite 170, 055 896 9484); take bus 91A from the station.

There are great bargains to be had in the city centre too, especially in via del Corso, via dei Neri and via Panzani. You'll pay a pittance for delicate crochet skirts and tops in jewel colours, and innovative knitwear from **Melo e Grano** (via della Scala-31r, Santa Maria Novella, 055 272 8990) and for hip streetwear for men and women at **The End** (via del Corso 39r & via Cerretani 9r, Duomo & Around, 055 212 785). In via Borgo San Lorenzo visit **Zini** for club clothes (26r; 055 289 850), **Desii** for menswear (4-6r; 055 211 222/055 292 321) and **Ritratto** for young, funky styles (53r; 055 295 091). Also try **Echo** (Via dell'Oriuolo 37r, Duomo & Around; no phone), whose excellent sweaters, skirts and eveningwear, made-to-order or off-the-rack, are incredibly cheap. Right in the middle of designerland,

And (Via della Vigna Nuova 81r, Santa Maria Novella, 055 284607) sells, at market prices, simple crisp linens and knits that wouldn't be out of place in one of the neighbouring designer emporia.

For sample lines from Kookai, Lui-Jo and Byblos, try **Stroll** (Via Romana 78r, Oltrarno, 055 229 144), if you can stand suffocating service, or have an easier time browsing through designer end-of-lines and past seasons' stock at **Il Guardaroba** (Borgo degli Albizi 85R, Santa Croce, 055 234 0271, & Via Nazionale 38, San Lorenzo, 055 215 482).

Market stalls are a good source of cheap and second-hand clothes; the Mercato Centrale is the main event, but the weekly Tuesday morning Cascine market is where Florentines search for bargains (*for both see p150* **Markets**). For second-hand clothes also try **La Belle Epoque** (Borgo degli Albizi 24r, Santa Croce, no phone), which has a mixed bag, including Levis and some antiquey items.

Peppe Peluso (Via del Corso 1/11r, Duomo & Around, 055 268 283) has a huge choice of ridiculously cheap men's and women's shoes and bags, in styles that can often be seen at twice the price at shops up the road. The chain **Bata** (Piazza Stazione 39r, Santa Maria Novella, 055283 112; & Via Calzaiuoli 110r, Duomo & Around, 055 211 624) also has a great selection of shoes, trainers and boots starting at around L120,000 (€62).

Your very best chance of finding real bargains is during the twice-yearly sales that are strictly planned by the local council to start and finish at the same time. The dates are decided year by year; they're usually held from mid January to mid February and for about six weeks from the beginning of August.

Pineider

Piazza della Signoria 13r, Duomo & Around (055 284 655). **Open** 3.30-7.30pm Mon; 10am-7.30pm Tue-Sat; 10am-2pm, 3.30-7.30pm Sun. **Credit** AmEx, DC, JCB, MC, V. **Map** p314 C4.
Stocks great paper, writing accessories and also leather goods.
Branch: via Tornabuoni 76r, Duomo & Around (055 211 605).

Zecchi

Via dello Studio 19r, Duomo & Around (055 211 470/www.azienda.com/zecchi). **Open** 8.30am-12.30pm, 3.30-7.30pm Mon-Fri; 8.30am-12.30pm Sat. Closed Aug. **Credit** AmEx, DC, MC, V. **Map** p314 B4.
Everything from pencils to gold leaf.

Handmade marbled paper

Giulio Giannini e Figlio

Piazza Pitti 36r, Oltrarno (055 212 621/www.giuliogiannini.it). **Open** 10am-7.30pm Mon-Sat. **Credit** AmEx, DC, MC, V. **Map** p314 D2.
Old family-run firm stocking marbled books, leather desk accessories and greetings cards.

Il Papiro

Via Cavour 55r, San Marco (055 215 262). **Open** 9am-7.30pm Mon-Sat; 10am-6pm Sun. **Credit** AmEx, MC, V. **Map** p314 A4.
Amazing marbled paper products and gifts.
Branch: Piazza del Duomo 24r, Duomo & Around (055 281 628).

Il Torchio

Via dei Bardi 17, Oltrarno (055 234 2862). **Open** 9am-7.30pm Mon-Fri; 9am-1pm Sat. Closed 2wks Aug. **Credit** AmEx, MC, V. **Map** p314 D3.
A pleasant place to watch bookbinding in action, and stock up on handmade paper boxes, stationery and albums.

Shipping

Fracassi

Via Santo Spirito 11, Oltrarno (055 283 597). **Open** 8.30am-12.30pm, 2.30-6.30pm Mon-Fri. **No credit cards. Map** p314 C2.
Not the cheapest in town, but very central and will move anything, anywhere.

Gondrand

Via Baldanzese 198, Outside the City Gates (055 882 6376/www.gondrand.it). Bus 92. **Open** 9am-12.30pm, 2-6.30pm Mon-Fri. **No credit cards.**
Reliable international or local shipping and moving, with free estimates.

Ticket agencies

When booking by phone, ensure all arrangements for collection or delivery are clearly specified.

Box Office

Via Alamanni 39, Santa Maria Novella (055 210 804). **Open** 3.30-7.30pm Mon; 10am-7.30pm Tue-Sat. **No credit cards. Map** p314 A1.
Sells tickets for concerts, plays and exhibitions in Italy and abroad. Go in person; phone lines are constantly engaged.
Branch: Chiasso de Soldanieri 8r, Duomo & Around (055 293 393/055 219 402).

Travel agents

Biemme

Via delle Belle Donne 4r, Santa Maria Novella (055 294 329). **Open** 9am-12.30pm, 3-6.30pm Mon-Fri; 9.30am-12.30pm Sat. **Credit** AmEx, DC, MC, V. **Map** p314 B2.
The staff here are experts at finding the best deal going for holidays and flights, as well as train and boat tickets.

CTS (Student Travel Centre)

Via dei Ginori 25r, San Lorenzo (055 289 570/www.cts.it). **Open** 9.30am-1.30pm, 2.30-6pm Mon-Fri; 9.30am-12.30pm Sat. **Credit** MC, V. **Map** p314 A3.
The official student travel service offering discounted (some student-only) air, coach and train tickets. Obligatory membership is L50,000 (€26) for non-students, L20,000 (€10.50) for students.

Intertravel

Via Lamberti 39r, Duomo & Around (055 217 936). **Open** 9am-6.30pm Mon-Fri; 9am-noon Sat. **Credit** AmEx, MC, V. **Map** p314 C3.
A busy and efficient place, with a full range of services, a currency exchange and a DHL service.

Lazzi Express

Piazza Adua/Piazza Stazione, Santa Maria Novella (055 215 155/www.lazzi.it). **Open** 9am-7pm Mon-Fri; 9am-6pm Sat. **No credit cards. Map** p314 A2.
Information and tickets for coach services within Italy and Euroline international services.

Video rental

Blockbuster

Viale Belfiore 6A, Outside the City Gates (055 330 542). **Open** 11am-11pm Mon-Thur, Sun; 11am-midnight Fri, Sat. **Credit** V.
Good number of films in English, plus cinema-style trimings of popcorn and ice-cream. Registration is L10,000 (€5.20); films cost L6,000-L8,000 (€3.10-€4.10) for 48 hours.
Branch: Via di Novoli 9/11, Outside the City Gates (055 333 533).

Punto Video

Via San Antonino 7r, San Lorenzo (055 284 813). **Open** 9am-8pm Mon-Sat. **Credit** AmEx, DC, MC, V. **Map** p314 A2.
Has over 500 titles in English to choose from. Membership is free and videos cost L6,000 (€3.10) per night.

Arts & Entertainment

Tuscany by Season

It's any excuse for a knees-up with the hedonistic Tuscans.

From elaborate historical festivals such as the Scoppio del Carro in Florence and the Giostra del Saracino in Arezzo, which are staged in medieval or Renaissance costume and accompanied by musicians and flag-throwers, to the simplest country *sagre* or rites, Tuscans like to make the best of things, which often means food, drink, music and dancing. While mainstream events usually draw large crowds, if you want to escape from your fellow tourists and get a taste of genuine country life, head out of town for one of the hundreds of festivals celebrating anything from the Virgin Mary or a local saint to sausages, wild boars or pine nuts. The point is to eat, drink and be merry, and outsiders are always welcome.

Phone numbers listed may be operational for the duration of the festival only, in which case the local tourist office is the best place to call.

Spring

Festa della Donna
Date 8 Mar.
Italy is one of the few countries where International Women's Day is celebrated: women are given sprigs of yellow mimosa by all and sundry, and in the evening restaurants and clubs are full of girl gangs out on the town (many places put on male strippers).

Holy Week
Date Mar or Apr.
Holy Week is celebrated in many small Tuscan towns with religious processions, many carried out in Renaissance costume. Some of the more important ones are Buonconvento (near Siena), Castiglion Fiorentino (near Arezzo) and Bagno a Ripoli (just outside Florence). In Grassina, near Florence, and San Gimignano, re-enactments of episodes from the life of Christ are staged on Good Friday.

Scoppio del Carro
Piazzale della Porta al Prato to Piazza del Duomo, Florence. Date Easter Sunday.
Easter Sunday, one of the most important days of the Florentine calendar, is the day of the Scoppio del Carro, an eccentric ritual dating back to the 12th century. A long parade of trumpeters, drummers, costumed dignitaries and flag-throwers escort a *carro* (tall, heavy wooden cart), pulled by four white oxen with garlands of flowers around their horns, through the streets. Spectators crowd the city centre, so be at Porta al Prato at 9.30am for a clear view. The

scoppio (explosion) happens at 11am, when a mechanical dove is 'lit' by a priest during mass, flies along a wire stretched from the altar to the *carro* outside and sets off fireworks. If all goes smoothly, it is said that the year's harvests will be good.

Settimana dei Beni Culturali
Florence. Information 055 290 832. Date 1wk early spring.
State museums (including the Uffizi, Accademia, Palatina and many more) allow a day's free entry.

Mostra Mercato di Piante e Fiori
Giardino di Orticoltura, Via Vittorio Emmanuele 4, Outside the City Gates, Florence. Bus 4.
Information 055 290 832. Date around 25 Apr-1 May and 6 & 7 Oct.
A spectacular plant and flower show attracting growers from miles around.

Mostra Mercato Internazionale dell'Artigianato
Fortezza da Basso, Outside the City Gates, Florence. Information 055 49721. Date 2wks late Apr/May.
This vast international craft fair embraces ceramics, glassware, fabrics and wood items of varying quality; ethnic goods are a highlight.

Maggio Musicale Fiorentino
Teatro Comunale, Santa Maria Novella, Florence. Information 055 211 158. Date late Apr-late June.
The highlight of the musical year, with opera, concerts and ballet featuring international artists.

Palio, Magliano in Toscana
Magliano in Toscana. Information 0564 592341. Date during 1st wk May.
A jousting match and *palio* in a lovely town in the Maremma. The evening before there's a torchlit procession through town and the horses are blessed. The race, held in a field on the town outskirts, is at 4pm, but teams gather and parade from 9am.

Mille Miglia
Florence. Information 030 280 036. Date Sat in early-mid May.
Some 350 vintage cars take part in this 1,000-mile (1,600km) race, which starts and finishes in Brescia

> ▶ More details on many of the cultural festivals listed are given in the **Arts & Entertainment** chapters. Major Tuscan events are listed here; smaller, local festivals are described in the relevant **Tuscany** chapter.

The eccentric **Scoppio del Carro** is an explosive date in the Florentine calendar. *See p154.*

in northern Italy. It passes through the centre of Florence in the early afternoon of the final day.

Festa del Grillo
Parco delle Cascine, Outside the City Gates, Florence.
Date 27 May.
Held on Candlemas, this ancient symbolic event has become, like many such, an excuse for a big general market. Until 2000, crickets, traditionally meant to woo sweethearts and given as gifts to cheer them up during separations, were sold in hand-painted cages, but animal rights activists have been trying to convince the authorities that this is cruel and the trade in live insects has been discouraged.

Cantine Aperte, Toscana
Information 0577 738 312 (guide available at tourist offices). **Date** last Sun in May.
Wine-producing estates (many not normally open to the public) put on tastings and nibbles.

Summer

Everyone comes out to play in the evening in summer, as the heat tends to be at its worst in the afternoon and long siestas become de rigueur. A variety of open-air venues emerge around the end of May, while restaurants and bars fill their outside spaces with tables (book if you want to eat al fresco at a popular eatery). In Florence, open-air cinemas show two films a night (*see chapter* **Film**), open-air bars doubling as live music venues run a full programme of events (*see chapter* **Nightlife**),

clubs move dancefloors outside and cloisters and squares host classical concerts. Piazzas and gardens, meanwhile, fill with locals chatting or playing cards.

Giostra del Saracino
Piazza Grande, Arezzo. **Tickets** standing L10,000 (€5.20); sitting (June only) L30,000-L70,000 (€15.50-€36). **Information** 0575 377 678/tickets 0575 377 262. **Date** June, Sept.
This reconstruction of an ancient jousting tournament between the four *quartieri* of Arezzo, held in the Piazza Grande on the penultimate Sunday in June and the first Sunday of September, originated in the 13th century and is accompanied by a parade of musicians and acrobatic flag-throwers dressed in the period garb of their team's colours. The first parade starts at about 10am, another starts at 2.30pm, and at 5pm the procession of horses, knights and their escort arrives in the Piazza, and the tournament begins.

Calcio in Costume
Piazza Santa Croce, Florence. **Information** 055 290 832. **Map** p314 C5. **Date** June, early July.
This violent variation on football, played in medieval costume on 24 June and three other days in June or early July (dates are pulled out of a hat on Easter Sunday), is one of the most colourful events in the Florentine year: four teams of strapping bare-chested lads representing the city's ancient quarters – Santa Croce, Santa Maria Novella, Santo Spirito and San Giovanni – parade through the streets accompanied by the local great and good and musicians,

Arts & Entertainment

Boys will be boys – **Calcio in Costume** always stirs local passions. *See p155.*

before settling old rivalries in a no-holds-barred version of football played over one hour by two teams of 27 men. Blood is often spilled. Check the venue: the event was moved in 2001 owing to residents' protests but organisers hope it will return.

Estate Fiesolana
Teatro Romano, Fiesole. **Information** 055 597 8308. **Date** mid June-mid Aug.
This festival of music, dance and theatre in an atmospheric setting has some worthwhile events.

Luminaria di San Ranieri
Pisa. **Information** 050 560 464. **Date** 16/17 June.
Tens of thousands of candles are lit and displayed along the Arno and on the buildings on the *lungarni*. The next day, at about 6.30pm, there's a boat race along the Arno between the town's four *quartieri*.

Festa di San Giovanni
Florence. **Date** 24 June.
A public holiday in honour of Florence's patron saint. In the evening a huge fireworks display is held near Piazzale Michelangiolo.

Il Gioco del Ponte
Pisa. **Tickets** L20,000 (€10.50). **Information and tickets** 050 910 393. **Date** last Sun June.
A kind of 'push-of-war' dating from the 13th century, with teams from Pisa and around fighting for supremacy on the Ponte di Mezzo (by pushing a metal construction on rails against the opposing team). Processions start near the Ponte di Mezzo at 4.30pm; the competition starts at 6.30pm.

Festa Internazionale della Ceramica
Montelupo. **Information** 0571 518 993. **Date** 8 days last wk June.
A celebration of Tuscan ceramics, a craft very much rooted in the past, with Renaissance music and costume, and demos of past and present techniques.

International Polo Tournament
Ippodromo delle Cascine, Outside the City Gates, Florence. Bus 17C. **Information** 0335 7536550. **Date** late June/July.
Top-flight sporting action for horsey types.

Pitti Uomo
Fortezza da Basso, Outside the City Gates, Florence. **Information** 055 36931. **Date** early July.
The summer instalment of the international men's ready-to-wear fashion fair.

Florence Dance Festival
Teatro Romano, Fiesole. **Information** 055 289 276. **Date** 3wks in July.
A global contemporary dance festival held in Fiesole's Roman amphitheatre in 2001 but probably elsewhere in 2002.

Incontri in Terra di Siena
La Foce, Chianciano Terme. **Information** 0578 69101. **Date** 10 days late July.
Rare chamber music performed by top native and global musicians in the incomparable settings of La Foce (the family estate of writer Iris Origo), Castelluccio di Pienza and surrounding villages.

Opera Festival

Batignano, near Grosseto. **Information** 0564 414 303 (Grosseto tourist office). **Date** July-Aug.
Little-known opera productions by global artists in an idyllic tiny hilltop town. A bit precious.

Puccini Opera Festival

Torre del Lago. **Information** 0584 359 322/fax 0584 350 277. **Credit** MC, V. **Date** July-Aug.
Puccini's lakeside villa is a magnificent setting for the staging of two or three of his operas. The stage is built out over the water, with the audience on the lake shore. Take mosquito repellent.

Palio, Siena

Piazza del Campo, Siena. **Information** 0577 280 551. **Date** 2 July & 16 Aug.
This controversial, often violent horse race around Siena's Piazza del Campo is Tuscan pageantry at its best. Trial races are run on the three days leading to the two main dates; the last takes place at 9am on the big days. In the early afternoon, each qualifying horse and jockey is blessed in their team's church. At around 4.30pm, the procession enters the Piazza del Campo and, after a display of acrobatic flag-throwing, the race is run at about 7pm. It's free to stand in the square, but you need to be in place early. Tickets for balconies overlooking the piazza are sold in bars and cafés on the piazza, but are hard to come by and expensive.

Effetto Venezia

Livorno. **Information** 0586 898 111. **Date** 10 days late July/Aug.
Evening shows and concerts in Livorno's 'Venetian quarter', so-called because of its canals. Restaurants stay open late to serve local delicacies; many set up street stalls. Try the Livornese fish soup *cacciucco*.

Medieval Festival

Monteriggione. **Information** 0577 304 810. **Date** 10 days late July.
A re-enactment of medieval life in the town of Monteriggione, just north of Siena, with food, drink and craft stalls, music and dancing, shops and performances. Action, which fills the main piazza and takes place in the costume of the day, focuses on the third weekend of July, but events take place during

The culinary year

While hothouses bring a tired year-round availability to the UK and US, Tuscan eating habits are, thankfully, still very much ruled by seasonal availability. Each arrival is treated with reverence and in country areas some are even celebrated in the form of 'sagre' festivals – steak in Cortona (mid August), grapes in Impruneta (late September) and truffles in San Miniato (late November), for example.

Spring is probably the food season that Tuscans look forward to most; the sense of excitement in the air is almost palpable when the first green asparagus or *bacelli* (broad beans to be eaten with pecorino cheese) appear. Lettuces and salad leaves are superb by the start of May, while courgettes (the skinny, ridged ones are best) and their blousy yellow flowers (the latter something of a delicacy to be deep fried or stuffed) start early and continue all summer. On the fruit front, cherries (especially the duroni, a fat juicy variety whose deep purple skin seems too tight for the pink flesh) are a real treat in late May.

With the long, hot days of high summer come the sensual, summer fruits – peaches, apricots, nectarines and melons – and the 'Mediterranean' vegetables: the sweetest red, green and yellow peppers, deep purple aubergines and the first, truly ripe tomatoes (round ones, long ones, knobbly ones, oval ones, cherry ones). Late summer sees a glut of sensual and fleshy figs; pair them with *salame Toscano*.

Early September heralds the 'vendemmia' or grape harvest, and towards the end of the month the first *vino novello* arrives, a light, fruity and slightly fizzy wine, traditionally accompanied by roasted chestnuts.

Porcini mushrooms are plentiful, too. Their wide, fleshy caps are grilled and drizzled with olive oil or (with their white stalks) they are chopped and flavoured with nipitella (a variety of wild mint) for pasta sauce. And then there is the new oil or *olio nuovo*, another much-anticipated arrival. It is sludgy green and peppery on the tongue.

Even winter is not without its culinary pleasures; cabbages in all varieties (including the typical Tuscan cavolo nero), pale green fennel bulbs, bright orange pumpkins, densely packed heads of broccoli and a wide range of crisp and slightly bitter winter salads. Artichokes come in several varieties, from the big, round mamme to spiky, purple-tipped morelli. Pears (often eaten with pecorino cheese) are particularly good through winter, but it is the oranges – aranci, mandarini, clementini – that crown the winter fruit stalls, reaching their zenith around January/February with the tarocchi variety which have the sweetest of blood-red flesh.

Arts & Entertainment

the following week and weekend. Torches are lit after dark. Visitors must change their cash into 'medieval' currency.

On The Road Festival
Pelago, 25km (16 miles) east of Florence. **Information** 055 832 6236. **Tickets** L12,000 (€6.20). **Date** 1 weekend (Thur-Sat) mid/late July, from 9pm.
A festival of street performers, artists, musicians, actors, mime artists and fire-eaters.

Autumn

Settembre Musica
Teatro della Pergola and various venues, Florence. **Information** 055 608 420. **Date** Sept.
A month of early-music concerts, by young or relatively obscure ensembles, with the odd bigger name.

Rassegna Internazionale Musica dei Popoli
Auditorium Flog, Outside the City Gates, Florence. *Bus 4,8, 14, 20, 28.* **Information** 055 422 0300. **Date** Oct-Nov.
An innovative world music festival.

Winter

Italians go for Nativity scenes in a big way, and many churches set up cribs, some *viventi* (with live animals). At Campese on Giglio island, there's even an underwater crib. The main ones in Florence are at San Lorenzo, Santa Croce, Chiesa di Dante and Santa Maria de' Ricci.

Florence Marathon
Florence. **Information** tel/fax 055 572 885. **Date** late Nov/early Dec.
A full and half marathon. Prize money is L7,000,000 (€3,616) and L500,000 (€258) respectively.

Florence Dance Festival Winter Edition
Teatro Goldoni, Florence. **Information** 055 289 276. **Map** p314 D1. **Date** late Nov/early Dec.
The winter session of the innovative festival organised by the Florence Dance Centre.

Christmas Concert
Teatro Verdi, Florence. **Information** 055 263 8777; tickets 055 212 320. **Map** p315 C5. **Date** 24 Dec.
Given by the Orchestra Regionale Toscana.

Christmas
A tad disappointing in terms of festivities, Christmas in Florence is marked mainly by longer shop opening hours, decorations (generally very tasteful) around town and events organised by the Comune, which vary from year to year. An atmospheric midnight mass is held in the Duomo. A few restaurants open on Christmas Day, but there's more choice on Boxing Day (Santo Stefano).

New Year's Eve
Many Florentines see in the New Year in at home (accompanied by lots of food and drink, of course), but lots of restaurants put on special 'Cene di Capo d'Anno' involving endless courses (including, traditionally, stuffed pigs' trotters and lentils), for which you'll pay through the nose. Alternatively, take to the streets – outdoor events have been on the up and up in the past few years, with street parties, both official and impromptu, all over town.

Sfilata dei Canottieri
Florence. **Date** 1 Jan.
A traditional parade of boats on the Arno.

New Year Concert
Teatro Comunale, Florence. **Date** 1 Jan. **Information** 055 597 851 (for free tickets).
Put on by the Scuola di Musica di Fiesole.

La Befana (Epiphany)
Date 6 Jan.
An Italian holiday on which smaller towns hold street parties. In Pisa, parachutists dressed as the Befana (a poor old woman) drop in and bring presents to children.

Pitti Uomo
Fortezza da Basso, Outside the City Gates, Florence. **Information** 055 36931. **Date** mid Jan.
The first of the year's international men's ready-to-wear fashion fairs, with leading global labels.

Carnevale
Date 10 days up to Shrove Tuesday, Feb.
Many Tuscan towns celebrate Carnevale; most events consist of parades with elaborate floats, fancy dress parties, and eating and drinking to excess. In Florence, children dress up and parade with their parents in the piazzas and along Lungarno Amerigo Vespucci, scattering confetti and squirting anything moving with aerosol foam. Elsewhere in Tuscany, Borgo San Lorenzo has a children's event with floats, street performances, costumes and mimes, Calenzano has revellers in medieval costumes and San Gimignano has floats, masks and costumes.

Viareggio Carnevale
Viareggio. **Transport** LAZZI bus from Piazza Adua, Florence (055 351 061) to Viareggio; train from Florence SMN (1478 88088) to Viareggio via Pisa. **Tickets** for all days L20,000 (€10.50); L36,000 (€18.50) & L40,000 (€20.50) in stands. **Information** 0584 963 501. **Date** 4 consecutive Suns in Feb (and possibly March).
The biggest Carnival celebrations in Italy outside Venice. The first three parades begin at about 2.30pm, the last at 5pm, finishing around 9.30pm. The latter, an OTT procession of gigantic floats, often lampooning political and public figures, is rounded off with a fireworks display and prize ceremony for the best float. Buy tickets at booths in the town from 8am on the day, or by phone in advance.

Children

It's not a conventional family spot, yet among its museums and ancient walls Florence has lots to interest the kids.

Children can get pretty bored in front of even the greatest masterpieces of Renaissance art, especially when combined with long visits to churches and museums. Luckily Florence has many child-friendly attractions: gardens with merry-go-rounds and swings, swimming pools and some curio-stuffed museums. In addition, the labyrinthine streets of the city itself are fun to explore, especially around piazza Santo Spirito, where you can peek into workshops to see artisans applying gold leaf, carving wood or polishing silver. Italians love children, so they're welcomed almost everywhere.

Florence's museums are of course, well, art-dominated, and there are no specialist kids' museums, but there are at least a handful displaying the kind of esoterica that seize children's imaginations: **Museo di Geologia e Paleontologia** (*see p91*), with its strange fossilised elephant and **La Specola** (*p100*), the zoology museum. Finally, there's the **Museo Archeologico** (*p91*), with its Egyptian tombs, complete with mummies. Three museums (Palazzo Vecchio, *p70*; Museo Stibbert, *p101*; and Museo della Storia della Scienza, *p73*) have special children's programmes involving experiments, games and costumed re-creations.

If your kids like nature there is plenty of easily accessible countryside near the city, and farmers usually tolerate a discreet invasion of their olive groves for walks and picnics, and the prospect of a day at the sea or the hot springs tends to make kids more tolerant about visiting monasteries and Etruscan tombs along the way.

For babysitting, ask at your hotel or check the noticeboards of the children's lending library in St James' American Church (*see p159*), the British Institute (*p288*), Paperback Exchange (*p135*) and Ludoteca Centrale (*see p161*).

Book & toy shops/rental

Città del Sole

Via Cimatori 21r, Duomo & Around (055 219 345). **Open** 3.30-7.30pm Mon; 9.30am-7.30pm Tue-Sat. Closed 2wks Aug. **Credit** AmEx, MC, V. **Map** p314 C4.
This sells well-made children's toys – the wooden ones are particularly nice – as well as a selection of board games and puzzles.

La Co-operativa dei Ragazzi

Via San Gallo 27r, San Lorenzo (055 287 500/www.libreriaragazzi.net). **Open** 9am-1pm, 3.30-7.30pm Mon-Sat. Closed Aug. **Credit** V. **Map** p314 A4.
A great shop with a large selection of books and an even better choice of toys.

Menicucci

Via Guicciardini 51r, Oltarrno (055 294 934). **Open** 9.30am-8pm daily. **Credit** AmEx, MC, V.
This sweet and charming place is a good all-round toy shop known for its window display of soft toys and wooden Pinocchios in all sizes.

Natura e...

Via dello Studio 30r, Duomo & Around (055 265 7624/www.naturae.it). **Open** *Summer* 9.30am-7.30pm Mon-Fri; 10am-2pm Sat. *Winter* 3.30-7.30pm Mon; 9.30am-7.30pm Tue-Fri; 10am-7.30pm Sat. **No credit cards. Map** p314 B4.
There is no doubt that this is a shop for little nature freaks, selling everything from scientific toys, experiments and optical illusions to outdoor trekking gear. It also has pamphlets on WWF activities and parks in Tuscany.

St James' American Church

Via Bernardo Rucellai 9, Outside the City Gates (info Kathy Procissi 055 577 527). Bus 17, 22. **Open** 10-11.30am, 3.30-5.30pm Wed; 10-11am, noon-1pm Sun. **Membership** *books* L15,000 (€7.80); *videos* L15,000 (€7.80); *books & videos* L25,000 (€13). **No credit cards.**
A friendly place with a good selection of English-language books, videos and games. On Saturdays before festivals children make and paint decorations and masks. The video/books section is undergoing restoration and is due to reopen in January 2002.

Festivals

During February's **Carnevale** (*see p158*), especially on Sundays, you'll see children in fancy dress in the *piazze* and on lungarno Amerigo Vespucci.

La Befana

In the past, it was at Befana (Epiphany), not Christmas, that children in Italy got their presents (that's when the magi brought theirs). The story goes that on the eve of 6 January a poor, tattered old woman (*la befana*) riding a donkey (or a broom) and carrying a sack full of toys, fills children's stockings with toys and sweets (or coal, if they've been naughty). On the eve of Befana children leave biscuits and milk out for the old lady and some hay for her donkey near where they have hung their stockings. Christmas is more celebrated now, but there is lingering affection for La Befana (there was uproar when this public holiday was cancelled a few years ago; it was rapidly restored). *See also p158.*

La Rificolona

One day in September every year, children make or buy paper candle lanterns. They gather in the evening either in piazza SS Annunziata in San Marco or along the river (posters give details of the gatherings). After dark, with their lanterns bobbing up and down on long bamboo poles, the children parade about singing. Traditionally, the boys use peashooters to blow paper darts into the little girls' lanterns to set them on fire. You'll often see a delighted boy and wailing girl holding a burning lantern, with onlookers laughing.

Food

Florentine mothers give fingers of *schiacciata all' olio* (white pizza with salt and olive oil) to babies to chew on and the taste clearly stays with them, since children buy big squares of it before school, stuffed with a little ham or mortadella. The taste for pizza among children, of course, is international.

Il Cucciolo

Via del Corso 25r, Duomo & Around (055 287 727). **Open** 7.30am-8.30pm Mon-Sat. Closed 2wks Aug. **No credit cards. Map** p314 B4.
This bar is famous among Florentine children because up in a first-floor room *bomboloni* (pastries, either plain or filled with cream, chocolate or jam) are made and then dropped down a tube to the bar below and served hot.

Mr Jimmy's American Bakery

Via San Niccolò 47, Oltrarno (055 248 0999/ www.mr-jimmy.com). **Open** 11am-8pm Tue-Sun. Closed July, Aug. **No credit cards. Map** p314 D5.
American-style apple pie, chocolate cake, cheesecake, muffins, brownies and bagels.

Pit Stop

Via F Corridoni 30r, Outside the City Gates (055 422 1437). Bus 14, 28. **Open** 12.30-2.30pm, 7.30pm-1am Mon, Wed-Sun. Closed 3wks Aug. **No credit cards.**
An amazing 128 different *primi* (starters) and 100 different kinds of pizzas.

Runner Time

Via dei Bardi 58r, Oltrarno (055 214 502/ www.runnertime.it). **Open** 10am-2am daily. **Credit** Amex, DC, MC, V.
This fast-food Internet café serving hamburgers and pizzas has a breathtaking view on to the Ponte Vecchio and a playroom for small children.

I Tarocchi

Via dei Renai 12/14r, Oltrarno (055 234 3912). **Open** 12.30-2.30pm, 7pm-1am Tue-Sun. **Credit** AmEx, DC, JCB, MC, V.
A friendly place that serves child-sized pizzas.

Gardens & parks

Boboli Gardens

For listings, see p99.
Labyrinths, grottoes, fountains, statues and hiding places: the Boboli offers plenty of diversions for children and magnificent views of the city.

Le Cascine

Florence's largest park, located to the west of the city along the river and the site of regular fairs and markets, is at its most animated on Sundays. Visitors will find that they can swim in the pool and rent rollerblades. Playgrounds dot the park, and there are snacks and balloons for sale.

Forte Belvedere

When not hosting an exhibition, Forte Belvedere along the northern perimeter of the old city is a wonderful place to go. It has a 360° view over the city and surrounding countryside and lots of grass to laze or play on. It's currently closed for restoration, with no firm reopening date.

Giardini d'Azeglio

With a merry-go-round, swings, slides and games, this shady park is peaceful during the day but fills up after school, at about 4.30pm. There's a small second-hand toys market and other activities.

Giardino di Borgo Allegri

A former parking lot near Santa Croce transformed by local senior citizens into a charming garden full of flowers, with games for small children.

Play centres

Canadian Island

Via Gioberti 15, Outside the City Gates (055 677 567). Bus 3, 6, 14. **Open** *June, July, Sept* 3.30-6.30pm Mon-Fri. *Oct-May* 3.30-6.30pm Mon-Fri; 9am-1pm Sat. Closed Aug. **Admission** L50,000 (€26) per afternoon. **No credit cards.**
Children can be left here for hours to play in an English-speaking environment and mix with Italian children learning English. English-speaking summer camps are also organised on farms and day camps at the Ugolino in the Chianti area.

Centro Giovani

Corner of via Pietrapiana and via Fiesolana, Santa Croce (055 276 7648/giovani.s.croce@comune.fi.it). **Open** 5-11pm Mon, Wed; 5-8pm Tue, Thur. Closed mid July-late Aug. **Map** p314 B5.
Youth centre that offers free access to computers (including the Internet), shows films and videos and has information on courses and events.

Kids can get into the act in Florence.

selling snacks and ice-cream for all, and a handy restaurant in the evening.

Piscina Bellariva
Lungarno Aldo Moro 6 (055 677 521). Outside the City Gates. Bus 14. **Open** *Summer* 10am-6pm, 8.30-11pm Mon-Fri; 10am-6pm Sat, Sun. *Winter* 8.30pm-11pm Tue, Thur; 9.30am-12.30pm Sat, Sun. **Admission** L11,000 (€5.70); L10,000 (€5.20) members. **No credit cards.**
Great for little ones: safe pools, grassy lawns, trees and a separate pool for older kids and adults.

Piscina Costoli
Viale Paoli, Campo di Marte, Outside the City Gates (055 623 6027). Bus 10, 17, 20. **Open** June-early Sept 2-6pm Mon; 10am-6pm Tue-Sun. **Admission** L11,000 (€5.70). **No credit cards.**
An enormous swirling water slide makes this pool a big hit with older kids.

Rowing on the Arno
Ponte San Niccolò, lungarno Pecori-Giraldi, Outside the City Gates.
From May to September the Lidò (055 234 2726) next to the tourist bus park hires out little rowing boats for L20,000 (€10.50) an hour.

Out of town

The best way of escape is by car, though buses and trains run to most major destinations: *see p101* **Outside the City Gates**. Another option is a one-day bike ride, organised by **I Bike Italy** (055 234 2371/0474 198 288).

Giardino Zoologico
Via Pieve a Celle 160, Pistoia (0573 911 219/ www.zoodipistoia.it). **Open** *Summer* 9am-7pm daily. *Winter* 9am-5pm daily. **Admission** L15,000 (€7.80); L11,000 (€5.70) 3-9-yr-olds; free under-3s. **No credit cards.**
Giraffes, rhinos, crocodiles, jaguars and a growing gang of Malagasy lemurs in a large park with palm and banana trees. No entrance after 6pm.

Parco Giochi Cavallino Matto
Via Po 1, Marina di Castagneto Donoratico, Livorno (0565 745 720). **Open** *Mar, Oct* 10am-7pm Sun; *April* 10am-7pm Sat, Sun; last 2wks Sept 10am-7pm Sat, Sun & hols; *May, June* 10am-7pm daily; *July, Aug & 1st 2wks Sept* 10am-midnight daily. **Admission** L23,000 (€12). **Credit** Amex, DC, MC, V.
The largest funfair of the coastal region.

Parco Preistorico
Peccioli Via Cappuccini 20, Pisa (0587 636 030/ 635430/www.parcsmania.it). **Open** 9am-noon, 2pm-sunset Mon-Sat; 9am-sunset Sun and public hols. **Admission** L8,000 (€4.10); L6,000 (€3.10) children; free tours in Italian (English info sheet). **No credit cards.**
This park, situated about 50 km (30 miles) from Pisa, has impressive life-size models of 18 different dinosaurs, a play area, bar and picnic facilities. The tour lasts an hour.

Ludoteca Centrale
Piazza SS Annunziata 13, San Marco (055 248 0477). **Open** 9am-1pm, 3-6.30pm Mon, Tue, Thur, Fri (Fri afternoons only young adults); 9am-1pm Sat. Closed 3wks Aug. **Map** p314 A5.
Free play centre with books and toys to borrow, play rooms, library and comfy sofas to fall into. One room is beautifully frescoed and next door is the Museo dello Spedale degli Innocenti (*see p92*).

Mondobimbo Inflatables
Parterre, piazza della Libertà, San Lorenzo (03392 885 586). **Open** 10.30am-midnight daily. **Admission** day ticket L8,000 (€4.10). **No credit cards.**
Under-tens can let off steam here on huge inflatable castles, whales, dogs and snakes. It's wise to bring spare socks (or you can buy some at the entrance).

Water fun

Le Pavoniere
Viale della Catena 2, Outside the City Gates (055 362 233/055 658 3501). Bus 17. **Open** 10am-6pm daily end June-mid Sept. **Admission** *adults* L11,000 (€5.70); *children* L8,000 (€4.10). **No credit cards.**
This peaceful pool in Cascine park is not suitable for toddlers unless they can swim. There is also a bar

Arts & Entertainment

Film

Who needs set designers when you've got Tuscany?

Admire the gilded lilies decorating Hannibal's lecture room in the Palazzo Vecchio, stay at the convent in Sant'Anna near Pienza where Juliet Binoche tended her English patient, gaze at the frescoes she illuminated at the church of San Francesco in Arezzo or do a wine course at Villa Vignamaggio where Ken and Em cavorted in *Much Ado about Nothing*. Thanks to strict planning laws, Tuscany is largely unspoiled, and the lure of cypress trees, Renaissance villas and *palazzi* has proven irresistible to many Italian, US and British filmmakers. (For a filmography, *see p299*).

But to non-Italian speakers, Tuscany's flourishing filmgoing scene is somewhat less accessible that its output: Italians are generally loath to sit through a subtitled film, and Italy has one of the biggest dubbing industries in the world.

Dubbed versions are sometimes given extra oomph when famous Italian actors are used, but this can also cause problems – when *Heat* was made with Robert de Niro and Al Pacino in leading roles, for example, film execs nearly went into cardiac arrest, since the unmistakably grainy tones of screen legend Ferruccio Amendola had been used for years to dub both.

The problem was only solved when the equally well-respected Giancarlo Giannini, who played the foolhardy police inspector in *Hannibal*, stepped in to dub Pacino's part.

Nonetheless several cinemas do now show international films in their original language (*versione originale* or 'VO') one night a week. More varied programmes are shown at cineclubs, often with subtitles.

If you speak Italian then you can take advantage of the cheaper matinées at many main cinemas on weekdays (before 6.30pm) or all day Wednesdays (L8,000/€4.10) as opposed to the standard price of L12,000-L13,000 (€6.20-€6.70). But be prepared for long queues for blockbuster English-language films. When the *posto in piedi* light is on, tickets being sold are standing room only.

For screening times check listings in newspapers such as *La Nazione*, *Il Giornale* and *La Repubblica*. Most bars display 'La Maschera', an info sheet on what's showing in cinemas and theatres. For information on festivals and other special events, the monthly *Firenze Spettacolo* is a good source.

Cinemas

Astra
Via Cerretani 54r, Duomo & Around (055 294 770/www.cinehall.it). **Shows** 3pm, 6.15pm, 8.30pm, 10.45pm Thur. Closed mid July-mid Aug. **Tickets** L13,000 (€6.70); L8,000 (€4.10) matinées. **No credit cards. Map** p314 B3.
Original-language films from around the globe are shown from September to March, sometimes with subtitles in English, sometimes in Italian or French.

Cinema Astro
Piazza di San Simone, Santa Croce (no phone). **Open** box office 6.30pm, shows 6.45-7.30pm, 10pm Tue-Sun. Closed early/mid May-early Sept. **Tickets** L10,000 (€5.20). **No credit cards. Map** p314 C5.
The only cinema showing only English-language films – mostly recent releases – six days a week.

Fulgor
Via Maso Finiguerra 22r, Santa Maria Novella (055 238 1881/www.cinemafulgor.it). **Open** box office times vary according to film. Closed 3wks Aug. **Tickets** L12,000 (€6.20); L8,000 (€4.10) Wed & matinées. Closed 2wks Aug. **No credit cards. Map** p314 B1.
Main-release English-language films are shown on Thursdays in this multi-screen. A ticket valid for ten entrances (L80,000/€41.50) can be used for several people to go to the same screening, and for Italian and English-language films.

Odeon Original Sound
Via Sassetti 1, Duomo & Around (055 214 068/ www.cinehall.it). **Open** box office times vary according to film. Closed late June-late Sept. **Tickets** L13,000 (€6.70). **No credit cards. Map** p314 B3.
On Mondays and Tuesdays this art nouveau cinema shows films on current release in English, sometimes with English or Italian subtitles. For a 30% discount, cut the voucher from Sunday's *Repubblica*.

Cineclubs & bookshops

Film clubs are cheap to join, especially for students, and the main cinemas sometimes offer discounts for members. Most clubs hold debates and presentations by local filmmakers.

British Institute Cultural Programme
Lungarno Guicciardini 9, Oltrarno (055 2677 8270). **Shows** 6pm Wed, 7.15pm Fri. Closed July, Aug. **Tickets** L15,000 (€7.80); L12,000 (€6.20) members. **No credit cards. Map** p314 C2.

Odeon Original Sound. See p162.

On Wednesdays the film shown is usually sandwiched between an introduction and a debate, all of them in English. On Fridays there's a film appreciation series, with retrospectives of famous directors or seasons of films by British authors, also followed by a discussion.

Centro Universitario Cinematografico

Cinema Alfieri Atelier, Via dell'Ulivo 6, Santa Croce (055 240 720). **Shows** 3.30-10.45pm Thur. Closed mid July-mid Aug. **Tickets** L5,000-L12,000 (€2.60-€6.20). **No credit cards. Map** p314 B5.
Films introduced by a lecturer or film critic. There are usually two themed screenings of classics, generally in Italian but sometimes VO or subtitled.

CineCittà

Via Baccio da Montelupo 35, Outside the City Gates (055 732 4510). **Bus** 6A. **Shows** 8.30pm, 10.45pm

Wed-Sun. **Tickets** L5,000-L7,000 (€2.60-€3.60), plus L9,000 (€4.70) membership. **No credit cards.**
Run by Casa del Popolo Fratelli Taddei community centre, CineCittà is 15 minutes' ride south-west of the centre. It shows Hollywood action pictures and also has festivals of obscure Italian films. Some VO/subtitled screenings.

Cineteca di Firenze

Via R Giuliani 374, Outside the City Gates (055 745 0749). **Bus** 2, 20, 28. **Shows** times vary. Closed June-Sept. **Tickets** L6,000-L7,000 (€3.10-€3.60), plus L5,000 (€2.60) membership. **No credit cards.**
Tributes to various actors, some original-language, a 20-minute bus ride north-west of centre.

Libreria del Cinema e dello Spectacolo

Via Guelfa 14r, San Lorenzo (055 216 416). **Open** 9.30am-1pm, 3.30-7.30pm Mon-Sat. **Credit** MC, V. **Map** p314 A4.
Cinema books and memorabilia. Also organises conferences and exhibitions and sponsors screenings. Great for finding out about upcoming film events.

Stensen Cineforum

Viale Don Minzoni 25a, Santa Maria Novella (055 576 551/fax 055 582 029). **Shows** 9.15pm Mon, Thur, Fri. Closed July, Aug. **Tickets** prices vary. **No credit cards. Map** p314 B2.
Italian and foreign films, shown in series, to season-ticket holders only (available on the door; the price depends on the number of films shown). Lectures, debates and presentations by filmmakers.

Seasonal cinema

There are two major international festivals in Florence and one in Fiesole, with films usually screened in their original language. The **Festival dei Popoli** (055 244 778/ www.festivalpopoli.org) of narrative and documentary films includes showings in various clubs and cinemas throughout Florence. The theme changes each year but always centres on a social issue.

France Cinema (055 214 053), usually held in November at the French Institute (Piazza Ognissanti 2; 055 239 8902) and at the Teatro della Compagnia (Via Cavour 50r; 055 217 428) has grown in importance, with a good turnout of French directors and stars.

The **Premio Fiesole ai Maestri del Cinema**, held in July in Fiesole's open-air Roman theatre, pays homage to a great director.

Many cinemas are now air-conditioned and some stay open throughout the summer, but a pleasant alternative for Italian-speakers (though some international films may be shown in their original language) or those wanting to sample a taste of local life are the open-air cinemas listed below, which show recent films

Cannibal culture

It was never going to be easy to persuade a population understandably in love with their beautiful city that it had been fairly chosen as the adopted home of the most notorious fictional mass murderer since Mr Hyde. And, sure enough, when *Hannibal* hit the screens, gone were the parasols and horse-drawn carriages of the Merchant/Ivory era and in their place was a dark, brooding, traffic-choked metropolis with murder in the streets and a disembowelled body strung from a Palazzo Vecchio balcony.

In May 2000, when the film was being shot, local gossip centred on the comings and goings of the cast and crew: where they were staying, which bar had the honour of making lunch for them, who had managed to get invited on to the set. What no one asked at the time was why the Florence of the book had been returned to an earlier age of torture and death.

Rumour has it that when author Thomas Harris came to Florence to research the new book, he had in mind a completely different plot. Meetings with an authority on medieval armaments and Renaissance history and a member of the Capponi family (owners of the Palazzo Capponi, home to Hannibal in the film), a penchant for a small osteria called the Cinghiale Bianco (White Boar) and the bronze statue of a boar, the 'Porcellino', that stands in the loggia of the Mercato Nuovo,

seem to have changed his mind. Few who have seen the film will forget the scenes of boars in a feeding frenzy, or the chilling images of Hannibal sizing up the police inspector from his grand medieval apartments in Palazzo Capponi.

It was left to Ridley Scott to re-create the atmosphere of the book in his inimitable style, and risk the wrath of locals in the process. Look closer, however, and you'll notice the camera lingering lovingly on a sunset over the Ponte Vecchio and peering down in awe at the Loggia dei Lanzi in Piazza della Signoria, and you'll get the sneaking suspicion that, in the end, even the heart of the director of *Alien* was melted by the charm of Florence.

---

from June to September. Some have bars and even restaurants, and a couple have double-screenings for die-hards (the second films finish at around 1am). Shows usually start at 9pm to 9.30pm. Programmes, which can be found at cinemas and some bookshops, usually cover at least a month's screenings.

Arena di Marte

Palazzetto dello Sport di Firenze, Viale Paoli (055 678 841). Outside the City Gates. Bus 10, 20, 34. **Dates** mid June-late Aug. **Open** 8pm (shows 9.30pm & 11pm) daily. **Tickets** L12,000 (€6.20). **No credit cards.**
Two screens, one showing cult and less mainstream films, some in original language with Italian subtitles, and the larger showing the previous year's hits.

Chiardiluna

Via Monte Oliveto 1, Outside the City Gates (055 233 7042/055 218 682). Bus 12, 13. **Dates** June-Sept. **Open** 8pm (shows 9.30pm) daily. **Tickets** L10,000 (€5.20). **No credit cards.**
Outdoor cinema between the Ponte alla Vittoria and Porta Romana, surrounded by the woodland of the *monte* and so cooler than the other cinemas (but do take some mosquito repellent). It concentrates on recent commercial releases, with some double screenings. Small snack bar.

Esterno Notte at the Poggetto

Via M Mercati 24b, Outside the City Gates (055 481 285). Bus 4, 8, 14, 20, 28. **Dates** mid June-mid Sept. **Open** 8pm (shows 9.30pm) daily. **Tickets** L10,000 (€5.20). **No credit cards.**
Films from the previous 12 months plus the occasional special screening. Poggetto is a 15-minute bus ride north of town and has a Japanese restaurant.

Raggio Verde

Palacongressi Firenze, Viale Strozzi, San Lorenzo (055 289 318). **Dates** late June-late Aug. **Open** 8pm (shows 9.30pm & 11.30pm daily). **Tickets** L10,000 (€5.20). **No credit cards. Map** p314 B3.
Nightly double screenings at a stunning amphitheatre-style cinema with the backdrop of a 16th-century villa, five minutes' walk from the main railway station. A simple restaurant in the gardens serves imaginative world cuisine.

Galleries

Hypnotic, chaotic, polychromatic: Florence's art scene is finally swinging.

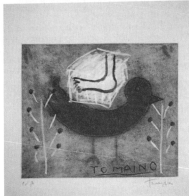

Giuliano Tomaino, at **Galleria Tornabuoni** (*see p166*).

Until a few years ago, artists, gallery owners and agents were continually bemoaning the fact that art funding was so concentrated on restoring the city's Renaissance heritage that little consideration was given to contemporary artists. Suddenly this trend is changing, as is confirmed by the continuing presence of lucrative showcase galleries in upmarket roads such as Via Tornabuoni at a time when many other long-standing independents are succumbing to the vice-like jaws of the international designer shops (*see p144* **Ousted**).

This small-scale revolution is thanks to the talent and perseverance of the artists, to the grit of a hard core of curators and galleries, and to the growing presence of collectors. Most of these are from the US, although many young Italians are starting to attend private views and show interest in contemporary artists.

The need among artists to go it alone, without sponsorship, a museum-space or the support of art critics, seems to have catalysed the boom, bringing hot talent from Italy and abroad into the galleries. Some, like Giuliano Tomaino, have even elicited interest from the public sector – his work has been chosen for a public museum exhibition at an as-yet top-secret venue. To date, the council's sole contribution remains the impressive collection at the Centro per L'Arte Contemporanea, Luigi Pecci, on the outskirts of Prato.

Gallery spaces

Base

Via San Niccolo' 18r, Oltrarno (055 215 273/679 378). **Open** 4-7pm Mon-Sat. **Map** p314 D5.
A centre of excellence for the installation and digital art scene. Light-box luminaries Pietro Sanguineti and Maurizio Nannucci's neons have lit up the faces of visitors to this tiny, non-profit-making exhibition space. Buyers are put in touch with the artists.

La Corte Arte Contemporanea

Via de'Coverelli 27r, Oltrarno (055 284 435/ www.members.xoom.it/arfarf). **Open** 4-7pm Tue-Sat. Closed 15 July-1 Sept. **No credit cards**. **Map** p314 C2.
Alice in Wonderland's hallucinogenic 'drink me' phials and 'eat me' cakes spring to mind when Rosanna Tempestini organises shows of 'gigantografia' (mammoth celluloid artworks) in this tiny gallery. A diverse range of local artists are showcased but the emphasis is on the experimental scene.

Galleria Biagiotti Arte Contemporanea

Via delle Belle Donne 39r, Santa Maria Novella (055 214 757/www.artbiagiotti.com). **Open** *Summer* 11am-7pm Mon-Fri. *Winter* 11am-7pm Tue-Sat. Closed Aug. **Credit** AmEx, MC, V. **Map** p314 B2.
Carole Biagiotti runs this stunning 15th-century converted atrium gallery like a fairy godmother, seeking out Cinderellas worthy of a golden carriage and watching over her brood of established princes and princesses of art. The result is a stream of innovative exhibitions of the best works by the mostly young artists, whose pieces often sell to collectors unviewed. Highlights from some of tomorrow's stars include the likes of Brigitte Kowantz's hypnotic neon morse-coded light-boxes and Maya Vukoje's discomfiting baby dolls.

Galleria Festina Lente

Via Condotta 18r, Duomo & Around (055 292 612). **Open** 10am-1pm, 4-8pm Mon-Sat. Closed Aug. **Credit** AmEx, DC, JCB, MC, V. **Map** p314 C4.
Rita Pedulla's loose, sultry nudes and tantric Indians engaged in contortionist Kama Sutra practices are the showstoppers in this consummately consumerist gallery-cum-shop, contrasting delightfully with her seductively pre-coital oils and colonial ginger-tea pots, Ganges-floating candles and white slip dresses. Argentine Virginia Moreno's comparatively chaste black-and-white nude photos take a worldly backseat. Strong temporary exhibitions of young ceramicists and sculptors complete the concoction.

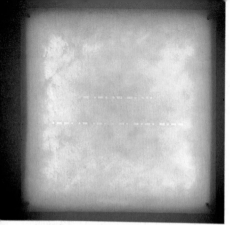

Brigitte Kowantz, at **Galleria Biagiotti**. *See p165.*

Galleria Masini

Piazza Goldoni 6r, Santa Maria Novella (055 294 000/www.masiniart.com). **Open** 9am-1pm, 3-7pm Tue-Sat. Closed 3wks Aug. **Credit** AmEx, DC, JCB, MC, V. **Map** p314 B2.

Masini boasts the largest collection of original modern paintings in Florence, but 'quaint' and 'picturesque' are words that spring to mind to describe warm landscapes such as Ballerini's *Camomile & Poppies* and Negri's *Wheat & Cornflowers*.

Galleria Pananti

Piazza Santa Croce 8, Santa Croce (055 244 931/fax 055 245 849). **Open** 10am-7pm daily. Closed July & Aug. **Credit** AmEx, DC, JCB, MC, V. **Map** p314 C5.

One of the most important galleries in town, with major contemporary Italian shows and retrospectives of internationally renowned modern artists.

Galleria Santo Ficara

Via Ghibellina 164r, Santa Croce (055 234 0239). **Open** 9.30am-12.30pm, 3.30-7.30pm Mon-Sat. Closed Aug. **Credit** AmEx, DC, JCB, MC, V. **Map** p314 C5.

Mostly well-established artists with an international market, including the 1950s abstract Gruppo Forma member Carla Accardi. Occasional shows pay lip service to up-and-coming young painters.

Galleria Spazio Tempo

Piazza Peruzzi 15r, entrance via Verdi 41r, Santa Croce (055 218 678/www.spaziotempo.com). **Open** 10am-1pm, 4-7.30pm Mon-Sat. Closed 3wks Aug. **Credit** AmEx, DC, JCB, MC, V. **Map** p314 C5.

Though Spazio Tempo is picky about the artists it showcases and keeps the number of exhibitions down, there's a permanent display of the comic-book-inspired neo-pop art of Luca Matti.

Galleria Tornabuoni

Via Tornabuoni 74r, Duomo & Around (055 284 720). **Open** 3.30-7.30pm Mon; 9.30am-1pm, 3.30-7.30pm Tue-Sat. **Credit** AmEx, DC, JCB, MC, V. **Map** p314 B2.

The prestigious permanent home to some of the best-known artists sold in the city – the roll of

honour includes Francesco Musante, whose whimsical story-book work sells as postcards beside Botticellis and Duomo views. Fabio Fornaciai also sells Tomaino's fabulous rocking horses.

Ken's Art Gallery

Via Lambertesca 15/17r, Duomo & Around (055 239 6587/www.mega.it/kensgallery). **Open** 10am-1pm, 3-8pm Mon-Sat. Closed Aug. **Credit** AmEx, DC, JCB, MC, V. **Map** p314 C3.

Walter Bellini's exciting gallery has several artists in residence and an exhibition programme with a rapid turnover. The fiercely contemporary works, all by Florentine residents, include Paolo Staccioli's Etruscan-inspired decorated urns and warrior busts.

Consumer art

One of the most important contributions to contemporary art in Florence comes from the many bars, restaurants and hotels that showcase the work of local artists, often commission-free. Potential customers are normally put in direct contact with the artist.

Capocaccia

Lungarno Corsini 12/14r, Santa Maria Novella (055 210 751). **Open** noon-2am Tue-Sun. **Map** p314 C2.

A stunning setting for talented young painters. The bar's main prerequisite in selection is colour with a twist – hence Diego Piccaluga's red and black canvasses that reveal X-rayed hearts and stomachs.

Dolce Vita

Piazza del Carmine, Oltrarno (055 284 595). **Open** *Summer* 10.30am-1.30am Mon-Sat; 6pm-1.30am Sun. *Winter* 6pm-1.30am daily. Closed 2 wks Aug. **Map** p314 C1.

Not content with displaying some of the most inventive and beautiful lamps you'll ever see, the polychromatic glass creations of Peppino Campanella, Dolce Vita also puts on week-long shows of both new and established artists.

Gallery, Hotel Art

Vicolo Oro 5, Duomo & Around (055 27263) **Open** for viewing 24hrs daily. **Map** p314 C3.

The innovative two-month art cycles in this avant-garde hotel dictate the decor, creating a continually mutating concept gallery. Young artists from all over the world, all new to the Italian scene, are chosen for their originality and outlandish styles. It might sound pretentious, but it works.

Momoyama

Borgo San Frediano 10r, Oltrarno (055 291 840). **Open** 8-11.30pm Tue-Sat; noon-3.30pm, 8-11.30pm Sun. **Map** p314 C1.

Everything at this Japanese restaurant is a work of art, from the dishes to the decor, so dedicating the small basement art space to local artists was an extension of Momoyama's design mentality. Shows have included Elisabetta Scarpini's manic texts on coloured parchments. *See also p119.*

Gay & Lesbian

Dance and drink yourself dizzy in city clubs and beachside bars.

Sometimes referred to as 'little San Francisco', Florence is one of the most evolved and welcoming cities in Italy from a gay perspective and has a thriving scene, both in terms of clubs and bars and in a political sense.

Florence has always had pulling power for gay and lesbian travellers, artists and writers, but it wasn't till 1970 that it got its first gay disco, **Tabasco** (*see p168*), in the heart of the historic centre. The venue was soon packed every weekend as Italians from every part of the boot came to kick up their heels. At around the same time, the Fronte Unitario Omosessuale Rivoluzionario Italiano or FUORI (Italian for 'out'), Tuscany's first gay/lesbian political organisation, was set up by members of the Radical party. Other landmarks included the opening of queer cultural space Banana Moon in borgo degli Albizi in 1977 and the founding of Arci Gay/Lesbica, the leading organisation for gay political initiatives in Tuscany, in the 1980s. In the mid '90s the latter split into two groups: **Ireos** is a social, cultural and info centre, while **Finisterrae-Azione Gay e Lesbica** focuses on political issues (*for both, see p286*).

As far as gay etiquette is concerned, there should be no problem with holding hands in the streets, but anything much more overt than this in public places is less acceptable. For gay men, there are lots of cruising areas, though some can be quite dangerous. The Parco delle Cascine, for instance, is active from sunset till late at night, but local cognoscenti warn against it. Another popular area is the Campo di Marte (in eastern Florence) where most of the cruising takes place in cars. The park at viale Malta is active too, but subject to frequent incursions from police checking IDs. In the historic centre, cruising is best around via Vaccherreccia, Ponte Vecchio, piazza della Repubblica and via Calimala most of the time, but especially at night.

The age of consent is 18, and clubs and bars are very strict about age checks, so bring ID along with you. Gay travellers should also note that membership is required for many Italian bars and saunas, though this is easily obtained at your first visit.

All of the places that have been listed below are good for both gay men and lesbians unless otherwise stated.

Homeless house: **Area Disco**. See *p168*.

Florence

Bars

Le Colonnine

Via dei Benci 6r, Santa Croce (055 234 6417).
Open 7am-1am daily. **Admission** free.
Credit AmEx, DC, JCB, MC, V. **Map** p314 C5.
Bar and restaurant with seating inside and out, plus a *tabaccheria*. A popular nocturnal meeting spot.

Crisco

Via S Egidio 43r, Santa Croce (055 248 0580/ www.crisco.it). **Open** 11pm-3am Mon, Wed, Thur, Sun; 10pm-6am Fri, Sat. Reduced opening 2wks Feb.
Membership free. **Credit** MC, V. **Map** p314 B5.
Bar with (mostly X-rated) videos, special events, parties and performances. Mixed crowd but especially popular among leathermen and bears.

Il Piccolo Caffè

Borgo Santa Croce 23, Santa Croce (055 200 1057/ www.piccolofirenze.com). **Open** 5pm-late daily.
Admission free. **No credit cards**. **Map** p314 C5.
Attracting a very mixed crowd, Il Piccolo gets especially crowded on Saturdays. In the week there are art exhibitions and frequent live shows.

Tin Box

Via dell'Oriuolo 19-21r, Santa Croce (055 246 6387/www.crisco.it). **Open** 3-11pm Tue-Fri, Sun; 3pm-midnight Sat. **Membership** free. **Credit** MC, V. **Map** p314 B5.

Affiliated with Crisco *(see p167)*, this is a men's bar for afternoon encounters. It features Internet access, video rooms and a labyrinth.

YAG B@r

Via de'Macci 8r, Santa Croce (055 246 9022/ www.yagbar.com). **Open** 9pm-3am Mon-Sat; 5pm-3am Sun. Closed Aug. **Admission** free. **Credit** AmEx, DC, MC, V. **Map** p314 C6.

This spacious dance-bar, with its futuristic feel, draws a young crowd of both genders. There's a full bar, Internet access and videogames. A popular first stop on the club-hopping route, it's a great place in which to hear the latest music.

Clubs

Alien

Piazza Matteucci 11, Campi Bisenzio, Outside the City Gates (0348 610 0838/www.discoalien.it). Bus 30 (until 12.30am). **Open** 11pm-4am Sat. Closed June-mid Sept. **Admission** L25,000 (€13). **No credit cards.**

Excellent DJs and a young, friendly crowd of men and women make Alien's gay night worth the long trip to the suburban hinterlands.

Tabasco Disco Bar

Piazza Santa Cecilia 3r, Duomo & Around (055 213 000/www.tabascogay.it). **Open** 10pm-late daily (bar only Mon, Tue, Wed). Obligatory drinks minimum L25,000 (€13). **Credit** AmEx, V. **Map** p314 C4.

Florence's first gay club *(see p167)*, Tabasco remains popular among both tourists and young locals of both sexes. The music is mostly techno, with some '70s-style disco.

Tenax

Via Pratese 46, Outside the City Gates (055 308 160/www.dada.it/tenax). Bus 29, 30. **Open** 10pm-4am Sat. Closed mid May-Sept. **Admission** L35,000 (€18). **Credit** AmEx, V.

Saturday nights at Tenax go by the name of 'Nobody's Perfect', but that doesn't stop an international fashion crowd going all out to look flawless *(see also p176 and p179)*.

Timida Godzilla at Auditorium Flog

Via M Mercati 24b, Outside the City Walls (055 240 397). Bus 4, 8, 14, 20, 28. **Open** 10pm-3.30am one Fri a month. **Admission** L18,000 (€9.30). **No credit cards.**

DJs, cabaret acts and bands mean that this megafest invariably draws a huge and diverse crowd out in support of the Associazione Azione Gay e Lesbica di Firenze *(see p286)*. It's a great place to get literature and information on all the latest goings-on in the local queer community.

Sauna

Florence Baths

Via Guelfa 93r, San Lorenzo (055 216 050). **Open** *winter* 2pm-1am daily; *summer* 3pm-1am daily. **Admission** L25,000 (€13). **Membership** L10,000 (€5.20) a year. **Credit** AmEx, MC, V. **Map** p314 A3.

Italian saunas hot up late afternoon/early evening. Florence's only sauna offers dry sauna and steam, Jacuzzi (always cold), bar, TV and private rooms. There's a very friendly mixed crowd. The steam room is one of the best anywhere.

Tuscany

The Versilia Riviera *(see p250)* is becoming somewhat of a gay mecca, with lots of clubs and bars, but gay beaches are numerous along the Tuscan coast *(see below)*. Pisa is also home to many clubs and organisations. Other groups and bars are scattered throughout Tuscany.

Pisa

Absolut

Via Mossotti 10 (050 220 1262). **Open** 8pm-late daily. **No credit cards.**

A mixed club with DJs and a modern, hi-tech look. Arci membership is needed.

Sauna Siesta Club 77

Via di Porta A Mare 25/27 (050 220 0146). **Open** *Sept-May* 3pm-1am daily; *June* 5pm-1am daily; *July & Aug* 9pm-1am daily; *Sept-May* 3pm-1am daily. **Admission** L20,000 (€10.50). **No credit cards.**

Bathhouse with sauna, steam, Jacuzzi, video and private rooms. Arci membership required.

Versilia, Viareggio & Torre del Lago

Area Disco

0335 538 2929 (www.discoarea.com). **Open** 11pm-5am Sat. **Admission** L30,000 (€15.50). **Credit** MC, V.

Check the website for the ever-varying location. A fashionable crowd of gays and lesbians follow popular local DJs Renzo Giannini and Francesco Belais.

Bar Notturno

Via Aurelia 220 (piazza del Popolo), Torre del Lago-Viareggio, Lucca Province (0584 341 359). **Open** 7am-3am Mon-Fri; 7am-6am Sat, Sun. **No credit cards.**

Coffee and breakfast after all-night dancing.

Barrumba Disco

Viale Kennedy 6, Torre del Lago, Lucca Province (0584 351 717). **Open** 10pm-4am Fri, Sat. Closed Oct-April. **Admission** L25,000 (€13). **No credit cards.**

An upbeat open-air dance spot surrounded by woods, with a live DJ and other entertainments. The mixed crowd is made up mainly of holidaymakers.

Arts & Entertainment

It's just a stage you're going through

In Florence, where many people begin their evening at the theatre before going clubbing, there's been a bit of a renaissance in gay theatre of late, with local theatres putting on plays and festivals that draw playwrights and performers from Britain, Germany and North America, as well as Italy itself. Under Barbara Nativi, **Il Teatro della Limonaia** (via Gramsci 426, Sesto Fiorentino, 055 440 852, closed July-Oct) has put on Italian performances of gay classics, including plays by Wilde and Artaud, plus some new works. Recent hits include Alessandro Baldinotti's production of Eduardo Mendicutti's *Seven vs Georgia* and Mark Ravenhill's *Shopping & Fucking*.

The annual Intercity Festival brings theatre from a different city each year and provides an opportunity for gay foreign artists to bring their works to Florence, perform, lecture and mingle with the crowds. **Teatro di Rifredi di Firenze** (via Vittorio Emanuele 303, 055 422 0362, closed June-Aug) also provides space for new productions and workshops, sometimes in tandem with Azione Gay e Lesbica. A recent series of workshops was dedicated to writer Pier Vittorio Tondelli, and the latest season ranged from a gay chatlines storyline to a campy tribute to Italian pop idol Raffaella Carrà.

Brutal comedy in **Shopping & Fucking**.

Boca Chica

Viale Europa, Torre del Lago-Viareggio, Lucca Province (0584 350 976). **Open** 10am-4am Tue-Sun. Closed 2wks Nov & Feb. **Admission** free. **Credit** MC, V.

A seafront bar with music. The garden fills quickly with a trendy young crowd.

Frau Marlene

Viale Europa, Torre del Lago, Lucca Province (0584 342 282/www.fraumarlene.com). **Open** *Summer* 10pm-4am Fri, Sat. *Winter* 10pm-4am Sat. **Admission** L25,000 (€13). **Credit** AmEx, MC, V.

Gays and lesbians of all ages consider a stop-off at Frau Marlene, which is one of Versilia's most established nightspots, to be an integral part of any summer night's itinerary.

Voice Music Bar

Viale Margherita 61, Viareggio, Lucca Province (0584 45814/www.galleriadeldisco.com). **Open** 9-30am-2am daily; *winter* 9.30am-2am Tue-Sun. **No credit cards**.

Voice Music is a friendly seafront bar that offers an eclectic selection of rare music, perhaps to match the very mixed crowd.

Beaches

Policemen, often in plain clothes, impose hefty fines on those who ignore the ban on nudism.

Carbonifera

North of Follonica; mostly gay and lesbian.

La Lecciona

Near via dei Tigli at Torre del Lago. The shaded pines nearby get cruisy in the late afternoon.

Le Marze

Between Castiglione della Pescaia and la Marina di Grosseto. Well-hidden but lovely pine-shaded beach.

Le Piscine

Mixed beach on the island of Elba, near Seccheto.

Rimigliano

South of San Vincenzo, this long, isolated beach is popular with gay men and women. As the afternoon wears on the pines get busy.

Sassoscritto

Exclusively gay and lesbian beach south of Livorno, accessible by bus from Livorno train station.

Arts & Entertainment

Music: Classical & Opera

Safe sounds.

For such a small city, Florence has a lively classical music scene, but don't come expecting to find much that is cutting edge – Florentines will pack the theatre night after night for *La Traviata* but only a handful will turn up to hear anything new. And don't you dare mess around with Verdi or Puccini; all but the most traditional of stagings are greeted with mutters, or even whistles, of resentment. The superb 1998 production of Alban Berg's *Wozzeck* by William Friedkin (director of *The Exorcist*) was one of the most interesting shows in recent years, yet the theatre was only ever three-quarters full. Symphonic or chamber concert programmes suffer from this conservatism too: big names, yes; innovative repertoire, not likely.

Lack of funds does nothing to help this situation, and nor does Florence's lack of a decent concert hall. Concerts and recitals are held in theatres, churches, small halls or outdoors, but none have the acoustics to host a big symphonic repertoire. If all goes according to plan, this will change: a site has been chosen on the ring road near the Fortezza da Basso for a 1,700-seater auditorium, and word has it that it will be up and running by 2004.

One of the best Florentine experiences is a visit to the opera. Opera-going here is interactive: shows can be held up for several minutes after an aria that has been particularly well (or badly) received, and the Teatro Comunale has an unofficial clique that leads audience vocals. A word of warning: check your programme to make sure you won't be watching the potentially mediocre 'B Cast', which in some productions is alternated with the 'A Cast' of big names.

Smaller events are promoted on fly-posters around town and in local papers and listings mags. From June to October, there are lots of concerts in churches and outdoor concerts at villas, gardens and museums, some free. They're not always well advertised, but tourist offices usually have information. Smaller events outside Florence include the **Metastasio Classic** season of chamber music and orchestral concerts at Prato's theatre (Dec-Apr; 0574 608 501); the **Estate Musicale Chigiana** series of courses and concerts in Siena and at such venues as the abbeys of San Galgano and Sant'Antimo (July-Aug; 0577 46152); the **Tavernelle Val di Pesa** concerts at Badia monastery in Passignano (late May; tourist office 055 807 7832); the **Barga Opera Festival**, combining music courses with little-known operas (July-mid Aug; 0583 723 250); the **Vaglia** summer concerts in the grounds of Villa Demidoff (*see p104*; June; tourist office 055 290 832); and the **International Choral Festival** in Impruneta (June; tourist office 055 231 3729).

For larger annual events in Florence and Tuscany, *see chapter* **Tuscany by Season**.

TICKETS

For main ticket agencies, *see chapter* **Shopping & Services**. Many hotels and travel agents also book tickets for the biggest venues.

Tickets for the Teatro Comunale can be hard to come by. Phone bookings and credit cards are accepted, but you have to pick up tickets in person within a week of booking. If you can't get a seat in advance, it's worth turning up on the night on the off-chance of a return (some restricted-vision seats are available an hour before the start, too).

For chamber music concerts and Orchestra Regionale Toscana concerts, tickets are usually available on the door half an hour beforehand, but the safest plan is to go to the box office in good time and with cash. Unless otherwise stated, box offices don't accept credit cards.

TICKET PRICES

At the Teatro Comunale, tickets for the opening night of an opera cost from L40,000 (€20.50) for a seat in the upper circle to L160,000 (€82.50) for a box or stalls seat. Repeat performances cost a little less. Symphonic concerts cost from L35,000 (€18) to L55,000 (€28.50) and ballets from L20,000 (€10.50) to L55,000 (€28.50). Restricted-view seats are L20,000 (€10.50).

Tickets for the Orchestra Regionale Toscana concerts at Teatro Verdi cost L20,000-L25,000 (€10.50-€13), while the Amici della Musica series at the Pergola costs L18,000-L35,000 (€9.30-€18) per seat. One-off concerts usually cost around L30,000 (€15.50) or less, and some outdoor events or concerts in churches are free.

Venues

Accademia Bartolomeo Cristofori

Via di Camaldoli 7r, Oltrarno (055 221 646 from 4.30-7pm Mon, Wed, Thur).
A fine private of early keyboard instruments, and a workshop for restoration and repair. Concerts and

Teatro Comunale hosts big-name conductors and soloists – and plenty of unknowns.

seminars from well-known early keyboard players are held in a beautiful little hall next door.

Chiesa Luterana

Lungarno Torrigiani 11, Oltrarno (information: tourist office 055 290 832). **Map** p314 D4.
Organ recitals and other chamber music, often involving early repertoire, all year. Usually free.

Scuola Musica di Fiesole

Villa la Torraccia, San Domenico, Fiesole (055 597 851). Bus 7, then 10min walk. **Open** 8.30am-8.30pm Mon-Sat. **Tickets** L10,000 (€5.20); concessions for students, OAPs.
Based in a 16th-century villa in large grounds. On June 24 the annual Festa della Musica, an 'open house', involves concerts and workshops by pupils, while the 'Concerti per gli Amici' series takes place in the 200-seat auditorium from September to June.

Teatro Comunale

Corso Italia 16, Santa Maria Novella (055 211 158/055 213 535/fax 055 277 9410/ www.maggiofiorentino.com). **Open** box office 10am-4.30pm Tue-Fri; 9am-1pm Sat; & 1hr before performance. **Tickets** *see p170.* **Credit** AmEx, DC, MC, V.
After a period of stability and a rise in the number of young orchestra and chorus members, the Teatro Comunale – now officially named the Teatro del Maggio Musicale Fiorentino – is on good form. Big-name guest conductors and soloists have recently included George Pretre, Misha Maisky and Seiji Ozawa, though these are padded out by plenty of unknowns for whom the orchestra (L'Orchestra del

Maggio Musicale Fiorentino) fails to pull out all the stops. The principal operatic line-up isn't star-studded, but emerging talents often get breaks here, and there's the odd diva. More opera has been promised.

The theatre's performing year is divided roughly into three parts: January to March is the concert season, with a new programme weekly; October to December is the opera and ballet season, with about four operatic productions, a couple of ballets and the odd concert; and the Maggio Musicale Fiorentino festival, one of the oldest in Europe (it was founded in 1933), runs for two months from late April/early May. The latter offers a mix of opera, ballet, concerts and recital programmes, generally with a theme, and culminates in two free open-air jamborees, traditionally held in Piazza Signoria but, in 2001, as an experiment, in Piazza Santa Croce.

The building itself, constructed in 1882 and renovated in 1957, is unexciting. Acoustics-wise, the best of the 2,000 seats are in the second gallery; they're the cheapest, too. But if you want to mix with the Florence 'Per Bene', then you have to fork out for an opening night in the stalls or one of the *palchi* (boxes).

Teatro Goldoni

Via Santa Maria 15, Oltrarno (055 210 804/Teatro Comunale 055 211 158). **Open** box office 1hr before performance. **Map** p314 D1.
This divine but underused little theatre, dating from the early 18th century and seating only 400 people, is used for sporadic performances of chamber music and small-scale operas and ballets (often under the auspices of the Teatro Comunale, *see above,* or Amici della Musica; *see p172*), which fit its intimate atmosphere.

Arts & Entertainment

Who they? The Florentine Camerata

Between about 1573 and 1587, a group of Florentine intellectuals, musos and literati frequenting the salon of Count Giovanni de' Bardi began experimenting with the setting of words to music, and in doing so became the fathers of the genre known as opera.

One of the musicians most closely associated with this group, known as the Camerata Fiorentina, was Vincenzo Galilei, father of the astronomer and a talented madrigal composer.

Galilei was one of the first people to play with a new way of setting words to music, derived from the Greek 'monody' – from 'monos' (alone) and 'aidein' (to sing). Vocals followed the natural accent and flow of speech to produce something between speech and song, and instruments were kept to a minimum (Galilei believed melody should enhance, not interfere with, the inflections of speech).

These rather austere ideas were expanded and elaborated on by successive, most notably the Florentines Jacopo Peri and Giulio Caccini, the latter allowing an element of improvisation into the melodic line in appropriate places, in the form of flowery embellishments that showed off the singers' vocal virtuosity. *Le Nuove Musiche* (The New Music), a collection of songs written in the 1590s by Caccini, are the earliest surviving compositions in the Florentine monodic style.

By the early 17th century, this monody was being used in all kinds of music. It had proved to be the missing link that made opera possible, by providing a means to convey dialogue and ideas efficiently but dramatically in music. *Euridice*, written by Peri and Caccini and performed in Florence in 1600 to celebrate the marriage of Henry IV of France and Marie de' Medici, is generally considered the first opera.

Teatro della Pergola
Via della Pergola 12-32, San Marco (055 226 4316). **Open** box office 9.30am-1pm, 3.30-6.45pm Tue-Sat; 10am-12.15pm Sun. **Season** Oct-Apr. **No credit cards. Map** p314 B5.
Set up in 1656, the Pergola is Italy's oldest theatre. Exquisite and intimate, it's ideal for chamber music and small-scale operas. Most of the Amici della Musica chamber concerts (*see below*) are held here, and the Teatro Comunale (*see p171*) uses it for small-scale opera and some ballets.

Teatro Verdi
Via Ghibellina 99, Santa Croce (055 212 320/ www.teatroverdifirenze.it). **Open** box office 4-6pm Mon; 10am-1pm, 4-7pm Tue-Fri; 10am-1pm Sat. **Season** Sept-June. **Map** p314 C5.
Florence's regular venue for the Orchestra Regional.

Tempo Reale
La Limonaia di Villa Strozzi, Via Pisana 77, Outside the City Gates (055 717 270/www.centrotemporeale.it). Bus 12, 13.
This centre for contemporary music in Monte Uliveto places an emphasis on music technology. Concerts, workshops and seminars are held.

Performance groups/ promoters

Amici della Musica
055 608 420/055 607 440.
An organisation promoting world-class chamber music concerts, most presented at the Teatro della

Pergola (*see above*), from September through to late April/early May. Some of the world's great string quartets (Borodin, Emerson, Alban Berg) and recitalists play, and there's the odd early-music ensemble too. Concerts are usually on Saturday and Sunday at 4pm or 9pm.

L'Homme Armé
Tel/fax 055 695 000.
A small, semi-professional chamber choir whose repertoire ranges from medieval to baroque. It gives about ten concerts a year in Florence and regularly runs excellent courses on aspects of early music.

Orchestra da Camera Fiorentina
055 783 374.
This young chamber orchestra plays a season of mostly baroque and classical concerts from February to September, with a break in August.

Orchestra Regionale Toscana (ORT)
055 281 792/www.orchestradellatoscana.iti.
This 40-strong chamber orchestra was founded in 1980 with the brief of taking classical music into Tuscany. During the season (November/December to May) it gives two or three concerts a month in Florence, and 35 to 40 in other Tuscan towns. Since the 1993 Uffizi bomb damaged Santo Stefano, its main venue has been the Teatro Verdi (*see above*). The management, artistic director and musicians are all relatively young, and this is reflected in the programming, which covers everything from baroque to modern, with emphasis on 19th-century works. International names frequently appear as soloists and conductors.

Music: Rock, Roots & Jazz

Florence may not spawn benchmark bands, but break out of the centre and you'll find some interesting fare.

When it comes to the contemporary, non-classical music scene, Florence is a one-horse town – inevitably, perhaps, for a provincial city that relies so much on its heritage for its identity. Yet there's more to live music here than Bob Dylan covers sung in an Italian accent – while you may encounter quite a few venues offering something of that ilk in the tourist areas, outside the city centre are some decent venues in which to hear quality home-bred sounds and better-known international groups.

Small Florence-based labels such as Contempo and Ultravox continue to churn out albums – most of them indie rock – but not since the likes of retro-rockers **Litfiba** and **Diaframma** made their mark in the mid 1980s has there been a Florentine group that stands out. The most notable recent local success has been alternative rockers **Malfunk**. The long-standing stress on alternative/indie rock is evidenced by the popularity of bands such as **Marlene Kuntz** and **Tortoise**, while the confused commercial output of the likes of **Frankie Hi Energy** – Italy's answer to hip hop – and the pop-punk of **Jovanotti** have a considerable following.

Beyond the venues that are listed in this chapter, a handful of places offer concerts and other special events, including art galleries, trade shows and cultural symposia. One such is the former Stazione Leopoldo at the Porta al Prato near the Parco delle Cascine, Florence's first train station. With its majestic vaulted ceilings and original brickwork dating back to 1848, the Leopoldo has become a hip venue catering to Florentine youth culture, most recently hosting a multimedia Internet festival. The Fabbrica Europa Festival also hosts live music events here yearly.

▶ For outdoor summer events, *see* chapter **Tuscany by Season**, and for ticket agencies, *see p152*. Some nightlife venues, notably **Anfiteatro** and **Le Murate**, also stage live music: *see* chapter **Nightlife**.

The city perks up from June to September, with open-air stages playing to crowds sipping cocktails as the sun goes down. Especially noteworthy is the summer stage in piazza Santo Spirito, which features different sounds almost every night, and the 'Rime Rampanti' series at piazza Poggi, with views over the Arno.

Auditorium Flog

Via M Mercati 24b, Outside the City Walls (055 490 437). Bus 4, 8, 14, 20, 28. **Open** Tue-Sat (call for details). **Admission** L10,000 (€5.20) approx. **No credit cards**.

A largeish student venue outside the city centre, Flog hosts concerts every Thursday, Friday and Saturday night, with Friday often dedicated to reggae and ska. On a good night the place, though acoustically not infallible, can be fun. Marlene

Lose the blues at **Jazz Club**. *See p176*.

Chill out at **Eskimo**, where nascent local bands jam to an appreciative audience.

Kuntz, local favourites Funk Off and Florentine indie rockers Elle are among the artists to have played here recently. Flog serves up a medley of genres, from hard rock and funk/R&B to Tex Mex. Enthused crowds keep on dancing after concerts wind down, when a DJ usually takes the helm. Keep an eye out early in the week for themed dance parties and other theatrical showcases as Flog expands its repertoire. It also hosts the excellent world music festival, the Rassegna Internazionale Musica dei Popoli, in November (*see p158*).

Be Bop

Via dei Servi, San Marco (no phone). **Open** times vary; usually 6pm-1am daily. **Admission** free. **No credit cards. Map** p314 A4.
Like many clubs in the city centre, Be Bop is a sweaty windowless underground cave. Though not the swinging joint it used to be, it attracts a bratpack of foreign students plus a handful of brooding artsy types. The varied music is rarely original: you might encounter a band doing Beatles covers or old Italian standards, or else a motley crew of Italian wannabe Rastafarians muddling their way through a set of reggae classics. Drinks are pretty expensive. Monday, when many other clubs are closed, can be a good night.

Cafe La Torre

Lungarno Cellini 65r, Oltrarno (055 680 643). **Open** 10.30am-3am daily. **Admission** free. **Credit** AmEx, DC, MC, V. **Map** p314 D6.
A well-known local hangout for an aperitif and late-night snack, this small riverside café has nightly live music, from campy polka to spicy Brazilian beats. *See also p181.*

Eskimo

Via dei Canacci 12, Santa Maria Novella (no phone). **Open** 6pm-4am daily. **Admission** annual membership L10,000 (€5.20). **No credit cards. Map** p314 A1/B1.
Communal wood tables burst with Italian uni students at this tiny joint founded on leftist principles, with its amateur expressionist art and open mike. Conjuring up images of an old speakeasy with its back-alley entrance and cheap beer, it's a gem if you're looking for a taste of the student music scene. Youth is definitely the keyword here – the artists are, at best, still in their infancy. But with Eskimo's unique charm, it's hard to resist swaying along with the exuberant crowd as local groups jam to the accompaniment of jolly, Santa Claus-like owner Lalo on the piano. There's live music at about 11pm every night, from jazz, blues and Neapolitan to staple rock cover bands. Happy hour is 6-9pm.

Girasol

Via Del Romito 1, Outside the City Gates (055 474 948). *Bus 14.* **Open** 8pm-2.30am Tue-Sun. **Admission** free. **No credit cards.**
Trying its best to be a 'Little Havana', complete with fake palm trees, Girasol is *the* place for live Latin sounds. Dim lighting and flamboyantly fruity cocktails transport you far from the incessant buzz of Florentine scooters, but though the Cuban, Brazilian, rumba, flamenco, Caribbean and Latin jazz rhythms tempt you to your feet, the tightly tabled room leaves no place to get your swerve on. Drink prices are a bit steep but include admission. A semi-chic Florentine crowd arrive in droves at about 11pm; so you should aim to arrive at 10.15pm to be sure of a table.

Hot to squat

Centri sociali autogestiti are a widespread feature of contemporary Italy; no major city is without at least one. These mega-squats are usually located in abandoned buildings and run by rebel ex-university students. They function as unofficial social and arts centres, putting on gigs, exhibitions, films and sometimes offering courses and counselling, though the vibe is generally a little tired and threadbare.

Florence's three *centri sociali* are all run on principles that have undergone little or no refinement since the protesting heyday of the 1960s. For reasons best known to themselves, they shun interaction or co-operation with each other, as well as any impetus to become anything even faintly resembling a commercial venture, preferring to keep the operation within 'the family'. Bologna's Link, which isn't afraid of making money, is far more successful, with a full and stimulating programme of concerts and happenings by artists from all over the world.

CSA Indiano and CPA Fi-Sud are both worth a visit, especially if you happen to pick a good night, but go often and you'll soon tire of seeing the same old faces. The **Indiano**, at the far end of the Cascine park, is more than 13 years old and the city's oldest *centro sociale*. It's always had the reputation of being more downbeat and less politically mannered than the others: bored by the limited options on offer in Florence, its founders wanted to have a good time on their own terms and give exposure to top punk and hard-core bands (particularly from the US). It now organises concerts, raves and occasional demos in support of political prisoners around the world. Every weekend it stages dance nights with local DJs running the gamut of techno, garage, drum 'n' bass and jungle. Gigs by Italian and foreign bands provide less thrilling entertainment on other nights. Entry is cheap, as are food and drinks.

At the time of writing **CPA Fi-Sud** (Centro Popolare Autogestito Firenze Sud) had just about managed to hold its own in the face of local big businesses hungry to expand on to the site. Located in south Florence, it's the biggest and most active of the *centri*, with a 1,000-capacity concert hall, known as the Spaceship, that's the largest alternative concert venue in the city.

Techno and dub usually provide the soundtrack on dance nights. The *centro* also has a vast range of other amenities, including a small library, a gym, a small cinema, three rehearsal rooms for local bands, a theatre where resident dance/theatre group Kinkaleri put together performances, various theatre and film clubs and a photography group. The worthiest project is the provision of shelter for homeless non-EU citizens. Concerts and parties are usually held at weekends, with both admisison and drinks great value; check out flyers for details.

Is the CPA Fi-Sud worth saving? A couple of years ago the answer would have been in the affirmative. Having invested in a sound system, overhauled the concert arena and arranged a three-day festival that attracted thousands of punters, things seemed to be looking up. But since then the place has been going downhill, with stray dogs starting to outnumber paying punters. Through its inability to attract a clientele that goes beyond diehard disciples, the centre has become more of a protest site than a live music venue. Yet on a good night CPA is still worth a visit.

The most politically engaged of Florence's centri, **CSA Ex-Emerson** maintains connections with the Autonomia Operaia, the Italian protest movement of the 1970s, and both its ideology and its style sense are stuck in a time warp – its inner sanctum of self-consciously scruffy, long-haired social outcasts sometimes seem so clichéd you begin to wonder when the punchline is going to arrive. A more low-key operation now than in the past (it doesn't put up flyers), it holds gigs every Friday and Saturday from about 9pm, usually by little-known Italian bands.

CPA Fi-Sud
viale Giannotti 79, Outside the City Gates (www.ecn.org/cpa). Bus 32, 31, 32. **No credit cards.**

CSA Ex-Emerson
via Niccolò da Tolentino, Outside the City Gates (http://utenti.tripod.it/cesexemerson). Bus 14B. **No credit cards.**

CSA Indiano
piazzale delle Cascine, Outside the City Gates. Bus 30. **No credit cards.**

The best Sounds

Latin

Loungey and loose **Girasol** (*see p174*).

Reggae

Auditorium Flog (*see p173*): reggae almost every Friday night in an atmosphere of raucous funked-out fun.

Jazz

Masterly music and a cool vibe at **Jazz Club** (*see p176*).

Local flavour

Tenax (*see p176*), an acoustically superior sound sanctuary for local and visiting acts alike.

Up and coming

Student and amateur acts play **Eskimo** (*see p174*) until their fingers bleed.

Jazz Club

Via Nuova de' Caccini 3, Santa Croce (055 247 9700). **Open** 9.30pm-2am Tue-Fri, Sun; 9.30pm-2.30am Sat. Closed June-Sept. **Admission** L5,000 (€2.60) visitor membership. **No credit cards**. **Map** p314 B5.

One of the few venues in Florence where you can hear live jazz regularly, this sophisticated basement venue is popular with large groups of thirtysomethings and beatniks, though there a few smaller tables for more intimate conversations. Live performers range from traditional bands to smoky fusion and contemporary experimental groups, with other evenings dedicated to musical styles such as blues, Latin folk and flamenco. Further novelties are a big band on Thursdays and the Jazz Club Gospel choir two Sundays a month. On Tuesday nights there's an open, and free, jamming session. Cocktails average L12,000 (€6.20), beer L8,000 (€4.10).

Loonees

Via Porta Rossa 15r, Duomo & Around (055 212 249). **Open** 8pm-3am Tue-Sun. Closed Aug. **Admission** free. **No credit cards**. **Map** p314 C3.

One of the few places offering live music without an admission fee, Loonees brims with tipsy foreign students, random punters and locals lurking for female prey. Crowds are usually elbow to elbow by 11pm, to sounds ranging from reggae and funk to rock covers and to Italian pop. Two easily accessible bars offering free shots with every beer may assuage those with a more critical ear. The vaulted ceiling captures the sound nicely but makes conversation virtually impossible. Depending on the night, you may find room to dance in front of the stage. On Saturday nights you can catch bluesman Jeff Jones, whose smooth tunes have garnered a following. Beer is L7,000 (€3.60), a spirit with mixer about L10,000 (€5.20), and there's a two-for-one happy hour every night (8-10pm).

Palasport

Viale Paoli, Outside the City Gates (055 678 841). Bus 3. **Open** box office 8am-8pm Mon-Fri; 8am-2pm Sat. **Tickets** L25,000-L60,000 (€13-€34). **No credit cards**.

Sting, Elton John and Eric Clapton have all made tour stops at this expansive arena near the football stadium at Campo di Marte, and these international headliners sell out fast, despite a seating capacity of about 7,000. The majority of concerts here, however, showcase Italian commercial pop stars such as Alex Britti and Eros Ramozzotti. Try to avoid the area left of the stage, which has a limited view, and feel free to indulge in the cheap beer (miraculously, there are no toilet queues).

Pinocchio Jazz

Viale Giannotti 13, Outside the City Gates (no phone). Bus 23 to Piazza Gavinana. **Tickets** L10,000-L22,000 (€5.20-€11.50). **No credit cards**.

Situated in the south-east corner of the city, this venue books recognisable international names as well as Italian artists, covering a variety of musical styles, including big band, traditional Tuscan folk, blues, Latin, experimental and classical jazz. As a venue it lacks cosiness and atmosphere, but the quality acts and friendly staff make up for this. A mellow, older set tend to fill up the small, amphitheatre like stage area at around 9.30pm. Call for concert info or check the well-circulated flyers.

Sala Vanni

Piazza del Carmine 14, Oltrarno (055 287 347). **Open** varies. **Admission** L20,000-L25,000 (€10.50-€13). **No credit cards**. **Map** p314 C1.

This large warehouse-like auditorium is by far the best place in town to hear good progressive jazz, showcasing a series of concerts organised by Musicus Concentus throughout the year.

Tenax

Via Pratese 46, Outside the City Gates (055 308 160/fax 055 307 101/www.dada.it/tenax). Bus 29, 30. **Open** 10.30pm-4am Thur-Sat. Closed mid May-Sept. **Admission** L15,000-L35,000 (€7.80-€18). **Credit** AmEx, MC, V.

The hip and happening Tenax offers a healthy stew of acts, from international artists as varied as Morcheeba, Tori Amos and Radiohead to Italian rock faves such as Ligabue and Hooverphonic. Bands touring Italy but not big enough to fill the arenas often stop off here. The spacious club boasts an enormous raised dancefloor and antechambers stuffed with computers, pool tables and bars. Upstairs are more bars, sofas and café-type seating areas with balconies to watch the action below. Gigs are followed by discos. Free buses are laid on from the town centre in piazza Indipendenza to the club; on concert nights they start at 7.30pm and make half-hourly round trips until close. *See also p179.*

Nightlife

They might be stuck in a bit of a time warp, but no one could say the Florentines don't know how to party.

Florence is blissfully ignorant of its distance from the cutting edge of the nightlife scene, and most club-goers remain convinced that they're gyrating to the hottest tunes. While London's done the '70s and '80s revivals and is stomping its way through a remixed, sampled '90s revival, '90s club music only recently landed in the Renaissance capital for the first time, and drum 'n' bass and jungle are finally hitting the headlines. Latin sounds continue to have a stranglehold on many clubs and bars, while the latest fad is a worrying breed of 1960s lounge music. But there are notable exceptions – some of the city's DJs are well travelled and have a talent for hotting things up with a hip mix of dance tunes, hip hop, house and 'nu-jazz' (the Italian take on acid jazz), and a few clubs invite big-name international DJs for one-nighters.

What the city lacks in avant-garde club beats it more than makes up for in style, and a crawl round the spirited bars will give you a dose of glamour to rival anything at Milan's fashion week. Whether you're looking for an aperitif with trimmings or a full night out, there's an effortless party feel about the bars and clubs.

Most clubs have a card system, whereby instead of being asked for an entrance fee you'll be given a small card, which you hand over whenever you're buying drinks and using the cloakroom. The card is stamped and returned to you, and then requested at the till when you leave; usually there's a minimum cost that includes the first drink.

Opening times and closing days of bars and clubs are notoriously vague and erratic, while phones that are answered are the exception, so be prepared to take a chance. Musical genres often vary with the day of the week, so check fliers or *Firenze Spettacolo*.

Clubs

Central Park

Via Fosso Macinante 2, Outside the City Gates (055 353 505). *Bus 1, 9, 16, 26, 27.* **Open** *Summer* 11pm-4am Tue-Sat. *Winter* 11pm-4am Fri, Sat. **Admission** L30,000/€15.50 (incl 1st drink). **Credit** AmEx, DC, MC, V.
Central Park comes into its own in summer, when it becomes L'Isola che C'e', a desert island complete with bamboo, palm trees and love-starved Man Fridays. Desert Island Discs consist of deep house

classics, techno, mediocre live acts or commercial hits, depending on which of the four music zones you've washed up on. Thursdays and Fridays are usually good bets, but Saturdays cater to the influx of out-of-townies (the hip crowd head to the beach). It can be worth the trek in winter if you're up for a big night; Thursdays feature some of the best drum 'n' bass in Italy. The card system can be excruciating when you want to leave and have to face the hordes bearing down on the coat desk and cash till. Drinks cost L15,000 (€7.80).

Club Blob

Via Vinegia 21r, Santa Croce (055 211 209). **Open** 6pm-3am daily. **Admission** free. **Credit** AmEx, DC, MC, V. **Map** p314 C4.
Hidden away on a sidestreet with an anonymous black door, Blob is generally mobbed by Florentine art students. The mezzanine seating area serves as a viewing gallery over the small dancefloor. The crowd is friendly, the measures generous and the opening hours long, leading to the place being

The best Bars & clubs

All-round bar
Capocaccia. See p181.

All-round club
Maramao. See p178.

Chic pre-club meeting place
Dolce Vita. See p182.

For big outdoor nights
Central Park. See p177.

For fantasy first-dates
Il Caffè. See p181.

For Guinness nostalgia
James Joyce. See p182.

For hip jazz
Astor Caffè. See p181.

For late-night dance beats
Soulciety. See p179.

Sight for sore eyes
Universale. See p180.

Arts & Entertainment

Maramao: will you pass muster?

known affectionately as 'the belly of the beast' (you enter a timeless dimension before being spat out into the streets to see the sun rise over the Arno). Beer is L7,000 (€3.60), G&T L10,000 (€5.20), but at happy hour (6-9pm) you get two drinks for the price of one.

Full-Up

Via della Vigna Vecchia 25r, Santa Croce (055 293 006). **Open** 11pm-4am Tue-Sat. Closed June-Sept. **Admission** free; L15,000 (€7.80) after midnight (incl 1st drink). **Credit** AmEx, MC, V. **Map** p314 C4.
This smoothies' paradise is generally full of sugar daddies who've watched too many Bond films sitting round the roulette, and mini-skirted models looking for a Mercedes ride home. Wednesdays have always been the exception to the steer-clear rule, with cool if flash Florentines enjoying hip hop and funk. Avoid Thursdays and Fridays (the very iffy 'Real Commercial' and 'College Party'). Drinks cost, on average, L12,000 (€6.20).

Maracana Casa di Samba

Via Faenza 4, San Lorenzo (055 210 298). **Open** *Club* midnight-4am Tue-Sun. *Restaurant* 8.30-11.30pm Tue-Sun. Closed June-Aug. **Admission** L15,000-L30,000 (€7.80-€15.50). **Credit** (restaurant only) AmEx, DC, JCB, MC, V. **Map** p314 A3.
A mix of samba, salsa and Earth, Wind & Fire. Give the place a wide berth if you can't stomach middle-aged suits dribbling lecherously over wiggling Brazilian bottoms – after the restaurant stops serving South American fare to mop up the long drinks, all decorum is shed. The central dancefloor is surrounded by poser platforms; balconies assure views of cleavages and bald patches. Bottled beers and

spirits cost L12,000 (€6.20), draught beer L10,000 (€5.20). Exhibitionists will love the video cameras freeze-framing shots of them on the huge screen.

Maramao

Via dei Macci 79r, Santa Croce (055 244 341). **Open** 11pm-3am Tue-Sat. Closed May-Sept. **Admission** L20,000/€10.50 (incl 1st drink). **Credit** AmEx, DC, MC, V. **Map** p314 C6.
Maramao doesn't figure on many of the 'what to do at night' leaflets, mags and guides for the city and would never stoop so low as to print invites, lending it the elusiveness that makes a club a Club. It's also the most Italian of the city's nightspots. Queues form soon after opening time, and bouncers scan the line of hopefuls; those deemed suitably sleek lose their street-cred by punching the air like beauty queens. Once you're inside, your prize is a heady mix of unleery camaraderie and fine tunes through the spectrum from house anthems and hip hop to St Germain-style jazzy lines. Drinks cost on average L10,000 (€5.20).

Meccanò

Viale degli Olmi 1, Outside the City Gates (055 331 371). Bus 1, 9, 16, 26, 27. **Open** summer 11pm-4am Tue-Sat; winter 11pm-4am Thur-Sat. Closed Nov. **Admission** L25,000/€13 (incl 1st drink). **Credit** AmEx, DC, MC, V.
Meccanò caters to the masses, who come out in force to play in its theme park atmosphere. The restaurant is just an excuse for a musical statues contest on the tables once diners have moved on, while it's easy to play hide-and-seek in the labyrinthine tangle of bars and dancefloors, especially when the

Arts & Entertainment

garden opens in summer, adding a fourth bar and dance area. Music is often commercial party stuff but there's a welcome sprinkling of hip hop and house. Drinks cost L10,000-L12,000 (€5.20-€6.20).

SottoSopra
Via dei Serragli 48r, Oltrarno (055 282 340).
Open 6.30pm-1.30am Mon-Thur; 6.30pm-2am Fri, Sat. Closed June-Sept. **Admission** free.
No credit cards. Map p314 D1.
The motto 'piu' sotto che sopra' ('more down than up') refers to this friendly club's mini bar area upstairs and the comparatively spacious cellar dancefloor. In-the-know locals give the place a neighbourly feel, and the music mix motivates even a half-full dancefloor into a party mood. Drinks cost from L5,000 to L10,000 (€2.60-€5.20).

Soulciety Club
Via San Zanobi 114a, San Lorenzo (055 830 3513).
Open 11.30pm-4am Tue-Sun; closed June-Sept.
Admission L10,000 (€5.20). **No credit cards.**
One of Florence's best-kept secrets, yet popular with weekend crowds who know a cool alternative to the huge mainstream clubs when they see one. The atmosphere is akin to a private party. Deep bassy sounds throb round the dancefloor at the back of the club, interspersed with slabs of funk, hip hop and soul. Beer is L6,000 (€3.10), a G&T L10,000 (€5.20).

Space Electronic
Via Palazzuolo 37, Santa Maria Novella (055 293 082/www.spaceelectronic.com). **Open** 10pm-4am daily; closed 3wks Nov. **Admission** L25,000 (€13).
Credit AmEx, MC, V. **Map** p314 B1.
1970s kitsch and Brits-abroad territory, with a miniature replica of a pub and a TV with Sky Sports. The massive dancefloors have great sound systems, though where the music's concerned it's a good idea to blunt your critical faculties with a few drinks first. Coach parties are welcomed with open arms, so you could find yourself face to face with a pack of lurching Vikings. Insistently lecherous Italian males are bounced. Drinks cost L7,000-L12,000 (€3.60-€6.20).

Tenax
Via Pratese 46, Outside the City Gates (055 308 160/www.dada.it/tenax). Bus 29, 30. **Open** 10.30pm-4am Thur-Sat. Closed mid May-Sept. **Admission** L15,000-L35,000 (€7.80-€18). **Credit** AmEx, MC, V.
The most warehousey of the Florentine clubs, Tenax has long held the record for best-known nightspot, especially as a live venue for big international bands (*see also p176*). Head for London lights DJs Harvey and Cosmo of 'Nobody's Perfect' on Saturday nights (house, big beat and drum 'n' bass) or the ultra-hip 'Bizzarro' on Friday nights (hip hop).

Summer nights

Between May and September the character of Florence nightlife changes entirely, with most clubs shutting down to avoid mass heatstroke and those that stay open using every inch of patio, garden or even pavement, and outdoor bars springing up in *piazze* and villas.

The best summer nightlife bars are Le Murate and Parterre. **Le Murate** (via dell'Agnolo, 0338 506 0253), the coolest of the summer bars is set in a former women's prison. It has a dancefloor, pizzeria and even a cinema three nights a week and hosts concerts, theatre, dance and other events.
Parterre (piazza della Liberta, no phone) is a precarious looking prefab built over a car park with a two-floor clubbing area inside. Venues for main summer musical and cultural events organised by the council (concerts are generally MOR Italian schmaltz), they're open from 9pm to late nightly, with free admission.

From mid June to August the **Anfiteatro Parco delle Cascine** becomes something of a small festival site, with thousands of people skinning up and chilling out on the surrounding parkland. If planning permission is granted (a recurring problem), the Anfiteatro hosts concerts most evenings among the old Roman stones, following them up with a disco that lasts into the small hours. Bar prices are pretty average. The Anfiteatro is difficult to get to without your own transport – you can get a bus there but they stop running at night, and it's not advisable to leave on your own.

For riverside seats, head for **Teatro sull'Acqua** (lungarno Pecori Giraldi, 055 234 3460, open 10am-late mid May-mid Sept) or **Lido** (*see p182*), sprawling bar-cum-clubs right on the river bank. Street bars are a recent summer phenomenon: **Le Rime Rampanti** (open 7pm-1am Tue-Sat) overlooking the river on the terraces above piazza Poggi has live bands and a bar, while piazza Santo Spirito, one of the most popular pre-club squares, comes alive with **Notti d'Estate** (open 7pm-1am nightly), which has a bar, live music and dance and theatre shows.

For jazz, head for **Jazz&Co** (0348 810 2501), live acts held in a Florence square decided year by year, or a new addition, **Le Terrazze di New Orleans** (Villa Fabbricotti, via Vittorio Emanuele 64, 7pm-late nightly), which is organised by the Jazz Club (*see p176*) in an enchanting 19th-century villa garden.

Everything under one roof at **Universale**.

Universale

Via Pisana 77r, Outside the City Gates (055 221 122/ www.universalefirenze.it). Bus 6.
Open 8.30pm-2am Tue-Sun. Closed June-Sept.
Admission free (L12,000/€6.20 drinks minimum).
Credit AmEx, MC, V.

This stunning, spanking-new club, converted from a 1950s cinema, is pure heaven for those who've grown tired of traipsing from one Florentine nightlife hotspot to another – it's an emporium of entertainment with restaurant, bar, video screen and club areas. Restaurant-goers peer over the balustrade of the magnificent double curved *Gone With the Wind* staircases towards a flash central oval bar. Wednesday is a mellow jazz and wine night; funky live bands or smooth-vibes session DJs take the rest of the week.

XO Disco Bar

Via Verdi 57r, Santa Croce (055 234 7880).
Open 10pm-3am Mon-Sat. Closed June-Sept.
Admission L15,000-L20,000/€7.80-€10.50 (incl 1st drink). **No credit cards. Map** p314 C5.

This newly restyled and renamed bar and club, the latest incarnation of a long-running venue, opens out onto the main street, its red hues casting a warm glow over the fresh-faced twentysomethings who lounge at the chrome tables in full view of passing traffic. Inside, a friendly mixed crowd hit the dancefloor to a selection of mainstream house sounds (Saturdays can be more adventurous). If you don't like school discos, make sure to stay away on Wednesday nights. Drinks cost between L10,000 and L12,000 (€5.20-€6.20).

Yab

Via Sassetti 5r, Duomo & Around (055 215 160).
Open 9pm-4am Mon, Wed-Sun. Closed June-Sept.
Admission free (L30,000/€15.50 drinks minimum Fri, Sat). **Credit** AmEx, DC, V. **Map** p314 B3.

Yab is an institution among Florentines, and the average age of the punters goes up each year. The powerful sound system has the mammoth dancefloor shimmying with fortysomething dancers, while wall-to-wall bars on raised platforms with seating areas cater to those whose feet have given up the ghost. The door policy can be heavy-handed if you're not a regular. The best nights are Mondays ('Smoove' hip hop) and Wednesdays ('Pearl of the Florentine' with guest house DJs from all over Italy). Drinks average L10,000 (€2.60).

Pubs & bars

Apollo

Via dell'Ariento 41r, San Lorenzo (055 215 672).
Open 10am-3pm, 6.30pm-3am Tue-Thur; noon-3pm, 6.30pm-3am Fri; noon-3pm, 4.30pm-3am Sat; noon-3pm, 9pm-3am Sun. Closed 2wks Aug.
Credit AmEx, DC, MC, V. **Map** p314 A3.

A pulsating, late-opening bar now run by the Maramao captains (*see p178*), who've never had a problem filling out their ships with see-and-be-seen Italians. By 11.30pm the bar is bursting at the seams, all conversation drowned out by the housey tunes of DJs André and Miguel, whose decks appear, as if by magic, when the banquet of aperitif snacks has disappeared down the hatches of the lively crowd. An aperitif costs L8,000 (€4.10).

Art Bar

Via del Moro 4r, Santa Maria Novella (055 287 661). **Open** 7pm-1am Mon-Sat. Closed 3wks Aug. **No credit cards. Map** 314 B2.

Battered French horns hanging from the ceiling and sepia photographs of blues and jazz musicians lend a Parisian beatnik air to this perennially popular bar. The ambience here is cosy but animated, with student types holed up in the brick cellar sipping at Long Island teas and potent Pina Coladas. Drinks cost L7,000 (€3.60) at happy hour (7-9pm), then beer is L9,000 (€4.70) and cocktails start at L13,000 (€6.70).

Astor Caffè

Piazza Duomo 20r, Duomo & Around (055 239 9000). **Open** 7am-1am Mon-Sat. Closed 2wks Aug. **Credit** MC, V. **Map** p314 B4.

This huge, new, international-style jazz bar with soft red lighting, a flash chrome bar and wall-mounted reliefs promises to pep up central Florence nights with live and DJ-piped dance-jazz played to an enthusiastic young crowd. Internet points provide distraction from the busy socialising under the skylight of the main bar. Happy hour is from 6pm to 10pm. *See also p127.*

Cabiria

Piazza Santo Spirito 4r, Oltrarno (055 215 732). **Open** 8am-1am Mon, Wed-Thur; 8am-1.30am Fri-Sun. **No credit cards. Map** p314 D2.

The grungiest of the pre-club bars, with a crowd that often overflows past the outside seating into the square and sometimes ends up in several happy heaps on the steps of nearby Santo Spirito. Inside, the principal congregating area is in the micro corridor alongside the bar, which leads into a back room where DJs start up at around 9pm, blasting out an eclectic selection of alternative sounds, reggae and jazz. Beers cost L7,000 (€3.60), a G&T is L9,000 (€4.70).

Cafe la Torre

Lungarno Cellini 65r, Oltrarno (055 680 643). **Open** 10.30am-3am daily. **Credit** AmEx, DC, MC, V. **Map** p314 D6.

Follow the river to the medieval tower beacon that signposts this late-night opening, nice 'n' easy bar. The post-clubbing music is mercifully mellow, but if you make it here earlier you can sway to the foot-tapping tunes of the various nightly (or almost) live acts (*see p174*). Beer is L6,000 (€3.10) before 6.30pm, L8,000 (€4.10) after; tapas and tortellini are served to assuage moonlight munchies.

Il Caffè

Piazza Pitti 9r, Oltrarno (055 239 9863). **Open** 11am-1.30am Tue-Sun. **Credit** MC, V. **Map** p314 D2.

Not the most happening of Florentine nightspots but without a doubt the most sophisticated. Wrought-iron lanterns lead the way across the burnished oak floors of the bar to a spiral staircase and two intimate balcony rooms, tiny love nests curtained off with white drapery. Hypnotic *Arabian Nights* music plays as the candlelit, canopied outside tables overlooking the grand Palazzo Pitti fill with beautiful people delicately sipping cognacs and discreetly eyeing one another up. Drinks cost about L10,000 (€5.20).

Capocaccia

Lungarno Corsini 12/14r, Santa Maria Novella (055 210 751). **Open** noon-2am Tue-Sun. **Credit** AmEx, DC, MC, V. **Map** p314 C2.

The most delightful atmospheric of Florence's evening bars. Sit in the packed bar room nursing a cocktail amid the fairy lights; dig the acid jazz and big beats in the central buffet room, where from 7pm onwards all drinks are L10,000 (€5.10) and there's a feast of snacks; chat in the amazing frescoed chill-out salon; or join half the population of cool Florence outside, blocking the traffic on warm summer nights. *See also p131.*

Chequers

Via della Scala 7/9r, Santa Maria Novella (055 287 588). **Open** 6.30pm-1am Mon; 6pm-1am Tue-Sat; 6pm-1.30am Sun. Closed 2wks Aug. **Credit** AmEx, DC, MC, V. **Map** p314 B2.

A huge watering-hole playing indie rock, frequented by military cadets from the nearby barracks and lost backpackers. Best visited during major football matches, when its big screen draws in the crowds. Half-price drinks at happy hour (6.30-8pm); otherwise beer is L8,000 (€4.10), G&T L10,000 (€5.20).

Capocaccia: big beats and chilled chat.

Arts & Entertainment

Enjoy a brew at the lively **James Joyce**.

Dolce Vita

Piazza del Carmine, Oltrarno (055 284 595/
www.dolcevitafirenze.it). **Open** *Bar* summer
10.30am-1.30am Mon-Sat; 6pm-1.30am Sun;
winter 6pm-1.30am daily. *Restaurant* 12.30-3pm,
7.30-11.30pm Mon-Sat. Closed 2wks Aug.
Credit AmEx, DC, JCB, MC, V. **Map** p314 C2.
Dolce Vita has stood the test of time to remain
Florence's number one wannabe bar. The interior,
with its sofas and beautiful crystal lamps, is much
less popular than the outside meeting area – to the
point that neighbours have invested in soundproof
windows. If you ever make it as far as the impos-
sibly busy bar, a beer is L4,000/€2.10 (L7,000/
€3.60 seated), a G&T costs L10,000/€5.20 (13,000/
€6.70 seated). *See also p132.*

Fiddler's Elbow

Piazza Santa Maria Novella 7r, Santa Maria Novella
(055 215 056). **Open** 3pm-1am Mon-Thur; 3pm-2am
Fri; 2pm-2am Sat; 2pm-1am Sun. **No credit cards**.
Map p314 B2.
The plus-points of this Italian chain pub are the
satellite TV showing sports on request, and the outdoor seating – a rare commodity for a central pub,
and worth forgoing a happy hour for on humid
nights. Beer is L7,500 (€3.90), G&T L7,000 (€3.60).

James Joyce

Lungarno B Cellini 1r, Oltrarno (055 658 0856).
Open 6pm-1am Mon-Thur; 6pm-2am Fri, Sat;
3pm-1am Sun. **No credit cards**.
The best of Florence's pubs in spring and summer,
thanks to its large enclosed garden with long wood-
en tables, JJ has a high-spirited vibe. Happy hour,

when drinks (beer L8,000/€4.10, G&T L9,000/€4.70)
come with free snacks, lasts till 9.30pm. There's
a small bookshop selling paperbacks, some in
English. Closes early on Sunday in winter.

JJ Cathedral Pub

Piazza San Giovanni 44r, Duomo & Around (055
280 260). **Open** 11am-1am daily. **Credit** AmEx,
DC, MC, V. **Map** p314 B3.
When this authentic Irish pub opens there's always
a frantic scrabble to get to the most coveted drinking table in the city, on the tiny Juliet balcony
overlooking the 11th-century Baptistery. If you're
thwarted in your aim, drown your sorrows in
a Guinness at one of the nearby tables, to the
occasional sound of fiddled jigs, or settle on a
downstairs bar stool with a Beamish (L8,000/€4.10
a pint) and an earful of the Corrs.

Lido

Lungarno Pecori Giraldi 1r, Santa Croce (055 234
2726). *Bus 12, 13, 14, 71.* **Open** 12.30pm-2am
Tue-Sat; 1pm-2am Sun. Lunch served 1-3pm daily.
Closed Jan, Feb. **Admission** free. **No credit cards**.
Large glass doors open from this bar to a garden
that extends down to the river bank, making it a
good bet for hot summer nights, when queues
inevitably form despite the ugly, uncomfortable
plastic chairs. The music is a thumping collection
of drum 'n' bass, R&B and the like, though the
dancefloor is entirely taken up by the queue for the
bar. Fridays are stomping deep house. Come early
if you want to hire a boat for a quick punt
(L15,000/€7.80 an hour). Beer is L7,000 (€3.60), and
long drinks L10,000 (€5.20).

Lion's Fountain

Borgo degli Albizi 34r, Santa Croce (055 234 4412).
Open 6pm-2am daily. Closed Aug. **No credit cards. Map** p314 B5.
One of many Irish pubs in town, but the atmosphere and homey decor make it a cut above the rest. Staff pull a fair pint of Guinness, snacks are served and the atmosphere is friendly. Beer is L8,000 (€4.10), a G&T L10,000 (€5.20). Two TVs show sport.

Loonees

Via Porta Rossa 15r, Duomo & Around (055 212 249).
Open 8pm-3am Tue-Sun. Closed Aug.
Admission free. **No credit cards. Map** p314 C3.
Popular with US students, this mainly live music bar (*see p176*) has a relaxed atmosphere that's partly due to the loud music, leaving punters with little to do but sway and take advantage of the free shot with every pint. A beer costs L8,000 (€4.10), a G&T is L10,000 (€5.20).

Montecarla

Via dei Bardi 2, Oltrarno (055 234 0259).
Open 9pm-3am Mon-Thur, Sun; 9pm-4am Fri, Sat.
Admission free. **No credit cards. Map** p314 D4.
Montecarla's reputation is built on Chinese whispers; the chief rumour is that it was once a brothel (it wasn't, but its low-slung leopardskin couches, hidden recesses and oriental drapery encourage the fantasy). Soft background music plays, a pile of board games is on hand and service is conspiratorial and intimate. The drinks, which are mainly cocktails, come in monster measures; the house special is Montecarla (gin, rum, Cointreau and orange). Non-alcoholic drinks cost L10,000 (€5.20), others are L12,000 (€6.20).

Porfirio Rubirosa

Viale Strozzi 38r, San Lorenzo (055 490 965).
Open 8am-2am Tue-Sun. Closed 2wks Aug.
Credit MC, V.
At night the elegant Rubirosa is recognisable from the Mercs, Ferraris and Audi TTs parked five-deep on the avenue. You'll find the owners inside, propping up the long marble bar and trying to live up to its namesake, a Brazilian playboy (*see p131*), while foot-tapping to *The Boy from Ipanema*. Cocktails are about L10,000 (€5.20).

Rex Caffè

Via Fiesolana 25r, Santa Croce (055 248 0331).
Open 5pm-1.30am Mon-Thur, Sun; 5pm-2.30am Fri, Sat. Closed June-Aug. **Credit** MC, V. **Map** p314 B5.
With more of a club than a bar atmosphere, Rex is the king of the east, filling up with loyal subjects who bow, scrape and sashay to the sounds of the session DJs playing bassy beats and jungle rhythms. Gaudí-esque mosaics decorate the central bar and columns, wrought-iron lamps shed a soft light and a luscious red antechamber creates seclusion for more intimate gatherings. Tapas are served during happy hour (5-9.30pm), and Rex prides itself on its cocktails (costing from L12,000/€6.20; wine starts at L5,000/€2.60).

Rose's

Via del Parione 26r, Santa Lorenzo (055 287 090).
Open 8am-1.30am Mon-Sat; 5pm-1.30am Sun.
Sushi bar 7-11pm Tue-Sun. Closed 2wks Aug.
Credit MC,V. **Map** p314 C2.
Daniele runs Rose's with the ease of a man whose sophisticated, relaxed bar has attracted the in-crowd for more than 15 years. His secret has been to move with the times; it's now the first sushi bar to grace town. When you're all raw-fished out, slap your palate back into shape with a house Caipirhina made with the Brazilian spirit cachaca, or the vodka Caipiroska. Cocktails are L10,000 (€5.20), wine or beer L5,000/€2.60 (L7,000/€3.60 after 9pm). *See also p129.*

La Rotonda

Via Il Prato 10/16r, Santa Maria Novella (055 265 4644). **Open** 7.30pm-1am daily. Closed 2wks Aug.
Credit AmEx, DC, MC, V.
This sprawling saloon-style pub cum pizzeria is decked out in tacky wood-panelling and inexplicably watched over from the upper-floor balcony by wooden models of jazz musicians. The DJ session music wavers from hip hop to mainstream; upstairs live bands drive you to drink from Thursdays to Sundays. The beer selection (L5,000/€2.60) is the La Rotonda's only saving grace, with Chimays and bottled Guinness, and the crowd is friendly, though there are often rowdy stag nights and birthday parties being held on the premises.

The William Pub

Via Magliabechi 7-11r, Santa Croce (055 263 8357).
Open 1pm-1am Mon-Thur, Sun; 1pm-2am Fri-Sat.
Credit AmEx, DC, JCB, MC, V. **Map** p314 C5.
British pub culture, complete with photos of English sporting heroes and quaint village scenes, has been transplanted into this most frescoed and Florentine of buildings. The identity crisis extends to the clientele, which runs from butch bikers to caressing couples. The downstairs bar is generally packed, the upstairs bar and the back room have space to sip a Newcastle Brown and munch on a late-night ploughman's. Stick to bottled beers rather than draught. Beer costs L8,000 (€4.20), a G&T is L12,000 (€6.20).

Zoe

Via Dei Renai 13r, Oltrarno (055 243 111).
Open 8am-1am Mon-Thur; 8am-2am Fri, Sat; 6pm-1am Sun. Closed 3wks Aug. **Credit** AmEx, MC, V.
Map p314 D4.
Siren Zoe's red neon signs have lured many a parched modern-day Odysseus into her clutches, where she plies them with lethal cocktails (try the Crimson Zoe – vodka, gin and Cointreau blended with fresh strawberries, sugar and crushed ice) and salty snacks. Most passing travellers are an easy catch and by midnight the crowd spills onto the street. There's seating in the green river bank square in summer. Beer is L7,000 (€3.60), a G&T L10,000 (€5.20). Happy hour is from 5pm to 10pm.

Theatre & Dance

It's tough on the Tuscan stage.

That Tuscany is spattered with beautiful old theatres – there are around 300 in the region, some dating back to the 15th and 16th centuries – reflects the fact that Italian theatre has a long and distinguished history. In the past every town in Tuscany had its theatre; some of the most interesting still remain, in Montalcino, San Casciano, Massa, Pescia, Pistoia, Prato, Montecarlo di Lucca, Lucca and Pisa. Florence itself has two historic theatres: **Teatro della Pergola** (*see p185*) and **Teatro Goldoni** (*see p184*). The former hosts a full season of plays, the latter is used principally for musical events. The city's **Teatro Verdi** (*see p172*) is not as picturesque but it does host a varied programme of productions. Still, though Florence is the regional capital, many new productions bypass the city in favour of the renowned Teatro Metastasio in Prato or the Teatro Manzoni in Pistoia, or skip Tuscany altogether.

The main problem with theatre in Tuscany is the reluctance on the part of funding bodies and producers to put on experimental or fringe events (seen as a risk) and a general lack of public curiosity. Safe, middle-of-the road productions guarantee the fullest houses, so these are the shows chosen for funding. Yet despite the chronic lack of cash for smaller initiatives, individual enthusiasm and hard graft continue to produce interesting projects.

Of course, most theatre productions in both Florence and Tuscany are in Italian and thus of limited interest to most visitors, but there's a fair amount of non-verbal theatre too. Musicals have undergone a huge revival in Italy in general, to the extent that the country is now a European leader in the genre in terms of the level of production. Many of the biggest hits have come through Tuscany in the past two years. Otherwise you can see anything from Pirandello, Goldoni and foreign classics (in Italian) to mainstream contemporary and even, occasionally, a radical fringe show.

The Tuscan theatre season is short, running from (roughly) September to April.

If Italian theatre suffers from lack of funding, dance has an even tougher time of it, though a recent change in the law may improve things a little over the next few years. The ministry of culture now has an office dedicated just to the promotion of dance in Italy, although funding is very hard to tap into and money will probably

go to mainstream, well-established projects. For the lucky few, however, a successful application will mean three-year funding – something that's never before been available in Italy. Despite this upswing, however, the Tuscan dance scene did suffer a great loss in early 2001 when the much-missed, excellent Balletto di Toscana went spectacularly bankrupt.

Full-length classical and contemporary productions by the group **MaggioDanza** are performed at the **Teatro Comunale** (or the Teatro del Maggio Musicale Fiorentino as it's now officially called; *see p175*); while modern work comes from the likes of the **Virgilio Sieni Dance Company**, the **Florence Dance Company** and other experimental companies, who perform all year. Summer brings events in beautiful venues such as the lovely **Boboli Gardens** and **piazzale Michelangiolo**. Just outside of Florence, look out for groups such as **Motus** from Siena, **Compagnia Xe** from San Casciano and **Giardino Chiusi** from San Gimignano. Other festivals are located even further afield including **La Versiliana** in Marina di Pietrasanta and the **Armunia Festival della Riviera** in Castiglioncello.

Organisations promoting dance in Tuscany include **ToscanaDanza** (formed several years ago to promote new performances by selected regional dance companies) and **Fondazione Toscana dello Spettacolo**, who recently began including dance in their promotion of theatrical events in small theatres in the region.

For upcoming events, see the monthly listings mag *Firenze Spettacolo* or local press.

Venues

Teatro Goldoni

Via Santa Maria 15, Oltrarno. For tickets, contact relevant organising body (*see below*) or buy on door 1hr before show. **Map** p314 D1. **No credit cards**. Tiny Teatro Goldoni has been used mainly for classical music until now (*see p171*), but a new project instigated in 2001 means dance events will play a major role from now on. The scheme, run by the city of Florence and the Maggio Musicale Fiorentino (*see p171*), hands over the theatre to four dance bodies (the Florence Dance Cultural Centre, MaggioDanza, Compagnia Virgilio Sieni and Versilia Danza; *see p184*) for certain periods of the year. There will also be workshops, choreography competitions, stages and promotional dance platforms.

Arts & Entertainment

The delightful **Teatro della Limonaia**.

Teatro della Limonaia
Via Gramsci 426, Sesto Fiorentino, Outside the City Gates (055 440 852). Bus 28A, 28B. **Open** for telephone bookings only 10am-6.30pm Mon-Fri. **No credit cards.**
A tiny, delightful space that could be in New York. Shows are mainly alternative. Look out for the Intercity Festival in *(see p186)*.

Teatro della Pergola
Via della Pergola 12-32, San Marco (055 226 4316). **Open** box office 9.30am-1pm, 3.30-6.45pm Tue-Sat; 10am-12.15pm Sun. **Season** Oct-Apr. **No credit cards. Map** p314 B5.
A full programme of productions from visiting companies. Catch anything from *King Lear* to Beckett's *Happy Days. See also p172.*

Teatro Puccini
Piazza Puccini, Outside the City Gates (055 362 067/www.teatropuccini.it). Bus 17, 22, 30, 35. **Open** box office 4-7.30pm Mon-Fri. Closed May-Sept. **No credit cards.**
Light opera, musicals and one-man variety shows fill the bill at this large Fascist-style building.

Teatro di Rifredi
Via Vittorio Emanuele 303, Outside the City Gates. (055 422 0361/www.toscanateatro.it). Bus 4, 14, 28. **Open** box office 4-7pm Mon-Sat; 30min before performance. **Season** Sept-May. **No credit cards.**
The Rifredi has come through a sticky couple of years, but funding has been confirmed – for now. Resident company Pupi & Fresedde offers a varied programme featuring productions from classical Pirandello and Shakespeare to contemporary and fringe shows. There's particular emphasis on young and up-and-coming playwrights and directors.

Teatro Studio di Scandicci
Via Donizetti 58, Outside the City Gates (055 757 348/ teatrostudio@scandiccicultura.org). Bus 16. **Season** Sept-June. **No credit cards.**
This small theatre in the suburbs is now possibly the best place to see alternative theatre on a regular basis in Florence. Though the resident Compania di

Krypton *(see below)* is now well established and no longer avant-garde, there are two new companies in residence, one of which, Kinkaleri, is making big waves with their shows involving dance, physical theatre and multimedia.

Fringe theatre companies

Compania di Krypton
Piazza Santa Croce 19, Santa Croce (055 234 5443). Bus 14, C5. Closed 2wks Aug.
Founded by Giancarlo and Fulvio Cauteruccio in 1982 and the resident company at the Teatro Studio di Scandicci *(see above)*, Krypton is well established and respected. Lighting, stage and sound techniques were avant-garde when it started out, and it still experiments with video, projections, lasers, microphones and other effects. Its 2000/2001 shows included reworkings and improvisations on classics including *The Tempest* and Pinter's *The Caretaker.*

Il Teatro delle Donne
Piazza Santa Croce 19, Santa Croce (055 234 7572). **Open** office hours 10am-4pm Mon-Fri. Season Oct-May. **Map** p314 C5.
All-female company promoting plays by women.

Pupi e Fressedde
A young company that does a lot of work with schools and has an eclectic repertoire. Contact via Teatro de Rifredi *(see above)*.

Dance companies

Compagnia Virgilio Sieni Danza
Via San Romano 13, Outside the City Gates (055 655 7435).
Dancer and choreographer Virgilio Sieni directs one of the few local avant-garde dance companies to have achieved international fame. Performances are often creative collaborations with instrumentalists, composers and designers. Among Sieni's latest work is an ongoing project on the theme of fairy-tales, involving composer Giorgio Batistelli (artistic director of the Orchestra Regionale Toscana; *see p172*).

Florence Dance Cultural Centre
Borgo della Stella 23r, Oltrarno (055 289 276). Closed Aug. **Map** p314 C1.
Directed by Marga Nativo and American choreographer Keith Ferrone, this eclectic centre offers a range of dance classes, from children's activities to advanced ballet at professional level, and organised the Florence Dance Festival *(see p186)*. There are daily open classes, so you can attend even on a short-term basis. The Florence Dance Company made their debut in July 2001 with Béjart's *Bolero.*

MaggioDanza
Teatro Comunale, Corso Italia 16, Santa Maria Novella (055 211 158/055 213 535).
Resident company at the Teatro Comunale (now officially the Teatro del Maggio Musicale Fiorentino,

Arts & Entertainment

Who they? Machiavelli

A complex and confusing character, Niccolò Machiavelli (1469-1527), the statesman, writer and political philospher was best known in his day for his plays, most notably *Mandragola*. Written in 1518, it's a fine classical comedy about a young man's successful plot to have his way with the beautiful wife of a wealthy merchant.

In many ways Machiavelli, a largely self-educated lawyer's son, was a product and beneficiary of the rebirth of classical learning, yet he had little esteem or affection for most of his contemporaries. Shrewd, sarcastic, arrogant and aloof, he believed that the achievements of the Renaissance were worth nothing if they were not backed by force. He'd been in Florence in 1494 when Charles VIII's troops had marched in, and had been horrified by the city's abject inability to oppose them. The theory of the pursuit and maintenance of power became his obsession.

Gaining political influence when his friend Piero Soderini was appointed as Florence's Gonfaloniere (the most powerful position in the administration) for life in 1502, Machiavelli shouldered responsibility for war, forming the Republic's first national militia. When Cardinal Giovanni de Medici (the future Pope Leo X) advanced toward Florence with Spanish troops in 1512, this militia garrisoned Prato, then lost its nerve and fled. Florence capitulated and Machiavelli's cynicism deepened.

Forced into exile at his villa at Sant'Andrea in Percussina, he wrote his most celebrated book, *The Prince*, a sort of handbook for rulers. By that time he'd become convinced that the best form of government was that provided by a strong leader and maintained by armed force. 'It is better to be feared than loved if you cannot be both,' he wrote.

see p175), MaggioDanza presents a range of ballet from *Swan Lake* and *Nutcracker* to contemporary works by visiting choreographers. In summer, performances are held in Boboli Gardens.

Festivals

For the **Estate Fiesolana** see p156.

Fabbrica Europa
Borgo degli Albizi 15, Santa Croce (055 248 0515/www.fabbricaeuropa.net). Date May/June. Map p314 B5.
The former Stazione Leopolda forms a huge and versatile space for the innovative programme of dance, music, theatre, circus and multimedia events presented by Fabbrica Europa.

Florence Dance Festival
Borgo della Stella 23r, Oltrarno (055 289 276/www.florencedance.org). Date June-Aug. Map p314 C1.

The only festival dedicated solely to dance in Tuscany and now in its 12th year, this summer event can be relied upon to bring some of the great names of contemporary, traditional and classical dance to Florence. The brainchild of Marga Nativo, Keith Ferrone and the Florence Dance Cultural Centre, it puts on six weeks of performances by acclaimed companies in Fiesole's Teatro Romano and dedicates several evenings to up-and-coming choreographers. Also features choreography contests, seminars and art exhibitions.

Intercity Festival
Teatro della Limonaia, Via Gramsci 426, Sesto Fiorentino, Outside the City Gates. (055 440 852). Date Sept, Oct.
A rare (in Florence) opportunity to see contemporary theatre performed in its mother tongue. Each year a city is chosen, and playwrights, actors and theatre companies from the country concerned are invited to participate. Berlin warrants a second year in 2001. Athens is under consideration for 2002.

Sport & Fitness

Whether you've eaten too many *biscotti* or want your fill of spectator sports, Florence has the recipe.

Florence is not a mecca for sports enthusiasts, but look between the Gothic façades and tiny artisans' shops and you'll find bustling modern gyms and sports complexes tucked behind ancient loggias guarded by centuries-old iron gates. If it's spectator sports you're looking for, *calcio* or football seems to be in the blood of every Italian, and whether you attend a game in the stadium or watch it in a local *tabacchi*, you're guaranteed a true Italian experience.

Spectator sports

Car & motorbike racing

Autodromo del Mugello
Near Scarperia (055 849 9111). Closed Dec-Feb.
Rates Formula 1 trials L10,000 (€5.20).
No credit cards.
Top-notch racing, including Formula 3 and motorcycle world championship competitions. If you can get your hands on a motorbike, you can take it for a spin on the test track for L10,000 (€5.20) per lap.

Football

Stadio Artemio Franchi
Campo di Marte, Outside the City Gates (055 579 743). Bus 11, 17. **Tickets** L33,000-L230,000 (€17-€119). **No credit cards.**
The home ground of Fiorentina (*see p189* **Who they?**). The season runs from August to May, with matches generally every other Sunday at 3pm. Tickets can be purchased at the 45,000-capacity stadium two to three hours prior to a match or pre-booked either at the Chiosco degli Sportivi outlet (via Anselmi near piazza della Repubblica, 055 292 363) or at the Box Office ticket agency (via Alamanni 39, 055 210 804/www.boxoffice.com).

Horse racing

Ippodromi e Città
Viale del Pegaso 1, Outside the City Gates (055 422 6076). Bus 17C. Closed Aug. **Admission** L7,000 (€3.60). **No credit cards.**
Florence's racecourse for *il trotto* (trotting), where the driver sits in a carriage behind the horse. The Premio Duomo in June is one of Tuscany's biggest racing events; look out for Enrico Bellei, one of Italy's best *trotto* drivers.

Ippodromo il Visarno
Via delle Cascine, Outside the City Gates (055 353 394/055 422 6076). Bus 17. Closed Aug. **Admission** L7,000 (€3.60). **No credit cards.**
Florence's *galoppo* (flat-racing) course. The season lasts from spring to summer, and you might spot leading Tuscan jockeys such as Muzzi and Colombi.

Active sports/fitness

Climbing/trekking

Galleria Dello Sport
Via Venezia 18/20, San Marco (055 580 611).
Open 3.30-7.30pm Mon; 9am-1pm, 3.30-7.30pm Tue-Sat. Closed last 3wks Aug. **No credit cards.**
Primarily a sporting goods shop, this houses a rare treasure in Florence – an eight-metre (26ft) climbing wall. With proper gear and a friend to spot you, you can flex your skills free of charge.

Guide Alpine Agai
Office at Libreria Stella Alpina, Via Corridoni 14, Outside the City Gates (055 411 688). Bus 14, 28.
Open 4-7pm Mon; 9am-1pm, 4-7pm Tue-Sat.
Credit AmEx, MC, V.
This mountaineering company organises courses for all levels. The five-day beginners' course costs L350,000 (€181), with the first day spent on a climbing wall in Montecatini. Guided excursions include hiking and rock- and ice-climbing. There are also personalised treks and expeditions throughout Italy.

Gruppo Escursionistico CAI (Club Alpino Italiano)
Via del Mezzetta 2, Outside the City Gates (055 239 8580). Bus 3, 6, 20. **Open** 3.30-7.30pm Mon-Fri. Closed Aug. **Rates** about L30,000 (€15.50) depending on group size. **No credit cards.**
Guided Sunday treks in Tuscany. Most hikes, on trails through gentle countryside, are rated easy to moderate. Prices include transport to and from the city centre but don't cover lunch, so pack a snack.

Cycling
See also p284 **Directory: Cycling.**

Veni Vidi Bici
Mobile 0328 118 0270/http://venividibici.dadacasa. supereva.it. Closed mid Nov-Feb. **No credit cards.**
This programme, run by a group of students and outdoor enthusiasts, offers a variety of bike tours around Florence and Tuscany. Prices (including

bike, insurance, meals and accommodation as needed) are L85,000 (€44) for a one-day tour in Tuscany, L400,000 (€206.50) for three days. Throughout the summer (rainy days excepted) there are bike tours around Florence for L40,000 (€20.50).

Golf

Circolo Golf Ugolino
Via Chiantigiana 3, Grassina (055 230 1009).
Bus 31. **Open** 8.30am-7pm daily. Closed Jan. **Rates**
18 holes L110,000 (€57) Mon-Fri; L140,000 (€72.50)
Sat, Sun. *9 holes* L95,000 (€49) Mon-Fri; L80,000
(€41.50) Sat, Sun. **Credit** AmEx, DC, JCB, MC, V.
The nearest course to the city (about 20 minutes south by bus), but it's not open during the frequent weekend tournaments. It's best to phone for reservations at least a week in advance.

Gyms

Body's New Wellness Center
Via Leonardo Bruni 11, Outside the City Gates
(055 688 117). Bus 23, 33. **Open** 8.30am-10.30pm
Mon-Fri; 8.30am-8.30pm Sat; 8.30am-12.30pm Sun.
Membership 1-month L210,000 (€108.50);
1-day L20,000 (€10.50). **No credit cards.**
Ultra hip and ultra expensive,this recently renovated gym has a sauna and massage centre and an expansive weight-training/cardio area. It also offers spinning, t'ai chi and various aerobics classes. In addition, it's the only Florence gym to offer Pilates.

Palestra Gymnasium ○
Via Palazzuolo 49r, Santa Maria Novella (055 293
308). **Open** 10am-10pm Mon-Fri; 10am-6pm Sat.
Closed 2wks Aug. **Membership** 1-day L20,000
(€10.50); 1-month L120,000 (€62); annual
L50,000/€26. **Credit** MC, V. **Map** p314 B1.
Equipped with free weights, machines and a sauna, which costs extra. There are also stretching, tae kwan do and various aerobics classes.

Palestra Porta Romana
Via G Silvani 5, Outside the City Gates (055 232
1799). Bus 11, 12, 36, 37. **Open** 9.30am-10pm Mon,
Tue, Thur, Fri; 12.30-10pm Wed; 10am-12.30pm Sat.
Membership 1-day L20,000 (€10.50); 1-month
L120,000 (€62); annual L30,000 (€15.50).
No credit cards.
Weights room, plus aerobics, step, boxing and spinning classes. There's also a specialised programme for karate and other martial arts.

Palestra Ricciardi
Borgo Pinti 75, Santa Croce (055 247 8462).
Open *Sept-July* 9am-10pm Mon-Fri; 9.30am-6pm Sat.
Aug 5-10pm Mon-Sat. **Membership** 1-month
L150,000 (€77.50); 1-day L20,000 (€10.50).
No credit cards. Map p314 A6.
One of the largest and most modern of Florence's gyms, and central, but one of the most expensive.

Zero Uno/Indoor Club
Via Bardazzi 15, Outside the City Gates (055
430 275/055 430 703). Bus 29, 30. **Open** 10.30am-
11pm Mon-Thur; 10.30am-10pm Fri; 10.30am-8pm
Sat. **Membership** 1-day L30,000 (€15.50).
No credit cards.
Sauna, indoor pool, weights and classes, including step, spinning and aerobics.

Horse riding

Maneggio Marinella
Via Di Macia 21, Travalli Calenzano (055 887
8066). Bus 28. **Open** 9am-1pm, 3-7pm daily.
Rates 1-hr ride L25,000 (€13). **No credit cards.**
Phone during the week to book a place on one of the daily rides. Lessons and special or group trips can be organised on request.

Rendola Riding
Montevarchi (055 970 7045/bawtree@ats.it). **Open**
9am-1pm, 3-6pm Tue-Sun. **Rates** *1-hr lesson* L30,000
(€15.50), *1-hr ride* L30,000 (€15.50). **No credit cards.**
This stable, which is located 30 minutes' drive south of Florence, bordering Chianti, offers one- to five-hour rides through the countryside. Lessons are available, as well as a package offering two hours of riding, full lunch and transport to and from the nearest train station. Reservations must be made a day in advance at the latest. There are also two- to three-day trips, with lodging provided at a neighbouring *agriturismo*.

Pool

Gambrinus
Via dei Vecchietti 16r, Duomo & Around (055 287
201). **Open** 1.30pm-1am daily. **Rates** *tables* L12,000
(€6.20) per hour. **No credit cards.**
The only pool hall in central Florence, Gambrinus offers nine pool tables and eight tables without pockets, where you can try your hand at *boccette* or *cinque birilli*. The clientele here is predominantly serious but non-hostile males.

Rowing

If you want to row on the Arno, you'll need to join a local club.

Società Canottieri Firenze
Lungarno Luisa dei Medici, Duomo & Around
(055 238 1010/055 211 093). **Open** 8am-8.30pm
Mon, Sat; 8am-9.30pm Tue-Fri; 8am-1pm Sun.
Membership annual L800,000 (€454.50); 3-month
L210,000 (€108.50); 1-month L120,000 (€62).
No credit cards. Map p314 C3.
This rowing society is blessed with a prime location on the bank of the Arno just below the Uffizi. It also offers gym facilities, a tank and showers. The first few trials are free of charge, which allows you to test out the waters without having to commit yourself beforehand.

Who they? Fiorentina

Sweet victory for Florence's home team in the 2001 Coppa Italia.

Dubbed the 'Viola' after their purple shirts, Fiorentina gave its obsessive fans reasons to be cheerful in June 2001 when it lifted the Coppa Italia by beating Parma in the two-leg final – sweet revenge for the defeat by Parma in the 1999 final, but small compensation for a season that had soured off the pitch.

It kicked off badly when Vittorio Cecchi Gori, the much-reviled club president, let star Argentine striker Gabriel 'Batigol' Batistuta go to Roma – who went on to rub salt into the wound by winning the only Italian competition that really matters, the Serie A, a prize that has eluded Fiorentina for some 30 years. The lucrative transfer failed to restore their finances and by the end of the season the club was in chaos: rumours of $140 million debts, court liquidation hearings, three of the best players touted for sale and the fans so incensed that Gori fled town among rumours of death threats.

Ultimately, Fiorentina will doubtless survive. They're the only team in town, for one thing, and not new to controversy. Their forays into Europe have been notoriously marred by

crowd trouble. They were banned from staging European ties after Barcelona's English coach Bobby Robson was hit by a bottle in a Cup Winners Cup tie in 1997. And in 1998 a firework that was thrown at an official in a match in Salerno against the Swiss team Grasshoppers got them thrown out of the UEFA Cup. The Viola have also earned an unpleasant reputation as having some of the most racist fans in Europe.

While it's not a major concern for most Florentine stadium-goers, crowd problems are more likely during matches with Juventus. A series of controversies between the two clubs over the past two decades has led to a fierce mutual dislike.

That said, a visit to the Stadio Artemio Franchi – also known as the Stadio Comunale – is well worth it. The intense passion of the spectators and the outstanding firework and choreographed crowd displays make for a memorable experience. Squeeze into the rowdiest section – the 'Curva Fiesole' – for the fully fired-up Viola experience.

'Dai Ragazzi!

Running

Most joggers head for the Parco delle Cascine or the Giardino dei Semplici, Bobolino.

Associazione Atletica Leggera
Viale Matteotti 15, Outside the City Gates (055 571 401/fax 055 576 616). Bus 8, 80. **Open** 9am-1pm, 3.30-6.30pm Mon-Fri.
Good source of info on running clubs and races.

Organizzazione Firenze Marathon
Casella Postale 597, 50100 Firenze (055 572 885).
Florence's marathon is usually run in late November.

Skating

There's a temporary rink in the Fortezza Da Basso from December to mid-January. You pay by the session (there are three or four a day); the last ends at about 11pm.

Le Pavoniere
Via della Catena 2, Parco delle Cascine, Outside the City Gates (0335 571 8547). Bus 17C. **Open** 3-8pm Mon-Fri; 10am-8pm Sat, Sun. Closed when raining. **Rates** L8,000 (€4.10) per hour. **No credit cards.**
Rollerblade hire. Glorious open path along the Arno, but avoid Sunday afternoon unless you want to weave through hordes of strollers.

Tennis Pattinaggio
Viale Michelangiolo 61, Outside the City Gates (055 681 1880). Bus 12, 13. **Open** 3-8pm daily. **Admission** L7,000 (€3.60). **No credit cards.**
Sports complex with a large rollerskating rink.

Skiing

See chapter **Massa Carrara & Lucca Provinces** for the Abetone Ski Area.

Squash

Centro Squash Firenze
Via Empoli 16, Outside the City Gates (055 732 3055). Bus 1. **Open** 10.30am-11pm Mon-Fri; 10.30am-6.30pm Sat. Closed Aug. **Rates** L28,000 (€14.50) for 45min court time. **No credit cards.**
Squash courts, gym, sauna and equipment rental.

Swimming

Many pools open in summer only. In winter some pools require at least a month's membership and may limit access to a few times a week.

Amici del Nuoto
Via del Romito 38b, Outside the City Gates (055 483 951). Bus 14 & 28. **Open** 11am-3pm Mon-Sat; 10am-noon Sun. **Membership** annual L60,000 (€34); 1-month L95,000 (€49.10). **No credit cards.**
Members can use this indoor pool thrice weekly.

Fiorentina Nuoto
Piscina Bellariva (indoor/outdoor)
Lungarno Aldo Moro 6, Outside the City Gates (055 677 541). Bus 14. **Open** *Summer* 10am-6pm, 8.30-11pm Mon-Fri; 10am-6pm Sat, Sun. *Winter* 8.30-11pm Tue, Thur; 9.30am-12.30pm Sat, Sun. **Admission** L10,000 (€5.50). **No credit cards.**
Piscina San Marcellino (indoor)
Via Chiantigiana 28, Outside the City Gates (055 653 0000). Bus 31, 32. **Open** 10am-9pm Mon-Sat; 9.30am-12.30pm Sun. **Membership** monthly L90,000/€46.50 (unlimited access). **No credit cards.**
Costoli (2 indoor/1 outdoor June-Sept)
Viale Paoli, Outside the City Gates (055 623 6027). Bus 3. **Open** 2-6pm Mon; 10am-6pm Tue-Sun. **Admission** *Winter* L7,000 (€3.60) per hour. *Summer* L11,000 (€5.70) per visit or 10 visits for L85,000 (€44). **No credit cards.**

Le Pavoniere
Via della Catena 2, Parco delle Cascine, Outside the City Gates (055 358 327). Bus 17C. **Open** 10am-6pm daily. Closed Oct-May. **Admission** L12,000 (€6.20). **No credit cards.**
Near the bank of the Arno in Florence's largest park. Late opening hours, small bar and pizzeria.

Tennis

Assi Giglio Rosso
Viale Michelangiolo 64, Outside the City Gates (055 681 0749). Bus 12, 13. **Open** 8am-10.30pm Mon-Fri; 8am-7pm Sat; 8am-1pm Sun. Closed 2wks Aug. **Rates** L22,000 (€11.50) 1-hr court rental. **No credit cards.**
Private club with six outdoor courts and city views.

Il Poggetto
Via M Mercati 24b, Outside the City Gates (055 484 465). Bus 4. **Open** 8am-10.30pm Mon-Fri; 8am-8pm Sat; 8am-1.30pm Sun. **Rates** *annual membership* L50,000 (€26) a year; *hourly court rental, outdoor* L16,000 (€8.30), *indoor* L24,000 (€12.50). **No credit cards.**
Seven-court complex offering instruction, private and group, and a restaurant. Reservations required.

Yoga

Centro Iyengar Di Yoga
Via San Gervasio 18, Outside the City Gates (055 582 821). Bus 17. **Open** 9am-9pm Mon-Fri (call for lesson times). Closed Aug. **Rates** lessons L20,000 (€10.50). **No credit cards.**
Classes taught by a well-known Iyengar teacher and others. Courses and workshops for all levels and off-site yoga retreats for members.

Yoga Centro
Via dei Bardi 5, Oltrarno (055 234 2703). **Open** 8am-9.30pm Mon-Fri. Closed 2wks Aug. **Rates** lessons L15,000 (€7.80). **No credit cards. Map** p314 D4.
One of the most important yoga centres in Italy. Four hour-long classes a day in various disciplines.

Arts & Entertainment

Tuscany

Introduction

More than just a pretty face.

While Milan may be its brain and legs, Rome its soul and Naples its creativity, Tuscany pulsates with Italy's history and is a microcosm of its geography like no other region.

Fuelled by endless infighting between its *comuni*, which climaxed between the 13th and 15th centuries, Tuscany gathered commercial strength, mustered military respectability and, most significantly, outpaced its neighbours both artistically and culturally. Eventually it imposed its language on the rest of the country and then produced an unmatched crop of everything from poets and scientists to explorers and architects. Tuscany's rulers also had the foresight to amass the greatest artistic wealth anywhere in Europe. To this day, the region has the single highest concentration of art anywhere in the country and – by extension – in the world, as Italy by most accounts holds more than half of the planet's artistic treasures.

Tuscany's geography also went a long way towards ensuring its overall unity amid constant internal squabbling – more than 90 per cent of its territory is mountainous or hilly, which leaves only small slivers of level ground around the rivers and along the coast.

AN OVERVIEW

Tuscany's popular image is of sunset-drenched and cypress-lined rolling hills. Needless to say, there's much more. The *Alpi Apuane* in the north-west and the Apennine peaks to the east set the region apart and provide a plethora of giddy, winding roads to explore by car, as well as ski resorts and high-altitude trekking. These, self-contained, forested valleys – such as the Garfagnana and Lunigiana, which stretch north from Lucca, and the Valtiberina, which branches east from Arezzo – have always provided both the basic ingredients for Tuscany's culinary tradition and the backdrop for many of its paintings.

In the deep south is the Maremma, a large expanse of sparsely populated and previously malaria-infested swampland that was once the region's poorest part but is now a playground for Italy's rich and famous. Etruscan remains are scattered all over this southern part of Tuscany, and inland a series of small, ancient towns, including Pitigliano, cling precariously to hillsides. Towards the northern end of the coast is the modern port of Livorno, Tuscany's historical melting pot, and the Versilia, with its

beach umbrellas and night spots. But despite all its other attributes, mainland Tuscany can hardly be considered ideal for a seaside holiday: its coast is dominated by grey-brown sand, heavy industry and large crowds.

The chapters that follow don't aim to provide exhaustive information on the towns and provinces of Tuscany so much as to lead you in the direction of the area's very best elements.

A SENSE OF PLACE

The region's identity, and that of its people, is permeated by a profound sense of belonging known as *campanilismo* – visceral attachment to one's city, town, village or even, as in the case of Siena's *contrade* (*see p255*), one's home district. Having foregone the habit of assaulting one another's walled enclaves, today's Tuscans re-enact their historical enmities mostly verbally, and often colourfully and musically.

Florence is generally despised, though this is on account of its historical arrogance and is directed at Florentines as a group rather than individual *Fiorentini*. The capital's two main challengers for regional supremacy have historically been Pisa and Siena. While Pisans are also universally disliked, it's the Sienese, conscious of being frozen in their medieval glory, who epitomise the idea of identification with place and history.

Prato commands respect for its wealth-generating entrepreneurial spirit, while Pistoia elicits the same for its sense of age. For its part, Montecatini too recalls the past, with its turn-of-the-19th-century parks and grandiloquent bathing establishments. A bit further west, Lucca, hermetically sealed by its chunky sixth-century walls, always managed to pay off would-be conquerors and now seems to have many more friends – even in Tuscany – than enemies. Bourgeois Arezzo has also kept a high standard of living while falling under Florentine dominion, and working-class Livorno has always been open-minded with loud-mouthed inhabitants and a pioneering spirit.

WHERE, WHEN, HOW

The best overall advice, especially if you only have a week or two, is to concentrate on one or two provinces or parts of the region, allowing at least two full days for major towns such as Siena or Lucca. Unless you want to dedicate your holiday to, say, wine tourism or art and

Best bathing spots

Montecatini Terme, See p200.
Cascaste Del Gorello, Saturnia. See p273.
Hotel Posta Marcucci, Bagno Vignoni.
See p238.
Elba, See p278.

Best events

Carnevale, Viareggio (Feb). See p250.
Luminaria di San Ranieri/Regatta, Pisa
(June). See p212.
Giostra del Saracino, Arezzo (June, Sept).
See p259.
Il Palio, Siena (July, Aug). See p255.
Bravo delle Botti, Montepulciano (Aug).
See p239.

Best frescoes

Legend of the True Cross (Piero della
Francesca), San Francesco church,
Arezzo. See p258.
Saint Benedict Cycle (Giovanni Antonio
Bazzi and Luca Signorelli), Monte Oliveto
Maggiore abbey. See p236.

Best hill towns

Barga, Lucca Province. See p253.
Pitigliano, Maremma. See p274.
Massa Marittima, South Tuscany.
See p272.
Anghiari, Arezzo Province. See p266.

Best sunsets

Cortona, Arezzo Province. See p269.
Pienza, Siena Province. See p238.
Montecatini Alto. See p200.

Best places to paint

Bagno Vignoni, Siena Province. See p238.
Anghiari, Arezzo Province. See p266.
City walls, Lucca. See p240.
Badia A Coltibuono Chianti. See p229.

Best unspoilt regions

The Maremma, South Tuscany. See p273.
Arezzo Province. See p263.
The Mugello, north-east. See p203.

Worth the climb

Torre del Mangia, Siena. See p219.
Torre Guinigi, Lucca. See p245.
Campanile, Pisa. See p205.

Grumpiest locals

Arezzo. See p256.
Pisa. See p204.

architecture, Tuscany invites you to be eclectic.
In other words, mix it up while you're here.
Visit and enjoy ornate churches and galleries in
moderation; try not to saturate your days with
perfect Tuscan hill towns or devote all your time
to long drives around the countryside. Instead
spend a day walking (*see below* **Outdoor
pursuits**) and try to sit down at least once each
day to a memorable Tuscan meal. If you need to
recuperate from sightseeing you could spend a
few hours at one of the region's many thermal
spas. Or, of course, another possibility is to
build your holiday around a language, cookery
or painting course (*see p194*).

Inevitably, in Easter and summer, many
places get horribly busy and you have to
weigh up whether they're worth fighting
through the hordes for. The gorgeous hill town
of San Gimignano, for instance, is like honey to
the tourist bees, so go in months either side of
the rush, such as May or September/October.
Winter is especially good for its lack of crowds
but many attractions and restaurants either
close or are open for limited hours only, and
the weather won't be as good.

In peak season you should book rooms in
advance, and even at other times you shouldn't
leave it until too late.

OUTDOOR PURSUITS

Tuscany offers endless possibilities for walkers.
One popular area to hoof it (partly because you
can pop into wineries) is to be found within the
gentle hills of Chianti. There are more serious
walks throughout the Apuan Alps (*see p253*)
and coastal tracks in the Maremma (*see p273*)
or on the island of Elba (*see p278*).

The news for cyclists is mixed. Major roads
are a no-no but there are some lovely if hilly
areas of Tuscany with backroads just ripe for
exploration. These include Chianti, the Crete
Senese (south-east of Siena) and the Maremma
(particularly inland). A bike is also a good way
to get round towns such as Lucca, Montecatini
Terme, Pisa and Arezzo.

It's worth considering booking a customised
trip or joining a group (*see below* **Specialist
holidays**) – having pre-booked accommodation
and luggage transfer cuts out a lot of slog.

TOURIST INFORMATION

The general tourist information website for the
Tuscany region is www.turismo.toscana.it

Specialist holidays

There are a number of companies that offer a
variety of tours, although just a few are listed
here. For Florence-based companies offering
cycling, walking and hiking tours, *see p187*.

Walking & cycling

The Alternative Travel Group

69-71 Banbury Road, Oxford OX2 6PE (01865 315 678/fax 01865 31 56 96/www.atg-oxford.co.uk)
Dates spring, summer & autumn.
Escorted walking and cycling trips (from £795, excluding flights) in groups of no more than 16, plus customised unguided walking trips with rooms in family-run hotels and luggage transfer (eight days from £369 B&B, flights not included).

Ramblers Holidays

Box 43, Welwyn Garden City, Herts AL8 6PQ (01707 331 133/fax 01707 333 276/ www.ramblersholidays.co.uk). **Dates** spring, summer & autumn.
Centre-based (Florence, Siena, Ronta or San Marcello) walking/sightseeing holidays from £422.

Art history

Prospect Art Tours

36 Manchester Street, London W1U 7LH (0207 486 5704/fax 0207 486 5868/sales@prospecttours.com). **Dates** spring, summer & autumn.
Music and art history holidays in Florence and Lucca, with concert tickets, museums and specialist guides. A six-day all-inclusive package costs £1,095.

Specialtours

2 Chester Row, London SW1W 9JH (0207 730 2297/info@specialtours.co.uk). **Dates** spring & autumn.
One-off tours of museums and gardens, with lectures by art historians, for £1,200 a week all inclusive.

Cookery schools

Italian Cookery Weeks

PO Box 2482, London NW10 1HW (0208 208 0112/fax 0207 627 8467/www.italian-cookery-weeks.co.uk). **Dates** May-Sept.
Excellent food and wine with daily tuition by cook Susanna Gelmetti, and occasional trips and excursions. Prices start at £1,249 a week including flights.

La Bottega Del 30

Via Nuova, Villa a Sesta, Castelnuovo Berardenga, Siena (tel/fax 0577 359 226/www.labottegadel30.it).
This is a popular course in Chianti cookery run by an expert: Helene Stoquelet, who used to have a successful restaurant. The price (L2,500,000/€1,290 for two people per week) also includes room and board, along with five half-day cookery lessons, trips and regular evening meals out.

Villa Delia

Via del Bosco 9, Ripoli di Lari, Pisa (0587 684 322/fax 0587 684 331). Reservations through Umberto Management Ltd, 13760 Hornby Street, Vancouver, BC V6Z 1W5 (604 669 3732/fax 604 669 9723/www.umberto.com). **Dates** April-Nov.

Nine nights' accommodation in a rustic 16th-century villa, plus food, classes by regional chefs and excursions to local markets, cultural centres and wine tastings for US$4,700, excluding flights.

Painting courses

Simply Tuscany

598 Chiswick High Road, London W4 5RT (0181 995 9323/fax 0181 995 3346). **Dates** May-Sept.
One- and two-week watercolour holidays led by landscape artist Sandra Pepys, with day-trips to Lucca and Florence. A week is £865 excluding flights.

Verrochio Art Centre

Via San Michele 16, Casole d'Elsa. Bookings through Rose Konstam, 37 Eaton Mews, Handbridge, Chester CH4 7EJ (tel/fax 01244 676 585). **Dates** May-Oct.
Specialist painting and sculpture courses in a hilltop village. Prices start at £570 for a two-week course (full board, excluding flights).

Language schools

See also p292 **Directory: Study.**

Cooperativa 'Il Sasso'

Via del Voltaia nel Corso 74, Montepulciano (0578 758 311/fax 0570 757 547).
Two- and four-week language courses for all levels, plus courses in art history and mosaics. Rooms can be arranged in hotels, flats or with families. Prices start at L520,000 (€268.50) for a two-week course.

Italian Cultural Institute

39 Belgrave Square, London SW1 8NX (0207 235 1461/www.italculture.org.uk).
Good source of info about language courses in Italy.

Farming holidays

WWOOF (Willing Workers on Organic Farms)

19 Bradford Road, Lewes, Sussex BN7 1RB (01273 476 286), or contact Elisa Grandis, Caslare Acquachiara, Via Vallicorati 11, Guardistallo Pisa.
Working holidays on organic farms, especially during the grape and olive harvests. Food and board are usually provided in exchange for about four hours work a day. You should find out about living and working conditions before you go. For a regular newsletter and list of farms you need to become a member. *See also p273.*

▶ For a **map** of Tuscany, see *p308*, and for information on **transport**, see *p280* **Directory: Getting Around**. The best festivals are rounded up in **By Season** (*see p154*), gay highlights on *p167* and children's attractions on *p161*.

Tuscany

Around Florence

Get a taste of Tuscany with quick trips into Florence's varied hinterland.

Prato's charming river-bank promenade.

Most towns around Tuscany's capital have something to offer – Prato's textile industry and shrewd business acumen has made it a place Florentines hop to for shopping, for instance, while Pistoia's immaculately preserved historical centre has been the setting for TV shows and films. Historic points of interest, from the birthplace of Leonardo da Vinci (the town of Vinci) to numerous Medici villas, all make pleasant day-trips from Florence.

West of Florence

Prato

Poor old Prato suffers from the little sister syndrome – Florence is so much more famous and beautiful that few visitors pay attention to its industrial sibling, devoted to the manufacture of worsted cloths. Florentines can be pretty snotty about it too, dismissing the Pratese as a bunch of nouveau riche Rolex-wearers, but don't let their prejudice put you off visiting. Prato has

a lively and upbeat feel to it these days – and a significant number of Florentines flirt with the idea of decamping here from the Big Smoke.

To make the best of a visit, hurry through Prato's unprepossessing outskirts to the walled city centre, where you will find most of its attractions within easy walking distance. Afterwards, step outside the walls again for a tasty, sociable lunch among local office-workers at the **Enoteca Barni** (see p197), walk it off on the banks of the picturesque Bisenzio and spend an afternoon at the **Museo d'Arte Contemporaneo Luigi Pecci** (see p197).

Like her big sister, Prato was a dynamic trading centre back in the Middle Ages. Accountancy was virtually invented here in the 14th century by one Francesco di Marco Datini, on whose meticulous accounts and private letters Iris Origo based her 1957 novel *The Merchant of Prato*. Prato honours its chief bean-counter with a large statue in piazza del Comune in the heart of the city.

The **Duomo** is a striking Romanesque-Gothic building in pinkish brick with a half-finished green-and-white striped marble façade. On one corner, canopied by what looks like a Chinese parasol, is the 15th-century Pulpit of the Sacred Girdle (Sacro Cingolo), designed by Michelozzo and carved with reliefs of dancing children and cherubs by Donatello (now replaced by casts). Inside are frescoes by Paolo Uccello and Filippo Lippi: the latter was responsible for the *Lives of Saints John the Baptist and Stephen* in the choir and apparently used his nun-lover Lucrezia Buti as a model for *Salome at Herod's Banquet*. The city's singular religious icon, the Sacro Cingolo, is paraded through the Duomo during the **Ostensione della Sacra Cintola** every Easter, 1 May, 15 August, 8 September and 25 December.

The **Museo dell' Opera del Duomo** (piazza Duomo 49, 0574 29339, closed Tue & Sun, admission with Museo di San Domenico & Prato castle L10,000/€5.20) is in Palazzo Vescovile to the left of the Duomo. Exhibits include Donatello's bas-reliefs of dancing *putti* that once decorated the pulpit, a fresco attributed to Paolo Uccello and works by both Filippo and Filippino Lippi. The **Museo di San Domenico** (piazza San Domenico, 0574 440 501, closed Tue, for admission see Museo dell' Opera del Duomo), sometimes called Museo di Pittura Murale, houses major works from the **Galleria Comunale**, including some Della Robbia terracottas, a Filippino Lippi tabernacle and Filippo Lippi's *Madonna del Ceppo* (1453) with its realistic portrayal of Prato merchant Datini. The church of **Santa Maria delle Carceri**, opposite the tourist office, is a masterpiece of early Renaissance architecture by Giuliano da Sangallo.

The **Museo d'Arte Contemporaneo Luigi Pecci** (viale della Repubblica 277, 0574 5317, closed Tue, admission free, exhibitions L12,000/€6.20) is on the outskirts of town, near the autostrada exit Prato Est. Lazzi and Cap buses from Florence stop close by in viale della Repubblica. Since its opening in 1988, it's established itself as Italy's leading centre of contemporary art. Initially it only held temporary exhibitions, but a permanent collection was added in 1998. The exhibits rotate but there are works by Italian artists Carlo Guaita, Daniela De Lorenzo and Fabrizio Plessi, along with a significant contingent of international artists, including Sol LeWitt and the French-born Anne and Patrick Poirier, whose *Exegi Monumentum Eere Perennius* dominates the sculpture garden.

Where to eat

Prato's Chinese community is one of the largest in Tuscany, so the city has some of the best Chinese food; **Hua Li Du** (via Marini 4, 0574 24163, closed lunch Tue, L25,000/€13), is one of

the foremost Chinese restaurants in the Florence area. Of the Italian places, **Enoteca Barni** (via Ferucci 22, closed lunch Sat, all Sun, average L20,000/€10.50 lunch, L70,000/€36 dinner), a family-owned spin-off from the 40-year-old deli next door, stands out; at lunch it's busy with locals ordering delicious pasta dishes straight from the kitchen, while dinner is a more drawn-out and even more mouthwatering affair. **Il Baghino** (via dell' Accademia 9, 0574 27920, closed lunch Mon, dinner Sun, lunch Sun in winter, L50,000/€26) serves local specialities such as stuffed celery, and **La Cucina di Paola** (via Banchelli 14, 0574 24353, closed Mon, L60,000/€31) offers top-notch local fare.

Where to stay

Top of the style heap is **Hotel Museo** (viale della Repubblica 289, 0574 5787, rates L300,000-L350,000/€155-€181) out near the Luigi Pecci Museum. More central, and cheaper, is **Hotel Flora** (via Cairoli 31, 0574 33521, L150,000-L260,000/€77.50-€134.50). **Hotel Giardino** (via Magnolfi 4, 0574 26189, rates L160,000-L220,000/€82.50-€113.50) is an agreeable place just behind the Duomo and, further out, characterful **Villa Rucellai** (via di Canneto 16, 0574 460 392, from L160,000/€82.50) is a lovely hillside villa with a medieval tower that's been home to the Rucellai family for generations.

Local hero **di Marco Datini**. *See p196.*

Tuscany

Tourist information

Agenzia per il Turismo
Via Santa Maria delle Carceri 15 (0574 24112).
Open *Summer* 9am-7pm Mon-Sat; 10am-1pm, 2.30-6.30pm Sun. *Winter* 9am-1pm, 3-6pm Mon-Sat.

Festivals
Prato hosts the **Annual National Comic Book Conference** in spring, while **Prato Estate** (July/Aug) is a series of concerts, films and open-air shows. The two largest and most prestigious theatres of Prato, Metastasio (probably the most important in Tuscany) and Fabbricone Theatre, kick off their season in November. The free listings mag *Pratomese* has more information.

Pistoia

If Prato is Florence's sparky little sister, Pistoia is its maiden aunt – it's an old-fashioned, slow-paced place that's remained in tune with the countryside. Circled by walls dating back to the 14th century, the quiet historic centre has some fine Romanesque and Gothic buildings leading in towards its elegant colonnaded cathedral.

Local goodies include *biroldo*, a spicy boiled sausage, *migliaccio*, a pancake made with pig's blood, pine-nuts, raisins and sugar, and *confetti*, small, spiky white sweetmeats. You can find the latter at Corsini in piazza San Francesco and Bertinotti in viale Adua. Try also the excellent bread baked in traditional wood-burning ovens at **Forno della Paura** in via N Sauro.

In 1864, when foundations were being laid for **Valiani Caffè Pasticceria** (via Cavour 55, 0573 23034, closed Tue & 1st 3wks Aug) on the site of a former oratory, frescoed walls from the school of Giotto were uncovered. The café's regulars have included the likes of Verdi, Rossini, Bellini, Leoncavallo, Giordano and Puccini. It also houses a private art gallery.

The **Duomo** has a simple Romanesque interior and a campanile with exotic tiger-striped arcades on top. Opposite is the octagonal 14th-century, green-and-white striped Baptistery. The **Museo Civico** (0573 371 296, closed Mon, admission L6,000/€3.10, free Sat afternoon) behind the Duomo has fine 14th-century paintings on the ground floor and some fairly dreadful late mannerist works two floors above. In the middle is a section on famous Pistoian Giovanni Michelucci (1891-1990), architect of Florence's Santa Maria Novella station. **Palazzo Tau** (corso Silvano Fedi 30, 0573 30285, closed Mon, admission L6,000/€3.10, free Sat afternoon)

Arcades in **Pistoia**'s piazza del Duomo.

houses Centro di Documentazione e Fondazione (0573 30285), devoted to the other Pistoian of renown, sculptor Marino Marini (1901-80). **Ospedale del Ceppo** is famous for its splendid Della Robbia ceramic frieze (1526-29). The parish church of **Sant'Andrea** has a magnificent carved stone pulpit (1298-1301) by Giovanni Pisano.

Where to eat

It's worth the journey ten kilometres north of Pistoia and up a narrow winding country road to the village of Castagno di Pitecchio to eat at **Il Castagno di Pier Angelo** in (0573 42214, closed lunch Tue-Sat, all Mon, L75,000/€38.50), situated in a chestnut wood. The menu has both traditional Tuscan dishes and creative dishes such as goose terrine with pistachios, fillet of sea bass with poppy seeds and deep-fried porcini mushrooms, and a divine coffee crème brulée.

Back in town, **Lo Storno** (via del Lastrone 8, 0573 26193, closed dinner Mon-Wed, all Sun, 3wks Aug, L30,000/€15.50) is a traditional *osteria* serving dishes such as tripe, spelt and bean soup, and salted cod with leeks. **La Bottegaia** (via del Lastrone 4, no phone, closed Sun & Mon, L10,000/€5.20) is a cellar with just a few tables, but the wines, the home-made flans and the local cheeses are all very good. For superb pizza, make sure you try **Tarabaralla** (via del Lastrone 13, 0573 976 891, closed Sun & Mon).

Where to stay

There's a country-house atmosphere and great food at the comfortable if slightly eccentric **Villa Vannini** (villa di Piteccio 6, Villa di Piteccio village, 0573 42031, L140,000/€72.50). More mainstream is the pleasant and central **Hotel Leon Bianco** (via Panciatichi 2, 0573 26675, L120,000-L170,000/€62-€88). **Hotel Piccolo Ritz** (via A Vannucci 67, 0573 26775, L80,000-L150,000/€41.50-€77.50) is utterly unremarkable but convenient for the station.

Tourist information

Agenzia per il Turismo
Piazza Duomo (0573 21622/fax 0573 34327). **Open** 9am-1pm, 3-5pm Mon-Sat.

Events
Arts & Crafts show and market of local products in the ex-Breda coach factory (May/June); **Pistoia Blues** music festival (July); **Giostra dell'Orso** procession and jousting tournament (25 July).

Who he? Leonardo

'In the normal course of events many men and women are born with various remarkable qualities and talents; but occasionally, in a way that transcends nature, a single person is marvellously endowed by heaven with beauty, grace and talent in such abundance that he leaves other men far behind, all his actions seem inspired, and indeed everything he does clearly comes from God rather than from human art.'

This quote from Vasari's *Lives of the Artists* (1452-1519) refers to Leonardo da Vinci, an *uomo universale* who, with Michelangelo and Raphael, is considered one of the three great artists of the High Renaissance. He's best known as a painter, though few of his works were ever finished, due to his impatience and low boredom threshold, and his drawings far outnumber his paintings. He was fascinated by science and the natural world, believing that to see was to know. He practically discovered the circulation of blood and the growth of the embryo in the womb. He was a keen geologist, botanist, musician and writer. He performed numerous dissections to gain a greater insight into anatomy, and designed buildings, fortifications, canals and locks.

Leonardo was born in Vinci and apprenticed to Verrochio's studio in about 1469. He helped on Verrochio's *Baptism* (now in the Uffizi; *see p78*) – you can see his hand in the angel on the left (he actually observed how the cloth would fall across the forms of the body) and in parts of the landscape.

Leonardo's earliest drawing, *Arno Landscape* (Uffizi), is dated 3741 – he was left-handed and often wrote right to left, perhaps as a game, but also so that his notes would not easily be copied. He soon gained a reputation and as early as 1481 received a commission from the monks of San Donato at Scopeto for the *Adoration of*

the Magi. The work was never finished, though the cartoon remains in the Uffizi. It's a masterpiece in itself, offering a wonderful insight into his working practices. The composition is geometrically mapped out; the figures and landscape are not separate but work together as a harmonious whole.

In 1482 Leonardo set off for Milan, where he produced a number of important works. Though few good examples of his original work survive in Vinci or even in Florence, it's worth visiting the Uffizi to see for yourself the great advances he made in painting and to experience a small part of his immeasurable genius.

LEONARDO
VINCI

So spa so good

Although there are thermal springs and baths all over Tuscany, nowhere is better endowed with them than the area around Montecatini Terme. Discovered back in 1387, the town's therapeutic waters became popular with ailing Tuscan grand dukes in the late 18th century. Now, with the new wave of interest in alternative therapies, they're hot property once more.

Thankfully, both Montecatini, with its nine 'terme', and nearby Monsummano, with its thermal caves, are more than ready for the onslaught, offering an extensive menu of potential health and beauty treatments. At the newly renovated Excelsior Centre (viale Verdi 61, 0572 778 509), the only spa in Montecatini that's open year-round, you can get anything from a good intestinal douching (L35,000/€18) or divine 'massage under rain' (a pummelling beneath a warm thermal shower; a bargain at L60,000/€31) to seven-day anti-stress (L580,000/€300) and anti-cellulite (L980,000/€506) packages.

At Monsummano Terme, you can take your health kick even further by living in at the spa at the plush **Grotta Giusti Hotel** (via Grotta Giusti 1411, 0572 51165, closed early Jan-early Mar). But be warned – if you do check in here, you'll be sent, for your own good, to the 'Inferno', an underground thermal cave where temperatures hover around 34°C (90°F).

For further info on Montecatini's thermal baths go to www.termemontecatini.it or phone 0572 7781/0572 778 487.

Montecatini Terme

Montecatini has a restrained elegance that's always charmed the European petite bourgeoisie. Times are a-changing, however: the town's historic thermal spas (*see p200* **So spa so good**) are attracting interest from a new generation of alternative health enthusiasts and its grand parks are packed at weekends with Tuscans enjoying Montecatini's Belle Epoque atmosphere. While this can mean that the town's 200-plus hotels cannot keep up with demand, it's still possible to escape the crowds.

A lovely way to do this, particularly on a balmy summer evening, is to ride the funicular railway (viale Alfredo Diaz, 0572 766 862, tickets L8000/€4.10) to **Montecatini Alto** for a drink and/or meal. Of several restaurants with outdoor tables grouped around Alto's main piazza, **La Torre** (piazza Giusti 8, 0572 706 50, L35,000/€18) is a good choice. Views over the town and the Nievole valley are great.

Where to eat

Back down in Montecatini, it's tougher deciding where to eat. **Gourmet Restaurant** (via Amendola 6, 0572 771 012, closed Tue, L95,000/€49) is good for fresh seafood but the atmosphere is a little precious. A lot more fun is **Egisto's** (piazza Cesare Battisti 13, 0572 78413, closed Tue, L40,000/€20.50), with its slick design and non-traditional pastas alongside Tuscan classics. **San Francisco** (corso Roma 112, 0572 79632, closed Tue, L60,000/€31) gets the louder crowd in from Florence. Its saving grace is wood-oven pizza (L25,000/€13) served until 4am. If you want to sample Tuscan wines, staff at **Il Chicco d'Uva Vineria** (viale Verdi 35, 0572 910 300, closed Mon) are laid-back experts. Stand at the bar for wine by the glass and home-made snacks, or lounge in the backroom.

Where to stay

The **Grand Hotel Bellavista Palace** (viale Fedeli 2, 0572 78122, L300,000-L500,000/€155-€258), with its indoor and outdoor pools and fading opulence, is the glitziest option. The recently refurbished **Hotel Savoia & Campana** (viale Cavallotti 10, 0572 772 670, L100,000-L130,000/€51.50-€67) is in one of Montecatini's oldest buildings, though most of its original character has been wallpapered over. The owners also run **Hotel Verena** (viale Cavallotti 35, 0572 72809, L50,000-L90,000/€26-€46.50), a gem of a *pensione*. You could also try the **Minerva Palace Hotel** (via Cavour 14, 0572 92811, L150,000-L250,000/€77.50-€129).

Up and away: **Montecatini Alto**. *See p200.*

Tourist information

Azienda Promozione Turistica (APT)
Viale Verdi 66 (0572 772 244). **Open** 9am-12.30pm, 3-6pm Mon-Sat; 9am-noon Sun.

Getting there

By bus
Lazzi (055 363 041) runs regular buses between Florence, Prato, Pistoia and Montecatini Terme. Florence–Prato and Florence–Pistoia take 45min and Florence–Montecatini about 1hr. **Cap** (055 214 637) also links Pistoia and Prato with Florence.

By car
Prato, Pistoia, Montecatini and nearby Monsummano are accessible off the east–west A11 *autostrada.*

By train
Regular trains on the Florence–Lucca line service Prato (journey time from Florence 25min), Pistoia (35min) and Montecatini (50min).

South-west of Florence

Carmignano

Carmignano seems untouched by the proximity of Florence's hubbub. The doors of the 13th-century church of **San Michele & San Francesco** on its main street remain unlocked even though one of Pontormo's most famous works, *Visitation* (1530), and paintings by Andrea di Giusto grace the interior.

The area is known for wines that marry Sangiovese, Canaiolo and Cabernet grapes. Nearby villa-farms that offer public tastings of Carmignano wines are **Capezzana** (via Capezzana 100, Seano, 055 870 6005, closed Sat & Sun, tours by appointment) and **Bacchereto** (055 871 7191, tours by appointment, closed 2wks Nov or Jan). The

latter also has a shop, restaurant (closed Mon, lunch Tue, average L60,000/€31) and rooms (L50,000-L150,000/€26-€77.50).

Fattoria di Artimino (viale Papa Giovanni XXIII, 055 879 2051, tours & tastings by arrangement) produces DOC and DOCG wines on its beautiful land. It also makes extra-virgin olive oil and grappa.

Where to eat & drink

Bar Ristorante Roberto (piazza Vittorio Emanuele, 055 871 2375) is a local legend. In the modest dining room the indomitable Fedora will ply you with delicious homely food (pasta with lamb *ragù*; salted cod cooked with wild leeks, onions, tomatoes and Swiss chard) and wine for only L15,000 (€7.80).

For a taste of the local wine, try **Il Poggiolo** (via Pistoiese 90, 055 871 1242, closed Sun) and **Castelvecchio** (via delle Mannelle 19, 055 870 5451, closed Sun, dinner Sat, 2wks Aug), two bars that carry their own elegant and well-balanced reds.

In the village of Artimino on the road from Carmignano to Florence is **Da Delfina** (via della Chiesa 1, 055 871 8074, closed Mon, Sun, Aug & 2wks Jan, L80,000/€41.50), an elegant restaurant overlooking the multi-chimneyed Medici villa of Artimino, which is an upmarket hotel. Try *sformato di ortiche* (a pale green mousse of wild leaves served with a purée of pumpkin) or *gnocchi alla parietaria* (featherlight gnocchi with butter and fresh herbs).

Montecatini's colourful viale Verdi (*p200*).

Vinci

As the birthplace of Leonardo da Vinci (*see p199* **Who he?**), this little town attracts a constant stream of visitors. The **Museo Leonardiano** (via la Torre 2, 0571 56055, admission L7,000/€3.60) displays models of machines and instruments devised by the Renaissance polymath.

Where to eat

To refuel, try **La Torretta** (via della Torre 19, 0571 56100, closed Mon, dinner Sun, average L40,000/€20.50) or **Leonardo** (via Montalbano Nord 16, 0571 567 916, closed Wed & 3wks Jan, L35,000/€18).

Montelupo

The people of Montelupo have been making glazed pottery since the Middle Ages. In 1973 an old public laundry in the Castello district was dismantled to reveal a two-metre-wide (6.5-foot) well that had been filled over the centuries with ceramic rejects and shards; many are now in the **Museo della Ceramica** (via Sinibaldi 34, 0571 51352, closed Mon, admission L5,000/€2.60).

The locals have never forsaken their vocation and every third Sunday of the month sell their products in the old cinema and surrounding stalls . The town also hosts a flower festival the first Sunday in April, an antiques market in May and the Festa Internazionale della Ceramica towards the end of June.

San Miniato

Snaking along the crest of a lofty hill, with views over to Fiesole and to the coast, the town of San Miniato dominated both the Pisa–Florence road and the via Francigena, which brought pilgrims from the north to Rome. In the 12th and 13th centuries the town was fortified and became one of Tuscany's foremost imperial centres, but it succumbed to Florence in the mid 1300s. Unfortunately, the interiors of both the 13th-century **Duomo** and the slightly later church of **San Domenico** were subjected to some heavy-handed baroque 'improvements'.

The spacious *loggiati* of San Domenico are used for an antiques and collectibles fair on the first Sunday of each month, an organic food market on the second, and an arts and crafts market on the third. The surrounding area is rich in truffles and November weekends (part of the Festa del Tartufo, the truffle festival) are devoted to tasting them.

Where to eat

Caffè Centrale (via IV Novembre 19, 0571 43037, closed 1st 2wks Sept, L15,000/€7.80) serves a delicious beetroot pasta and other light lunch dishes, and has music at night. The family-run **L'Antro di Bacco** (via IV Novembre 13, 0571 43319, closed Sun, dinner Wed, average L40,000/€20.50) also serves good food and drink, while just outside town there's **Il Convio** (via San Maiano 2, 0571 408 114, closed Wed, 2wks Jan or Feb, L50,000/€26), run by Luciano Ciulli. Even more *simpatico* is **La Trattoria dell' Orcio Interrato** in nearby Montopoli Val d'Arno (piazza San Michele 2, 0571 466878, closed Mon, dinner Sun in winter, L65,000/€33.50), which has a summer terrace. Thorough research has gone into unearthing the ancient recipes used here, which include such flavour combinations as tripe with egg and saffron, and roast suckling pig with quinces.

Tourist information

Ufficio di Turismo

Piazza del Popolo (0571 42745). **Open** *Summer* 9.30am-1pm, 3.30-7.30pm daily. *Winter* 10am-1pm, 3-7.30pm Mon-Sat.

Certaldo Alto

This settlement's main claim to fame is that Giovanni Boccaccio (1313-75, author of *The Decameron*) was born and died here. Its historic centre monopolises a stunning view over the Val d'Elsa, looking over to Volterra. During the first week in August the town is bathed in candlelight for the Mercantia – a festival aimed at re-creating the atmosphere of the town as it was before electricity. The **Palazzo del Vicario** (piazzetta del Vicario, 0571 661 219, admission L5,000/€2.60) is worth a visit for its beautiful frescoed rooms.

Where to stay & eat

Osteria del Vicario (via Rivellino 3, 0571 668 228, closed early to mid Dec, rates L150,000/€77.50) has a dining room and a wisteria-clad portico where you can enjoy inventive dishes devised by Enzo Pette (closed Wed, lunch Sat & Sun in Jan, L80,000/€41.50). **Il Castello** hotel and restaurant (via G della Rena 6, 0571 668 250, restaurant & hotel reception closed Fri, hotel & restaurant closed Nov, rooms L90,00-L150,000/€46.50-€77.50, average L40,000/€20.50) has a funicular that can carry up to 30 passengers (tickets L2,500/€1.30) to the terrace, where candlelit tables surround a 17th-century fountain. The roasted meats rubbed with rosemary are exceptional. Antique Russian samovars and Tuscan shields and swords sustain the medieval atmosphere inside.

Getting there

By car
Montelupo and, further west, San Miniato are both just off the main Florence–Livorno road. The quickest way to Certaldo is to turn south off this road onto the SS429 between the two towns near Empoli. To reach Vinci you also turn off this main road near Empoli heading north in the direction of Pistoia.

By train
Carmignano, Montelupo and San Miniato are on the Florence/Empoli/Pisa train line. Journey times are Florence–Carmignano 25min (irregular service), Florence–Montelupo 30min and Florence–San Miniato 45min. Certaldo can be reached from Florence by changing at Empoli (journey time about 1hr) or from Siena on the same line (35min).

North-east of Florence: the Mugello

The Mugello covers the area north to north-east of Florence, towards the border with Emilia-Romagna. It's divided into the Sieve Valley, Mugello and Upper Mugello. Space-loving Medici adored its gentle hills and valleys and built villas all over it. In fact, the six balls on the Medici coat of arms are attributed to the legend that a Carolingian knight named Averardo (one of the first Medici) clashed with a giant, whom he defeated, not far from Scarperia. In battle, he suffered six blows, each represented by a ball (*see p86* **Who they? Mark-makers**).

Scarperia

This pleasant little town in the rolling Mugello countryside was founded in 1306 as the northernmost military outpost of the Florentine Republic, and because of its strategic location enjoyed considerable prosperity until the 18th century, when the main road over the Apennines to Bologna opened further west. It's most famous for producing the traditional bone-handled pocket knives that older people in Italy sometimes use on their farms and that have a particular prestige at the table. Each is considered an individual masterpiece that waits until its true owner claims it. The **Conaz** factory (via G Giordani 2, 055 846 197, closed Mon morning, tours free) outside the walled

nucleus of the town holds knifemaking demonstrations, but true artisans are a dying breed. There's an international knife exhibition during the first half of September.

In the spacious central square is the **Palazzo dei Vicari**, built in the 13th century to designs by Arnolfo di Cambio. Distinctly reminiscent of the Palazzo Vecchio in Florence, it was the residence of the Republican governors, whose coats of arms decorate the façade. Inside are frescoes dating back to the 14th to 16th centuries, including a *Madonna and Child with Saints* by the school of Ghirlandaio.

Near Scarperia, in the Sieve valley and ringed by mountains, **Borgo San Lorenzo** is a busy market town with an attractive historic centre.

Where to eat

For Mugello cuisine, try **Il Torrione** (via Roma 78/80, 055 843 0263, closed Mon, L35,000/€18) or **Fattoria il Palagio** (viale Dante, 055 846 376, closed Mon & 3wks Aug, L50,000/€26) just outside the walls.

Locals swear by a restaurant by the A1 exit for Barberino di Mugello, **Cosimo de' Medici** (055 842 0370, closed Mon, L50,000/€26). The cuisine here makes up for the unprepossessing location. Another popular place is **Il Paiolo** (via Cornocchio 1, Barberino di Mugello, 055 842 0733, closed Tue, Aug & from late Dec to early Jan, L60,000/ €31), which specialises in grilled meat.

Tourist information

Ufficio Promozione Turistico
Via P Togliatti 45, Borgo San Lorenzo (055 849 5346). **Open** 8.30am-1.30pm Mon, Wed, Fri; 8.30am-1.30pm, 3-5.30pm Tue, Thur.

Getting there

By bus
Both **Sita** (055 214 721) and **Cap** (055 214 637) run bus services to Borgo San Lorenzo. Journey time is 1hr. From there, there are connections to Scarperia.

By car
Borgo San Lorenzo can be reached via one of two roads from Florence: the SS65 (the old road to Bologna) or the more winding SS302 (the old road to Faenza). For Scarperia, take the former and pick up the SS503 at San Piero a Sieve. It takes about 45min to get to Borgo; Scarperia is 10min further on.

By train
There's a regular service from Florence's Campo di Marte station to Borgo San Lorenzo. Journey time is 45min. There's also a train from Santa Maria Novella via Pontassieve but it takes longer.

Tuscany

Pisa & Livorno

There's little to hold you in these twin towns once you've seen the lean.

If you're going to Tuscany, neither Pisa nor Livorno, 20 kilometres (12.5 miles) apart, are priorities. After taking in Pisa's Campo dei Miracoli, where it's elbow-room only in summer, and snapping a cheesy pic of a friend/lover/relative holding up the now not-so-Leaning Tower, most visitors head somewhere more compelling, while low-key Livorno's polyglot population is the most interesting thing about it.

Pisa

Pisa has not one but three leaning towers. It also claims two New Years per year: when the rest of Europe opted for the Gregorian calendar (introduced in Tuscany in 1749 by ducal decree) that starts on 1 January, Pisa stuck to 25 March, the zodiacal new year and the widely accepted date of the Annunciation (when the angel delivered the results of Mary's unsolicited pregnancy test). This means Pisans reached a new millennium before everyone else.

Though Pisa's days of glory are gone, the attitude isn't. Ask 'How could Pisa have been a maritime republic if it isn't on the coast?' and you'll drive a Pisan insane. But at least now there's a decent reply, since in 1998 the original

harbour was discovered only 500 metres from the Leaning Tower. An excited Italian government minister described the site as the marine equivalent of Pompeii and by April 2001 as many as 16 2,000-year-old ships had been found, eight of which have been extensively excavated. A museum is planned; in the meantime some of the discoveries are on show at the **Arsenale Medicio** (lungarno Simonelli, 050 21441, admission L5,000/€2.60).

The city of Pisa, which straddles the River Arno, is enclosed within the remains of its medieval walls. Between piazza della Stazione and the Arno, the Mezzogiorno (south) part of the city contains few sights. The main focus for visitors is north of the river in Tramontana, especially around the Campo dei Miracoli.

Sightseeing

Campo dei Miracoli

It's a miracle that the 'Site of Miracles' is still in evidence at all. Not one structure on this expanse of grass and stone – reclaimed from the marshes and built on between the 11th and 13th centuries – could pass a safety test today, each tilting in a different direction.

The view along the **Arno**.

Tuscany

The layout of the Duomo, Baptistery, Leaning Tower and Camposanto seems haphazard to say the least. Perhaps realising that future generations would not understand it, 13th-century court astrologer Guido Bonatti detailed its cosmological symbolism, attributing it to the theme of Aries.

General information

050 560 547. Bus 1 from train station to piazza del Duomo. **Admission** L19,000/€9.80 (all sights); L16,000/€8.30 (any four sights, without Duomo); L10,000/€5.20 (any two sights, without Duomo). **No credit cards.**
The ticket offices are in the south-east corner of piazza del Duomo, sharing a room with the entrance to the Museo dell'Opera del Duomo, a shop and tourist info office.

Duomo

Open *Spring-autumn* 10am-7.40pm Mon-Sat; 1-7.40pm Sun. *Winter* 10am-12.45pm Mon-Sat; 3pm-4.45pm Sun. **Admission** L3,000/€1.60. **No credit cards.**
Pisa's cathedral is one of the earliest and finest examples of Pisan Romanesque architecture. Begun in 1063 by Buscheto, the delicate, blindingly white marble four-tiered façade incorporates Moorish mosaics and glass within the arcades (examples can be more closely inspected in the Museo dell'Opera del Duomo; *see below*). Buscheto's tomb is set in the wall on the left side of the façade. The brass doors (touch the lizard for good luck) by the school of Giambologna were added in 1602 to replace the originals, destroyed in a fire in 1595. The main entrance facing the Leaning Tower is called the Portale di San Ranieri and features bronze doors by Bonanno da Pisa (1180), which survived the fire. After the fire, the Medici family came to the rescue and immediately began restorations, but at the time nothing could be done for Giovanni Pisano's superb Gothic pulpit (1302-11), which was all but incinerated and lay dismembered in crates until the 1920s. Legend has it that the censer suspended near the now-restored pulpit triggered Galileo's discovery of the principles of pendular motion, but it was actually cast in 1587, six years later. Crane your neck to admire the Moorish dome decorated by a vibrant fresco of the Assumption by Orazio and Giralomo Riminaldi (1631). Behind the altar is a mosaic by Cimabué of Saint John (1302).

Baptistery

Open *Summer* 8am-7.40pm daily. *Spring & autumn* 9am-7.40pm daily. *Winter* 9am-4.40pm daily.
The marble Baptistery was designed by Diotisalvi (meaning 'God save you') in 1153 but not finished until 1395, when the 12-sided pyramid that first topped it was covered by a more harmonious, onion-shaped dome. Nicola Pisano's pulpit of 1260 was the first of the commissions, setting the style for the rest, but most of the precious artwork has been shuffled off to the Museo dell'Opera del Duomo for safekeeping. Before you leave, tip a guard to make him sing – the echoes turn the voice of a soloist into what sounds like an ethereal chorus of angels.

Leaning Tower

Located in the south-east corner of the *campo*, the famous tower has a seven-tiered campanile that was begun in 1173 (the commemorative plaque says 1174 because of the offbeat Pisan New Year) and started to lean almost as soon as it was erected. The top level, housing the seven bells (not rung since 1993), was added in 1350. In 1989, the last year before the tower was closed to the public, more than a million visitors scrambled up its 293 steps. After years of restoration work (*see p211* **Bonanno's banana**), it was due to reopen in November 2001, with visits restricted to groups of 30 paying L25,000 (€13) a head for a restricted guided tour, but check with the info office for the latest details. If you don't manage to get one of the coveted tickets, the best views of the campanile are from the courtyard of the Museo dell'Opera del Duomo. But be warned – according to Pisan superstition, seeing the tower before an exam will bring disastrous results.

Museo dell'Opera del Duomo

Open *Summer* 8am-7.20pm daily. *Spring & autumn* 9am-5.20pm daily. *Winter* 9am-4.20pm daily.
This museum contains works from the Baptistery, the Campo Santo and the Duomo itself. Highlights include a lanky wooden Christ on the cross by Borgognone; vibrant concentric mosaics from the Duomo parapet; and a clutch of works by Giovanni Pisano, notably his ivory *Madonna & Crucifix* and *Madonna & Child*. There's a mixed bag of paintings, *intarsia* (meticulous 16th-century mosaic woodwork), costumes and relics on the first floor.

Campo Santo

Open *Summer* 8am-7.40pm daily. *Spring & autumn* 9am-5.40pm daily. *Winter* 9am-4.40pm daily.
The Campo Santo (Holy Field) centres on a patch of dirt that, according to legend, was carried from the Holy Land to Pisa by the Crusaders. Lining the Gothic cloisters around the edge of the field are the gravestones of VIP Pisans buried in holy soil. On the west wall hang two massive lengths of chain that were once strung across the entrance to the Pisan port to keep out enemy ships. Stolen, the chains were only returned in 1848 and 1860, by Florence and Genoa respectively. In 1944 an Allied bomb landed on the Campo, destroying frescos and sculptures, including a reportedly fabulous cycle by Benozzo Gozzoli. A few survived, though, including *Triumph of Death*, *Last Judgment* and *Hell*, hammering home the transitory state of worldly pleasures.

Museo delle Sinopie

Open *Summer* 8am-7.40pm daily. *Spring & autumn* 9am-5.40pm daily. *Winter* 9am-4.40pm daily.
The 1944 bombings and subsequent restoration work had the effect of uncovering *sinopie* from beneath the frescos in the Campo Santo, though

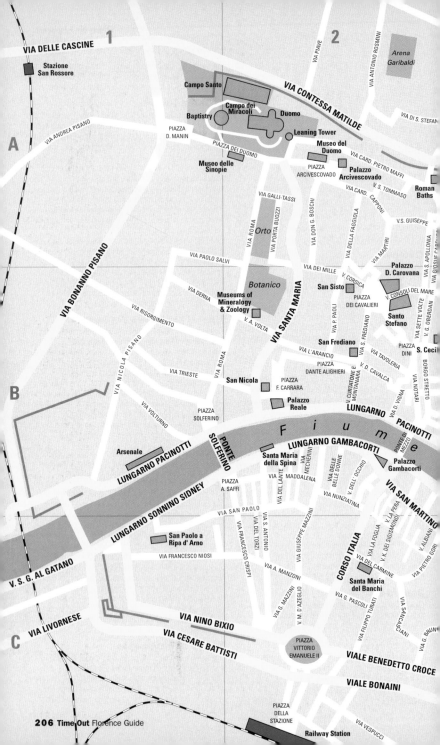

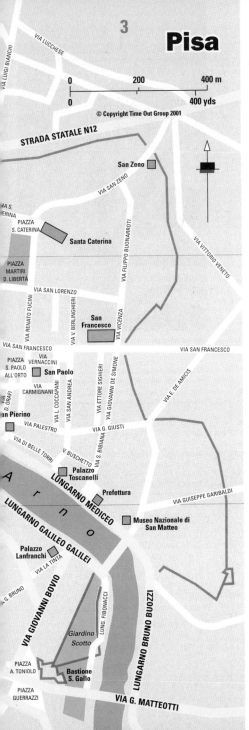

3

Pisa

STRADA STATALE N12

San Zeno

VIA SAN ZENO

VIA LUCCHESE

VIA LUIGI BIANCHI

0   200   400 m

0   400 yds

© Copyright Time Out Group 2001

PIAZZA
S. CATERINA

Santa Caterina

PIAZZA
MARTIRI
D. LIBERTÀ

VIA SAN LORENZO

VIA FILIPPO BUONARROTI

VIA VITTORIO VENETO

VIA RENATO FUCINI

VIA V. BERLINGHIERI

VIA VICENZA

San
Francesco

VIA SAN FRANCESCO

VIA SAN FRANCESCO

PIAZZA
S. PAOLO
ALL'ORTO

VIA VERNACCINI

San Paolo

VIA
CARMIGNANI

VIA L. COCCAPANI

VIA S. ANDREA

VIA ETTORE SIGHIERI

VIA GIOVANNI DE SIMONE

VIA E. DE AMICIS

an Pierino

D. ORAFI

VIA PALESTRO

VIA G. GIUSTI

VIA DI BELLE TORRI

V. BUSCHETTO

VIA S. BIBIANA

Palazzo
Toscanelli

Prefettura

VIA GUISEPPE GARIBALDI

LUNGARNO MEDICEO

Museo Nazionale di
San Matteo

LUNGARNO GALILEO GALILEI

Palazzo
Lanfranchi

VIA LA TINTA

A r n o

G. BRUNO

VIA GIOVANNI BOVIO

LUNG. FIBONACCI

LUNGARNO BRUNO BUOZZI

Giardino
Scotto

PIAZZA
A. TONIOLO

Bastione
S. Gallo

PIAZZA
GUERRAZZI

VIA G. MATTEOTTI

these reddish-brown preliminary sketches were meant to be hidden forever after the artist covered the original *arriccio* (dry plaster on which the sketches were made) with a lime-rich plaster called *grassello*. This museum has two floors of 14th- and 15th-century *sinopie* by Buffalmacco, Traini (a Pisan), Gaddi, Antonio Veneziano and Spinello Aretino. On the first floor is an enormous *Christ Holding the Circle of Creation*, with nine layers of angels, the zodiac, stars, moon, fire and air, surrounding the centre of the world, divided into Asia, Europe and Africa.

Torre di Santa Maria

Open 10.30am-6.30pm daily. **Admission** L4,000/ €2.10. **No credit cards.**
This is the place to head to in order to get a good overview of the Campo dei Miracoli and access to a small portion of the city walls.

Other sights

Museo Nazionale di Palazzo Reale

Lungarno Pacinotti 46 (050 926 539). **Open** 9am-2.30pm Mon-Fri; 9am-1.30pm Sat. **Admission** L6,000 (€3.10). **No credit cards.**
Housed in a Medici palace dating from 1583, this museum shows many works donated by private collectors of Medici and Savoy pieces. Portrait paintings represent members of various European dynasties depicted as Madonna-like figures, angels and kings, with some striking Pisan backdrops.

Museo Nazionale di San Matteo

Piazza San Matteo in Soarta, lungarno Mediceo (050 541 865). **Open** 9am-7pm Tue-Sat; 9am-2pm Sun. **Admission** L8,000 (€4.10). **No credit cards.**
This 12th- to 13th-century building, which once housed the convent of the Sisters of San Matteo, now contains a collection of Pisan and Islamic medieval ceramics and paintings by Masaccio and Fra Angelico, a *Madonna & Child with Saints* by Domenico Ghirlandaio and a bust by Donatello. There's authentic Gioco del Ponte gear, the garb worn by medieval Pisans when they locked heads on the Ponte di Mezzo, here too.

Orto Botanico

Via L Ghini 5 (050 911 374). **Open** 8am-1pm Mon-Fri; 8am-1pm Sat. **Admission** free.
Founded by Luca Ghini in 1543, then replanted in different parts of the city, the oldest university botanical garden in Europe found its permanent home on this site in 1595. It was originally used to study the medicinal values of plants. Look out for the 200-year-old myrtle bush the size of a tree, and a clump of papyrus reeds in the arboretum. Groups of ten or more must have an appointment.

Piazza dei Cavalieri

Pisa's second most important piazza houses Palazzo dei Cavalieri, the seat of one of Italy's most esteemed universities, the Scuola Normale Superiore

Santa Maria della Spina. *See page 209.*

established by Napoleon Bonaparte in 1810 (his mum was of Pisan descent). The piazza has long been a focal point of the city: the Romans used it as their forum, and Cosimo I based his religious-military order, the Cavalieri di Santo Stefano, here.

Vasari designed most of the piazza's buildings in the 16th century, including the Chiesa dei Cavalieri, Palazzo della Conventuale (opposite the church), erected as home to the Cavalieri of Santo Stefano, and Palazzo del Consiglio dell'Ordine and Palazzo Gherardescha. Palazzo Gherardescha occupies the site of a medieval prison: in 1288 Count Ugolino della Gherardescha and three of his male heirs were condemned to starve to death there for engaging in covert negotiations with the Florentines. It took Ugolino nine months to die (he allegedly snacked on his own kids). Dante, seizing the chance to get at the Pisans, depicted the count gnawing on someone's head for eternity in hell (Canto XXXIII, *Inferno*).

You'll see the Maltese Cross everywhere in this piazza but nowhere else in Pisa; Cosimo wanted to hammer home the parallel between his new Cavalieri of Santo Stefano and the crusading Knights of Malta. Elsewhere you're likely to spot the Pisan cross, with two balls resting on each point.

San Nicola

Via Santa Maria 2 (050 24677). **Open** 8am-noon, 5-6.30pm Mon-Sat; 9am-noon, 5.30-6.30pm Sun. **Admission** free.
Dating from 1150, the church of San Nicola is dedicated to one of Pisa's patron saints, San Nicola da Tolentino. In one of its chapels is a painting

showing the saint protecting Pisa from the plague in around 1400. The campanile is built on unstable ground and hence leans.

Santa Maria della Spina

Lungarno Gambacorti. **Open** *June-Aug* 11am-1.30pm, 2.30pm-6pm Tue-Fri; 11am-1.30pm, 2.30-8pm Sat, Sun. *Apr, May & Sept* 10am-1pm, 2.30-5pm Tue-Fri; 10am-1.30pm, 2.30-7pm Sat, Sun. *Oct-Mar* 10am-2pm Tue-Sun. **Admission** L2,000 (€1). **No credit cards.**
This gorgeous, tiny Gothic church on the bank of the Arno is now open again after years of restoration. Originally an oratory, it took its present form in 1323. It gets its name from the fact that it used to own what was claimed to be a thorn (*spina*) from Christ's crown, brought back by Crusaders.

Where to eat & drink

Restaurants

Cèe alla Pisana (eels) has been one of Pisa's culinary assets for centuries (*cèe* comes from *ciechi* or 'blind ones'). Sadly, the poor little creatures have been fished almost to extinction, and few venues now serve the costly winter delicacy. When they are available, the eels are fished out of the Arno and tossed in warm oil, garlic and sage, then sautéed and served seconds after they cease wriggling.

Bruno

Via Luigi Bianchi 12 (050 560 818). **Open** noon-2.30pm Mon; noon-2.30pm, 7.30-10.30pm Wed-Sun. **Average** L70,000 (€36). **Credit** AmEx, DC, MC, V.
Bruno concentrates on typical Tuscan cooking; try the *ribolita*, supposedly the best this side of the Arno, and the *baccalà alla Pisana*.

Cagliostro

Via del Castelletto 26-30 (050 575 413/fax 050 973 256/cagliostro@csinfo.it). **Open** 12.45-2.30pm, 8pm-1am, Mon, Wed, Thur, Sun; 12.45-2.30pm, 8pm-2am Fri, Sat. **Average** L25,000 (€13) lunch, L45,000 (€23) dinner. **Credit** AmEx, DC, MC, V.
This intriguing *enoteca* and restaurant, which is located off via Ulisse Dini close to piazza dei Cavalieri, is named after a Sicilian count who masqueraded as an alchemist in France and Italy during the 18th century. The extensive wine list here complements the eclectic menu, which draws on recipes from all over Italy.

La Mescita

Via Cavalca 2 (050 544 294). **Open** 8-10.30pm Tue, Wed; 1-2.15pm, 8-10.30pm Thur-Sun. Closed Aug. **Average** L40,000 (€20.50). **No credit cards.**
Run by the Bantis, La Mescita is a pretty, tranquil restaurant that's set right in the heart of Vettovaglie market (on the right after the *loggia*). The wine list is enormous, the *sformati* of cheese and vegetables delicious.

Osteria dei Cavallieri

Via San Frediano 16 (050 580 858). **Open** 12.30-2pm, 7.45-10pm Mon-Fri; 7.45-10pm Sat. Closed late July-late Aug. **Average** L55,000 (€28.50). **Credit** AmEx, DC, MC, V.
One of Pisa's best eateries, especially for the money, serving typical Tuscan dishes with a touch of fantasy, such as chick-pea soup with mussels and clams. Noteworthy wine list.

Re di Puglia

Via Aurelia Sud 7, Pisa (050 960 157). **Open** 8-10pm Wed-Sat; 1-3pm, 8-10pm Sun. Closed 2wks Jan. **Average** L45,000 (€23). **No credit cards.**
Slabs of succulent meat are grilled in front of your eyes at the open fire that's the focus of this rustic restaurant a few kilometres south of Pisa on the Livorno road. Mixed antipasti include *bruschette* and vegetable *sformati*, and there are good pasta dishes, but it's the meat (mostly organic) that reigns supreme here. In summer you can eat outdoors.

Il Ristoro del Vecchio Macelli

Via Volturno 49 (050 20424). **Open** 12.30-3pm, 7.30-10pm Mon, Tue, Thur-Sat; 7.30-10pm Sun. Closed 2wks Aug. **Average** L75,000 (€38.50). **Credit** AmEx, DC, MC, V.
Loved by Pisan sophisticates, this place is known for its quality ingredients and stunning presentation. The Vanni family make a meal around your choice: *di terra* (meat) or *di mare* (seafood). The fact that the building is a restored 15th-century slaughterhouse doesn't put people off; booking is advised.

Il Vecchio Dado

Lungarno Pacinotti 21/22, nr ponte di Mezzo (050 580 900). **Open** 12.30-3pm, 7.30pm-12.30am Mon, Tue, Fri-Sun; 7.30pm-12.30am Thur. **Average** L40,000 (€20.50). **Credit** AmEx, DC, MC, V.
A warm atmosphere and a river view are the two main draws of this Tuscan pizzeria next to the Royal Victoria hotel. Reservation is advisable.

Bars, cafés & *gelaterie*

Bar Duomo

Via Santa Maria 114 (050 561 918). **Open** 8am-7.20pm Mon-Wed, Fri-Sun. **No credit cards.**
Join the crowd thronging to one of the busiest bars in the city to sip a prosecco at an outside table facing the Campo dei Miracoli.

Pasticceria Salza

Borgo Stretto 46 (050 580 144). **Open** 7.45am-8.30pm Tue-Sun. **No credit cards.**
The most distinguished café in Pisa – anyone who is anyone comes here for an aperitif or cappuccino.

Pizzicheria Gastronomia a Cesqui

Piazze delle Vettovaglie 31 (no phone). **Open** 7am-1.30pm, 4-8pm Mon, Tue, Thur-Sat; 7am-1.30pm Wed. **No credit cards.**
Part the beaded curtains and stock up on cheeses, pastas, wines and takeaway hot snacks.

Tuscany

Nightlife

It's worth stopping in Pisa to get away from the manic crowds of Florence without losing the Arno, sparkling lights and charm.

Borderline

Via Vernaccini 7 (050 580 577). **Open** 9pm-2am Mon-Sat. **Admission** free-L20,000 (€10.50) Wed-Sat. **No credit cards**.
Good for late drinks or the occasional live gig. A beer costs L7,000 (€3.60), as does a gin and tonic.

Dottorjazz

Via Vespucci 10 (050 985 233). **Open** 9pm-2am Tue-Sat. Closed June-Sept. **Admission** free-L20,000 (€10.50). **No credit cards**.
With its small candlelit tables and pictures of jazz greats on the walls, this jazz venue attracts folk from in and out of town, bonded by a love of turtlenecks and black-rimmed glasses.

Teatro Verdi

Via Palestro 40 (050 941 111/fax 050 941 158). **Open** box office 4-7pm Mon-Sat & 1hr before events; phone bookings (050 542 600) 11am-1.30pm Mon-Fri. Closed Aug. **Credit** MC, V.
Come here to enjoy an evening of dance, drama or music, but don't be late or you won't be let in.

Shopping

Most of the main shops, especially the more expensive ones, are on corso Italia, including **Mellani** (No.44) with its amazing crystal, silver and porcelain. Across the ponte di Mezzo is a funkier shopping zone starting at the *loggia* of borgo Stretto. Where borgo Stretto meets the ponte di Mezzo you'll find the Mercatino Antiquario on the second weekend of every month. The Mercato Vettovaglie is the fruit and veg market, held every morning.

Where to stay

Make sure to reserve during high season, and well in advance for major festivals.

Consorzio Turistico Pisa È (Booking Centre)

Via Carlo Cammeo 2 or PO Box 215, Pisa 56125 (050 830 253/fax 050 830 243/ www.traveleurope.it/pisa.htm). **Open** 9.30am-1pm, 2-6.30pm Mon-Sat.
This tourist agency and booking centre offers a free room-booking service.

Albergo Galileo

Via Santa Maria 12 (tel/fax 050 40621). **Rates** *single* L70,000 (€36); *double* L95,000 (€49). **No credit cards**.
It's illegal to employ Galileo Galilei's full name for commercial purposes in Pisa, but this *pensione*

manages to get away with using half of it. Five of Albergo Galileo's nine rooms are decorated with 17th-century frescos.

Albergo Gronchi

Piazza Arcivescovado 1 (050 561 823). **Rates** single without bath L36,000 (€18.50); double L62,000 (€32); triple L84,000 (€43.50). **No credit cards**.
Gronchi is pleasant and clean, and ideal if you've dreamed of spending the night under the tower. There's a midnight curfew in force.

Camping Internazionale

Via Litoranea in Marina di Pisa 7 (050 36553). **Rates** L12,000 (€6.20); children L9,000 (€4.70); tent L11,000-L17,000 (€5.70-€8.80); camper van L12,000-L17,000 (€6.20-€8.80); car L8,000 (€4.10). **Open** May-Sept. **Credit** MC, V.
With its private beach, bar and pizzeria, there's never any need to leave this upbeat campsite. No reservations are taken, but staff claim that there's always a pitch. To get here take the ACIT bus from piazza della Stazione to Marina di Pisa/Tirrenia and ask for the *campeggio*.

Casa della Giovane

Via F Corridoni 29 (050 43061). **Rates** per person double/triple L30,000 (€15.50). **No credit cards**.
This boarding house close to the station caters mostly to students so it's usually packed in term-time. The curfew is 10.30pm.

Centro Turistico Madonna dell'Acqua

Via Pietrasantina 15 (tel/fax 050 890 622). Bus 3. **Open** office 6-11pm. **Rates** per person double L38,000 (€19.50); triple L34,000 (€17.50); quadruple or bigger L27,000 (€14). **Credit** MC, V.
The only youth hostel in Pisa. If you're feeling penitent you can attend Sunday mass in the little church of Madonna dell'Acqua nearby.

Grand Hotel Duomo

Via Santa Maria 94 (050 561 894/fax 050 560 418). **Rates** single L225,000 (€116); double L325,000 (€168); suite L380,000 (€196.50). **Credit** AmEx, DC, MC, V.
Like an ageing aunt who's known better days, the Grand hints at bygone opulence but is now somewhat frayed around the edges. You can't fault its location though, nor the sweeping views it offers over the Campo dei Miracoli from its fourth-floor terrace. If you arrive by car, make sure you ask for a parking permit for via Santa Maria.

Royal Victoria

Lungarno Pacinotti 12 (050 940 111/fax 050 940 180). **Rates** single L155,000 (€80); double L185,000 (€95.50). **Credit** AmEx, DC, MC, V.
This elegant hotel has been run by the Piegaja family since 1839. The building, some parts of which are more than 1,000 years old, has been carefully preserved. Many rooms face the Arno; river breezes make up for the absence of air-conditioning. Make sure to book in advance.

Bonnano's banana

Pisa's emblematic campanile was an early leaner. When construction began on the bell-tower in 1173, it rapidly became clear that local architect Bonnano Pisano had neglected to do his groundwork: the sand and clay beneath the new structure simply could not support it.

By the time the third storey was completed the tower was tilting markedly northwards, and in 1178 work was suspended to allow the ground to settle. It was nearly 100 years before construction resumed, during which time the tower had begun veering to the south, its present direction, using what little firm soil that existed beneath it as its fulcrum. By the second half of the 14th century, despite all attempts to correct the impression of a curve as further tiers were added, the world's most famous leaning tower was finally completed.

If the quirky tower was ever a cause of embarrassment to Pisans, its merits as a tourist attraction (and source of revenue) made up for that. But even as many of those millions of visitors made the unnerving climb

of the tower's 293 steps, so the campanile continued to tilt, until in 1989, close to its maximum discrepancy from the vertical of 4.47 metres (15 feet), it was deemed to be in danger of collapse.

A complex rescue operation, involving enormous counterweights and suspenders and a reduction in the depth of the soil between the north and south sides of the tower, swung slowly into action. The aim was never to straighten the tower entirely (who'd come and visit it then?) but to correct its tilt by 40 centimetres (18 inches). At one point, in around 1995, the scheme threatened to go pear-shaped as the lean increased fractionally. By 2001, however, the then Minister of Public Works, Nerio Nesi, could declare the 55 billion-lire project a triumph, with the monument now safeguarded for at least the next 250 years.

The decrease in lean is too little to discern with the naked eye, but those who are that way inclined can now get inside the campanile for the first time in more than a decade.

Essentials

Getting there & around

By air

Galileo Galilei airport (050 0707) is Tuscany's major international airport (though Florence has pretty much caught up), with flights from around Europe. For full details, *see* **Directory**. There are frequent trains into Pisa and Lucca (*see below*).

By bus

Lazzi (piazza Vittorio Emmanuelle 2, 050 46288) operates a regular service to Lucca (journey time 50min), with onward connections to Florence, as well as buses to Viareggio (50min).
CPT (piazza Sant Antonio, 050 505 511) covers the area around Pisa and runs buses to nearby areas such as Livorno and Marina di Pisa.

By taxi

Call Radio Taxi on 050 541 600, or there are taxi ranks at piazza Stazione and piazza Duomo.

By train

Pisa is on a main train line to Rome (journey time 3hrs Intercity, 4hrs otherwise) and Genoa (2hrs). There are also frequent trains to Florence via Empoli (80min), Livorno (15min) and Lucca (25min). Some trains also stop at Pisa Aeroporto and San Rossore. The train station is Pisa Centrale Piazza della Stazione (050 28117, train info 84 8888 088, ticket office open 24hrs daily).

Tourist information

Azienda Promozione Turistica (APT)

Via Pietro Neni 24 (050 970 433/fax 050 929 764/ www.pisa.turismo.toscana.it). **Open** 8am-2pm Mon-Fri.
Branches piazza della Stazione 11 (050 42291); via Cameo 2 (050 560 464).

Festivals

On 16 June every year, on the eve of San Raniero (patron saint of Pisa), the **Luminaria** takes place, with candles outlining the roofs along the Arno and the porticoes of the Leaning Tower. The following day the city hosts a regatta to celebrate its past maritime glories, with a parade and boat displays by representatives from its ancient quarters. Pisa is one of the four Italian maritime republics that take it in turns to host another **regatta**, usually on the first Sunday in June, in which they battle it out against each other. Pisa is hosting it in 2002. *See chapter* Tuscany by Season *and* www.turismo.toscana.it for further information on festivals in Pisa.

Useful addresses

Hospital

Santa Chiara *Via Roma 67 (050 992 111)*.

Police station

Vigili Urbani *Via del Moro 1 (050 800 111/ 050 502 626)*.

Post office

Piazza Vittorio Emmanuele II 8 (050 5194).
Open 8.15am-7pm Mon-Fri; 8.15am-noon Sat.

Outside Pisa

Marina di Pisa

About five kilometres (three miles) out of Pisa towards the beach you'll come across the 11th-century church of San Pier in Grado. This area used to sit on Pisa's river estuary, but the Arno altered its course and left the church out on a limb. Built on the spot where St Peter is said to have first set foot off the boat from Antioch, it now has a conspicuous lack of water. Vibrant 14th-century frescos depicting the lives of Peter and Paul sit above 24 columns. An excavation to the rear of the church revealed a pillar from the first century.

For a meal right on the coast looking out to the island of Gorgona (used as a prison), **Cliff** (via Repubblica Pisana 4, Lungomare, Marina di Pisa, 050 36830, closed Mon in winter, average L40,000/€20.50) has an attractive, covered outdoor area. The bar attracts a drinking-only crowd at weekends, when the place stays open later than usual.

Tirrenia

Still on the coast, south of Marina di Pisa and towards Livorno, Tirrenia has a number of private beaches, a US military base, a zoo and the flashy **Grand Hotel Continental**, which sits directly on the beach (largo Belvedere 26, 050 37031, rates L155,000-L320,000/€80-€165.50). It boasts 200 luxury rooms, an Olympic-size pool, tennis courts, beach access and parking. Book well in advance in summer.

San Rossore park (via Aurelia Nord 4, 050 525 500) offers guided walks, bike tours, horse treks and jaunts in horse-driven carriages.

Casciana Terme

Tucked away in the Pisan hills, this spa town (which was known as Castrum ad Aquas to the Romans) was destroyed in World War II and rebuilt in the 1960s. With a modern pool and drinking fountains, **Terme di Casciana** (piazza Garibaldi 9, 0587 64461) is less popular and hence less crowded than its Tuscan cousins such as Montecatini and Saturnia. Check out the beautiful **La Speranza** hotel (via Cavour 44, 0587 646 215, rates L110,000-L140,000/€57-€72.50) down the street from the thermal waters, or the greener **Villa Margherita** (via Marconi 20, 0587 646 113, rates L100,000-L120,000/€51.50-€62), which has a garden and a bar where you can get your hands on a mean martini.

A kilometre east of Calci, **Certosa di Pisa** (050 938 430, closed Mon, Sun afternoon, admission L8,000/€4.10) is a vast complex that was originally a monastery. From 1366 it was used on and off until being definitively abandoned by the Carthusian monks in 1969. The interior includes a 14th-century church, various cloisters and gardens and a view of the Campo dei Miracoli to the west. The former granaries, carpenters' workshops and cellars in the grounds here now house the **Natural History Museum** of the University of Pisa (via Roma 103, 050 936 193, closed Mon, admission L8,000/€4.10), which was founded in 1591 by the Grand Duke Ferdinando I. It is considered one of the top three natural history museums within Italy.

Livorno

Livornese like to quip that they're like their local dish, *cacciuco* – not, literally, a steamy dish of sea-beast parts cooked in wine, but rather a mix of people from different places who, together, form a lively whole. A look in the local directory is telling: letters usually passed by in Italian (J, H, K and W) are more common here than in other regions.

The Livornese are among the most left-wing of all Italians, with an abundance of industrious fishermen and factory workers. Native flavours are strong, fresh and warming; *il torpedino* is a short coffee with a chilli and locally produced rum. Wild boar head, drained of its blood for three days, emptied, spiced, then restuffed and stitched up is another speciality.

Livorno came into being when Pisa was in a pinch: the Arno silted up and the maritime republic of Pisa found itself without any sea, so Cosimo I pounced on this tiny fishing village in 1571. In 1593 a far-sighted constitution allowed foreigners to reside in the city regardless of nationality and religion, instantly endowing it with a cosmopolitan mentality.

The Porto Mediceo, with the red-brick bastion of the Fortezza Vecchia designed by Sangallo the Younger in 1521, quickly became the focus of city life. From here the canals of Venezia Nuova (or I Fossi) extend, tracing the pentagonal perimeter of Francesco I's late-16th-century plan for an ideal city.

Blanket bombing during World War II did away with most of Livorno's historic monuments, and post-war reconstruction finished the job: Buontalenti's piazza Grande was cut in two and all that remains of the 16th-century Duomo is Inigo Jones's fine portico.

Where to eat, drink & stay

Osteria da Carlo (viale Caprera 43/45, 0586 897 050, closed Sun & 3wks Sept, average L35,000/€18) is run by Carlo himself, who as well as helping to manage Livorno's rugby team has been serving traditional dishes since 1963. Try the *cacciuco*, a medley of fish and crustaceans cooked with wine and chilli and served with garlic bread, which supposedly originates from a Turkish recipe ('kuzuk' meaning 'small' in Turkish). Otherwise, try the excellent **La Chiave** across the moat from Fortezza Nuova (scali delle Cantine 52, 0586 888 609, closed lunch, closed dinner Wed, average L50,000/€26). Other great spots to sample typical Livornese dishes are **L'Antica Venezia** (via dei Bagnetti 1, 0586 887 353, closed Sun & last 3wks Aug, average L40,000/€20.50) and **Il Sottomarino** (via de' Terrazzini 48, 0586 887 025, closed Tue, Wed & 2wks Aug, average L55,000/€28.50), where portions are generous.

Disco-pubs are flourishing on Livorno's canals; **The Barge** (scali delle Anchore 6, 0586 888 320, closed Sun), which was built in the bow of an old mast ship, puts on live music on Saturdays and offers Livornese tapas. **Sotto Costa** at Quercianella outside Livorno is a raucous dance-on-the-table restaurant/bar, while **Pappafico** in Marina di Pisa is a true disco-pub where the Pisans and Livornese actually get along together.

If you've stayed too late to make it back to Pisa, try the central, three star **Hotel Gran Duca** (Piazza Micheli 16, 0586 891 024, rates L150,000-L200,000).

Getting there

By car
Livorno is just off the coastal SS1 and a 20min drive south of Pisa along the same road. The A12 autostrada also runs past the city.

By train & bus
The main station (on Piazza Dante) is on the main Rome/Pisa train line, a 12min journey from Pisa. Trains also run to and from Florence (journey time 1hr 20min) via Pisa and Empoli. **Lazzi** buses connect Livorno with Pisa, Lucca, Viareggio and Florence. Livorno is also a major port with departures to Sardinia and Corsica, among other islands.

Tourist information

APT
Piazza Cavour 6 (0586 898 111/ info@livorno.turismo.toscana.it). **Open** 9am-1pm Mon, Wed, Fri, Sat; 9am-1pm, 3-5pm Tue, Thur.

Tuscany

Siena

Whose medieval past is never far away.

The gloriously sweeping **piazza del Campo**. *See p215.*

A fountain adorned with marble goose heads, a giraffe poster, a tiny ceramic caterpillar plaque on a wall – these zoological road signs reveal the proud tradition that has defined Siena for more than seven centuries. They map out three of the city's 17 *contrade* (*see p219* **Whose side are you on?**) and illustrate the fiercely independent identities of their citizens. Babies are baptised in the fountain of their *contrade*, and the dead are buried with their *contrade* flag.

This well-preserved medieval city perches on three hills flanked by two fertile valleys, and its red-brick skyline stands out against a backdrop of vines, olive trees and fields. The historic centre is divided into three districts: **Terzo di Città** includes piazza del Campo and the Duomo; **Terzo di Camollia**, the religious heart of the city, with churches and basilicas; and the **Terzo di San Martino** to the south-east is the most unspoiled area.

SOME HISTORY

Siena's history is shrouded in mystery: who founded this ancient city and where does its name originate? Some traces of Bronze Age

fortifications suggest its geographic vantage point has always been highly contested. The Etruscans settled here, creating an important trading colony with Volterra, and one theory is that the city was named after the prominent Etruscan Saina family. The city was refounded as a Roman colony, Saena Julia, by Emperor Augustus and it was another 1,000 years before it become an independent republic.

What really put Siena on the map was via Francigena, a trade and pilgrim route that spanned the whole of Tuscany and was heavily trafficked throughout the Middle Ages. Siena became an important station along this route and thus acquired political weight. By 1125, the young city had amassed enough self-confidence to pick fights with its neighbours – it embarked on a plan to expand its territory, a move that didn't go unnoticed by Florence.

The hatred between Tuscany's sister cities over the following century was one of history's more malevolent rivalries. Things came to an explosive climax on 4 September 1260, when Siena won the bloody Battle of Montaperti. A 15,000-strong Sienese army killed 10,000

Florentine soldiers and captured 15,000. The jubilant Sienese danced on the bodies of the fallen Florentines with nails in their shoes to hammer home the victory.

It was short-lived: nine years later the two cities clashed again in Colle di Val d'Elsa, and Florence came out on top. This 1269 defeat marks a profound shift in Siena's social and political identity that paradoxically forged the way for its prosperous golden age.

With their minds off expansion, the Sienese channelled their creative juices into commerce. Gradually, successful merchants and bankers gave rise to a wealthy middle class. Trade with France and England brought in cash and also nourished a flourishing wool industry. Siena's civic infrastructure developed, and in 1287 its governing body, the Council of Nine, was first established, in friendship with Florence. The city's most important public works occurred under the Council: much of the **Duomo**, the **Palazzo Pubblico**, the **Torre del Mangia** and **piazza del Campo** (divided into nine brick sections to represent the Council).

Siena's golden age came to an abrupt halt in 1348, when the Black Death struck, with brutal force. Its vicious impact slashed the population from 100,000 to 30,000 in less than a year. After that, the city never fully recovered; internal fighting ensued, bringing down the Council of Nine in 1355. Forty-four years later Siena fell under the control of Gian Galeazzo Visconti, Grand Duke of Milan, until his death in 1402. He was followed by the tyrannical, exiled nobleman, Pandolfo Petrucci.

In 1552 Spain's Charles V besieged the city, but three years later a popular insurrection against the Spanish left Siena open to Cosimo I de' Medici. Reduced to 8,000 inhabitants, the city could not defend itself. A group of Sienese nobles tried to keep their republic alive in exile for a few years in nearby Montalcino, but the effort proved fruitless. The definitive end of the Sienese Republic came in 1559.

Following that period, once again, Siena poured its energies into commerce, this time building on its earlier achievements. One of the world's oldest banks, the Monte dei Paschi di Siena, founded in 1472 as a protectionist measure against Florence's heavy taxes, matured into an economic powerhouse. But one of the most spectacular institutions to be born from the 1600s was Siena's **Palio** (*see p219* **Whose side are you on?**).

In 1859 Siena became the first major Tuscan city to join a united Italy. Two years later, it was plugged into Italy's budding rail system, allowing faster communication and commerce with the rest of the country. More importantly, it launched a lucrative tourist trade.

Piazza del Campo

One of Italy's most beautiful squares, built on the site of an ancient Roman forum, this shell-shaped piazza lies at the base of Siena's three hills and curves downward on the southern side to the Palazzo Pubblico and Torre del Mangia. It was paved in 1347 and its nine sections pay homage to the city's Council of Nine.

The Fonte Gaia, designed by Jacopo della Quercia (built 1408-19), sits on the north side of the piazza. In 1868 the eroded marble panels of the basin were replaced by copies; what's left of the originals can be seen in the loggia of the Palazzo Pubblico. The fountain's basin serves as a terminus for the elaborate network of underground wells and aqueducts (totalling 25km/15 miles throughout the province) developed by Siena. According to legend, before the Fonte was built, a construction team uncovered a perfectly preserved antique marble statue of Venus. When the Black Death struck, the Sienese blamed the treasure, which was smashed to pieces. The fragments were buried in Florentine territory.

Palazzo Pubblico

This elegant example of Gothic architecture was built between 1288 and 1342. The brick and stone building housing the town hall and the Museo Civico (*see p221*) is a symbol of medieval Siena's mercantile wealth. Its façade – with its she-wolf and Medici balls – reads like a history book of the city.

The medieval **Torre del Mangia**.

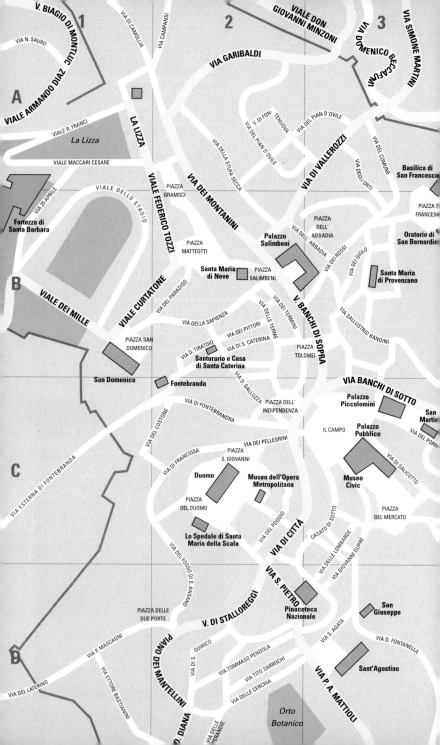

Siena

4 **5**

VIA DUCCIO DI BONINSEGNA

VIA BALDASSARRE PERUZZI

Santo Spirito

VIA DI PANTANETO

VIA DEI PISPINI

VIA DEL RIALTO

VIA S. MARTINO

V. D. OLIVIERA

VIA DI SALICOTTO

VIA DEL SOLE

Palazzo San Galagno

VIA ROMA

VIA DELLE CANTINE

VIA DEI SERVI

VIA DI PORTA GIUSTIZA

Basilica di Santa Maria dei Servi

0   200 m

0   200 yds

© Copyright Time Out Group 2001

Torre del Mangia
0577 226 822. **Open** *mid Mar-Oct* 10am-7pm
daily. *July & Aug* 10am-11pm daily. *Nov-mid Mar*
10am-4pm daily. **Admission** L10,000 (€5.20).
No credit cards.
Architects Minuccio and Francesco di Rinaldo were
instructed to build their tower as tall as possible, and
what they completed in 1348 was, in fact, medieval
Italy's tallest tower at 102m (330ft). With views over
much of Siena province, Torre del Mangia is named
after one of its first bell-ringers, the pot-bellied
'Mangiaguadagni' ('eat-profits'), who bulked up at
the local trattoria, never burning off excess fat
despite a daily climb up the tower's 503 steps. Only
15 visitors are allowed up at any one time, and tickets sell out quickly, so try to get here early in the
morning. At the foot of the tower is the Gothic
Cappella di Piazza, finished in 1352 to commemorate
the end of the plague.

Churches

The tourist office offers a L14,000 (€7.20)
combined ticket (also sold at the Duomo) that
includes admission to the Libreria Piccolomini,
Battistero, Museo dell' Opera Metropolitana and
Oratorio di San Bernardino.

Basilica di San Domenico
Piazza San Domenico (0577 280 893). **Open** 7am-
1pm, 3-6.30pm daily. **Admission** free.
This soaring brick edifice was one of the earliest
Dominican monasteries in Tuscany. Begun in 1226
and completed in 1465, unfortunately it has not been

Whose side are you on?

If you're staying in or around Siena at the
time of the Palio, you'll be encouraged by
locals to lend your support to the *contrade*
that represents the area in which you're
staying. Then again, you could just form an
arbitrary allegiance. Here are your choices:
Tartuca (tortoise), Onda (wave), Lupa
(she-wolf), Oca (goose), Nicchio (shell),
Istrice (porcupine), Drago (dragon), Civetta
(owl), Chiocciola (snail), Pantera (panther),
Aquila (eagle), Bruco (caterpillar), Leocorno
(unicorn), Montone (ram), Giraffa (giraffe),
Selva (forest), and Torre (tower).

treated kindly by history – fires, military occupa-
tions and earthquakes have all wreaked havoc, and
what you see today is largely the result of an extensive mid 20th-century restoration. Luckily, a few
things of interest have survived intact; at the end of
the nave is a *Madonna Enthroned* attributed to
Pietro Lorenzetti, while halfway down on the right
is the restored chapel of Siena's patron saint,
St Catherine. Inside, in a container, is her head (her
body was chopped up by heretics after her death and
various Italian cities made off with pieces, but her
birthplace got the grand prize).

Fire, war, earthquakes: **Basilica di San Domenico** has had a tough life.

14 suites
Accurate balance of confort,
tradition and design

Tht restautant
The cooking of
" the tuscan lineages",
in conformity with old recipes
of family, prepared with the
products of our farm.

Stok of vintage wines
A "strict selection" of
tuscan wines.

In any season relax
and welfare are insured:
fitness center, covered and
warming swimming-pool.

Residence, Restaurant; Stock of vintage wines and fitness center
Lupompesi 53016 Murlo, Siena (Italy) tel.039(0)577814605
www.boscodellaspina.com - bsturist@boscodellaspina.com

The jagged gothic edges of the **Duomo**.

The result is Gothic in style but Romanesque in spirit. Even in its more modest state, the Duomo is an impressive achievement. The black and white marble façade was started in 1226, and 30 years later work began on the dome, one of the oldest in Italy. The lower portion of the façade and the statues in the centre of the three arches were designed by Giovanni Pisano (built 1284-96). Inside, the cathedral's polychrome floors are its most immediate attraction – if you can see them. Worked on by more than 40 artists between 1369 and 1547, the intricately decorated inlaid boxes are usually covered by protective planks (they're visible mid Aug-mid Sept). The most impressive are those beneath the dome by Domenico Beccafumi, who single-handedly created 35 of the 56 scenes (1517-47). In the apse there's a splendid carved wooden choir (14th-16th centuries) and above this is a stained-glass rose window (7m/22ft across), one of Italy's earliest, made by Duccio di Buoninsegna in 1288. It depicts the life of the Virgin in nine sections. The tabernacle has Bernini's *Maddalena* and *San Girolamo* statues.

Another highlight is the pulpit (1266) by Nicola Pisano, with the help of his son Giovanni and a young pupil, Arnolfo di Cambio. The Piccolomini altar includes four statues of saints by a young Michelangelo (carved 1501-04), and above that is a *Madonna* attributed to Jacopo della Quercia.

At the far end of the left aisle a door leads to the Libreria Piccolomini (admission L2,000/€1), built in 1495 to house the library of Sienese nobleman Aeneas Silvius Piccolomini, the Renaissance humanist who became Pope Pius II. This vaulted chamber was constructed at the behest of his nephew (who became Pope Pius III for 28 days) and frescoed by Pinturicchio (1502-9; his last work), reportedly assisted by a young Raphael. The vibrant frescoes depict ten scenes from Pius II's life, including a scene in which he meets James II of Scotland.

Basilica di San Francesco

Piazza San Francesco (0577 289 081). **Open** 8.30am-12.30pm, 3-6pm daily. **Admission** free.

The Franciscans built this grand, somewhat severe church of Gothic origins in 1326. Little of its original artwork survived a big fire in 1655 – the mock Gothic façade is a 20th-century addition. One work that does remain is Pietro Lorenzetti's *Crucifixion* (1331) in the first chapel of the transept. In the third chapel are two frescoes by his brother Ambrogio.

Battistero

Piazza San Giovanni (no phone). **Open** *Summer* 9am-7.30pm Mon-Sat. *Autumn-Spring* 9am-1pm, 2.30-5pm daily. Closed for mass 9am & 10am daily. **Admission** L4,000 (€2.10). **No credit cards**.

Squeezed under the Duomo's apse is the oddly rectangular Baptistery (most are octagonal). Its unfinished Gothic façade includes three arches adorned with human and animal busts. On the inside, colourful frescoes by various artists, mainly Vecchietta, fill the room. The focal point is the central font (1417-34); designed by Jacopo della Quercia and considered to be one of the masterpieces of early Renaissance Tuscany, it features a gilded bronze bas-relief by Jacopo, Donatello and Lorenzo Ghiberti.

Duomo

Piazza del Duomo (0577 47321). **Open** *Summer* 7.30am-7.30pm Mon-Sat. *Winter* 7.30am-1pm, 2.30-5pm daily. Closed for mass 9am & 10am daily. **Admission** free.

The Siena Duomo was one of Italy's first Gothic cathedrals. Construction started in 1150 on the site of an earlier church, but plans for what was to have been a massive cathedral had to be abandoned because of the Black Death of 1348 and technical problems from an unlevelled foundation.

Oratorio di San Bernardino

Piazza San Francesco (0577 283 048). **Open** *Mid Mar-Nov* 10.30am-1.30pm, 3-5.30pm daily. Closed Dec-Feb. **Admission** L4,000 (€2.10). **No credit cards**.

To the right of San Francesco, this oratory was built in the 15th century on the site where St Bernard used to pray. On the first floor is a magnificent fresco cycle (1496-1518) by Beccafumi, Sodoma and their lesser contemporary, Girolamo del Pacchia.

Museums

Museo Civico

Palazzo Pubblico, piazza del Campo (council cultural office 0577 292 230/ticket office 0577 292 263). **Open** *Summer* 10am-7pm daily. *Winter* 9am-1.30pm daily. **Admission** L12,000 (€6.20). **No credit cards**.

Access to this museum is through the courtyard of Palazzo Pubblico and up an iron staircase. Its first four rooms house work dating from the 16th to 19th centuries. The Sala del Risorgimento pays homage to the fact that Siena was one of the first cities of the

Tuscany

region to embrace a united Italy. In the Sala del Concistorio are frescoed vaults (1529-35) on a judicial theme by Domenico Beccafumi and a marble portal sculpted in 1448 by Bernardo Rossellino.

In the *anticappella* you can admire Taddeo di Bartoli's (1362-1422) frescoes, which reflect his fascination with Greek and Roman antiquity and mythological heroes, plus a *Madonna and Child with Saints* by Sodoma at the altar of the Cappella del Consiglio. The Sala del Mappamondo was decorated by Ambrogio Lorenzetti around 1320-30, and its barely visible cosmological frescoes depict the universe and celestial spheres. This room also houses one of Siena's most cherished jewels: the *Maestà* fresco painted by Simone Martini in 1315, thought to be one of his earliest works. It is also considered one of the first examples of 'political painting', because the devotion to the Virgin Mary depicted is said to represent devotion to the Republic's princes. The faces of the main figures are repaints, as Martini got a second inspiration following a visit to Giotto's masterpiece frescoes in the Basilica di San Francesco in Assisi. The equestrian *Il Guidoriccio da Fogliano* (1328) is also attributed to Martini and celebrates a victorious battle in Montemassi.

Museo dell'Opera Metropolitana

Piazza del Duomo 8 (0577 283 048). **Open** *Mid Mar-Sept* 9am-7.30pm daily. *Oct* 9am-6pm daily. *Nov-Mar* 9am-1.30pm daily. **Admission** L10,000 (€5.20). **No credit cards.**

The museum occupies the never-completed nave of the Duomo and displays works taken from the cathedral. On the ground floor is a large hall divided in two by a stunning 15th-century wrought-iron gate. Along the walls you can enjoy a better view of Giovanni Pisano's 12 magnificent marble statues (carved 1285-97) that once adorned the façade of the Duomo. In the centre of the room is the bas-relief of the *Madonna and Child with St Anthony* by Jacopo della Quercia, commissioned in 1437 and probably not quite completed when the artist died in 1438.

On the first floor is the *Pala della Maestà* (1308-11) by Duccio di Buoninsegna, used as the high altar of the Duomo until 1506. The front has a *Madonna with Saints* and the back depicts 26 religious scenes; all in dazzling colours on a gold background. A climb to the Facciatone (the unfinished nave) affords a beautiful view of the city.

L'Ospedale di Santa Maria della Scala

Piazza del Duomo 2 (0577 224 811). **Open** *Summer* 10am-6pm daily. *Winter* 10.30am-4.30pm daily. **Admission** L10,000 (€5.20).

This museum in progress is set in a former hospital: Siena was an important stopover for pilgrims on the via Francigena, and this hospital, founded in the ninth century and named after the Duomo's marble staircase, was considered the finest of its time. Funded by donations from local noble families, it was one of the first to ensure disinfected medical equipment and bug-free cots. It was still taking in

patients until relatively recently, and author Italo Calvino died here in 1985. From 1440 to 1443, the Pellegrinaio (pilgrim's room), an emergency care unit, was embellished by, among others, Domenico di Bartolo, with the elaborate frescoes that depict the history of the hospital. The Museo Archeologico is also housed here and has several rooms devoted to Etruscan and Roman artefacts.

Pinacoteca Nazionale

Palazzo Buonsignori, via San Pietro 29 (0577 281 161). **Open** 8.30am-1.30pm Mon; 8.15am-7.15pm Tue-Sat; 8.15am-1.15pm Sun. **Admission** L8,000 (€4.10). **No credit cards.**

One of Italy's foremost art collections, holding more than 1,500 works of art in a lovely 15th-century *palazzo*. It's renowned for its Sienese *fondi d'oro* (paintings with gilded backgrounds). The second floor is devoted to Sienese masters from the 12th to 15th centuries, including Guido da Siena, Duccio di Buoninsegna, Simone Martini and the Lorenzettis. Don't miss Lorenzetti's cubist-in-feel *A City by the Sea*, one of the first examples of landscape painting.

The first floor features works by the Sienese Mannerist school of the early 1500s, including Sodoma and Beccafumi. The large room on the third floor is devoted to the Spannocchi Collection: works by northern Italian and European artists of the 16th and 17th centuries.

Monuments

Fonte Branda

Via di Fontebranda.

It's a steep walk down from via di Città to this monumental 12th-century spring. Housed in a red-brick structure with three arches, the fountain is fed by the miles of underground aqueducts across Tuscany. In its day it supplied half the city with water and powered numerous flour mills.

Fortezza Medicea

Viale C Maccari.

This huge red-brick fortress slightly outside the city, is a sore reminder of Siena's troubled past. Charles V of Spain forced the Sienese to build a fortress here in 1552, but as soon as his reign ended they celebrated by demolishing it. A few years later Cosimo I de' Medici annexed the city and demanded the fortress be rebuilt. When Florentine rule finally came to an end, Siena named the square within the fortress walls piazza della Libertà. These days, with its views over Siena, it's a good place for an evening stroll or for a drink at the Enoteca Italiana (*see p223*).

Piazza Salimbeni

A beautiful square flanked by three of Siena's most glorious *palazzi*: Tantucci, Spannocchi and Salimbeni. The latter serves as the HQ of one of the world's oldest banks, the Monte dei Paschi di Siena (founded by shrewd Sienese in 1472, to protect themselves and their savings from hefty levies and taxes imposed on them by Florence).

Handwritten margin notes (top): Trecento-Quattrocento transition. Pupil of Bartoli di Fredi. Perugia + Pisa. Out of gothic, realistic representation, clear gestures, depth.

Handwritten margin notes (left): influence Giotto; Simone Martini workshop; Count of Naples, frescoes in Assisi, Founder of school; as something regarded as forerunner of renaissance.

Shopping

The main shopping street is via di Città, which forks above the Campo: banchi di Sotto heads down and banchi di Sopra climbs up to piazza della Posta. Just before sunset, locals emerge for the *passeggiata* (stroll through town).

Siena's fantastic **general market** (8am-1pm Wednesday) stretches from piazza La Lizza to the Fortezza; get there early. The third Sunday of the month sees an **antiques market** at piazza del Mercato behind the Campo.

Consorzio Agrario
Via Pianigiani 5 (0577 2301). **Open** 8am-7.30pm Mon-Sat. **Credit** MC, V.
A local co-operative where farmers sell their goods in the big city; quality and freshness can't be beat.

Dolci Trame
Via del Moro 4 (0577 46168). **Open** 3-8pm Mon; 9.30am-7.45pm Tue-Sat. **Credit** AmEx, DC, JCB, MC, V.
Hip women's clothing at the back of piazza Tolomei.

Enoteca San Domenico
Via del Paradiso 56 (0577 271 181). **Open** 9am-8pm daily. **Credit** AmEx, DC, MC, V.
Fine wines, grappas and local sauces and jams.

Libreria Senese
Via di Città 62-66 (0577 280 845). **Open** 9am-8pm daily. **Credit** AmEx, DC, MC, V.
A family-run bookshop with plenty on local art and history, including publications in English.

Morbidi
Via Banchi di Sopra 73 (0577 280 268) & via Banchi di Sotto 27 (0577 280 541). **Open** 8.15am-1.15pm, 5-8pm Mon-Fri; 8.15am-1.15pm Sat. **Credit** AmEx, DC, JCB, MC, V.
A long room full of savoury Tuscan treats.

La Nuova Pasticceria di Iasevoli
Via Giovanni Dupré 37 (0577 40577). **Open** 8am-12.30pm, 5-7.30pm Tue-Sat; 9am-12.30pm Sun. **No credit cards.**
Choose from the fine selection of Sienese baked confectionery such as *cantuccini, pan dei santi* (bread with raisins and walnuts made for All Saint's day), *cavallucci* (dry bread buns spiced with aniseed), *panforte* and *ricciarelli* (almond biscuits).

Where to eat & drink

Restaurants

When the Sienese taste a winning combination, they stick with it: thus many recipes commonly used in the region today have survived since medieval times, including *pici* (noodle-like pasta with breadcrumbs) and *panzanella* (dried bread soaked in water, then blended with basil, onion,

and tomato). Popular Sienese desserts include *panforte* (a dense slice of nuts, candied fruits and honey) and *ricciarelli* (almond biscuits topped with powdered sugar).

Al Marsili
Via del Castoro 3 (0577 47154). **Open** 12.30-2pm, 7.30-10.15pm Tue-Sun. **Average** L60,000 (€31). **Credit** AmEx, DC, MC, V.
The place to go if you're dressed up and in need of a splurge. The food is classic Tuscan, from crostini to *faraona alla Medici* (guinea fowl with pine nuts, almonds and plums). Next door, Enoteca Marsili is filled with sumptuous wines stashed in a cave carved out of stone that dates back to the Etruscans.

Antica Osteria da Divo
Via Franciosa 25-29 (0577 284 381). **Open** noon-2.30pm, 7-10pm daily. **Average** L45,000 (€23). **Credit** AmEx, DC, JCB, MC, V.
Cellars, vaulted ceilings and niches carved in tufa stone give this *osteria*, run by Iolanda Ibelli – a Libyan who's lived here for 15 years – a distinctly archaeological feel. The food is fresh and delicious and the welcome friendly. Try *pici* with wild boar and ravioli with mushrooms and pecorino.

Cane e Gatto
Via Pagliaresi 6 (0577 287 545/fax 0577 270 227). **Open** noon-3pm, 8-11pm Mon-Wed, Fri-Sun. **Average** L90,000 (€46.50). **Credit** AmEx, DC, MC, V.

The lovely **piazza Salimbeni**. *See p222.*

This is a family-run restaurant with a *menu degustazione* (L110,000/€57) that will teach you virtually everything you could ever wish to know about Sienese cooking. The decadent lunch menu offers risotto and champagne.

Hosteria il Carroccio
Via del Casato di Sotto 32 (0577 41165).
Open noon-2.30pm, 7.30-10pm Mon, Tue, Thur-Sun. **Average** L35,000 (€18). **Credit** MC, V.
A small restaurant run by Renata Toppi and her children. Try the *tegamate di maiale*, pork cooked in a ceramic bowl, based on an old Sienese recipe that's virtually extinct today.

Nuovo Ristorante Tullio ai Tre Cristi
Vicolo di Provenzano 1 (0577 280 608).
Open 10.30am-2.30pm, 7.30-10pm Mon, Wed-Sun. **Average** L35,000 (€18). **Credit** MC, V.
Founded in 1830, this is the traditional eaterie of the giraffe *contrade* – witness the banners and symbols on every available bit of wall space. In a lively neighbourhood atmosphere, Tullio cooks up specialities such as potato *gnocchetti* with asparagus, or warm steak marinated with spices.

L'Osteria
Via de' Rossi 79/81 (0577 287 592). **Open** 12.30-2.30pm, 7.30-10.30pm Mon-Sat. **Average** L35,000 (€18). **Credit** AmEx, DC, MC, V.
This informal students' haunt serves up simple, well-cooked Tuscan food at wooden tables.

Osteria Castelvecchio
Via Castelvecchio 65 (0577 49586). **Open** 12.30-2pm, 7.30-9.30pm Mon, Wed-Sun. **Average** L40,000 (€20.50). **Credit** AmEx, DC, MC, V.
Just a few steps from the Panoteca Nazionale in former horse stables, Castelvecchio stands out. The *fusilli verdi al limone* (green corkscrew pasta with lemon) makes an excellent first course. Mauro and Simone offer vegetarian dishes at least twice a week.

Osteria la Chiacchera
Costa di Sant'Antonio 4 (0577 280 631).
Open noon-3pm, 7pm-midnight daily.
Average L25,000 (€13). **Credit** MC, V.
A charming spot for traditional Sienese recipes, friendly service and decent house wine.

Osteria Le Logge
Via del Porrione 33 (0577 48013). **Open** noon-3pm, 7.15-11pm Mon-Sat. **Average** L60,000 (€31). **Credit** AmEx, DC, MC, V.
This is a popular and conveniently central *osteria* with good food and setting.

La Taverna del Capitano
Via del Capitano 6/8 (0577 288 094). **Open** noon-3pm, 7-10pm Mon, Wed-Sat. **Average** L50,000 (€26). **Credit** AmEx, MC, V.
This place oozes Siena, from the vaulted ceilings to the dark wood furnishing. On Fridays try *baccalà* (salt cod), a Sienese speciality. Great house wine.

Bars, enoteche & gelaterie

Bar Gelateria Nannini
Piazza Salimbeni 95/99 (0577 281 094).
Open 7.45am-8.30pm daily. **Credit** MC, V.
A small haven for both Italian ice-cream fanatics and those in search of an afternoon aperitif.

La Costarella
Via di Città 33 (0577 288 076). **Open** 8.30am-midnight Mon-Wed, Fri-Sun. **No credit cards**.
If you've hoofed it up the steep hill from the Fonte Branda, the excellent ice-cream and home-made *cornetti* (similar to sweet croissants) are your prize.

Enoteca Italiana
Fortezza Medicea (0577 288 497). **Open** noon-8pm Mon; noon-1am Tue-Sat. **Credit** AmEx, MC, V.
A refreshing surprise for those who thought anything run by the fumbling Italian government can't amount to much, Italy's only national wine cellar is located in the massive vaults of the fortress. The *enoteca* stocks more than 1,000 wines from all over the country (400 from Tuscany). There are group tastings and occasional evening concerts.

Enoteca i Terzi
Via dei Termini 7 (0577 44329). **Open** 11am-4.30pm, 6.30pm-1am Mon-Sat. **Credit** AmEx, DC, MC, V.
This wine cellar, run by the knowledgeable Michele, also serves light snacks.

Where to stay

Siena doesn't have enough hotels to meet the demand, so book in advance. It's worth considering staying somewhere in the outskirts with a bus service into town.

Hotels Promotion Service
Piazza San Domenico 2 (0577 288 084/fax 0577 280 290/www.hotelsiena.com).
Info and booking service with user-friendly website that includes accommodation listings for Siena and nearby towns. It can be hard to get through by phone around public holidays.

Antica Torre
Via di Fieravecchia 7 (tel/fax 0577 222 255).
Rates single L170,000 (€88); double L200,000 (€103.50). **Credit** AmEx, DC, JCB, MC, V.
Siena's most eclectic hotel, set in a well-restored 16th-century tower, is so sought after that it gets booked up weeks in advance (there's just two rooms per floor round a central staircase).

Centrale
Via Cecco Angiolieri 26 (0577 280 379/fax 0577 42152). **Rates** double L125,000 (€64.50). **Credit** MC, V.
Located one block north of piazza del Campo on a quiet street, this small, pleasant hotel has seven large, comfortable rooms.

Tuscany

The Palio

More than just a horse race, the Palio is the explosive culmination of centuries-long neighbourhood rivalries and the moment that defines the social, cultural and political fabric of urban Siena each year.

There's a single objective: to win at all costs. Cheating, biting, putting doses of laxatives in a horse's food the night before the race (a recent phenomenon) are all admissible. The bareback jockeys, who are dismissed as mere mercenaries, often come from Sardinia; others are rented horsemen or 'cowboys' from the 'wild west' of southern Tuscany, the Maremma. Many fall off their horses before the end. The horse, unlike the jockey, is adored, receiving special rites and banquets to motivate it for the race. The winning horse brings year-long glory to its *contrade*.

The *contrade* (*see 219* **Whose side are you on?**) that contest the Palio are districts of Siena that trace their roots back to the 12th century and vaguely represent the military groups that once protected it. At the head of each was a mayor and a central governor (*podestà*) flanked by councillors. Originally the city was divided into 42 *contrade*, but the numbers shrank to the current 17 in 1729, and of these eight are selected by lottery to participate in the race.

Each *contrade* is symbolised by an animal or an object, and you'll see little plaques and colourful flags on street corners marking their territories. Each district also has its own church and a museum.

The Palio takes place in the piazza del Campo. Twice a year, commemorating the feast of the Virgin Mary on 2 July and the Assumption on 16 August, the square is carpeted with dirt and tall protective walls padded with mattresses are erected. On the perimeter, there are balconies and stands for spectators (usually wealthy tourists) willing to shell out L500,000 (€258) or more to watch the race in comfort. The majority of the Sienese – up to 30,000 of them – stand under the blazing sun in the jam-packed centre of the square, where the real action is. The square is divided into sections representing each *contrade* and their supporters stick together wearing *contrade* colours, waving banners and singing.

The Palio starts in the late afternoon with a parade of drummers and flag-carriers dressed in medieval costumes. The horses charge three times around the square; the first one over the line wins the Palio and earns a banner of the Virgin Mary as a trophy. Such is the tension of the occasion that there are often false starts – at one race in the 1980s there were so many of these that the race itself had to be postponed and run on another day – but the event is normally over in a startlingly brief 90 seconds.

The reactions of the Sienese, depending on their allegiance, range from weeping and hair-tearing to rapturous kissing and embracing. Banquets and festivities sponsored by the winning *contrade* last well into September and animosity between the first and second placed teams lasts until the following year.

Certosa di Maggiano
Strada di Certosa 82 (0577 288 180/fax 0577 288 189). **Rates** double L600,000-L900,000 (€310-€465). **Credit** AmEx, DC, MC, V.
Raised from the ruins of a 13th-century monastery, this is Siena's most luxurious (and expensive) hotel. Located just south of the city, it is known for its stunning garden. It is also sought after because of its extensive amenities, including tennis courts, swimming pools and even a heliport.

Chiusarelli
Viale Curtatone 15 (0577 280 562/fax 0577 271 177). **Rates** (incl breakfast) single L125,000 (€64.50); double L185,000 (€95.50). **Credit** AmEx, DC, JCB, MC, V.
Reasonably priced for a three-star hotel on the edge of the historic centre. The unexceptional rooms have all the necessities. Ask for a quiet room at the back.

Duomo
Via Stalloreggi 38 (0577 289 088/fax 0577 43043). **Rates** single L150,000 (€77.50); double L220,000 (€113.50). **Credit** AmEx, DC, MC, V.
It has a location that can't be beat, but its sterile, sober rooms certainly could be. Ask for one of the two rooms with a small balcony that overlook the Duomo and have a view of Siena's characteristic red roofs. Service is informal and friendly.

Grand Hotel Villa Patrizia
Via Fiorentina 58 (0577 50431/fax 0577 50442). **Rates** double L380,000 (€196.50). **Credit** AmEx, DC, MC, V.
This 'grand' hotel on the northern side of the city has known better days but it's still got some things going for it. Among the offerings that keep guests coming back are its outdoor pool, friendly service and peaceful and attractive gardens.

Tuscany

Pensione Palazzo Ravizza

*Pian dei Mantellini 34 (0577 280 462/fax 0577
221 597)*. **Rates** (incl breakfast) double with bath
L320,000 (€165.50). **Credit** AmEx, DC, JCB, MC, V.
Owned by the same family for more than 200 years,
this 1800s *palazzo* still has its original furnishings.
Many of the 38 rooms overlook a charming, well-
kept garden; others have a view of the city.

Piccolo Hotel Etruria

*Via delle Donzelle 3 (0577 288 088/fax 0577
288 461)*. **Rates** single L75,000 (€38.50); double
L120,000 (€62). **Credit** AmEx, DC, JCB, MC, V.
This is a 12-room hotel located just off Siena's commercial artery, banchi di Sotto.

Tre Donzelle

*Via delle Donzelle 5 (0577 280 358/fax 0577 223
933)*. **Rates** single L50,000 (€26); double L100,000
(€51.50). **Credit** MC, V.
With 27 spacious rooms, this is handy if the Piccolo
Hotel Etruria next door (*see above*) is full, though it
does have a midnight curfew.

Villa Scacciapensieri

*Via di Scacciapensieri 10 (0577 41441/fax 0577 270
854)*. **Rates** single L225,000 (€116); double L390,000
(€201.50). **Credit** AmEx, DC, JCB, MC, V.
As the name ('squish your thoughts') suggests, you
can leave your worries behind once you're at this
family-run hotel. It's 3km (2 miles) north of the city
– follow the signs up a private tree-lined drive to the
crest of the hill. There's an excellent restaurant, a
tennis court and a swimming pool.

Camping

Colleverde

Strada Scacciapensieri 47 (0577 280 044). Closed
Dec-Feb. **Rates** adults L15,000 (€7.80); children
L8,000 (€4.10). **No credit cards**.
The closest campsite to the city (3km/2 miles) and
one of southern Tuscany's most attractive.

Essentials

Getting there & around

By bike & moped

For the pedal-powered variety contact **DF Bike** (via
Massetana Romana 54, 0577 271 905). For mopeds
try **Automotocicli Perozzi** (via del Romitorio 5,
0577 223 157).

By bus

If you're reliant on public transport, the bus is the
way to go in Siena, especially if you're travelling to
or from Florence. Siena's major bus terminal is at the
edge of the historic centre at piazza Gramsci; the
main ticket office (0577 204 246) is underground.
Most buses leave from the adjacent via Frederico
Tozzi or nearby piazza San Domenico. **Tra-in**, the
principal bus company serving Siena and beyond

(same phone as ticket office), has departures every
30 min for Florence (direct service takes 75 min)
as well as services to Arezzo and to Grosseto,
and most regional towns of interest. The excellent
www.comune.siena.it/train gives full timetable info
on all services.

By car

The SS2 links Florence and Siena (journey time
around 1 hr). The historic centre of Siena is mainly
traffic-free so you have to park on the outskirts
and walk in; there are big car parks at the Stadio
Comunale and near the Fortezza Medicea, but even
these can fill rapidly on weekends, public holidays
or around the time of the Palio.
To hire a car try **Avis** (via Simone Martini 36, 0577
270 305) or **Hertz** (viale Sardegna 37, 0577 45085).

By taxi

Call **Radio Taxi** (0577 49222) or go to one of the
taxi ranks at piazza Stazione (0577 44504) or piazza
Matteotti (0577 289 350).

By train

There are some direct trains to and from Florence,
but more often you'll have to change at Empoli
(journey time up to 2hrs). For Pisa, change in Empoli.
Siena's train station is at the bottom of the hill on the
east side of the city (piazza Fratelli Rosselli, 0577 280
115). From here a local bus makes the short journey
up to piazza Gramsci, close to the historic centre.

Tourist information

Centro Servizi Informazioni Turistiche Siena (APT)

*Piazza del Campo 56 (0577 280 551/fax 0577 270
676/www.siena.turismo.toscana.it)*. **Open** 8.30am-
7.30pm Mon-Sat; 9am-3pm Sun.

www.comune.siena.it

A website jam-packed with info (in Italian).

Festivals

The **Palio** (*see p225*) is held on 2 July and 16 Aug.
Siena Jazz (0577 271 401) is a major summer event
with international musicians (late July-early Aug).
The **Settimana dei Vini**, a showcase of regional
wines, takes place in the Fortezza Santa Medicea in
early June. The music conservatory **Accademia
Chigiana** (0577 46152) organises an outdoor concert
cycle in June and has a classical concert season
(Oct-Mar). **Teatro dei Rinnovati** (0577 292 265)
runs a lively theatre season (Nov-late Mar).

Useful addresses

Hospital

Viale Bracci, north of the city (0577 586 111).

Police station

Via del Castoro (0577 201 111).

Post office

Piazza Matteotti 37 (0577 42178).

Chianti & Siena Province

Fall under the spell.

The magic of this part of Tuscany lies in its perfect blend of elements: stunning, unspoiled countryside, excellent food and wine, a rich cultural heritage and proximity to Florence. Its most inebriating effect is an unshakeable desire to just settle down and live there, and many visitors, Italians and foreigners alike, do just that, buying and restoring crumbling 15th-century farmhouses. Others leave reluctantly, haunted by their glimpse of paradise.

Chianti

The ultimate Tuscan dreamscape, Chianti's punch is twofold: breathtaking natural beauty and plenty of wine. Vine trellises outline the sensual curves of the land and restored stone farmhouses perch picturesquely.

Chianti is best experienced at leisure in your own transport, though there's a regular **SITA** bus service (055 214 721/800 373 760) from Florence to Greve (50min) and Panzano (70min) and some buses continue on to Radda (90min) and Gaiole (2hrs). A car will also allow you to explore La Chiantigiana and the SS222, which wiggles its way south of Florence to Siena through hilltop towns such as Panzano and Castellina. This section is organised along the north to south route of the SS222.

Around San Casciano in Val di Pesa

Only 17 kilometres (10 miles) south of the Florence Certosa autostrade junction (where the main roads to Siena and Rome begin), this bustling little market town would be gobbled up by sprawling cement suburbs if it existed in another part of the world. Yet, despite its proximity to the Tuscan capital, San Casciano is nestled safely in full-blown Chianti country. Inside the stone village is the 14th-century Gothic Santa Maria del Prato church, with a painted crucifix allegedly by Simone Martini.

Seven kilometres (4 miles) north is the tiny hamlet of Sant'Andrea in Percussina, where Machiavelli lived while writing his despot's handbook *The Prince*, in between furious card games with the local gravedigger. His house is now the Antica Fattoria Machiavelli, a winery.

South of here, near Montefiridolfi, is the **Fattoria La Loggia** (via Cassiano 40, 055 824 4288, rates L200,000/€103.50), an agricultural estate with restored medieval apartments and small private houses for hire.

Nearby, one of Tuscany's most highly rated restaurants is north-west of San Casciano, in the village of Cerbaia. **La Tenda Rossa** (piazza del Monumento 9/14, 055 826 132, closed Sun,

The 11th-century abbey **Badia a Passignano**. See p228.

lunch Mon, average L140,000/€72.50), has two Michelin stars, and serves authentic country fare in a formal atmosphere that's more than made up for by the cooking, service and exceptionally broad-ranging wine list.

Greve in Chianti

Greve makes a lovely base from which to explore the surrounding area. Its triangular-shaped main square, piazza Matteoti, with its cream-painted, green-shuttered buildings and arcaded perimeter is particularly attractive. On Saturday mornings the square's wine bars and appealing food shops heave with locals gossiping and stocking up on supplies. Giovanni da Verrazzano hailed from these parts before discovering New York harbour in 1524, as the statue in the square testifies.

Another pioneer, Amerigo Vespucci, the 16th-century explorer who gave his name to America, was born in nearby **Montefioralle**. A tiny road of hairpin turns leads up to it from Greve's northern side. One of Tuscany's best rustic restaurants, can be found in the family-run **La Taverna del Guerrino** (via Montefioralle 39, Montefioralle, 055 853 106, closed Mon, lunch Tue & Wed, 2wks Feb, L40,000/€20.50) in this ancient walled village. The plain, wholesome food is not exceptional, but the place feels as if it was left behind by

One of Chianti's jewels: **Radda**. *See p229.*

another age, and therein lies its charm. The short menu of Tuscan standards has hardly changed for the past 15 years – there's *ribollita*, *pappa al pomodoro*, grilled meats (try the spicy *salsicce*, *rosticciana* or fat pork chops) and corn fed chicken (if you order it in advance).

If you're looking for a room back in Greve, the best option is probably **Albergo Giovanni da Verrazzano** (055 853 189; rates L140,000-L160,000/€72.50-€82.50) on the main square, with an attractive restaurant on its geranium-lined second-floor terrace.

Tourist information

Ufficio Turistico
Viale G da Verrazzano 59 (055 854 6287/fax 055 854 4149). **Open** 9.30am-1.30pm, 3.30-7.30pm Mon-Fri; 9.30am-1.30pm Sat.

Panzano in Chianti

Another seven kilometres (4 miles) south (either along the SS222 or the road from Montefioralle) is the fortified village of Panzano. With stunning views of the Conca d'Oro Valley, it is probably best known today as the home of Dario Cecchini, the renowned traditionalist butcher.

Right of the church, is the **Enoteca Il Vinaio** (via Santa Maria 22, 055 852 603, closed dinner Tue & Nov-Mar, average L20,000/ €10.50), which serves up hearty *pappa al pomodoro* and *ribollita* accompanied by a vast selection of local wines all served on a vine-covered terrace. For restaurant fare, try nearby **Il Vescovino** (via Ciampolo da Panzano 9, 055 852 464, average L50,000/€26), which does a fine roast duck in orange juice which it serves up on a large terrace with a wonderful view.

On an eroded dirt road about eight kilometres (five miles) north-west of town, the **Badia a Passignano** was once a centre of the wealthy Vallombrosan order. The 11th-century abbey, which looks, from afar, like a Tuscan dish served up on a bed of cypress trees, is now in private hands, but the church can be visited. On the road to the Badia is another dirt road turn-off for **La Cantinetta di Rignana** (via Rignana, Greve, 055 852 601, closed Tue, average L45,000/€23). Set among ancient farmhouses, it's the quintessential Tuscan restaurant, with the kind of extraordinary food and views from which fantasies are made. The entire experience is fantastic. In season, meals start off with sensational steamed artichokes, followed by classic *primi* such as *papardelle* with rabbit sauce and ending with succulent grilled meats. La Cantinetta is one of Chianti's best-kept secrets, possibly because it really is so hard to get to.

Get friendly with the locals in rustic **Gaiole**.

A sudden bend in the SS222 brings the hilltop town of **Castellina** into postcard-perfect view. The surrounding hills marked the battlefront between the armies of Siena and Florence, hence the town's heavy fortification. Its main square, piazza del Comune, is in the shadow of the imposing Torre (now the town hall), and a covered walkway evokes a chilly 14th-century feel. But there are plenty of places to taste/buy wine, and one of Chianti's top wineries, **Castello di Fonterutoli** (*see p232* **Visiting wineries**), is nearby.

If you're staying, **Colle Etrusco Salivolpi** (via Fiorentina 89, 0577 740 484/fax 0577 740 998, rates L165,000/€85), up a steep hill from the village, is a restored farmhouse-turned-country club with an outdoor pool.

About 200 metres (220 yards) away is **Ristorante Albergaccio** (via Fiorentina 63, 0577 741 042, closed Sun, lunch Tue-Thur, average L70,000/€36), where Francesco Cacciatori and Sonia Wisman offer two 'Taste of Tuscany' fixed menus. Just north of town on the Chiantigiana in Pietrafitta is the terraced **Bar-Ristorante Pietrafitta** (0577 741 123, closed Wed, L40,000/€20.50), which looks like a truck stop but is a fantastic spot for lunch.

Around Radda in Chianti

About a kilometre before Castellina, a fork in the road indicates the direction (N429) for Radda, yet another Chianti jewel. In it's early days, Radda was the capital of the medieval League of Chianti, a chain of Florentine defensive outposts against Siena that included Castellina and Gaiole.

There are compelling reasons to extend your stay in this charming town. The first is to enjoy a meal in the elegant but simple **Ristorante Vignale** (via XX Settembre 23, 0577 738 094, closed Thur & Dec-late Mar, average L50,000/€26), with its beautifully presented Tuscan dishes and home-made bread and pasta. And it's hard not to be tempted to put your head down at the soothing **Relais Fattoria Vignale** (via Pianigiani 8, 0577 738 300, rates L230,000-L700,000/€119-€361.50), owned by the same people, with its broad terraces and pool overlooking the green valleys below, plus its own *enoteca* and taverna (closed Wed).

Beyond Radda, the Etruscan tomb-rich area around Volpaia, seven kilometres (4 miles) to the north, is worth exploring. An enchanting option for accommodation just outside Volpaia is the *agriturismo* **Podere Terreno** (via della Volpaia, 0577 738 312, rates L170,000/€88 per person), a stone farmhouse surrounded by oak groves and chestnut trees. The rate includes an excellent dinner (with wine) around a long table. Fine wine is produced here.

Tourist information

Ufficio Informazioni Turistiche

Piazza Ferucci 1 (0577 738 494). **Open** 10am-1pm, 3-7pm Mon-Sat; 10am-1pm Sun.

Around Gaiole in Chianti

On the steep eastern edge of Chianti, surrounded by the Monti dei Chianti, the area around Gaiole is wild and rustic yet well explored. Gaiole itself was a bustling market in the Middle Ages but is quieter now. It makes for a pleasant stop on the way to the nearby wineries (*see p232* **Visiting wineries**) and castles.

The **Badia a Coltibuono**, four kilometres (three miles) north of Gaiole, is a Vallombrosan abbey magnificently situated amid cedar forests; it makes a great starting point for hikers. Its restaurant (0577 749 031, closed Mon Mar-May, closed mid Nov-early Mar, average L60,000/€31) specialises in game. In summer you can eat at tables in the beautiful gardens.

For somewhere to stay, continue south to the hamlet of San Sano, just off SS408, where the friendly **Hotel Residenza San Sano** (0577 746 130, rates L200,000-L250,000/€103.50-€129) has a pool set among old stone houses.

Tourist information

Ufficio Informazioni Pro Loco

Via Antonio Casbianca (0577 749 411/fax 0577 749 375). **Open** *Apr-Oct* 10am-12.30pm, 3.30-7.30pm Mon-Sat. Closed Nov-Mar.

Tuscany

Castelnuovo Berardenga

An alternative to continuing along the SS408 from Gaiole toward Siena is to branch off to the east on the SS484, which eventually leads you to this southern offshoot of Chianti. Before you get to the town, which dates back to the 9th century, you'll come to one of the region's best-known castles, **Castello di Brolio** – largely a 19th-century reading of what a castle should look like (the original was wrecked by Spanish troops in 1478 and completely destroyed by the Sienese 50 years later). It was rebuilt by Baron Bettino Ricasoli, who was responsible for pushing Chianti's wine industry into the major league. The **Barone Ricasoli** vineyard remains one of the best, along with nearby winery **Felsina** (*for both, see p232* **Visiting wineries**).

A more surprising find, given the distance from the sea, is **Da Antonio** in Castelnuovo Beardanga (via Fiorita 38, 0577 355 321, closed Mon, lunch in winter, set meal L100,000/€51.50), considered by many to be Tuscany's best fish restaurant. Owner Antonio Farina makes dawn trips to the coast to bring back the freshest of catches for his fixed menus, which always have interesting antipasti, *primi* (maybe with a sauce of baby squid) and a *secondo* of the day's catch, grilled or baked.

West of Siena

The Poggibonsi exit of the Si-Fi (Siena-Florence) *autostrada* quickly gives access to western Siena Province and the Etruscan town of Volterra in Pisa Province. As is the case with the Chianti region, driving is the easiest option, though **SITA** (055 214 721) runs buses from Florence to San Gimignano (via Poggibonsi, 70min) and to Volterra (1hr 50min) via Colle di Val d'Elsa (1hr). From Siena, **Tra-in** (0577 204 111) runs a regular service to San Gimignano (1hr) via Monteriggioni (30 min).

Poggibonsi is an ugly commercial centre with eyesore cement buildings and factory-dotted suburbs, but nearby **Colle di Val d'Elsa** is an excellent base from which to explore San Gimignano, Monteriggioni and the Elsa Valley. The birthplace of Arnolfo di Cambio (who was the architect responsible for Florence's Duomo and the Palazzo Vecchio), its medieval core is certainly worth exploring.

Another good reason for staying in the town is **Da Arnolfo** (via XX Settembre, 0577 920 549, closed Tue, lunch Wed, L140,000/€72.50), which boasts two Michelin stars. Its typical offerings include steamed shrimp with candied tomatoes, and pigeon stuffed with chicken livers, followed by extraordinary desserts.

Views of **San Giamignano**. See p232.

Tuscany

San Gimignano

For Italy's best skyline, head to San Gimignano, nicknamed Tuscany's Medieval Manhattan because of its 13 stone towers (although, at its political and financial peak in the 12th and 13th centuries, it had 72). Its good fortune and wealth came from its strategic position on the via Francigena trade route, which passes through the perfectly preserved medieval city.

Tourism has brought it more wealth, and masses of day-trippers. Its narrow streets are often congested with sightseers who bottleneck between the two main squares. It's best to visit early morning, when *la città delle torri* is at its most magical, or in the off season, otherwise it can seem worse than Manhattan in rush hour.

It makes sense to buy a combined museum ticket (L20,000/€10.50; L18,000/€9.30 per person for families), which allows you entry to the city's main sights (those listed below plus the Museo Archeologico, Museo Ornitologico and Museo d'Arte Sacra/Museo Etrusco).

Cars are not allowed inside the walls of the city, to which there are two main entrances: through Porta San Matteo to the north and up via San Matteo, or through Porta San Giovanni to the south and up via San Giovanni. Both lead up a steep incline to the heart of the medieval city: the piazza della Cisterna and the adjacent piazza del Duomo. **Piazza della Cisterna** has a functioning 13th-century well in its centre and the Torre del Diavolo ('Devil's Tower') looming overhead. The tower earned its name when its

Visiting wineries

This area contains three of Tuscany's wine making havens – the Chianti area in the north, and around Montalcino and Montepulciano to the south. One of the best Tuscan whites, Vernaccia, is also produced here, in the hills surrounding San Gimignano. Almost all the wineries you pass, from the humble to the huge, will welcome the public, though the facilities range from guided tours and tasting rooms to nothing but a barrel out of which to slosh you a glass.

For more on Tuscan wines, *see chapter* **Tuscan Wines**. Here we've listed our choice of the prominent wineries as a starting point.

Chianti

The heartland of Chianti Classico is best defined by the towns of **Radda**, **Castelnuovo Berardenga**, **Gaiole**, **Castellina Greve** and **Panzano**. The wineries below are given in north–south order. All times listed are for the outlets. Visits of the wineries and tasting are by appointment only.

Castello di Fonterutoli

Fonterutoli, Castellina in Chianti (0577 740 476). **Open** 8am-1pm, 2-5.30pm Mon-Fri. **Credit** AmEx, DC, MC, V.
This is run by the handsome scions of a family that competes with the Antonori for aristocratic panache. There's a country residence to match.

Badia a Coltibuono

Gaiole in Chianti (0577 749 498/shop 0577 749 479). **Open** Early Apr-early Nov 9.30am-

1pm, 2-7pm daily. *Mid Feb-early April, early Nov- Dec* 2-6.30pm Mon; 9.30am-1pm, 2-6.30pm Tue-Sat. **Credit** MC, V.
In a 700-year-old abbey (*see p229*).

Barone Ricasoli

Brolio, Gaiole in Chianti (0577 7301). **Open** 8am-7pm Mon-Fri; 11am-7pm Sat, Sun. **Credit** AmEx, DC, MC, V.
Producers of the famous Castello di Brolio.

Felsina

SS 484, near Castelnuovo Berardenga (0577 355 117). **Open** 8.30am-5.30pm Mon; 8.30am-7pm Tue-Sat. **Credit** MC, V.
Located at Chianti Classico's southernmost border. This winery is the producer of some of the region's best wines, including the SuperTuscan Fontalloro.

Further information

Consorzio Chianti Classico
(*055 82285/www.chiantinet.it*).

owner convinced his neighbours that it had grown taller on its own. **Piazza del Duomo** is the town's cultural and political hub. If you face the so-called Duomo (technically it's the Collegiata), Palazzo del Popolo (home to the town hall, Museo Civico and Torre Grossa) is to your left and Palazzo del Podestà behind you.

The plain Romanesque façade of the **Collegiata** or cathedral (0577 940 316, closed Sun morning, closed late Jan-early Mar except services, admission to dome L6,000/€3.10) is in stark contrast to the glorious interior. Almost every inch of wall space is frescoed; on the left wall is an Old Testament fresco by Bartolo di Fredi, flanked by an expressive New Testament cycle (1333), probably by Lippo Memmi, on the right wall. Before the altar is the waxy body of

Santa Fina (the patron saint of San Gimignano, she spent most of her short life lying on planks in a dark rat-infested room, after her mother scolded her for accepting an apple from a boy who was in love with her) and to the right is the Cappella di Santa Fina.

The **Museo Civico** (piazza del Duomo, no phone, closed late Jan-mid Feb, admission L12,000/€6.20) houses the masterpiece by Lippo Memmi, the *Maestà* (1317), as well as Taddeo di Bartolo's *Scenes from the Life of St Gimignano* (1393), showing the saint holding the city in his lap against a golden background. Access to the **Torre Grossa** is through a courtyard in the museum. Trekking to the top is worth it for the fantastic views, but it can be a crowded journey back down at weekends.

Chianti Rufina

This comprises the towns of Pontassieve and Rufina. Its wineries are protected by low mountains and enjoy a dry microclimate.

Fattoria Selvapiana
Via Selvapiana 43, Rufina (055 836 9848). **Open** 9am-1pm, 3-7pm Mon Fri. **Credit** AmEx, DC, MC, V.
The pick of the Rufina wineries.

Montalcino

One of Italy's top wines, **Brunello di Montalcino** (DOCG), is produced around this hilltop town 40 kilometres (25 miles) south of Siena, and standards are kept high. There are a number of *enotecha* in town (*see p237*) and nearly 30 vineyards in the area where you can sample Brunello.

Biondi Santi
Tenuta Il Greppo 183, Montalcino (0577 848 087). **Open** 8am-noon, 2-4pm Mon-Fri. Closed Aug. **Credit** AmEx, DC, MC, V.
The historic estate where Brunello originated, thanks to the enterprise of Ferruccio Biondi-Santi in the early 20th century.

Fattoria dei Barbi
Podere Novi village 170, Montalcino (0577 84827). **Open** 10am-1pm, 2.30-6pm Mon-Fri; 2.30-6pm Sat, Sun. **Credit** AmEx, DC, MC, V.
In addition to a variety of wines, the Fattoria also sells oil, grappa and cheese and has its own restaurant.

Further information
Consorzio Del Vino Brunello di Montalcino
Costa del Municipio 1, Montalcino (0577 848 246/www.consorziobrunello dimontalcino.it).

Montepulciano

Wine has been made here since the sixth century, and the Vino Nobile di Montepulciano was among the first Italian wines to achieve the prestigious DOCG status in 1981, hot on the heels of neighbouring Montalcino.

Avignonesi
Via Colonica 1, Valiano di Montepulciano (0578 724 304). **Open** 9am-6pm Mon-Fri. **Credit** AmEx, DC, MC, V.
The main Avignonesi vineyard, Le Cappezzine, is about 23 kilometres (14 miles) outside Montepulciano and has tastings and tours on weekdays. There's also a small cellar in town (via di Gracciano nel Corso 91).

Poliziano
Via Fontago 11, Montepulciano (0578 738 171). **Open** 8.30am-12.30pm, 2.15-6pm Mon-Fri. Closed wks Dec & Aug. **Credit** AmEx, DC, MC, V.
Vineyards on three different sites. Produces three different types of Vino Nobile, two of which are single-vineyard varieties.

Further information
Consorzio Del Vino Nobile di Montepulciano
Piazza Grande 7, Montepulciano (0578 757 812).

Tuscany

Where to stay

Because this is not a particularly big town, there is not a wide selection of hotels here. Luckily, there is a sprawling network of *affittacamere* (rooms for rent in private houses) in the city and *agriturismi* in the surrounding countryside, although these can vary in quality and price, so it's always a good idea to ask around before you choose one. In town is the **Hotel L'Antico Pozzo** (via San Matteo 87, 0577 942 014, rates L160,000-L280,000/ €82.50-€144.50). This is one of the classiest, with its own well and frescoed rooms. **Hotel La Cisterna** (piazza della Cisterna 24, 0577 940 328/fax 0577 942 080, rates L125,000-L205,000/€64.50-€105) in an ivy-covered 14th-century *palazzo* is pleasantly peaceful.

Where to eat

For regional cooking with an alternative slant, head for the northern side of town, to **Osteria delle Catene** (via Mainardi 18, 0577 941 966, closed Wed, average L45,000/€23). One of San Gimignano's more elegant places, **Ristorante Dorandó** (vicolo dell'Oro 2, 0577 941 862, closed Mon, average L90,000/€46.50) serves food based on a variety of Etruscan, medieval and Renaissance recipes; try *pici* with mint pesto washed down with a local white wine.

For a treat at any time of day, **Gelateria di Piazza** (piazza della Cisterna, 0577 942 244, closed Nov-Feb); its claims to sell the best ice-cream in the world seem to be backed up by Tony Blair, if the framed photo and letter inside are anything to go by.

X marks the spot

It's definitely worth straying off the well-worn path to visit **La Frateria di Padre Eligio**, just off the wiggly road between the quaint medieval towns of Sarteano and Cetona in the south-easternmost reaches of Siena province, close to its borders with Umbria.

Run by reformed drug addicts under the umbrella of the Mondo X communities (of which there are 35 throughout Italy, providing caring homes for troubled young people), La Frateria is both a restaurant and an away-from-it-all haven. Housed in a 12th-century monastery, lovingly restored over 15 years by the community's first members, this place inspires in all aspects, from the fresh mountain air and the fabulous countryside views to the nurturing environment.

But don't imagine that La Frateria di San Francesco (as it's alternatively known) is merely a Priory-like retreat with a half-decent canteen – as much care goes into the food here as went into the restoration of the building, with around 80 to 90 per cent of the food produced by the community itself and little more than sugar and flour brought in from outside. Talented chef Walter and his dedicated team serve memorable tasting menus of up to nine courses.

Despite having a strict no-alcohol policy for the community itself, the Frateria has a huge, dusty wine cellar full of local goodies. Should you be so inclined, you can even retire to the monastery's former prison (where they once incarcerated wayward monks for heaven knows what) and have a post-prandial bevvy.

La Frateria di Padre Eligio
Convento di San Francesco, Cetona (0578 238 261/fax 0578 239 220/ www.mondox.it). **Lunch** served 1-3pm daily. **Dinner served** 8-11pm daily. **Rates** L380,000-L500,000 (€196.50-€258) including breakfast. Set meal L150,000 (€77.50). Bookings essential. **No credit cards.**

Tourist information

Pro Loco Ufficio Informazioni Turistiche
Piazza del Duomo 1 (0577 940 008/fax 0577 940 903). **Open** 9am-1pm, 3-7pm daily.

Festivals
February's Carnival procession is the best time to visit in the off-season, along with 12 March, the day of patron saint Fina, when museum entrance is free. In July the Festival Internazionale series of daily concerts includes classic piano recitals and opera.

Volterra

Volterra stands proudly on a 531-metre (1,750-foot) peak between the Cecina and Era valleys in Pisa Province. Traces from the Neolithic period were discovered here, but it wasn't until the fifth century BC that Etruscan culture flourished and Volterra's population grew to 25,000 – it became one of the 12 Etruscan states. Velathri (its Etruscan name) put up a hearty resistance to the expansionist Romans and was the last Etruscan city to fall to the Empire in 260 BC, when it was renamed Volaterrae.

The town as it appears today was built in the 12th and 13th centuries and virtually all traces of the Etruscans have been erased, save patches of the fortified walls that reveal its Etruscan foundations. Etruscan buffs shouldn't miss the **Museo Etrusco Guarnacci** (via Don Minzoni 15, 0588 86347, closed afternoons and early Nov-mid March, admission L13,000/€6.70 with Volterra's other two museums), which houses one of the world's most complete collections of artefacts discovered from this mysterious ancient population, including the celebrated 'evening shadow' statuette familiar from cheap souvenir copies. The long thin statue was found by a local farmer and used as a firestoker until someone recognised its importance.

Since Etruscan times, Volterra's most important industry has been the production of alabaster artefacts (the area around the city contains one of Italy's largest deposits of the stone). Once used to adorn abbeys and palaces, alabaster is now turned into everything from thimbles to life-sized horse heads – anything that can be carted away in a tour bus.

Where to stay & eat
For rooms, **Villa Rioddi** (Rioddi village, 0588 88053, L100,000-170,000/€51.50-€88) just outside Volterra is a 15th-century villa with modest prices, a pool and a lovely garden. **Trattoria del Sacco Fiorentino** (piazza XX Settembre, 0588 88537, closed Wed, Jan & Feb,

L35,000-L45,000/€18-€23) near the Etruscan museum is a cosy restaurant serving seasonal goodies such as gnocchi with spring vegetables, tagliatelle with courgettes and basil and rabbit with garlic. There's a good choice of cheeses and an excellent wine list.

Tourist information

Associazone Pro Volterra
Via Giusto Turazza 2 (0588 86150/ fax 0588 90350). **Open** *Spring-Autumn* 9am-12.30pm, 3-6.30pm daily. *Winter* 9am-12.30pm, 3-6.30pm Mon-Sat.

Monteriggioni

Whichever way you approach it on the Si(ena)-Fi(renze) *autostrada*, Monteriggioni stands out as one of Tuscany's most surreal visions – the 14 stone towers built on thick walls encircling the tiny medieval hamlet make it look like a crown on top of a grassy hill. In *The Divine Comedy* Dante described it as an enormous well filled with horrible giants. One of Tuscany's earliest examples of military architecture, it's a perfectly preserved walled city. The walls – with a perimeter of 570 metres (1,770 feet) – were built by Siena (1213-19) and reinforced half a century later to protect Siena's northern territories from Florence's armies.

There's not much here beside a bar, a few homes and the Romanesque-Gothic Pieve di Santa Maria. It takes less than five minutes to get a sense of the town and walk its length.

Where to stay & eat

On the corner of the main square, the same family has been serving up delicious Tuscan staples for nearly four decades at **Ristorante Il Pozzo** (piazza Roma 2, 0577 304 127, closed Sun dinner, Mon, average L80,000/€41.50). It's still a good choice for a lingering lunch or dinner in a convivial atmosphere. Slightly cheaper is **Il Piccolo Castello** (via I Maggio 2, 0577 304 370, average L60,000/€31), which has an attractive garden. If you're inclined to stay within the village walls, the four-star **Hotel Monteriggioni** (Via I Maggio 4, 0577 305 009, rates L200,000-L360,000/€103.50-€186) has 12 rooms, a pool and a garden.

Abbazia di San Galgano

This abandoned abbey is worth a detour even if you've overdosed on Tuscan churches. Located in the Valdimerse, midway between Siena and Roccastrada on SS73, it's like something out of a fairytale – or a nightmare. Built between 1218

Tuscany

and 1288, it was a Cistercian powerhouse until the 14th century. Its monks devised compex irrigation systems and sold their services as doctors, lawyers and architects (helping to build Siena's cathedral). But the abbey was sacked one time too many and eventually abandoned. The ruins retain an atmosphere of eerie spirituality.

Saint Galgano Guidotti lived in a hut on a hilltop next to the abbey where the **Cappella di Montesiepi** now stands. A knight from a local noble family, he renounced his warlike ways to become a Cistercian hermit. When fellow knights persuaded him to revert to his old self in 1180, he defiantly stabbed a stone and his sword slid in. The (alleged) sword in the stone is now on display in the centre of this curious circular Romanesque chapel, which has fading frescoes by Ambrogio Lorenzetti.

South-east of Siena

No sooner does the red Sienese skyline vanish behind you as you travel south on the via Cassia (SS2, which traces an ancient trade route used by the Romans) than the landscape dramatically changes: the wooded hills of Chianti give way to rolling hills of open fields, with machine-perfect rows of budding crops disturbed by the occasional lone cypress tree.

The quieter secondary southern route (N438) to Asciano passes through the rippled core of the Crete Senesi, an area of white clay hills and deep gullies resembling a stylised *quattrocento* drapery. **Asciano** is a pleasant town in the heart of the Crete Senesi. Here, the main action takes place around its pleasant central piazza which is called the Garibaldi.

About three kilometres (two miles) north of this is the riotous **La Pievina** (via Lauretana 9, La Pievina, 0577 718 368, closed Mon & Tue, average L70,000/€36), a unique place staffed by three flirty elderly ladies who stuff visitors with home-cooked goodies.

As far as getting around is concerned, driving gives you the most freedom, though some of the slower trains on the main train line between Rome and Florence do stop at Chiusi to the very east, from where you can pick up local trains to Montepulciano and Asciano (on the Siena line). Local buses run from Chiusi to Montepulciano, while **Tra-in** (0577 204 111) operates a regular service between Siena and Montalcino (1hr) and another regular service between Siena and Montepulciano (via Pienza; 90min).

If you do come to Siena Province by train and get off at Chiusi, don't miss the **Museo Archeologico Nazionale** (via Porsenna 7, 0578 20177, admission L8,000/€4.10), with its wonderful Etruscan artefacts.

Local colours at the **Bravio delle Botti**. *See p239.*

Monte Oliveto Maggiore

The red roof of Italy's most-visited Benedictine monastery (0577 707 611) seems to scream out in Technicolor brilliance against the white gullies of the Crete Senesi and surrounding pine forests. Once you're in its grounds, where a signpost welcomes you 'to silence and prayers', all that gives way to a calm spirituality.

Founded in 1313 by Bernardo Tolomei, a scion of one of Siena's richest families, the monastery began as a solitary hermitage in an area so arid it was referred to as a *deserto*. But Bernardo soon drew a large following, and the Olivetan order was recognised by the Pope in 1344. Expanded territory brought wealth that was channelled into embellishing the buildings and creating a library (sadly closed to the public since the theft of some priceless volumes, but you can peek through the exquisite carved wooden doors), though the biggest project was the Saint Benedict fresco cycle. Ghostly white-robed monks greet you as you enter the arcaded cloister, where the Technicolor kicks in again. The panels were painted by Giovanni Antonio Bazzi, better known as Il Sodoma, and Luca Signorelli. The frescoes are fascinating for what you can read between the brushstrokes – Sodoma was a colourful character with a taste for exotic pets and young boys (if Vasari and his nickname are to be believed). Notice the backside views of the saint's younger helpers and other renditions of human anatomy. Outside, a Benedictine gift shop sells home-brewed *amaro* drinks and herbal medicines.

Montalcino

Montalcino produces one of Italy's premier wines, the robust Brunello di Montalcino, whose consistent quality has earned it Italy's highest wine honour: the DOCG seal. Brunello ages in oak for five years to acquire its body and aroma; look out for the 1995 vintage and the highly anticipated 1997 vintage, ready in 2002. If you want younger and less solemn, try the year-old Rosso di Montalcino.

The existence of a hilltop town here can be traced to AD 814, when it was ceded to the nearby Abbey of Sant'Antimo. Under Siena's rule in the 13th century, four families dominated the town's political identity and are represented today in Montalcino's four *contrade*. The town's proudest moment came in 1555, when it became the temporary seat of power of the Sienese Republic (a group of exiled Sienese nobles held out here when Siena fell to Cosimo I de' Medici). Soon after, Montalcino fell on hard times and plague, and until the late 1950s was one of Tuscany's poorest corners. Tourism, olive oil and the mighty Brunello have turned its luck.

All roads in Montalcino lead to piazza del Popolo, the peculiar triangle that marks the heart of the town. This is where you'll find the shield-studded **Palazzo Comunale** (with the tall tower), modelled after Siena's Palazzo Pubblico in 1292. Around the corner, annexed to Sant'Agostino church, is the **Museo Civico** (via Ricasoli 31, 0577 846 014, closed Mon, admission L8,000/€4.10, L10,000/€5.20 with Rocca). Opened in 1997, it features Sano di Pietro's *Madonna dell'Umiltà*, in which the virgin is portrayed kneeling. The Gothic-Romanesque Sant'Agostino (1360) has superb frescoes by Bartolo di Fredi. For a change of pace head to the downright neo-classic **Duomo** (1818-32), built on the site of an older church.

Montalcino may not be quite as stunning as other nearby hilltop towns but it has a laid-back feel and views that extend all the way to Siena on a clear day. Its most rewarding attraction is the **Rocca** (0577 849 211, closed Mon, L5,000/€2.60, L10,000/€5.20 with Museo Civico); built in 1361 on Sienese orders, this fortress remains one of Tuscany's best examples of military architecture. Tickets are sold in the *enoteca* inside the fortress walls, which also offers a wide selection of Brunellos.

Where to eat

Montalcino is where *pici* (thick, flourless, hand-rolled spaghetti) originated. Also try *ossi di morto* – flat almond biscuits that crumble like brittle bones – and, of course, some Brunello. Two top spots for this are the *enotecha* **Fiaschetteria Italiana** (piazza del Popolo 6, 0577 849 043, closed Thur in winter, average L25,000/€13), which is also great for people-watching, and **Bacchus** (Via G Matteotti 15, 0577 847 054, closed Tue, average L20,000/€10.50), which serves plenty of tasty titbits to go with the wine. **Trattoria Sciame** (Via

Ricasoli 9, 0577 848 017, closed Tue, L40,000/€20.50) is especially renowned for its *zuppa di fagioli* (bean soup topped with slivers of red onion and Parmesan).

Where to stay

On the southern edge of town, the three-star **Hotel Vecchia Oliviera** (Porta Cerbaia, 0577 846 028, L160,000-L450,000/€82.50-€232.50) has a pool, a terrace and lovely views over the valley. In town, the **Albergo Il Giglio** (via S Saloni 5, 0577 848 167, rates L80,000-L120,000/€41.50-€62) is a family-run place with 12 frescoed rooms in its main building and an additional five (no bath) next door. The **Hotel Residence Montalcino** (via S Saloni 31, 0577 847 188, L90,000-L150,000/€46.50-€77.50) has clean, comfortable apartments with kitchens.

Tourist information

Ufficio Informazioni
Costa del Municipio (0577 849 331). **Open** 10am-1pm, 2-6pm Tue-Sun.

Abbazia di Sant'Antimo

Sant'Antimo is reached by one of three roads radiating south of Rocca. The sensational country lane snakes through ten kilometres (six miles) of unspoiled landscape and is best appreciated if you have three hours to walk it, leads to an isolated valley.

The Benedictine abbey is built of creamy travertine with translucent alabaster highlights, and it stood empty for 500 years before a handful of French Premonstratensian monks – a Cistercian branch – moved here in 1979. Its founding is attributed to Charlemagne in 781, and it is said to be the first of more than 20 abbeys established by the emperor. In 1118, funds were granted to construct the present church and additional monastic buildings that have since fallen to rubble. This grant was so important that it was literally written in stone – engraved in the steps of the altar.

Thanks to the via Francigena trade route, Sant'Antimo soon grew into a true regional powerhouse, but by the 15th century financial mismanagement saw the beginning of its demise. Over the subsequent years, it fell, leaving Siena to divide up its territory. In 1462 Pope Pio II evicted the remaining monks, citing moral degeneration.

Inside are carvings in onyx and alabaster; don't miss *Daniel in the Lion's* Den (second column from the right of the nave) by an unknown mysterious Spanish carver.

Tuscany

Ancient walls of **Montepulciano**. *See p239.*

Bagno Vignoni

Bagno Vignoni, just south of San Quirico
d'Orcia, has to be seen to be believed. Piazza
delle Sorgenti – its main square – has a large
pool of thermal water at its centre flanked by
a ragged collection of houses along a low
Renaissance loggia. Featured in a memorable
scene in Tarkovsky's *Nostalgia*, it's been off
limits since 1979, after crowds grew too big, but
there's a stream of thermal run-off 200 metres
(220 yards) south that's perfect for soaking tired
feet. The thermal swimming pool of Hotel Posta
Marcucci (*see below*) is open to non-residents.

Where to stay & eat

It's worth coming to Bagno Vignoni just to eat
at the outstanding **Osteria del Leone** (piazza
del Moretto, 0577 887 300, closed Mon, closed
Tue lunch winter, average L45,000/€23). The
popular restaurant has a cosy, rustic feel with
chunky wooden tables, friendly staff and a
daily changing menu that sometimes includes
an excellent suckling pig with fennel flowers.

The choice of hotels is less impressive,
though the modern **Hotel Posta Marcucci**
(via Ara Urcea 43, 0577 887 112, rates L130,000-
L235,000/€67-€121.50) does have an open-air
thermal pool with views across the valley.
Access for non-guests is L12,000 (€6.20) for
a half day; it's especially good at sunset.

Pienza

Pienza was built as an 'ideal humanist city'
and in many ways still is one, though Aeneas
Silvius Piccolomini, the Renaissance humanist
who was elected Pope Pius II in 1458, probably
had something more imposing in mind when he
first gave architect Bernardo Rossellino *carta
bianca* to build here in 1449. Born in backward
Corsignano, Piccolomini apparently had an
inferiority complex because of his insignificant
home town, and dreamed of transforming it into
a utopia of Renaissance principles.

With a lovely setting above the Val d'Orcia
and an intricate series of alleyways, including
several with schmaltzy names such as via di
Bacio ('of kisses') and via del Amor ('of love'),
Pienza is a place to linger.

The focal point is **piazza Pio II**. Stand in its
centre and slowly spin around: everything you
see was either built or reconstructed between
1459 and 1462. The travertine **Duomo** contains
works by Vecchietta and Sano di Pietro in the
side chapels, and a marble altar by Rossellino.
Sadly, in order to grant Pius II's wish of a
luminous south-facing church, it was built on
sandstone and is thus dangerously tilted on
the far end. **Palazzo Piccolomini** (0578
748 503, closed Mon, admission L5,000/€2.60)
was reserved for the pope and modelled after
Alberti's Palazzo Rucellai in Florence. There
are tours of Pius II's lavish private apartments.

Pienza's art collection is kept in the new
Museo Diocesano (0578 749 905, closed
Tue, admission L8,000/€4.10). Highlights are a
golden *Madonna and Child* altarpiece by Pietro
Lorenzetti and some Flemish tapestries.

Where to stay & eat

If you're looking for a place for an unhurried
lunch or dinner, you're likely to be well taken
care of at **Ristorante Il Prato** (viale Santa
Caterina 1/3, 0578 749 924, closed Tue, average
L60,000/€31) just outside the town gates, or
Trattoria Latte di Luna (via San Carlo 6,
0578 748 606, closed Tue, average L45,000/€23)
at the other end of town. The latter has an
outdoor terrace and was a favourite of the
crew during the filming of *The English Patient*.
For a quick refuel, try **Albergo Ristorante il
Garibaldi** (Santa Quirico d'Orcia, 0577 898 315,
closed Wed) in Val d'Orcia. Its unprepossessing
venue – actually, a petrol station – belies its
tasty, simple and reasonably priced cuisine.
It's best offerings are its excellent fish antipasti
and soup at the weekend.

If you weren't thinking of staying the night,
you might change your mind once you've seen
the gorgeous **Hotel Relais Il Chiostro di
Pienza** (corso Rossellino 26, 0578 748 400,
closed early Jan-late Mar, rates L200,000-
L400,000/€103.50-€206.50), housed in a 15th-
century convent overlooking the Orcia valley
and with an inviting pool and a restaurant
(closed lunch Mon, average L100,000/€51.50)
offering refined modern Tuscan cuisine.

Tourist information

Ufficio Informazioni
Palazzo Publico, piazza Po 11 (0578 749 071).
Open 9.30am-1pm, 3-6.30pm daily.

Montepulciano

It's hard to imagine anyone ever voluntarily pushing heavy oak wine barrels up a steep two-kilometre (1 mile) cobblestone in the torrid heat of August, but that's what Montepulciano's proudest menfolk do each year in the highly anticipated Bravio delle Botti (*see below* **Festivals**). During this festival, eight rival *contrade* battle it out for the honour of being the first to roll their barrel to the town's highest point: the best easily complete the task in under ten minutes. The winner is doused in the local wine, Vino Nobile di Montepulciano, and brings glory to his *contrade*.

Montepulciano oozes the philosophy 'no sweat, no glory' – something that's worth keeping in mind during the unrelenting uphill climb (in more like 30 minutes) to the town's core. Your prize is a cool drink on the piazza Grande, where most of the buildings are the legacy of the town's boom years following 1511, when it finally declared its allegiance to Florence after vacillating between it and Siena for more than a century. Eminent architects of the time, including Antonio da Sangallo the Elder and Vignola, were brought in to rework the town's medieval fabric, and some lasting Renaissance monuments were put up. Sangallo was especially active, rebuilding many of the buildings on the central square before excelling himself down at San Biagio.

The best way to see the town is by huffing it up the steep **via di Gracciano del Corso**, which starts near Montepulciano's northern entrance, Porta al Prato. Along the way, the Roman and Etruscan marble plaques cemented into the base of Palazzo Bucelli (No.73) are worth a look. A bit further up, on piazza Michelozzo, you can't help but notice the towering Torre Pulcinella, a clock tower topped by a mechanical Punch. This Bavarian touch was apparently the warped artistic vision of an exiled Neapolitan noble with time on his hands.

Further up, your efforts will be rewarded when you reach **piazza Grande**. This is the town's highest and most beautiful point. The spacious square carpeted with chunky stones is reminiscent of Pienza's 'ideal city' layout. Don't let the rough brick façade of the **Duomo** put you off. Inside is a treasure trove: there's a fine Gothic *Assumption* by Taddeo di Bartolo over the altar (1401), and towards the top of the left of the nave a *Madonna and Child* by Sano di Pietro. Don't overlook, while you're there, the *Ciborium*, a rare marble sculpture by fresco artist Vecchietta. It's tucked away on the right. Finally, though, the highlight of the Duomo is the delicately carved tomb of humanist Aragazzi (1428) by Michelozzo.

Also in the square are Sangallo's Palazzo Tarugi, with loggia; the 13th-century Palazzo Comunale, which deliberately echoes Palazzo Vecchio in Florence; and Palazzo Contucci across the square. Whatever else you see, the pilgrimage church of **San Biagio** 20 minutes' walk from Porta al Prato is a must. Designed by Sangallo and built between 1518 and 1545, this Bramante-influenced study in proportion is a jewel of the High Renaissance.

Where to stay & eat

For drinks or light midday snacks, don't miss **Antico Caffè Poliziano** (via di Voltaia nel Corso 27, 0578 758 615, L65,000/€33.50), an art deco institution and great place to sample Vino Nobile. Below town in San Biagio, there's more substantial fare at **La Grotta San Biagio** (0578 757 607, closed Wed, average L70,000/€36), a former 14th-century staging post where Sangallo ate when working on the church.

Montepulciano doesn't have a huge choice of accommodation. Of those in the centre the **Albergo Il Marzocco** (piazza Savonarola 18, 0578 757 262/fax 0578 757 530, L115,000-L160,000/€60-€82.50), just inside the Porta al Prato in a 16th-century *palazzo*, has some of the most spacious rooms, a few with terraces.

Tourist information

Ufficio Informazioni Pro Loco

Via del Corso 59A (0578 757 341). **Open** *Summer* 9.30am-12.30pm, 3-8pm Mon-Sat; 10am-12.30pm Sun. *Winter* 9.30am-12.30pm, 3-6pm Mon-Sat; 9.30am-12.30pm Sun.

Festivals

In August the **Cantiere Internazionale d'Arte** is a modern music/festival workshop with poetry readings and amateur opera night. The last Sunday in August is the day for barrel-pushing at the **Bravio delle Botti** (*see above*).

Montepulciano's **Antico Caffè Poliziano.**

Lucca

Lucca's sleepy surface belies its stormy history.

The 12th-century **San Frediano**. *See p242.*

Sunken and sheltered behind its magnificently preserved 16th- to 17th-century walls, Lucca is a mystery right up until the moment you walk through one of its six gates. More than in any other Tuscan city, its walls and ramparts are intrinsic to its identity, constantly reminding us of its past glory and reinforcing the lingering mental insulation and traditionalism of the Lucchesi. Healthy neutrality, commercial vigour and careful husbandry have all kept the city in a time warp and ensured that it's one place in Tuscany that other Italians consistently lavish with praise.

But a city can only be commended for so long before it becomes crowded, and though it may not particularly want to take its place on Tuscany's clogged tourist trail – and though queues are still shorter and prices less exorbitant – Lucca is in danger of becoming the region's next big thing.

For the moment, however, a stroll through the pedestrianised streets – the Lucchesi prefer

bicycles to cars – is very rewarding, with a surprise at every corner. The ornate white façades of the Romanesque churches – overplayed **San Michele in Foro**, the glistening mosaic of **San Frediano**, the asymmetrical **Duomo di San Martino** – all appear unexpectedly. The colourful piazza dell'Anfiteatro, which has retained the oval hape of the ancient Roman amphitheatre, opens up through a gate, while the tree-lined ramparts and oak-topped **Torre Guinigi** afford splendid views of the cityscape.

Lucca's flatness and relatively simple grid plan make everything easily accessible. A lovely way to get your bearings is to hire a bike and cycle the four kilometres (2.5 miles) along the top of the city walls (*see p249*).

SOME HISTORY

Possibly the site of a Ligurian and then an Etruscan settlement, Lucca acquired political significance as a Roman municipium in 89BC and hosted the signing of the first triumvirate between Pompey, Caesar and Crassus in 56BC. It was crucially positioned at the crossroads of the empire's communications with its northern reaches, and controlled the Apennine passes along the Serchio valley.

Despite Rome's fall the city continued to maintain its supremacy in Tuscany, first as capital of Tuscia under Lombard rule then as the seat of the Frankish Margravate from AD 774. By the turn of the millennium Lucca had grown into Tuscany's largest city and consolidated itself as a commercial powerhouse thanks to the wool and silk trades and to its command of a strategic juncture of the via Francigena. Wealth engendered commercial rivalry with its upstart neighbours, which soon turned into open military clashes with Pisa and a gradual loss of political dominance to Florence during the drawn-out Guelph/Ghibelline conflict.

The 14th century was turbulent for Lucca: a short-lived heyday as the capital of a mini-empire in western Tuscany under the helm of the *condottiere* Castruccio Castracani (1320-28) soon gave way to a series of set-backs leading to domination by Pisa from 1342. In 1369 Lucca was granted autonomy and independence by Emperor Charles IV of Bohemia; this was to last, unbroken, until 1799.

Lucca

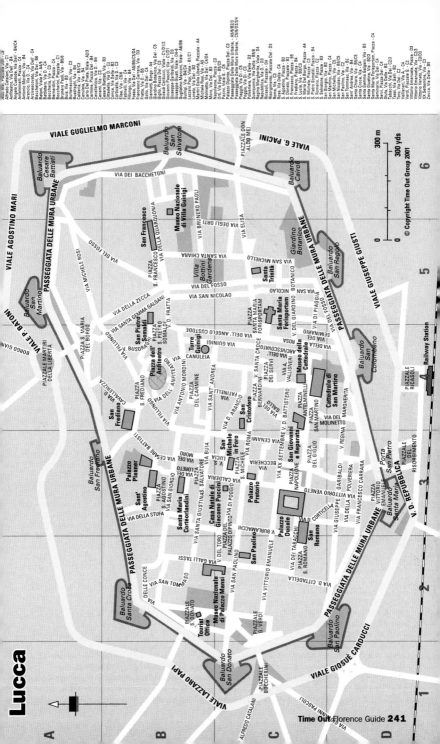

© Copyright Time Out Group 2001

300 m
300 yds

Having renounced claims to regional leadership, Lucca moved into relative obscurity and turned in on itself. An oligarchy of ruling families, foremost among them the Guinigi, tightly controlled all public offices and private wealth and set about enlarging the medieval urban nucleus. In 1805 Lucca passed under the direct rule of Elisa Baciocchi, Napoleon's sister, and then in 1817 to the infanta Maria Luisa di Borbone of Spain. Both did much to recast the city architecturally and patronised a brief but intense period of artistic ferment. In 1847 Lucca was ceded to the Grand Duchy of Tuscany and then joined a united Italy in 1860.

The city's almost uninterrupted history as an opulent, free *comune* has left it largely unaffected by outside developments, both architecturally and psychologically. Indeed, by very literally minding their own business the Lucchesi have stayed both safe and prosperous: in their own, telling, words 'a minuscule and fragile republic entirely dedicated to commerce and defenceless against the uproar of war'.

Sights

Churches

Duomo di San Martino
Piazza San Martino (0583 957 068). **Open** *Summer* 7am-7pm daily. *Winter* 7am-5pm daily. *Sacristy* 10am-5.45pm Mon-Fri; 9.30am-7pm Sat; 9-10am, 1-5pm Sun. **Admission** L3,000 (€1.60). **No credit cards**.
At first glance Lucca's Romanesque cathedral seems somewhat out of kilter and unbalanced. A closer look reveals why: the oddly asymmetrical façade has the arch and the first two series of *logge* on the right literally squeezed and flattened by the campanile. Nobody is really to blame (or commend) for this, as the Lombard bell-tower was erected before the rest of the church in around 1100 and completed only 200 years later. It predates the Duomo, on which work only began in earnest in the 12th century. The asymmetry of the façade, designed by Guidetto da Como, only adds to the overall effect of exuberance and eccentricity provided by the carvings of beasts, dragons and wild animals in the capitals and in the multi-chrome columns.

San Martino's dimly lit interior is broken up midway up the left nave by Matteo Civitali's octagonal marble *Tempietto* (1484), home to a dolorous wooden crucifix known as the *Volto Santo* (Holy Visage), perpetually surrounded by candle-holding worshippers in rapturous devotion. The effigy (what we see is a copy) was supposedly begun by Nicodemus and finished by an angel, set on a pilotless ship from the Orient in the eighth century and brought into Lucca on a cart drawn by steer. This miraculous arrival quickly spawned a cult following and the relic soon became an object of pilgrimage throughout Europe. Nowadays it is draped in silk and gold garments and

ornaments and marched through Lucca's streets in night-time processions on 13 September.

The Duomo's Sacristy contains the other top attraction: the tomb of Ilaria del Carretto (1408), a delicate sarcophagus sculpted by Sienese master Jacopo della Quercia representing the young bride of Paolo Guinigi, Lucca's strongman at the time.

San Francesco
Via della Quarquonia (no phone). **Open** 7.30am-noon, 3-6pm daily. **Admission** free.
The eerie grey interior of this 14th-century barn-shaped church is only slightly lit by light streaming in from the rose window in the façade. San Francesco houses the tombstone (but according to the parish priest not the body) of one of Lucca's greatest sons, 14th-century adventurer Castruccio Castracani, who gave the city its brief glorious age of conquest in the early 1300s. There is also a plaque to Giacomo Puccini; its rather dusty and overblown inscription reads 'artistic great and genius whose exquisitely human art moved and will forever move the entire world'.

San Frediano
Piazza San Frediano (no phone). **Open** 7.30am-noon, 3-6pm daily; 9am-1pm, 3-6pm public hols. **Admission** free.
San Frediano's strikingly resplendent Byzantine-like mosaic façade is unique in Tuscany, rivalled only by that above the choir of San Miniato al Monte in Florence. On this site, a church was founded by Fredian, an Irish monk who settled in Lucca in the sixth century and converted the ruling Lombards by allegedly diverting the River Serchio and saving the city from flooding. This miracle put the finishing touches on Christianity's hold on Lucca and earned Fredian a quick promotion to bishop, eventually leading to canonisation. A few centuries later, in the 1100s, he had this singular church built for him.

Apart from the mosaic, the façade of San Frediano is in the Pisan-Romanesque style of many of Lucca's other churches and was the first to face east. The façade's mosaic is an Ascension in which a monumental Jesus is lifted by two angels over the heads of his jumbled apostles. Inside, immediately on the right, is a small gem: the *fonte lustrale*, or baptismal font, carved by unknown Lombard and Tuscan artists who surrounded the fountain with scenes from the Old and New Testaments. Behind it is a glazed terracotta Ascension by Andrea della Robbia. In the chapel next to it is another of Lucca's revered relics, the miraculously conserved though somewhat shrivelled body of Saint Zita, a humble servant who was canonised in the 13th century and whose mummy is brought out for a close-up view and a touch by devotees on 27 April.

San Giovanni e Reparata
Via del Duomo (0583 490 530). **Open** *Apr-Oct* 10am-6pm daily. *Oct-Apr* call for details. **Admission** L2,000 (€1); L9,000 (€4.70) with Museo

della Cattedrale; L4,000 (€2.10) excavations.
No credit cards.
Originally Lucca's cathedral, the 12th-century basilica of San Giovanni, now part of the Duomo, is on the sight of a pagan temple and according to some also rests on Roman thermal baths. Apart from its magnificently ornate ceiling, the church's main draw is the architectural remains uncovered by excavations in the 1970s, ranging from a mosaic dating back to Imperial Rome to a fifth-century early Christian basilica.

Santa Maria Corteorlandini

*Piazza Giovanni Leonardi (no phone).***Open** 7.30am-noon, 3-6pm daily; 9am-1pm, 3-6pm public hols.
Admission free.
This overwhelming late baroque church is Lucca's odd man out. Its *trompe-l'œil* frescoed roofs, an abundance of coloured marble and the gilded and ornamented tabernacle by local artist Giovanni Vambre (1673) provide a break from the stark and grey interiors of the city's other churches.

Santa Maria Forisportam

Piazza Santa Maria Forisportam (no phone). **Open** 7.30am-noon, 3-6pm daily. **Admission** free.
Set on the square known to Lucchesi as *piazza della colonna mozza* (referring to the truncated column at its centre), Santa Maria takes its name from its location just outside Lucca's older set of walls. The unfinished marble façade dates mostly from the 12th and 13th centuries and is a slightly toned down version of the Pisan-Romanesque style present throughout the city, with lively carvings in the lunettes and architraves above the portals.

San Michele in Foro

Piazza San Michele (no phone). **Open** 7.30am-12.30pm, 3-6pm daily. **Admission** free.
San Michele's façade is a feast for the eyes. Set on the site of the ancient Roman forum, Lucca's consummate take on the Pisan-Romanesque style is one of the city's most memorable sights. Each element lightly plays off against the other: the knotted, twisted and carved columns with their psychedelic geometric designs, the fantastical animals and fruit and floral motifs in the capitals. The façade culminates in a winged and stiff Saint Michael precariously perched while vanquishing the dragon. San Michele's sombre interior contrasts sharply with its façade. On the right as you enter is a *Madonna and Child* by Matteo Civitali – a copy of the original is on the church's right-hand outside corner. Further on is Filippino Lippi's *Saints Jerome, Sebastian, Rocco and Helena*, all of whom helped the Madonna deliver Lucca from the plague in 1480.

San Paolino

*Via San Paolino (no phone).***Open** 7.30am-6pm daily.
Admission free.
Giacomo Puccini received his baptism of fire here in 1881, with his first public performance of the *Mass for Four Voices*. San Paolino had, in fact, always been the Puccini family's second home, with five generations of them serving as its organists. Built from 1522 to 1536 for Lucca's patron St Paulinus, who allegedly came over from Antioch in AD 65 and became the city's first bishop and whose remains are buried in a sarcophagus behind the altar, it's Lucca's only example of late Renaissance architecture.

The memorable **San Michele in Foro** is on the site of the ancient Roman forum.

Museums

Casa Natale di Giacomo Puccini

Corte San Lorenzo 9, off Via di Poggio (0583 584 028). **Open** *Mar-May & Oct-Dec* 10am-1pm, 3-6pm Tue-Sun. *June-Sept* 10am-6pm daily. *Jan & Feb* Closed. **Admission** L5,000 (€2.60); L3,000 (€1.60) under-14s and groups of 10 and over. **No credit cards**.

The birthplace of Lucca's most famous son (*see p244*) has been turned into a charming museum that offers some interesting insights into his sheltered youth, turbulent private life and artistic genius. The rooms include such memorabilia as the original librettos of his early operas *Mass for Four Voices* and *Symphonie Caprice*, his private letters on subjects both musical and sentimental, the piano on which he composed *Turandot* and the gem-encrusted costume used in the opera's American debut in 1926.

Museo della Cattedrale

Via Arcivescovado (0583 490 530). **Open** *May-Oct* 10am-6pm daily. *Nov-Apr* 10am-2pm Mon-Fri; 10am-6pm Sat, Sun. **Admission** L6,000 (€3.10); L9,000 (€4.70) including San Giovanni. **No credit cards**.

Many of the treasures from the Duomo di San Martino and from nearby San Giovanni (*see p242*) have been transferred and arranged in strict chrono-logical order in this well-curated museum displaying everything from the cathedral's furnishings, its gold and silverware to its sculptures, including Jacopo della Quercia's splendid *Apostle*.

Museo Nazionale di Palazzo Mansi

Via Galli Tassi 43 (0583 55570). **Open** 9am-7pm Tue-Sat; 9am-2pm Sun. **Admission** L8,000 (€4.10); free concessions; L12,000 (€6.20) including Villa Guinigi. **No credit cards**.

The 16th- to 17th-century *palazzo* that hosts this collection of mostly Tuscan art is Lucca's most remarkable example of baroque exaggeration. While the frescoed Salone della Musica and the neo-classical Salone degli Specchi are still light on the eye, the overindulgence climaxes in the Camera della Sposa, an over-the-top bridal chamber with a *baldacchino* bed. The largely uninspiring artwork includes samples from the Venetian school with lesser-known works by Tintoretto and Tiziano and some Flemish tapestries. Perhaps Palazzo Manzi's best draw is Pontormo's Manneristic portrait of his nasty patron Alessandro de' Medici.

Museo Nazionale di Villa Guinigi

Via della Quarquonia (0583 496 033). **Open** 9am-7pm Tue-Sat; 9am-2pm Sun. **Admission** L8,000

Who they? Puccini

Though in recent times Lucca has played up its link with Giacomo Puccini of *La Bohème*, *Tosca* and *Madama Butterfly* fame, the great composer was not always seen in a favourable light by his fellow citizens. Born in nearby Celle in 1858 but raised in Lucca, Puccini had a restlessness that kept him elsewhere for most of his career, and his non-conformist attitude, artistic unpredictability and unrepentant womanising made him enemies among Lucca's staid upper echelons.

A recalcitrant student, he was persuaded to study composing through spending time with his music teacher and surrogate father Carlo Angeloni, though their conversations revolved more around wildlife hunting (Puccini's other great passion). When he went to study at Milan's conservatoire in 1880 his secluded petit-bourgeois lifestyle – he was the last in a long family line of organists and composers –

quickly turned to bohemian poverty, but, following some flops, he had a big break in 1893, when he committed to music the tragedy of Manon Lescaut.

The success put him on his feet financially, allowing him to create a private hunting Eden at Torre del Lago on Lake Massaciuccioli, where he remained for most of the rest of his life. Creative serenity brought box-office hits flowing from his fingertips, but emotionally his life was a roller-coaster: he fathered a son with a married woman, Elvira Bonturi, and continued to depend upon her despite countless other escapades, including a notorious love affair with flashy German baroness Josephine von Stangel, which was consummated in the pine forests of his beloved Torre del Lago.

He wrote libretti right up until his death in Brussels in 1924, when he was still working on the unfinished *Turandot*.

Say cheese! The **Cacioteca** is the place to head for an aromatic Pecorino. *See p246.*

(€4.10); L4,000 (€2.10) concessions; L12,000 (€6.20) with Palazzo Manzi. **No credit cards**.

This porticoed pink-brick villa (1403-20) surrounded by greenery was erected at the height of rule by Lucca's 'enlightened despot' Paolo Guinigi and now houses art from Lucca and its region. The first floor has a recently expanded selection of Roman and Etruscan finds and some 13th- and 14th-century capitals and columns by Guidetto da Como taken from the façade of San Michele in Foro (*see p243*). The rooms upstairs start with 13th-century painted crucifixes and wooden tabernacles. The highlights, though, are Matteo Civitali's *Annunciation*, impressive altarpieces by Amico Aspertini and Fra Bartolomeo and the *intarsia* panels by Ambrogio and Nicolao Pucci.

Monuments

Ramparts

Lucca's defining landmark, *le nostre mura* – as the Lucchesi adoringly call them – are among Italy's best-preserved and most impressive city fortifications. Built in the 16th and 17th centuries, they're 12m (40ft) in height and 30m (100ft) across, with a circumference of just over 4km (2.5 miles), and are punctuated by 11 sturdy bastions, meant to ward off the most heavily armed of invaders. A proper siege, though, has never occurred, and the only real use the ramparts got was in 1812 when they allowed the city to hermetically close itself off to floodwaters. Soon after, Maria Luisa di Borbone turned them into a public park and promenade, dotting them with plane, holm-oak, chestnut and lime trees. Today, Lucchesi flock there to picnic, cuddle or stroll and take in the views.

Torre Guinigi

Via Sant'Andrea 42 (0583 48524). **Open** *Nov-Feb* 10am-4.30pm daily. *Mar-Sept* 9am-7.30pm daily. *Oct* 10am-6pm daily. **Admission** L6,000 (€3.10); L4,000 (€2.10) concessions. **No credit cards**.

The 14th-century, 44m (145ft) high Torre Guinigi offers spectacular panoramic views over Lucca's rooftops and on to the countryside past the walls.

Parks & gardens

Giardino Botanico

Via del Giardino Botanico 14 (0583 442 160). **Open** *Summer* 9am-1pm Mon-Fri; 9am-1pm, 3.30-6.30pm Sat, Sun. *Winter* 9am-1pm Mon-Sat. **Admission** L5,000 (€2.60); free-L3,500 concessions. **No credit cards**.

The Giardino Botanico are set up against the city walls. The greenhouse and arboretum are planted with a wide and imoressive range of Tuscan flora and provide Lucca's greenest and most exotic spot for a romantic stroll.

Palazzo Pfanner

Via degli Asili 33 (0583 491243). **Open** *Mar-mid Nov* 10am-6pm daily. *Nov-Feb* by appointment. **Admission** L3,000 (€1.60); free under-8s.

The statues in this *palazzo*'s interior courtyard are a well-known Luccan landmark, as is the open-air marble staircase. Both can also be viewed from the walls above. The 18th-century palazzo itself, though, is perennially under restoration.

Shopping

Lucca's main shopping artery is via Fillungo, a twisting showcase of art nouveau façades.

The town's general market is held on via dei Bacchettoni by the eastern wall on Wednesdays and Saturdays, selling clothes, food, flowers and household goods.

There's an antiques market in piazza San Martino and surrounding streets on the third weekend of each month and a crafts market (*arti e mestieri*) in piazza San Giusto on the last weekend of the month.

La Bottega di Mamma Rò

Piazza Anfiteatro 4 (0583 492 607). **Open** 3.30-8pm Mon; 9.30am-8pm Tue-Sat & 3rd Sun of month. **Credit** AmEx, DC, JCB, MC, V.

Hand-painted ceramics, hand-dipped candles and bright country cotton fabrics.

Tuscany

Cacioteca

Via Fillungo 242 (0583 496 346). **Open** 7am-1.30pm, 3.30-8.30pm Mon, Tue, Thur-Sat; 7am-1.30pm Wed. **Credit** MC, V.

An intense waft of seasoned cheese emanates from this inconspicuous but well-known specialist. Typical products from the Garfagnana include the pecorino *in barile* (in a barrel).

DelicaTezze di Roberto Isola

Via San Giorgio 5 (0583 492 633). **Open** 7am-1pm, 3.30-7.30pm Mon, Tue, Thur-Sat; 8am-1pm Wed. **Credit** AmEx, DC, MC, V.

This excellent deli has a great selection of home-made ravioli and tortelli, olive oils, *farro*, porcini and cheeses. There's also a constant choice of wine, cheese and cold cuts ready for tasting.

La Grotta

Piazza Anfiteatro 2 (0583 467 595). **Open** 8am-2pm, 4.30-8.30pm Mon-Fri; 8am-2pm Sat. **Credit** AmEx, MC, V.

Among Lucca's oldest *insaccatori* ('sausage baggers'), La Grotta is located in what used to be salt storage caves. Peppered Tuscan prosciutti are lined up alongside a Lucchese peculiarity known as *birol-do* – salami made of pig's blood with raisins. Closes on Wednesday afternoon out of season.

Panificio Amedeo Giusti

Via Santa Lucia 18/20 (0583 496 285). **Open** 7am-1pm, 4-7.45pm Mon, Tue, Thur-Sat; 7am-1pm Wed. **No credit cards.**

The city's best bakery is an institution, with customers elbowing each other to get to both savoury and sweet confections. Closes early and on Saturday afternoons in summer.

Vini Liquori Vanni

Piazza del Salvatore 7 (0583 491 902). **Open** 4-8pm Mon; 9am-1pm, 4.30-8pm Tue-Sat. **Credit** AmEx, DC, MC, V.

This enoteca's seemingly endless cellar, recently renovated for the first time in 30 years, is a treasure for those seeking out Lucca's better vintages. Call ahead and book a wine lesson and *degustazione*, plus a mini-tour of this 13th-century *cantina*. Local wines to sample from the Colline Lucchesi and Montecarlo regions include Maiolina, Tenuta da Valgiano, Michi and Fattoria Colleverde.

Vintage Lucca – **Vini Liquori Vanni**.

La Buca di Sant'Antonio

Via della Cervia 3 (0583 55881). **Open** 12.30-2.30pm, 7.30-11pm Tue-Sat; 11am-3pm Sun. **Average** L50,000-L60,000 (€26-€31). **Credit** AmEx, DC, MC, V.

A Lucca fixture, La Buca is located in a restored 19th-century hostelry steps away from San Michele and serves traditional fare with the occasional innovative touch. Soups include a Lucca classic *mines-tra di farro alla Garfagnana*, while among the primi is *tordelli lucchesi* (huge tortelloni). The *capretto allo spiedo* (spit-roasted kid) is a handsome *secondo*.

Da Giulio in Pelleria

Via della Conce 45 (0583 55948). **Open** noon-3pm, 7-10.30pm Tue-Sat & 3rd Sun of month. **Average** L30,000 (€15.50). **Credit** AmEx, DC, MC, V.

One of Lucca's best-known haunts, Da Giulio is a vast trattoria with a huge following, though its staff are not always the most courteous. Typical, good-value Tuscan dishes include the age-old Lucchese dish *la concia* (chitterlings) and more mainstream primi such as *gnocchetti al pomodoro* and a *rustic pollo al mattone* (brick-roasted chicken).

Da Guido

Via Cesare Battisti 28 (0583 467 219). **Open** noon-2.30pm, 7.30-10pm Mon-Sat. **Average** L20,000 (€10.50). **Credit** AmEx, MC, V.

'Prezzi modicissimi' ('unbeatable prices') is Da Guido's watchword, but this wood-panelled trattoria is a Lucca favourite more for its reliably good food and the warm welcome proffered by the Barsotti brothers. Dishes such as *Zuppa di farro*, home-rolled *tortelli al ragú* and *coniglio alla cac-ciatora* (roast rabbit) fill the belly without voiding the wallet. For dessert, try the Lucchese *torta di verdure* (sweet spinach cake).

Where to eat & drink

Restaurants

The nearby Garfagnana valley contributes many prime ingredients to Lucca's cuisine, including chestnut flour, river trout, olive oil and above all *farro,* the spelt grain made into soup, which pops up on every menu. The signature sweet is *buccellato*, a doughnut-shaped sweet bread flavoured with aniseed and raisins and topped with sugar syrup.

Da Leo

Via Tegrimi 1 (0583 492 236). **Open** noon-2.30pm, 7.30-10.30pm Mon-Sat. **Average** L30,000 (€15.50). **No credit cards.**

Da Leo's din can be heard in the street. The regulars squeezed into its main room are well served by a changing menu with *primi* such as *farinata Garfagnana* (similar to a *ribollita* with cornflour) and *secondo* such as *rosticciana in umido* (small chunks of stewed pork and olives in a tomato sauce). Don't worry if while you're devouring the delicious fruit tiramisù you feel a paw on your lap – Da Leo's black dog Nerina does the rounds at dessert time.

Gli Orti di Via Elisa

Via Elisa 17 (0583 491 241). **Open** 12.30-2.30pm, 7.30-10.30pm Mon, Tue, Fri-Sun; 7.30-10.30pm Thur (pizzeria till 11.30pm). **Average** L25,000 (€13). **Credit** AmEx, MC, V.

A good lunch spot if you're at Lucca's eastern end, with a self-service salad bar, simple but filling pastas and pizzas and odd grilled meat *secondi*.

Locanda Buatino

Borgo Giannotti 508, nr piazzale Martiri della Libertà (0583 343 207). **Open** noon-2pm, 7.30pm-10pm Mon-Sat. **Average** L25,000 (€13). **Credit** MC, V.

If you only have time for one meal, step outside Lucca's walls into this *locanda*, the city's most memorable inn and eaterie. Il Buatino originally fed farmers from the Garfagnana in town for the local agricultural market. Today, owner Giuseppe Ferrua serves inventive Tuscan food at great value for money. There's the odd ethnic food night, too.

La Mora

Località Ponte a Moriano, Via Sesto di Moriano 1748, Sesto di Moriano (0583 406 402). **Open** noon-2.30pm, 7.30-10pm Mon, Tue, Thur-Sun. **Average** L65,000 (€33.50). **Credit** AmEx, DC, MC, V.

Culinary heavyweight Sauro Brunicardi has turned this old post-house 10km (6.25 miles) north of Lucca into a regionally renowned osteria where you can eat outside in refined surroundings. Look out for *cacciucco di pesce d'aqua dolce* (freshwater fish chowder), *piccione in casseruola* (pigeon casserole) and some terribly tempting desserts. La Mora also has a good list of wines from the nearby Lucchese hills.

Osteria Baralla

Via Anfiteatro 5-9 (0583 440 240). **Open** 12.30-2.30pm, 7.30-10.30pm Mon-Sat & 3rd Sun of month. **Average** L30,000-L35,000 (€15.50-€18). **Credit** AmEx, DC, MC, V.

Recently re-opened, Baralla is a hit with the locals, offering lighter fare such as an antipasto of *spuntini Toscani* or a *minestra frantoiana* (with mixed veg and herbs) and excellent grilled meats. To finish off there's a crumbling dark chocolate *crostata*.

Ristorante Puccini

Corte San Lorenzo 1/2, off Piazza Cittadella (0583 316 116). **Open** *Summer* noon-3pm, 7-10.30pm Mon, Thur-Sun; 7-10.30pm Tue, Wed. *Winter* noon-3pm, 7-10.30pm Mon, Thur-Sun; 7-10.30pm Wed. **Average** L65,000 (€33.50). **Credit** AmEx, DC, MC, V.

Set in the city's 'Puccini corner', this classy restaurant with outdoor seating is Lucca's best bet for fish.

Pizza

Tuscany isn't really known for its pizza, but Lucca's tradition of immigrants from the south has spawned two places worthy of mention: **Da Felice** (via Buia 12, 0583 494 986, closed Sun) close to San Michele is great for a crispy, tasty slice on the run, while **La Sbragia** (via Fillungo 144/146, 0583 492 641, closed Mon) towards the top end of Lucca's main shopping artery is popular for both sit-down and takeaway pizza.

Bars, cafés & *gelaterie*

If you're in Lucca for the nightlife, you'll be disappointed: the big nightspots are out towards the Versilia coast. The closest is **Riva Marina** (Bar Casina Rossa, via Sarzanese 1978, 4km towards Viareggio, 0583 327 732), an expansive 1960s disco with eaterie and swimming pool that has recently reacquired its past fame.

Antico Caffè della Mura

Piazzale Vittorio Emanuele 2 (0583 467 962). **Open** 12-2.30pm, 8-10pm Mon, Thur-Sun; 8-10pm Wed. **Average** L70,000 (€36). **Credit** AmEx, JCB, MC, V.

Overlooking Lucca from its ramparts, the Antico Caffè have a slightly stuffy atmosphere but wonderful outdoor tables, and it's open late in summer.

Bar San Michele

Piazza San Michele 1 (0583 55387). **Open** *Summer* 7.30am-8pm daily. *Winter* 7.30am-8pm Mon-Sat. **No credit cards.**

Facing San Michele and the morning sun, this bar is great for people-watching.

Caffè di Simo

Via Fillungo 58 (0583 496 234). **Open** *Bar* 7.30am-midnight Tue-Sun. *Restaurant* noon-3pm Tue-Sun. **Average** L30,000 (€15.50). **Credit** AmEx, MC, V.

Lucca's ultimate belle époque *café-pasticceria*, whose early 20th-century habitués included poet Pascoli and composers Mascagni and Puccini, is worth the expense. There's a clubby feel and excellent pastries.

Casali

Piazza San Michele 40 (0583 492 687). **Open** *summer* 7am-11pm daily. *Winter* 7am-8.30pm Tue, Thur-Sun. **Credit** MC, V.

With a view across the piazza, Casali is perfect for aperitifs outdoors in the early evening.

Gelateria Veneta

Chiasso Barletti 23 (0583 493 727). **Open** 11am-midnight Mon, Wed-Sun. **Closed** Jan & Feb. **No credit cards.**

This venerated gelateria has set Lucca's ice-cream standards for 150 years.
Branch: Via Vittorio Veneto 74 (0583 467 037).

Tuscany

Where to stay

You can count the hotels within Lucca's walls on the fingers of one hand, and there are no signs that this is going to change in a hurry, since Lucchesi like it that way and have no intention of turning their precious city into an appendage of the overcrowded Versilia coast.

Diana

Via del Molinetto 11 (0583 492 202/fax 0583 467 795). **Rates** single L70,000 (€36); double L105,000 (€54). **Credit** AmEx, DC, MC, V.
Small but conveniently located between the cathedral of San Martino and the train station, Diana is a good option if you're looking for something within easy walking distance of the sights.

Locanda Buatino

Borgo Giannotti 508 (0583 343 207/fax 0583 343 298). **Rates** *single* L50,000 (€26); *double* L75,000 (€38.50). **Credit** MC, V.
Even in a land as tradition-bound as Tuscany and a city as set in its ways as Lucca, the *locande* (hostelries that used to provide well-deserved rest and food for local farmers) have gradually disappeared, leaving just the Buatino. A few minutes to the north of the city walls, its five rooms are as welcoming as they come, and there's the bonus of a terrific restaurant downstairs (*see p247*). For breakfast try the pastries at L'Angolo Dolce (closed Mon) just across the street.

Locanda L'Elisa

Via Nuova per Pisa 1952, Massa Pisana (0583 379 737/fax 0583 379 019/locanda.elisa@lunet.it). **Rates** *single* L330,000-L360,000 (€170.50-€186); *double*
L450,000-L520,000 (€232.50-€268.50); *suite* L490,000-L790,000 (€253-€408). **Credit** AmEx, DC, MC, V.
In a league of its own, this elegant five-star hotel 4km (2.5 miles) south of Lucca is one of the region's best. The villa's current appearance dates back to 1805, when Napoleon's sister and Lucca's ruler Elisa Baciocchi had the interiors and gardens refashioned. Highlights include a restaurant modelled after an English conservatory, 18th-century furnishings, revamped gardens and a large swimming pool.

La Luna

Corte Compagni 12 (0583 493 634/fax 0583 490 021). **Rates** *single* L120,000 (€62); *double* L180,000 (€93); *suite* L280,000 (€144.50). **Credit** AmEx, DC, MC, V.
Easily the best bargain in this price range, with a great location at the upper end of busy Via Fillungo and 30 welcoming rooms, La Luna is set in two 17th-century *palazzi* facing each other across a courtyard.

Palazzo Alexander

Via Santa Giustina 48 (0583 583571/fax 0583 583610/info@palazzoalexander.it). **Rates** single L200,000 (€103.50); double L290,000 (€150). **Credit** AmEx, DC, V, MC.
New upmarket B&B promising comfort and elegance.

Piccolo Hotel Puccini

Via di Poggio 9 (0583 55421/fax 0583 53487). **Rates** *single* L100,000 (€51.50); *double* L140,000 (€72.50). **Credit** AmEx, DC, MC, V.
Paces away from Puccini's boyhood home, this is a wonderfully cosy *pensione* with helpful English-speaking staff, great views from most rooms and, of course, Puccini memorabilia. Book ahead.

Reflecting badly

There's one proverb that sums up the communal rivalries that form the backbone of Tuscan history and identity better than any other: 'meglio un morto in casa che un Pisano all'uscio' ('better a death in the family than a Pisan on your doorstep'). The macabre expression was coined in Lucca, though it's been happily adopted in Livorno, Florence and elsewhere. Its origins are unclear, but there's a historical anecdote that would seem to justify it.

In 1288, following decades of taunts and threats, Lucca lashed out in an uncharacteristic fit of aggression and conquered the Pisan fort of Asciano, erecting four massive mirrors on its walls so that the Pisans could reflect on their defeat. Pisa got its own back in 1313 when Ghibelline leader Uguccione della Faggiuola besieged Lucca and called a truce before invading so that he

could set up two huge mirrors of his own on Lucca's walls, to the same ends.

Lucca's Guelph leadership was relieved to have avoided an invasion and swallowed the humiliation, but the squabbles didn't stop there: the terms of the truce required Lucca to embrace all its Ghibelline outcasts. Among these was Castruccio Castracani, a long-exiled, canny adventurer in search of a power base. His rise to power required ridding Lucca of its Guelph dominion, so he struck a Trojan horse-style secret deal with Uguccione and opened up Lucca's gates one night.

What followed was a week of rampaging and bloodshed in which Lucca's Guelphs were all but eliminated. Setting aside any Ghibelline loyalties, Castracani went on to subdue Uguccione and most of western Tuscany. Never again did a Pisan pass through Lucca's gates unnoticed.

Rex

Piazza Ricasoli 19 (0583 955 443/fax 0583 954 348). **Rates** *single* L130,000 (€67); *double* L180,000 (€93). **Credit** AmEx, DC, MC, V.

Just outside the walls by the train station, this modern hotel has air-conditioned rooms, minibars, cable and satellite TV and unfriendly staff.

Universo

Piazza del Giglio 1 (0583 493 678/fax 0583 954 854). **Rates** *single* L160,000-L220,000 (€82.50-€113.50); *double* L260,000-L290,000 (€134.50-€150). **Credit** MC, V.

The choice in Lucca for many years, the Universo feels like it belongs in an Eastern European capital, yet even the crumbling fixtures and confused staff don't detract from its retro charm.

Essentials

Getting there & around

By air

Lucca has its own small airport (0583 936 062) but it's more easily reached from Tuscany's main airport at Pisa, which has a train link (journey 30/50mins).

By bicycle

The largest concentration of bike hire shops is in piazza Santa Maria; try **Cicli Bizzarri** at No.32 (0583 496 031) or **Poli Antonio** at No.42 (0583 493 787). Elsewhere, there's **Barbetti** at via Anfiteatro 23 (0583 954 444). Standard hire rate is L4,000 (€2.10) per hour, L20,000 (€10.50) per day.

By bus

The bus station is at piazzale Guiseppe Verdi. **CLAP** operates buses to towns in Lucca province (0583 587 897). **LAZZI** run buses to Florence, Pisa, Bagni di Lucca, Montecatini and Viareggio (0583 584 876). At least one bus an hour leaves Florence for Lucca (first 5.58am; last 8.15pm) and from Lucca to Florence (first 6.25am; last 7.45pm). The journey takes around 1hr 15min.

By car

To hire a car contact **Europcar** (0583 464 590), **Hertz** (via Catalani 59, 0583 53535) or **Nolo Auto Pittore** (piazza Santa Maria 34, 0583 467 960). Within the city walls parking is expensive, and free only for hotel guests, but there's a spacious free car park just outside the walls past Porta San Donato.

By taxi

There are radio taxi ranks at piazza Napoleone (0583 492 691) and the train station (0583 494 989).

By train

Lucca's train station is at piazza Ricasoli (0583 467 013), 2mins' walk from the southern gate, Porta San Pietro. Trains from Florence to Viareggio stop at Lucca (as well as Prato and Pistoia). The trip from Florence takes about 1hr 20min, with trains leaving almost every hour from early morning to 10pm. For train info phone 848 888088.

Tranquil side streets abound in Lucca.

Tourist information

Azienda di Promozione Turistica (APT)

Piazza Santa Maria 35 (0583 91991/ www.lucca.turismo.toscana.it). **Open** 9am-7pm daily. The useful 'My Guide' audio commentary on the city, which has a suggested itinerary, costs L10,000 (€5.20) for three and a half hours.

Branch: piazzale Giuseppe Verdi, near Vecchia Porta San Donato (0583 419 689; recorded info in English).

Festivals

Notable festivals include the **Santa Zita** flower show and market (4 days end Apr); a **summer music festival** in piazza Anfiteatro (July); the **Luminara di San Paolino**, a torchlit procession celebrating Lucca's patron saint (11 July); the **Luminara de Santa Croce** procession of the Volte Santo (13 Sept), the cultural, religious and sporting events of **Settembre Lucchese** (Sept, Oct) and the **Natale Anfiteatro** Christmas market.

What's on

The English-language monthly *Grapevine* has news and info on what's happening in the Lucca area.

Useful addresses

Hospital

Campo di Marte hospital on Via dell'Ospedale (0583 9701) has an emergency department.

Police station

Viale Cavour 38, near the train station (0583 4541).

Post office

Via Vallisneri 2, near the Duomo.

Tuscany

Massa-Carrara & Lucca Provinces

From bump and grind on the coastal strip to the tranquil valleys behind.

Massa-Carrara and Lucca provinces couldn't be further apart in spirit, though they sit side by side, with only the Alpi Apuane mountain range between them. Massa-Carrara is a stretch of all-night discos, bikini-clad bodies, bumper-to-bumper traffic and industry. Ancient trade routes such as the via Aurelia have been on the map since Roman times, and today much of the Italian peninsula's north–south traffic passes through here. Lucca, meanwhile, an Alpine wonderland with snow-capped peaks and valleys full of chestnut trees, is one of Italy's least-explored regions.

Fishy goings on at **Viareggio**.

The Versilia Riviera

This belt of sand, bathing establishments and traffic, which extends from the Ligurian border (north) to Viareggio (south), is heavily industrialised and littered with huge blocks of unfinished Carrara marble awaiting export.

For info on Verisilia's gay scene, *see p169*.

Viareggio

Viareggio's main attractions are its beach and palm-tree lined promenade flanked by art deco villas and outdoor cafés. Summer nights pulsate to the sound of techno, and party-goers crowd the mega-clubs; Florence's club scene virtually transplants itself here in summer. By day the *stabilimenti balneare* (bathing establishments) are full of sun-worshippers. One of Europe's first *stabilimenti*, the Balena, was founded here in 1827: it was recently modernised to include a bigger pool, massage rooms and an underground sports centre. The 130-year-old *carnevale*, held around February, is one of Italy's wildest (*see p158*). A new **Carnival Town** (Magazeno village, 0584 962 568) was due to open out towards Camaiore during 2001, featuring hangars full of old *carnevale* floats, an arena for shows, a multimedia museum and a papier mâché school. Ring for opening times or check out www.viareggio.ilcarnevale.com.

Six kilometres (four miles) south of town is the reed-fringed Lago di Massaciuccoli. On its

shore is **Torre del Lago Puccini**, where the composer spent his summers. The villa is open to visitors (0584 341 445, closed Mon, L7,000/€3.60), but it contains little of interest. During the first week of August the town hosts an outdoor Puccini festival (*see p156*).

Nightlife

A good meeting spot for pre-club drinks is **Il Giardino** (via IV Novembre, Forte dei Marmi, 0584 81462, closed Tue); it's popular with twentysomething *figli di papa* (rich kids who cruise around in Daddy's car) but the garden makes up for this. A beer at the bar is L4,000 (€2.10); seated it's L6,000 (€3.10).

La Capannina (viale Franceschi, Forte dei Marmi, 0584 80169, closed Mon-Thur & Sun spring & autumn, Mon-Fri & Sun winter, L40,000/€20.50 including 1st drink) attracts clubbers of all ages. Next to the sea (but without access to the beach) and Versilia's oldest and most revered club, it has two dancefloors that are packed all summer. **La Cannicia** (via Unità d'Italia 1, Marina di Pietrasanta, 0584 745 685, closed Mon-Wed in summer, Mon-Thur & Sun in winter, L30,000/€15.50 including 1st drink) has a huge garden, walkways, a lake and a dancefloor under a gazebo. There are three bars and a late-night restaurant. Located on the beach, **Seven Apple** (viale Roma, Marina di Pietrasanta, 0584 20458, closed Mon-Thur, L30,000/€15.50 including 1st drink), is Versilia's trendiest club. There's an outdoor bar with tables straddling a swimming pool, and two floors of dancing.

Where to stay & eat

Viareggio has more than 100 hotels, but rooms are hard to find in high season. Try via Vespucci, via Leonardo da Vinci and via IV Novembre, which run from the station down to the sea. Places that stand out are **Hotel Garden** (via Ugo Foscolo 70, 0584 44025, rates L125,000-L200,000/€64.50-€103.50), a glorious Liberty-style building with 40 rooms, and **Hotel Plaza et de Russie** (piazza d'Azeglio 1, 0584 44449/fax 0584 44031, rates L225,000-L430,000/€116-€222), offering *fin de siècle* luxury in a refurbished 19th-century building with chandeliers and a roof garden.

With its huge portions and low prices, fish restaurant **La Darsena** (via Virgilio 150, 0584 392 785, closed Sun, L45,000/€23) in the backstreets behind the boatyards, attracts dock workers and other locals. The mixed antipasti consists of piscine delights such as stuffed mussels, while *primi* include taglierini with red mullet. **Osteria No.1** (via Pisano 140, 0584 388 967, closed Wed, L35,000/€18) is another fantastic fish joint on a quiet street on the outskirts of town, towards Torre del Lago. Dishes include the unique *seppie stufate con le bietole* (squid stuffed with a sour, spinach-like vegetable) and giant grilled shrimps.

Gelateria Mario (via Petrolini 1, 0584 961 349, closed Mon-Fri in winter) is deservedly popular – it serves the best ice-cream in town, plus superb fruit-based sorbets.

Pietrasanta

Carrara is home to the raw material itself but Pietrasanta ('holy stone') is where artists transform the famous marble. In fact, this beach town is full of studios where sculptors work with marble, bronze and clay and in summer piazza Duomo becomes an open-air exhibition space for artists to display work against the splendid backdrop of the 13th-century cathedral and the Rocca Arrighina (the citadel up the hill). Wandering through the backstreets you'll see modern-day Michelangelos with newspaper hats (which absorb sweat but filter fine marble dust).

Try the speciality *Bersagliere* (white wine with a splash of Campari) while you're here.

Massa & Carrara

Locked between the sea and the Apuane Alps, these twin cities are barely distinguishable from the mesh of industry and traffic that congest the area, but where Massa is of little interest, Carrara is a marble mecca for sculpture enthusiasts. Throughout the year, the steep ridges of the mountains flanking the town glow brilliant white with the world's largest concentration of pure marble. The ancient Romans mined here and built most of their Imperial City with it, while these days Carrara marble lines the lobby of the World Trade Center in New York.

Michelangelo considered Carrara's marble the purest and whitest in the world. Its greatest asset, according to artists, is that it reflects light off its thinnest outer layer, giving the stone a translucent, wax-like lustre. Carrara mines less marble these days, but about 1.5 million tonnes are extracted from the nearby hills each year.

The town itself has a downbeat feel. **Piazza Alberica**, its most attractive square, is lined with pastel-coloured buildings and has a lion fountain in the middle. Off its north-east end, via Ghibellina opens up to a seductive view of the 11th-century Duomo with its Pisan façade and 14th-century rose window carved from a single slab of marble.

For the quarries, take the scenic route, marked *Strada panoramica per le cave*, towards Colonnata. Three kilometres (two miles) out of town in the village of Stadio, the **Museo Civico del Marmo** (viale XX Settembre, 0585 845 746, closed Sun, L6,000/€3.10) has displays on marble history and production.

Essentials

Getting there

By bus

CLAP buses (0584 53704) service Viareggio and link the city several times a day with Pietrasanta and Lucca. **LAZZI** buses (0584 46234) run between Viareggio and Florence (journey time 2hrs).

By car

Both the main A12 coastal autostrada and via Aurelia (SS1, very busy in summer) run through the entire Versilia area, and Viareggio, Pietrasanta and Carrara are all accessible via the autostrada. Another autostrada (A11) in turn links the Versilia with Lucca (about 30min) and other cities inland.

By train

Viareggio is linked to Florence (100-120min) by regular trains on the Lucca (20min) line. Trains between Pisa and Genoa also pass through the Versilia, stopping at Viareggio (20min from Pisa), Pietrasanta (35min) and Carrara-Avenza (a bus ride from Carrara, 50min from Pisa).

Tourist information

Agenzia per il Turismo (APT)

Viale Carducci 26, Viareggio (0584 962 233/ www.versilia.turismo.toscana.it). **Open** *Summer* 9am-1pm, 4-7pm Mon-Sat. *Winter* 9am-1pm, 3-6pm Mon-Sat (plus 4 Sun afternoons during Carnevale).

Tuscany

East of Lucca

East of Lucca on the SS435, in the region of the border of Lucca province, are two towns that are well worth a visit.

Collodi

Collodi is the birthplace of the author of Italy's most cherished fairytale character (*see p255* **Who he? Pinocchio**), who fuels a micro economy that supports this otherwise minor town. The surrounding area is plastered with advertisements for **Pinocchio Park** (0572 429 342, L13,000/€6.70 or L8,000/€4.10 under-14s), which opened in 1956 and features a walk-through maze and Pinocchio statues, including one by Emilio Greco, plus a colourful mosaic-lined courtyard by Venturino Venturi.

The nearby **Giardino Garzoni** (piazza della Vittoria 1, 0572 429 590, L10,000/€5.20) are attractive baroque gardens that took more than 170 years to complete after the construction of the Garzoni residence in 1633. Designed by the Marquis Romano di Alessandro Garzoni, they're a masterpiece of perspective and symmetry, though they could do with a little more TLC.

Pescia

Set in a protective valley and straddling the humid Pescia river, the town of Pescia is the hub of Italy's budding flower industry, cultivating and auctioning everything from chrysanthemums to bonsai olive trees, and exporting them for an international market. The hills surrounding the town are studded with greenhouses, and flower merchants gather for Pescia's international fairs. You can smell the results of the industry at the Centro di Commercializzazione dei Fiori just south of the train station.

Collodi's sumptuous **Giardino Garzoni**.

Getting there

By bus: CLAP (0583 587 897) buses connect Lucca with Pescia (journey time around 45min) and less regularly with Collodi.
By car: head east of Lucca along the SS435 toward Montecatini Terme.
By train: Pescia is served by regular trains on the line from Florence (60-75min) to Lucca (20min).

The Garfagnana

As you head north through the Lower Serchio Valley from Lucca, you'll see that the cultivated flat land radiating from Lucca's circular walls soon piles up into the mighty Apuane Alps. Within an hour's drive you'll be in a mountain paradise of snowy peaks and river valleys lined with chestnut trees and wild flowers.

Before you head for the hills (or on your way back), try to stop at **La Mora** restaurant just off the SS12, 10 kilometres north of Lucca (*see p247*).

Abetone

If you don't want to fork out for the northern ski resorts and are willing to try gentler slopes, head for Abetone – just 85 kilometres (53 miles) from Florence, it's easy to get to for the weekend or even a day trip. Wide runs make it ideal for beginners and intermediate skiers. Ski-boot hire costs L20,000 (€10.50) per day and ski passes are L42,000 (€21.50) per day Monday to Friday, L50,000 (€26) at the weekend.

If you want to stay over, the one-star **Noemi** (via Brennero 244, 0573 60168, L50,000-L95,000/€26-€49) has 26 rooms, seven of which have a bath.

For tourist information call 0573 60231, for information about the slopes 0573 60001. Regular buses serve Abetone in season.

Bagni di Lucca

It's hard to believe that this tiny spa village buried in the narrow reaches of the Lima valley once attracted the intellectual elite – Puccini, Heine, Shelley and Byron all visited for its saline and sulphurous thermal waters. Elisa Bonaparte Baciocchi (the Grand Duchess of Tuscany and Napoleon's sister) had a summer home here (now Hotel Roma; *see below*), but once her brother had fallen the place was taken by Grand Duke Carlo Ludovico, under whose reign Europe's first licensed casino opened in 1837. Today the casino entrance is weed-choked and the building in dire need of a lick of paint.

Tuscany

Ponte della Maddalena: the devil's work?

Bagni's lustre is long gone and so is much
of its population – many emigrated to America
after World War II – though the town continues
to attract a Brit contingent each summer.

To have a soak, visit the externally dingy
Terme di Bagni di Lucca above the river
(Bagni Caldi village, 0583 87221, closed Dec-
Mar except 2wks Christmas), which offers a
range of services, including mud treatments
and hydro massage. Admission varies
according to the treatments chosen.

Hotel Roma (via Umberto I 110, 0583
87278, rates L65,000-L85,000/€33.50-€44) is
marvellously old-fashioned, with a drop-dead
decadent style. Or try **Locanda Maiola** in
Maiola di Sotto, if only to eat at its restaurant
(0583 86296, rates L100,000/€51.50, average
L40,000/€20.50). Owner Enrico Franceschi
travels the region seeking out the best cheeses
and cold meats to serve with specialities
such as baby river trout.

On the SS12 from Lucca, eight kilometres
(five miles) south of Bagni, the **Ponte della
Maddalena**, nicknamed the Devil's Bridge,
spans the Serchio river. It was built in the
11th century by (according to legend) Beelzebub
himself, in return for the soul of the first person
who crossed it. The locals sent a dog.

Barga

This perfectly preserved medieval city looks
majestic against the mountainous landscape
and lush Serchio river valley. Red roofs climb
to its highest point, dominated by a grassy
square and the brilliant sunlit façade of the 11th-
century Duomo. The cathedral was built in a pale
local stone called Albarese di Barga; its most
striking feature is its pulpit, carved by Como

Massa-Carrara & Lucca Provinces

sculptor Guido Bigarelli in the 13th century and
supported by carved lions and dwarves, the
latter a symbol of crushed paganism.

If you come when the flea market is on (the
second Sunday of the month), visit **Vecchia
Enoteca Puccini** (via di Mezzo 46), which is
open only with the market and has an extensive
collection of ancient wine bottles, with labels
faded by years of humidity. The collector's
widow, Eda Puccini, opens this magical place
to any adventurer patient enough to dust off
the bottles in the quest for a priceless vintage.

For a late-afternoon aperitif, head to the
central **Caffè Capretz** (piazza Salvo Salvi,
0583 723 001, closed Tue), an antique café
founded in 1870 with outdoor tables beneath
a wood-beam *loggia* that used to host the
town's vegetable market. The trendy **Osteria
Angelio** (piazza Angelio 13/14, 0583 724 547,
closed Mon, average L30,000/€15.50) serves
Tuscan fare to (occasionally live) jazz.

In summer Barga hosts a slew of cultural
activities, the most worthwhile being the jazz
festival in mid August. For further info on the
town, visit the fun www.barganews.com, which
is run by a local Irish musician.

L'Eremo di Calomini

This monastery, set on the other side of the
Serchio river valley from Barga, is built into
a vertical cliff and seems to hang in mid-air.

At its outdoor **Antica Trattoria
dell'Eremita** (0583 767 020, closed Nov-Feb,
L30,000/€15.50) there's grilled trout fresh
from the Serchio river and spaghetti with a
fine trout sauce, served on a shady, sycamore-
lined terrace with great views.

There are rooms to rent in the monastery
(ask in the trattoria), plus a little shop selling
herb syrups and extracts of medicinal plants.

Grotta del Vento

Seven kilometres (4.5 miles) of hairpin
bends and steep ridges from L'Eremo di
Calomini lead to the semi-abandoned town
of Fornovolasco and to Tuscany's geological
wonder, the **Grotta del Vento** or 'wind
cave' (0583 722 024, closed Oct-Mar, L12,000-
L28,000/€6.20-€28), which is packed with
stalactites, stalagmites and underground
lakes. Cold air that blows from the cave's
entrance gave it its name and a practical
purpose: it was used as a refrigerator until the
17th century. It wasn't until 1898, when local
bullies forced a little girl to go in and she
came back out describing the wonders inside,
that scientists became aware of its existence.
There are one-, two- and three-hour tours.

Tuscany

Barga's majestic **Duomo**. See p253.

Vagli di Sotto

Another valley pass into the Apuane Alps leads
to the artificial lake of Vagli, fed by the Edron
river. When Vagli was formed, the tiny stone
town of Fabbriche di Careggine had to be
abandoned, but every ten years the lake is
emptied for maintenance (the next time is 2004)
and the ruins of the ghost town can be seen.

Castelnuovo di Garfagnana

Garfagnana's capital makes a decent base from
which to explore the area. Encased by ancient
walls and dominated by a 13th-century castle,
its historic centre is a pleasant place to refuel
and pick up supplies, despite the nasty traffic
junction at its centre.

For daytime and early-evening snacks,
Il Vecchio Mulino (via Vittorio Emanuele
12, 0583 62192, closed Sun, average L30,000/
€15.50), run by brother and sister team
Andrea and Cinzia Bertucci, is a wine bar
with top-notch salamis and cheeses. For rooms
try **Hotel-Ristorante Ludovico Ariosto** (via
Francesco Azzi 28, 0583 62369, rates L80,000-
L120,000/€41.50-€62).

Parco Orecchiella

This park (0583 619 098/058365169, closed
Mon-Fri June-Sept, Mon-Sat spring & Oct,
all winter, museum L3,000/€1.60) is perhaps
the loveliest part of the Alpi Apuane.
Abundant rain gives the area lush forests
and meadows, and wildlife includes deer,

boar, goats, predatory Apennine wolves and
more than 130 species of bird, including the
eagles that are Orecchiella's symbol. Hiking
and biking paths of varying length and
difficulty criss-cross the park, which is best
visited in late spring or early autumn.

Essentials

Getting there

By bus

CLAP (0583 587 897) operates buses to Barga and
Castelnuovo di Garfagnana from Lucca.
LAZZI (0583 584 876) runs several buses a day from
Lucca to Bagni di Lucca.

By car

Take the SS12 north out of Lucca; it follows the
Serchio river valley and branches off toward Bagno
di Lucca just beyond Borgo. At the same intersection
you can take the winding hill road (SS445) toward
Barga (there's a turn-off after a few kilometres) and
Castelnuovo di Garfagnana. This is the main route
through the Garfagnana region and smaller roads
fan off from it towards highlights such as the Grotta
del Vento (turn off near Barga to the south) and the
Parco Orecchiella park. It also leads, eventually, to
the SS63 (and then the SS62), which go through the
Lunigiana region to the far north. The drive through
the mountains is very scenic but you should allow
plenty of time (at least a day from Lucca) and
perhaps aim to stop over somewhere en route.

By train

An irregular but very scenic rail service (848 888
088) goes through this area between Lucca and
Aulla in the north, with stops at Bagni di Lucca
(30min), Castelnuovo di Garfagnana (60min) and
piazza al Serchio (75min).

Tourist information

The tourist office at Castelnuovo di Garfagnana
(piazza delle Erbe 1, 0583 644 242/fax 0583 648
435, closed Mon in winter) has info on walking
and other activities in the Apuane Alps.

The Lunigiana

Named after the Luni, the area's aboriginal
population, the Lunigiana is Tuscany's least-
explored region – the Cisa pass (where the
A15 autostrada runs) and the area surrounding
Pontrémoli and Aulla (the hub for buses and
transport to the rest of the area) are way off
most tourist itineraries. The people of the
Lunigiana don't identify with either Tuscany
or nearby Liguria or Emilia Romagna but are a
curious blend of all three – a fact that's reflected
in the dialect and cuisine.

Tuscany

Who he? Pinocchio

The Adventures of Pinocchio has been published in so many editions and languages that only the Bible and the Koran beat it. Or at least that's what the official Pinocchio fan club in Collodi would have you believe.

Carlo Lorenzini, its author, took Collodi as his nom de plume after his mother's birthplace. Lorenzini himself was born in Florence in 1826 and gained fame as a journalist and writer of educational children's books who incorporated music in his writing, often inventing sing-song names for characters. Soon after witnessing the unification of Italy, he began writing for one of Italy's first children's magazines, Il Giornale per i Bambini. His main contributions were instalments of the story of Pinocchio, which soon had a base of young fans. Just as the final episode was published in the magazine, The Adventures of Pinocchio was published as a complete book and was soon translated into English for sale in Britain and the States.

Lorenzini died in 1890 and is buried in San Miniato al Monte cemetery, Florence, but Pinocchio's incarnation in a Walt Disney cartoon in 1940 secured his immortality.

Fosdinovo

Lunigiana hasn't always been Tuscany's most isolated corner – for more than ten centuries from prehistory and the Romans to the heyday of the traffic-heavy via Francigena trade route, the region was of utmost geographic significance. The river valleys that slice into the Apuane Alps form important passageways between the northern and central sections of the Italian peninsula.

With prime location comes fortification and this region is dotted with more than 100 castles and towers. **Fosdinovo** (0187 68891 for tour times, L8,000/€4.10) is one of Lunigiana's best examples of a feudal residence, with impressive strategic views of mountains and sea. It was built by local warlords, the Malaspinas, some of whose heirs still live here 800 years later.

Fivizzano

This is a tranquil, isolated place. On piazza Medicea (also called piazza V Emmanuele), the regional branches of two Italian political parties (the DC and the PCI) that folded shortly after the fall of the Berlin Wall are still a gathering place for wrinkled old men. There's also a fountain with four marble dolphins – a gift from Cosimo III in 1683, when the town served as the Medici government's Lunigiana capital. Behind it is the church of San Jacopo and San Antonio, built on the site of a 13th-century church.

Caffè Elvetico (0585 926 657, closed Thur in winter) has tables spilling into the square. The elegant **Hotel Il Giardinetto** (via Roma 151, 0585 92060, rates L40,000-L70,000/€20.50-€36) attracts clientele that looks like they comes from a different era. There's a restaurant too (closed Oct, Mon Nov-June, L35,000/€18).

North-east of town on the SS63, Castello della Verrucola was also built by the Malaspinas, who controlled the area from here to Carrara.

Pontrémoli

Pontrémoli is the Lunigiana's biggest town, though only 11,000 people live here. Its wealth grew from its position as an important station on the via Francigena trade route and the Cisa pass. It boasts the 14th-century Torre del Campanone, built by Castruccio Castracani and set amid quaint, narrow, arched streets.

The tourist office has closed. **Hotel Napoleon** (piazza Italia 2, 0187 830 544, L90,000-L140,000/€46.50-€72.50), the better of the two hotels, is bland and overpriced, though staff are friendly and the food good. **Trattoria del Giardino di Bacciottini** (via Ricci Armani 4, 0187 830 120, closed Mon, closed dinner Sun in winter, L45,000/€23) is the saving grace, serving an excellent version of local speciality testaroli with pesto.

The main attraction is the 19 prehistoric stele statues in the **Museo del Comune** (Castello di Piagnaro, 0187 831 439/0187 460 111, closed Mon, L6,000/€3.10). Found nearby and dating from the third millennium BC, they're fascinating for their sophistication and simplicity – Henry Moore was apparently transfixed by them. Though it's known they were made by the ancient Ligurian-Apuani tribes, their purpose remains a mystery.

Tuscany

Arezzo

Look hard and you will find in initially unprepossessing Arezzo.

Arezzo has never seemed quite as glamorous as its Tuscan neighbours to the north and west. In fact you can't help feeling that the city hasn't moved on that much since Dante called the Aretini people *botoli ringhiosi* (growling and waspish), in spite of the fact that they sheltered him in exile. Though in the 20th century Arezzo has prospered economically – asserting itself as a manufacturing and gold-producing centre – there remains something determinedly grim about the place. To appreciate this city, you have to embrace its simplicity and its comparative lack of crowds and step inside its grey exteriors. It might not be a *città d'arte* as Florence and Siena are, but it has produced and hosted eminent artists and is home to Piero della Francesca's extraordinary fresco cycle.

HISTORY

Strategically built at the intersection of four fertile valleys – the Casentino, Valdarno, Valtiberina and Valdichiana – Arezzo has seen much external conquest and only a brief period of city-state independence. In the seventh century BC, the settlement of Arretium was a significant member of the Etruscan federation. It soon caught the eye of upstart Romans moving north and became a military stronghold and economic outpost. By 89 BC, its people were granted honorary Roman citizenship, which brought with it an amphitheatre, baths and fortified walls. But with the glory came decadence; Arezzo's trade routes were supplanted and its territory overrun by waves of Barbarians. The darkest days came under the Lombards in the sixth century, but gradually a feudal economic system began to pull the city from its slump and paved the way for Arezzo's 'golden age' in the 1200s.

The turning point came in 1100, when the emerging merchant class started to question its subservience to Arezzo's clerical-feudal overlords. Secular power began to shift to the budding bourgeoisie, and in 1192 the Commune was established. There was extensive building and Arezzo began to take on its current urban contours. However another foreign power, this time Florence, set its sights on the city. The two clashed in the Battle of Campaldino in 1289, from which Arezzo never fully recovered. The city was eventually sold to Florence in 1384.

Political submission did not, however, equal artistic or cultural paralysis; it just meant that Arezzo's natives went elsewhere to achieve

Arezzo's inspiring **Duomo**.

success. Most notable were Giorgio Vasari (1511-74), the Medicis' official architect and historiographer (*see p106*), and Pietro Aretino (1492-1556), a court poet and satirist. Henceforth, in fact, the city's artistic and cultural achievements were carried out under the Medici and then the Lorraines. Foreign domination meant Arezzo's population turned in on itself, growing rural and conservative. These days, however, it has regained some sense of identity, predicated largely on the reputation of its goldsmiths and jewellers.

Sights

Churches

Duomo

Piazza Duomo (0575 23991). **Open** 7am-12.30pm, 3-6.30pm daily. **Admission** free.
Arezzo's Gothic Duomo was started in 1277 but the finishing touches were made only in the early 1500s and it was a further 300 years before its campanile

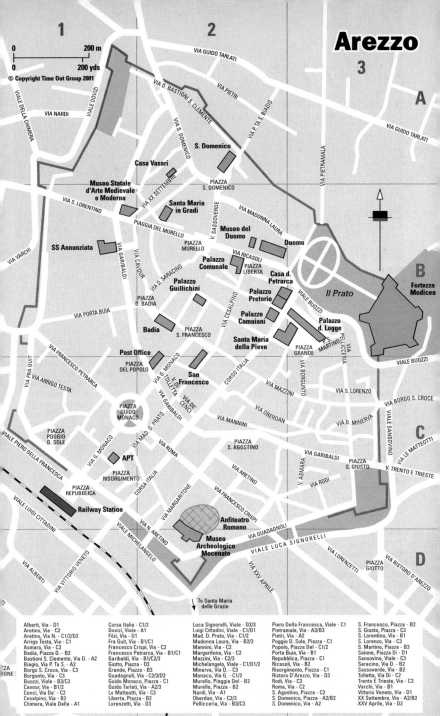

Arezzo

3

0 200 m
0 200 yds
© Copyright Time Out Group 2001

VIA GUIDO TARLATI

VIA PIETRI

VIA P.TA S. BIAGIO

VIA GUIDO TARLATI

VIALE DELLA CHIMERA

VIA NARDI

VIALE DOVIZI

VIA D. BASTIONI S. CLEMENTE

VIA S. DOMENICO

S. Domenico

Casa Vasari

PIAZZA S. DOMENICO

VIA PIETRAMALA

Museo Statale d'Arte Medievale e Moderna

VIA S. LORENTINO

VIA XX SETTEMBRE

Santa Maria in Gradi

VIA MADONNA LAURA

V. SASSOVERDE

PIAGGIA DEL MURELLO

Museo del Duomo

Duomo

SS Annunziata

VIA GARIBALDI

VIA CAVOUR

VIA D. SARACINO

PIAZZA MURELLO

VIA RICASOLI

PIAZZA LIBERTA

Palazzo Comunale

Casa d. Petrarca

Il Prato

Fortezza Medicea

VIA VARCHI

Palazzo Guillichini

Palazzo Pretorio

VIA CESALPINO

VIALE BUOZZI

VIA PORTA BUIA

Badia

PIAZZA D. BADIA

PIAZZA S. FRANCESCO

Palazzo Camaiani

Palazzo d. Logge

P.S. MARTINO

VIA PELLICCERIA

VIALE BUOZZI

VIA FRANCESCO PETRARCA

Post Office

PIAZZA DEL POPOLO

VIA G. MONACO

VIA TOLLETTA

Santa Maria della Pieve

PIAZZA GRANDE

VIA S. LORENZO

VIA FRA GUIT

VIA ARRIGO TESTA

San Francesco

VIA DE' CENCI

CORSO ITALIA

VIA MAZZINI

VIA BORGUNTO

VIA BORGO S. CROCE

PIAZZA GUIDO MONACO

VIA GARIBALDI

VIA MAD. D. PRATO

VIA MANNINI

VIA OBERDAN

VIA D. MINERVA

VIALE SANSOVINO

PIAZZA POGGIO D. SOLE

VIA ROMA

PIAZZA S. AGOSTINO

V. ASMARA

VIA GARIBALDI

VIA LE MATTEOTTI

VIALE PIERO DELLA FRANCESCA

APT

PIAZZA RISORGIMENTO

CORSO ITALIA

VIA ARETINO

VIA RODI

PIAZZA S. GIUSTO

V. TRENTO E TRIESTE

PIAZZA REPUBBLICA

VIALE LUIGI CITTADINI

Railway Station

VIA VITTORIO VENETO

VIA N. ARETINO

VIA MICHELANGELO

VIA MARGARITONE

VIA FRANCESCO CRISPI

Anfiteatro Romano

Museo Archeologico Mecenate

VIALE LUCA SIGNORELLI

VIA GUADAGNOLI

VIA LORENZETTI

VIA RISTORO D'AREZZO

PIAZZA GIOTTO

VIA ALBERTI

VIA XXV APRILE

To Santa Maria delle Grazie

The once-mighty **Anfiteatro Romano** was plundered by Cosimo I. *See page 259.*

was erected. The effect of its size and the vertical thrust of its ogival vaulted ceilings is inspiring, though there's barely enough light to appreciate it. The little there is comes through the exquisite stained glass windows (c1515-20) by Guillaume di Marcillat. The Duomo's real attractions are along the left aisle: screened off from the rest of the church the Cappella della Madonna del Conforto guards a terracotta Madonna, while just beyond is Vasari's grandiose choir stall and nearby, almost hidden, Piero della Francesca's *Mary Magdalene* (c1465).

Pieve di Santa Maria

Corso Italia (0575 22629). **Open** 8am-6pm daily. **Admission** free.

A striking example of Romanesque architecture built mostly in the 12th and 13th centuries. The façade is of chalky sandstone so weathered that the *loggie* look about to crumble. They're ordered in three increasingly busy layers above five arcades. The ornate columns holding them up, all 68 with an eccentric motif, reach a climax in the bell-tower, the *delle cento buche* ('of the 100 holes').

San Domenico

Piazza San Domenico (0575 22906). **Open** 9am-7pm daily. **Admission** free.

San Domenico was started by Dominicans in 1275, around the same time as their Franciscan brothers were getting underway with San Francesco. It faces a simple, open square and has an attractive quaintness about it, accentuated by its uneven Gothic campanile with two 14th-century bells.

San Francesco

Piazza San Francesco (0575 20630). **Open** 8.30am-noon, 2.30-6.30pm daily. **Admission** free.

This unassuming church has had a convoluted history: begun by Franciscan friars in the 1200s, its interior was adorned with frescoes, chapels and shrines throughout the 1500s thanks to the largesse

of Arezzo's merchant class. By the 19th century, however, it had been deconsecrated and was being used as a military barracks.

No visit to Arezzo is complete without stepping inside San Francesco to see Piero della Francesca's magnum opus, *The Legend of the True Cross* (c1453-64). The fresco cycle – considered to be one of the most important ever produced – was begun in 1453, the year Constantinople fell to the Ottoman Turks, and portrays the fear this induced in the Christian world. In the 1980s, state-of-the-art restoration techniques were employed on it (there's a fascinating exhibition on the restoration in Monterchi; *see p266*). Miraculously, some might say, the frescoes have survived fire, earthquake and the destruction of chapels.

Santa Maria delle Grazie

Via Santa Maria (0575 323 140). **Open** 8am-noon, 4-6.30pm daily. **Admission** free.

On the site of an ancient sacred spring, the Fonte Tecta, to Arezzo's south, the religious complex built around Santa Maria delle Grazie is known for housing the Renaissance's first porticoed courtyard. Started in 1428, the religious buildings were imposed by San Bernardino of Siena on the recalcitrant Aretini. In a well-publicised gesture he marched over from San Francesco, brandishing a wooden cross, and destroyed the spring site, replacing it with a *Madonna della Misericordia* by local artist Parri di Spinello. Fortunately, the enlightened Antonio da Maiano, who created the *loggia* and was one of the Renaissance's foremost architects, reconciled the church's late-Gothic, essentially medieval design (partly by covering it up) with the then-emergent classical style.

Santissima Annunziata

Via Garibaldi (0575 26774). **Open** 8am-12.30pm, 3.30-6.30pm daily. **Admission** free.

A miracle in which a statue of the Madonna wept before a passing pilgrim is reputed to have occurred on this site in 1460, in an oratory belonging to the company of Santissima Annunziata. The owners lost no time in capitalising on the event and began building a church the same year.

Museums

Casa Vasari
Via XX Settembre 55 (0575 409 040).
Open 9am-7.30pm Mon, Wed-Sat; 9am-1pm Sun.
Admission free.
A good example of an unpromising Arezzo exterior concealing riches within. The city's own Medici insider, Giorgio Vasari, bought and decorated this house in extravagant style before entering Florence's big league in 1564. Today it houses the Archivio e Museo Vasariano, which boasts a number of contemporary paintings by the master's school, various artefacts and a rear garden. The star attraction is definitely the *piano nobile*, with its richly decorated Sala del Trionfo della Virtù (Room of the Triumph of Virtue).

Museo Archeologico Mecenate
Via Margaritone 10 (0575 20882). **Open** 9am-2pm Mon-Sat; 9am-1pm Sun. **Admission** L8,000 (€4.10); free concs. **No credit cards.**
A sense of dusty abandonment pervades this assortment of mostly Roman and Etruscan artefacts. The Etruscan collection comprises votive figurines, vases and funerary urns in terracotta, alabaster and travertine, plus a unique coin collection. More noteworthy are the ceramics, which include some ancient Roman vases that date back as far as the first century BC.

Museo Statale d'Arte Medievale e Moderna
Via San Lorentino 8 (0575 409 050). **Open** 8.30am-7.30pm Tue-Sat; 9am-7.30pm Sun. **Admission** L8,000 (€4.10); free concs. **No credit cards.**
Arezzo's main art museum doesn't really live up to its name, offering little medieval and nothing modern. The ground floor has an assemblage of Romanesque capitals, stone carvings and fragments of sculptures found in the area. The baroque vestibule on the first floor is dominated by Vasari's *Wedding Feast of Ahasuerus & Esther* (1548), and just past this are rooms with some 13th- to 17th-century glazed ceramics and a number of terracottas from the Della Robbia school.

Landmarks

Anfiteatro Romano
Accessible from via Margaritone or via Crispi (no phone). **Open** *Apr-Oct* 7am-8pm daily. *Nov-Mar* 7.30am-6pm daily. **Admission** free.
In the second century this amphitheatre would, on occasion, be packed with up to 10,000 people. Its travertine and sandstone blocks were plundered by Medici grand duke Cosimo I for the Fortezza Medicea (*see below*) following the Florentines'

decision to strengthen their hold on Arezzo in 1531. Today its elliptical shape and the stage can be made out, plus parts of what must have been the stands.

Fortezza Medicea
No phone. **Open** *Apr-Oct* 7am-8pm daily; *Nov-Mar* 7.30am-6pm daily. **Admission** free.
When the Medici finally decided to turn Arezzo into a duchy in 1531, they set about improving the city's defences, and the introduction of cannons prompted them to embark on another (the eighth) stint of wall-building. The final perimeter is visible in sections round the city and dominated by the architecturally revolutionary Fortezza Medicea (1538-60). Its pentagonal form, punctuated by four doors and seven bastions, was designed by Antonio da Sangallo the Elder and required the razing of towers, alleys and medieval *palazzi* in the hills of San Donato.

Piazza Grande
This sloping piazza is a visual feast of architectural irregularity resulting from its growth from peripheral food market to political heart of the city. The jumble of styles includes the arcaded, rounded back of the Romanesque Pieve di Santa Maria at the square's lowest point, the baroque Palazzo del Tribunale and next to it the Palazzo della Fraternità dei Laici, designed mostly by Bernardo Rossellino. Unsurprisingly, Vasari also had a hand in piazza Grande – his is the typically arcaded Palazzo delle Logge, which presides over the assortment of medieval homes around the rest of the square.

Like Siena, Arezzo holds its own historic event in its main square. The **Giostra del Saracino** (June, Sept), one of Italy's more famous jousting tournaments, claims to be rooted in raids carried out by and against the Saracens during the Crusades in the 1200s, although the first Giostra historically took place in 1535 (*see p155*).

Parks & gardens

Il Prato
Arezzo's only park, between the Duomo and the Fortezza Medicea, has views over the town and by day is a pleasant place for a stroll. On summer nights locals flock to **La Casina del Prato** bar (*see p261*).

Shopping

As you climb corso Italia, mainstream shops peter out to make way for a proliferation of antiques shops around piazza Grande; stray off the corso if you're looking for something more.

On Saturdays a general market sells clothes, food, flowers and household goods. On the first Sunday of the month and the previous Saturday the city centre is taken over by a huge and important antiques fair; the APT (*see p262*) has a handy Italian-English glossary and a map with listings to get you round the maze of stores and stands.

Piazza Grande: antiques heaven. *See p259.*

L'Artigiano
Via XXV Aprile 22 (0575 351 278). **Open** 9am-
1pm, 3-8pm daily (ring bell). **No credit cards.**
One of Arezzo's last goldsmiths to carry on the tradition of *mosaico fiorentino* – intricate pendants and
picture frames inlaid with mosaics.

Casa della Renna
Piazza San Michele 15 (0575 356 774). **Open** 9am-
1pm, 3.30pm-7.30pm Mon-Sat. **Credit** MC, V.
Custom-made buckskin and calf leather jackets,
natural and treated, are this shop's trademarks.

Libreria Einaudi
Via Oberdan 31 (0575 353 085). **Open** 4-8pm
Mon, Fri; 10am-1pm, 4-8pm Tue, Thur, Sat.
No credit cards.
Arezzo's outlet for Italy's best-known publishing
house and a space for exhibitions and events.

Macelleria-Gastronomia Aligi Barelli
Viale della Chimera 20 (0575 357 754). **Open** 8am-
1pm, 4.30-8pm Mon, Tue, Thur, Fri; 8am-1pm Wed,
Sat. **Credit** DC, MC, V.
Justly renowned *macelleria* with mouthwatering
salamis from the Casentino and a range of ready-
made meat-based dishes.

Mondo Antico I Coloniali
Via Cavour 24/26 (0575 21801). **Open** 4-7.30pm
Mon; 9.30am-1pm, 4pm-7.30pm Tue-Sat.
Credit AmEx, DC, MC, V.
An exotic and colourful Indonesian furniture store
with perfumed textiles, woven bamboo recliners and
lampshades made from banana and corn leaves.

Pane e Salute
Corso Italia 11 (0575 20657). **Open** 7.30am-1.30pm,
4-8pm Mon-Sat. **No credit cards.**
This shop sells traditional Tuscan breads, including
schiacciate (flattened bread peppered with rosemary), plus oven-baked sweets.

Pasticceria de'Cenci
Via de' Cenci 17 (0575 23102). **Open** 9am-1pm,
4-8pm Tue-Sat; 9am-1pm Sun. **No credit cards.**
This pâtisserie is chock full of elegant delights such
as *bigne' al limone* (lemon cream puff).

Where to eat & drink

Restaurants

Arezzo's culinary specialities draw heavily
on the products of the four rich valleys that
encircle it. First courses almost always include
pasta dishes with *funghi porcini* (ceps) or
tartufo nero (black truffle). For main courses,
no self-respecting *osteria* in Arezzo is without
a local Chianina steak on its menu, and oddities
such as *grifi* (stewed cheek of veal) and *zampucci*
(pig leg) occasionally feature.

Antica Osteria L'Agania
Via Mazzini 10 (0575 295 381). **Open** noon-2.30pm,
7-10.30pm Tue-Sun. **Average** L35,000 (€18).
Credit AmEx, DC, MC, V.
This cosy two-level hideaway, with its traditional
decor and no-frills service, exudes warmth. The
primi are more mainstream than the *secondi*, which
include *grifi con polenta*.

Il Cantuccio
Via Madonna del Prato 76 (0575 26830).
Open 12.30-2.30pm, 7-10.30pm Mon, Tue, Thur-Sun.
Average L40,000 (€15.50). **Credit** AmEx, DC,
MC, V.
The vaulted cellar here is the city's most rustic.
Home-made pasta dishes include *tortelloni alla
Casentinese* (with potato filling) and *tagliolini in pas-
sato di fagioloni* (a bean-based sauce).

Osteria dei Mercanti
Via Ser Petracolo 9 (0575 24330). **Open** noon-
2.30pm, 7.45-11.30pm Mon-Fri; 7.45pm-midnight Sat.
Average L30,000 (€18). **Credit** MC, V.
Conveniently located near the lower end of corso
Italia, the atmospheric Osteria dei Mercanti with
its outside tables is an excellent spot for pizza or a
bowl of home-made pasta.

Sbarbacipolle
Via Garibaldi 120 (0575 299 154).
Open 7.30am-8pm daily. **Average** L15,000 (€7.80).
No credit cards.
A colourful corner deli with a good choice of *panini*
and cold dishes. Great for a quick bite and always
immensely popular with the locals.

Il Torrino
Località Il Torrino 1 (0575 360 264). **Open** noon-
3pm, 7-10pm Tue-Sun. **Average** L45,000 (€23).
Credit AmEx, DC, MC, V.
Up a winding road off the Arezzo-Sansepolcro
route, Il Torrino is a vast, bright dining hall,
unnervingly reminiscent of the hotel in *The
Shining*. Luckily, the food is anything but creepy;
try *tagliolini al tartufo bianco* (with white truffles)
and *cappelli d'alpino* (large ravioli stuffed with
ricotta, spinach and herbs in cream sauce). For *secondo* we recommend the *filetto alla ghiotta* (steak
on a bed of porcini mushrooms).

Tuscany

Who he? Piero della Francesca

Born in about 1420, Piero della Francesca was a reclusive low-key painter who spent much of his life around peripheral noble courts such as the Este in Ferrara and the Montefeltro in Urbino and, of course, Arezzo.

His work is perhaps best known for its precision and quasi-maniacal obsession with detail. Perspective, proportion, light and shade, colour and shape all needed to be portrayed, said the artist, according to strict and unchanging mathematical and geometric laws. These in turn derived from a superior rational order that regulates a universal cosmic harmony.

Though his approach was highly humanist and rationalist, Piero's subject matter remained almost exclusively sacred, with only the odd commissioned portrait of a patron. He was influenced by Flemish and Northern European art, and, in turn, had a profound influence on 20th-century Cubist and metaphysical painters

such as Cézanne, Seurat and De Chirico.

During a period crammed with exhibitionists and polemicists, his modest lifestyle was refreshing. Piero's legacy is one of lasting innovation. His quiet death in Sansepolcro on 12 October 1492 coincided with another event taking place across the ocean: the discovery of the New World.

THE WORKS

Arezzo *Legend of the True Cross* (1455-6), church of San Francesco; *Santa Maria Maddalena* (1460), Duomo.
Florence Portraits of Battista Sforza and Federico da Montefeltro (1465-72) and *Triumphs of Federico da Montefeltro* and *Battista Sforza* (1465-75), Uffizi (pictured).
Monterchi *Madonna del Parto* (1455-60), Museo Madonna del Parto.
Sansepolcro *Madonna della Misericordia* (1445-60) and *Resurrection* (1460), both in Museo Civico.

Trattoria Il Saraceno

Via Mazzini 6A (0575 27644). **Open** 12.30-3pm, 7-11pm Mon, Tue, Thur-Sun. **Average** L45,000 (€23). **Credit** AmEx, DC, MC, V
Fine food, including a porcini soup, *pici al cinghiale* (egg pasta in wild boar sauce with pine nuts and juniper) and *fagioli cannellini all'uccelletto* (white beans in tomato sauce).

Bars, *enoteche & gelaterie*

Wines produced in Arezzo's hinterland have always been held in lower esteem than their famous counterparts from Chianti and Siena, but this is changing, with acknowledgment of the quality of Colli Aretini vintages and a resulting growth in the number and standard of Arezzo's wine bars.

Caffè dei Costanti

Piazza San Francesco 19-20 (0575 21660). **Open** *Oct-May* 7am-9pm Tue-Sun. *June-Sept* 7am-midnight Tue-Sun. **Credit** AmEx, DC, JCB, MC, V.
The oldest café in Arezzo, this is a popular meeting place. After featuring in the Oscar-winning *La Vita è Bella*, it named an ice-cream after the film and covered the barfront with Roberto Benigni memorabilia.

La Casina del Prato

Via Palagi 1, Il Prato park (0575 299 757).
Open 10am-2am Mon, Wed-Sun. **No credit cards**.
An open-air summer hotspot overflowing with the hipper Aretini crowd. Some snacks are available.

Enoteca La Torre di Gnicche

Piaggia San Martino 8 (0575 352 035). **Open** noon-3pm, 6pm-1am Mon, Tue, Thur-Sun. **Credit** DC, MC, V.
A tastefully decorated bar with a superb selection of local wines, including its standard-bearers Bricco di Gnicche and Bigattiera di Val d'Ambra, and a number of Gratena reds. Hot food is served.

Enoteca VinoDivino

Via Cesalpino 19 (0575 299 598). **Open** 10am-10.30pm Tue-Sat; 10am-4pm Sun. **Credit** AmEx, DC, MC, V.
The interior here is covered in tastefully restored frescoes. A rotating 15-wine *degustazione* list includes some smooth Galatrona and Gratena reds.

Fiaschetteria de'Redi

Via de' Redi 10 (0575 355 012). **Open** 11.30am-3.30pm, 7.30pm-12.30am Tue-Sat, 1st Sun of month; 7pm-midnight Sun rest of month. **Credit** DC, MC, V.
A bustling wine bar just off corso Italia, with cosy dark wood and tan walls and a good wine selection to boot. *Osteria*-style food is served.

Tuscany

Il Gelato

Via dei Cenci 24 (0575 300 069). **Open**
Summer 11am-midnight Mon, Tue, Thur-Sun.
Winter 11am-1pm, 2.30-8pm Mon, Tue, Thur-Sun.
No credit cards.
An unassuming and constantly busy ice-cream par-
lour. The *pinolata* (with pine nuts) and *arancello al
liquore* (liqueur orange) are worth a try.

Where to stay

Accommodation here is mostly in uninteresting
middle-of-the-range hotels. For better options,
try outside the city walls.

Cavaliere Palace Hotel

*Via Madonna del Prato 83 (0575 26836/fax 0575
21925).* **Rates** single L160,000 (€82.50); double
L240,000 (€124). **Credit** AmEx, DC, MC, V.
Beyond the cramped lobby, this recently renovated
four-star hotel is the best choice inside Arezzo.

Val di Colle Residenza di Campagna

Località Bagnoro (tel/fax 0575 365 167). **Rates**
single L260,000 (€134.50), double L310,000 (€160).
Credit AmEx, DC, MC, V.
The urge to splurge may bring you to this refined,
recently refurbished 14th-century country residence
4km (2.5 miles) from the town (beyond the stadium
on the south side). The eight rooms are a delight.

Villa Burali

*Località Policiano SS71, 154 (0575 979 045/fax
0575 979 296).* **Rates** single L175,000 (€90.50);
double L184,000-L193,000 (€95-€99.50).
No credit cards.
Though not exactly a bargain, this is a great option
if there's a group of you. The 17th-century villa has
been divided into 11 apartments and is well situated
on the road to Cortona, about 7km (4 miles) from
Arezzo. Its swimming pool is another draw.

Villa Severi Youth Hostel

*Via dei Cappucini, or via Redi 13 if coming
by bus (tel/fax 0575 299 047).* **Rates** dorm
L25,000 (€13); single L40,000 (€20.50); double
L60,000 (€31); breakfast L3,000 (€1.60).
No credit cards.
Good value for money and a relaxed atmosphere.
Rooms sleep up to 10 people. Take bus 4 from
outside the station towards Ospedale Vecchio,
alighting at the Ostello della Gioventù.

Essentials

Getting there & around

By bus

Bus services to Florence are slow and irregular,
so it's better to take the train. **LFI** (La Ferrovia
Italiana; 0575 39881) has direct buses to Siena
(90min) and Cortona (1hr, via Castiglion Fiorentina).

Other bus companies covering the Arezzo region
include **Lazzi** (055 919 922) and **Sita** (for
Sansepolcro; 0575 74361). Buses leave from the
terminal opposite the train station. For info and
tickets for local routes call **ATAM Point** in the
same square (0575 382 651).

By car

Arezzo is a few kilometres off the A1 (Florence–
Rome) autostrada. Journey time from Florence is
around 1hr, though the autostrada experiences big
jams on summer weekends and public holidays.
The SS73 links the city with Siena to the west
(about 1hr) and Sansepolcro to the north (30min).
Finding a parking space can be difficult and
expensive in Arezzo. The tourist office (*see below*)
has a list of free places to park outside the city walls.
To hire a car, there's both **Avis** (piazza della
Repubblica, 0575 354 232) and **Hertz** (via
Calamandrei 97/D, 0575 27577).

By taxi

Radio-taxi (0575 20245).

By train

Regular InterCity and InterRegionale trains link
Arezzo with Florence (50-60min) and Rome (90min).
The train station is located at piazza della
Repubblica (0575 27353).

Tourist information

Azienda di Promozione Turistica (APT)

*Piazza della Repubblica 22 (0575 377 678/fax
0575 20839/info@arezzo.turismo.toscana.it).*
Open *Oct-Mar* 9am-1pm, 3-6.30pm Mon-Sat; 9am-
1pm 1st Sun of month. *Apr-Sept* 9am-1pm, 3-7pm
Mon-Sat; 9am-1pm Sun.

Festivals

June, September: Giostra del Saracino, Arezzo's
heated jousting tournament (*see p155*).
Early July: Arezzo Wave (0575 911 005), a vibrant
festival of indie music in the stadium.
August: The Concorso Polifonico Internazionale
Guido d'Arezzo international choral competition.

Useful addresses

Hospital

There's an emergency department at the **San
Donato Hospital** (viale Alcide de Gasperi 17,
0575 3051).

Internet point

The **Phone Centre** (piazza Guido Monaco 8/B,
0575 371 245, closed 2wks Aug) has a couple of
computer terminals that you can rent at L6,000
(€3.10) per half-hour.

Police

For thefts or lost property reports, your best bet
is the Questura state police office (via Poggio del
Sole, 0575 23600).

Arezzo Province

Abbeys, Apennine peaks and other eastern delights.

The four valleys that make up Tuscany's eastern province branch out like spokes in a wheel along the Arno, Tiber and Chiana rivers from the city of Arezzo at its centre. This chapter is divided along these lines, beginning with the Valdarno (west of Arezzo), continuing with the Casentino (to the north) and the Valtiberina (east of Arezzo), and ending with the Valdichiana in the south.

The Valdarno

Encased between the imposing Pratomagno Apennine range to the north and the gentler Chianti hills to the south lies the **Valdarno**, a largely industrial region connecting Florence to Arezzo. North-east of the Arno, the Setteponti ('seven bridges') route along the Pratomagno foothills crosses the Arno's tributaries amid olive and chestnut groves – less direct that the autostrada but more interesting.

Getting there

By car: There are several routes through this area, including the Florence–Rome autostrada (A1 – use Montevarchi exit), the slower A69, which runs through San Giovanni and Montevarchi and on to Arezzo, or the Setteponti route (described below) through the country.
By train: Local trains on the Florence–Arezzo line stop at Montevarchi. Journey time from Florence is 45min, from Arezzo 25min. Timetable information 848 888 088.
By bus: **Lazzi** (055 919 9922) has regular buses linking Montevarchi, Terranuova Bracciolini and Loro Ciuffena with Arezzo. **Sita** (0575 382 651) runs regular buses from Arezzo to Montevarchi and other points in Arezzo province.

Tourist information

APT, Arezzo (see p262).

Castelfranco di Sopra & Loro Ciuffenna

There are a few worthwhile stops along the Setteponti route. The first is **Castelfranco di Sopra**, founded as a Florentine military outpost in the late 13th century. Just outside it is the **Badia di San Salvatore a Soffena**, a 12th-century abbey with a bright interior sporting an *Annunciation* and other pastel-coloured frescoes. The second is the town of **Loro Ciuffenna**, precariously set on the edge

Loro Ciuffenna and its Ponte Vecchio.

of a gorge over the roaring Ciuffenna torrent. Loro grew up around an ancient *borgo* (hamlet), and has its own Ponte Vecchio.

A couple of kilometres outside Loro on the Arezzo road, a dirt path twists off towards the stark and simple church of **San Pietro a Gropina**, a Romanesque parish church dating back to the ninth century. The carved detail on the capitals and knotted columns on the pulpit, with stylised human figures, grapes, knights and hunting eagles, are a pre-Christian rendition of the circle and knot of life.

The Setteponti's last attraction before reaching Arezzo is **Ponte a Buriano**, a harmonious 13th-century bridge that is the Arno's oldest, pre-dating the Ponte Vecchio in Florence by almost 100 years.

The Val d'Ambra

The Val d'Ambra, technically Chianti's easternmost reach, is nestled against the Monti del Chianti, past the Valdarno's two

Tuscany

main cities, San Giovanni Valdarno and Montevarchi, both leather manufacturing and leather centres. Hidden away are places of note such as Cennina, where a crumbling castle is sentinel to the sprawling Valdarno below, and Civitella in Val di Chiana, a perfectly preserved medieval village.

One of the highlights of Val d'Ambra is off the road between Montevarchi and Mercatale Valdarno. The well-signposted **Osteria di Rendola** (via di Rendola 78, 055 970 7490, closed Wed & Thur lunch, average L75,000/€38.50) is at the helm of Tuscany's gastronomic avant-garde. Alberto Fusini and young owner and chef Francesco Berardinelli have created a welcoming space with Cubist artwork and jazz *sottofondo*; their innovative dishes strike a delicate balance with their Tuscan roots.

Also near Montevarchi (to the east, just off the Florence-Rome autostrada) is the **Hostaria Costachiara** (via Santa Maria 129, Badiola, Terranova Bracciolini, 055 944 318, closed dinner Mon, all Tue, average L50,000/€26), one of the region's best farmhouse restaurants, with a groaning antipasto table and open-fire roasts.

The Casentino

The Casentino is abruptly closed off to the north by some of the Apennine's highest peaks. It has always been a peaceful area, with one bloody exception: the Battle of Campaldino in 1289, which saw Arezzo's capitulation to Florence. Today, serenity emanates over the valley from the monastery of Camáldoli and the sanctuary of La Verna.

Getting there

By car: This is easily the best way to see the Casentino, and there are thrilling mountain roads to explore, but progress, even on major roads, is slow, and snow can be a problem between October and April. The region's main arteries are the SS70, which threads south to Poppi and Bibbiena, and the SS71, which heads north from Arezzo. More circuitous minor roads lead off these to points of interest.
By train: A tiny train line run by La Ferroviaria Italiana (LFI) links Pratovecchio (journey time 1hr), Poppi (40min) and Bibbiena (30min) to Arezzo, with departures roughly every hour during the day.
By bus: Irregular LFI buses (0575 39881) serve Camáldoli and Chiusi Verna from Bibbiena station.

Tourist information

APT, Arezzo (see p262).

Poppi & Camáldoli

Poppi slopes down through arcaded streets from the 13th-century **Castello dei Conti Guidi** (0575 520 516, closed weekdays

Oct-Mar, admission L5,000/€2.60), which bears a close resemblance to Florence's Palazzo Vecchio and offers a staggering view of the Casentino region. Dante is said to have stayed in the castle for a few months while writing a minor work, and there's a noble-looking statue of him outside.

Across the square and a good base from which to explore the region is homely **Albergo Casentino** (piazza della Repubblica, 0575 529 090, rates L90,000-L130,000/€46.50-€67) with its own little enclosed garden and a restaurant (closed Wed, average L25,000/€13). A rustic alternative, just off the road to Camáldoli, is **Il Rustichello** (via del Corniolo 14, 0360 514 111, rates L100,000-L140,000/€51.50-€72.50).

In the wooded hills north-east of Poppi, in the midst of the **Foreste Casentinesi** national park, are the monastery and hermitage of Camáldoli. Romualdo, an itinerant Benedictine monk, set up the Camaldolite congregation within the larger Benedictine order in 1012, and his followers still meditate in the splendid isolation of the holy retreat, surrounded by fir trees, their individual cells visible only through a gate. Romualdo's original cell, with its wooden panelling and cot, is open to visitors, as is the baroque church, which is in stark contrast to the ascetic exterior.

Stop-off for Dante: **Castello dei Conti Guidi.**

Grim reapers of **Sansepolcro**.

Three kilometres (two miles) downhill, the monastery is the Camaldolites' link to the outside world. Its church contains some early Vasaris, including a *Madonna and Child* and *Nativity* (the young artist took refuge here from 1537 to 1539, after the murder of his patron Alessandro de' Medici).

The dark wood *farmacia* just around the corner has an interesting selection of monk-made soaps and liqueurs.

If you have time, it's worth taking the small road that twists up to Pratovecchio from the hermitage – the views over the Arno valley from up here are superb.

La Verna

A little further south, close to the town of Chiusi, this is an even more important monastic complex. In 1214 St Francis's vagabondage brought him to La Verna, an isolated peak at 1,129 metres (3,670 feet), where he and some followers were inspired to build some cells for themselves. Ten years later, Italy's most famous saint received the stigmata here and since then this evocative spot has been a must-see on the Franciscan trail.

The basilica contains a reliquary chapel with the saint's personal effects, while, in the walkway towards the stigmata chapel, a door leads to the place St Francis used to rest – a humid cavern the rocks of which miraculously split apart at the moment of Christ's death. The sanctuary also contains what must be the highest concentration of Andrea della Robbia glazed terracottas anywhere.

This impressive religious compound of interconnected chapels, churches, corridors and cloisters inevitably attracts large numbers of visitors, but on a quiet weekday the stunning sight of a sunset over the Casentino can still stimulate meditative silence.

The Valtiberina

The **Valtiberina**, Tuscany's easternmost fringe, takes its name from the Tiber as it flows down from the Apennine peaks. You'll be constantly reminded by its inhabitants that this valley marks the border between a land that has produced the likes of Michelangelo and Piero della Francesca and the less sophisticated Umbrians and Marchegiani next door.

Getting there
By car: From Arezzo take the SS73, heading north-east toward Sansepolcro. Monterchi and, further on, Anghiari are signposted off this road, a few kilometres before Sansepolcro.
By bus: Sita (0575 74361) runs buses between Arezzo and Sansepolcro (journey time 1hr) that also stop in Anghiari (45min) and sometimes Monterchi.

Tourist information
Piazza Garibaldi 2, Sansepolcro (0575 740 536).
Open 9am-1pm, 3-6.30pm daily.

Sansepolcro

The Valtiberina's largest town, Sansepolcro has its origins in (and gets its name from) the relics of the Holy Sepulchre brought here in medieval times. Today it sits at an important crossroads between Tuscany, Umbria and the Marche, its surrounds an unattractive centre for light industry and food production, especially pasta – even before you reach the walled centre, the sprawling Buitoni pasta factory, founded more than 150 years ago, leaps into view. Once you're through the Porta Fiorentina, however, you'll find the town pleasant enough, with its pedestrianised main thoroughfare (via XX Settembre), curving its way among *palazzi* interspersed by the odd medieval tower.

Sansepolcro is best known as the birthplace of the early Renaissance maestro of perspective and proportion **Piero della Francesca** (*see p261*), whose works are prominently displayed in the excellent **Museo Civico** (via Aggiunti 65, 0575 732 218, admission L10,000/€5.20). Works on display include the important *Madonna della Misericordia* (c1445), in which della Francesca overturns the laws of proportion by depicting an all-encompassing, monumental Madonna dwarfing the faithful and protecting them with her mantle. The fatalism in her expression and stance echo those of the *Madonna del Parto* in Monterchi (*see p266*), painted around the same time. Della Francesca can't resist placing himself among the Virgin's followers, facing us, to her left. There's another self-portrait in *The Resurrection* (c1460), in which a muscular Christ steps from his own tomb, carrying with him a renewal of life, reawakening the somnolent soldiers at his feet. Della Francesca again faces us, among them, to the left of Christ. The Casa di Piero della Francesca, the painter's base for most of his life (today it houses the artist's foundation), is nearby but isn't open to the public.

The 14th-century Romanesque Duomo contains on its left altar an imposing wooden crucifix known as the Volto Santo, probably brought to Sansepolcro from the Orient, and very similar to its better-known and more revered equivalent in Lucca's Duomo di San Martino.

Local events include a torchlit Easter procession on Good Friday and a traditional crossbow tournament known as the Palio della Balestra, held the second Sunday in September.

There are central though somewhat sterile rooms at the **Albergo Fiorentino** (via L Pacioli 60, 0575 740 350, rates single L80,000-L120,000/€41.50-€62) on the corner of Via XX Settembre. The **Ristorante da Ventura** (via Aggiunti 30, 0575 742 560, closed Sat, average L70,000/€36) probably provides the town's best meal, at a price; top it off, or warm up to it, at the **Enoteca Guidi** (via L Pacioli 44, 0575 741 086, closed lunch Sat & Sun, all Wed, average L25,000/€13), where you can sample local red or white Terra di Piero della Francesca or a glass of home-made Vin Santo.

Monterchi enveloped in valley mist.

Monterchi

No Tuscan town craves to be as associated with a single piece of art as this cluster of hilltop homes on the road between Arezzo and Sansepolcro does with della Francesca's delicate *La Madonna del Parto*, with the creation of a multimedia centre, the **Museo Madonna del Parto** (via Reglia 1, 0575 70713, admission L5,000/€2.60), in the local school for the study of Sansepolcro's famous son.

Centre stage, of course, is the rotund Madonna, one hand protectively and proudly rested on the slit in her dress revealing her pregnant state, circled symmetrically by angels lightly drawing back a canopy. This sublime rendition of a sacred yet rustic maternal figure is the only one of its kind in Renaissance art. The exhibit also contains a fascinating display about the restoration of some of Piero's pieces, including his masterpiece *The Legend of the True Cross*, displayed in the church of San Francesco in Arezzo (*see p258*).

Monterchi began life as Mons Ercules, a centre for the cult worship of the pagan figure of Hercules. For an atmospheric meal head up to **Ristorante Al Travato** (piazza Umberto 1, 0575 70111, closed Mon Apr-Oct, Mon-Thur & dinner Fri-Sun Nov-March, average L25,000/€13) in part of Monterchi's fortress.

Anghiari

Perched on a hill overlooking the Valtiberina and Sansepolcro from the south, Anghiari's dominant position and impressive walls made it a stronghold from which Florence could control Tuscany's far east, following its victory over the Milanese Visconti family in the Battle of Anghiari in 1440. Leonardo consigned the event to posterity in his (unfinished) rendition on display in the Palazzo Vecchio in Florence. Today, with its maze of vaulted alleys and abundance of flower-strewn doorways it's a peaceful and pleasant place to wander around.

The town has also become renowned for its wood-crafting and antique furniture restoration. It hosts the annual Valtiberina crafts market in late April and an antiques fair on the third Sunday of every other month. The **Museo Statale di Palazzo Taglieschi** (piazza Mameli 16, 0575 788 001, closed Mon, admission L4,000/€2.10) is essentially a crafts museum displaying numerous local artefacts, a polychrome terracotta by della Robbia and a striking wooden sculpture of the Madonna by Jacopo della Quercia.

Across the road is the Istituto Statale d'Arte, a training school for furniture and wooden antique restorers. The products can be seen in

Florentine bastion **Anghiari**. *See p266.*

with Chianina beef, an even leaner, more tender and flavoursome variety of its northern cousin, La Fiorentina. The valley west of the Chiana river is dotted with self-contained outposts such as Monte San Savino and Lucignano, but it's to the east of the river that Arezzo province shows off its very best, in splendid sandstone Cortona.

Getting there

By car: The A1 autostrada passes right through the Valdichiana, with exits for Monte San Savino and Val di Chiana (for Cortona, off the main SS75 to Perugia). From Arezzo, Castiglion Fiorentina and Cortona are reached via the SS71.

By train: Cortona has 2 train stations: Camucia-Cortona, 5km (3miles) away, and Terontola-Cortona, 11km (7miles) from town. Castiglion Fiorentina is on the same line. Trains from Arezzo take 15min to Castiglion, 22min to Camucia and 27min to Terontola. Slow trains between Florence (journey time to Terontola roughly 90min) and Rome (Terontola 80min) also pass through all 3 stations. A regular bus service links Cortona with its 2 stations. Timetable information 848 888 088.

By bus: **LFI** (0575 39881) runs regular buses between Cortona (from piazzale Garibaldi) and Arezzo, which also stop in Catiglion Fiorentina.

Tourist information

Via Nazionale 42, Cortona (0575 630 352/fax 0575 630 656). **Open** *May-Sept* 9am-1pm, 3-7pm Mon-Sat; 9am-1pm Sun. *Oct-Apr* 9am-1pm, 3-6pm Mon-Sat.

the workshop of Mastro Santi (Via Nova 8), a carving and marquetry specialist.

Anghiari's other big traditional and commercial draw is its woven and naturally dyed textiles, exemplified by the **Busatti** store-cum-factory (via Mazzini 14, 0575 788 013, closed Sun). The deafening shuttle looms in its workroom, some of them almost a century old, produce everything from wedding lace to curtain fabrics, using only natural fibres.

The popular **Locanda Castello di Sorci** (0575 789 066, closed Mon, set meal L31,000/ €18), on the estate of a 15th-century castle just off the main Arezzo–Sansepolcro route, is guaranteed to fill you up without emptying your wallet. Owners Primetto and Gabriella want to serve 'the masses tired of fast foods the taste of natural products and fresh air', which include mixed antipasti, plates of meats cooked *alla griglia* and home-made cake to finish.

The Valdichiana

Etruscan heartland and modern-day agricultural flatland, the Valdichiana whetted the appetites of Arezzo, Siena and Florence over the centuries, with the Medici eventually appropriating or buying control of virtually all of it by the late 15th century. Its name today is synonymous

Monte San Savino

Typically circular and enclosed, Monte San Savino is a prominent town provincially, though its Renaissance heyday was brief, coinciding with the commercial patronage and religious power exercised by the Di Monte family in the late 1400s and 1500s. Its main architectural attractions, both bearing the family's imprint, face each other along the Corso Sangallo.

The quintessentially Renaissance Palazzo Di Monte, today **Palazzo Comunale**, was designed between 1515 and 1517 by Antonio Sangallo the Elder and contains an arcaded courtyard in its interior; via it you reach hanging gardens and an open-air theatre overlooking a cypress-dotted landscape. Across from it is the Vasari-like **Loggia dei Mercanti**, attributed to architect and sculptor Andrea Sansovino, Monte San Savino's most eminent son. His hand also retouched the nearby Piazza di Monte and helped embellish the church of Santa Chiara with two terracottas – the Madonna and Saints Lawrence, Sebastian and Rocco.

The Estate Savinese event includes open-air concerts and films in July, the Festival Musicale in the first half of August and the

Tuscany

Sagra della Porchetta all-you-can-eat roast suckling pig celebration in mid-September.

The town is known for its engraved pottery, designed in delicate floral motifs and on display at the **Ceramiche Artistiche Lapucci** (Corso Sangallo 8/10, 0575 844 375, ring bell for entry).

Six kilometres (4.5 miles) west of town the medieval **Castello di Gargonza** (0575 847 021, rates L155,000-L195,000/€80-€100) has been turned into furnished mini-apartments with modern facilities.

Lucignano

Tiny Lucignano is as classically Tuscan as Tuscan towns come. A stroll along its concentric alleys inevitably leads up to the crumbling staircase of the church of the Collegiata di San Michele. Behind it is the 13th-century church of San Francesco, barn-like in its simplicity.

Next door, inside the Palazzo Comunale, the **Museo Civico** (Piazza del Tribunale 22, 0575 838 001, closed Mon & Wed, admission L5,000/€2.60) exhibits Lucignano's symbol, the Albero di San Francesco large late-Gothic golden reliquary representing a cross, along with wooden panels by Signorelli and a triptych by Bartolo di Fredi.

Within a few metres is the **Albergo e Osteria Da Totó**, a delightful family-run hotel with competitive prices (piazza del Tribunale 6, 0575 836 763, rates L90,000-L110,000/€46.50-€57). Set in a converted monastery, it has a small swimming pool. Owner and chef Lorenzo Totó takes pride in his herb-based cooking. There are three multi-course menus at L25,000 (€13), L35,000 (€18) and L45,000 (€23), and an impressive range of 54 fruit-, flower- and root-based *grappe*.

Foiano della Chiana

Foiano's buildings and steeples are distinguished by the warm, reddish tones of their *cotto* bricks. Its oval shape centres on piazza Cavour, dominated by the Palazzo delle Logge, formerly a Medici hunting lodge. Today, it houses the Fototeca Furio del Furia, an engrossing display of early 20th-century snapshots of rural life in Italy.

Just outside the walls is Foiano's other main draw, the neo-classical Collegiata di San Martino, which houses a vintage Andrea della Robbia glazed terracotta, the *Madonna of the Girdle*, and Signorelli's last work, *Coronation of the Virgin* (1523), which was heavily influenced by della Francesca.

Lucignano – as Tuscan as they come.

Castiglion Fiorentino

Castiglion Fiorentino (formerly Castiglion Aretino and, briefly, Castiglion Perugino) is a bustling mid-sized town set against the lower Apennines and overlooked by its impressive Cassero tower, situated in a quiet corner at the town's highest point.

Its Etruscan origins were reaffirmed by recent excavation of walls and the discovery of artefacts dating to the fifth century BC, now on display in the crypt of the Chiesa di San Angelo al Cassero. Above this is the **Pinacoteca Comunale** (via del Cassero, 0575 657 466, closed Mon, admission L5,000/€2.60), which displays paintings by Giotto's godson and follower Taddeo Gaddi and 15th-century artist Bartolomeo della Gatta along with some gold and bronze relics.

Castiglion Fiorentino's most pleasant spot, from which you overlook the Valdichiana, is the **Loggiato Vasariano** in the piazza del Municipio. Just past the Loggiato you'll find the minuscule **Panificio Melloni** (via San Michele 48) with its alluring bakery products piled up behind a tiny wooden door.

At the lower end of town, near the Porta Fiorentina and next to the 13th-century church of San Francesco, **Da Muzzicone** (piazza San Francesco 7, 0575 658 403, closed Tue, average L45,000/€23) is your best bet for refuelling.

On the way south to Cortona, standing imperiously on top of a hill, is the Castello di Montecchio, which once belonged to the famously successful English mercenary and battle strategist John Hawkwood.

Cortona

Both refined Tuscan and rustic Umbrian in feel, architecture and dialect, Cortona is in a league of its own: its jumble of irregular, angular buildings, its windswept city walls, its layered urban development and its strategic position dominating the Valdichiana distinguish it among central Italy's historic cities.

Probably founded as an Umbrian fortress, Cortona grew into an important Etruscan outpost around the eighth century BC and then passed under Roman rule. Following its depredation by the Goths, it thrived as a free community from the 11th century on, and though sacked by Arezzo in 1258, it bounced back and was taken over and quickly sold by the King of Naples to Florence in 1411. Since then, it has prospered safely behind its walls.

Today it's a quintessential *città d'arte* that carefully balances tradition and innovation. Local authorites have chosen to healthily channel its constant foreign presence, even inserting events by foreign study groups into its cultural calendar. Cortona also provides a spectacular venue for the final days of the Umbria Jazz Festival in late July and for the sizzling Sagra della Bisteccha in mid August, a Chianina beef feast.

The town is best absorbed from the steps leading up to the crenellated clock tower of the heavy-set Palazzo Comunale, overlooking uneven piazza della Repubblica, where town life inevitably centres. Adjacent is piazza Signorelli, containing the arcaded Teatro Signorelli, both honouring Cortona's foremost offspring, high Renaissance artist Luca Signorelli (c1445-1523).

On the piazza, in the Palazzo Casali, is the small but eccentric **Museo dell'Accademia Etrusca** (0575 630 415, closed Mon, admission L8,000/€4.10), which spans history all the way from ancient Egyptian remnants to visionary Futurist pieces by Gino Severini (1883-1966), another of Cortona's natives. It includes local Etruscan findings, such as a bronze lamp decorated with sirens and satyrs.

Cortona – in a league of its own.

A few steps on is the piazza del Duomo, which opens on to a picture-book view of the valley. Facing the rather bland Duomo is the **Museo Diocesano** (0575 62830, closed Mon and Oct, admission L8,000/€4.10), home to Beato Angelico's glorious *Annunciation* and works by Signorelli and Pietro Lorenzetti.

More of Cortona's rewarding sights climb via Berrettini towards the Fortezza Medicea. Among these is the 15th-century church of **San Nicolò** with its delicate courtyard and baroque-roofed interior containing a Signorelli altarpiece. Also worth the schlep is the **Chiesa di Santa Margherita**, with its vivid ceilings, and the fort itself, just above it, from where there are views to Lake Trasimeno.

Cortona's only flat surface is lively Via Nazionale, dotted with antiques and wood-crafting stores. At No.54, Giulio Lucarini's laboratory showcases traditional terracottas in typical yellow-red sunflower patterns. Aromas emanate from the *pasticceria* at number 64, which makes sublime pastries.

Where to stay

The **Albergo Athens** (via Sant'Antonio 12, 0575 630 508, rates L45,000-L80,000/€23-€41.50) is the only budget option within Cortona's walls, with dorm-like rooms at unbeatable prices; the newly renovated **Hotel Italia** (via Ghibellina 7, 0575 630 254, rates L115,000-L170,000/€60-€88), offering rooftop views from top-floor rooms and terrace, is one of the best lower-end hotels. The **Hotel San Luca** (piazza Garibaldi 1, 0575 630 460, rates L110,000-L170,000/€57-€88) is generic and modern but has spectacular views over the valley. If you're looking for something central and classy, the **Hotel San Michele** (via Guelfa 15, 0575 604 348, rates L160,000-L250,000/€82.50-€129) boasts a unique 1700s ceiling in its breakfast room.

Where to eat

The **Osteria del Teatro** (via Maffei 5, 0575 630 556, closed Wed, average L45,000/€23) offers good food in an operatically themed setting. **Preludio** (via Guelfa 11, 0575 630 104, closed Mon, lunch Nov-May, average L50,000/€26) serves great gnocchi with chestnuts or funghi porcini. **Tonino** (piazza Garibaldi 1, 0575 630 500, average L55,000/€28.50) is good for Tuscan *antipastissimo* and has lovely views over the valley. For the same view but cheaper, quicker nosh (bruschette and omelettes), try its outdoor Belvedere terrace. **Trattoria Dardano** (via Dardano 24, 0575 601 944, closed Wed, average L30,000/€15.50) is a locals' haunt that serves home cooking at reasonable prices.

Grosseto & Southern Tuscany

Though it hides its light under a bushel, this is the perfect region for lovers of the great outdoors.

This area has been backward in coming forward, and even the region known as the Maremma managed to barely be touched by the '80s development boom that suddenly boosted tourist earnings elsewhere in Tuscany and Italy as a whole.

With the exception of popular resorts such as **Orbetello** (*see p275*) – which are inevitably just as crowded as the French Riviera in the August high season – and excluding also such yachting crowd favourites as **Porto Ercole** (*see p276*) and **Porto Santo Stefano** (*see p276*) – which tend to draw in the boat crowd in droves during the summer months – the majority of the region is relatively unexplored. Yet it has much to offer, be it hiking through the woods, viewing its awesome 2,500-year-old Etruscan necropolises, trekking through one of the huge WWF nature reserves sheltering wildlife that's disappearing from other parts of Tuscany, or sailing to one of the islands.

Getting there & around

By bus
There are about 10 buses a day connecting Grosseto, the region's main town, and Siena (journey time 90min). Buses leave from in front of Grosseto's train station. For further information on buses serving regional towns such as Piombino and Pitigliano call **Rama** on 0564 25215.

By car
The main coast road (E80/SS1) links Grosseto with Livorno to the north and the Maremma to the south. The SS223 is the main route down from Siena, though it's not well signposted in and around Siena. The region's most scenic road is the SS74, which branches inland off the SS1, north of Orbetello, and winds toward Manciano and Pitigliano.

By train
Grosseto is on the main train line between Rome and Pisa. From Rome the journey takes at least 90min, from Pisa about 80min. Trains on this line also stop at Capalbio and Orbetello (for Monte Argentario) to the south, and San Vincenzo and Cecina to the north. A local train links Grosseto with Siena (around 80min).

Grosseto

The largest Tuscan town south of Siena, Grosseto is the capital of the province of Southern Tuscany. During the Middle Ages it represented civilisation for inhabitants of the malaria-ridden swamplands. Bombing in World War II destroyed almost everything in the city centre but left the 16th-century walls intact.

If you're driving to Grosseto along the SS223 from Siena, stop for food at **Le Milandre** (0564 900 683, closed Wed, average L35,000/€18) near Civitella Marittima. The main room features reproductions of photos of Maremma cowboys, while outside there are tables overlooking the family's olive grove.

A interesting stop is **Roselle**, just off the SS223 about eight kilometres (five miles) north-east of Grosseto. Here you'll find the excavated ruins of an Etruscan city, which was conquered by Rome in the third century.

Grosseto itself is hardly one of Tuscany's most attractive towns, but it does trace its history back to the fifth century, when it was an Etruscan settlement. That history can be seen in detail at the **Museo Archeologico e d'Arte della Maremma** and the **Museo d'Arte Sacra del Diocesi di Grosseto** (piazza Baccarini 3, 0564 488 750, closed Mon, admission L10,000/€2.60).

Down an inconspicuous sidestreet, close to a deliciously shady-looking Irish pub, the cosy **Trattoria Il Bavaro** (via Fucini 15, 0564 28673, closed Sun, average L30,000/€15.50) has the added attraction of a charming roof terrace with a pergola. The elegant but relaxed **Buca San Lorenzo** (viale Manetti 1, 0564 25142, closed Sun, average L60,000/€31) attracts the diamonds and pearls set of Grosseto as well as sailors on a spending spree.

It's unlikely that you'll want to stay overnight in Grosseto; if you do, the tourist office (*see below*) can recommend hotels. A much better bet accommodation-wise is to head to **Monte Argentario** (*see p276*) on the Maremman coast a half-hour drive south.

Just another day's work for the fishermen of **Porto Santo Stefano**. *See p276.*

Tourist information

Agenzia per il Turismo (APT)
Viale Monterosa 206 (0564 462 611). **Open** 8.30am-1pm Mon-Fri.
There's also an information office on via Fucini 43c near the station (0564 414 303), open 9am-1pm and 3-5pm Mon-Fri, 9am-noon Sat.

The Etruscan Riviera

The stretch of coastline between Livorno and Piombino has, as well as pricey, parasol-stabbed beaches overrun by holidaymakers, a number of discreet, sandy coves surrounded by dunes and pine groves. A little further inland, between the coast and the Colline Metallifere to the east, is the northern section of the Maremma; stretching between Cecina and Follonica, this section is known as the Pisan Maremma.

Cecina

One of the best things to do while in this area is to indulge in a seaside picnic. Stop in Cecina and pick up supplies at the **Rosticceria** at viale Galliano 5 (closed Nov-Mar), then head for Marina di Cecina. The beaches here are free and tend not to get too crowded.

After lingering over an Italian style lunch out in the open, you can head just south of Cecina to an area set aside as Italy's first World Wildlife Fund (WWF) nature reserve. Called the **Oasi di Bolgheri**, it provides a haven for rare ducks, geese and storks.

San Vincenzo

This former watchtower base is about halfway between Livorno and Grosseto on via Aurelia. It's historic role is clear in the ruins left behind. In particular, a Pisan tower from 1304 still stands here as it has for 700 years.
Many visitors come to San Vincenzo to eat at the Michelin-starred **Gambero Rosso** (piazza della Vittoria 13, 0565 701 021, closed Mon & Tue, average L140,000/€72.50). Eating here is as much about status as appeasing your appetite, but even so, the food is very good. If you're not in a mood to face the snobbery, try popping in next door instead to **Il Bucaniere** (viale Marconi 8, 0565 705 555, closed lunch, all Tue and Oct-May, average L70,000/€36), which serves simpler fare in a more humble atmosphere. In particular, its fish ravioli earns raves from regulars.
About 20 kilometres (13 miles) north of San Vincenzo there's a left turning off the via Aurelia leading up to **Bolgheri**, where the Romantic poet Giosuè Carducci (1835-1907) grew up and where the stunning medieval Gherardesca castle still stands.

Tuscany

Steam yourself in **Saturnia**. *See p273.*

Piombino & around

Not the first stop on your itinerary in its own
right, Piombino is the place from which to catch
ferries to various destinations on Corsica, Elba
(*see p278*) and Pianosa.

The stretch of coastline north of Piombino
up to the ruins of Etruscan Populonia is sandy
and rocky by turns. This area is replete with
mystifying rock formations, necropolises and
unspoiled waters. The easiest beach to get to is
Cala Moresca – leave the car in Piombino's
main car park and follow the signs, which will
take you along a series of tiny trails that follow
the coastline to the Golfo di Baratti.

Populonia, with its Etruscan necropolis,
perches high above the little fishing port of
Baratti. The remains – which include evidence
of both pre-Roman and Roman towns – are
across the road from the car park, just outside
the village. Admission is free and official guides
can be contacted through the **Uffizio Turismo**
(*see below*). Within the village walls there's a
small Etruscan museum and a tower to visit.

If you opt for the coastal road south from
Piombino to Grosseto, it's worthwhile to stop
in at **Castiglione della Pescaia**. This
bustling fishing port offers a good choice of
hotels and eateries. Or go inland to **Massa
Marittima**, an unexpected enclave of art,
history and civic pride.

Tourist information

Uffizio Turismo
Torre Comunale, via del Ferruccio (0565 225 639).
Open summer 9am-3pm, 5-11pm.

Massa Marittima

Massa's position, together with its mineral
wealth and fresh water supply, helped it to
survive as an independent city state for 110
years before being taken over by Siena in
1335. Back then, Massa dominated the high
southern ranges of the Colline Metallifere, a rich
source of the iron, copper and other minerals that
were one of the economic driving forces behind
the early Renaissance. But, after the mines were
closed in 1396, Massa's boom years were over,
and were followed by half a millennium of
neglect, until a small-scale return to mining,
along with the draining of the surrounding
marshes turned the tide in the middle of the
19th century. Today, the town has preserved
one of the most uniform examples of 13th-
century town planning anywhere in Tuscany.

Recent restorations have put a new polish
on the town's Duomo, Le Fonti
dell'Abbondanza and Museo Civico
Archeologico. The **Duomo** harmoniously
blends Romanesque and Gothic details and its
bare stone interior includes a Baptistery famous
for its 13th-century bas-reliefs by Giroldo da
Como.

In the second half of the 13th century *la fonte
nova* was the hub of town life, and the saviour
of the community when war and extensive
surrounding social chaos forced the townsfolk
to hole up for extended periods. Named **Le
Fonti dell'Abbondanza** (fountains of
abundance), the basins suffered neglect for
several centuries before restoration work
opened up the original source to allow the
waters to flow from the fount once again.

In the 13th-century Palazzo del Podestà
on piazza Garibaldi is the interesting **Museo
Civico Archeologico** (0566 902 289, closed
Mon, admission L5,000/€2.60), which has an
expanded Etruscan collection and a marvellous
1330 *Maestà* by Ambrogio Lorenzetti. Up via
Moncini is the Città Nuova or 'new town'
(that is, the 14th-century bit rather than the
12th/13th-century bit) with a fine Sienese arch.
You can climb the arch for L3,000 (€1.60) or
walk around the side for equally good but free
views over the rooftops of town.

Another Massa draw is the **Balestro del
Girifalco** festival on the first Sunday after 22
May, the feast day of San Bernardino of Siena,
who was born here. The Renaissance costumes
are dazzling, the *sbandieratori* (flag-throwers)
are faultless and the final contest – when teams
from the town's three *terzieri* attempt to shoot
down a mechanical falcon with their crossbows
– is a truly fascinating sight.

If you fancy staying overnight, opt for the
three-star **Sole** (corso Libertà 43, 0566 901 971,

Tuscany

rates L90,000-L125,000/€46.50-€64.50) in an old *palazzo*. As for food, **Da Tronca** (vicolo Porte 5, 0566 901 991, closed lunch, all Mon & Wed, average L35,000/€18) is a cheap *osteria* in the town centre serving creative regional fare. Also try **Enoteca Grassini** (via della Libertà 1, 0566 940 149, closed Sun, average L30,000/ €15.50) for a plate of local food such as the town's famous lentil and pheasant soup, or put together a picnic at the counter.

Tourist information

Ufficio Turistico
Via Norma Parenti 22 (0566 902 756/fax 0566 940 095). **Open** *Winter* 10am-12.30pm, 3.30-6pm Mon-Sat. *Summer* 9.30am-12.30pm, 3.30-7pm Mon-Sat; 10am-12.30pm Sun.

The Maremma

The Maremma (as distinct from the Pisan Maremma; *see p271*) covers the coastal strip south of Piombino and the inland region between Grosseto and the Tuscan border with Lazio. Its people have seen centuries of cruel overlords and dynasties – 'mangiavamo pane con la nostra miseria' ('we ate bread with our misery') is a local saying. The area's past struggles have lent it a distinct character and cuisine that have little to do with the gentle, privileged image of the rest of Tuscany.

Most of the Maremma's southern hilltop towns have a view of the sea but no seaside culture. Only recently, with a slight increase in tourism, has seafood been introduced to inland towns such as Capalbio. Some may call this underdevelopment, others respect for the environment. Whatever it is, the end result is that the air seems fresher, the sun warmer and the sky a touch bluer over the unspoiled terrain.

Consorzio L'altra Maremma
Piazza Vittorio Veneto 8, Saturnia (0564 601 280/ www.laltramaremma.it). **Open** *Summer* 9am-1pm, 3-7pm Mon-Sat. *Winter* 10am-4.40pm Mon-Sat.

Inland Maremma

Saturnia

Were it not for its proximity to the small tributary of Albenga, there would be little reason to stray as far as this off the beaten track, but you'll find relaxing in the hot waters here sheer bliss – once you've got accustomed to the steamy stench of sulphur. Either pay through the nose for a luxurious experience at the thermal pools of the **Hotel Terme** (0564

Agriturismo

As you drive round this unspoiled southern part of Tuscany, you'll come across a lot of signposts pointing up the small country lanes to the working farms offering tourist accommodation. These *agriturismo* properties are becoming increasingly popular among both visitors to this region, for the authentic experience of Tuscan life that they afford, and farmers themselves, as a way of boosting their incomes. To become an official *agriturismo* a place has to derive a certain percentage of its income from the land, and its revenue from tourism mustn't exceed a certain amount.

Many places offer a week's minimum stay, especially in high season. The farms are often family-run, and some offer the opportunity of dining with your hosts or getting involved with day-to-day tasks on the farm. The properties vary enormously, ranging from small, rustic villas to castles or lavish farmhouse complexes with vast swimming pools, but are usually peacefully set in the midst of the countryside.

Farm stays are available throughout Tuscany (and indeed much of the rest of Italy), but if you're looking to get away from the tourist masses, finding a place here in the south should fit the bill.

There are a few websites that give information on the sort of properties available, including www.agriturist.it, the site of Florence-based Agriturist Toscana (055 287 838), and the US-based website www.italyfarmholidays.com. There are also catalogues available in bookshops throughout Tuscany.

601 061, rates L350,000-L600,000/€181-€310 incl breakfast), which also offers mud treatments, fitness classes and massage therapy; or follow the procession of camper vans further down the road (in the direction of Manciano) to Montemerano and bathe (for free) in the pretty **Cascate del Gorello** falls and pools, where the rocks are stained green – on a warm, clear night, this is magical. According to legend, Saturn, to punish those who thought only of war, sent down a thunderbolt that split the earth open, causing steamy water to pour forth. In this liquid the disobedient earthlings found rejuvenation and became calm again.

The closest restaurants to Saturnia are in Montemerano, six kilometres (3.5 miles) south. **Da Caino** (via Canonica 4, 0564 602 817, closed all Wed, Thur lunch in low season, average L150,000/€77.50) offers local pheasants with seasonal side dishes. A cheaper option is **Osteria Passaparola** (via del Bivio 16, 0564 602 827, closed dinner, all Thur, 2wks July & 2wks Feb, average L50,000/€26); its owners have another nearby restaurant that serves dinner (**Passaparola nel Antico Frantoio**, via dell Mura 21, 0564 602 835, closed all Thur, 2wks July & 2wks Feb, average L50,000/€26).

Manciano

The massive grey walls of Manciano loom up defensively out of the landscape but its coat of arms bears an outstretched hand in a gesture of friendship. This is the administrative centre of the Maremma, with a hospital and post office, and connecting buses between Grosseto and the surrounding Etruscan sights. Manciano is a quiet haven with views all over the surrounding countryside and plenty of outdoor cafés. It also offers the **Museum of Prehistory & Protohistory** (via Corsini, 0564 629 227, closed all Mon, Sun afternoon, L3,000/€1.60).

Il Poderino (0564 625 031, rates L95,000/ €49 per person incl breakfast, *agriturismo* rooms L60,000-L110,000/€31-57), is a country inn off SS74 shortly before you reach Saturnia; 20 minutes from La Giannella and La Feniglia beaches at Monte Argentario (*see p276*).

Pitigliano

At dusk, with its lights twinkling against the reddish tufa limestone, the higgledy-piggledy town of Pitigliano looks like something out of an Arthurian tale. It sits on a high plateau surrounded by steep cliffs and was dubbed the Eagle's Nest by the Etruscans. The dramatic drop into the valley below is accentuated by an immense aqueduct, built in 1545, that connects the lower and upper parts of town. The tower of the church of **Madonna delle Grazie** (1527) provides a great vantage point over the surrounding countryside.

The Orsinis built up the town's grandeur in the 14th century. They were preceded by the Aldobrancescas, who ruled over the Maremma for about 500 years. Both coats of arms are still on display in the Orsini family's palace courtyard on piazza Orsini.

The Jewish community that was attracted here by increasing Medici tolerance in the 16th century either left or was forced out during World War II. All that's left of it today is a small Museum of Jewish History, housed in the former synagogue in via Zuccarelli, and a pâtisserie around the corner, which still makes a local Jewish pastry called *sfratti* ('the evicted').

The **Museo Civico Archeologico** (piazza Orsini, for info call council on 0564 616 322, closed Wed, admission L5,000/€2.60) has a small but well-presented collection of Etruscan and Roman artefacts from the area.

Tucked away in an alleyway is the homely and award-winning **Il Tufo Allegro** (vicolo della Constituzione 2, 0564 616 192, closed Tue, average L40,000/€20.50) carved into the tufa walls of the town. As well as the excellent seasonal food – try the unusual *zuppa di ricotta*, the sublime papardelle with juniper-spiked *cinghiale* sauce, or rabbit with wild fennel – it serves one of Tuscany's best white wines, Bianco di Pitigliano, under a variety of labels. **Trattoria dell'Orso** (piazza San Gregorio VII 14/15, 0564 614 273, closed Thur in winter, average L30,000/€15.50) is extremely friendly and serves wonderful artichokes.

Sovana

North-west of Pitigliano, four miles by road, lies this now semi-abandon`ed but once important Etruscan town. Between the ninth and 12th centuries it was a thriving bishopric under the dominion of the wealthy Aldobrandini family. One of the clan's most famous scions, the great reforming pope Gregory VII (after whom the calendar is named), was born here in around 1020. There's a small museum of local history in the 13th-century **Palazzo Pretorio**, next door to the arched Loggetta del Capitano. At the other end of town, down a cobbled track lined with cypress trees, is the **Duomo**, a Lombard Romanesque structure with a cool, unfussy interior and a fine carved portal on the left side.

Back in the centre, medieval **Santa Maria** is one of the most beautiful churches in Tuscany. It's a blend of the Romanesque and Gothic, with a ciborium from the eighth or ninth century and a series of 15th-century Siena-school frescoes.

Sovana has two of the best places in the area to dine: **La Taverna Etrusca** (piazza del Pretorio 16, 0564 616 183, closed Mon, average L60,000/€31), where the pasta and the *agnelli con capperi* (lamb with capers) are consistently good and the ricotta-based desserts outstanding, and **Scilla** (via Rodolfo Sidiero 1/3, 0564 616 531, closed Tue, average L40,000/€20.50). Both have rooms should you find the village's sense of peace irresistible – a double with breakfast is L140,000 (€72.50) at La Taverna Etrusca, L160,000 (€82.50) at Scilla.

In a valley below the town to the west is one of the most completely preserved Etruscan necropolises, a series of tombs cut into the tufa walls of the Fosso Calesina. Among the tombs is the second-century BC Tomba Ildebranda, complete with pedestal and sculpted columns.

Hit the dizzying heights of imposing **Sorano**.

Sorano

This village of dark, greyish tufa, perched precariously high above the Lente river as you head north-east from Sovana towards the Umbrian border, is a dizzying sight. Under the Orsini empire Sorano was a defence post, but at times its geology was more dangerous than the rampaging enemies. A series of deadly landslides encouraged a slow but steady exodus of people. Masso Leopoldino, a giant terraced tufa cliff, peers down on the town.

If you like the idea of staying in a medieval Tuscan fortress, **Della Fortezza** (piazza Cairoli, 0564 632 010, rates L180,000-L231,000/ €93-€119) is good value and has excellent views over the town.

The Maremman coast

Parco Naturale della Maremma

This WWF-protected nature reserve, which encompasses Monti dell'Uccellina, has some great hikes. Birds, both migratory and resident, thrive here – ospreys, falcons, kingfishers, herons and the rare Knight of Italy can all be spotted. The terrain ranges from the mudflats and umbrella pines of the estuary to the untouched woodland of the hills, taking in gorse, rosemary, dwarf pines and cork oaks.

Cars are not allowed in the park – there's a car park in the square near the reserve headquarters at Alberese, where the main entrance is located. There's a train service from Grosseto to Marina di Alberese; from the station, take a bus or walk the four kilometres (2.5 miles) to the entrance. The main attraction is the beach, which can be reached from Marina di Alberese but takes more time and effort. To the north of the park, Marina di Alberese beach 'resort' and the salt marshes are open every day from 9am until one hour before sunset. Not as pristine as the bay in the park itself, the waters are still very clean. The Visitors' Centre is at via del Fante (0564 407 098, closed afternoons Nov-April). Admisson to the park is L4,000-L15,000 (€2.10-€7.80).

Talamone

At the southern edge of the nature park is the quiet, unspoiled port town of Talamone, which offers the only accommodation for miles. **Hotel Capo d'Uomo** (via Cala di Forno, 0564 887 077, closed Nov-March, rates L120,000-L220,000/ €62-€113.50) is a three-star hotel overlooking the bay. In town there's **Telamonio** (piazza Garibaldi 4, 0564 887 008, rates L95,000-L250,000/€49-€129).

La Buca di Nonno Ghigo (via Porta Garibaldi 1, 0564 887 067, closed Mon in winter, average L40,000/€20.50) serves up steamy plates of *cozze* (mussels with garlic and olive oil), with a lightly sparkling local white.

Orbetello

In the middle of the most central of the three isthmuses that connect Monte Argentario to the mainland, Orbetello has remnants of Spanish fortifications dating from the 16th and 17th centuries, when this was the capital of the Stato dei Presidi, a Spanish enclave on the Tuscan coast. There's a small antiquarium with some uninspiring Etruscan and Roman exhibits, and the cathedral has a Gothic façade, but Orbetello is really more about atmosphere than it is about sightseeing. Join the evening *struscio* (promenade up corso Italia) before dining on a plate of eels (fished from the lagoon) at one of the town's simple *trattorie*. **Osteria del Lupacante** (corso Italia 103, 0564 867 618, closed Tue in winter, average L50,000/€26) also serves good spaghetti with sea urchins.

Of the town's three least expensive hotels,the best is **Piccolo Parigi** (corso Italia 169, 0564 867 233, rates L70,000-L120,000/€36-€62).

Ansedonia

This is the Beverly Hills of the Etruscan Riviera – not much is left that really reflects its ancient history. Roman ruins from 170 BC overlook villas with flower-draped walls, and the nearby Museo di Cosa displays artefacts from the area. Daily trains from Grosseto stop at Capalbio station; from there it's three kilometres (about two miles) down to the beach alongside the Lago di Burano lagoon (now a WWF reserve).

The coastline stretching southward from Ansedonia offers 18 kilometres (11 miles) of beach with heavenly clear water. There are several campsites; try **Campeggio Chiarone** at Chiarone (0564 890 101, closed Oct-April, rates L10,000-L18,000/€5.20-€9.30 per tent, L10,000-L16,000/€5.20-€8.30 per person).

Monte Argentario

A mountain rising abruptly from the sea, Monte Argentario is the Tuscan coast at its most rugged. If it looks as though it should be an island, that's because it was until the 18th century, when the two long outer sand-spits created by the action of the tides finally reached the mainland. It has two attractive port towns, Porto Ercole and Porto Santo Stefano.

Porto Ercole

On the south-east corner of Argentario lies this exclusive town; the place where the painter Caravaggio died drunk on the beach in 1610. As with Orbetello and Santo Stefano, Easter and August holidays see this small bay full to the gills. The hotel with the best view in town is the three-star **Don Pedro** (via Panoramica 7, 0564 833 914, rates L220,000-L250,000/€113.50-€129), which overlooks the harbour; the two-star **Hotel Marina** (lungomare Andrea Doria 30, 0564 833 055, rates L130,000-L200,000/€67-€103.50) is more central. If you can afford it, splash out on the secluded **Il Pellicano** (Sbarcatello village, 0564 833 801, closed Nov-March, rates L605,000-L1,115,000/€312-€550), about three kilometres (two miles) out of town, which numbers Charlie Chaplin and the king and queen of Spain among past guests. With

a private rocky beach, terraces overlooking the sea and the relaxed feel of a country house, it's one of the most glamorous and luxurious hotels in Tuscany. You'd be hard pressed to find a more divine breakfast anywhere in Italy.

Porto Santo Stefano

The place to get a ferry for the Isola del Giglio (*see p278*), this is also an atmospheric little port where you'll find fishermen mending nets on the quay and fresh seafood stalls.

It's certainly worth pausing here for a meal, particularly at **Dal Greco** (via del Molo 1/2, 0564 814 885, closed Tue, average L80,000/€41.50), a seafood restaurant with a terrace overlooking the quay. At the lower end of the price scale is **Trattoria/Pizzeria Il Moletto di Amato & Figli** (via del Molo, 0564 813 636, closed Wed, average L50,000/€26), which serves pizza and seafood and has views over the bay. The prawn and pine nut risotto is recommended, as is the *tonnarelli*.

In Porto Santo Stefano, the seafront is lined with a string of bars. One of the hipper ones is **Il Buco** (lungomare dei Navigatori 2, 0564 818 243, closed Tue), where the well-dressed and darkly tanned take their Camparis and Martinis. Join them if you dare.

The **tourist office** is at corso Umberto 55a (0564 814 208, closed afternoons in winter).

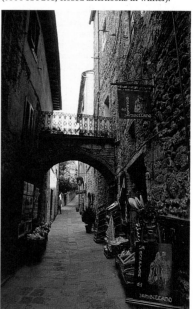

Massa Marittima. *See p272.*

Exile on Elba

When the French emperor Napoleon Bonaparte was exiled in 1814, he must have felt that salt was being rubbed into his wounds – the great conqueror's dreams of a vast world empire had been reduced to the reality of a tiny chunk of Tuscany, the island of Elba. He had been exiled to his origins.

Looking west on a clear evening, he would have seen his birthplace, Corsica, looming up out of the sea in front of the setting sun. Looking east, just ten kilometres (six miles) from the main town of Portoferraio, he would have seen mainland Tuscany, the land of his father's ancestors – the Buonaparte family were already established there, in San Miniato (*see p202*), in the 12th century, at a time when the town was an important administrative centre for the Holy Roman Empire. As Florence became the dominant power in northern Tuscany, the family naturally became Florentine nobles. There are still Buonaparte tombs in the cathedral at San Miniato, as well as other name references including the piazza Buonaparte in the town, with relics that once belonged to Napoleon's family.

With the decline of the Florentine economy in the 16th century, the family moved to Corsica. Just before Napoleon's birth, Genoa, then the island's owner, sold it to France. This made the Corsicans technically French, though many, including Napoleon's parents, who were leaders of a resistance, objected. Being French meant that Corsican children of wealthy families could be sent to French military schools – as Napoleon was. So Napoleon, really half-Tuscan, half-Corsican, eventually became a French officer; first consul in 1799, and emperor.

Italians, especially those who grew up on the island, have a particularly dry sense of humour towards the French, and many tell the following story, which may well be true: After Napoleon made himself emperor in 1804 and placed the Iron Crown upon his own head, he turned to his Italian aide and complained 'Tutti gli italiano sono ladri' ('All Italians are thieves'). The aide, who probably lost his head later on in the day, replied, 'Non tutti, Imperatore...' ('Not all, Emperor...'), '...solamente la buona parte' (...'only most of them').

Beaches

There are two wonderful beaches making up the sand-spits that join Monte Argentario to the mainland – **La Giannella** to the north and **La Feniglia** to the south. Access to the former is along the main Talamone–Argentario road; to get to the latter you have to park at the western end and walk. The further you walk, the less crowded it is. Both beaches have the odd paid *bagno*, but the rest is free beach. You can also hire a bicycle and cycle through the protected pine woods that back on to La Feniglia.

Capalbio

Close to the Lazio border, Capalbio is a magnet for Rome's poets, musicians and politicians. What brings most people here is its proximity to the beach that stretches all the way from Chiarone to Ansedonia.

Trattoria la Torre da Carla (via Vittorio Emanuele 33, 0564 896 070/0564 896 617, closed Thur, average L50,000/€26) serves robust Tuscan cuisine; its terrace looks over the forest where your *cinghiale* (wild boar) was probably shot. The renegade bandit Tiburzi ate here before he was strung up in 1896; his photo adorns one of the restaurant's walls.

Hotel Valle del Buttero (via Silone 21, 0564 896 097, rates L45,000-L140,000/€23-€72.50) is a three-star hotel on the first turn up the hill to Capalbio. **Trattoria da Maria** (via Comunale 3, 0564 896 014, closed Tue spring-autumn, early Jan-early Feb) also rents double rooms (L80,000/€41.50); call in advance. **Agriturismo Ghiaccio Bosco** (via della Sgrilla 4, 0564 896 539, closed early Jan-Easter, rates L70,000-L100,000/€36-€51.50 per person), just outside of Capalbio has ten pleasant rooms.

Il Giardino dei Tarocchi (Tarot Garden)

Garavicchio Capalbio (0564 895 122). **Open** 2.30-7.30pm daily. Closed late Oct-mid May. **Admission** L20,000 (€10.50), free-L12,000 (€6.20) concessions. **No credit cards.**
This amazing walled garden to the south-east of Capalbio was founded in 1976 by Anglo-American artist Niki de Saint Phalle. She has created more than 20 massive sculptures of splinters of mirror, coloured tiles and sculpted stone to represent the main characters from the tarot deck: the *High Priest* and *Priestess*, the *Moon*, *Sun* and so on. Some of the sculptures house four-storey buildings, which you can enter. The artist herself made her home in the immense *Empress* for a while: she slept in the right breast and ate in the left.

The Islands

The Tuscan Islands can be the welcome antidote to Tuscany's largely unappealing coast, particularly tiny, tranquil Isola de Giglio west of Orbetello, though the largest and most popular island, Elba, is inundated with beach junkies in season. The islands and the sea in which they are set make up the Parco Nazionale Arcipelago Toscano, Europe's biggest protected marine park; for information call 0565 919 411 or visit www.islepark.it.

Isola del Giglio

A tortuously winding road connects the island's three villages – Giglio Porto, where the ferry docks, Campese on the other side and Giglio Castello on the ridge between the two, with its medieval walls and steep narrow lanes. But most people find the precipitous journey well worth the effort.

Overlooking Giglio Porto, the three-star **Castello Monticello** (via Provinciale, 0564 809 252, rates L90,000-L230,000/€46.50-€119) occupies a crenellated folly. For the ultimate sun and sea experience, head to **Pardini's Hermitage** (cala degli Alberi, 0564 809 034, full board L185,000-L260,000/€95.50-€134.50), in a secluded cove accessible only by foot or by boat (staff will fetch you).

Another local stalwart is **Tony's** (0564 806 452, closed Nov-Feb), located on the north end of the beach in Giglio Campese below the tower. It can be relied on for everything 'from a cappuccino to a lobster'. Pizzas start at L8,000 (€4.10). Tanned yachters and kids frequent **I Lombi Disco** at Giglio Castello (0564 806 001, closed Mon-Fri & Sun Sept-June, admission L15,000/€7.80), which also has a quieter piano bar (open from 9.30pm).

The **tourist office** is at via Umberto 1, Pro Loco Isole di Giglio (0564 809 400).

Getting there

Toremar (0564 810 803) and **Maregiglio** (0564 812 820) have several sailings a day from Porto Santo Stefano (*see p276*) in summer.

Elba

Part of the Tuscan archipelago, Elba is Italy's third largest island, with 142 kilometres (82 miles) of coastline. Be prepared for crowds, however, it seems that everybody heads to Elba in the summertime. In fact, it can be unbearable by August, when its resident population of 30,000 swells to almost a million.

Portoferraio is the island's capital and the focus of Napoleonic interest (*see p277* **Exile on Elba**); and there is plenty to see here if you can drag yourself from the beach. Napoleon's town residence, the Palazzo dei Mulini, is worth a visit for its views and Empire-style furnishings, incongruous in this Mediterranean setting. However, more difficult to get to at more than six kilometres (3.5 miles) south-west of town, off the road for Marciana, is his summer retreat, the neo-classical Villa Napoleonica di San Martino. This is strictly for pilgrims.

Choosing between Elba's many seaside village resorts can be a problem. One unusual option for accommodation is just out of town – the *agriturismo* at the **Monte Fabbrello** winery (Schiopparella village 30, 0565 933 324, L80,000-L180,000/€41.50-€93 a night for 4-bed apartments) gives guests discounts on wines.

If you head west from Portoferraio, passing through Sorgente and Punta Aquaviva, you'll come to Capo d'Enfola jutting out into the waters; between here and Biòdola are the best options for rooms, food and clean beaches.

Pretty Marciana Marina in the west has **Rendez-Vous**, on the buzzing piazza della Vittoria (0565 99251, closed Wed in winter, average L60,000/€31), which has a variety of Elban specialities such as roasted potatoes stuffed with seafood salad.

Casa Lupi right outside Marciana Marina (Ontanelli village, 0565 99143, rates L50,000-L130,000/€26-€67) is a modest one-star hotel. Marciana itself offers an array of fine medieval and Renaissance quarters. It's the starting point for the ascent of Monte Capanne.

In Marmi di Procchio is Smania, the biggest Elban producer of *limoncino*, which – like its cousin *limoncello*, produced on the Amalfi coast – is a yellow liqueur made from lemon peel and a perfect *digestifo* on a hot day.

On the east side of Elba, particularly in the area that stretches from Porto Azzuro to Capoliveri you'll find the main wine production area of the island. **La Laterna** (via Vitaliani 5, Porto Azzuro, 0565 958 394, closed Mon & Nov, L40,000/€20.50) offers a decent choice of local wines and a mean *torta bria'a*, a dessert containing Aleatico wine.

The **tourist office** is at calata Italia 26, Portoferraio (0565 914 671, closed Sun).

Getting there

Most ferries run from Piombino (*see p272*) to Portoferraio. There are frequent ferries every day; ticket outlets for the ferry companies – **Etruria Shipping** (0586 263 319), **Moby** (0565 918 101) and **Toremar** (056 531 100) – are at the port.

Directory

Directory

Getting Around

By air

If you're travelling by air, you'll most likely land at Pisa's **Galilei Airport,** Bologna's **Marconi Airport** or the smaller but nonetheless busy **Vespucci Airport** west of Florence at Peretola.

Amerigo Vespucci, Florence

Vespucci Airport, Peretola (055 373 498/24hr flight info 055 306 1702/www.safnet.it).
A small airport handling more than 70 scheduled flights a day. About 5km (3 miles) west of central Florence, it's linked to the city by an airport bus service, the **Volainbus,** which runs half-hourly, costs L6,000 (€3.10) and stops in the SITA bus station in via Santa Caterina da Siena 15 (*see p282*). Buy tickets on the bus. A taxi to central Florence costs about L30,000 (€15.50), extra for luggage and nights/public holidays. The journey takes about 20 minutes.

Galileo Galilei, Pisa

Galilei Airport (flight info 050 500 707/www.pisa-airport.com).
South of Pisa and 84km (52 miles) west of Florence, this handles national and international scheduled and charter flights.
To get to Florence by car, take the Firenze-Pisa-Livorno dual carriageway, which goes to the west of the city. The direct train service to Florence's Santa Maria Novella station takes just over an hour. Buy tickets (L8,600/€4.40) at the info desk immediately to the right of arrivals in the main airport concourse. Train times are not co-ordinated with flight arrivals; they run roughly every hour from 10.30am to 5.45pm, with an inconvenient two-hour gap at lunchtime. After 5.45pm there are very few trains and after about 10pm none. There's another service to Florence via Lucca, but trains on this line are even less frequent and the journey time is nearly two hours – check the departure board before taking the

first train (fast trains usually leave from the platform on the left).
Trains run further into the night from Pisa Centrale, with the last departure at around 11.30pm. A taxi into Pisa costs about L15,000 (€7.80), and CPT bus 5 leaves for Pisa city centre and station every quarter of an hour. Tickets and timetables are available at the info desk.
In the other direction, the first train to Pisa airport from Florence Santa Maria Novella is at 6.47am, and trains run almost every hour between 11.05am and 5.05pm. There's a check-in facility on platform five for most flights (not Ryanair). The minimum check-in time is 15 minutes before your train to Galilei airport is due to leave, five with only hand baggage, but there may be queues. Tickets cost L2,000 (€1) more than the normal fare if bought here. A flight info service is also provided (055 216 073).

Marconi, Bologna

Marconi Airport (051 647 9615).
Open 5am-midnight daily.
This is 10km (6 miles) north-west of Bologna, with two terminals. Charter flights, go and British Airways fly here. There's a shuttle between the terminals and an airport bus stops outside terminal A (arrivals); it leaves for Bologna train station every 15 minutes and costs L7,000 (€3.60). Get tickets from the machine in the terminal building or on board; the trip takes about 20 minutes, less at quiet times. A taxi to the station costs about L30,000 (€15.50).
From Bologna Centrale, trains to Florence are frequent and take anything from 50 to 90 minutes; ticket prices also vary widely. The fastest and most expensive trains are the Eurostars; tell the ticket vendor which train you want to catch. They run regularly from 6.30am to about 9.45pm daily (7.15am-10.20pm back to Bologna from Florence). A single second-class ticket is L24,700 (€13). The Intercities are less regular but cost just L15,000 (€7.80) and are reasonably fast. On a Friday or Sunday, taking a Eurostar may be a problem: reservations are required and trains are usually full (consider booking on www.trenitalia.com). For travel on these days, buy your return ticket from Florence back to Bologna a day in advance.

If you hire a car, the trip to Florence takes about 90 minutes, south on the A1.

Major airlines

Alitalia 055 27881/www.alitalia.it.
British Airways 050 501 838/www.britishairways.com.
go 848 887 766/www.go-fly.co.uk.
Ryanair 050 503 770/ www.ryanair.com
Meridiana 055 230 2314/info & bookings 199 111 333/ www. meridiana.it.

By rail

Train tickets can be bought from the ticket desks or cash-only vending machines in the station, from **Ticket Point** (*see p281*) or travel agents displaying the **FS** (Ferrovie dello Stato – state railways) logo. Before boarding a train in any Italian city, stamp (*convalidare*) your ticket and any supplements in the small yellow machines at the head of the platforms. Failure to do this may result in a fine.

Taxis serve Florence's main **Santa Maria Novella** station on a 24-hour basis, and many city buses stop here. If you're travelling light, it's only a 15-minute walk into central Florence. Otherwise, head for the taxi rank or one of the buses or night buses stopping here. Trains arriving during the night go to **Campo di Marte** station to the north-west of the city, where buses 67 and 70 also stop. Note that train strikes are common.

Campo di Marte

Via Mannelli, Outside City Gates (055 235 4130/disabled assistance 055 242 934). Bus 12, 70.
Florence's main station when SMN is closed during the night. Many long-distance trains stop here. The ticket office is always open.

Santa Maria Novella

Piazza della Stazione, Santa Maria Novella (055 235 2061). **Open** 4.15am-1.30am daily; information office 7am-9pm daily; ticket office 5.45am-10pm daily. **Map** p314 A2.

Train information

(055 2351/www.trenitalia.com) **Open** 7.45am-5.15pm daily.
The centralised info service of the state railways (FS – Ferrovie dello Stato) provides details on national and international routes. Some English is spoken.

Disabled enquiries

(055 235 2275). **Open** 7am-9pm daily. English spoken.
There's a disabled assistance desk on platform five at Santa Maria Novella (open 7am-9pm daily).

By bus

If you come to Florence by bus, you'll arrive at either the **SITA** or the **Lazzi** bus station, both near Santa Maria Novella station. *See above.*

Ticket Point

Piazza della Stazione 3r, Santa Maria Novella (055 215 155/ www.ticket point.it). **Open** 9am-7pm Mon-Sat. **Credit** (train tickets only) AmEx, DC, MC. V. **Map** p314 A2.
Sells tickets for Lazzi, Eurolines coaches and Ferrovie dello Stato.

Public transport

Florence is a small city and while the council consider subway and tram systems, its only public transport is the bus network. Run by **ATAF**, it covers most of the city, though strikes are a regular fixture and at weekends you can wait a very long time.

Information

ATAF

Information desk, Piazza della Stazione, opposite north-east exit of train station, Santa Maria Novella (freephone 800 424 500/www. ataf.net). **Open** 7am-1.15pm, 1.45-7.30pm Mon-Fri; 7.15am-1.15pm Sat.
The main ATAF information desk has English-speaking staff, but on the phone, you may not be so lucky. Here you can buy a variety of bus tickets and get a booklet with details of all routes and fares.

Fares & tickets

Except on night buses (*see below*), all tickets must be bought in advance. Drivers cannot sell them. They're available from the ATAF office in Piazza della Stazione (except for season tickets), a few machines, *tabacchi*, newsstands and bars displaying an orange ATAF sticker. When you board, stamp the ticket in one of the validation machines. If you are using a ticket for two consecutive journeys, stamp it on the first bus only, but keep it till you complete your journey, and if you go beyond the time limit, stamp another. Plain-clothes inspectors circulate frequently and anyone without a valid ticket is fined L75,000 (€38.50) plus the ticket price, on the spot.
60min ticket (*biglietto 60 minuti*) L1,500 (78c); valid for an hour of travel on all buses.
Multiple ticket (*biglietto multiplo*) L5,800 (€2.80); four tickets, each valid for 60 minutes.
3-hour ticket (*biglietto 3 ore*) L2,500 (€1.30); valid for three hours.
24-hour ticket (*biglietto 24 ore*) L6,000 (€3.10); great-value one-day pass that must be stamped at the beginning of the first journey.
Monthly pass (*abbonamento*) Ordinary: L53,000 (€27.50), student: L36,000 (€18.50). The ordinary pass can be bought without ID or photos from the ATAF office at Santa Maria Novella station, or from any of the normal outlets displaying an 'Abbonamenti ATAF' sign. For the student pass, go to the Ufficio Abbonamenti in Piazza della Stazione (open 7am-1.15pm, 1.45-7.30pm Mon-Fri; 7.15am-1.15pm Sat). You will need ID and two passport photos.

Daytime services

Most ATAF routes run from 5.30am to 9pm with a frequency of between 10 and 30 minutes. Don't take much notice of the timetables posted on many bus stops – on most routes they're over-optimistic to say the least. After 9pm, there are four night services (*see below*). The orange and white *fermata* (bus stops) list the main stops along the route; each stop has its name indicated at the top.

Useful tourist routes

7 from Santa Maria Novella station, via Piazza San Marco to Fiesole
10 to and from Settignano
12, 13 circular routes via Santa Maria Novella station, Piazza della Libertà, Piazzale Michelangiolo and San Miniato.

ATAF has recently introduced a network of environmentally friendly electric buses, which runs four routes: **A**, **B**, and **C** plus a smaller version of the diesel buses, the **D**. Small enough to cope with narrower streets, they make wonderful unofficial sightseeing tours, taking in most of the important sights north and south of the river. They also have a special 30-day season ticket for only L25,000. Routes are detailed in ATAF's booklet and marked on our map on page 314.

Night buses

Three bus routes operate until 12.30am/1am (the 67, 68 and 71), but only one, the 70, runs all night. It leaves Santa Maria Novella every hour, passes through the centre of town, goes north, calls at Campo di Marte station and returns to Santa Maria Novella via a long, circular route. Tickets are usually available on board for L3,000, double the normal cost, though you will need the correct change, and some drivers don't carry the tickets, so it's always best to buy them first if possible.

Disabled services

New buses (grey and green) share routes 3, 7*, 9, 12, 13*, 16, 23*, 27, 28, 30, 31, 34, 36 with the old (all orange), and are fully wheelchair accessible with an electric platform at the rear door; an asterisk denotes the routes with the most new buses. The small bus route D, which goes through the centre of town, is also fully equipped.

Transport in Tuscany

Tuscany is made for touring by car or motorbike, with roads that thread invitingly through an ever-changing landscape. Having your own wheels is the only practical way of getting to and around out-of-the-way places such as the Casentino, the Maremma, Grosseto and southern Tuscany and the Garfagnana. It will also help you achieve more on better-worn paths, such as Chianti and the south of Siena province.

On the down side, progress on winding country roads is slow and parking in even the bigger towns is difficult, so the train can be a relaxing (and economical) alternative. There are few parts of Tuscany that

Directory

you can't reach via the efficient rail system. One particularly helpful line, with regular services all day, links Florence with the cities to its west – from Prato to Lucca and continuing onto Viareggio or, alternatively, Pisa. There are also lots of small local lines. You will need to buy a decent train timetable, available at large stations, newsagents and newsstands.

Tuscany's bus network is pretty extensive too, with a number of companies, including **Tra-in** (out of Siena) and **Lazzi** (out of Florence), operating around major towns. Note that in most remote villages, buses are timed to coincide with the school day, leaving early in the morning and returning at lunchtime.

Information

For train information, consult FS-Ferrovie's centralised service, which has an excellent website (*see p281*). The bus companies are poorer at providing information: only two – Lazzi and Tra-in – have useful websites. Major Tuscan bus companies include:
CAP *Via Nazionale 13, Santa Maria Novella, Florence (055 214 627/055 214 537)*. **Map** p314 A2.
Lazzi *Piazza della Stazione 4, corner of Piazza Adua, Santa Maria Novella, Florence (055 351 061/www.lazzi.it)*. **Map** 314 A2.
Rama *Via Topazo 12, Grosseto (0564 454 169)*.
SITA *Via Santa Caterina da Siena 15, Santa Maria Novella Florence (055 483 651)*. **Map** 314 A2.
Tra-in *Piazza San Domenico, Siena (0577 204 111/www.comune.siena.it/train)*.

Taxis

There are scandalously few taxis in Florence (one per 653 inhabitants, compared to one per 364 in London), so finding a cab can be a nightmare, especially during rush hour, at night or if there's a trade fair. Licensed cabs are white with yellow graphics, with a code name of a place plus ID number on the door; for example,

Londra 6. If you have problems, make a note of this code.

It's practically impossible to flag a cab down in the street. For important appointments, book several hours before with a phone cab company (though even this is no guarantee, as you will sometimes be told there are no cars available, and to call when you're ready to go).

Fares & surcharges

Taxis are expensive in Florence, but fares are standard. When the taxi arrives, the meter should read L4,500 (€2.30) during the day, L7,700 (€4) on Sundays and public holidays, and L9,800 (€5) at night. The fare increases at a rate of L1,440 (€7) per kilometre. Lone women pay ten per cent less after 9pm – if you ask.

Phoning for a cab carries a surcharge of L3,200 (€1.70). There is an overall minimum fare of L7,100 (€3.65). Each item of luggage in the boot costs extra, and destinations beyond the official city limits (Fiesole, for example) cost considerably more. For details, see the tariff card that cabs are legally obliged to display.

Taxi ranks

Ranks are indicated by a blue sign with TAXI written in white, but this is no guarantee any cars will be waiting, or will arrive in your lifetime. There are ranks in piazza della Repubblica, piazza della Stazione, piazza di Santa Maria Novella, piazza del Duomo, piazza San Marco, piazza Santa Croce and piazza di Santa Trinità.

Phone cabs

When your call is answered, give the address where you want to be picked up, specifying if the street number is *nero* or *rosso* (*see p284*). If a cab is available, you will be given its code and a time; for example, 'Londra 6 in tre minuti'. Otherwise, the operator will tell you to call back.
Taxi numbers: 055 4390; 055 4798; 055 4242; 055 4386.

Driving in Florence

In one word: don't. Florence is easily and pleasantly walkable, and the bus service is a good complement. The traffic is notorious, parts of the centre off limits and parking difficult and expensive.

The air quality is so poor that when pollution levels reach a certain limit, cars that use diesel or leaded fuel are banned from within a large radius of the city (though hire cars and cars with foreign plates are excluded). Digital notices above the main roads into town give notice of these bans. An extraordinarily Stone Age warning system is also in place: streetlights go on for 15 minutes at noon, 2pm and 4pm of the day prior to a ban.

In addition there are the permanent Traffic Free Zones (ZTL). These areas (lettered A-E) include the *centro storico* and are gradually expanding. Only residents or permit-holders can enter from 7.30am to 7.30pm, Monday to Saturday. This is usually extended in the summer to exclude cars from the centre in the evenings from Friday to Sunday. Access to hotels on arrival and departure is permitted, and foreign-plated cars are again excluded.

Breakdown services

It's advisable to join a national motoring organisation such as the AA or RAC in Britain or the AAA in the US before taking a car to Italy. They have reciprocal arrangements with the **Automobile Club d'Italia (ACI)**, which will tell you what to do in case of a breakdown, and provide useful general information on driving in Europe. Even for non-members, the ACI is the best number to call if you have any kind of breakdown (though you'll be charged, of course).

Automobile Club d'Italia (ACI)

Viale Amendola 36, Outside the City Gates (055 24861/24hr information in English 055 064 477/24hr emergency line 116). *Bus 8, 14, 31*. **Open** 8.30am-1pm, 3-5.30pm Mon-Fri. The ACI has English-speaking staff, and charges reasonable rates. Members of associated organisations are entitled to basic repairs free, and to other services at preferential rates.

Car pounds

If your car's not where you left it, it's probably been towed. Phone the municipal police (Vigili Urbani) on

055 32831, or the central car pound (Depositeria Comunale) on 055 415 781. The pound is open 24 hours daily at via del Olmatello (take bus 62). Charges vary.

Parking

Parking is a major problem and is severely restricted in the centre of town. Wheel clamping has just been introduced and carries a hefty fine.

In unrestricted areas, parking is free in most side streets, while most main streets are strictly no-parking zones. No parking is allowed where you see Passo Carrabile (access at all times) and Sosta Vietata (no parking) signs. Disabled parking spaces are marked by yellow stripes. Blue lines indicate pay-parking; an attendant will issue you with a timed ticket, to return to them when you return to your car. A Zona Rimozione (tow-away area) sign at the end of a street is valid for its entire length.

Most streets are washed once every one or two weeks, usually in the small hours. Vehicles have to be removed or they will be towed. It is easy to get caught out, but signs tell you when cleaning takes place.

The safest place to leave a car is in one of the underground car parks, such as Parcheggios **Parterre** and **Piazza Stazione**, which both have surveillance cameras.

Garage Lungarno *Borgo San Jacopo 10, Oltrarno (055 282 542).* **Open** 7am-midnight daily. **Rates** L10,000 (€5.16) 2 hrs; L38,000 (€19.63) 24hrs. **Map** p314 C3.

Garage Europa *Borgo Ognissanti 96, Santa Maria Novella (055 292 222).* **Open** 6am-2am daily. **Rates** L10,000 (€5.16) 2hrs; L35,000 (€18.08) 24hrs; L165,000 (€85.22) week.

Parcheggio Parterre *Via Madonna delle Tosse 9, Outside the City Gates (055 500 1994).* Bus 8, 17, 33. **Open** 24hrs daily. **Rates** L2,000 (€1) hr; L20,000 (€10.50) 24hrs; L70,000 (€36) week. Just off piazza della Libertà.

Parcheggio Piazza Stazione *Via Alamanni 14/Piazza della Stazione 12/13, Santa Maria Novella (055 230 2655).* **Open** 24hrs daily. **Rates** L3,000 (€1.60) hr; L2,500 (€1.30) hr 9pm-7am Mon-Thur; L140,000 (€72.50) 5 days. **Map** p314 A2.

Petrol

Most petrol stations sell unleaded petrol (*senza piombo*) and regular (*super*). Diesel fuel is *gasolio*. All offer a full service on weekdays; many offer a discount for self-service. Pump attendants don't expect tips.

There are petrol stations on most of the main roads leading out of town, and their normal opening hours are 7.30am to 12.30pm, 3pm to 7pm Monday to Saturday. There are no permanently staffed 24-hour petrol stations in Florence; the nearest are on the motorways. The following AGIP stations have 24-hour self-service machines that accept good-condition notes: Via Bolognese, Via Aretina, Viale Europa, Via Senese, Via Baracca.

Roads

There are three motorways in Tuscany that you have to pay a toll to use. They are the autostrade A1 (Rome-Florence-Bologna), A11 (the coast-Lucca-Florence) and A12 (Livorno, along the coast to the north). Autostrade are indicated by green road signs. As you drive on to one, you pick up a ticket from one of the toll booths; hand it in when you come off. As an idea of price, it costs L35,000 (€18) to drive the 270km (169 miles) from Rome to Florence. You can pay in cash, with a Viacard (a swipe-card available from the ACI and newsagents) or by credit card.

Vehicle hire

Car hire

Branches of most major car hire companies are near the station, around borgo Ognissanti. Shop around for the best rates; prices given below are an indication, but they vary according to season (as do opening times).

Avis *Borgo Ognissanti 128r, Santa Maria Novella (055 213 629).* Bus B. **Open** 8am-7pm Mon-Fri; 8am-1pm, 3-6pm Sat. **Credit** AmEx, DC, MC, V. **Map** p314 B1.
The cheapest grade B car costs around L300,000 (€155) for a (three-day) weekend and L600,000 (€310) for the week.
Branches: Peretola Airport (055 315 588); Pisa Airport (050 42028).

Europcar *Borgo Ognissanti 53/55, Santa Maria Novella (055 290 438/055 290 437).* Bus B. **Open** 8am-1pm, 2.30-7pm Mon-Fri; 8am-1pm Sat. **Credit** AmEx, DC, MC, V. **Map** p314 B1.
A Fiat Punto is about L180,000 (€93) for a weekend and L600,000 (€310) for a week. This branch is open on Sundays in summer.
Branches: Peretola Airport (055 318 609); Pisa Airport (050 41017).

Chauffeur-driven cars

Sunny Tuscany (055 400 652/0335 605 2001) provides chauffeur-driven cars for tours of Florence/Tuscany.

Golf carts

It might sound eccentric, but it's actually a very practical and pleasant way to see Florence (see p64 **Electric dreams**). Hire costs L30,000 (€15.50) for an hour up to (€103.50) for a full day. Prices include delivery of the car and insurance. Contact **Biancaneve** on 055 713 4270/0339 871 9125.

Cycling

Cycling in Florence is a form of Russian roulette. There are cycle lanes on the main *viali* but that's no guarantee they'll only be used by bikes, and cyclists should take particular care of roadside car doors being opened (a bad local habit), and of mopeds speeding and monopolising cycle lanes.

Moped & bike hire

To hire a scooter or moped (*motorino*) you need a credit card, ID and cash deposit. Helmets must be worn on all mopeds. Cycle shops normally ask you to leave ID rather than a deposit.

Alinari

Via Guelfa 85r, San Lorenzo (055 280 500). **Open** 9.30am-1pm, 2-7.30pm Mon-Fri; 9.30am-7.30pm Sat; 10am-7pm Sun. **Credit** MC, V. **Map** p314 A3/4.
Rental of *motorino* (for use of one person only) L50,000 (€26) per day.

Florence by Bike

Via San Zanobi 120r, San Lorenzo (055 488 992). **Open** *Mar-Oct* 9am-7.30pm daily. **Credit** AmEx, MC, V.
Bike hire costs L4,000 (€2.10) per hour, L20,000 (€10.50) per day. Guided tours are also available, and English is spoken.

Walking

The easiest and quickest way to get around. Part of the historic centre is pedestrianised, though beware of bicycles and mopeds. Don't be surprised if you meet two-wheeled vehicles coming the wrong way up a one-way street, don't expect cars to stop instantly at lights, and do expect them to ignore red lights when making right turns from side streets.

Resources A-Z

Addresses

Addresses in Florence are numbered and colour-coded. Residential addresses are 'black' numbers (*nero*), and most commercial addresses are 'red' (*rosso*). This means that in any one street there can be two addresses of the same number, but different colours, sometimes far apart. Some houses are both shops and flats and could have two different numbers, one red and one black. Red numbers are followed by an 'r' when the address is written.

Age restrictions

In Italy there are official age restrictions, but it's very rare for anyone to be asked to show ID in bars or elsewhere, other than in gay bars and clubs. Beer and wine can legally be drunk in bars and pubs from the age of 16, spirits from 18. It's an offence to sell cigarettes to children under 16. Mopeds (50cc) can be driven from the age of 14; cars from 18; only those over 21 can hire a car.

Business

Conventions & conferences

Firenze Expo *Piazza Adua 1, San Lorenzo (055 26025/fax 055 211 830)*. **Map** p314 A2.
This centre includes Palazzo dei Congressi in the Fortezza da Basso and Centro degli Affari Firenze. It specialises in hosting international meetings and can accommodate parties from five to 1,000.

Couriers & shippers

CAI Post courier service *Via Alamanni 20r, Santa Maria Novella (055 216 349/055 238 1065)*. **Open** 8.15am-7pm Mon-Fri; 8.15am-12.30pm Sat. **Map** p314 A1.
This express letter and parcel service is run by the Poste Italiane. Within

Europe, delivery is guaranteed in between one and three days and costs L30,000 (€15.50)up to 500g to the UK; 500g takes between two and four days to the US and costs L46,000 (€24). Within Italy the service is called Post'Accelere Interno and costs L12,000 (€6.20). You can track your package on the web (www. poste.it) or by phone (800 009 966).
Branch: Via Pellicceria 3 (in main post office) (055 216 122).
DHL *Freephone 800 345 345*. **Open** 24 hours daily. **No credit cards**. Letters (up to 150g) cost L63,000 (€33) to the UK; L61,000 (€6.20) to the US (guaranteed delivery within 48 hours). A 5kg package is L201,000 (€104) to the UK (guaranteed delivery 24 hours); L229,000 (€118.50) to the US (guaranteed delivery within two to three days). Free same-day pick-up is offered if you phone before 3pm.
Federal Express *Freephone 800 123 800*. **Open** 8am-7pm Mon-Fri. **No credit cards.**
Letters (up to 500g) cost L75,000 (€38.50) (plus tax) to the UK; L53,100 (€27.50) to the US. A 5kg package is L160,700 (€83) (plus tax) to the UK; L194,900 (€100.50) to the US. Next-day service is guaranteed for all deliveries placed before 10am (except on Friday). Free pick-up.
Mail Boxes Etc *Via della Scala 13r, Santa Maria Novella (055 268 173/fax 055 212 852)* **Open** 9am-1pm, 3.30-7pm Mon-Fri; 10am-1pm Sat. **Credit** AmEx, JCB, MC, V. **Map** p314 B2.
Various services offered, including packaging, shipping at good rates, and of course mailboxes (L30,000/€15.50 per month). English spoken.
UPS *freephone 800 877 877*. **Open** 8am-7pm Mon-Fri; 8.30am-1pm Sat. **Credit** MC, V. Letters are L60,500 (€31) (plus tax) to the UK and about the same to the US (guaranteed delivery by 10.30am the next day). A 5kg package costs L167,500 (plus tax) to the UK, L224,500 (€86) to the US (guaranteed delivery within two days). Free same-day pick-up is offered if you phone before 1pm.

Packing & removals

Oli-Ca *Borgo SS Apostoli 27r, Duomo & Around (055 239 6917)*. **Open** 9am-1pm, 3.30-7.30pm Mon-Fri; 9am-1pm Sat. **Map** p314 C3.
For full preparation (all materials and labour included) of a 70x40x 25cm box, the cost is L15,000 (€7.80). No mailing service, but the main post office is only two blocks away.

Translators & interpreters

Emyservice *Lungarno Soderini 5/7/9r, Oltrarno (055 219 228/fax 055 218 992/emynet@ emynet.com)*. **Open** 9.30am-1.30pm, 3-7pm Mon-Fri. **Map** p314 C1.
Full written and spoken translations in 'all' languages.
Interpreti di Conferenza *Via Faenza 109, San Lorenzo (055 239 8748/fax 055 293 204)*. **Open** 9am-1pm Mon-Fri. **Map** p314 A2.
Interpreters for business meetings.

Useful organisations

Camera di Commercio, Industria, Artigianato e Agricoltura (Chamber of Commerce) *Piazza Giudici 3, Duomo & Around (055 27951/fax 055 279 5259)*.**Open** 8am-3.30pm Mon-Fri. **Map** p314 C4.
Provides information on all elements of import/export and business in Italy, and on Italian trade fairs.
Commercial Office, British Consulate *Lungarno Corsini 2, Duomo & Around (055 289 556)*. **Open** 9.30am-12.30pm, 2.30-4.30pm Mon-Fri. Telephone enquiries 9am-1pm, 2-5pm Mon-Fri. **Map** p314 C2.
Commercial Office, United States of America Consulate *Lungarno A Vespucci 36/38/40 Outside the City Gates (055 211 676/055 283 780) Bus B*. **Open** 9am-12.30pm, 2-3.30pm Mon-Fri.

Consumer

Shops are unlikely to take back purchases for a refund, unless the goods are faulty. The best you can hope for is an exchange or credit note. If you feel hard done by, contact the organisation below.
Associazione Italiana per la Difesa Consumatori e Ambiente *Via Ricasoli 28, San Marco (055 216 180)*. **Map** p314 A4.

Customs

EU nationals don't have to declare goods imported into or exported from Italy for their personal use, as long as they arrive from another EU country. US citizens should

check their duty-free allowance on the way out. Random checks are made for drugs. For non-EU citizens the following import limits apply:
● 400 cigarettes or 200 small cigars or 100 cigars or 500g (17.6oz) of tobacco
● 1 litre of spirits (over 22% alcohol) or 2 litres of fortified wine (under 22%)
● 50 grams (1.76oz) of perfume. There are no restrictions on the importation of cameras, watches or electrical goods. Visitors are also allowed to bring in up to L20 million (€10,330) in cash.

Disabled

Disabled facilities are not great, but they are improving. All new public offices, bars and restaurants must be equipped with full disabled facilities. Many museums are wheelchair-accessible with lifts, ramps on steps and toilets for the disabled.

Most new buses are equipped with ramps and a wheelchair area (see p281). Trains that allow space for wheelchairs in the carriages and have disabled loos have a wheelchair logo on the outside, but there is no wheelchair access up the steep steps – call the information office for assistance (055 235 2275, English spoken). Taxis take wheelchairs, but tell them when you book. There are free disabled parking places throughout Florence, and disabled drivers displaying the sticker have access to pedestrian areas of the city. There are wheelchair-accessible toilets at Florence and Pisa airports and Santa Maria Novella train station, as well as in many of Florence's main sights.

The Provincia di Firenze produces a booklet (also in English) with disabled-aware descriptions (how many steps on each floor, wide doorways and so on), of

venues throughout Florence province, available from tourist offices. For more info, call 800 437 631 (some English spoken).

Drugs

Drug-taking is illegal in Italy and if you are caught in possession of drugs of any type, you may be taken before a magistrate.

If you can convince him or her that your stash was for purely personal use, then you may be let off with a fine or ordered to leave the country. Anything more than a tiny amount will push you into the criminal category: couriering or dealing can land you in prison for up to 20 years. It is an offence to buy or sell drugs, or to give them away. Sniffer dogs are a fixture at most ports of entry into Italy; customs police take a dim view of visitors entering with even the smallest quantities of narcotics, and they could be refused entry or arrested.

Electricity

Most wiring systems work on one electrical current, 220V, compatible with British and US-bought products. A few systems in old buildings are 125V. With US 110V equipment you will need a transformer. Buy two-pin travel plug converters before leaving, as they will be hard to find in Italy. Adapters for different Italian plugs can be bought at any electrical shop.

Embassies & consulates

There are no embassies in Florence; there are some consular offices, which offer limited services.
Australian Embassy Via Alessandria 215, Suburbs-North, Rome (06 852 721).
British Consulate Lungarno Corsini 2, Duomo & Around (055

284 133/fax 055 219 112). **Open** 9.30am-12.30pm, 2.30-4.30pm Mon-Fri. Telephone enquiries 9am-1pm, 2-5pm Mon-Fri. **Map** p314 C2. Outside these hours, a message will tell you what to do.
Canadian Embassy Via GB de Rossi 27, Suburbs-North, Rome (06 445 981).
Irish Embassy Piazza Campitelli 3, Ghetto, Rome. (06 697 9121).
New Zealand Embassy Via Zara 28, Suburbs-North, Rome (06 441 7171).
South African Consulate Piazza dei Salterelli 1, Duomo & Around (055 281 863). **Map** p314 C3. No office; call to make an appointment.
United States of America Consulate Lungarno A Vespucci 38, Outside the City Gates (055 239 8276/fax 055 284 088). Bus B. **Open** 9am-12.30pm, 2-3.30pm Mon-Fri.
In case of emergency call the above number and a message will refer you to the current emergency number.

Emergencies

Thefts or losses should be reported immediately at the nearest **police station** (see p291). You should report the loss of your passport to your embassy or consulate (see above). Report the loss of a credit card or travellers' cheques to your credit card company (see p290 **Money**) immediately.

Emergency numbers

Emergency services & state police Polizia di stato 113
Police Carabinieri (English-speaking helpline) 112
Fire service Vigili del Fuoco 115
Ambulance Ambulanza 118
Car breakdown Automobile Club d'Italia (ACI) 116
City traffic police Vigili Urbani 055 32831

Gay & lesbian

For HIV and AIDS services, see p286 **Health**.
Azione Gay e Lesbica Circolo Finisterrae c/o SMS Andrea del Sarto, via Manara 12 (055 671 298). **Open** 6-8pm Mon-Fri. Closed 3wks Aug.
Formerly part of Arci Gay Arci Lesbica, this group has been independent since 1997. In addition to the Timida Godzilla parties it runs,

it maintains a library and archive, facilitates HIV testing and provides community info.

IREOS-Queer Community Service Center *Via del Ponte All'Asse 7, Outside the City Gates (055 353 462/ireos@ freemail.it).* **Open** 5-8pm Mon-Thur, Sat.
Formerly part of Arci Gay Arci Lesbica, Ireos hosts a social open-house every Wednesday evening, offers referrals for HIV testing, psychological counselling and self-help groups. It also organises hikes and outings. All Santa Maria Novella station buses pass nearby.

Queer Nation Holidays *Via del Moro 95r (055 265 4587/fax 055 265 4560/www.queernation holidays.com).* **Open** 9.30am-7.30 pm, 10am-6:30pm Mon-Sat.
Credit MC, V.
Individual and group travel, plus referrals to other gay/lesbian organisations to aid the traveller.

Health

Emergency healthcare is available free for all travellers through the Italian national health system. EU citizens are entitled to most treatment for free, though many specialised medicines, examinations and tests will be charged for. To get treatment you need an E111 form (*see p287*). For hospital treatment, go to one of the casualty departments listed below. If you want to see a GP, go to the state health centre (**ASL**) for the district where you are staying, taking your E111 form with you. ASLs are listed in the phone book and usually open 9am to 1pm and 2pm to 7pm Monday to Friday.

Consulates (*see p285*) can provide lists of English-speaking doctors, dentists and clinics, and they are also listed in the *English Yellow Pages* (available for purchase from larger bookshops).

Non-EU citizens are recommended to take out private health insurance.

Accident & emergency

If you need urgent medical care, it's best to go to the *Pronto Soccorso* (casualty) department of one of the

hospitals listed below; they're open 24 hours daily, or call 118 for an ambulance (*ambulanza*).
To find a doctor on call in your area (emergencies only), call 118. For a night (8pm-8am) or all-day Sunday emergency doctor's home visit call the Guardia Medica for your area (west central Florence 055 287 788; east central Florence 055 233 9456).

Santa Maria Nuova *Piazza Santa Maria Nuova 1, Duomo & Around (055 27581).* **Map** p314 B4.
The most central hospital in Florence. There is also a 24-hour pharmacy directly outside.

Ospedale di Careggi *Viale Morgagni 85, Outside the City Gates (055 427 7111). Bus 2, 8, 14c.*

Ospedale Torregalli *Via Torregalli 3, Outside the City Gates (055 719 2447). Bus 83.*

Ospedale Meyer (Children) *Via Luca Giordano 13, Outside the City Gates (055 56621). Bus 11, 17.*

Ospedale Santa Maria Annunziata (known as Ponte a Nicchieri) *Via Antella 58, Bagno a Ripoli, Outside the City Gates (055 24961). Bus 32.*

Complementary medicine

Most pharmacies sell homoeopathic and other complementary medicines, which are quite commonly used in Italy. Herbalists sell herbal but not homoeopathic medicines; some can refer you to alternative health practitioners.

Antica Farmacia Sodini *Via dei Banchi 18/20r, Santa Maria Novella (055 211 159).* **Open** 9am-1pm, 4pm-8pm Mon-Sat. **No credit cards. Map** p314 B2.
The English-speaking staff at this homoeopathic pharmacy are very helpful. They carry a huge range of medicines and make up prescriptions as well as giving advice.

Ambulatorio Santa Maria Novella *Piazza Santa Maria Novella 24, Santa Maria Novella (055 280 143).* **Open** 3-7.30pm Mon; 9am-1pm, 3-7.30pm Tue-Fri. **No credit cards. Map** p314 B2.
This is a large group practice where several homoeopathic doctors have consulting rooms and offer a range of alternative health services. Some English is spoken. Call first for an appointment.

Contraception & abortion

Condoms and other forms of contraception are widely available in pharmacies and some supermarkets. If you need further

assistance, the **Consultorio Familiare** (family-planning clinic) at your local USL state health centre (in the phone book under Azienda Sanitaria di Firenze) provides free advice and information, though for an examination or prescription you need an E111 form or insurance. An alternative is to go to a private clinic like those run by AIED.

The morning-after pill has been sold legally in Italy since October 2000; it must be taken within 72 hours, and to obtain it you need a prescription – *see below* **Doctors**.

Abortion is legal in Italy and is performed in hospitals, but the private clinics listed below can give consultations and references.

Santa Chiara *Piazza Independenza 11, San Lorenzo (055 496 312/055 475 239).* **Open** 8am-7pm daily by appointment.
This private San Lorenzo clinic offers gynaecological examinations and physicals. Call for an appointment.

AIED *Via Ricasoli 10, San Marco (055 215 237).* **Open** 3-6.30pm Mon-Fri. **Map** p314 B4.
The clinics run by this private organisation provide help and information on contraception and related matters and medical care at low cost. Treatment is of a high standard and service is often faster than in state clinics. An examination will usually cost around L60,000 (€31) plus L20,000 (€10.50) compulsory membership, payable on the first visit and valid for a year.

Dentists

The following dentists speak English. Call for an appointment.

Dr Sandro Cosi *Via Pellicceria 10, Duomo & Around (055 214 238/ 0335 332 055)* **Open** 9am-5pm Mon-Fri. **Map** p314 C3.

Dr Maria Peltonen Portman *Via Teatina 2, Duomo & Around (055 218 594).* **Open** 9.30am-6.30pm Mon-Fri. **Map** p314 B3.

Doctors

Dr Stephen Kerr *Via Porta Rossa 1, Duomo & Around (055 288 055/0335 836 1682).* **Surgery** by appointment 9am-1pm Mon-Fri; drop-in clinic 3-5pm Mon-Fri. **Credit** AmEx, MC, V. **Map** p314 C3.
This English-speaking GP practises privately in Florence. He charges L80,000-L100,000 (€41.50-€51.50) for a consultation in his surgery.

IAMAT (Associated Medical Studio) *Via Lorenzo il Magnifico 59, Outside the City Gates (24hr line 055 475 411). Bus 8, 13.* **Clinic open** 11am-noon, 5-6pm Mon-Fri; 11am-noon Sat.

A private medical service that organises home visits by doctors. Catering particularly for foreigners, it will send an English-speaking GP or specialist out to you within an hour and a half for between L120,000 and L150,000 (€62-€77.50). IAMAT also runs a clinic.

Hospitals

For emergencies, see p285.

One of the obvious anxieties involved with falling ill when you're abroad is the language problem. If you need a translator to help out at the hospital, contact:
AVO (Association of Hospital Volunteers) 055 425 0126 (24hrs)/055 234 4567 (24hrs). **Open** office hours 4-6pm Mon, Wed, Fri; 10am-noon Tue, Thur.
A group of volunteer interpreters who help out with explanations to doctors and hospital staff in 22 languages. They also give support and advice.

Opticians

For eye-tests and prescription glasses and contact lenses see the optician listings on p147.

Pharmacies

Pharmacies (farmacia), which are identified by a red or green cross hanging outside, function semi-officially as mini-clinics, with staff able to give informal medical advice and suggest non-prescription medicines. Normal opening hours are 8.30am-1pm and 4-8pm Monday to Friday, 8.30am-1pm Saturday, but many central pharmacies are open all day. At other times there's a duty rota system. A list by the door of all pharmacies indicates the nearest one open outside normal hours, also published in local papers. At duty pharmacies there's a surcharge of L5,000 (€2.60) per client (not per item) when only the special duty counter is open – usually midnight to 8.30am. The following pharmacies provide a 24-hour service without a supplement for night service.
Farmacia Comunale no.13 Inside Santa Maria Novella train station, Santa Maria Novella (055 216 761/055 289 435). **Open** 24 hours daily. **No credit cards.** **Map** p314 A2. English spoken.
Farmacia Molteni Via Calzaiuoli 7r, Duomo & Around (055 215 472/055 289 490). **Open** 24hrs daily. **Credit** AmEx, MC, V. **Map** p314 C3. English spoken.
Farmacia all'Insegna del Moro Piazza San Giovanni 20r, Duomo &

Around (055 211 343). **Open** 24hrs daily. **Credit** V. **Map** p314 B3. Some English spoken.

Prescriptions

Prescriptions are required for most medicines. Some prescription medicines are free, for others you will be charged the full price.

STDs, HIV & AIDS

Clinica Dermatologica Piazza Brunelleschi 4, San Marco (055 275 8684). **Open** 8am-noon Mon, Wed, Fri; 8-11am Tue, Sat; 8am-2pm Thur. **Map** p314 A4.
Examinations, tests, treatment and counselling for all sexually transmitted diseases including HIV and AIDS. Some are free, others are state-subsidised. An examination costs L36,000 (€18.50) for those with an E111. Some staff speak English.

AIDS centres

Ambulatorio Malattie Infettive, Ospedale di Careggi Viale Morgagni, Outside the City Gates (055 427 9425/055 427 9426). Bus 2, 8, 14C. **Open** 9am-12.30pm, 3-6pm Mon-Fri; 9am-12.30pm Sat. AIDS centre with info, advice and testing. Call for an appointment. Some English spoken.
Consultorio per la Salute Omosessuale Via San Zanobi 54r, San Lorenzo (055 476 557). Run by the ARCI gay organisation, this centre provides various services relating to AIDS and HIV. Telephone counselling is offered from 4pm to 8pm Monday to Friday, and counsellors are also available in person. AIDS tests are carried out on Wednesdays 4pm to 5.30pm. Staffed by volunteers, these services are free. English spoken.

Helplines

Alcoholics Anonymous St James' Church, via Rucellai 9, Santa Maria Novella (055 353 6254 winter; 055 294 417 summer). **Map** p314 A1. This English-speaking branch of AA is affiliated to the American Church. Meetings are held on Tuesdays and Thursdays at 1.30pm and Saturdays at 5pm. These are also open to anyone with drug-related problems.
Drogatel Freephone 800 016 600. **Open** 9am-9pm daily.
A national help centre with some English speakers who can refer you to the correct number to call in Florence if you should need help. They also give advice on alcohol-related problems.

Samaritans 06 7045 4444/06 7045 4445.
Staffed by native English speakers, this confidential help and counselling line was set up for Rome's diplomatic and expatriate community.

ID

You're required by law to carry photo ID at all times. You'll be asked to produce it if you're stopped by traffic police (who will demand your driving licence, which you must have on you whenever you are in charge of a motor vehicle). ID will also be required when you check into a hotel.

Insurance

EU nationals are entitled to reciprocal medical care in Italy, provided they have an **E111** form, available in the UK from health centres, post offices and Social Security offices. This will cover you for emergencies, but involves having to deal with the Italian state health system, which can be overwhelmingly frustrating. The E111 will only cover partial costs of medicines. For short-term visitors it's advisable to get private travel insurance. Non-EU citizens should take out medical insurance for all eventualities before leaving home.

Visitors should also take out adequate property insurance before setting off for Italy. If you rent a car, motorcycle or moped, unless your home insurance covers you make sure you pay the extra for full insurance, and sign the collision damage waiver.

Internet & e-mail

Italy started late, but now it's going all out to catch up with the rest of the Western world in getting wired. Even most budget hotels will allow you to plug your modem into their phone system and the more upmarket establishments will probably have dataports in every bedroom.

Some Italian phone plugs are different from US and UK versions, though in modern hotels the standard US Bell socket is often used. Check in advance so you can buy one on your way over.

A number of Italian providers offer free Internet access, including **Caltanet** (www.caltanet.it), **Libero** (www.libero.it), **Tiscali** (www.tiscalinet.it), **Kataweb** (www.kataweb.com), **Telecom Italia** (www.tin.it) and **Wind** (www.inwind.it).

Internet access

Internet points have been springing up all over the city. Most cost around L10,000 (€5.20) per hour, often with discounts for students.
Internet Train *Via dell'Oriuolo 25A Santa Croce (055 263 8968).* **Open** 10am-10.30pm Mon-Fri; 10am-8pm Sat; 3pm-7pm Sun. **Credit** MC, V. **Map** p314 B5.
The first Internet shop in Italy started off with four PCs and now has 14 shops in Florence. Friendly English-speaking staff.
Intotheweb *Via de' Conti 23r, San Lorenzo (055 264 5628).* **Open** 10am-midnight daily. **Credit** MC, V. **Map** p314 B3.
Friendly centre with 18 PCs and Macs. It also sells international phone cards, sends and receives faxes and rents out mobile phones.
The Netgate *Via Sant'Egidio 10r, Santa Croce (055 234 7967/www.the netgate.it).* **Open** *Summer* 11am-9.45pm Mon-Sat. *Winter* 11am-9pm Mon-Sat; 2-8pm Sun. **Map** p314 B5.
A spacious work centre with 35 computers. For more branches, see the website.
Virtual Office *Via Faenza 49r, San Lorenzo (055 264 5560)* **Open** 10am-midnight Mon-Wed; 10am-1am Thur-Sat; noon-1am Sun. **Credit** MC, V. **Map** p314 A3.
Webcams on every PC, DVD players and a range of office services on offer, including shipping and money transfers. Also runs Internet courses. **Branch**: Via Ginori 59r (055 239 9376).

Language

English is spoken in many central shops, and all main hotels and restaurants, though

in some family-run shops and restaurants, and in the smaller villages of Tuscany, it may be trickier to communicate – taking a phrase book is a good idea. For basic Italian vocabulary, *see p297*.

Left luggage

There's a left luggage point in **Santa Maria Novella** train station, on platform 16.

Legal help

Your first stop should be your embassy or consulate (*see p285*). Staff will be able to supply you with a list of English-speaking lawyers.

Libraries

British Institute Library
Lungarno Guicciardini 9, Oltrarno (055 2677 8270/fax 055 2677 8252/info@ britishinstitute.it). **Open** 9.45am-1pm, 3-6.30pm Mon-Fri. **Map** p314 C3.
The British Institute's library requires a membership fee, but offers a reading room that overlooks the Arno, an extensive collection of art history books and Italian literature and well-informed staff.
Kunsthistorisches Institut in Florenz *Via G Giusti 44, Santa Croce (055 249 111/fax 055 249 1155).* **Open** 9am-8pm Mon-Fri. **Map** p314 A6.
One of the largest collections of art history books in Florence is held by the German Institute. You'll need your passport and a photo.
Biblioteca Marucelliana *Via Cavour 43-45, San Marco (055 27221/marucelliana@cesit1.unifi.it).* **Open** 9am-7pm Mon-Fri; 9am-1pm Sat. **Map** p314 A4.
A diverse range of books including some in English. ID is needed.

Lost property

For property lost elsewhere than in planes, trains and taxis, contact the council's lost property office (*below*). For lost passports, contact the police (*see p290*).
Ufficio Oggetti Rinvenuti *Via Circondaria 17B, Outside the City Gates (055 328 3942). Bus 23, 33.* **Open** 9am-noon Mon-Sat.

Airports

Vespucci airport: 055 308 023; Pisa's Galilei airport: 050 44325; Bologna's Marconi airport: 051 647 9615.

Buses

Anything left on a bus should turn up at the lost property office (*see above*).

Trains

FS/Santa Maria Novella (SMN) Station *Interno Stazione SMN, Santa Maria Novella (055 235 2190).* **Open** 8am-noon, 2-6pm daily. **Map** p314 A2.
Articles found on state railways in the Florence area are sent to this office on platform 16, next to the left luggage. Minimal English.

Taxis

If you leave something in a cab, call the taxi company quoting the car's code (place name and number) if you can remember it. Or contact the *vigili urbani* police (055 212 290), where anything left in cabs will be taken by honest drivers.

Media

Magazines

Many newsstands sell *Time*, *Newsweek*, *The Economist* and glossy English-language mags. For Italian speakers, Italian mags worth checking out are *Panorama* and *Espresso*, weekly current affairs and general interest rags whose full-frontal style covers do little justice to the high-level journalism and hot-issue coverage. There are also some useful booklets with listings of events in Florence:
Firenze Spettacolo Monthly listings and local interest mag with an English-language section called Florencescope.
Florence Concierge Information Found at tourist offices and most hotels, this freebie gives events, useful information, timetables and suchlike in English.

Newspapers

Foreign dailies
Many newsstands and newsagents sell foreign papers, which usually arrive the next day (the same evening in summer, except Sundays). You'll find the widest range around piazza Duomo, piazza della Repubblica, via Tornabuoni and SMN station.

Who they? Massimo Sestini

'Paparazzo: a freelance photographer who specialises in candid shots of famous people and often invades their privacy to obtain such photographs.' (OED)

Such is Massimo Sestini, the legendary Florentine sharp snapper. Dubbed 'the Man with the Golden Lens' by the *Sunday Times* some years back in a double-page spread feature on him, he is quick to defend the fierce criticism that has been directed at himself and colleagues, a subject that was brought sharply into focus with the death of Dodi and Diana.

Sestini, now 38, started taking photographs at the age of 17, and shortly afterwards began to dabble in *paparazzate*, as the business is known in Italy. At first, it was an excuse to spend time at the beach; he realised that the Versilia coast was full of celebrities sunning themselves in summer, and that he could actually have a holiday *and* make big money out of it. He then expanded his activities to the more exclusive and lucrative hunting grounds of the VIP haunts of Sardinia and the South of France.

A good paparazzo has to be ingenious and outwit his competitors to get the best, most exclusive shot. To this end, Sestini has become a master of disguise, frequently donning false beard, moustache and wig to gain access to forbidden territory. He also has a range of 'costumes' that allow him to transform into anything from a doctor to the man reading the gas meter at the drop of an eyepatch. By various devious means, he has managed to worm his way into weddings (including David Bowie's Florence bash), funerals (including Stefano Casarighi's to take a shot of weeping ex, Caroline of Monaco) and other situations where security has been 'watertight'; 'impenetrable' is a word that has no meaning for the man.

His biggest 'hit' was Princess Diana in Sardinia in a bikini in 1991, a shot for which he earned some L80,000,000 (about £26,000). Sestini admits that it is a foul job in many ways, that he is always *a rompere i coglioni agli altri* (busting everybody's balls) and that the paparazzi are generally despised by a large slice of society, but he doesn't seem over-concerned about invasion of privacy, believing that lots of the celebrities he hounds are asking for it. It's a question of supply on demand; the tabloids and the *stampa rosa* (or 'pink press' as they call the gossip rags in Italy) pay astronomical sums for gossip and juicy photos because that's what their readers want. He also feels that his *mestiere* or skill is perfectly valid photo journalism resulting in shots that can potentially make history. 'No one recalls my shot of Riccardo Muti on the cover of some glossy weekly, but everybody will remember the photos of Dodi and Diana's Sardinia kiss for years to come'. Besides, he enjoys it.

Italian dailies

Only one Italian in ten buys a daily newspaper, so the press has little of the clout of other European countries, and the paper is generally a simple vehicle for information rather than a forum of pressure for change. Most papers publish comprehensive listings for local events. Sports coverage in the dailies is extensive and thorough, but if you're not sated there are the mass-circulation sports papers **Corriere dello Sport** and **La Gazzetta dello Sport**.
La Nazione Selling some 160,000 copies daily, this is the most popular newspaper in Tuscany. Founded in the mid 19th century by Bettino Ricasoli, it's also one of Italy's oldest. Basically right-wing and gossipy, it consists of three sections (national, sport and local), and each province has its own edition.
La Repubblica One of the youngest of Italy's major papers. It's centre-left, with strong coverage of the Mafia and Vatican issues, but has an unfortunate tendency to pad the news section out with waffle and gossip. The Tuscan edition has about 20 pages dedicated to local and provincial news.

Radio

Controradio (93.6 MHz) Dub, hip-hop, gangster rap, drum 'n' bass and indie rock feature heavily on this station.
Nova Radio (101.5 MHz) No ads: run by volunteers and committed to social issues, Nova Radio broadcasts a very good mixture of jazz, soul, blues, reggae, world music, hip hop and rap.
Radio Diffusione Firenze (102.7 MHz) Mainstream pop, house and clubbing music.
Radio Montebeni (108.5 MHz) Classical music only.

Television

Italy has six major networks. Of these Mediaset channels, **Italia 6** shows familiar US series, Brazilian soaps, Japanese cartoons and adventure films; **Rete 4** spews out an awful lot of cheap gameshows and *Colombo* repeats but also shows top nature documentaries; and **Canale 5** is the top dog, with the best films, quiz shows, live shows and the most popular programme on Italian TV, the scandal-busting, satirical *Striscia la Notizia*. Programmes are riddled with ad breaks. **RAI** channels are known for their better-quality programming but generally much less slick presenting, and there is still a relentless stream of quiz shows and high-kicking bikini-clad bimbettes. When these have bored you, there are numerous local stations featuring cleaning demos, dial-a-fortune-tellers (surprisingly popular), prolonged

Directory

adverts for slimming machines and
late-night trashy soft porn.

Sky and **CNN** broadcast news in
English in the early hours of the
morning on TVL (local TV) and
TMC. French channel **Antenne 2**
is also accessible in Tuscany.

Of the many satellite and cable TV
subscription channels, the best are
Stream and Telepiù. Some of their
packages include BBC and major US
channels, but even the best hotels
have a limited selection.

Money

From 1 January 2002 the
Italian lira makes way for the
euro (€), going out of
circulation on 28 February
2002. There are euro banknotes
for €5, €10, €20, €100, €200
and €500, and coins worth €1
and €2 plus 1, 2, 5, 10, 20 and
50 cents (c). €1 is equivalent to
L1,936.27. Leftover lire can be
exchanged for euros in banks.

Florence is not generally
expensive for tourists –
restaurants, bars and public
transport are fairly priced.

ATMs

Most major banks have 24-hour
cashpoint (Bancomat) machines, and
the vast majority of these also accept
cards with the Maestro and Cirrus
symbols. To access the cashpoint
lobby, you have to insert your card in
the machine outside. Most machines
will dispense the daily limit of
L500,000/€258.23; older ones may
only let you have L300,000/€154.94.
Your home bank will make a charge.

Banks

Bank opening hours are generally
from 8.20am to 1.20pm and from
2.35pm to 3.35pm Monday to Friday.
All banks are closed on public
holidays and staff work reduced
hours the day before a holiday,
usually closing at around 11am.

Expect long queues even for
simple transactions, and don't
be surprised if the bank wants to
photocopy your passport, driving
licence and last exam essay as proof
of ID. They even try to photocopy
credit and debit cards in some banks
– refuse if this happens. Some banks
will give cash advances on credit
cards (though not all), so if in
doubt, ask before joining the queue.
Branches of most banks are found
around **Piazza della Repubblica**.

Bureaux de change

Changing your money in a bank
usually gets you a better rate than in
a private **bureau de change**
(*cambio*) and will often be better than
back home, but if you need to change
money out of banking hours there's
no shortage of *cambi*. Commission
rates vary considerably: you can pay
from nothing to L10,000 (€5.16) for
each transaction. Watch out for 'No
Commission' signs; the exchange
rate will almost certainly be worse.
Main post offices also have exchange
bureaux, where commission is L5,000
(€2.58) for all cash transactions
(maximum L2,000,000/€1032.90).
Travellers' cheques are not accepted.

Some large hotels also offer an
exchange service, but again, the
rate is almost certainly worse than
in a bank. Always take ID for any
financial transaction. Many city-
centre bank branches have automatic
cash exchange machines, which
accept notes in good condition in
most currencies.

Agency Prime Link *Via Panicale
18, San Lorenzo (055 291 275)*.
Open 9.30am-1.30pm, 3-7pm daily.
Map p314 A3.
The quickest if not the cheapest way
to send money across the world.

American Express *Via Dante
Alighieri 22r, Duomo & Around
(055 50981)*. Bus 23. **Open** 9am-
5.30pm Mon-Fri; 9am-12.30pm Sat.
Map p314 B4.
Also has a travel agency.

Change Underground *Piazza della
Stazione 14, interno 37, Santa Maria
Novella (055 291 312)*. **Open** 9am-
7.30pm Mon-Sat; 9am-1.30pm Sun.
Map p314 A2
In the mall underneath the station.

Thomas Cook *Lungarno Acciaiuoli
6/12, Duomo & Around (055 289
781)*. **Open** 9am-7pm Mon-Sat;
9.30am-5pm Sun. **Map** p314 C3.
One of the few exchange offices open
on a Sunday. No commission for cash
withdrawal via MasterCard or Visa.

Western Union *(freephone 800
464 464)*. *Agenzia STS, via Zanetti
18, San Lorenzo (055 284 183)*.
Open 9.30am-1pm, 3.30-7pm Mon-
Fri. **Map** p314 B3.

Credit cards

Italians have an enduring fondness
for cash, but nearly all hotels of two
stars and above, and most shops and
restaurants now accept at least some
of the major credit cards, though
surprisingly few attractions do.

Lost/stolen

Most lines are freephone (800)
numbers, have English-speaking
staff and are open 24 hours daily.

American Express card
emergencies 06 72282/gold card
holders 06 722 807385.
Diner's Club 800 864 064
Eurocard/CartaSi (including
MasterCard and Visa) 800 018 548
MasterCard 800 870 866
Visa 800 877 232

Tax

Sales tax (**IVA**) is applied to all
purchases and services at 4%, 10%
and 20% in an ascending scale
of luxury, but is almost always
included in the price given. At some
luxury hotels it's added on, but prices
will be clearly stated as *escluso IVA*.

By law, all non-EU residents are
entitled to an IVA refund on
purchases of L300,000 (€155) and
over (plus tax, of course) at shops
participating in the 'Tax-free
shopping' scheme, identified by a
purple sticker. On presentation of
your passport, they will give you a
'cheque' that can be cashed at the
airport desk (look for signs after
Customs) on your way home. You'll
need to show your passport and the
unused goods, and there's a three-
month time limit. Sadly, IVA paid
on hotel bills cannot be reclaimed.

Travellers' cheques

Travellers' cheques can be changed
at all banks and bureaux de change
but are only accepted as payment (in
any major currency) by larger shops,
hotels and restaurants.

Police

Italian police forces are divided
into four colour-coded units.
The *Vigili Urbani* and *Polizia
Municipale* (municipal police)
wear navy blue. The *Vigili*
deal with all traffic matters
within the city, and the *Polizia
Municipale* with petty crime.
The two forces responsible
for dealing with crime are
the *Polizia Statale* (state
police), who also wear blue
but have paler trousers, and
the normally black-clad
carabinieri, part of the army.
Their roles are essentially the
same. The *guardia di finanza*
(financial police) wear grey and
have little to do with tourists.

In an emergency go to
the nearest *carabinieri* post

(*Commissariato*) or police station (*Questura*), in the phone book. If you have had something stolen, say you want to report a *furto*. A *denuncia* (statement) will be taken, which you'll need for an insurance claim. Lost or stolen passports should also be reported to your embassy or consulate.

Commando Regione Carabinieri
Borgo Ognissanti 48, Santa Maria Novella (055 24811). **Open** 24hrs daily. **Map** p314 B1.
A carabinieri post near the town centre; the best place to report the loss or theft of personal property.

Questura Centrale *Via Zara 2, San Lorenzo (055 49771).* **Open** 24hrs daily; Ufficio Denuncie 8.30am-8pm daily.
To report a crime, go to the Ufficio Denuncie, where you will be asked to fill in a form.

Tourist Aid Police *Via Pietrapiana 50, Santa Croce (055 203 911).* **Open** 8.30am-7.30pm Mon-Fri; 8.30am-1.30pm Sat. **Map** p314 B6.
Interpreters are on hand to help report thefts, lost property and any other problems.

Postal services

Improvements have been made recently in Italy's notoriously unreliable postal service, and you can now be more or less sure that the letter you sent will arrive in reasonable time, though some problems still remain with receiving mail from abroad.

Stamps (*francobolli*) can be bought at *tabacchi* or post offices. A 20 gram or less letter or postcard to any EU destination costs L800 (40c approx); to the US both cost L1,300 (65c approx) air mail. Most post boxes are red and have two slots, Per la Città (for Florence) and Tutte le altre Destinazioni (everywhere else). There are also blue post boxes with the EU star symbol for European Union mail only. A letter takes about five days to reach the UK, eight to the US. Mail can be sent *raccomandata* (registered, L4,000/€2.10 extra) or *assicurata* (insured, L6,400/€3.30 extra) from post offices.

The new equivalent to first-class post, *posta prioritaria*, generally fulfills its delivery promise of within 24 hours in Italy, three days for EU countries and four or five for the rest of the world. A letter weighing 20 grams or less going to Italy or any EU country costs L1,200 (62c approx) by *posta prioritaria*; outside the EU the cost is L1,500 (77c approx); special stamps can be bought at post offices and *tabacchi*.

Heavier mail is charged according to weight. A one kilogram parcel to the UK costs L30,700/€16 (air mail); L33,300/€17 to the US. Italian postal charges are notoriously complicated depending on whether you are sending a letter, an open parcel, a sealed parcel and so on, so be prepared for variations.

For guaranteed fast delivery, use a courier or the CAI-Post' Acelere service (*see p283*).
Postal information *(160).* **Open** 8am-7pm Mon-Fri; 8am-1pm Sat.
This phoneline (some English spoken) answers queries on the postal system. A call costs L600 (30c).

Post offices

Local post offices (*ufficio postale*) in each district generally open from 8.15am to 1.30pm Monday to Friday and 8.15am to 12.30pm on Saturdays. The main post office has longer opening hours and a range of additional services.
Posta Centrale *Via Pellicceria 3, Duomo & Around (055 27361).* **Open** 8.15am-7pm Mon-Fri; 8.15am-12.30pm Sat. **Map** p314 C3.
This is the main city post office. A vast building on two floors, it's always busy and offers a full range of postal and telegram services. There is a CAI Post courier office here (*see p284*), and a Telecom Italia mobile phone centre.

Other post offices
Via Pietrapiana 53, Santa Croce. **Open** 8.15am-6pm Mon-Fri; 8.15am-12.30pm Sat. **Map** p314 B6.
Via Cavour 71r, San Marco. **Open** 8.15am-1.30pm Mon-Fri; 8.15am-12.30pm Sat. **Map** p314 A4.
Via Barbadori 40r, Oltrarno. **Open** 8.15am-1.30pm Mon-Fri; 8.15am-12.30pm Sat. **Map** p314 C3.

Poste restante

Poste restante (general delivery) letters (in Italian, *Fermo Posta*) should be sent to the main post office (*see above*), addressed to **Fermo Posta Centrale, Firenze**. You need a passport to collect mail and you may have to pay a small charge. Mail can also be sent to any Mail Boxes Etc branch (*see p284*).

Religion

There are Roman Catholic churches all over the city, and a few churches still sing mass. Catholic mass is held in English at Santa Maria del Fiore (the **Duomo**) on Saturday afternoons at 5pm and at the **Chiesa dell' Ospedale San Giovanni di Dio** (Borgo Ognissanti 20) on Sundays and holidays at 10am.

American Episcopal Church
St James, Via Rucellai 9, Santa Maria Novella (055 294 417). **Services** (in English) 9am, 11am Sun.

Anglican
St Mark's, Via Maggio 16, Oltrarno (055 294 764). **Services** 9am (Low Mass), 10.30am (Sung Mass) Sun; 6pm (Low Mass) Thur; 8pm (Low Mass) Fri. **Map** p314 C2.

Islamic
Moschea Islamica, Via Baccio Bandinelli 11, Outside the City Gates (055 711 648). Bus 1, 9, 16 (15min from centre).

Jewish
Comunità Ebraica, Via Farina 4, Santa Croce (055 245 252/055 245 253). **Services** 8.30/8.45am Sat. Call for details of Fri and Sat evening services; times vary. **Map** p314 B6.

Methodist
Chiesa Metodista, Via dei Benci 9, Santa Croce. **Services** 11am Sun. **Map** p314 C4.

Safety & security

Crime is on the increase in Florence, causing great concern among residents, but for visitors the main risk is from pickpockets and bag-snatchers. Buses, shops, bars

Directory

and other crowded areas are petty criminals' hunting grounds: take the usual precautions.

● Don't keep wallets in back pockets – a pickpockets' favourite, especially on buses.
● Wear shoulder bags diagonally and facing away from the road to minimise the risk of *scippi* – bag-snatching from mopeds.
● Never leave bags on tables or the backs of chairs in bars;
● Keep an eye on valuables while trying on clothes.

Also watch out for 'baby-gangs' of children who hang around the tourist spots and create a distraction by flapping newspaper or card while trying to slip their hands into bags or pockets. If you are approached, keep walking, keep calm and hang on to your valuables.

Serious street crime is rare in Florence, and it remains a relatively safe city to walk in, but take care at night; stick to the main well-lit streets and, lone women particularly, avoid the station area.

Smoking

Cigarettes are on sale at *tabacchi* and *bar tabacchi*; both are recognisable by the blue/black and white sign outside. Smoking is not permitted in any public offices or on public transport. There is also a law that bans smoking in all public places without adequate air filtering, but this is widely ignored: you're likely to find people smoking in food shops, banks, even hospitals.

There are a few bars and restaurants with no-smoking areas and **Capocaccia**, **Rose's** and **Latteria Moggi** (for all, *see p131*) all have smoke-free rooms.

Study

With over 20 US university programmes and countless language schools and art courses, many of which have international reputations, the city's student population rivals its residents' at some times of the year.

To study in Florence, you will need a *permesso di soggiorno per studio*. The same requirements apply as for the *permesso di soggiorno* (*see p296*), plus a guarantee that your medical bills will be paid (an E111 form will do), evidence that you can support yourself and a letter from the educational institution.

Art, design & restoration courses

Il Bisonte *Via San Niccolo 24, Oltrarno (055 234 7215).* **Map** p314 D5.
Located among the artisans' workshops in the former stables of Palazzo Serristori, the school has specialist courses and theoretical/practical seminars in the techniques of etching and printing by hand.

Charles H Cecil Studios *Borgo San Frediano 68, Oltrarno (tel/fax 055 285 102).*
The Church of San Rafaello Arcangelo was converted into a studio complex in the early 19th century. It now houses one of the more charismatic of Florence's art schools, which is heavily frequented by Brits. It gives a thorough training in the classical techniques of drawing and oil painting. Twice a week the school hosts life-drawing classes for the general public. For a bit of extra cash, models are always needed at the school either for portraits or as nude figure models.

L'Istituto per l'Arte e Il Restauro *Palazzo Spinelli, Borgo Santa Croce 10, Santa Croce (055 246 001/fax 055 234 3701/www.spinelli.it).*
Map p314 C5.
Widely considered one of the best art restoration schools in Italy, Palazzo Spinelli offers a multitude of courses in the restoration of frescoes, paintings, furniture, gilt objects, ceramics, stone, paper and glass. Courses last between one and three years; one-month courses are held from July to September in the same disciplines.

Oro e Colore *Via della Chiesa 25, Oltrarno (tel/fax 055 229 040/www.oroecolore.com).* **Map** p314 D1.
Month- to year-long courses in art restoration, gold leaf restoration and other techniques. No previous experience is needed, however places on courses are limited and are all taught in Italian.

Studio Art Center International (SACI) *Via San Gallo 30, San Lorenzo (055 486 164/fax 055 486 230/info@saci-florence.org).*
SACI offers five specific credit programmes for graduates and undergraduates. These include both academic and practical courses in the arts, ranging from museology to batik design. There is an entry requirement for certain courses.

Università Internazionale dell'Arte *Villa il Ventaglio, Via delle Forbici 24/26, Outside the City Gates (055 570 216/fax 055 570 508/www.vps.it/propart/uia). Bus 7.*
Courses cover restoration and preservation, museum and gallery management and art criticism.

Language classes

There are no end of language and culture courses in Florence, including many intensive one- or two-month courses, which should provide an adequate everyday grasp of the language. Prices refer to a standard four-week course with four hours' tuition a day.

ABC Centro di Lingua e Cultura Italian *Via dei Rustici 7, Santa Croce (055 212 001/fax 055 212 112/www.abcschool.com).* **Price** L1,000,000 (€515). **Map** p314 C4.
Language teaching at six levels and preparatory courses for the entrance exam to the University of Florence.

British Institute *Piazza Strozzi 2, Duomo & Around (055 267 781/fax 055 2677 8223/info@british institute.it/www.britishinstitute.it). Library and Cultural Centre Lungarno Guicciardini 9 (055 2677 8270).* **Price** L1,455,000 (€746). **Map** p314 B3.
Short courses in Italian language, history of art, drawing and cooking.

Centro linguistico italiano Dante Alighieri *Via dei Bardi 12, Oltrarno (055 234 2984/fax 055 234 2766); Piazza della Repubblica 5 (055 210 808/fax 055 287 828).* **Price** L1,050,000 (€542), plus L100,000 (€51.50) enrolment. **Map** p314 D4.
Eleven language levels; opera and literature courses.

Istituto Lorenzo de' Medici *Via Faenza 43, San Lorenzo (055 287 143/fax 055 239 8920/LDM@dada.it).* **Price** L950,000 (€490). **Map** p314 A3.
Four different courses in Italian as well as classes in cooking, Italian cinema and art history.

Scuola Leonardo da Vinci *Via Bufalini 3, Duomo & Around (055 294 420/fax 055 294 820/www.scuolaleonardo.com).*

Price L900,000 (€465) plus L135,000 (€70) enrolment. **Map** p314 B4. Versatile languages courses for all levels. Classes in history of art, fashion, drawing, design, cooking and wine are also on offer.
Scuola Machiavelli *Piazza Santo Spirito 4, Oltrarno (055 239 6966/055 280 800/machiavelli. firenze@agora.stm.it)*. **Price** L780,000 (€403). **Map** p314 D1. One of the smaller language schools in the city, this co-op offers Italian, pottery, fresco, mosaic, *trompe-l'oeil* and book-binding classes.

Universities

To study alongside Florentine undergraduates, contact an Italian consulate to apply to do a *corso singolo*, or one year of study at the University of Florence. Register at the Ufficio per Studenti Stranieri at the beginning of November. The fees for a *corso singolo* (maximum five subjects) is approximately L1,950,000 (€1,010). To complete a degree course, you must have studied to university level. For details see www.unifi.it. There are also exchange programmes for EU students.
Several US universities, including **Georgetown**, **Middlebury**, **Sarah Lawrence**, **New York** and **Syracuse**, have Florence outposts, open to students from any US university (for the semester and summer courses).
Università di Firenze: Centro di Cultura per I Stranieri *Via Vittorio Emanuele 64, Outside the City Gates (055 472 139/ www.unifi.it/ccs)*. Bus 4, 12, 13, 25. **Open** 9am-noon Mon-Fri. Offers language and cultural courses.

Useful organisations

Student Point *Viale Gramsci 9a, Outside the City Gates (055 234 2857/fax 055 234 6212)*. Bus 8, 12, 13. **Open** 2-6pm Mon, Wed, Fri. The tourist board has established this office to help foreign students with orientation in Florence. Staff advise on accommodation, getting a *permesso di soggiorno*, study courses, doctors and events.
Council of International Education Exchange (CIEE) *205E 32nd Street, New York, NY 10017, USA (212 666 4177/ fax 212 822 2699)*.
Institute of International Education *809 UN Plaza, New York, NY 10017-3580, USA (212 883 8200)*.
Italian Cultural Institute *39 Belgrave Square, London SW1X 8NX, UK (0207 235 1461/ fax 0207 235 4618)*.

Telephones

Although competition has led to some price cuts, the biggest and most commonly used Italian telephone company, Telecom Italia, still operates one of the most expensive phone systems in Europe, particularly for international calls. Tarrifs are still more expensive if you're calling from a public phone and often higher still from a hotel: you're usually better off buying an international phone card (*see below*), though they don't offer anything approaching the same level of discount as in the UK and US. Calling from a phone centre costs the same as from a payphone, but is more convenient.

Dialling & codes

The international code for Italy is 39. To dial in from other countries, preface it with the exit code: 00 in the UK and 011 in the US. All normal Florence numbers begin with the area code 055. The code for Siena is 0577, for Pisa 050. As with all Italian codes, these must always be used in full, including internationally.
To make an international call from Florence, dial 00, then the country code (Australia 61; Canada 1; Irish Republic 353; New Zealand 64; United Kingdom 44; United States 1), followed by the area code (for calls to the UK, omit the initial zero) and individual number. The same pattern works to mobile phones.
All numbers beginning 800 are free lines (*numero verde*). Until recently, these began 167: you may still find old-style numbers listed, in which case replace the prefix with 800 or call 12 – directory enquiries – for the new number. For numbers that begin 840 and 848 (147 and 148 until recently) you will be charged one unit only, regardless of where you're calling from or how long the call lasts. These numbers can be called from within Italy only; some only function within one phone district.

Public phones

Since the popular mobile phone revolution, many public phones in Florence have disappeared, especially in less central areas, and those that remain tend to be in areas where the traffic makes it impossible

to hear. However, many bars have payphones. Most public phones only accept **phone cards** with magnetic strips (*schede telefoniche*); a few also accept major credit cards and some accept coins only. *Schede telefoniche* are available from *tabacchi*, some newsstands and some bars, as are the pre-paid phone cards offering access via an 800 number to both domestic and international calls.
To use a card phone, lift the receiver and wait for the tone, then insert the card (with the perforated corner torn off), and dial. To use a coin phone, lift the receiver and insert the minimum, then dial. There are no beeps to warn you that your money is about to run out, so it's best to overdo the coins. Unused coins will be refunded, but change isn't given from half-used coins so keep small ones in hand.

Operator services

To make a reverse charge (collect) call, dial 170 for the international operator in Italy. To be connected to the operator in the country you want to call, dial 172 followed by a four-digit code for the country (hence 172 00 44 for the UK and 172 00 1 for the US) and you'll be connected directly to an operator in that country. If you are calling from a phone box, you will need to insert a coin, which will be refunded after your call.
The following services operate 24 hours daily.
Operator and **Italian directory enquiries** 12.
International operator 170.
International directory enquiries 176.
Problems on national calls 182.
Problems on international calls 176.
Wake-up calls 114; an automatic message will ask you to dial in the time you want your call, with four digits on a 24-hour clock, followed by your phone number.
Tourist information 110 (Italian).

Phone centres

Telecom Italia *Via Cavour 21r, San Lorenzo*. **Open** 8am-9.45pm daily. **Map** p314 A4.
At this Telecom Italia office, you are allocated a booth and can either use a phone card or pay cash at the desk after you have finished making all your calls. It also has phone books for all of Europe, information on telephone charges and phone cards.

Telephone directories

All hotels and most bars and restaurants have phone books

and Yellow Pages (ask to see the *elenco telefonico*).

Mobile phones

Italian mobile phone numbers begin with 3. Note that until mid-2001 they began 03.

Owners of GSM phones can use them on both 900 and 1800 bands; British, Australian and New Zealand mobiles enabled for roaming work fine on a local network. US mobiles use a different frequency and cannot be used in Italy. You'll need to use + and your country code to dial home.

Pay-as-you-go mobiles can be bought from any of the many phone shops from L200,000 (€103.50), including the SIM card and L50,000 (€26) of calls of all kinds (both international and within Italy). Top-up cards are available from all *tabacchi* and some newsstands. This could be an option for longer or business stays or if you visit Italy frequently, since even if your UK mobile works here you will pay pumped-up rates.

Some Internet points hire out phones; try **Intotheweb** or **Internet Train** (*see p288*). These mobile phone shops are central:

Spazio Omnitel *Via Panzani 33r, Santa Maria Novella (055 267 0121)*. **Open** 3.30-7.30pm Mon; 9.30am-7.30pm Tue-Sat. **Credit** AmEx, MC, V. **Map** p314 B2.

Il Telefonino (TIM) *Via Pellicceria 3, Duomo & Around (055 239 6066)*. **Open** 3.30-7.30pm Mon; 9.30am-7.30pm Tue-Sat. **Credit** AmEx, MC, V. **Map** p314 C3.

Faxes

Faxes can be sent from most large post offices (*see p291*), which charge per sheet sent. Rates are L2,500 (€1.30) per page in Italy or L9,860 (€5.10) for Europe. Faxes can also be sent from some photocopying outlets and Internet points though at higher rates, and at most hotels. DIY fax/phones can be found in airports and main stations.

Telegrams

These can be sent from main post offices. The telegraph office at the Posta Centrale (*see p291*) is open 8.30am to 7pm Monday to Friday and 8.30am to 12.30pm Saturday. Alternatively, you can dictate telegrams over the phone. Dial 186 from a private or hotel phone and a message in Italian will tell you to dial the number of the phone you're phoning from. You will then be passed to a telephonist who will take your message (some speak English).

Time

Italy is an hour ahead of London, six ahead of New York and eight behind Sydney. Clocks go forward an hour in spring and back in autumn, in line with other EU countries.

Tipping

The 10-15 per cent tip customary in many countries is considered generous in Florence. Locals sometimes leave a few coins on the counter when buying drinks at the bar and, depending on the standard of the restaurant, L2,000 (€1) to L10,000 (€5) for the waiter after a meal. Many of the larger restaurants now include a 10-15 per cent service charge. Tips are not expected in smaller restaurants, although they are always appreciated. Taxi drivers will be surprised if you do more than round the fare up to the nearest L1,000 (50c).

Toilets

Florence has very few public loos. The most useful of them are in Santa Maria Novella station, Palazzo Vecchio, the Palazzo Pitti, the coach park to the west of Fortezza da Basso and piazzale Michelangiolo. It's usually easiest to go to a bar (obliged by law to let you use their facilities). Ask for the *bagno*; in some bars you'll be given the key: bar loos are often kept locked to discourage use by drug addicts.

Tourist information

To be sent an information pack in advance of your visit, get in touch with ENIT, the Italian tourist board (UK: 020 7498 1254/fax 020 7493 6695/enit lond@globalnet.co.uk; US: 212 245 5618/fax 212 586 9249/ www.italiantourism.com). Tell them where and when you're going and any special interests.

Florence's provincial tourist board, the **Azienda Promozionale Turistica**, or APT, and the council-run **Ufficio Informazione Turistiche** have helpful multilingual staff who do their best to supply reliable information – not easy as museums and galleries tend to change their opening hours without telling them. There's no central information service for the Tuscany region; you have to contact the APT in each district (listed in this guide under the relevant area).

The *English Yellow Pages*, from principal bookshops, lists English-speaking services and useful numbers.

A good street map is available free from APT offices. Telecom Italia supplies subscribers with *TuttoCittà*, a detailed street atlas covering the whole urban area; most bars and hotels keep one.

APT Firenze *Via Manzoni 16, Santa Croce (055 23320)*. **Open** 9am-1pm Mon-Sat.
This is the APT headquarters. The most central office, however, is at via Cavour 1r (open 8.15am-7.15pm Mon-Sat); there are also offices in Florence and Pisa airports. The APT provides information and brochures on attractions and events in Florence and the surrounding province (not all of Tuscany). As well as free maps, it publishes a brochure, *Firenze per i Giovani*, aimed at young people, with listings for language courses, Internet services, clubs, bike hire, hostels and so on. APT provides hotel lists but not a booking service. **Branches:** Via Cavour 1r (055 290 832); Piazza Mino 37, Fiesole (055 598 720).
Ufficio Informazione Turistiche *Borgo Santa Croce 29r, Santa Croce (055 234 0444)*. **Open** *Summer* 9am-7pm Mon-Sat; 9am-1.45pm Sun. *Winter* 9am-5pm Mon-Sat. **Map** p314 C5.
Run by the city of Florence, these offices provide tourist information, free maps, restaurant and hotel lists. **Branch:** Piazza della Stazione (055 212 245).
Tourist Help Open *Easter-Sept* 8am-7pm daily.
This useful service is run by the *vigili urbani* from two vans, one in Piazza della Repubblica and one just south of the Ponte Vecchio in Via Guicciardini. APT personnel and the

Directory

Average monthly climate

Month	High temp	Low temp	Rainfall	Relative humidity
Jan	50° F (10°C)	30°F (-1°C)	2.5in (64.1mm)	75%
Feb	54°F (12°C)	34°F (1°C)	2.4in (61.5mm)	72%
Mar	59°F (15°C)	41°F (5°C)	2.7in (69.4mm)	72%
Apr	68°F (20°C)	46°F (8°C)	2.8in (70.5mm)	72%
May	75°F (24°C)	52°F (11°C)	2.9in (73.3mm)	71%
June	84°F (29°C)	57°F (14°C)	2.2in (56.4mm)	64%
July	93°F (34°C)	64°F (18°C)	1.3in (34.2mm)	66%
Aug	90°F (32°C)	57°F (14°C)	1.8in (46.9mm)	71%
Sep	82°F (28°C)	55°F (13°C)	3.3in (8.4mm)	76%
Oct	73°F (23°C)	52°F (11°C)	3.9in (99.1mm)	81%
Nov	61°F (16°C)	39°F (4°C)	4.1in (103.4mm)	81%
Dec	55°F (13°C)	39°F (4°C)	3.1in (79.4mm)	73%

municipal police provide practical help and information. This is also where to register complaints about abusive restaurant or hotel charges.

Visas & immigration

Non-EU citizens and Britons require full passports. EU citizens are permitted unrestricted access to Italy and citizens of the US, Canada, Australia and New Zealand do not need visas for stays of up to three months. In theory, all visitors to Italy must declare their presence to the local police within eight days of arrival. If you are staying in a hotel, this will be done for you. If not, contact the **Questura Centrale** (*see p291*), the main police station, for advice and the requisite bureaucracy.

Weights & measures

Italy uses only the metric system; remember that all speed limits are in kilometres. One kilometre is equivalent to 0.62 mile (1 mile = 1.6km). Petrol, like other liquids, is measured in litres: one UK gallon = 4.54 litres; 1 US gallon = 3.79 litres).

A kilogram is equivalent to 2.2 pounds (1 pound = 0.45kg). Food is often sold in 'ettos' (sometimes written 'hg'); 1 *etto* = 100 grammes (3.52 ounces), so in delicatessens, you should ask for multiples of *etti* (*un'etto, due etti*, etc).

What to take

Any prescription medicines should always be obtained before leaving, and should be enough to cover the entire period of your stay, as not all US and UK medicines are available in Italy, and even when they are, they can be much more expensive.

When to go

Climate

The hills surrounding Florence mean it can be cold and humid in winter and very hot and humid in the summer. In July and August, temperatures often soar to 40°C (104°F), and don't often fall below 30°C (86°F) between May and September. During the summer take the sun seriously – every year doctors in Florence warn about the number of visitors who are hospitalised with serious burns from spending

too much time in the sun, going out in the middle of the day (Italians stay in whenever they can during the hottest hours) and not using high enough SPF suncreams. The short spring and autumn can be very warm, though not without the risk of rain, particularly in March, April and September. Between November and February you cannot rely on good weather, and might come across either a week of rain, or crisp, bright (sometimes even warm) sunshine but will see a comparative scarcity of fellow tourists. For full climate information, *see above* **Average monthly climate**.

Public holidays

On public holidays (*giorni festivi*), virtually all shops, banks and businesses are shut, though most bars and restaurants stay open.

The public holidays are: New Year's Day (*Capo d'anno*) 1 January; Epiphany (*La Befana*) 6 January; Easter Monday (*Lunedì Pasqua*); Liberation Day (*Venticinque Aprile*) 25 April; May Day (*Primo Maggio*) 1 May; Saints' Day (*San Giovanni*) 24 June; Feast of the Assumption (*Ferragosto*) 15 August; All Saints' (*Tutti Santi*) 1 November; Immaculate Conception (*Festa dell'Immacolata*) 8 December; Christmas Day (*Natale*) 25 December; Boxing Day (*Santo Stefano*) 26 December.

As this guide went to press there was uncertainty as to whether the 2

Directory

June holiday, which was reinstated in 2000, would continue in the wake of the election of a new government.

There is limited public transport on 1 May and Christmas afternoon. Holidays falling on a Saturday or Sunday are not celebrated the following Monday, but if a holiday falls on a Thursday or Tuesday many people make a long weekend of it, and take the intervening day off as well. Such a weekend is called a *ponte* (bridge); beware the 'rientro' or homecoming, when the roads are packed. Many people also disappear for a large chunk of August, when *chiuso per ferie* (closed for holidays) signs appear in shops and restaurants, with the dates of closure. These closures are co-ordinated on a rota system by the city council, so there should be something open in each area at any given time.

However, if you should find yourself in Florence, or many other Tuscan towns, on the Ferragosto (festival of the Assunta; 15 August) the chances are that your only company will be other tourists wandering the baked streets in search of something to do or somewhere to eat. The Florentines desert the city like rats from a sinking ship and are likely to stay away for several days either side. So stock up on provisions and count the hours until life returns to normal. Exceptions to this rule are holiday resorts such as coastal towns where, although shops and public offices may close, the infrastucture doesn't completely collapse.

For a calendar of Tuscany's traditional and modern festivals, *see chapter* **Tuscany by Season**.

Women

Tuscany, while not one of the worst places for women travellers, still has its hassles. Visiting women can feel daunted by the sheer volume of attention they receive, but most is friendly and men are unlikely to become pushy or aggressive if given the brush-off. It's normally a question of all talk and no action, but if ignoring unwanted advances doesn't work, using a few sharp words and a withering glance usually will. Be aware of who's around you – it's quite common to be followed by hopefuls; if things get too heavy, go into the nearest shop or bar and wait or ask for help.

The notorious bum-pinching is uncommon, but not unknown, especially on buses. As in Anglo-Saxon countries, it's an assault and a criminal offence, and recent prosecutions and convictions show that it's being taken seriously.

Network

Villa Rossa, piazza Savonarola 15, Outside the City Gates (Kelly Stevens 055 575 299/Sandy Nolan 055 899 8089/brusca@cesitl.unifi.it). Bus 10, 11, 13, 17.
A professional women's organisation geared mainly towards residents whose first language is English. It aims to improve communication, exchange ideas and information among the English-speaking community. Meetings (a small charge for non-residents) are generally on the second Wednesday of the month.

Women's health

Women suffering gynaecological emergencies should head for the nearest **Pronto Soccorso** (accident & emergency) (*see p286*). Tampons (*assorbenti interni*) and sanitary towels (*assorbenti esterni*) are cheaper in supermarkets, but you can also get them in pharmacies and some *tabacchi*.

Careggi hospital (*see p286*) has a clinic for women who have suffered a sexual assault, offering them examinations, treatment, counselling and liaison with the police. Some English is spoken.

For information on contraception, abortion and other health matters, *see p286* **Health: Contraception & abortion**.

Clinica Ostetrica *Reparto Maternità, Ospedale di Careggi, Viale Morgagni, Outside the City Gates (055 427 7111/427 7493). Bus 2, 8, 14C.* **Open** 24hrs daily.
Female victims of sexual assault should come here for medical attention. Legal services and counselling are available 9am to 1pm, 3pm to 5pm Monday to Friday at Viale Santa Maria Maggiore 1, Careggi (055 284 752) .

Working in Florence

Finding a job in Italy is not simple, as the work market isn't particularly mobile. Most jobs available are connected to tourism, although there are a few multinationals that

occasionally advertise for native English speakers. The classified ads paper *La Pulce* has job listings, and it's worth looking in the local English-language press.

The bureaucracy involved isn't easy, either. Anyone intending to stay in Italy longer than three months has to acquire a bewildering array of papers to get a *permesso di soggiorno* (permit to stay), and if they plan to work, they'll alos need a *permesso di soggiorno per lavoro*. EU citizens should have no trouble getting documentation once they are in Italy, but non-EU citizens are advised to enquire at an Italian embassy or consulate in their own country before travelling.

All non-EU citizens and EU nationals who are working in Italy should register with the police within eight days of arrival and apply for their permits. There is a useful computer at the Questura that prints out lists (in various languages) of the documents you need for every type of *permesso*. You'll also need a residency permit to perform certain transactions, including buying a car. To apply, contact your local *circoscrizione* office.

Administration and permit offices *Comune di Firenze (Florence council) Palazzo Vecchio, Piazza Signoria, Duomo & Around (switchboard 055 27681/freephone 800 831 133)* **Open** 8.30am-1.30pm Mon-Wed, Fri, Sat; 8.30am-6.30pm Fri mar. **Map** p314 C4.
For residence enquiries, ask for the Ufficio Circoscrizione; give your address and this office will give you the number you need to call.
Questura Centrale (central police station) *Via Zara 2, San Lorenzo (055 49771).* **Open** 24hrs daily; *Ufficio Stranieri* 8.30am-12.30pm Mon-Fri.
To apply for your documents, go to the Ufficio Stranieri (Foreigners' section) early in the day (there are often long queues) where English-speaking staff are usually available. There is a number system (take a ticket from the dispenser when you arrive), and applications are dealt with at one of eight desks.

Italian Vocabulary

Any attempt at speaking Italian will always be appreciated, and is often necessary; away from services such as tourist offices, hotels and restaurants popular with foreigners, the level of English is not very high.

When entering a shop or restaurant, it is the practice to announce your presence with '*buongiorno*' or '*buona sera*', and in the street, feel free to ask directions. People often go out of their way to help.

Italian is spelled as it is pronounced, and vice versa. Stresses usually fall on the penultimate syllable. There are three forms of the second person – the formal **lei**, to be used with strangers, the informal **tu**, and the plural form **voi**. Men and masculine nouns are accompanied by adjectives ending in 'o', women and female nouns by adjectives ending in 'a', though there are many nouns and adjectives that end in 'e', which can be masculine or feminine.

PRONUNCIATION
Vowels
a – as in **a**sk
e – like **a** in **a**ge (closed e) or **e** in s**e**ll (open e)
i – like **ea** in **ea**st
o – as in h**o**tel (closed o) or in h**o**t (open o)
u – as in b**oo**t

Consonants
c – before an a, o or u is like the **c** in **c**at
c – before an e or an i is like the **ch** in **ch**eck
ch – like the **c** in **c**at
g – before an a, o or u is like the **g** in **g**et
g – before an e or an i is like the **j** in **j**ig
gh – like the **g** in **g**et
gl – followed by an i is like **lli** in mi**lli**on
gn – like **ny** in ca**ny**on
qu – as in **qu**ick
r – is always rolled

s – has two sounds, as in **s**oap or ro**s**e
sc – like the **sh** in **sh**ame
sch – like the **sc** in **sc**out
z –has two sounds, like **ts** and **dz**
Double consonants are always sounded more emphatically.

USEFUL PHRASES
hello and **goodbye** (informal) – *ciao*
good morning, good day – *buongiorno*
good afternoon, good evening – *buona sera*
I don't understand – *Non capisco/non ho capito*
Do you speak English? – *Parla inglese?*
please – *per favore*
thank you – *grazie*
you're welcome – *prego*
When does it open? – *Quando apre?*
Where is... ? – *Dov'è…?*
excuse me – *scusi* (polite), *scusa* (informal)
open – *aperto*
closed – *chiuso*
entrance – *entrata*
exit – *uscita*
left – *sinistra;* **right** – *destra*
car – *macchina;* **bus** – *autobus;*
train – *treno*
bus stop – *fermata dell'autobus*
ticket/s – *biglietto/i*
I would like a ticket to... – *Vorrei un biglietto per…*
postcard – *cartolina*
stamp – *francobollo*
glass – *bicchiere*
coffee – *caffè*
tea – *tè*
water – *acqua*
wine – *vino*
beer – *birra*
the bill – *conto*
single/twin/double bedroom – *camera singola/doppia/ matrimoniale*
booking – *prenotazione*
Monday *lunedì;* **Tuesday** *martedì;* **Wednesday** *mercoledì;* **Thursday** *giovedì;* **Friday** *venerdì;* **Saturday** *sabato;* **Sunday** *domenica*
yesterday *ieri;* **today** *oggi;* **tomorrow** *domani*
morning *mattina;* **afternoon** *pomeriggio;* **evening** *sera;* **night** *notte;* **weekend** *fine settimana, weekend*

THE COME-ON
Do you have a light? – *Hai da accendere?*
What's your name? – *Come ti chiami?*
Would you like a drink? – *Vuoi bere qualcosa?*
Where are you from? – *Di dove sei?*
What are you doing here? – *Che fai qui?*
Do you have a boyfriend/ girlfriend? – *Hai un ragazzo/ una ragazza?*

THE BRUSH-OFF
I don't smoke – *Non fumo*
I'm married – *Sono sposato/a*
I'm tired – *Sono stanco/a*
I'm going home – *Vado a casa*
I have to meet a friend – *Devo andare a incontrare un amico/una amica*

INSULTS
shit – *merda*
idiot – *stronzo*
fuck off – *vaffanculo*
dickhead – *testa di cazzo*
What the hell are you doing? – *Che cazzo fai?*

NUMBERS & MONEY
0 *zero;* **1** *uno;* **2** *due;* **3** *tre;* **4** *quattro;* **5** *cinque;* **6** *sei;* **7** *sette;* **8** *otto;* **9** *nove;* **10** *dieci;* **11** *undici;* **12** *dodici;* **13** *tredici;* **14** *quattordici;* **15** *quindici;* **16** *sedici;* **17** *diciassette;* **18** *diciotto;* **19** *diciannove;* **20** *venti;* **21** *ventuno;* **22** *ventidue;* **30** *trenta;* **40** *quaranta;* **50** *cinquanta;* **60** *sessanta;* **70** *settanta;* **80** *ottanta;* **90** *novanta;* **100** *cento;* **1,000** *mille;* **2,000** *duemila;* **100,000** *centomila;* **1,000,000** *un milione.*
How much does it cost/is it? – *Quanto costa?/quant'è?*
Do you have any change? – *Ha da cambiare?*
Can you give me any discount? – *Si può fare uno sconto?*
Do you accept credit cards? – *Si accettano le carte di credito?*
Can I pay in pounds/dollars? – *Posso pagare in sterline/dollari?*
Can I have a receipt? *Posso avere una ricevuta?*
Is service included? *E compreso il servizio?*

Art & Architecture Glossary

Annunciation – depiction of the Virgin Mary being told by the Angel Gabriel that she will bear the son of God

Attribute – object used in art to symbolise a particular person, often saints and martyrs

Baldacchino – canopied structure, in paintings holding an enthroned Madonna and child

Banderuola – small forked flag bearing an inscription, held in Renaissance art by angels or *putti*

Baptistery – building for baptisms, usually octagonal to symbolise new beginnings, as seven is the number of completion and eight the start of a new cycle

Baroque – sumptuous art and architectural style from the 17th to mid 18th century

Byzantine – spiritual and religious art of the Byzantine Empire (fifth-15th century)

Campanile – bell-tower

Cartoon – full-scale sketch for painting or fresco

Cenacolo – depiction of the Last Supper

Chiaroscuro – painting or drawing technique using shades of black, grey and white to emphasise light and shade

Classical – ancient Greek and Roman art and culture

Corbel – brackets jutting from a roof

Cupola – dome-shaped structure set on a larger dome or a roof

Deposition – depiction of Christ taken down from the cross

Diptych – painting made of two panels

Fresco – technique for wall-painting where pigments bind with wet plaster

Golden mean – Renaissance art theory, with division of proportions by ratio of 8:13, considered to create perfect harmony

Gothic – architectural and artistic style of the late Middle Ages (from the 12th century), characterised by the integration of art forms, with pointed arches and an emphasis on line

Grotesque – ornate artistic style derived from Roman underground painted rooms (*grotte*)

Hortus conclusus – garden around Madonna and child symbolising their uncontaminated world of perfection and contentment

Iconography – study of subject and symbolism of works of art. For example, in Renaissance art, a **dog** symbolises faithfulness to a master, usually the Medici; an **egg** is a symbol of perfection; a **peacock** symbolises the Resurrection; a **giglio** (lily of Florence) is often found in Annunciations to symbolise the purity of the Madonna; a **sarcophagus** (stone or marble coffin) symbolises the death of an important person; and the colour **blue** sometimes symbolises divine peace.

Illumination – miniature painted as an illustration for manuscripts

Loggia – covered area with one or more sides open, with columns

Lunette – half-moon painting or semicircular architectural space for decoration or window

Madonna of Mercy – Madonna with her cloak open to give protection to those in need

Maestà – depiction of the Madonna on a throne

Mandorla – almond-shaped 'glory' surrounding depiction of holy person

Mannerism – 15th-century Italian art movement, characterised by exaggerated perspective and scale, and complex compositions and poses

Palazzo (*palazzi*) – large and/or important building, not necessarily a royal palace

Panel – painting on wood

Panneggio – style of folded and pleated drapery worn by figures in 15th- and 16th-century painting and sculpture

Pietà – depiction of Christ lying across the Madonna's lap after the crucifixion

Pietra dura – inlaid gem mosaics

Polyptych – painting composed of several panels

Putto (*putti*) – small angelic naked boys, often depicted as attendants of Venus

Relief – sculpted work with three-dimensional areas jutting out from a flat surface

Renaissance – 14th- to 16th-century cultural movement based on the 'rebirth' of classical ideals and methods

Romanesque – architectural style of the early Middle Ages (c500-1200), drawing on Roman Byzantine influences

Secco – the finishing off or retouching of a fresco, carried out on the dried plaster (*intonaco*)

Sinopia – preparatory drawing for a fresco made with a red earth mix or the red paint itself

Tempera – pigment bound with egg, the main painting material from 12th to late 15th century, before oils took over

Tondo – round painting or relief

Triptych – painting composed of three panels

Trompe-l'oeil – painting designed to give illusion of three-dimensional reality

Vanitas – objects in art symbolising mortality, such as skulls, hourglasses and broken columns

Votive – offering left as a prayer for good fortune or recovery from illness, usually as a painting or a silver model of the limb/organ to be cured

Further Reference

Books

Non-fiction

Luigi Barzini *The Italians*
Hilarious (dated) portrait of the Italians.

Julia Conaway Bondanella & Mark Musa
Introduction to the major Italian writers & influential thinkers of the Renaissance
Famous names and a few surprises.

Thomas Campanello
A Defence of Galileo, the Mathematician from Florence
Life, times and influence of Florence's most famous heretic.

Leornardo Castellucci
Living in Tuscany
Account of restoration efforts that turned Tuscan abbeys, castles, villas and farmhouses into homes.

Paul Ginsbourg
A History of Contemporary Italy: Society and Politics 1943-1988
Comprehensive modern history.

Frederick Hartt *The History of Italian Renaissance Art*
The definitive work.

Christopher Hibbert *The Rise and Fall of the House of Medici*
Very readable history tome.

Ross King
Brunelleschi's Dome: The Story of the Great Cathedral
Fascinating account of the building of Florence's magnificent dome.

Monica Larner and Travis Neighbor *Living, Studying and Working in Italy*
Everything you need to know to live in the *bel paese*.

Mary McCarthy
The Stones of Florence
McCarthy's loving portrait of Florence as an arts city.

Iris Origo *Images and Shadows; The Merchant of Prato*
Historical and autobiographical accounts of Florence old and new.

Thomas Paloscia
Accadde in Toscana (Vol III)
A beautifully illustrated who's who of Tuscany's contemporary artists.

Laura Raison
Tuscany: An Anthology
A collection of writings and illustrations about Florence and Tuscany from the classics to contemporary writers.

Leon Satkowski
Giorgio Vasari: Architect & Courtier
Biography of the most famous Italian art chronicler.

Matthew Spender
Within Tuscany
The son of Stephen Spender writes a witty account of growing up in an unusual family in Tuscany.

Fiction

Italo Calvino *The Florentine*
One of Calvino's 'folktales' collection of short stories. Tells of the misery of a Florentine who has nothing to boast of and longs to travel.

Jack Dann *The Memory Cathedral – A Secret History of Leonardo da Vinci*
Mystery and intrigue in 15th-century Florence.

Michael Dibdin *A Rich Full Death*
Amusing thriller with insight into 19th-century Florence.

EM Forster *A Room With a View; Where Angels Fear to Tread*
Superb social comedy from the master.

Robert Hellenga *The 16 Pleasures*
A young American woman goes to Florence and feels obliged to act out 16 'pleasures' from a book of erotica.

W Somerset Maugham
Up at the Villa
Temptation and fate in wartime Florence.

Frances Mayes
Under the Tuscan Sun, Bella Tuscany
Ubiquitous *Year in Provence*-style expat dreams and nightmares.

Magdalena Nabb
The Monster of Florence
Thriller based on a serial-killer who murdered 16 campers in the 1980s.

Michael Ondaatje
The English Patient
Booker-winning novel turned Oscar-winning film, partly set in Tuscany.

Davina Sobell *Galileo's Daughter*
A study of the life of Galileo seen in the context of his relationship with his daughter.

Sally Stewart
An Unexpected Harvest
London yuppie moves to Tuscany to help grandparents save family estate.

Food & wine

Leslie Forbes
A Table in Tuscany
A personal account of the author's Tuscan food experiences, with recipes from local restaurants.

Slow Food and Gambero Rosso
Italian Wines Guide
The English edition of possibly the most reliable guide to Italian wines; updated annually.

Film

The English Patient (1996)
Tragic World War II story starring Ralph Fiennes and Juliette Binoche, partly set in Tuscany.

Hannibal (2000)
Creepy sequel to *Silence of the Lambs* shows Anthony Hopkins' serial killer travelling to Florence.

Life is Beautiful (La Vita e' Bella) (1997)

Roberto Benigni's bittersweet comedy about wartime Tuscany.

Much Ado about Nothing (1993)
Kenneth Branagh's fanciful interpretation of Shakespeare's comedy, filmed in Tuscany.

Portrait of a Lady (1996)
Jane Campion directs Nicole Kidman in this adaptation of Henry James's story of a New World woman in Old World Italy.

A Room with a View (1985)
Merchant and Ivory flick in which Helena Bonham Carter learns of love and loss in 19th-century Florence.

Stealing Beauty (1995)
Bernardo Bertolucci directed this Tuscan-based film that brought the world Liv Tyler.

Up at the Villa (2000)
Sean Penn plays a cynical American who proves innocent in comparison to his European companions.

Music

Giacomo Puccini
Gianni Schicchi
Delightful comic one-act opera set in medieval Fucecchio, a small town west of Florence.

Peter Ilich Tschaikovsky
Souvenir of Florence
String sextet written while the composer was living in via San Leonardo in Florence.

Websites

www.boxoffice.it Info and online booking for concerts and shows. Italian only.

www.comune.it Official council site with what's-on page, weather forecasts and useful info about visas, permits and tax.

www.cultura.toscana.it Official Regione Toscana site for info on museums, exhibitions and libraries in all of Tuscany.

www.fionline.it Shopping online, job search site and useful entertainment info.

www.firenze.net Useful site with info on Florence and Tuscany cinemas, nightlife, music, art, traffic and weather and a booking service for museums, hotels and farm holidays.

www.firenzespettacolo.it
The monthly listings mag website with constantly updated whats-on info, reviews and much more – you can even order a pizza here.

www.florenceonline.it/www.fol.it Useful info on health, travel, sports, hotel bookings and business.
www.lapulce.it Online version of the small-ads mag; free insertions.

Index

Advertisers' Index

Please refer to the relevant sections for
addresses/telephone numbers

Regional Border	‑‑‑‑
Province Border	‑ ‑
Autostrade	▬▬
City Wall	▬
Place of Interest and/or Entertainment	▢
Railway Station	▢
Park	▢
Hospital/University	▢
Ancient Site	▨
Car Park	P
Tourist Information	i
Predestrianised Area	▢
Bus Routes	12, 13
Electric Bus Routes	A

Maps

Targasys.

A world of services.

Targasys is always with you, ready to assure you all the tranquillity and serenity that you desire for your journeys, 24 hours a day 365 days a year.

Roadside assistance always and everywhere, infomobility so not to have surprises, insurance... and lots more.

To get to know us better contact us at the toll-free number **00-800-55555555**.

...and to discover Targa Connect's exclusive and innovative integrated infotelematic services onboard system visit us at:

www.targaconnect.com

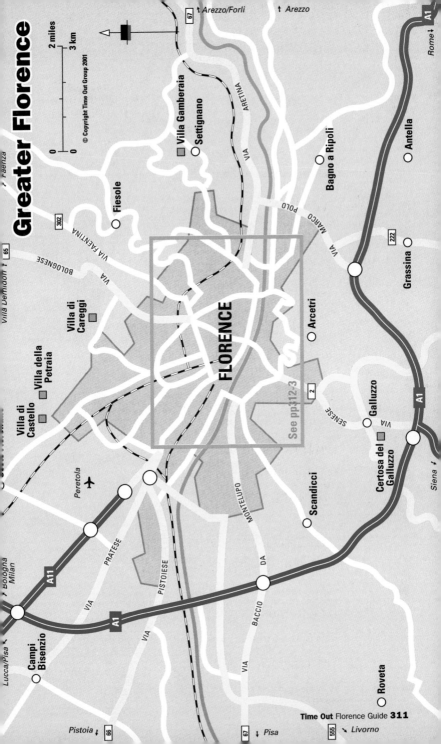

Greater Florence

© Copyright Time Out Group 2001

2 miles
3 km
0

↑ Faenza
↑ Arezzo/Forli   67   ↑ Arezzo
VIA ARETINA
Villa Gamberaia ■ ● Settignano
VIA
Fiesole
Bagno a Ripoli ●
● Antella
VIA MARCO POLO
302
VIA FAENTINA
VIA BOLOGNESE
↑ Villa Demidoff
222
65
Grassina ○
Villa di Careggi ■
Villa della Petraia ■
FLORENCE
● Arcetri
Villa di Castello ■
See pp312-3
2
Rome ↓
A1
SENESE
Galluzzo ■
Peretola ✈
VIA
A11
↑ Bologna
↑ Milan
VIA PRATESE
VIA PISTOIESE
Certosa del Galluzzo ■
Siena ↓
Scandicci ●
MONTELUPO
A1
↙ Lucca/Pisa
VIA
A1
● Campi Bisenzio
VIA DA BACCIO
VIA
Roveta ○

Pistoia ↓   66
67   ↓ Pisa
555   ↘ Livorno

62 to Airport

VIA DI NOVOLI

VIA FRANCESCO BARACCA

V. ENRICO FORLANINI

VIA G. FILIPPO MARITI

VIALE FRANCESCO REDI

VIA MARAGLIANO

V. F. CORRIDONI

VIA CIRCONDARIA

PIAZZA
P. LEOPOLDO

V.S. BANDINI

VIA VITTORIO

Museo
Stibber

IL ROMITO

VIA DEL ROMITO

Stazione
Statuto

V. D. STATUTO

PIAZZA
GIACOMO PUCCINI

S. JACOPINO

V. FILIPPO STROZZI

Tiro a Segno

VIA DELLE CASCINE

VIA DEL PONTE ALLE MOSSE

V. BEN. MARCELLO

Fortezza
da Basso

VIA

PIAZZA
DELLE
CASCINE

Ippodromo
Delle Cascine

V. FILIPPO STROZZI

VIALE BELFIORE

62

PONTE AL L'INDIANO

Le Cascine

VIALE DEGLI OLMI

Porta
Al Prato

VIA VALFONDA

7, 10, 36, 37, 62

VIA XXV

VIALE ABRAMO LINCOLN

Stazione della
Porta al Prato

Porta
Al Prato

VIA L. ALAMANNI

Stazione di
S. Maria Novella

VIA GUELFA

LUNGARNO DEI PIOPPI

PIAZZA
VITTORIO
VENETO

VIALE F.LLI ROSSELLI

VIA DELLA SCALA

PIAZZA
DELLA
STAZIONE

San
Lorenzo

VIA DEL SANSOVINO

PONTE DELLA
VITTORIA

IL PRATO B. OGNISSANTI

VIA DE'
CERRETAN

VIA BRONZINO

PIAZZA
TADDEO
GADDI

LUNGARNO AMERIGO VESPUCCI

VIA DE'
TORNABUONI

PIAZZA
DELLA
REPUBBLICA

VIA DEL

V. A. DEL POLLAIUOLO

PIAZZA
PIER VETTORI

Porta
S. Frediano

PONTE
A. VESPUCCI

VIA PISANA

VIA PISANA

Santa
Trinità

Uffizi

MONTE
ULIVETO

VIALE A. ALEARDI

BORGO SAN FREDIANO

F
i
u
m
e

VIA DELL' OLIVUZZO

VIA DI SOFFIANO

VIA DE SERRAGLI

PIAZZA
DE'PITTI

Palazzo Pitti

BELLOSGUARDO

VIALE PETRARCA

VIA ROMANA

Boboli
Gardens

Forte
di Belvedere

Pon
Sa
Gior

Porta
Romana

Istituto
d'Arte

BOBOLINO

PIAZZALE
DELLA PORTA
ROMANA

VIALE NICCOLO

0   200   400 m

0   400 yds

© Copyright Time Out Group 2001

36, 37

VIA SENESE

VIALE DEL POGGIO IMPERIALE

11

MACHIA

PIAZZALE
GALILEO

12, 13

German
Institute

VIALE TORRICELLI

Florence Overview

VIA BOLOGNESE

ANUELE

VIA FAENTINA

VIA FRANCESCO

PIAZZA DELLE CURE

↑ 7 To Fiesole

VIA SAN DOMENICO

To Fiesole →

A XX SETTEMBRE

7

Russian Church

Porta San Gallo

PIAZZA DELLA LIBERTÀ

VIA DON G. MINZONI

N LAVAGNINI

VIALE ALESSANDRO VOLTA

V. AUGUSTO RIGHI

V. CALATAFIMI

PIAZZA V. FARDELLA DI TORREARSA

VIA GIACOMO MATTEOTTI

VIALE DEI MILLE

VIA CAMILLO CAVOUR

PRILE

PIAZZA SAN MARCO

VIA DEGLI ALFANI

Giardino della Gherardesca

VIA D. ARTISTI

VIA MASACCIO

V. MANFREDO FANTI

Stadio Comunale

V. PASQUALE PAOLI

VIA EDMONDO DE AMICIS

10 to Settignano →

FILAROCC

English Cemetery

PIAZZA DONATELLO

VIALE MALTA

VIA GABRIELE D'ANNUNZIO

omo

V. DEL PROCONSOLO

10

VIA DELLA COLONNA

Cenacolo di Andrea del Sarteo

Psychiatric Hospital

PIAZZA C. BECCARIA

Porta Alla Croce

VIA VINCENZO GIOBERTI

PIAZZA L.B. ALBERTI

VIA ARETINA

MADONNONE

V. G. LANZA

VIA PIAGENTINA

V. QUINTINO SELLA

LUNG. ALDO MORO

PONTE ALLE GRAZIE

LUNG. D. ZECCA VECCHIA

L. DEL TEMPIO

LUNGARNO C. COLOMBO

PONTE G. DA VERRAZZANO

LUNG. B. CELLINI

Porta San Niccolò

PONTE SAN NICCOLÒ

A r n o

LUNG. FRANCESCO FERRUCCI

PIAZZA RAVENNA

VIA DI VILLAMAGNA

Porta San Miniato

ee pp314-5

PIAZZALE MICHELANGIOLO

PIAZZA F. FERRUCCI

V. COLUCCIO SALUTATI

VIALE DONATO GIANNOTTI

VIA ERBOSA

12, 13

RICORBOLI

VIA DI RIPOLI

VIALE GALILEO

San Miniato al Monte

12, 13

VIALE MICHELANGIOLO

V. TRAVERSARI

VIALE EUROPA

Central Florence

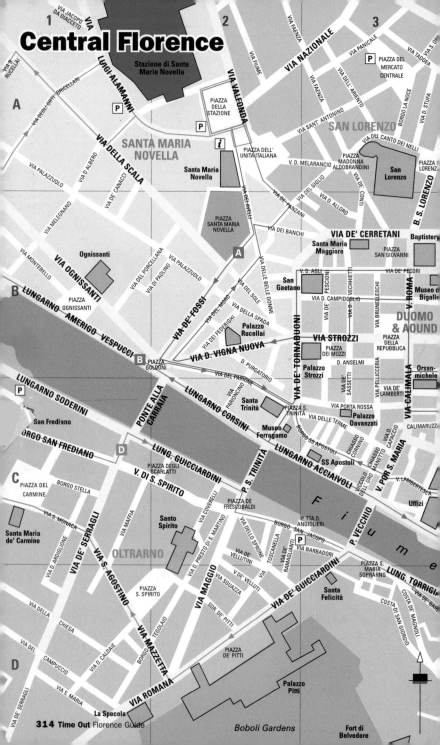

1 VIA JACOPO DA DIACETO VIA
2 VIA FAENZA
3

Stazione di Santa
Maria Novella

VIA NAZIONALE

VIA PANICALE

P PIAZZA DEL
MERCATO
CENTRALE

VIA S. OR

VIA DELLE PORTE NUOVE/BRICCELLARI

LUIGI ALAMANNI

P

PIAZZA
DELLA
STAZIONE

VIA FIUME

VIA DELL' ARIENTO

VIA TADDEA

BORGO LA NOCE

VIA LA NOCE

VIA S. ANTONINO

SAN LORENZO

VIA DELLA SCALA

SANTA MARIA
NOVELLA

P

i

PIAZZA DELL'
UNITA ITALIANA

V. D. MELARANCIO

VIA DEL CANTO DEI NELLI

PIAZZA
MADONNA
ALDOBRANDINI

San
Lorenzo

PIAZZA S.
LORENZO

B. S. LORENZO

A

VIA PALAZZUOLO

VIA DE' PANZANI

VIA DEL GIGLIO

VIA D. ALLORO

VIA D. CONTI

Santa Maria
Novella

VIA DE AREN

PIAZZA
SANTA MARIA
NOVELLA

VIA DEI BANCHI

VIA DE' CERRETANI

Santa Maria
Maggiore

PIAZZA
SAN GIOVANNI

Baptistery

VIA MONTEBELLO

VIA OGNISSANTI

Ognissanti

VIA DEL PORCELLANA

VIA PALAZZUOLO

VIA DI PAOLINO

VIA DELLE BELLE DONNE

VIA DEL SOLE

San
Gaetano

V. D. AGLI

PESCIONI

VIA DE' PECORI

VIA DE' VECCHIETTI

V. ROMA

Museo d
Bigalle

B

PIAZZA
OGNISSANTI

LUNGARNO AMERIGO VESPUCCI

VIA DE' FOSSI

VIA DEL MORO

VIA DELLA SPADA

VIA DE' FEDERIGHI

Palazzo
Rucellai

VIA D. CAMPIDOGLIO

VIA DI

VIA DE' BRUNELLESCHI

DUOMO
& AROUND

VIA D. VIGNA NUOVA

D. PURGATORIO

VIA STROZZI

PIAZZA
DEI MOZZI

PIAZZA
DELLA
REPUBBLICA

PIAZZA
GOLDONI

VIA DEL PARIONE

VIA DEL PARIONCINO

Palazzo
Strozzi

D. ANSELMI

VIA DE'
SASSETTI

VIA DE'
LAMBERTI

Orsan-
michele

VIA CALIMALA

LUNGARNO SODERINI

P

San Frediano

PONTE ALLA CARRAIA

LUNGARNO CORSINI

Santa
Trinità

PIAZZA S.
TRINITA

VIA PORTA ROSSA

VIA DELLE TERME

Palazzo
Davanzati

CALIMARUZZ

BORGO SAN FREDIANO

LUNG. GUICCIARDINI

Museo
Ferragamo

BORGO SS APOSTOLI

LUNGARNO ACCIAIVOLI

CHIASSO
CORSINO

SS Apostoli

CHIASSO
DEL ORETO

VICOLO
DELL' ORO

VIA D.
CATACCIO

V. POR S. MARIA

V. LAMBERTESCA

C

D

PIAZZA DEGLI
SCARLATTI

V. DI S. SPIRITO

PIAZZA DEL
CARMINE

BORGO STELLA

VIA S. MONACA

Santo
Spirito

VIA COVERELLI

P. S. TRINITA

PIAZZA DE
FRESCOBALDI

P. TTA D.
ANGIOLIERI

BORGO
SAN JACOPO

P

Uffizi

F

I

U

VIA DELLO SPRONE

VIA D. PRESTO DI S. MARTINO

Santa Maria
de' Carmine

VIA D. ARDIGLIONE

VIA DE' SERRAGLI

VIA S. AGOSTINO

VIA MAFFIA

TUSCANELLA

P. VECCHIO

P

VIA BARBADORI

PIAZZA S.
MARIA
SOPRARNO

m

e

OLTRARNO

PIAZZA
S. SPIRITO

VIA MAGGIO

VIA DELLO SPRONE

VIA DEL
VELLUTINI

VIA DE' VELLUTI

V DE PITTI

VIA DE' GUICCIARDINI

LUNG. TORRIGI

VIA DE' BARI

COSTA DI SAN GIORGIO

COSTA DE MAGNOLI

D

VIA DELLA
CHIESA

VIA DEL
CAMPUCCIO

VIA S. MARIA

VIA MAZZETTA

BORGO TEGOLAIO

VIA D. CALDAIE

VIA SGUAZZA

SDR DE PITTI

PIAZZA
DE' PITTI

Santa
Felicità

VIA DE' SERRAGLI

VIA ROMANA

La Specola

Palazzo
Pitti

Boboli Gardens

Fort di
Belvedere

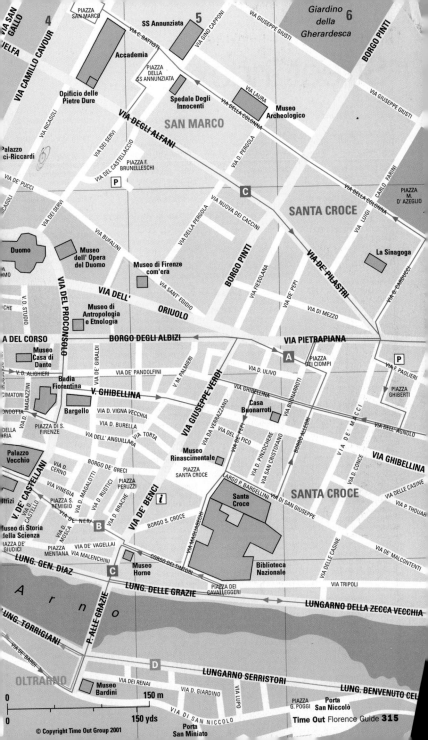

Street Index